Corporate Financial Crisis in Ireland

Corporate Financial Crisis in Ireland

Edward Cahill

Gill & Macmillan

Gill & Macmillan Ltd
Goldenbridge
Dublin 8
with associated companies throughout the world
© Edward Cahill 1997
0 7171 2024 4
Index compiled by Helen Litton
Print origination by Carole Lynch
Printed in Malaysia

All rights reserved. No part of this publication may be copied,
reproduced or transmitted in any form or by any means,
without permission of the publishers.

A catalogue record is available for this book from
the British Library.

1 3 5 4 2

Contents

Acknowledgments	xi
Preface	xiii
List of tables	xvii

Chapter 1: Introduction — 1
- Corporate health and pathology — 1
- Organisational decline, distress, failure and crisis — 5
- Rates of failure and age of failed companies — 6
- Economic context and corporate performance — 9
- Bad management and mismanagement — 11
- Corporate collapse is not unique to Irish organisations — 12
- Bankers, stockbroker analysts and accounting — 15
- The nature of this study — 16

Chapter 2: Causes of Corporate Financial Distress and Failure — 19
- Introduction — 19
- Analytical perspectives — 20
- Reasons for collapse: a management perspective — 21
- Some accounting views — 26
- Life-cycle theory as an organising framework — 27
- The problems of adolescence — 29
- The financial problems of growth — 34
- The problems of mature organisations — 35
- Downward spirals and blindness — 39
- Syndromes of failure patterns — 41
- Aggressive and cosmetic accounting — 42
- Financial ratio predictive models — 43

Chapter 3: Goodman International: Overambitious Expansion — 48
- The crisis erupts — 48
- Background — 51
- The 'dealer' becomes a processor — 53
- Acquisitions and turnarounds — 55
- Diversification and a new strategic objective — 57
- Financial performance — 58
- Organisational structure and management culture — 67

The entrepreneurial trader, the accountants and risk	75
Business and politics: oil and water?	77
The reasons for the financial collapse	78
A 'historical event' in the life of Larry Goodman	83
The banks and the restructuring	84
Accounting and auditing issues	86
Reflections	91

Chapter 4: Kentz Corporation and the Failed Management Buyout — 94

Kentz Corporation: an unexpectedly sudden collapse?	94
Background	97
Financial performance	102
Comparing Kentz with Jacobs Engineering	104
Product/market strategy	106
Board and ownership structure	109
Management structure, style and culture	110
Financial control	113
Overtrading: capital structure and working capital	115
Accounting issues	117
External governance and regulatory issues	125
The consequences	127
Reflections	128

Chapter 5: Xtra-vision: A Stock Exchange Shooting Star — 131

Introduction	131
Xtra-vision plc: a suitable firm for the Stock Exchange?	132
Background	135
Stockmarket flotation and rapid expansion	137
Board and management structure	138
Business and marketing strategy	139
Financial performance	140
The first financial crisis	142
The inadequate second rights issue and second financial crisis	143
Bailout by Cambridge	145
The third financial crisis, examinership and reorganisation	146
Financial reporting issues	147
Stockbroker analysts and their reviews	152
The strengths and weaknesses of Xtra-vision	153

The role of DCC	154
Reflections	155

Chapter 6: GPA: A Case Study in Market Share Fixation — 157

What was different about GPA?	157
Background	160
Product/market strategy and competitive position	166
Financial performance	171
Shareholders and board: the changing power structure	177
Management, organisation and culture	182
Growth, cash flow and financing shortfalls	184
Capital structure and gearing	186
Did GPA overtrade?	190
Bank covenants	192
Internal plans and profit expectations	193
Dividend policy	195
Aggressive accounting policies	197
The efficiency of stockbroker analysts	203
Stockbroker analysts' reviews in advance of the IPO	205
Reasons for the flotation failure	206
Who lost money in GPA?	215
Reflections	217

Chapter 7: Arthur Guinness and P. J. Carroll: Diversification and Decline of a Core Business — 222

Introduction	222

Arthur Guinness Son and Company Limited — *222*

Background	222
Product, market and competitive position	225
The Dublin efficiency and capacity dilemma	228
The Guinness culture	229
Financial performance	231
Guinness's strategic weaknesses in the UK	234
Cash flow profile	235
The failed diversification strategy	235
The fundamental causes of Guinness's problems	238
The Saunders turnaround and transformation of Guinness	240

P. J. Carroll	244
Background	244
Marketing and financial performance	248
Performance of the core tobacco division	251
The strategic dilemma	252
The 'marketing driven' diversification strategy	255
The twin new ventures: aquaculture and direct marketing	256
The disastrous outcome to the diversification strategy	259
Cash flow profile	259
Scapegoats and responsibilities	262
Comparing P. J. Carroll with Gallaher (Dublin)	264
The strategic and tactical errors	266
Board structure	270
Accounting and financial policies and management information breakdowns	272
Reflections on Guinness and P. J. Carroll	275
Chapter 8: Irish Press and Waterford Wedgwood: The Clash Between Culture, Craft and Change	**278**
Introduction	278
Irish Press	*280*
Background	280
The legacy of the Irish Press group's political origins	282
The influence of history and culture on the 'product'	284
Product/market and competitive position	286
Financial performance	288
Corporate reorganisation: ring-fencing the newspapers	291
Reasons for the collapse of the Irish Press group	294
Endgame and the wrong partner?	305
Appointment of examiner and the failed rescue	307
Waterford Wedgwood	*308*
The rebirth of a tradition	308
Adolescence and maturity	314
Labour costs, competitiveness and the dollar	316
The sale of the McGrath family equity to Globe: a new management and a new strategic plan	322
The Wedgwood acquisition	325
The crystal division's redundancy and accounting disasters	328

The failed turnaround	332
The second turnaround	334
Reflections on Irish Press and Waterford Wedgwood	337

Chapter 9: Irish Shipping: A Vessel Without a Chart or Compass — 340

The collapse of Irish Shipping: a national scandal	340
Background	344
Trading and financial performance	348
Organisation and management	350
The Tempany report on the causes of failure	352
The big project and a weak partner	354
Defects in internal governance and control	358
Financial reporting and finance issues	363
External governance defects	368
The liquidation and some consequences	372
Government responsibility	374
Reflections	375

Chapter 10: Conclusions — 377

Introduction	377
Age patterns	378
The extent and speed of the profit reversals	378
Themes and patterns of adolescent firm distress and failure	380
Themes and patterns of mature firm distress and failure	386
An analytical framework of management	390
Financial reporting issues	391
Public interest issues	396
The business cycle	397
Recognising and preventing possible financial distress and failure	398
The relevance of the corporate regulatory system	400
Bankers, analysts and investment institutions	401

Appendix 1: The Research Sample	**403**
Appendix 2: Outcome to the Financial Crises in the Eighteen Cases	**406**
Notes	**407**
Index	**435**

Acknowledgments

In the course of this study I interviewed over 170 people. I am deeply indebted to all those who gave generously of their time and advice. Almost all wished to remain anonymous. This is not surprising in view of the organisational research issues and the close social and business context in a small country. Interviewees included chairmen, chief executives, non-executive directors, financial controllers and management of the research sample. They also included some bankers, accountants and civil servants as well as stockbroker analysts and portfolio/fund managers in investment institutions (in Dublin and London). Many helped with contacts and pointed to (or provided) relevant documentation. A number commented on draft and restructured chapters and their continued encouragement in the project was much appreciated. They must remain 'unsung heroes'. I am in special debt to one senior analyst with whom I had many lively discussions. He reviewed some early draft chapters and was influential in the decision to adopt a case study framework in presentation — 'lest my colleagues and the next generation forget the lessons', as he put it. He will recognise himself.

It cannot have been easy for many of the executives to review a most difficult and traumatic period in their corporate life. During some 'interviews' there were moments of tension as sensitive issues were raised and probed by this author. Remarkably few tried to skirt the key issues. Some were surprisingly candid in their reflections on mistakes made and 'if I could do it again I would have . . .' (Of course both they and I acknowledged that we had the benefit of hindsight.)

Staff seminars in the mid stage of the research, in the Department of Accounting, Finance and Information/Systems in University College Cork and in the School of Business Studies in Trinity College Dublin, generated many fruitful comments, ideas and references for which I am most grateful.

I particularly wish to acknowledge the help of three departmental colleagues in University College Cork. Professor Ted O'Leary, Dr Ciaran Murphy and Dr Ray Donnelly read draft chapters and made constructive comments. Discussions with Ted and Ciaran and their solid encouragement tipped the balance in the weaker moments. My departmental colleagues were most tolerant and supportive during late 1995 and early 1996 when I focused on finalising the manuscript. Joanne Geary helped with Datastream and other stockmarket and financial data search and analysis in the early stages. Margaret Healy and Simon Quinn, both doctoral students in the department, not only helped in checking incomplete references but also offered many useful comments on the final manuscript. Maire Kavanagh provided sensitive administrative and secretarial back-up with the many research contacts with unparalleled discretion and good humour. Suzanne Buckley efficiently assisted in many of these secretarial activities. An early version of the manuscript benefited from very helpful suggestions of two anonymous reviewers. Jonathan Williams gave me most useful advice on writing style when he reviewed some early chapters. The manuscript undoubtedly benefited from the careful and comprehensive editing of Finbarr O'Shea.

I am grateful to University College Cork for leave of absence for a three-month period in 1993. This enabled me to embark on the project in some depth. Research over a three-year period — involving numerous visits to Dublin, and a number to London together with information searches which stretched to the USA and Hong Kong — could not have been undertaken without extensive financial support. This came from a combination of sources: use of my Dean's personal stipend from University College Cork and some research funds advanced by Irish Life Assurance plc and CRH plc.

I made fruitful use of four libraries: University College Cork (particularly the inter-library loan section), Trinity College Dublin, the well-organised Business Information Section of the Ilac Centre Library (Dublin Corporation) and the Institute of Chartered Accountants in Ireland. Their library staff were unfailingly professional and helpful.

I am heavily in debt to Professor Dermot Keogh, my close college colleague from the department of History. Dermot was a constant and sympathetic mentor in discreetly ensuring a focus to and completion of the project.

Another major debt is owed to Michael Gill, managing director of Gill & Macmillan. Michael not only responded positively to the original project proposal but patiently endured a delay in the manuscript submission with constructive encouragement.

Finally, above all others, this book could not have been written without the active support and forbearance of my wife, Angela and children, Peter, Helen, Joan and Susan. Books are not written during standard office hours. Angela was an active collaborator from the start of the project through file searches in the Companies Office, Dublin, through to proof-reading the final manuscript.

Edward Cahill
Cork
May 1997

Preface

It is never easy to pin down the origins of a research project. The genesis in this case probably occurred in April 1989 when Aileen O'Toole (then) of *Business & Finance* asked me to write a piece on the 'accounting errors' in Waterford Crystal. To the surprise of the stockbroker analysts Waterford's year-end profit was well below their expectations and the share price plummeted. The chairman had just resigned. It was a unique public event in Irish corporate history. Waterford's problems were associated with a major investment project which failed to deliver the productivity projected.

I had recently moved to University College Cork from Trinity College Dublin, so I hurriedly rummaged through my old notes on a short Waterford case study which I had used with the Trinity MBAs. Writing the article for Aileen prompted an initial reflection on the variety of issues which face a labour-intensive mature organisation and the problems of change.

Little over a year later, in June 1990, P. J. Carroll, the long-established cigarette manufacturer with an excellent track record, suffered a similar fate — announcing a net loss, the size of which caught many stockmarket analysts unawares. The share price fell sharply and the chairman resigned. I returned to old 'notes' of mine on a Carroll case study I had given in 1987. Two months later, in late August, the dramatic financial crisis of Goodman International, the largest agri-business in Ireland, occurred. It was quickly followed by the financial problems of two relatively new Stock Exchange companies — Xtra-vision, the country's largest video rental organisation, and Yeoman International, a large leasing group. In June 1992 we witnessed the financial crisis of Ireland's largest quoted property company, Power Corporation, followed within months by the financial distress of GPA, the world's largest aircraft leasing company with assets of over $6 billion. In September 1993, amidst some controversy, a consortium of banks appointed a receiver to the Cambridge Group, another quoted leasing company. The examinerships of Kentz Corporation, Ireland's largest engineering contractor, and of the two companies publishing the three Irish Press newspapers followed in 1994 and 1995.

This series of corporate setbacks stimulated my curiosity about the determinants of financial crisis in entrepreneurial as compared to mature organisations. Were the causes different in each type of organisation and could they be pinpointed — or were there common explanatory themes?

Not only did there appear to be issues of governance, strategic direction, organisational structure and management but also the reliability of management accounting and information systems was raised. In addition, there were questions about the efficiency of external financial reporting and regulation. These phenomena certainly made the research questions relevant to society.

At an early stage, I decided to undertake detailed personal research on a series of case studies on specific organisations, rather than solely using survey questionnaires or seeking the opinions of bankers, accountants and business advisers. The individual organisation's context and internal circumstances seemed fundamental to understanding the issues. The objective was to determine the causes of financial crisis and collapse in organisations within three stages of their possible life-cycle: birth (start-up), adolescence and maturity. This proved to be a three-year campaign in a search for information and evidence. A holistic perspective was adopted in order to understand the variety of interrelated issues which combine to trigger a crisis and collapse — or camouflage the symptoms for a period. The investigation involved interviews of directors and managers in the organisations, archival search together with internal (where available) and external documentation analysis as a basis of field studies. The process proved longer, messier and more complex than I anticipated. I certainly underestimated the difficulties in gaining research access to (perceived) sensitive materials. Drawing boundaries and mapping the links was not easy. The 'start-up' sample of companies had to be reluctantly abandoned. I had already gone down the road quite a bit with a couple of cases, particularly with the De Lorean debacle in Northern Ireland and the USA. The research was altered to focus on those organisations that had already made it to the adolescent stage and beyond. After all, they were up and running. In theory, financial crisis should have been less common. In practice, many leading Irish business organisations encountered financial problems and stakeholders suffered heavy losses. I wondered about the roles of directors, management, accountants and auditors. Why did some organisations in a particular industry collapse and others survive in the same period of the economic cycle?

The response rate, following many letters and telephone calls, averaged about one in three. The 170 interviews with chairmen, chief executives, non-executive directors, senior and middle level managers, bankers, stockbroker and investment institutions analysts and investment fund managers not only proved illuminating and instructive but also changed my perspectives on business organisations and their dynamics. The singularly powerful role of the chief executive who at the same time was chairman and a large shareholder — and the contrasting potentially weaker position of the financial director operating with inadequate internal information and without the support of strong and independent directors — was a significant finding. The feedback loop of audited financial statements and the quality of accounting policies adopted proved to have critical relevance to business strategy and governance — with implications for organisational power balance and sources of finance.

Apart from interviews, the documents and evidence in the High Court in the case of the examinerships of Goodman International, Kentz Corporation, Xtra-vision and Irish Press Newspapers, together with the examiners' reports, were most useful sources of corroborative information. In addition, the published report of the Tribunal of Inquiry into the beef-processing industry and the daily transcripts of the evidence provided helpful insights in the Goodman International analysis. In the case of Irish Shipping, the official liquidator's reports to the High Court were an important additional information source.

The adoption of the concept of an organisational life-cycle as a general analytical framework as well as comparative case study analysis may require some explanation. My own experience and the literature on organisations indicated that there were differences in the internal and external dynamics and environment between younger and older firms. Family firms seemed to have special characteristics which distinguished them from other managerially dominated mature firms. A qualitative methodology built around case studies was justified because of the absence of an accepted body of research constructs and theory in the area of financial crisis, distress and failure. I was aware of the debate on research method issues of validity, control and generalisability with regard to case studies. Though the work was difficult, it did reward this writer with a richness of experience and insights that were worth the effort. I have to thank colleagues Ted O'Leary and Ciaran Murphy for their encouragement and commitment to case study research as one of the methodological thrusts of the Department of Accounting, Finance and Information Systems in University College Cork.

The project investigation went beyond exploration and description of organisational and financial phenomena to a degree of explanation. Certain common themes and pathologies emerged. The outcomes and broad framework proposed can be used to generate models and theories which can be tested by future scholars. The findings can be put to practical use by shareholders, bankers, boards of directors, senior management and other stakeholders in entrepreneurial adolescent and mature organisations. The Achilles' heel of the former tends to be overtrading. While in the latter complacency often leads to hyperactivity. There are also serious issues for accounting and auditing standards and regulation arising out of the research findings.

Pinpointing symptoms of financial crisis early enough and taking corrective action can usually prevent collapse in most instances. The prize, apart from reducing economic losses to stakeholders, is that critical resources are not dispersed and heavy job losses and social disruption are avoided.

List of Tables

1.1	Company liquidations in Ireland	7
1.2	Age pattern of failing firms	8
1.3	Ten largest industrial organisations on the Dublin Stock Exchange in 1983 and their subsequent experience	9
1.4	Causes of business failure in the USA and Japan	12
2.1	Argenti's 'A score' failure prediction model	23
2.2	McKiernan's analysis of reasons for relative decline	24
2.3	Jackson and Crawford's causes of business failure	27
2.4	Mills' examples of bad management	28
2.5	Examples of entrepreneurial and professional cultures	30
2.6	Hambrick and D'Aveni's model of organisational decline as a downward spiral	40
2.7	Variables in US failure prediction models	45
2.8	Variables in Irish, UK and Australian failure predication models	46
3.1	Financial performance analysis: Goodman International and Kerry Group	60
3.2	Goodman International: consolidated profit and loss account	63
3.3	Goodman International: consolidated balance sheet	64
3.4	Goodman International: cash flow summary	66
3.5	Goodman International: the cost of the strategy	82
3.6	Goodman International: the bank restructuring deal	85
3.7	Goodman International: estimate of how much the banks lost	86
4.1	Kentz Corporations: key financial figures	102
4.2	Kentz Corporations: key financial ratios	103
4.3	Capital structure and working capital comparisons for Kentz Corporation and Jacobs Engineering	106
4.4	Kentz profit projections and the subsequent reality	118
4.5	Kentz Corporation: adjustments of accounting figures for 1992 on basis of more prudent accounting policies	124
5.1	Xtra-vision: financial performance	141
5.2	Xtra-vision: new video purchases to turnover	144
5.3	Xtra-vision: net cash flow to total debt	146

5.4	Xtra-vision: asset structure	149
6.1	Estimated market share of aircraft operating lessors (post-1985 Stage 3 aircraft)	169
6.2	GPA: early and late adolescent trading performance	171
6.3	GPA: gross profit margins	172
6.4	Financial performance analysis: GPA and ILFC	174
6.5	GPA: shareholding structure	179
6.6	Total asset and profit growth: GPA and ILFC	185
6.7	GPA: summarised cash flow analysis	187
6.8	GPA: fixed financial charges to leasing revenue	191
6.9	GPA: the overtrading configuration index	191
6.10	Total amount of dividends paid by GPA and ILFC	195
6.11	Dividends paid on GPA's A ordinary shares	196
6.12	Dividends declared on GPA's A preference shares	197
6.13	Comparison of GPA net profit under Irish and US GAAP	199
6.14	Comparison of GPA shareholders' funds under Irish and US GAAP	200
6.15	Comparison of GPA net profits under alternative accounting policies and regulatory standards	201
6.16	Davy and NCB 1992 forecasts for GPA	204
6.17	GPA's IPO share price financial statistics	208
6.18	GPA: larger equity and preference shareholders	216
7.1	Guinness: financial performance	232
7.2	A comparison of brewers' profit margins	233
7.3	Guinness: trading profits	235
7.4	Guinness: cash flow profile	236
7.5	P. J. Carroll: financial performance	249
7.6	P. J. Carroll: some conventional financial ratios	250
7.7	P. J. Carroll: tobacco division performance	251
7.8	P. J. Carroll: operating profits	253
7.9	P. J. Carroll: the changing investment profile	259
7.10	P. J. Carroll: divisional analysis of financial performance	260
7.11	P. J. Carroll: cash flow profile	261
7.12	Comparison of the profitability and dividend policy of P. J. Carroll and Gallaher	265
7.13	The changing gross profit margin profile of P. J. Carroll and Gallaher	265
7.14	P. J. Carroll's mistakes	267

List of Tables

8.1	Circulation of Irish Press and domestic competitors' newspapers	288
8.2	Profit/(loss) performance of Irish Press and its main domestic competitors	289
8.3	Irish Press: financial performance	290
8.4	Trading performance of Irish Press Newspapers	292
8.5	Waterford Wedgwood: trading performance	316
8.6	Waterford Wedgwood: some critical financial ratios	317
8.7	US dollar/Irish pound exchange rates	319
8.8	Comparison of the financial performance of Waterford Crystal and Wedgwood	327
8.9	Waterford Wedgwood: cash flow profile	335
8.10	Waterford Wedgwood: gross profit margins	336
9.1	Irish Shipping: trading performance	349
9.2	Irish Shipping: financial analysis	250
9.3	Irish Shipping: cash flow profile	351
9.4	The Tempany 'causes of failure' of Irish Shipping	353
9.5	Irish Shipping: divisional analysis of profitability	355
9.6	Irish Shipping: increasing deep-sea tonnage capacity	358
10.1	The extent of the profit/reversals in the crisis firms	379
10.2	Elements of mismanagement: adolescent firms	381
10.3	Elements of mismanagement: mature firms	387
10.4	Analytical framework of mismanagement	392
10.5	Financial reporting matters	394

Chapter 1

Introduction

> *From symbols and shadows to the truth.*
> Cardinal John Henry Newman's epitaph[1]

Corporate health and pathology

Tony Ryan, chairman of GPA, was proclaimed 'Man of the Week' by *Business & Finance* in April 1989. He had just announced a $17 billion deal with leading aircraft manufacturers for 308 aircraft.[2] It was the largest order in the history of civil aviation.

The fact that an Irish company could have the vision, courage and apparent creditworthiness to make such a huge commitment was testimony to the remarkable achievements of its management in building a 'world class' aircraft leasing organisation. Five weeks later, record net profits of $152 million were announced for 1988/89. A number of Irish and overseas investment institutions subscribed in a private placement of new equity. Shareholders in GPA could almost be described as the 'who's who' of the international investment community.[3] A 'grey' market operated in its shares with occasional trades.[4] Davy Stockbrokers provided regular valuations for institutional portfolios. Three years later, GPA's continued success seemed confirmed by peak profits of $279 million in late spring 1992. By early summer 1992 Davy valued GPA's equity at about $3 billion.

With the aim of raising $850 million, GPA issued a prospectus dated 9 June 1992 for an international public offer and multiple Stock Exchange listings. Investors were sought in New York, London, Tokyo and Dublin. Goldman Sachs and Nomura International were looking after the USA and Japan. Schroders was responsible for Britain and Ireland. All were leading banking and investment houses. In view of the size of the issue, GPA would become the largest quoted company on the Dublin Stock Exchange. Its market value would be double that of Allied Irish Banks and 50% greater than the Smurfit Group. Stockbroker analysts forecast increases in GPA's profits in 1993 and 1994, making it 'Ireland's most profitable company by a comfortable distance'.[5]

Two of the three start-up shareholders, Aer Lingus and Air Canada, remained among the largest shareholders. GPA's founder and executive chairman, Tony Ryan, and a number of his long-serving top management team also commanded a significant holding. Tony Ryan's was estimated to be worth $234 million.[6] Maurice Foley, Colm Barrington and Jim King were reported to hold shares valued at $18 million, $13 million and $6 million respectively. Well-known non-executive directors, Sir John Harvey-Jones, Garret FitzGerald and Peter Sutherland also owned valuable holdings.[7]

To the consternation of the capital markets, in the middle of the flotation process, the offer and listing plans were aborted. There was insufficient demand for GPA's shares in the four stockmarkets — particularly London and New York. There were wider ramifications to the debacle. It contributed to the 35.7 point fall in the FT 100 Index to 2562.7.[8] The following week the Dublin market suffered, with the ISEQ Index falling 31 points to 1331 (2.3%) on 26 June 1992.[9]

By early September there were reports that GPA shares were being offered at reduced prices[10] and that the US credit-rating agencies — Standard and Poor's, and Moody's — had downgraded their rating of GPA's senior debt and commercial paper in New York markets. A $350 million convertible preference share issue and a $750 million aircraft securitisation issue were abandoned. By November GPA admitted it was in discussion with over one hundred bankers and the aircraft manufacturers. A financial crisis was looming up. One newspaper carried the ominous headline 'GPA too big to be allowed fail'.[11] The economic reality was that GPA was now perilously close to a High Court examinership.

A net loss of $1 billion for 1992/93 followed a lengthy and costly debt restructuring. Many investment institutions valued GPA's shares at zero for portfolio purposes by December 1993. The rescue plans agreed three months earlier involved General Electric Capital Corporation of the USA injecting over $1 billion in cash in purchasing new aircraft at prices less than GPA's book value, taking over a large part of operational management, and having an option to acquire a controlling interest. There were sweeping board and management changes, with Tony Ryan, Colm Barrington and almost one-third of the staff departing GPA.

GPA's sudden fall from grace was not unique. It had been preceded two years earlier by the Goodman International saga. In late August 1990, Dáil deputies and senators were recalled from their holidays to urgently consider new company legislation. Broadly similar to the Chapter 11 bankruptcy regulations in the USA, this would permit the appointment of an examiner to companies in financial difficulties and place them under the protection of the court. The urgency for the new legislation was created by the imminent financial collapse of Goodman International — the largest meat-processing organisation in Europe. The group accounted for about 3% of Ireland's GNP. Beef processing was approaching its peak season with implications for employment and supplier-farmers. Thirty-three Irish and foreign banks, almost all of whom were unsecured, were owed over £500 million. Peter Fitzpatrick was appointed the first Irish examiner by the High Court, and a restructuring of the group's debt was agreed with the banks, allied to board and management changes. Subsequently the banks suffered almost £400 million in bad debt write-offs.

In January 1994, a striking confrontation erupted between the Kentz Corporation and its bankers, which ended up in the High Court with the former seeking the appointment of an examiner and the latter a receiver. The Kentz collapse and restructuring under an examiner resulted in heavy write-offs for the banks as well as for suppliers and the taxation authorities.

Each of these events had public concern consequences. There were losses of employment, the opportunity costs of further business development (GPA had been instrumental in setting up Shannon Aerospace), losses of taxation, and supplier and bank bad debts. In GPA the primary losers were its investors. Indeed, the enigma is how $3 billion in supposed market value could evaporate in months. The investment write-off of over £100 million had a dramatic impact on the balance sheet and capital needs of Aer Lingus.

The liquidation of the newspaper subsidiaries of the Irish Press group in the autumn of 1995, and the near death of Waterford Wedgwood a few years earlier, were lengthy and painful affairs. They followed years of financial losses, industrial strife and a weakening market position. The crisis in P. J. Carroll, provoked by loss-making diversifications and a progressive loss of market share in its core business over some years, was of a different pattern. Similarly, the decline of Irish Shipping was evident for some years in advance of its liquidation in 1984.

Perhaps we could describe the apparently sudden collapses of GPA, Goodman International and Kentz as 'corporate coronaries'. The metaphor of 'corporate cancer' might more suitably capture the more prolonged illnesses of Irish Press, Waterford Wedgwood, P. J. Carroll and Irish Shipping. Coronaries and cancer can prove fatal, but if they are detected in time, corrective treatment and some luck can lead to recovery.

External events are often blamed for a crisis, but there may have been decisions, processes and lifestyles which were the true internal cause. In most of the cases the symptoms of deteriorating corporate fitness were not recognised and preventative measures were never considered. In biological terms, some plants must die to create space and opportunities for new species to blossom. It is similar with business organisations. New entrepreneurial firms and innovations have replaced older ones to satisfy market needs. Biological and life-cycle analogies are attractive in explaining aspects of an organisation's development and death. An ecological framework also helps explain the phenomenon from an 'overcrowding' perspective.

In theory, a difficult environment might be thought to be the primary reason for decline. In practice, the evidence suggests that distressed organisations suffer from self-inflicted injuries which lead to differing degrees of infection depending on the company's internal health and the state of the external environment. The concept of 'organisational disease' informs a pathological examination of the causes of crisis. We might view organisations as experiencing processes and changes in their fitness and health due to a simple cause or set of causes which in turn can yield a series of observable consequences.

All man-made organisations are subject to extinction sooner or later. We know that the majority of business start-ups collapse within three years. The progression from birth, infancy and childhood to adolescence and maturity implies that an organisation has generated a series of learning experiences, resources and linkages which enable it to continue. Young and adolescent organisations are, generally, very much an extension of the founder's personality. This sets the culture, direction, activity, resources and risk profile of the organisation. The range of management, customer, process and financial problems which threaten survival in the formative years have been described as the 'liabilities of newness'.[12] Having reached adolescence, the organisation has demonstrated a series of product and market competencies and has established some niche in its industry. Generally, at this stage, the firm is less prone to failure because it remains adaptable. Yet in the 1980s and 1990s, many successful adolescent organisations collapsed in Ireland. What are the fatal flaws in some adolescent entrepreneurial firms which propel them into decisions and actions that lead to self-destruction? Are there also 'liabilities of adolescence'?

There are exceptions to the biological, life-cycle and ecological theories. Many Irish firms have survived successfully for over a century. Examples from the brewing sector are Guinness in Dublin, Smithwick's in Kilkenny and both Beamish & Crawford and Murphy's in Cork; though the last three firms were acquired, they continued activity in contrast to other smaller breweries in Ireland. In the newspaper industry, the Irish Independent, the Irish Times and the Cork Examiner have had long lives in contrast to the Irish Press group. Why is it that some companies in a sector continue to cope and adapt to a changing environment while others fall by the wayside? After all, the legal form of the limited company provides an institutionalised framework for an indefinite life, once there is a will, and resources are sufficient.

Organisational decline, distress, failure and crisis

Clearly some state of decline must occur if a firm falls into financial distress or failure. According to Weitzel and Jonsson, organisations enter the state of decline 'when they fail to anticipate, recognise, avoid, neutralise, or adapt to external or internal pressures that threaten the organisation's long-term survival'.[13] Some definitions of organisational failure and distress provide a starting-point to the objectives and themes of this study. Concepts of failure can be viewed from economic, managerial, financial and legal perspectives.[14]

Economic failure occurs when the organisation is unable to earn sufficient profits to enable it to service its capital structure with an appropriate market rate of return. Examples include the reduction or cessation of dividend or a financial reorganisation with bankers on the payment of principal or interest. Firms can limp along in a twilight zone between possible decline and recovery. They may just have sufficient resources to pay their creditors for current operations and perhaps service bank interest. However, there can be insufficient earnings to pay dividends or to plough funds back into a competitive investment renewal. Consequently, when compared with their competitors, the value of their equity shares would be low (often below book value), leaving them vulnerable to a takeover.

Managerial failure reflects the top management and board of directors' poor performance, when benchmarked against others in the same industry. It can follow faulty design or implementation of strategy and/or inefficient operations from product, market and competitive position perspectives. Signals are a loss of market share, lower profit margins and a lower price/earnings ratio in relation to industry benchmarks. Profits may have reached a plateau or be declining. Management often attribute the slack performance to a variety of external causes.[15]

Financial failure or distress occurs when the firm is unable to meet its cash flow obligations to its creditors, bankers or other debt securities. If distress is due to an ill-judged expansion or an unfortunate new investment project, but the company has a profitable core business with good future prospects, then a financial, managerial and business reorganisation, and perhaps an infusion of new equity and senior management personnel, could restore its fortunes. On the other hand, if the firm has a pattern of decline and losses for some years and a heavy level of debt and weak liquidity, then, depending on the industry situation, the failure may represent a more permanent condition in terms of expected future cash flows and financial obligations. Therefore, the terms distress and failure can be associated both with temporary and with more long-term profitability performance and financial conditions.

Financial distress or failure will generally lead to financial restructuring or the official disposal of assets through the appointment of a receiver by a bank on foot of security, or the appointment of a liquidator by the shareholders, creditors or the court. The terms insolvency and bankruptcy are also used. Technically, corporate insolvency or bankruptcy occurs when the firm is unable to meet its financial obligations as they fall due for payment. A deficit between assets and liabilities suggests insolvency but if the firm can demonstrate that future cash flows will meet its obligations and will not result in any further erosion of its asset values then it would be difficult to deem it insolvent.

Legal failure occurs when a receiver or liquidator is appointed, or when an examiner is appointed by the courts to advise on the prospects for a financial restructuring and continuance of operations.

When the major goals of the organisation are threatened and its survival is in jeopardy, the firm is said to be in a crisis. It restricts the time available for response because of the element of surprise. A crisis induces high levels of stress, resulting in inefficient behaviour and decision-making as management moves from motivation to anxiety. Researchers have noted the common outcome of 'the paranoid reaction characteristic of crisis behaviour'.[16]

The foregoing suggests a continuum starting with management decline and failure, moving on to economic failure, then financial distress, crisis and, finally, legal failure.

Rates of failure and age of failed companies

In 1993, according to Dun & Bradstreet, 670 limited companies in Ireland went into liquidation.[17] There were 110 receiverships.[18] This was the largest number of corporate failures since 1980. Receiverships are of concern because they reflect a scale of assets which makes it worthwhile for banks to act on foot of their security. This high level of corporate failure occurred despite an increase in GDP and exports, and low inflation of only 3%. Many were small new businesses in which, Dun & Bradstreet suggested, 'many of the entrepreneurs did not have the full range of skills to run a business successfully'.[19] Many were adolescent and mature companies which had established a track record and had been profitable for some years before their collapse — but made mistakes.

The summary of company liquidations to 1994, as shown in Table 1.1, is a tombstone statistic which measures a toll on economic resources. There was a consistent increase throughout the period 1980 to 1993. In the early 1980s the number of insolvency liquidations was less than half the 1990s levels. The number of failures in relation to annual company births — there were 15,503 new registrations in 1994 — may seem small. However, this statistic has to be treated with caution because of the inclusion of a large number of specialist companies formed for investment and taxation planning purposes. Also, a sizeable number of limited companies have been struck off the register by the Registrar of Companies in various years — 14,338 in 1989 alone.[20]

Table 1.1:	Company liquidations in Ireland
1990	525
1991	630
1992	619
1993	670
1994	634

Source: Dun & Bradstreet, Dublin.

There is a consistent body of data which confirms, not unexpectedly, that a much greater proportion of younger companies than older companies fail. Based on an analysis of 1993 Irish data, Dun & Bradstreet[21] issued the findings on the age of failing firms which are summarised in Table 1.2. In the USA, studies indicate broadly similar age patterns for failures. The proportion of firms failing within five years of birth ranged from 53% to 60%. Another 20% of the original births failed to survive beyond eight years. Thereafter the failure rate fell appreciably. Thus, about 75% of start-ups collapsed within eight years, and 82% within ten years.[22] Clearly there is a short time space between the birth and death of most young organisations.

Table 1.2: Age pattern of failing firms

Age (years)	% of firms failing	Cumulative position (%)
0–3	31	31
4–5	23	54
6–10	24	78
10+	22	100

Source: Dun & Bradstreet, Dublin.

A 1980 study by Colbert and McCarthy showed that between 1950 and 1979 the number of companies listed on the Irish Stock Exchange fell from 136 to 92.[23] These raw statistics mask the scale of movement, with 98 new entrants and 142 departures. Over 50% of the decline occurred during the 1970s, mainly in traditional industries such as clothing and textiles, food and drink, and building services. Takeovers, mergers, insolvency or financial difficulties accounted for their departure. Unfortunately, Colbert and McCarthy's predictions of the continuing decline of listed companies on the Dublin Stock Exchange proved accurate. Fitzgibbon, analysing the period 1973–93, found that fifty-five of the top seventy-five industrial companies on the stockmarket had lost their listing through receivership, liquidation or takeover.[24] He attributed this corporate disappearance to 'bad management'. Each of these organisations was large enough to be quoted on the Dublin Stock Exchange. Each had survived the start-up stage and so the probability of financial failure or distress should have been low.

Suggesting that size was no protection, the ten largest organisations listed on the Dublin Stock Exchange at the end of 1983 mirrored a similar experience. During the ensuing decade five encountered some form of financial crisis, while others were taken over. The outcome was that, by the mid-1990s, only four — Jefferson Smurfit, CRH, Independent Newspapers and Waterford Wedgwood — remained in the top group (with Waterford recovering from major financial problems and reorganisation). Details are shown in Table 1.3.

Even in the financial sector, the two largest organisations, Allied Irish Banks and Bank of Ireland, suffered self-inflicted setbacks through unsuccessful acquisitions (Insurance Corporation of Ireland and New Hampshire Bank, respectively). These involved a heavy cost in provisions, losses and write-offs, and had an adverse impact on their shareholders' funds and share price.

Table 1.3: Ten largest industrial organisations on the Dublin Stock Exchange in 1983 and their subsequent experience

Company	Outcome
1. Jefferson Smurfit Group	Progress
2. Cement Roadstone Holdings	Progress
3. Carroll Industries	Decline and acquired
4. Waterford Glass	Decline and recovery
5. R. & H. Hall	Decline and acquired
6. Irish Distillers	Acquired
7. Brooks Watson Group	Acquired
8. James Crean	Decline
9. Abbey	Decline and recovery
10. Independent Newspapers	Progress

Source: *Irish Times*, 29 December 1983; size is measured by turnover. Updated by author.

Economic context and corporate performance

The decade to 1983 was a difficult economic period. Ireland's entry into the European Community in 1973 brought turbulence to some sectors and was beneficial for others. The recession from 1974 was brought on by the oil embargo by Arab nations combined with the overheating of many economies in the early 1970s; this resulted in high inflation and high interest rates. Despite some economic recovery from 1977, high inflation and high interest rates continued and culminated in the 1980–83 recession. Many 'household names' such as Boland's Bakery, Arklow Pottery, Sunbeam Wolsey and Dubtex Clothing disappeared due to inefficiencies built up over decades of trade protection, particularly in the textiles and clothing sector. Inflation, interest rates and recessions played a secondary part.

Every era seems to throw up its fashion in company activity which attracts investor interest. The wave of 'shell' companies in the 1970s, which copied the 'conglomerate' fashions of the late 1960s and early 1970s in the USA and UK,[25] proved to be a managerial pipedream in Ireland. The majority of these companies were small or near dormant firms with a Stock Exchange quotation which were cheaply acquired and recapitalised (often with excessive debt) so that their quoted shares could be used as 'paper' for takeovers. The business concept was that modern management practices and financial engineering (i.e. bootstrapping earnings per share through leverage and low price/earnings takeovers[26]) could be implemented over a diversified range of technologies, products and markets under the one parent company.

Most of these newly created groups did not have the management depth or expertise to cope with the complexity they created. Generally, they were directed from a short-term financier perspective. Of the ten groups which emerged at the time, six failed, two were acquired and, by the mid-1990s, only two — Fitzwilton and James Crean — remained, though with indifferent performances for shareholders. Among the failures were Barrow Milling,[27] Brittain Group and TMG Group. Fitzwilton's exploits in the 1970s are cited by Fitzgibbon.[28] It made a bewildering series of acquisitions in textiles, fertilisers, newspapers, building materials, property, bottling, insurance and retailing. Within three years Fitzwilton was in financial crisis through overexpansion and excessive bank borrowing. Following boardroom changes and a series of asset disposals, its financial position was restored.[29] In contrast, the long-established textile and clothing industries were unable to adapt to changing markets and technology. Each was a different profile of 'bad management'.

The two largest insurance companies in their sectors, PMPA and the Insurance Corporation of Ireland, needed to be rescued in 1984 and 1985. There were costs to taxpayers of over £100 million. Two minor merchant banks/finance houses also collapsed. These events are surprising in view of the regulatory responsibilities of a government department and the Central Bank.

If the 'vogue' companies of the 1970s were the 'shell' operations, then their successors in the 1980s were the leasing groups such as GPA, Cambridge, Yeoman and Woodchester. It is remarkable how badly the first three of these companies fared in economic returns. All three experienced business failure; GPA and Yeoman survived through bank support and restructuring but Cambridge went into receivership. Only Woodchester escaped unscathed.

These organisations may represent a biased sample because most were quoted on the Stock Exchange. There were also hundreds of large private companies which collapsed or were acquired, and many multinational subsidiaries were closed. The decline of many Irish firms resulted in reduced employment and regional setbacks. The effect of joining the European Community was no longer an excuse by the mid-1980s. Kennedy, Giblin and McHugh noted that there were 12% fewer people employed in the 1980s than in the 1920s.[30] They concluded that Ireland's rate of economic progress was 'mediocre' and, except for Britain, below that of the rest of Europe. Ireland's indigenous industry was viewed as still weak with specific defects in marketing. Mjøset discussed in some considerable detail the historical, economic policy, sociological and cultural reasons for Ireland's high unemployment and its poor economic performance in comparison with a number of other small countries.[31] A comparison with Denmark illustrated many Irish defects and policy mistakes. A 1994 study of fast-growth small firms operating in Ireland, by Kinsella and others, highlighted management areas in need of strengthening.[32] The authors listed accounting systems, planning and control against objectives, quite apart from the expected problems of financing and management capability.

A small open economy with high unemployment, high state borrowings and relatively high levels of taxation cannot afford a high level of corporate failure. Corporate collapse represents a loss of economic and social resources. In a larger economy, a substitute firm would probably be established within the region. Because it has an exceptionally open economy, failure in Ireland has a higher economic and social cost than in most other European Union countries or in North America. The rate of failure and the poor performance of indigenous firms raise questions about the education, training, effectiveness and culture of Irish management.

Bad management and mismanagement

A 1996 survey of insolvency practitioners in Ireland indicated that in 62% of the cases of corporate insolvency, internal management failure was the cause of collapse.[33] Market factors primarily accounted for the remaining 38% of cases. As Table 1.4 shows, Altman found that two leading bankruptcy statistics publishers, Dun & Bradstreet in the USA and Tokyo Shoko Research in Japan, listed quite different categories of causes.[34] We could deduce from this that managerial incompetence and inexperience result in weak sales. If an organisation cannot achieve a certain level of sales in relation to its investments, capital and overheads, it will be uneconomic. But this explanation does not fit well with the characteristics of fast-growing entrepreneurial firms. It is more relevant to a young organisation or a mature firm which is not adapting to market demand and conditions. These 'causes' are too vague. A more detailed understanding of what is meant by 'managerial incompetence' or 'unbalanced experience' is required if we are to understand the reasons for business failure, link them to identifiable behaviours in organisations and take preventative action. We need to be able to detect the mismanagement patterns in advance, before valuable resources and jobs are lost.

In 1987 Aileen O'Toole, a leading Irish business journalist, discussed the business histories and people behind ten small and large Irish organisations, which she described as 'the pacesetters'.[35] All were viewed as extremely progressive in their sectors and some were designated 'world class'. Within six

Table 1.4: Causes of business failure in the USA and Japan

Cause	% of failures
USA	
Managerial incompetence	47
Lack of managerial experience	27
Unbalanced experience	18
Neglect, fraud and unknown	8
	100
Japan	
Slowdown of sales	41
Irresponsible management	23
Directly — other bankruptcies	12
Indirectly — other bankruptcies	8
Undercapitalisation	6
Bad debts	4
Excessive equipment investments	3
Other	3
	100

Source: Edward I. Altman, 'The Success of Business Failure Prediction Models: An International Survey', *Journal of Banking and Finance 8* (1984), p. 175.

years, the three largest firms had experienced severe financial difficulties. Mahon & McPhillips of Kilkenny, one of the country's largest civil engineering and contracting firms, went into receivership in 1990; GPA underwent a restructuring in 1993; and M. F. Kent (by then Kentz Corporation) of Clonmel, the country's largest electrical, mechanical and instrumentation engineering contractor, collapsed in January 1994. The lessons are that it takes a balanced and skilful management to survive a recession.

Peters and Waterman of the USA suggested some principles of progressive management practice based on a survey of twenty companies in the early 1980s.[36] Each had been selected because of its 'success' characteristics. Within a few years many firms in the sample had encountered problems and some of these 'best practices' had lost their credibility. This points to the fragility of business health and success.

Corporate collapse is not unique to Irish organisations

There were a number of spectacular collapses or cases of financial distress in the 1980s and 1990s in the UK, Continental Europe, North America and

Australia.³⁷ Examples in Britain were Polly Peck International, British and Commonwealth, Brent Walker, Colorall, Heron and the Queen's Moat House which was the second largest hotel group. The two largest advertising agencies in Britain, Saatchi & Saatchi and WPP, underwent financial restructuring and reorganisation.

The collapse of the Bank of Credit and Commercial International (BCCI) in 1992 and the long-established blue-blood Barings Bank in 1995 demonstrated that important elements of the financial system were not immune to mismanagement. Bower argued, from the evidence in the Maxwell group of companies' misuse of pension funds, that there were many internal and external corporate regulatory weaknesses involving professional firms and financial institutional practices.³⁸

UK Department of Trade and Industry investigations were instituted in a number of these cases because of public concern regarding their governance and management and the reliability of financial information provided. The inspector's report on Atlantic Computers plc, a major subsidiary of British and Commonwealth, indicated that poor management by a domineering chief executive, who wished to achieve growth at almost any price, allied to inappropriate accounting policies and weak auditing, contributed to the company's collapse.³⁹ Interestingly, the Accounting Standards Board in London has since issued new financial reporting standards which tighten up lease accounting.

The financial problems of Euro Disney and Credit Lyonnais in France, the Metallgesellschaft industrial group and the Schneider property empire in Germany, and the Ferruzzi-Montedison industrial group in Italy have been extensively publicised. Large organisations in Canada that encountered problems include Dome Petroleum, Massey-Ferguson and, in 1992, Olympia & York. A secretive private company controlled by the Reichmann brothers of Toronto, Olympia & York grew in twenty-five years, with many daring and innovative developments, to become the world's largest property developer. Its liquidity problems, mainly brought on by the enormous Canary Wharf project in London, seemed to come as a shock to many capital markets on 15 May 1992. Its bankers were owed $12 billion. The collapse had a negative impact on stockmarket prices in the USA, UK and Canada, and on banking and property company shares.⁴⁰

The rescue of Continental Illinois Bank, the eighth largest bank in the USA, by the Federal Deposit Insurance Company (FDIC) in 1984 was the largest ever support package mounted in the USA. The FDIC took over

$3.5 billion in non-performing debt. This proved to be a prelude to the scandals of the 'savings and loan crisis' during which several savings banks failed, with losses to depositors and others. The bailout of many of these institutions by the FDIC was estimated to have cost the US taxpayer up to $100 billion. Apart from reports of unscrupulous directors and management, there were allegations by the FDIC of misleading financial statements and negligent auditing.[41] It has filed over forty lawsuits against public accounting firms for damages as high as $560 million. Already, some 'Big 6' firms have made financial settlements.[42]

Australia has produced a number of well-publicised instances of collapse and distress associated with a dominant entrepreneurial personality. These include Rupert Murdoch of News Corporation, Alan Bond of Bond Corporation, Robert Holmes-à-Court of the Bell Group and John Elliott of Elders. All energetically built up a large domestic business, initially by internal marketing-led growth, and later by acquisitions funded by bank loans. Finally, they went international with an acquisitions and debt driven strategy. Many of these corporate excesses have been associated with poor internal governance, external regulatory weaknesses, and questionable accounting and auditing. Bond Corporation was a particular example of dubious accounting policies, optimistic profits and asset valuations, and off balance sheet financing.[43]

Family firms have their own unique ownership and organisational characteristics which can be central to their survival in the second and third generations of the family involvement. We have only to read the histories and biographies of leading family organisations such as Ford or IBM to learn of the nature of family involvement, and their very real and deep sense of obligation, honour and responsibility to employees and others to continue the family business tradition and name. However, intrigues and conflicts can also occur; many treat the business as a personal fiefdom, and it is difficult for the professional outsider-manager to resist family pressures.

The continuing grip of family members on power in an organisation and the belief in their right to control its affairs and future destiny should not be underestimated. Chandler pointed to many examples of the 'birthright' and 'identity' syndrome such as Du Pont and Ford in the USA.[44] The reaction of the young Du Pont cousins when they heard that their elderly uncles proposed selling the firm to its friendly competitor in 1902 is illustrative. Eugene du Pont had died unexpectedly, and no senior family member seemed to have the experience to take over:

Alfred du Pont disagreed. Young and energetic he was shocked at the thought of selling the company, his 'birthright', to outsiders. If he could get the support of his cousin Coleman du Pont, once his roommate at the Massachusetts Institute of Technology, he would buy it himself. Coleman immediately gave Alfred his backing, but he insisted that they must get Pierre, another cousin, to 'handle the finances'. A long-distance telephone call brought Pierre's acceptance.[45]

Bankers, stockbroker analysts and accounting

Money is the lifeblood of business and companies, and is often secured from banks. Bankers make loan decisions on criteria which usually include the character and competence of the people involved, the industry, the stage in the business cycle and the sales prospects of the firm. Above all, in looking to the return of its money, a bank will assess the financial gearing, liquidity and servicing ability of the company. A careful analysis of past financial statements, cash flows and ratios, and a sceptical view of future projections, also help. Despite the foregoing, could we say that many banks tend to lend excessively to fast-growing, larger, undercapitalised organisations? The Irish banks, like their counterparts in Britain and the USA, incurred heavy bad debt write-offs in the 1990s.[46] Goodman International, GPA and Xtra-vision had no difficulty obtaining large levels of bank facilities in relation to their size.

The quality of the accounting figures helps the review of financial performance and the evaluation of the loan risk by the bank. If the accounting concept of 'prudence' is supposed to be fundamental to the preparation of financial statements, then optimistic accounting might be viewed as a symptom or a cause of financial distress. Misleading feedback and the nourishing of managerial 'self-delusion' suggest that optimistic accounting is flawed information. It is a cause of crisis because it contributes to inefficient decision-making.

This raises the matter and validity of the principal–agent relationship of the shareholder and the manager, and the position of debt. The board and the auditor are supposed to be monitoring mechanisms under this model, so that management, as the agent, meets objectives. If internal governance and accounting information breaks down, then the efficiency of the firm and its potential for self-sustaining viability weaken.

Some stockbroker analysts in Dublin and London often seem to be just as inefficient as bankers in analysing financial statements and forming expectations of future prospects. The claims by Terry Smith about some stockbroking houses' and analysts' practices and customer constraints on their objectivity are of concern.[47] They tend to 'overshoot' in their forecasts of the earnings growth, financial stability and management capacity of fast-growing organisations — whereas many drown in a sea of bank debt. Corporate finance models expect adolescent organisations to have investment funding shortfalls, whereas mature organisations are expected to generate cash surpluses.[48] Mature organisations may be less dependent on bank finance, but they may have become rather stagnant from product and marketing perspectives.

The nature of this study

This book presents nine cases illustrating the interconnecting themes which contribute to financial crisis. The objective is to determine the causes of the crisis and to analyse patterns of mismanagement so that lessons can be derived to help recognise and anticipate problems. Avoidance and preventative measures could then be initiated, in order to minimise resource losses and adverse consequences for stakeholders and society. The framework distinguishes between two distinct groups — 'adolescent' fast-growing organisations and 'mature' slower growth or declining organisations. It is proposed that though there are some common reasons for the crises in adolescent and mature organisations, we can differentiate between the two categories and mark out some alternative patterns and characteristics.

This empirical investigation is justified on the grounds that in other areas of life, such as air disasters, investigations endeavour to find the causes of problems and present lessons to improve our knowledge and future practices. In medicine, pathological analysis is an accepted element in understanding the causes and symptoms of illness, disease and death.

In the fields of organisation theory, corporate finance and accounting, researchers accept that no integrated theory of corporate failure currently exists; nor is there an acceptable conceptual framework of corporate decline which is fully amenable to empirical testing.[49] Present knowledge is inadequate in helping top management, directors, shareholders, bankers, analysts, regulators and academic researchers to identify strategies that may help to prevent or reverse decline and failure. This is partially explained by the fact that research and information access has not proved easy. Based on US experience, Weitzel and Jonsson commented:

> The empirical study of decline is much more difficult than the study of expansion. Leaders of expanding organisations welcome the chronicler of organisational events, while those in charge of

organisations suffering declining performance or liquidation usually have little time and no interest in working with administrative scientists; their concern is survival.[50]

The unfortunate concerns of stigma, shame and anger make directors and managers avoid further discussion of failure issues.

The findings of this study suggest that many adolescent and mature company failures could have been prevented and much of the financial, economic and social cost could have been greatly reduced. In most cases, symptoms of mismanagement were evident before the firm's collapse. The financial collapse of many indigenous Irish firms, due to mismanagement, has contributed to the country's economic and employment problems. It is the purpose of this exploratory study to trace the causes and nature of mismanagement or bad management. Understanding the reasons why organisations decline and collapse, and the nature of the management defects and mistakes, may help prevent the future loss of scarce organisational and societal resources.

The puzzle is that successful adolescent organisations, which had survived the difficult 'birth' and early 'youth' years to become leaders in their industry, often encounter a serious financial crisis. Their apparent success was confirmed by their ability to borrow substantial funds from banks. Some also obtained injections of equity funds through a quotation on the stockmarket. How could they collapse so suddenly when they appeared to be vibrant and growing? In contrast, mature firms seem to decline gradually without corrective action or become hyperactive in new activities or diversifications which often drain their resource base.

The cases presented are drawn from an investigation of eighteen Irish organisations. Several include benchmarking comparisons with competitors or equivalent organisations. A brief description of the methodology adopted and the research sample is shown in Appendix 1. Dealing with the subject of corporations in crisis, Smith noted that 'at such times truth is hard to come by. Guilt, confusion, and self justification conspire to conceal the facts, while the wide diversity of viewpoints stretches the writer on the rack of judgement.'[51] These difficulties were considered in the design and execution of the research methodology and the analysis of findings in this study. A summary of the financial crisis outcomes in the firms studied is shown in Appendix 2.

Chapter 2 summarises what has been written about company failure and its causes and symptoms. This provides an analytical framework for the empirical investigation. Chapter 3 presents the first of the adolescent entrepreneurial cases — Goodman International. Chapters 4, 5 and 6 examine Kentz Corporation, Xtra-vision and GPA. Chapter 7 initiates the second part of the study on the findings on mature companies. Guinness and P. J. Carroll are taken together as the first of the 'family' companies who experienced diversification problems and a decline in the primary product. Chapter 8 brings together cases on Irish Press and Waterford Wedgwood as they share issues of succession and industrial relations strife. Chapter 9 presents the findings on the causes of liquidation in a different form of mature company — Irish Shipping, a state-sponsored body. Finally, Chapter 10 offers a synthesis of the dominant issues to emerge. It highlights common and differing causes, patterns and symptoms of financial distress and failure; what could be done to prevent such crisis; and the implications for corporate governance, management, financial control, financial reporting and the external regulatory system.

Chapter 2

Causes of Corporate Financial Distress and Failure

I found a main reason for failure of a company was lack of communication on the part of directors sideways among themselves, downwards and upwards to and from their staff. There was a lack of awareness about life in general, of how things and people operate. They so often seemed to live in a closed-circuit world of their own. They let products get out of date without a thought of replacing them. They so often failed to see, until it was too late, that they could not make a profit if the volume of sales fell. Over-trading with inadequate profits and cash was as common a cause as any. Sheer incompetence at board level was the basis of almost every failure. Luckily it was rare.

Sir Kenneth Cork[1]

Introduction

Organisations fail because they run out of money: they are unable to pay their bills as they fall due and a crisis ensues. But why and how do firms 'suddenly' appear to encounter a cash shortage? It is understandable in young firms, where the conflicts between undercapitalisation, growth, profitability, cash flow and poor accounting systems can, not unexpectedly, lead to crises. Adolescent and mature firms have been through a learning curve in coping with previous business setbacks. They develop a set of routines, systems, resources and networks which makes a serious financial crisis less likely. After all, after a life-span of eight years or so, the probabilities of collapse are low. Also, mature firms' growth and financing needs should be less demanding.

The firm can be visualised as a reservoir of liquid assets, which is supplied by inflows and drained by outflows.[2] The reservoir operates as a buffer against variations in the flows. If the reservoir runs dry, a financial crisis occurs and the firm could hover on the brink of technical insolvency. Shortages of money in firms, like water for living organisms, can be life threatening. In a firm, the equilibrium dynamics rest on six elements: the size of the reservoir buffer itself; the size of the liquidity inflows from operational activity; the size of the liquidity outflows from operational activity; the variability of these inflows and outflows; liquidity outflows through investments; and the size of bank debt and other financial commitments which would be a potential drain on the reservoir. Effective management of these causal elements of demand and supply of the reservoir flows and its level is essential if life-threatening scarcity is to be avoided.

The moral of this metaphor is that the first law of business is the availability of cash to facilitate operations. The more difficult issue is to determine what causes a disequilibrium in cash flows, resulting in the reservoir running dry. In business it shows up as a shortage of working capital, with insufficient cash to pay wages or suppliers. At one end of the spectrum of causes, there would be the steady drain of trading losses. Then there would be the impact of insufficient sales to convert stock into liquidity and pay for overheads. At another point in the continuum, scarce cash resources could have been tied up in capital expenditures. Cash shortages are symptoms of fundamental management problems, because they represent the impact of earlier management decisions and actions — which can be described as 'mismanagement'. Rarely is the external environment the only cause.

Analytical perspectives

Not only is there an absence of an integrated theory of organisational failure, but even the elements of a potential theory are debatable,[3] as is an acceptable conceptual framework due to the paucity of empirical studies.[4] Thus the questions of cause and effect remain unclear, despite the development of recent models. Researchers also accept that differing models for small and large firms may be more worthwhile.[5]

To achieve a balance, this study adopts two analytical frameworks: a management and organisational viewpoint, and an accounting and finance perspective. A firm is a system of interconnected elements. It would be myopic to look at the various aspects in isolation. Taking the firm as a bundle of elements, the accounting and finance perspective focuses on aspects such as information systems, valuation, level and volatility of returns, cash flow, asset structure, capital, debt and liquidity. Appraisals of market and book values, changes in market price, profit margins, various ratios, accounting policies, notes in the financial statements and auditors' reports — all provide clues to financial health and the propensity for financial distress.

The methodology and language are quite different in the organisation literature. Leadership, vision, strategy, products, markets, environment, structure, culture, power, politics, decision processes, information cognition and change, together with entrepreneurs and managers, are all associated with this framework. The accounting representation of the economic performance of the firm is an outcome of these internal and external organisational and product/market interactions. To a narrow extent this is true, but there are more complex and subtly symbiotic connections and influences between the two frameworks.

From both behavioural and feedback perspectives, there is the role of accounting information on strategy confirmation, corrective actions, power distribution and the commitment of resources. Moreover, finance is a critical resource which links to ownership and power. The capital structure decision also intersects with accounting information in risk and default analysis, decision-making and compliance with covenants. Consequently, financing decisions can have an unexpected ascendancy over other elements if they are inefficient, or if the organisational economic performance does not meet the cost of capital. Crossing both the accounting and organisation perspectives is the 'systems' model of an organisation — particularly the cybernetic focus which takes information and its scanning and perception as a prime determinant of goals, actions and control of behaviour.

All the foregoing takes the unit of analysis as the individual organisation, primarily from an internal perspective. If the frame of reference is widened to an industry from an ecological perspective, then the unit of analysis widens to populations of organisations.[6] The environment may be harsh or favourable for these populations. A Darwinian model suggests that some organisations will survive, others will die to make room for new ones; there will also be contractions in industry demand and change. Organisations will face a form of 'natural selection' by external selection agents — banks, customers, suppliers, government agencies and acquirers. Thus selection, through retention, rejection and the creation of new enterprises, will transform the composition and nature of whole populations in a sector.

Reasons for collapse: a management perspective

New theoretical frameworks have proposed more precise linkages between cause and effect. Much of the focus has been on mature organisations, but some work has also emerged on the adolescent crisis.[7]

Smith had no doubt that the ultimate crisis was long in the making and was the result of procrastination and an unwillingness to face up to mistakes or to write off failures.[8] There was rarely one single cause, but usually a central one with links to a series of others. Apart from the chief executive, he singled out the board for blame. Ross and Kami extended the analysis, particularly for large firms.[9] Both they and Smith pointed to 'one man rule', weak management and cost controls, and resistance to change. Ross and

Kami added an inactive board, an absence of unified strategy and communication, inadequate organisation structure, lack of management depth, overlooking the customer, accounting manipulations and computer information breakdowns. They argued that companies fooled themselves with accounting manipulations in their financial statements, even when they knew they were covering up on poor management performance. Such practices tended to introduce a climate of manipulation generally.

Perhaps the most quoted work on corporate collapse is that of Argenti.[10] He noted a dearth of management-derived models of corporate failure up to the 1970s, which he attributed to academics and management specialists being 'far too busy studying the much happier subject of success and growth'. He was struck by the many conflicting opinions on reasons for failure among authors, bankers and accountants. He acknowledged that ratio prediction models have a use, but argued that companies in financial distress will delay the issuance of financial statements and that creative accounting will tend to undermine the relevance of the ratios. Argenti trenchantly asserted that chief executives 'almost without exception . . . will resort to any device to hide their company's true position'.[11]

Creative accounting is one of the devices used. Of concern is that the concealment can approach the point of fraud. Argenti refined his earlier work to produce an 'A score' model of forecasting financial failure in 1983. This model is based on non-financial signs of failure. It brought together his designation of the elements of 'bad management' with a subjective interpretation. When taken together with financial statements, ratios, a visit to the firm, meeting its directors and examining its products, he claimed the model provided definite signals — with tests suggesting a misclassification rate of only 5%. The underlying proposition was that, 'as a general rule, most companies fail for broadly similar reasons and in a broadly similar manner'.[12] The sequence often takes at least five years, and falls into three stages. First, certain specific defects occur in management. Second, because of these inherent defects management makes mistakes which lead to failure. Third, financial and non-financial signs and symptoms of failure begin to appear. His model is set out in Table 2.1. The higher the number of marks awarded, the higher the probability of failure. A mark of 25 or over should be a cause for concern. The model's research evidence suggests that many companies which are at risk have a score between 35 and 70 — an unusually wide zone of risk. Argenti admitted that smaller companies, because of their risk characteristics, often have a high score; this would recommend a further examination before jumping to conclusions. Small

Table 2.1: Argenti's 'A score' failure prediction model

	Weighting score	Total
Defects		
Autocrat	8	
Chairman and chief executive	4	
Passive board	2	
Unbalanced skills	2	
Weak finance director	2	
Poor management depth	1	
No budgetary control	3	
No cash flow plans	3	
No costing system	3	
Poor response to change	15	
Total for defects		43
Mistakes		
High leverage	15	
Overtrading	15	
Big project	15	
Total for mistakes		45
Symptoms		
Financial signs	4	
Creative accounting	4	
Non-financial signs	3	
Terminal signs	1	
Total for symptoms		12
Total overall		100

Source: John Argenti, 'Predicting Corporate Failure', *Accountants' Digest* No. 138, London: ICAEW Summer 1983.

firms tend to be riskier than larger firms but they may also be more dynamic and responsive to change.

What is striking about Argenti's predictive model is that four elements (poor response to change, high leverage, overtrading and a big project), reflecting one defect and three mistakes, account for 15 marks each. Weak financial control and its consequences are particularly penalised. Having an autocratic chief executive who also holds the dual roles of chairman and chief executive adds an extra 12 points. It is not difficult to reach a danger zone with just three of these constituents. Though not empirically tested, much of Argenti's work remains an important breakthrough, particularly his framework of defects, mistakes and symptoms.[13] His differentiation of failure trajectories, in which he suggested three patterns of decline, and his suggestion that some distressed firms do not necessarily fail after decline, have been acknowledged by US researchers.[14]

Writing from a management perspective on strategies for recovery and growth in mature firms, McKiernan suggested that 'internal' causes — categorised into management defects, errors of omission and errors of commission — accounted for 67% of the reasons for decline.[15] A summary is shown in Table 2.2. Slatter reviewed collapse from a corporate 'turnaround' perspective and pinpointed many reasons similar to Argenti.[16] He emphasised marketing, competitiveness, acquisitions diversification, commodity prices and interest rates. Slatter also investigated small high-technology firms and found more specialist causes.[17] These included price competition, and manufacturing and operating problems — both of which reflect the relative youth of the firm. Technology, change in the industry and the fact that a smaller firm would not have a dominant market share also contributed. The dependence of these small firms on large contracts, and their impact if lost, were also identified as factors.

Table 2.2: McKiernan's analysis of reasons for relative decline

Internal
1. *Management defects:* autocratic leaders, poor succession programmes, lack of balance in top teams (e.g. too many engineers), lack of middle management depth, lack of participative boards
2. *Management errors of omission:* lack of budgetary and cost controls, price not reflective of cost base, failure to respond to market changes — especially competitive ones
3. *Management errors of commission:* overexpansion of products, facilities and personnel beyond firm's resources

External
1. Decline in government demand or change in regulations
2. Increased foreign competition
3. Economic variables, e.g. inflation, interest rates
4. Changes in product technology
5. Changes in demographic/social variables

Source: Peter McKiernan, *Strategies of Growth: Maturity, Recovery and Internationalisation*, London: Routledge 1992, p. 73.

Perhaps Sir Lewis Robertson, then a 69-year-old Scottish company doctor, was in a special position to present a definitive view of the causes of corporate failure.[18] Drawing on his wide experience, he stated in 1991 that the fundamental cause was 'feeble management'.[19] He put financial control and management accounting systems at the top of his list. They were either too weak, overdetailed or inadequate — in which case they were discredited and the board was paying no attention to them. The character of the finance director was important if a strong stance was to be taken against corner-cutting or too much optimism. This defect can be linked to the multiple banking relationship syndrome (implying an excessive reliance on borrowings) and the careless acceptance of bank covenants (such as interest cover), which leave the company vulnerable to the least accommodating bank in a situation where no strong relationship history or commitment has existed. The fact that so many banks provided such levels of credit often meant that they made the facility available in good times in the economic cycle without making an in-depth examination of the company and the nature of other borrowings made against the same cash flow and security.

The need to keep up with changes in customer demands and technology was critical. Robertson noted that it was very hard to win customers back once they had moved to a new supplier. Often the original management team was unable to grow in competence to cope with a much larger organisation or conglomerate business of separate operations. He held that the composition and balance of the board were far more important than he himself had realised when he was a young chief executive. This principle of balance also applied to the separation of the positions of chairman and chief executive. The issue of internal problems arising out of family politics or the difficulty of achieving transition from family to professional management was something which arose in four of his seven rescues. He was extremely critical of larger institutional shareholders, concluding that they 'bear a responsibility which they too often do not bestir themselves to discharge'. Robertson felt shareholders should be more interventionist.

Taking the regularity of business cycles as a framework in examining management decisions, strategy and timing, Houston argued that there is a business downturn approximately every seven years.[20] After a five- to six-year period of growth, there is a surge in inflation and interest rates, following an excess of credit. Recessions occur close to the time that short-term interest rates exceed long-term rates. Different investment strategies are more efficient at each of the three periods in the cycle. Consequently, if a firm gets the timing wrong and invests — and borrows — heavily in the final period of the cycle, it is taking a very high risk. If its balance sheet is weak, then it is very vulnerable.

Some accounting views

Like Argenti, this writer found experienced accountants and bankers offering a variety of causes of failure.[21] The opinions of practising experts are largely formed by their discipline and experience. This can lead to biases. Accountants tended to emphasise bad management and poor planning, a reliance on short-term debt, weak financial controls and cost/profitability analysis, and an absence of cash flow planning. They believed that accounting systems and records were often inadequate and information was delayed. Examples of bad management cited by accountants included ineffective marketing, lack of product development, a feeble approach to cost control and a high cost structure, weakening productivity, and an inability or unwillingness to face up to industrial relations and trade union bargaining problems where work practices and costs had eroded competitiveness. They felt that tough decisions tended to be avoided until it was too late, and that an unwarranted optimism and creative accounting were associated with some management styles. This was often used to conceal or delay exposure.

Bankers emphasised overtrading, debt, business and cash flow planning, and large projects. One banker pointed to the issues of management succession and internal conflict in many mature family businesses and an insufficient depth of outside professional management. Inflation and high interest rates had been a problem some years earlier, as was the downturn in the economic cycle, particularly in sectors such as construction, property and retailing.

Ray Jackson, an experienced liquidator, and John Crawford of KPMG Stokes Kennedy Crowley suggested a list of causes of failure for small and larger businesses which is set out in Table 2.3.[22] This list is useful because it links external forces to internal management, adaptation to change and weak marketing. It also highlights the management style and organisation structure. The emphasis on the need for independent views in the two areas of risk-taking and uninformed decision-making is relevant.

When reviewing a director's role and responsibilities, Mills drew on a Big 6 accounting firm's own analysis of twenty cases of collapse to summarise examples of 'bad management'.[23] This is shown in Table 2.4. In view of the earlier discussion on accountants' perceptions and biases,

> **Table 2.3: Jackson and Crawford's causes of business failure**
>
> **External**
> 1. Changes in the economy: interest rates, inflation
> 2. Changes in production technology: competitiveness, people and industrial relations issues
>
> **Internal**
> 3. General management and organisation deficiencies: delegation, assigning responsibilities, focus; role of chief executive
> 4. Weak marketing
> 5. Lack of adaptation and planning for new conditions
> 6. Absence of outside views and objectivity; no watchdogs when high risks being taken
> 7. Undercapitalisation
> 8. Uninformed decisions; lack of sound judgment; absence of independent advice

Source: Ray Jackson and John Crawford, *Why Businesses Fail*, Dublin: KPMG Stokes Kennedy Crowley 1992.

perhaps it is not surprising that the Mills/Big 6 examples of bad management emphasise gearing, costing, financial issues and overtrading.

Life-cycle theory as an organising framework

A weakness of much of the research reviewed is that it has spawned a series of 'lists' which tend to view the organisation from a static viewpoint. The reality is that individual organisations form part of a larger population ecology which is constantly changing, depending on the state of its internal and external environments. The life-cycle perspective provides a more dynamic framework for analysis because, unlike living organisms, firms do not have to eventually decline or die, if they adapt to their environment.

The idea of conceptualising an organisation as a living organism derives from nineteenth-century economic theorists.[24] During the 1950s, Boulding[25] and Penrose[26] took opposite views on the usefulness of life-cycle theory, but it was an arid debate in the absence of evidence. Organisational and social scientists developed the model further with the results of new empirical research in the 1980s. They argued that life-cycle theory can be summarised in the five stages of 'birth', 'growth', 'maturity', 'decline/revival' and 'death'. These stages offer a distinctive and useful typology in terms of phases,

Table 2.4: Mills' examples of bad management

Problem	Number of instances in 20 cases
High gearing	11
No financial projections	9
Poor costing	8
Overtrading	7
Not reading economic signs	6
Excessive overheads	6
Not selling production	6
Selling too cheap	5
Excessive R&D	5
Extravagance	4
Sales mix problems	4
Raw materials shortages	3
Labour shortages	2
Overstocked	2
Engineering problems	2
Poor production planning	2
Fixed price contacts	1

Source: Geoffrey Mills, *On the Board*, London: George Allen & Unwin 1985, p. 189.

themes, situations and changes in the organisation.[27] An accepted weakness of the model is that all organisations do not progress sequentially through the various stages. Some never reach maturity, but go from birth or adolescence directly to death. Others never die.

Certain critical distinguishing organisational characteristics and transformations have been identified with the differing life-cycle stages. These have implications for future success or failure. The various stages cannot be measured by reference only to time, because some firms expand their activities (turnover, employees or assets) much more rapidly than others. Reasons include the growth in the market, technological innovation, the personal attitudes of the founders and capital availability. The various stages may last between four and ten years. Despite its imperfections in fully reflecting and predicting organisational traits and metamorphoses, the model has some utility in distinguishing managerial characteristics. For example, Quinn and Cameron found that the criteria for organisational effectiveness seem to change over the different stages of the life-cycle, due to greater complexity.[28] Miller and Friesen reported contrasts in information processing (including management control and communication systems), decision-making styles and innovation rates between successful and unsuccessful organisations over the four stages following birth.[29] This supports earlier anecdotal and single case study material.

The problems of adolescence

The potential for crisis and the need to successfully cope in moving from one stage to the next, from birth to growth to maturity, have been found to be critical.[30] Management problems are a product of the organisation's history, age, growth rate, size and industrial environment. At the initial creative stage there can be leadership problems, because the founders are usually technically or entrepreneurially oriented. Formality in management procedures, structures and communications is disdained. An absence of staff involvement in decision-making and responsibility is the next problem. As growth and size accelerate, there is a potential crisis of control if managers operate their own activities and divisions without suitable co-ordinating plans and management information systems with feedback to top management linked to an overriding corporate purpose. At the mature stage, creeping bureaucracy emerges as the top management extends the variety of planning and control systems. Proliferation of procedures leads to a red-tape crisis. The emphasis on procedures tends to overwhelm people's innovation, problem recognition and efforts at resolution.

The 'growing pains' of transition from a founder/entrepreneur management style to a professionally managed, more formal structure were explained by Flamholtz.[31] Conflicts can arise as a result of the organisation's need for more discipline and structure in its growth phase in order to ensure survival. He illustrated the 'divorce' between the founder and the organisation with examples from firms in the computer industry. Many founder/entrepreneurs find it difficult to make the change, and consequently their organisations often lose their way. The paradox is:

> . . . this is a time the very personality traits that made the founder/entrepreneur so successful initially can lead to organizational demise. Most entrepreneurs have either a sales or a technical background, or they tend to know a particular industry very well. Entrepreneurs typically want things done in their own way. They may be more intelligent or have better intuition than their subordinates, who come to rely on their bosses' omnipotence. Typical entrepreneurs tend to be 'doers' rather than managers, and most have not had formal management training. . . . They like to be

free of 'corporate restraints'. They reject meetings, written plans, details of time and budgets as the trappings of bureaucracy. Most insidiously, they think, 'We got here without these things, so why do we need them?'[32]

A summary of contrasts between entrepreneurial and professional cultures is set out in Table 2.5.

Table 2.5: Examples of entrepreneurial and professional cultures

Values	We value 'fire fighters'.
	versus
	We value planners.
Beliefs	Our success is based on our ability to respond rapidly to changes in our environment.
	versus
	Our success depends on our ability to anticipate and plan for changes in our environment.
Norms	We do not plan; we react.
	versus
	We know what direction we are going in at all times.
Heroes	The Arsonists and the Fire Fighters
	versus
	The Planners

Source: Eric G. Flamholtz, *Growing Pains*, San Francisco: Jossey-Bass 1990, p. 306.

Changes in management systems and organisational structures are essential at each stage of growth — if a crisis is to be avoided. There is the need to move from entrepreneurial opportunism to more formal processes of planning, first from the top and later through a 'bottom-up' approach. The organisation will develop from the semi-chaotic form to a more functional structure; eventually, if greater product/market complexity evolves, then a divisional form may be created with changes in accounting, management control and information systems.

Corporate culture is a powerful force in influencing behaviour and change. Culture expresses the shared values, beliefs and social ideals which define identity and meaning. Pettigrew referred to the less rational 'more expressive social tissue around us' which gives the rational everyday tasks and objectives some meaning.[33] Culture is a form of 'social or normative glue that holds an organisation together'.[34] It is a system of terms, forms, categories and images which helps people in the firm to interpret their situation for themselves. This general sense of orientation and patterning manifests itself in symbols, language, ideology, beliefs, rituals and myths. Ceremonies, legends and a specialist language are devices of expression of these socialising processes. Larger organisations may contain multiple subcultures and countercultures; clearly the issue is complex. Kotter and Heskett categorise organisational culture into two aspects — its degree of visibility and its degree of resistance to change.[35] At the less visible level are the shared values in a group which persist over time, even when the group membership changes. The culture reflects what the members care deeply about — which can vary between organisations. It might be about technological innovation, deal-making or achieving incentive targets and money. Thus, strategy and change have to be compatible with culture. In the birth and adolescent stages, the vision and philosophy of a strong founder will be a major influence on values. Though 'strong' cultures have often been identified with good economic performance, Kotter and Heskett suggest culture can be a force for good or bad:

> Cultures can have powerful consequences, especially when they are strong. They can enable a group to take rapid and co-ordinated action against a competitor or for a customer. They can also lead intelligent people to walk, in concert, off a cliff.[36]

Culture marks out an organisation's essence and role. The need to make alterations and communications at each stage of the life-cycle is fundamental. The critical issue is the effectiveness and adaptability of the chief executive as a leader and a manager. The introduction of experienced professional, rather than entrepreneurial, management is crucial to sustainable growth. In addition management has to have considerable strength of character and interpersonal skills in coping with the entrepreneurially driven founder and creating more formal structuring. Greiner saw it as a difficult transition:

> . . . the founders find themselves burdened with unwanted management responsibilities. So they long for the 'good old days', still trying to act as they did in the past. The conflicts between the harried leaders grow more intense. . . . Who is to lead the company out of this confusion and solve the managerial problems confronting it? . . . But this is easier said than done. The founders often hate to step aside even though they are probably temperamentally unsuited to be managers.[37]

Adizes points to the four roles — technical, administrative, entrepreneurship and integration — which require differing skills combinations and emphasis at each stage of the life-cycle.[38] Managing the balance and changing emphasis for each of the roles in achieving a safe 'passage' to the next stage in the transformation of the organisation is the overriding responsibility of management. Two major dangers in the 'go-go' and 'adolescent' stages were the 'founder's trap' (the personification of the managerial process) and undercapitalisation.

Three international examples illustrate the issues — Apple Computer, Amstrad and Slater Walker Securities.

Founded in 1976, Apple Computer achieved a turnover of $8 million in two years and $583 million in six years.[39] It produced net profit margins of more than 10% and good cash flow. Raising external equity on the stockmarket allied to cash flow enabled Apple to sustain fast growth to the adolescence stage and introduce the second-generation product range around the 'Macintosh'. A recurring series of internal political conflicts and crises at founder/partner, top management and board levels led to setbacks in performance and the timing of new products. Turnover reached $1.8 billion by 1985 but margins and profits fell. An early co-founder/partner, Stephen Wozniak, and others resigned, and subsequently the charismatic and unconventional co-founder, Steve Jobs, was forced to resign by the board. The recruitment of outside professional management led to more disciplined organisation structures and systems. Under the new management, Apple achieved a turnover of $5 billion by 1990. It was a classic illustration of the structure, culture and management process problems experienced by brilliant entrepreneurs who are unable to make the role transition to the next stage in an organisation's life-cycle. It took a boardroom revolution to ensure survival.

In contrast, Alan Sugar, the founder/entrepreneur of Amstrad, survived. His audio and hi-fi equipment company went public on the stockmarket in London in 1980 when turnover was just Stg£9 million. By 1988 it had rocketed to Stg£626 million and was extraordinarily profitable, with pre-tax profit margins on turnover averaging 25%. A halving of margins to 12% in 1989 was the first signal of an impending crisis. Alan Sugar had been performing most management tasks. He had been aggressively pushing sales, product innovation and new markets by 'riding the tiger' of growth. This heady expansion led to overheads rising faster than sales. There were unknown build-ups of inventories in its European subsidiaries, and clearly management information systems, planning and financial control were inadequate. The Amstrad organisation survived — but not without extensive trauma and pain. Alan Sugar admitted:

> There was no financial policing within the organisation. There was no proper forecasting of overseas subsidiaries. There was no proper inventory control. There was no real head-count plan. It was a phenomenon brought about by the fact that we had been hot selling the products. . . . When you're in that kind of gi-normous growth trend, you tend to forget about the instinctive things you used to worry about in a much smaller business — looking after the pennies, making sure you're not spending too much, that your expenses are not running away, that you're not employing too many . . .[40]

The entrepreneurial management style of Alan Sugar, who was driven by a 'sales mania', was a classic illustration of the growing pains which emerge at the later adolescent stage in a fast-growing organisation's structure and management systems. However, because of Amstrad's strong previous profitability and limited debt, it had the time and resources to reorganise.

The rise and fall of Slater Walker Securities was one of the 'financial phenomena' of the UK in the twentieth century. It illustrated not only the problems of overtrading and the inability to cope with cyclical downturns but also the adverse effects of incentives and pressures to perform — particularly on ethical behaviour. Developed primarily by Jim Slater, a chartered accountant with extensive industrial and stockmarket investment experience, the business concept was novel in that it was a merchant bank, a holding company specialising in industrial 'turnaround' situations, a property company, and an insurance company. In its life-cycle from 1965 to 1975 it became one of the largest companies on the London Stock Exchange, mainly through acquisitions. At the start of the recession in the mid-1970s, it had to be rescued, amidst some controversy, by the Bank of England. Slater and his young executives found it was one thing to grow during a period of easy credit, strong demand and a bull stockmarket but it required a very different set of management skills to survive a recession, a bear market and a heavy debt burden. Much of its 'business efficiency' was an illusion and some questionable transactions, improprieties, operational weaknesses and misleading financial reporting were revealed.[41] In his autobiography[42] Jim Slater admitted that there were many lessons:

> . . . in the early years we achieved too much too soon, as a result of which I had to recruit executives too quickly. . . . I think the overall calibre of management would have been better if we had grown a

> little more slowly and, in certain instances, we would have attracted a better type of manager. The speed and informality of our management style had great advantages, but it had also disadvantages. . . . A more structured company would have formalised the incentive scheme . . . in a more careful and deliberate way administratively. At the time we were busy conquering the world and were not too worried about red tape.[43]

Despite Jim Slater's investment brilliance, the entrepreneurial psyche dominated the prudent accounting intellect. He felt 'the early success of Slater Walker . . . created a monster that was beyond my personal control'.[44] He pinpointed the absence of experienced and strong non-executive directors as a fatal flaw.

The financial problems of growth

Peter Drucker, with his extensive consulting experience and widely acknowledged writings, expressed some concern as far back as 1973 on the mistaken perceptions of analysts and managers on the effects of growth on a firm:

> The securities market would be well advised to put a discount on growth stocks and growth industries rather than a premium, for growth is a risk. . . . The idea that growth by itself is a goal is a delusion. There is no virtue in a company getting bigger. The right goal is to become better. Growth, to be sound, should be the result of doing the right things. By itself, growth is a vanity and little else.[45]

The fact that the internal cash flow profile generally involves deficits during the birth and growth stages but a surplus at the mature stage of the organisational life-cycle has been recognised in financial analysis.[46] The concept of a 'sustainable growth rate' depends on a match between on the one hand internal cash flows and/or external equity and on the other hand the rate of expansion and investment outlays. It shows up in a stable set of financial ratios involving the net sales margin, the turnover of assets to sales, the level of equity to assets, and the earnings retention/dividend policy. These vary over industries and individual companies, depending on their profit and asset efficiency as well as financial policies. A soundly based capital structure with sufficient working capital underpins financial equilibrium. Underlying the rate of 'sustainable growth' is the level of profitability and cash flow retained in the business in relation to its incremental investment in fixed assets and working capital. Any deterioration will result in a financing shortfall. The founder/entrepreneur is then faced with a capital structure decision which also links to control and risk issues. Debt is the soft option; it tends to be more easily available than equity. Debt also avoids any immediate dilution of ownership but in a fast-growth firm it usually leads to financial risk being added to high levels of business risk. Raising equity is much more demanding. The accountant's investigations and searching questions about the business and its management are perceived as intrusive and difficult by the entrepreneur.

In a US study of 795 'threshold' (early adolescent) companies for McKinsey & Co., management consultants, Clifford found that fast growth was often associated with a variable profit record, much higher levels of debt, weaker interest coverage and weak working capital.[47] It was a riskier stage than maturity, and profit margins tended to be lower. These 'threshold' companies had a competitive drive and vitality but they were also very volatile. Their ability to successfully negotiate the passage to the next stage of the life-cycle depended on their effectiveness in coping with increased product/market complexity and the changes that were required in management style and systems. Clifford pointed to the tensions between the founder's management competence and the pressures created by growth, new structures and styles. Financial problems often became the catalyst to firing the founder because he was unwilling or unable to adapt his role.[48]

The problems for a firm of maintaining a suitable organisational infrastructure and avoiding 'choking on its own growth' when this is in the range of 25% to 50% per annum become intense.[49]

The problems of mature organisations

Larger long-established companies suffer from an ageing process which can be distinguished from the decline of smaller entrepreneurial companies. Many chief executives blame problems on uncontrollable elements in the external environment. While true to some extent, this only partially explains decline. It is possible to take preventative measures to counteract decline. The primary cause is usually internal due to an inability or refusal to recognise problems, thus increasing the negative effect over time.

Lorange and Nelson identified five organisational features which contribute to mature company decline:

1. self-delusion and blindness
2. focus moves from basic business demands to hierarchical politics
3. cultural rigidity and excess bureaucracy

4. emphasis on acceptance and conformity — 'no rocking the boat'
5. emphasis on consensus and compromise.[50]

It is a paradox that competitive success can often result in complacency. An almost wilful blindness to the market, basic business needs and change links to organisational politics, separate empires, complex layers of management structures and diffused core business responsibilities. The earlier cycle of success breeds a more rigid culture. Organisational politics and bureaucracy dominate decision-making, processes and structures as the culture becomes more inward in its orientation. Major change is resisted. The extent of change in the marketplace will decide the size of the eventual problem — subject to the processes adopted by the organisation in strategy formulation, structure and decision-making. If top management discourages alternative views, a narrow 'group-think' culture comes to pervade the organisation with a political focus which will often filter out conflicting information and research.

Nine 'early warning' signals should be monitored systematically:

1. excess personnel and levels of management
2. tolerance of incompetence
3. bureaucratic paperwork, slow decision-making
4. large head office staff with excessive power
5. replacement of substance with form
6. scarcity of clear goals and decision criteria
7. fear of embarrassment, conflict and mistakes
8. ineffective communication and information flows
9. outdated organisation structure.[51]

These signals reflect a firm's greater internal focus and the decoupling of management concern from its external environment of customers, products, technology and the need to adapt. Internal preoccupations and managerial 'kingdoms' with their own agendas will blur the company's identity, goals and vision. Increasing overheads will depress profit margins and an absence of product innovation will result in a decline in market share. The eventual scale and timing of decline and crisis will vary, depending on the benevolence in the 'carrying capacity' of the market.

An example of these issues was IBM's complacency, lost opportunities and wrong decisions on personal computers in the early 1990s, which have been well documented.[52] Remarkably, it was not the first major crisis for this leading US computer firm. In his autobiography, Thomas J. Watson Jr, son of the founder of IBM, admitted that despite its sales and marketing culture, complacency crept in as IBM fell behind in product technology in the early 1960s.[53] It lost market share because new competitors had introduced more powerful mid-sized computer systems. Sorting out the problems in a new generation of software proved slow and costly. System 360 became a 'big project', which almost bankrupted IBM — but also saved it. Watson admitted that it was touch and go — IBM was fortunate that it was so rich in capital and human resources with technical brilliance.[54] He also revealed that IBM's management accounting information systems had broken down during the 'big project', and a cash flow crisis revealed incorrect valuations of stocks and work-in-progress with a 'black hole' in the accounting figures.

The classic accounts of Michael Edwardes[55] and Lee Iacocca,[56] who were brought into British Leyland and Chrysler respectively in the 1980s to achieve a 'turnaround', provide insights into the problems of long-established organisations which have not changed with the times. According to Edwardes, British Leyland's problems started at board level, with few independent directors. Management had lost the will to manage, and was overcentralised and bureaucratic. There was a high direct cost and overheads base allied to poor productivity. Almost a quarter of annual production was lost through labour disputes and industrial relations problems. Operating management had little authority and had lost control in many areas of personnel practices. There were weak costing and stock control systems. British Leyland had not updated its products or factories in keeping with its main competitors; not surprisingly, it had lost market share and was heavily loss-making.

The distinguishing culture of established family companies was illustrated by Thomas J. Watson Jr. He described the influence of his father (and the conflicts), his relationship with his younger brother Dick, and their roles in the organisation. He also admitted to a different relationship with the most senior 'non-family' professional manager, stating that 'inside and outside the company I wanted to establish that Tom Watson Jr meant IBM, and I guarded my power carefully'.[57]

Research by Channon on leading British companies showed that many families attempted to maintain managerial control over their companies through generations. Most of these family companies operated with a narrower product range and were slower to adopt new strategies and structures than non-family companies.[58] The family firms, over time, often became 'dynastic systems' which led to stagnation and the maintenance of the original product/market scope of the firm. Where the founder had been an autocratic entrepreneur, the second-generation family members faced very different tasks in administration and structural reform. The behaviour of family firms differs from that of others through the role and power of a 'founding family' in its culture and traditions, which, in turn, influence decisions and actions. In firms where ownership and control are separate, a professional management group may pursue quite different objectives.[59]

However, not all family companies remain stagnant within a simple product/market scope. Some become hyperactive in later generations, as illustrated by the overseas expansion by acquisition of Smurfit Group in Ireland and News Corporation in Australia. As sons of the founders, both Michael Smurfit and Rupert Murdoch went on to build successful international businesses. They focused on a range of core products. In each, the power of the family name held sway. In many ways the strategy of Rupert Murdoch mirrors that of Michael Smurfit except that Smurfit avoided a crisis by means of a more stable capital structure and stronger management control through Howard Kilroy.[60]

Though quoted on the stockmarket, News Corporation remained a 'family' company because Rupert Murdoch was a second-generation controlling shareholder. With worldwide assets in print and broadcast media valued at A$20 billion, News Corporation has been described as 'a unique phenomenon in modern capitalism'.[61] With newspaper publishing experience in Australia, Murdoch moved to Britain in the early 1980s, buying a number of newspapers, increasing circulation and reducing publishing costs through the aggressive adoption of new computer-driven technology. Then relocation to the USA resulted in a number of media acquisitions, the largest being Twentieth Century Fox film studios. There was also the expensive innovation of Sky satellite television. Despite its apparent success and reported profitability, it experienced a major financial crisis in late 1990. The rate of expansion and the heavy dependence on bank debt prompted the *Financial Times* to observe later:

> In the Autumn of 1990, News Corporation was almost overwhelmed by its debts of more than US$7.6 bn. Nearly 150 banks had to be persuaded to rollover the debt and come up with a new US$600 million loan. . . . The restructuring was a long and tortuous process.
>
> It is unlikely that Mr Murdoch will forget the experience, or the mistakes that made it necessary.[62]

Reflecting on the crisis in 1992, Rupert Murdoch admitted: 'We just got caught running when we should have been walking and that was sufficiently unpleasant to make you swear you are not going to let it happen to you again.'[63] He felt he should have spent less money on Sky, given it one less channel and phased it in more slowly. Over-rapid and unnecessary modernisation of four Australian newspaper printing plants proved costly. He agreed he paid too much for a number of acquisitions and had financed much of the new investment by way of short-term debt. High interest rates and a tightening in money markets and bank credit made rolling over the loans more difficult. News Corporation was not generating sufficient cash flow and liquidity to pay off the maturing debt. There were also accounting and bank covenant issues. How did Murdoch and News Corporation survive? One leading banker commented: 'Murdoch helped to ease the crisis by reacting swiftly. . . . Murdoch is an arrogant bugger, but he wasn't so arrogant that he didn't know when he was in trouble.'[64]

Asset disposals raised A$2.4 billion. The most bitter pill was the selling of equity which reduced the Murdoch family holding to 40%. Remaining businesses were reviewed with the objective of improving profit margins. Bankers' fees, redundancy payments and related reorganisation costs amounting to A$714 million — an expensive exercise. A revised group management structure gave full authority to Gus Fischer as chief operating officer. Costs were reduced and loss-making activities were eliminated, resulting in net profits soaring by 65% to A$531 million by 1992. The share price recovered from a low of A$3.80 at the time of the financial crisis to A$23.50. Murdoch was also lucky, because interest rates fell by half in the post-crisis period. News Corporation survived because there were a number of well-established and profitable businesses and product brands within the group. There was a reasonably coherent strategic vision which was focused on newspaper and magazine publishing, broadcast media and, more recently, the film industry which require broadly similar forms of managerial expertise. Murdoch could be viewed as a visionary 'builder' of a media empire, rather than an expansionist 'deal-maker'.

Downward spirals and blindness

The dynamics of failure of large firms were characterised as a 'downward spiral' process by Hambrick and D'Aveni.[65] Testing four central hypotheses — corporate strategic behaviour, environmental carrying capacity, resources slack and performance — they found the downward spiral could be divided into four distinct stages over a decade.[66] These are summarised in Table 2.6.

Table 2.6:	Hambrick and D'Aveni's model of organisational decline as a downward spiral
1. Origins of Disadvantage (pre t–10)	Deficient potential slack and performance
2. Early Impairment (t–10 to t–6)	Further deterioration of potential slack and performance Strategic extremism and vacillation
3. Marginal Existence (t–6 to t–3)	Neutral/buoyant environment Satisfactory working capital Marginal potential slack and performance
4. Death Struggle (t–2 to t)	Strategic extremism and vacillation Sudden environmental decline Sharp deterioration of slack and performance Failure

Note: t–10 = ten years before death.
Source: Donald C. Hambrick and Richard A. D'Aveni, 'Large Corporate Failures as Downward Spirals', *Administrative Science Quarterly* 33 (1988), pp. 13–14.

Remarkably, the research evidence suggested signs of weaknesses ten years before collapse. The strategic actions in the last four to five years were as much the effects of decline as its causes. This points to the possibility that 'weakness leads to even greater weakness' with the downward spiral reflecting the dynamics. Behaviour which varied between inertia and extreme risk-taking ('going for broke') was observed. Thus actions could be characterised as inaction and hyperaction. The phenomenon of 'delusion' about problems, performance and false encouragement was evident in a variety of forms, such as 'creative accounting' and unreal perceptions of reality through 'fantasising' and 'wishful thinking' — which resulted in judgment errors. A most useful concept to emerge was the state of the environment, its carrying capacity and changes in its needs specifications. Moving from a benign to a harsh environment affected the frail firms in their opportunities to recover.

In an elaboration, Weitzel and Jonsson proposed a model of decline founded on a continuum of five stages of a progressive process of organisational problems and weakening environmental support.[67] The consequences of the five stages — initial blindness, inaction, faulty decisions, faulty actions and implementation — eventually result in crisis and possible collapse, depending on the state of the environment. In an interesting one-case application of the model, McGrath found it offered useful explanatory insights, though the stages proved less distinct.[68]

Syndromes of failure patterns

Instead of a cause and effect analysis, Miller presented findings based on the more holistic concept of syndromes or configurations of common neuroses or behaviour patterns found in distressed firms.[69] He described the four most common syndromes, which accounted for 80% of his sample, as 'The Impulsive Syndrome: Running Blind', 'The Stagnant Bureaucracy', 'The Headless Firm' and 'Swimming Upstream: The Aftermath'.

The first two patterns involve power-hoarding dominant chief executives. The first pursues overambitious strategies with bold decisions and the second operates with a mind-set rooted in the past, which will not change. One demands a pace of growth which overtaxes the financial and managerial resources; 'the seat of the pants' style explains the lag in information systems and poor delegation. The other falls behind customer, market and technology changes. Internal bureaucracy and routines shift preoccupations from the external environment to the internal.

The third syndrome focuses on large firms which suffer from a leadership vacuum. The chief executive plays a figurehead role. The absence of a clear strategy results in the firm drifting aimlessly. Internally, the firm may have splintered into independent managerial fiefdoms. Weak internal and external intelligence systems may mean that top management do not realise what changes are occurring in markets and internal control needs. The consequence is inadequate adaptation. The fourth cluster of neuroses are found where the firm, possibly due to some of the problems mentioned earlier, is in a weak condition in products, equipment, and financial and managerial resources. Possibly a new chief executive is trying to attempt a 'turnaround' with a new set of lieutenants — brought in over the heads of some existing management. Co-operation, information and distrust are issues. Bold and impulsive decisions by the new team overtax the firm, and because of information blockages, the problems are not realised until it is too late.

More recently, Miller identified four alternative configurations in 'The Icarus Paradox' which described the character, values and orientations of entrepreneurial companies which had been growing successfully until an abrupt change in their strategic focus led to a trajectory which led to crisis and financial distress.[70]

Aggressive and cosmetic accounting

Terry Smith, a former analyst with stockbrokers UBS Phillips & Drew of London, disclosed how a number of very large British publicly quoted companies, audited by 'Big 6' firms, used a variety of dubious accounting methods to massage their profits and financial position. He concluded that 'much of the apparent growth in profits that occurred in the 1980s was the result of creative accounting rather than genuine economic growth'.[71] Within two years a number of the companies pinpointed by Smith had encountered various forms of crisis and change. Whether the market was efficient in seeing through the accounting smokescreens and making suitable pricing adjustments was questioned. Accounting and finance academics were not surprised. Almost a decade earlier, Brealey and Myers commented:

> There are . . . occasions on which managers seem to assume that investors suffer from financial illusion. For example, some firms devote enormous ingenuity to the task of manipulating earnings reported to stockholders. This is done by 'creative accounting' — that is choosing accounting methods which stabilise and increase reported earnings. Presumably firms go to this trouble because management believes the stockholders take the figures at face value.[72]

In theory, the efficiency of the market, through the analysis of sophisticated analysts, should 'see through' the variety of accounting techniques used to artificially adjust earnings or financial condition. In practice, there must be doubts, in view of the adjustment, after the Smith revelations, to some companies' share prices. The case study by Gwilliam and Russell into the published accounts and accounting policies of Polly Peck International, stockbroker reports and share price (it had a market capitalisation of £1.5 billion) raises many doubts about analysts' efficiency in London.[73] Further financial analysis by Pijper, and discussion of that case and other issues in respect of accounting regulation, suggests considerable scope for accounting manipulations in Britain and Ireland, because of the ambiguity and discretion in accounting standards, the role of auditing and the effectiveness of regulation.[74] He shows how many firms 'window dress' their balance sheets as well as their profit and loss accounts. A very considerable literature is emerging on the issues of 'earnings management', 'aggressive accounting', 'income smoothing' and accounting policy choices, which has reopened the question of financial analysis efficiency by stockbroker analysts and bankers.[75]

Financial ratio predictive models

Since the 1930s recession, many accounting and finance academics have attempted, with varying degrees of success, to compute financial ratios and predictive models based on ratios which would help predict the distress or failure of a firm. After all, a ratio is a powerful tool in portraying a picture of performance and health characteristics in the relationships it captures.[76] The profit to sales margin may be a cue to managerial efficiency and product competitiveness. The interest cover and equity capital to debt help form an opinion about gearing and financial strength. Absolute levels and trends of ratios provide useful information about a firm's health, particularly when they are compared to similar firms or industry data. As they represent a thermometer reading or pulse count of a firm, as a living organism, they also require some expert interpretation at critical points. There is extensive evidence that financial ratios are used by accountants, auditors, bankers and stockmarket analysts in evaluating firms.[77] Managements and their boards often use financial ratios in their objective setting and monitoring framework. Bankers also use a small number of key ratios in loan covenants, as part of a risk-controlling mechanism.

An extensive body of research has been conducted in constructing 'failure prediction models', particularly in the USA from the 1960s and 1970s as statistical computing methodologies and data became more accessible. Beaver and Altman were early pioneers.[78] Ohlson took the inquiry a stage further with refinements in methodology.[79] Elsewhere, there has been much less published work. In the UK, Taffler,[80] Marais[81] and Robertson[82] produced findings in the 1970s and 1980s. Cahill[83] and Clarke[84] have examined the financial ratios of Irish firms.

Beaver's univariate study of 1966 found two ratios out of seven — cash flow to total debt and net income to total assets — which discriminated to a high degree of accuracy when used individually, several years before failure. Total debt to total assets was a close third. Misclassification rates fell to 21% and 13% in the final two years. Altman and subsequently Altman, Haldeman and Narayanan innovated with multivariate modelling, using discriminant analysis, which produced a set of ratios that combined to determine a 'Z score' and a Zeta value respectively. In Altman's first model, the cluster of ratios was unconventional. The Zeta model and Ohlson's probabilistic model claimed less misclassifications, in failed and non-failed firms, and therefore greater accuracy some years in advance. In a rigorous review and study, Zmijewski concluded that bankrupt firms:

- were less profitable
- were more highly leveraged from balance sheet, income and cash flow cover of fixed charges
- had lower equity share returns and higher return variability.[85]

Surprisingly, liquidity and activity ratios did not particularly help early classification, though they did have some value when combined in a cluster with other ratios in some of the models. A summary of selected US model variables is shown in Table 2.7.

Findings from Ireland, the UK and Australia are taken together, in view of the similarity of their accounting traditions and capital market structures. Details are shown in Table 2.8. Similar to the US experience, a variety of variables emerged. Cahill's findings from a small sample — operating profit to total assets, cash flow to total debt and interest cover — were found elsewhere. Also, the ratio of current liabilities to total assets followed Taffler's findings in the UK.

The bulk of the ratio predictive model research has been conducted on large Stock Exchange companies. Some of the models include stockmarket material (quoted value of equity) or stockmarket indexes as a proxy for general economic conditions, which has helped their discriminatory power in separating matched samples of failed from non-failed firms. To date, most models have been sufficiently accurate only to the first or second last year — when it may often be too late to take corrective action. A criticism is that researchers have tended to take vast numbers of financial ratios and 'number crunch' them through increasingly refined statistical methodologies to derive a set of ratio variables for classification purposes. There has been only limited consistency between the variables chosen in the various studies, yet there has been little difference in the results achieved.[86] There is some concern about misclassification of surviving firms and the instability of the variable sets prior to the year before failure. A variety of definitions of the failure or distress 'event' has contributed to the dispersal of findings and their practical applicability. However, apart from being of interest to bankers, creditors and investors as a screening device, the failure prediction models have utility for auditors in their risk assessment of the 'going concern' status of the firm. The introduction of revised auditing standards increases the auditors' responsibility, but research from the USA continues to indicate that auditors fail to qualify or signify uncertainty in the majority of corporate bankruptcies — in contrast to the predictions of ratio models in these cases.[87]

Table 2.7: Variables in US failure prediction models

Measure	Beaver (1966)	Altman (1968)	Altman et al. (1977)	Ohlson (1980)
Profitability				
PBIT/TA	–	yes	yes	–
NI/TA	yes	–	–	yes
Rt Ea/TA	–	yes	yes	–
Cash flow				–
CF/TD	yes	–	–	yes
Gearing				
Mkt Eq./TD	–	yes	yes	–
TD/TA	yes	–	–	yes
Interest cover	–	–	yes	–
Liquidity				
WC/TA	–	yes	–	yes
CA/CL	–	–	yes	yes
Other				
S/TA	–	yes	–	–
Size/TA	–	–	yes	yes
Earnings volatility	–	–	yes	yes
Losses	–	–	–	yes
Neg. equity	–	–	–	yes

Note: PBIT = profit before interest and taxes; NI = net income; TA = total assets; Rt Ea = retained earnings; CF = cash flow; TD = total debt; Mkt Eq. = stockmarket value of equity; WC = working capital; CA = current assets; CL = current liabilities; S = sales (turnover).

Source: William H. Beaver, 'Financial Ratios as Predictors of Failure', *Empirical Research in Accounting, Supplement to Journal of Accounting Research* 4 (1966), pp. 71–111; Edward I. Altman, 'Financial Ratios, Discriminant Analysis and the Prediction of Corporate Bankruptcy', *Journal of Finance,* September 1968, pp. 589–609; Edward I. Altman, R. G. Haldeman and P. Narayanan, 'Zeta Analysis: A New Model to Identify Bankruptcy Risk of Corporations', *Journal of Banking and Finance,* June 1977, pp. 29–54; James S. Ohlson, 'Financial Ratios and the Probabilistic Prediction of Bankruptcy', *Journal of Accounting Research,* Spring 1980, pp. 109–31.

Table 2.8: Variables in Irish, UK and Australian failure prediction models

Measure	Cahill (Irl) (1981)	Taffler and Tisshaw (UK) (1977)	Marais (UK) (1979)	Izan (Aus) (1984)	Houghton and Woodliff (Aus) 1987
Profitability					
PBIT/TA	yes	–	–	yes	yes
PBT/CL	–	yes	–	–	–
Cash flow					
CF/TD	yes	–	yes	–	yes
CF/CL	–	–	–	–	–
CF ops/TD	–	–	yes	–	–
Gearing					
CL/TA	yes	yes	–	–	–
Mkt Eq./TD	–	–	–	yes	–
Bank/SF	–	–	–	yes	yes
Interest cover	yes	–	yes	yes	–
Liquidity					
No credit interval	–	yes	–	–	–
CA/TD	–	yes	–	–	–
CA/TA	–	–	yes	–	–
CA/CL	–	–	–	yes	–
QA/CL	yes	–	–	–	yes
Other					
Dividend cover	–	–	–	–	yes
Size/TA	–	–	yes	–	–

Note: PBIT = profit before interest and taxes; TA = total assets; PBT = profit before taxes; CL = current liabilities; CF = cash flow; TD = total debt; CF ops = operating cash flow; Mkt Eq. = stockmarket value of equity; SF = shareholders' funds; CA = current assets; QA = quick assets.

Source: Edward Cahill, 'Irish Listed Company Failure, Financial Ratios, Accounts and Auditors' Opinions', *Irish Business and Administrative Research* 3, 1 (1981), pp. 19–31; Richard Taffler and H. Tisshaw, 'Going, Going, Gone — Four Factors which Predict', *Accountancy*, March 1977; D. A. J. Marais, *A Method of Quantifying Companies' Relative Financial Strength*, Bank of England Discussion Paper No. 4, 1979; H. Y. Izan, 'Corporate Distress in Australia', *Journal of Banking and Finance* 8, 2 (1984), pp. 303–20; Keith Houghton and D. Woodliff, 'Financial Ratios: The Prediction of Corporate Success and Failure', *Journal of Business Finance and Accounting* 14 (1987), pp. 537–54.

Generally, US models have not proved accurate when used elsewhere. Different variable sets have emerged in Britain, Australia, France and Japan.[88] This is explained by the different accounting regulations, financial characteristics, business and capital market structures, and economic conditions in different countries. Different internal sets of financial ratios have also emerged in models in Britain, Australia and Ireland, as shown in Table 2.8. One constant to emerge was the usefulness of incorporating stockmarket data (as a 'lead indicator') into the models, particularly in improving timeliness of information.

The performance difficulties of financial ratio models, and the problems of timeliness of available data for small and medium-sized private firms, have prompted research into using 'qualitative' (non-financial) information.[89] This follows earlier successful qualitative research in Germany.[90] Distinguishing distribution and service firms from manufacturing, and focusing on industry sectors with their unique characteristics, has proved rewarding. The work on the construction and the oil and gas industries, for example, is promising.[91]

Cash flow based models, after disappointing initial work, have made a recovery.[92] Volatility has proved a critical criterion. Cash flow models appear to be a strong and earlier predictor in firms that have subsequently failed, but they can misclassify surviving firms. The successful growth firm which, though strained financially, survived tends to be misclassified in both cash flow and ratio models.

The incompleteness of the research to date is, to an extent, explained by the samples, the structure of the retrospective research methodology and the different times and economic conditions. A fundamental weakness is the dependence on tools of a *post hoc* pattern recognition nature, rather than constructing a model based on a theory of failure and testing it.[93] The absence of an acceptable theory of failure and its processes, as already noted from the management literature, has left much accounting and finance research in this field problematical, with limited dependability and practical application.

Thus, an aim of the qualitative case study based investigation by this author is to contribute towards a deeper understanding of distress and failure, so that relevant theory may be formulated for research and practical applications.

Chapter 3

Goodman International: Overambitious Expansion

A man of large wealth . . . always thinks . . . 'I have a great income. . . . If things go on as they are I shall certainly keep it; but if they change, I may not keep it.' Consequently, he considers every change of circumstance a 'bore'. . . . But a new man, who has his way to make . . . knows that such changes are his opportunity; he is always on the look-out for them, and always heeds them when he finds them. The rough and vulgar structure of English commerce is the secret of its life.

Walter Bagehot, *Lombard Street*, 1873

The crisis erupts

The Goodman International financial crisis in August 1990 was certainly unexpected by commentators and most of the thirty-three banks who advanced the group over £500 million in unsecured facilities. Less than three months earlier, the *Sunday Times* reviewed the widespread activities and growth of the group.[1] There was speculation that Larry Goodman was about to bid for either Berisford International or Unigate, both substantial companies on the London Stock Exchange. Goodman International was described as Europe's largest meat processor with a turnover of more than £900 million in 1989. It was said to be the leading supplier of beef to such UK supermarket multiples as Sainsbury and Tesco, as well as supplying most of the other supermarket groups including Marks and Spencer, and Asda.

The *Sunday Times* noted the diversification of the Goodman group into dairy processing, grain and malting, and the creation and launch of its subsidiary covering these non-meat activities, Food Industries plc, as a quoted company on the Dublin Stock Exchange. This was viewed as the springboard for a major diversification move away from beef and into a wider, more internationally based food business. Already, Goodman International was thought to account for about 30% of Ireland's agri-economy and 3% of the country's GNP.

The build-up of a 13% equity stake through stockmarket purchases in Berisford International, the UK commodities trading, sugar-processing and property group, was viewed as a prelude to a bid — despite an 8% shareholding in Unigate, the quoted dairy group. According to the *Sunday Times*:

[Berisford's] ownership of British Sugar makes it particularly attractive. The problem, however, for Goodman, as for all other would-be bidders for Berisford, is Berisford's American property division. 'Black Holes' have been found in its accounts, and the full extent of losses will not be known until Berisford reports its results at the end of next month.[2]

The *Sunday Times* wondered whether the group was sufficiently wealthy to acquire a large UK quoted public company and speculated about Larry Goodman's plans because 'his preference for privacy has been interpreted as a need for secrecy'.[3] There was speculation of losses of about Stg£20 million on Berisford shares because of its price decline to Stg127p. In response to the suggestion that a bid price of Stg170p was possible, Larry Goodman was quoted as replying 'We're not about to pay thirty shillings for a pound . . . When we go into battle we go in to win.'[4]

Commentators viewed Goodman International as a successful growth organisation which was dominated by an entrepreneurial, able and secretive founder with ambitions to transform it into a major international food company. It was thought to have the financial capacity to undertake a Stg£1 billion acquisition through a combination of its own resources, partners and leading international banks.

The disposal of the Goodman group's shareholding in Unigate for an estimated Stg£57 million on 17 August 1990 was widely reported in British and Irish newspapers. Tom Walsh, the group treasurer, was reported to have resigned. The media speculated about whether the Goodman group was financially stretched because of unsettled political developments in the Middle East or whether it was clearing the decks in preparation for a bid for Berisford, which was expected to fetch close to Stg£1 billion.[5] A group spokesman stressed that the Goodman companies were financially robust.[6] Berisford's share price had now fallen to Stg50p. It had just announced six-month losses of Stg£144 million. The Goodman group was thought to be 'nursing paper losses of the order of £50 million'.[7] The prey was now felt to be within financial reach, particularly as a Japanese bank was said to be in support.

Just three days later, Goodman International issued a press statement indicating that it was in discussions with its bankers, which were precipitated by the situation in the Middle East and the United Nations sanctions on Iraq. The following day the share price of Food Industries plc fell from 170p to 110p, despite reassurances that it was a strong and profitable group which was totally separate from Goodman International.

The Dublin stockmarket experienced its worst one-day fall in share values since the famous 'Grey Monday' of mid-October 1989. Newspapers referred to 'frenzied selling'.[8] There was concern about the exposure of the banks to the Goodman group of companies. Shares in the Smurfit Group fell by 45p to 495p, along with many other leading industrial quoted companies, because it was thought that Larry Goodman needed to dispose of his personal investment portfolio.[9]

The Taoiseach, Charles Haughey, called a special cabinet meeting to consider the group's problems and the consequences for farmers and the Irish agricultural industry. The Dáil was recalled from holidays for an emergency session to approve a Companies Bill which had been in the legislative pipeline for some years. The aim of this legislation was to permit the High Court to provide temporary protection to financially distressed companies by appointing an examiner to evaluate a company's potential for recovery and restructuring arrangements — broadly on the lines of the USA's Chapter 11 corporate bankruptcy legislation. The Dáil and Seanad approved the urgently prepared bill during 28 and 29 August. On the latter night, immediately after the legislative formalities, the President of the High Court, Mr Justice Hamilton, in an in camera sitting in his home, approved the appointment of Peter Fitzpatrick of Coopers & Lybrand as the examiner of Goodman International, at the request of its directors. In parallel to these moves, difficult discussions were being conducted in secret with Goodman International's bankers in London and Dublin. Richard Hooper of the Investment Bank of Ireland, the doyen of corporate financiers in Dublin, was appointed to advise and assist in the negotiations.

The speed of the financial crisis was striking. The most recently issued audited financial statements, signed off eighteen weeks earlier with a 'clean' audit report, reported a pre-tax profit of £34 million for 1989. It was remarkable that such a long-established and apparently profitable group could suddenly find itself unable to pay its debts as they fell due. The Goodman group pointed to the Iraqi invasion of Kuwait on 2 August 1990 as the primary cause of the group's liquidity predicament. Undoubtedly, this was a serious unexpected external circumstance which did have adverse financial consequences. Nevertheless, did internal managerial decisions and actions, which could be described as 'mismanagement', play a role? It would be exceptional for a well-managed organisation to founder so quickly because of one external event. Had the company's strategy left it dangerously vulnerable, and was the evidence already visible in its audited financial statements?

Background

The growth, crisis and restructuring of Goodman International is summarised in the following 'critical points history'.

Key events in the life of Goodman International

Birth and start-up years

1954 — Larry Goodman, aged sixteen, commences trading skins, hides and offal in Dundalk area.

1961 — Goodman purchases Dundalk Bacon Company.

1966 — Goodman purchases derelict Anglo-Irish Meat Company plant in Ravensdale, Dundalk. Enters beef processing directly.

Development years: first phase

1973 — Ireland joins European Community. UK market progress.
Goodman buys Cahir Meat Packers factory, Tipperary.

1980 — Goodman buys first Northern Ireland meat factory.
Acquisition of small grain and malting interests.
Build-up of retail trade with British and European food multiple groups.
Turnover £75 million. Ireland's fifth-largest indigenous company.

Development years: second phase — domestic market dominance

1983 — Group turnover £192 million.

1983–84 — Goodman buys Silvercrest meat factories in Dublin.

1985 — Goodman buys former Clover Meats Co-op factory in Waterford.

1985–86 — Goodman buys four meat plants in England and EuroScot meat plant, Scotland.

1986 — Change of name of group from Anglo-Irish Beef Processors to Goodman International.
Group turnover £500 million approx.

1987 — Group announces with government ministers £260 million beef industry investment plan.
Iraqi contract for $134 million in July.

1987–88 — Group purchases six meat plants in Ireland and the UK.

Development years: third phase — diversification

1988 — Acquisition of Bailieboro Co-operative and Westmeath Co-operative (dairying diversification).
Acquisition of Minch Norton and Merchants Warehousing — listed public companies: millers, malsters, warehousing and storage.
Group turnover £784 million.

cont.

Key events in the life of Goodman International *cont.*

1988–89	Creation of Food Industries plc and its flotation on Dublin stockmarket; group holds a 68% stake.
	Additional Iraqi contracts — $325 million in total. Seeks increased export credit insurance cover from government.
	Purchase of Unigate and Berisford shares on London stockmarket.

The beginnings of the crisis

1989	Group turnover £926 million.
	Purchase of more Unigate and Berisford shares.
	Desmond O'Malley, Minister for Industry and Commerce, voids export credit insurance in October.
1989–90	More factory acquisitions in Ireland and the UK.
1990	Purchase of more Unigate and Berisford shares.
	Berisford shares fall heavily in July — margin calls by banks.

The crisis erupts

1990	Iraq invades Kuwait on 2 August. United Nations applies economic sanctions to Iraq.
	Bank pressure on Goodman International; liquidity crisis by 20 August; banks owed over £500 million in unsecured loans.
	Taoiseach Charles Haughey calls special cabinet meeting in late August. Dáil and Seanad recalled from holidays. Company Law (Amendment) Act (examinership legislation) passed.
	Peter Fitzpatrick appointed examiner of Goodman International.
	Group turnover falls to £814 million; net loss £417 million.

The restructuring

1991	Examiner concludes core business is viable. High Court approves financial restructuring scheme.
	Banks approve restructuring, obtain security and 60% of equity.
	New board structure; Larry Goodman remains as managing director.
	Some repayments to banks (approx. £70 million).
	Beef Tribunal established.
1992	Revised restructuring with banks. More payments (approx. £20 million).
1994	Media reports of negotiations to buy banks' equity and loans.
	Beef Tribunal Report issued. Extensive media coverage.
1995	Buy-back of equity and approx. £350–400 million loans from banks for £40 million by Larry Goodman and backers in March.

The 'dealer' becomes a processor
The background to the entrepreneurial deal-making personality

The rise and fall, successes and failures, and more recent recovery of Goodman International can be viewed as an extension of the personality, energy and ambitions of its founder, Larry Goodman. The change of company name in 1986, the negotiations with the banks and examiner during the restructuring, his continuance as managing director after the crisis and the subsequent 'buy-back' from the banks in 1995 — all are evidence of the interweaving of the person and the organisation. Consequently, in examining the organisation's product/market strategy we are primarily reviewing the interests, the growth of expertise and the learning experience of the founder, the dominant personality who gave the organisation its direction and culture.

The evolution of the business was quite straightforward. Larry Goodman, the enterprising young trader in hides and skins, did not move into direct production until 1966 — almost twelve years after he started out. He was then twenty-eight. His father and grandfather were meat traders in the Dundalk area. In his early years Goodman is reported to have obtained meat contracts in Britain and subcontracted the processing to Dublin factories. Buying and selling meat — the 'craft' of finding and making deals — were his early skills.

He gained some meat-processing experience with the purchase of the Dundalk Bacon Company in 1961. A stronger business expertise was achieved with the acquisition in 1966 of the abattoir and plant of Anglo-Irish Meat Company, a sizeable beef-processing operation in Ravensdale, Dundalk. It was the real birth of the organisation. Efficient and profitable operation demanded new management skills and provided a vital business education and experience for Larry Goodman — who was quick to pick up the new skills. He was extremely hard-working, with an ability to focus on problem solving and money-making opportunities.

An illustration of his business commitment was provided in evidence to the Beef Tribunal in the early 1990s.[10] Larry Goodman explained that, following telephone discussions on Christmas Day 1987 about possible Iraqi beef contracts, he caught a plane to Baghdad the next day to pursue the matter.[11] This provides an insight into the work ethic and the dedication to 'doing a deal'. He has been described as 'taciturn, soft-spoken, utterly dedicated to his work, deeply distrustful of publicity. He neither drinks nor smokes, and cultivated an almost spartan image, once telling a trade-union negotiator who asked him "How would you like to live on £96 a week?", "But I do live on £96 a week."'[12]

The meat-processing industry is labour intensive. It is a harsh activity that has its own style and practices which have a long tradition. The culture of the industry is considered 'rough and tough'.[13] Up to the 1970s it was a traditional business with limited modernisation. It was dominated by a number of 'meat baron' families, including the Tunneys and the Horgans. It was also heavily unionised. The industry's culture and way of doing business were very different from the dairying industry, which was dominated by co-operatives. In the 1960s, there were different sets of supplier and customer relationships. Dealers or middlemen bought the cattle from farmers for the factory and live trade. Factory sales were, to an extent, arranged through the concept of a 'deal' rather than a constant relationship with a customer.

Goodman's innovations

Goodman broke the mould in a number of different areas. First, unlike his competitors and the meat co-operatives, he paid the farmers on the same day as the delivery and weighing of the cattle. Others took a week or longer to settle. The farmer was invited to observe the weighing and a relationship of trust and a fair price was built up, in contrast to the culture of the travelling cattle buyers and fairs of an earlier era. Second, any form of demarcation of work practices or featherbedding was unacceptable in the group's factories. Workers, supervisors and managers were expected to do almost any task. Larry Goodman's reply to Eoin McGonigal SC in evidence to the Beef Tribunal provides an insight:

> The whole industry was plagued with demarcation at floor level and with high overheads at management level. So we set about putting this right and we put in tremendous efforts into rearranging the whole production area and we categorised people by their skill rather than any other way. We paid them accordingly, but everyone had to do every job in the factory . . .
>
> There were some notable exceptions . . . but it is against that background that the other factories we bought seemed to have been in trouble, like Cahir in 1973.[14]

Third, tough production and efficiency targets were set and performance was demanded with no excuses. Modern processing and packaging methods were introduced, and stocks were not allowed to build up since there was a tight relationship between cold stores and daily output. The management team who purchased the cattle also had to achieve their sale. The factory management would automatically know the relationship and yields between cost inputs and selling price, what could be afforded and the consequent performance. It was a simple and effective system. Managers were paid on results. Operational costs and overheads were tightly controlled under an annual budgeting system, which monitored actual performance with plan on a simple but effective weekly input–output analysis.

Product and market innovations
From the late 1960s, instead of selling meat as a commodity into the wholesale meat markets in London, Liverpool and Birmingham or using commission agents, Goodman slowly broke into the smaller supermarket groups. Later the group penetrated the leading multiples and, in a decade, became one of their largest suppliers. Ireland's accession to the European Community in 1973 provided new market opportunities as well as 'intervention' purchase of processed meat output. The Goodman organisation helped modernise Irish meat processing, making it more marketing and customer oriented. More added value remained in Ireland than heretofore, because of the introduction of vacuum-packed lines to supermarkets. By the early 1980s it had won access to multiples in France and Germany. This penetration of the Continental European market was testimony to the group's quality standards and efficiency. In an extremely competitive business, it was an excellent management and sales achievement that many commentators have overlooked.

The product market comprised three constituencies: large retail multiples in Ireland, the United Kingdom and Continental Europe; European Community intervention support schemes for excess production of beef; and 'third countries', especially Iran and Iraq which offered extensive meat contracts to suppliers to support their armies during their lengthy war. Production of beef far exceeded demand in the EC. Larry Goodman told the Beef Tribunal that the group sold substantially less into EC intervention than any other meat supplier in Ireland and than most in Europe.[15] Output sold into intervention between 1987 and 1990 was about 11% of turnover, whereas commercial sales to multiples varied between 64% and 70% of turnover and the balance (between 19% and 25%) went to seventy-seven 'third countries'. He admitted that after the Gulf war in late 1990 (and the BSE restrictions) intervention sales rose to 19%, commercial sales were maintained at 68% and just 13% went to 'third countries'.

Acquisitions and turnarounds
Goodman made the transition from sales and deal-making to efficient factory production management, with a speciality in achieving high meat

yields. However, his skill in finding and closing large and profitable deals and coping with the risks involved was to help build the business.

The purchase of the Cahir Meat Packers plant in Co. Tipperary in 1973 was a pivotal event which set a pattern that was later to be repeated: it was a modern grant-aided plant which Goodman bought cheaply. It would appear that poor management and alleged labour problems resulted in heavy losses under its previous owners. The business had declined to a small workforce. Cahir provided Goodman with its first challenge and experience of a 'turnaround' situation. The returns were good, with an investment payback of close to eighteen months. Insights into practices on acquisition and turnaround emerged in Larry Goodman's response to questions from Eoin McGonigal SC at the Beef Tribunal:

> *McGonigal:* What is your first priority when you are taking over any plant?
>
> *Goodman:* We would assess its viability under various headings and we work under five key headings [procurement; production efficiency and costs; sales and marketing; finance and administration; and transportation] and we analyse the figures and . . . how the company was performing under the five headings and decide whether we could straighten out the problems in the plant, whether it needed medication, surgery, or whether it needed intensive care, or whatever. We would act accordingly.
>
> *McGonigal:* Did it sometimes result in the workforce that had been in the plant at the time that you took over, having to be reduced or a change in their work practices having to be brought about?
>
> *Goodman:* I think it would be in the early days, fair to say it would have resulted in major changes at management level, rather than just at floor level and we would have assessed the situation under the five headings.
>
> *McGonigal:* I think there has been a suggested criticism that the company was antagonistic to workers?
>
> *Goodman:* No, I wouldn't accept that. It's a question of having an operation to have long term viability and we would be tougher on management and there has been a lot of evidence that the company wouldn't have any frills or there would be no management cars, no management perks, but we would tend to pay the competitive salary and pay on results, so what we would be doing at each location is we would be doing the same top to the bottom, rather than just picking

out any particular sector and the object would be to make that operation successful.[16]

This 'turnaround' expertise and tough no-nonsense management style became the basis of the profitable purchase of almost seventy meat factories in Ireland, Britain and as far away as Brazil by 1991. An understanding with trade unions was also established. Apart from the acquisition of a few small milling plants, more by accident than design, the dominant activity continued to be beef processing.

Diversification and a new strategic objective

The group primarily remained within a core competence and product for two decades until 1987. By then red meat consumption was declining in Europe, because of diet and health perceptions of white meat. Margins were low and the EC Common Agricultural Policy support schemes for excess beef and dairy output were coming under budgetary pressure. Goodman's response was the opportunistic move in 1988 into dairy processing, where margins were higher, through first the controversial acquisition of the financially distressed Bailieboro Co-operative in Cavan and later the acquisition of the neighbouring Westmeath Co-operative. The group had entered a different, but related, product range which was more capital intensive. It had acquired a strategic 'milk pool' of forty-four million gallons per annum. This was a rational move, with farmers as the same supplier group. The cost reduction and 'turnaround' efficiency techniques were put to good advantage in Bailieboro. The larger dairy co-operatives subsequently became fiercely resistant to further dairy acquisitions.

In 1987 and 1988 Goodman acquired Merchants Warehousing and Minch Norton (malsters), smallish public companies. It folded them together with the dairying activities into a separate group, Food Industries plc. In an extraordinary achievement, within eighteen months, this new organisation was successfully launched on the stockmarket in 1989. This experience brought a new understanding to buying companies, improving performance, floating on the stockmarket and extracting a capital gain. The experience also stimulated the confidence to pursue the objective of becoming one of the largest food-processing organisations in Europe and achieve higher profit margins. The 'low cost' processing competence of the Goodman organisation was felt to be a competitive advantage which could be transferred to related food-processing industries. Interestingly, each of the primary areas of attempted diversification related to EC quotas and some form of intervention support scheme.

It is not difficult to understand the reasons why Goodman International set its sights on dairy and sugar processing in Britain in 1988 with its first secretive purchases of shares on the stockmarket in Unigate and Berisford International, the owner of British Sugar. The Irish diversification activity was minor in relation to meat processing, which accounted for 86% of the group's £926 million turnover in 1989. Following an internal strategic planning exercise in 1986, the group became aware of the constraints and the future prospects in the meat industry, and the need to widen its product range. How to achieve the crossover was the issue. There was little opportunity in other food-processing areas in Ireland. An expressed interest in buying one of Siúicre Éireann's beet-processing factories was rebuffed. The UK was an obvious location because of Goodman's existing operations there and its access to the food multiples.

Financial performance
Financial benchmarking against Kerry Group

The external picture portrayed by the Goodman group was one of profitability and financial health. This seems to have been accepted by the financial markets, if their actions can be taken as evidence. An interpretation of the financial facts indicates a different conclusion. Benchmarking the group's performance and financial position against Kerry Group, as summarised in Table 3.1, shows similar performances up to 1989. However, Goodman's Iraqi credit policy and the London share investments depended on an unsustainable level of risky short-term debt. The ratio analysis of the financial statements clearly signalled that the group was running out of control by late 1989 — nearly a year before the collapse.

Kerry is justified as a benchmark because it too was a young, entrepreneurially oriented food processor; it celebrated its first decade in 1983. Though primarily a dairy-based operation at the time, it faced similar constraints to Goodman in terms of growth and low margin prospects in its sector. Kerry adopted a similar 'growth by acquisition' strategy. It diversified into red, white and convenience meats by a series of acquisitions between 1985 and 1988.[17] By far the largest acquisition was that of Beatreme Foods Inc. of the USA for $130 million. This brought Kerry into food ingredients and contributed higher added value and profit margins. There were also linkages to Kerry's own R&D activities. Kerry focused on brand development through its acquisitions and the launch of new names such as

'Dawn', 'Dawn Light' and 'Hi and Lo'. By 1989 meat processing almost equalled dairying at 40% of turnover, with food ingredients and other activities making up the balance.

Kerry's five-year business plan for the period 1986–90 aimed at 'real growth of 20% per annum in sales and profits'.[18] The group's objective was 'to build an international food organisation'.[19] This ambition triggered the pioneering move of new group structures, under which the co-operative raised external equity for its operating subsidiary through a quotation on the Dublin Stock Exchange in October 1986. This resulted in a dilution of ownership and control, just like a private company, quite apart from the greater disclosure and regulatory requirements. Kerry's earnings per share were 5.0p in 1985 and 6.0p in 1986. By 1990 the earlier targets were surpassed, with earnings reaching 12.6p per share and sales more than doubling. Kerry's share price rose to 190p by the end of 1989, compared with the public issue price of 52p in 1986. Market capitalisation was £285 million, which was nearly double the size of the next largest quoted Irish co-operative food group.

Growth rates

In 1980 Kerry was the larger of the two groups, with an £80 million turnover compared to £75 million for Goodman. At a 36% and 38% compound rate of growth in turnover, in the two periods to 1986, Goodman International was growing at a faster rate. By 1983, Goodman passed out Kerry and between 1986 and 1987 it expanded so rapidly that its turnover became almost twice that of Kerry. Despite Kerry's 28% growth rate in the later period, its turnover was £560 million compared to £926 million for Goodman in 1989.

The real difference was in reported profits: they both attained profits of about £3 million in 1980, but by 1989 the Goodman group reported a pre-tax profit of £34 million compared to £19 million for Kerry.

Profitability

Goodman International seemed to achieve superior profitability returns to Kerry Group because of its higher pre-tax profit margins on turnover and on capital employed. In 1988 and 1989 Goodman achieved returns on equity of 17.2% and 16.7%, compared with 14.1% and 12.5% for Kerry. Even the margin of cash flow to turnover in 1988 and 1989 was similar for both organisations. In its industry the Goodman group was also very profitable: it earned about treble the sales/operating profit margin of Clover Meats Co-operative in the five years 1980–84.[20]

Table 3.1: Financial performance analysis: Goodman International and Kerry Group

Measure	Goodman	Kerry
Growth/profitability		
Turnover growth rates (compound p.a.)		
1980–83	36%[e]	24%
1983–86	38%[e]	19%
1986–89	23%	28%
Pre-tax profit margins		
1988	4.2%	3.3%
1989	3.7%	3.4%
1990	neg.	3.6%
Pre-tax return on equity		
1988	17.2%	14.1%
1989	16.7%	12.5%
1990	neg.	12.8%
Cashflow/turnover margins		
1988	5.0%	4.8%
1989	4.4%	5.0%
1990	neg.	5.0%
Gearing		
Debt/total assets		
1988	66%	67%
1989	69%	52%
1990	142%	55%
Interest cover		
1988	3.7 times	3.6 times
1989	2.7 times	2.6 times
1990	neg.	2.9 times
Cash flow/interest		
1988	4.2 times	4.9 times
1989	3.2 times	3.3 times
1990	neg.	3.7 times
Debt/turnover		
1988	46%	46%
1989	50%	30%
1990	76%	35%
Oper. cash flow/debt		
1988	neg.	10.5%
1989	neg.	14.0%
1990	neg.	21.1%

cont.

Table 3.1:	Financial performance analysis: Goodman International and Kerry Group *cont.*	
Measure	**Goodman**	**Kerry**
Liquidity		
Current ratio		
1988	1.6:1	1.3:1
1989	1.2:1	1.5:1
1990	0.8:1	1.3:1

e   Estimate of the author, derived from information given in evidence at the Beef Tribunal hearings.

Source: Annual reports.

The surge in Goodman's absolute profits did not occur until around 1985.[21] Making adjustments to the accumulated profits of £147 million and the share capital of £40 million, it is estimated that almost £110 million of this retained profit figure was achieved in the five years to 1989. Ignoring grants and capital reserves through revaluations, this implies that almost 60% of the earned shareholders' funds were achieved in the five-year period 1985–89. This analysis indicates the scale of expansion in operations and reported profitability in the critical transformation period to 1989. Goodman International declared modest dividends in relation to reported profits in 1988 and 1989 (£0.9 million and £1.6 million). Up to 1987 most of its growth was financed by retained profits and modest levels of government grants.

The quality of reported profits

The quality and sustainability of Kerry's profit stream were superior to those of the Goodman group. Kerry had created a portfolio of franchises and products on the foundation of milk quotas, brands, R&D and food ingredients. It was professionally managed, with an aggressive marketing emphasis. The basis and potential volatility of the Goodman profit stream suggest it was weaker. Without Iraqi sales of £296 million in the 1987–89 figures, the Goodman group's profit record would have been less impressive. The 1989 financial statements did not disclose separately the foreign currency gains of £7.8 million in the reported profits, in contrast to the 1990 accounts which disclosed a £10.7 million foreign currency loss. This was a 'swing' of £18.5 million, which implied sizeable currency risk on trading contracts and borrowings.

Gearing and liquidity

From income gearing criteria, interest cover is also a close match in both firms in 1988 and 1989. A deeper analysis of gearing, from cash flow criteria, reveals some structural and earnings weaknesses in Goodman International. Total debt to total assets at 66% in 1988 is similar to Kerry. However, this 1988 ratio was at a peak for Kerry because of the Beatreme Foods acquisition in October 1988. Kerry's debt ratio was reduced the following year to 52.5%, whereas Goodman's debt ratio continued to increase, reaching 69.4%. It was a definite warning signal, which was not heeded in 1990. Because of its quotation, Kerry was able to make a rights issue.

The difference in financial risk is more starkly highlighted by the total debt to turnover ratios. Both organisations started with the same figure, 46% in 1988. In 1989 Goodman International expanded to 50.1% in contrast to Kerry Group's reduction to 30%. Servicing this level of debt in relation to turnover would require much higher profit margins; otherwise it would not be sustainable. The only other source of funds (in a private company) was the conversion of assets into liquidity (i.e. the Iraqi debt). By 1990 the Goodman group's total debt rose to 76% of turnover: this was not sustainable, because it could not be serviced from operations with such a low profit margin. Goodman International's interest bill jumped from £12 million in 1988 to £20 million in 1989 and £48 million by 1990.

Another signal of Goodman International's financial deterioration was the decline in the current ratio from 1.6:1 to 1.2:1 between 1988 and 1989. In contrast, Kerry strengthened from 1.3:1 to 1.5:1. In parallel, the working capital to turnover ratio in Goodman International weakened dramatically between 1988 and 1989. This was despite the fact that the 1989 figures were bolstered by the accounting treatment of the Iraqi debt. A more prudent valuation, in view of the loss of the export credit insurance and the consequent risk, would have produced a much less favourable picture. Moreover, the Iraqi credit period was extended from twelve to eighteen months. Any Iraqi valuation provisions could have turned the profit figure reported in 1989 into a loss.

Goodman International did not overtrade so much as overexpand in investment commitments in 1990. Kerry's more controlled growth rate indicates superior planning and financial control linked to a much more balanced series of objectives. Growth and market share became key Goodman objectives — almost ends in themselves — in the 1980s. The objective of becoming the largest meat processor in Ireland was achieved by 1980. The second objective of becoming the largest in Britain and Ireland was accomplished by 1986. From then on it was a much wider and more ambitious canvas, with diversification into non-meat activities as a priority.

Goodman International appears to have copied Kerry, to some degree, in objectives and broad business strategy. It wanted to be an international food group and diversify away from its low-margin core activity to higher added value processes. This explains the subsequent risky aspiration to control British Sugar through the Berisford speculation. The problem was how to finance the strategy and remain a private company. Larry Goodman wanted full control and secrecy at the parent level, which posed conflicts for financial risk. Food Industries plc did not have the financial capacity to take on the London speculations, nor could they have remained secret for long.

Warning signals in the financial statements

Signals of and trends in the rapid collapse of Goodman International were reflected in the profit and loss accounts, balance sheets and cash flows for 1988–90, which are summarised in Tables 3.2, 3.3 and 3.4.

Table 3.2: Goodman International: consolidated profit and loss account (£m)

	1988	1989	1990
Turnover	784	926	814
Gross profit	99	108	76
Operating expenses	55	54	75
Operating profit	44	54	1
Bank interest	12	20	48
Extraordinary provisions/write-offs etc.	–	–	370
Net profit/(loss)	32	34	(417)

Source: Audited financial statements.

The increased turnover of £926 million in 1989 did not lead to an equivalent increase in profit because of lower gross profit margins and the sharp increase in bank interest. The gross profit margin fell from 12.6% to 11.6%. The net profit margin declined from 4.1% to 3.6%. By 1989, interest cover fell to 2.7 times, which was precarious for an industrial firm. The small operating profit of just £1 million in 1990 was due to the further fall in gross profit margins to 9.4% because of the BSE scare, the loss of Iraqi contracts, and the impact on the business of the examinership. The additional direct bankruptcy costs associated with examinership also took their toll. There was insufficient profit to cover the high bank interest charges of £48 million. The burden of servicing such heavy bank debt pushed Goodman into deficit. Provisions against Iraqi debtors of £158 million and intercompany losses, owing to the commitments arising on the share investments in Berisford and other items, resulted in an 'extraordinary' charge of £370 million and a net loss for 1990 of £417 million. The consequence was a negative equity position of £223 million in relation to total assets of £425 million.

Table 3.3: Goodman International: consolidated balance sheet (£m)

	1988	1989	1990
Fixed assets	108	124	98
Financial assets	–	8	128
	108	132	226
Current assets			
Stocks	88	94	35
Debtors	256	345	114
Cash	90	89	50
Investments	14	9	–
	448	537	199
Total assets	556	669	425
Financed by:			
Bank loans	250	366	547
Creditors	100	84	90
Government capital grants	14	16	11
Shareholders' equity	192	203	(223)
	556	669	425

Source: Audited financial statements.

In the balance sheet, the critical items were that bank borrowing jumped from £250 million in 1988 to £547 million in 1990. Shareholders' equity was £192 million in 1988 and it did not increase sufficiently to support the riskiness of the firm's activities. The fact that all the bank debt of £366 million was short-term by 1989 made the liquidity position extremely vulnerable. There was thus a dangerous combination of excess debt and weak liquidity. This was a change in financing policy because a quarter had been medium-term facilities the previous year. This change in borrowing structure broke all prudent financing principles and left the group dangerously exposed.

The combination of deteriorating debt and liquidity figures, together with Note 22 'Contingencies' which referred to off balance sheet guarantees for related companies, should have prompted the users of the financial statements to probe much more deeply. The additional off balance sheet 'debt' which subsequently emerged through the cross-guarantees (the Berisford and Unigate speculations) ultimately undermined the existing weak financial structure. The accounting principles and disclosure required careful consideration, because the 'Notes' to the accounts were extremely relevant. These figures did not include other facilities in excess of £150 million which were discounted against EC official support scheme payments.

In contrast, Kerry generated more internal resources and raised external equity through the stockmarket three times between 1986 and 1990. There was a real difference in funding policies and the strategic capital structure decision. Kerry also took a large investment 'breather' in 1989 and 1990, which enabled it to consolidate its financial position.

Put another way, banks and suppliers were financing almost 70% of the Goodman group's assets in 1989 and this did not include any off balance sheet obligations in respect of related company and group bank guarantees. Kerry's reliance on bank debt was proportionately much lower. Total debt fell to just 52% of assets. In contrast to Kerry, the Goodman group kept up its hyperactive pace of spending and borrowing in 1990. It was the combination of dynamic and structural weaknesses in Goodman that increased both its business and its financial risk profile.

The analysis demonstrates that Goodman International had compromised a long-established track record by late 1989. Its vulnerability and riskiness were evident in the 1989 financial statements, despite the apparently optimistic accounting policies. How can we explain such risky future commitments which bankrupted the company?

The cash flow profile, as set out in Table 3.4, clearly reveals the risky investment strategies, credit policies and financing of the group. Positive operating cash flows became negative with the impact of the rising working capital needs, mainly the Iraqi long-term credit. The consequence was that negative net free cash flows of £103 million and £80 million were generated in 1988 and 1989. Net investment spending was relatively low in 1988 and so the financing gap was £108 million. This 'gap' increased to £122 million in 1989 with the impact of the negative net cash flow and investment spending. It was out of control in 1990, with a positive net cash flow of £73 million being overburdened with net investment spending of £311 million, primarily on the related company share investment outlays.

Table 3.4: Goodman International: cash flow summary (£m)

	1988	1989	1990
Net operating flows	38	39	(12)
Working capital change	(141)	(119)	85
Net cash flow	(103)	(80)	73*
Investment outlays (net)	5	42	311
Financing shortfall	108	122	238
Annual increase in bank borrowing	108	122	238
Cumulative bank debt position	250	366	547

*   Could be taken as negative, depending on the classification of items included in 'investment outlays'.

Note: Bank borrowing defined as the gross bank debt position as shown on the face of the balance sheets. It does not include any off balance sheet obligations or intercompany or related group company guarantees. Most of these obligations 'crystallised' during 1990 and were incorporated in the 'investments' figure in the 1990 cash flows.

Source: Audited financial statements; data recomputed by author because of changes in financial statement layout and structure before 1990.

Thus, the 1990 financing shortfall escalated to £238 million — all of which was funded by risky short-term bank debt.

The combined financing shortfalls in the cash flow analysis over the three years 1988–90 came to £468 million. Since there was no new equity introduced into the organisation, this shortfall was funded by bank borrowings. It was a remarkable change in the company's previously prudent policies. The implications for the operating activities owing to the related and intercompany bank guarantees were particularly relevant. Investments were financed from internal cash flows and IDA grants. Bank borrowing had previously been modest because it was primarily used for seasonal working capital. With the rate of growth in investment outlays, the Goodman group's cash flow was negative for three consecutive years to 1989. This proved to be massively negative in 1990. The cash flow profile proved to be the fundamental distinguishing financial characteristic between the Goodman and Kerry organisations.

The sharp swing in cash flows and short-term debt was a signal of the emergence of a less cautious 'corporate personality' with a new risk profile. The Goodman organisation took almost thirty years to reach less than £100 million in bank borrowing. In three years this escalated to £547 million. This was what led to the financial self-destruction of the organisation.

Organisational structure and management culture
Board structure
Goodman International was a private family company with just three statutory directors: Larry Goodman, his wife and his brother Peter.[22] Larry Goodman was both chairman and chief executive. Brian Britton was company secretary until his resignation in late September 1990. Larry Goodman was reported to control 95% of the equity. Senior executives with the title 'director' were not directors of the parent company.

There were defects at board level. First, there was no experienced 'outsider' to provide some element of check and balance. Second, there was no full-time finance director with full board status. For a company of its size, increasing diversity of operations, and such dependence on unsecured bank borrowings, it was remarkable that the banks did not seek to correct this governance flaw earlier. This weakness signalled the status of the finance function in this large privately owned entrepreneurial firm. If there had been independent experienced non-executive directors, there may have been stronger management planning and control, with some reining back of the speculative Berisford and Unigate investments on the basis of short-term borrowings. A freezing or renegotiation of the Iraqi contracts after the export credit insurance cover was voided in December 1989 would also have been more likely, with implications for the London investments. Indeed, it is doubtful that independent directors would have approved the signing of the 1987 $134 million Iraqi contract, or any other large contracts, without written advance confirmation of insurance cover. In contrast, Kerry Group had a separate chairman and its three top executives were full members of the board, along with other farmer-suppliers and representatives of Kerry Co-operative.

The fact that the Goodman group's financial restructuring and corporate reorganisation agreed with the banking consortium required the appointment of an experienced independent chairman (Ian Morisson), two independent directors and a new financial controller indicates the bankers' views about the role of internal governance structures in the group's recovery. Management control was linked to the composition of the board and the separation of the chairman and chief executive roles, along with strengthened financial control.

Organisation structure
Until the mid-1980s the group operated with a simple management and organisation structure. For many years there was a direct line from Larry

Goodman to the factory managers. Each factory was a separate profit centre with its own buying, selling (under direction) and transportation scheduling. Each operated with its own accountant, who reported to the factory manager and also to head office in Ardee, Co. Louth under targets set in the annual budget. Head office staffing was extremely lean under this decentralised structure. Larry Goodman, assisted by his brother Peter or by Gerry Thornton, the chief executive of the meat division, made regular visits to plants to review operations and performance. Brian Britton, the former deputy chief executive–finance, in giving his impressions of when he was first recruited to Eoin McGonigal SC in Beef Tribunal evidence, provided an insight into the group's management culture and style:

> I joined a group which I believe was one of a typical entrepreneurial growth. Mr Goodman, as the chief executive and owner, had tried to control all aspects of operations. He had a finance director, Tom McAndrew, working with him but he recognised that trying to keep his finger on the pulse in all 17 different operations was no longer possible . . . the group had a turnover of approximately £190 million.[23]

The seventeen different operations in 1983 included five meat factories, six grain companies, three by-product companies and a large farming feed lot. The management arrangements up to 1986 were that each plant was responsible for all aspects of activities except where output was directed to the large multiple supermarket groups in the UK, Europe or wider international sales; this output was sold to the international division which marketed the product abroad.[24]

With the scope of new acquisitions now extending to Britain, the chain of command and responsibilities was altered by the creation of a divisional group structure in 1986.[25] The new organisation consisted of six divisions:

- meat-processing division (Ireland)
- UK processing division
- international division
- by-products division
- grain division
- finance division.

A subsequent revision of this structure was necessitated by the introduction of a dairy activity through the acquisition of Bailieboro Co-operative in 1988 followed by Merchants Warehousing and Minch Norton. This led to the spin-off of these non-meat activities into the newly formed Food Industries plc.

The rapid pace of these new initiatives stretched group management resources to the limit by 1988. There was an insufficient depth of senior management to cope effectively with operational, strategic and political/public affairs issues. For example, Brian Britton explained to the Beef Tribunal that in a five-month period between late 1987 and early 1988, he attended 104 meetings in connection with the development and flotation of 32% of the equity of Food Industries plc on the Dublin Stock Exchange. He pointed out that there were many other meetings relating to the acquisition of Bailieboro and other companies.[26] The management resource gaps were evident when it became necessary to appoint a young chartered accountant Aidan Connor, who had been financial controller in the finance division only since January 1986, to head the international division in September 1987.

This lack of management depth proved to be the organisation's Achilles' heel. Proper attention could not be given to public relations or to the management of the risk exposure on the Iraqi debt and the decision options on the Unigate and Berisford investments while senior management were also coping with operational issues. Growth and new diversity created a complexity which left top management overstretched. This shortage in managerial resources certainly contributed to the firm's financial crisis. Larry Goodman admitted as much, when discussing the investment in Unigate in response to a question from Mr Justice Hamilton, chairman of the Tribunal:

> . . . at one stage, in fact when we decided we had too much exposure when Minister O'Malley voided the insurance, we delegated the sale of Unigate to some of our advisors and at that stage Unigate was showing a profit of twenty two million pounds . . . and, unfortunately, by the time it was dealt with, we missed the boat.[27]

Larry Goodman admitted this management flaw more directly when replying to Eoin McGonigal SC:

> *McGonigal:* You identify, in the latter half of the 80s, a problem that arose as a result of management being overstretched, what was that?
>
> *Goodman:* Based on what I was saying, I suppose, in hindsight, maybe management was usually overstretched but, at the same time, this is a situation I think I am referring to here, where, yes, our attention to the media wouldn't have been what it should have been,

and I am saying here that the request for information from the media — and this resulted in a poor relationship . . . and the result of these developments was that some politicians found it easy to project the views that they had that had been projected to them, perhaps, from some of our competitors.[28]

The continued involvement in most aspects of decision-making by Larry Goodman seems to have been pervasive. Veronica Guerin's detailed account of the missing £25 million associated with the 'Cyprus transaction' was an example. It seems that Brian Britton, as deputy chief executive–finance, was bypassed. To his horror, he appears to have learned of the transaction and the problems relating to it on Friday 16 June 1990. The transaction appears not to have taken place as planned, with appropriate security, and the money had 'gone missing'.[29] The 'Cyprus transaction' also offered an insight into the risky 'deal-making' culture which was attracted to a profitable 'turn' on borrowed money. For a food-processing group with high borrowings, this was an unusual activity. The investigations to secure the return of the money, together with associated court actions and media publicity, continued to haunt the organisation in subsequent years.

Kerry Group operated with a stronger and deeper management structure. Though its growth tends to be identified with Denis Brosnan, as the entrepreneurial managing director, there was a top management team of three which included Denis Cregan in operations and Hugh Friel in finance and administration as well as Brosnan. Both Cregan and Friel joined the co-operative in its formative years soon after Denis Brosnan and both had been appointed deputy managing director by 1986. All three were also substantial shareholders in Kerry Group after its stockmarket quotation. Kerry also had a strong group of senior and middle level managers reporting to this top management team.

Financial control, management and internal control systems

For a company of Goodman's size, the weaknesses in financial controls were evident by the early 1980s as a result of acquisitions and the rapid organic growth. Turnover jumped from £75 million in 1980 to £192 million in 1983. Larry Goodman personally monitored and controlled operations, productivity and yields through a combination of simple (but reasonably effective) weekly physical and financial measures. The diversity and expansion demanded skilled financial management with the increasing working capital requirements, particularly in the heavy 'killing' season for cattle from

September to late winter. An illustration of the financing problems of the organisation and the need for more rigorous financial control was provided by Brian Britton, a chartered accountant, in Tribunal evidence. He was in his early thirties when he joined the organisation and his briefing from Larry Goodman in his first two weeks in the job was: 'Brian, we want you to ensure, number one, we have enough finance; number two, we get the best rate; number three, you make the best use of it.'[30]

Brian Britton provided a compelling insight into the group's management accounting and control systems at the time, when replying to Eoin McGonigal SC:

> *McGonigal:* I think, initially in 1983 when you joined and for a lot of 1984 . . . you spent a lot of that time putting in a system of financial controls and reporting procedures?
>
> *Britton:* That is correct. When I joined the group . . . I would like to draw a distinction between financial and management controls — the group was somewhat lacking in the area of financial controls whereas the management controls, the day to day running of the individual operations, I observed them as being very strong.[31]

The pace of acquisitions and growth created weaknesses in the accounting, finance and administrative sides of the organisation. By late 1985, there was a shortage of middle management personnel. Brian Britton disclosed that 'at different times in the growth of the group we were left in a situation where there were not enough people, to the extent of the work necessary to be done'. A programme of computerisation of financial accounting/finance reporting was initiated. He explained that the group was becoming unwieldy, from the accounting/financial control point of view. By the end of 1985, the number of operations had expanded from seventeen to twenty-five. Britton commented, 'we had, from memory, 96 sets of financial accounts'.[32]

The dominance of the entrepreneurial culture over administrative procedures was also highlighted by Niall O'Carroll, the Goodman audit partner in KPMG Stokes Kennedy Crowley.[33] In his evidence to the Tribunal he indicated that the group's monthly management accounts in 1986 and 1987 were not what one would expect in a large company.[34] He also implied that the group's systems did not match those of other multinational clients:

> . . . comparing them to other multinational clients where I might have had an involvement as auditor, generally the procedures,

accounting systems in well established large corporations would be very well documented and very well established and understood and fully debugged . . . In the Goodman group, as I have said, it had grown very substantially by acquisition mostly and it was in its nature that the administration was always trying to keep up with the pace of activity which Mr Goodman and the people involved in the group set so that the exercise of carrying out an audit and producing annual accounts required a certain degree of pragmatism to get a relatively timely and accurate result.[35]

The ineffective financial control was demonstrated by the enormous changes in the group's gearing levels allied to the extensive commitments to volatile asset values (Stock Exchange securities in Berisford and Unigate), the weakening interest cover (bank interest rose from £12 million to £48 million between 1988 and 1990) and the decline in liquidity. The combination represented a very high risk exposure and a deterioration in working capital and liquidity. The complete dependence on short-term bank borrowing and its link to intercompany and related company guarantees was very imprudent financial management and capital structure policy. The foregoing suggests weak cash flow projections, and ineffective planning and control of future financial commitments within a sustainable resource capacity.

Though Brian Britton's title had been changed to deputy chief executive–finance, by 1988 he had become much more involved with corporate development initiatives than with financial control. He worked virtually full-time on acquisitions in 1987 and 1988. With some verve and almost single-handedly, he successfully implemented the Food Industries plc merger of companies and helped bring together a new board and management. In his Tribunal evidence he described 1987 as 'a very hectic year'. The creation of Food Industries 'took up sixty to sixty five percent of my total time'. The group had insufficient depth of financial management to effectively support its new scale and complexity. The promotion of Aidan Connor to management of the international division in September 1987, after a short spell as the financial controller, left a senior vacancy for nine months in a vital function for a fast-expanding group until John McLoughlin was appointed financial controller in mid-1988.[36]

An internal auditor was appointed in 1986, but his role did not turn out as planned. Instead of carrying out internal audits and reviewing specific controls of the group, he ended up dealing with urgent problems in different areas. Though Goodman heeded the advice of his auditors in the early 1980s and recruited a new financial controller and a number of accountants (many came from the audit firm), nevertheless there were too few senior accounting personnel with industrial experience. Apart from each division having its own accounting team (the UK division had its own financial director), there were a number of younger accountants and others appointed in group functions such as internal financial controls, computerisation, financial planning, special projects and capital expenditure, and a group treasury function. The shortage of senior finance/administrative personnel was a continuing issue in the group. After all, by 1988 group turnover was approaching £800 million and there were dozens of plants in Ireland and the UK. Brian Britton noted, when discussing the financial controller vacancy in 1987–88 in his Tribunal evidence: 'So that reflects on the problems we had at different times where we didn't have enough people to fill the key positions that we required them for.'[37]

In effect, wider management needs exposed gaps and these were made good by 'raiding' the financial management and control function and putting the two most senior chartered accountants primarily into general management duties. Brian Britton was also given responsibility for the difficult public relations brief in 1989 following adverse publicity about alleged irregularities in a Dublin plant. Of course it is debatable whether a strong financial director would have been able to prevent the signing of the 1987 and 1988 Iraqi contracts, or the London share investments, bearing in mind the strong personality of Larry Goodman as well as the fact that he was the owner/manager.

The Goodman organisation claimed to have tight performance control systems with weekly measurement against budget on a physical basis and periodic financial reporting. Brian Britton elaborated on the planning and control systems:

> From the outset, the motivation of the group, or object of each of the operations in the group, was to make profit and every operation in the group was run as a profit centre. The manager for each operation was responsible for all aspects of that operation and he would essentially, following annual reviews, which looked at budgets, he would be operating to those budgets and key management figures were produced by those operations and they were to help the managers assess their performance, from a management point of view and then financial accounts were prepared, initially in the early days they were prepared quarterly; but latterly they were produced monthly, and following review by the divisions, they were given to

> head office. Essentially, management was by exception. . . . if someone was operating to budget, you left them alone and left them to get on with the running of their business, but if targets were not being met, they received attention initially from division and at the end of the year, if targets were not being met, we wanted to know why at head office . . . [38]

Annual meetings with management over a two-week period, with two to four hours devoted to each operation by Larry Goodman, his brother Peter and Brian Britton, indicate how seriously Larry Goodman personally took the process of controlling management performance. Goodman explained:

> We had developed, because of the pressures of time, a system of identifying the key areas where factories were operating very well or very poorly and I would have all that on a spreadsheet and I would have the meetings cut down to two hours or maybe, at the most, four or five hours for each operation and I would meet with the head of the division, the manager and his financial people and maybe his production person and we would have all these key figures identified prior to that and marked in terms of how that factory had performed vis-à-vis its budget, not just financially, but in terms of overheads or any sort of cost and anything that was above target in terms of cost would be in a red mark and anything that was below it would be in green. So, we could see straight away, against target, where they stood, so it cut things down and we had to deal with it in that way . . . [39]

This direct personal contact with managers in such a large group was an indication of the management style and leadership where the founder/entrepreneur remained very much involved in most aspects of the business. The difference between Larry Goodman and many other entrepreneurs was the methodical use he made of measurement of figures related to the group's productivity, performance and planning. Whereas the Goodman organisation had a reasonably effective operational planning and control system, at the strategic financial control level it was defective. This was the result of the entrepreneurial risk-taking propensity of Larry Goodman which, in this writer's view, between 1987 and 1990 reached a level that seemed out of character with his previous track record.

The group undoubtedly had good operational management linked to a reasonably efficient management and financial control system for day-to-day operations. This reflected well on Brian Britton's earlier influence on the organisation's operational activities before being drawn into acquisitions, strategic implementation and, later, public relations. The lack of depth in other senior management areas, apart from accounting and finance, meant that the small number of senior executives were trying to handle on a 'fire fighting basis' potentially serious group problems, as well as co-ordinate and integrate the acquisitions. It would appear to this writer that Brian Britton was overinfluenced by the entrepreneurial culture and this left little restraint on Larry Goodman in view of the board's structural weaknesses.

Despite the group's claims about its strong management controls, the proposed terms of the restructuring with the banks appear to have included a provision that the banks were to be satisfied that there were improved management controls and reporting mechanisms and a commitment by the Goodman organisation to adopt any recommendations in this respect by Coopers & Lybrand. The examinership seems to have revealed weaknesses in controls and accounting systems which the banks wished to see remedied while they remained tied into the group.

The entrepreneurial trader, the accountants and risk

An emphasis on growth, market share and the customer dominates the interest of the trader/entrepreneur, whereas finance staff are much more conscious of stability, order and risk. Though the finance people in Goodman International put their concerns about the large Iraqi contracts in memos to Larry Goodman, he still went ahead without written confirmation of export credit insurance. The first big contract was for $134 million in July–August 1987. Insurance cover for these contracts was not in place. Following completion of this contract, the group negotiated $325 million in new Iraqi contracts for delivery in 1988 and 1989. Application for additional insurance cover was made by October 1988. The insurance cover arrangement seems to have been for 80% of the value of the contract at a premium of 1%. The credit period had been extended from twelve months to eighteen months, during the course of a trade mission led by a minister.

Without insurance cover the risk of a bad debt was very real. The contracts were large in comparison with the group's working capital and net worth. Signing such contracts, therefore, was a serious financial commitment. Brian Britton and Aidan Connor, the two senior chartered accountants in the group, were concerned and both expressed their apprehension to Larry Goodman in verbal and written form.

The conflict between the approach adopted to business and financial risk by the founder/chief executive and the professional accountants was brought out starkly in the following exchange between Adrian Hardiman SC and Larry Goodman at the Beef Tribunal. This part of the dialogue focused on the credit risk and the Iraqi contracts, particularly since a second large contract was being negotiated in December 1987, which would relate to the 1988 season. This was for $105 million on top of the earlier August contract for $134 million.

> *Hardiman:* In order to commit yourselves to a very large contract for the following year, the 1988 season, you required an assurance in relation to export credit?
>
> *Goodman:* We would have been looking for it. It would have been helpful.
>
> *Hardiman:* Isn't it a little more than that in respect of the previous contract, the $134 million, the one notified on the 31 August, both Mr Connor and Mr Britton have confirmed that your company would not have entered into a contract at that size without export credit, that must be the same for the large contract in December 1987?
>
> *Goodman:* More or less, not actually. Sometimes the accountants would look at it different than the traders. The traders are trying to capture the market. The accountants are trying to count the figures. Different people see it in different ways.[40]

The difference between the two views, as Larry Goodman so succinctly put it, was that the 'trader' was trying to capture the market and 'mind the customer', whereas the accountant was 'minding the figures'. The implied meaning was that one course of action could supersede the other, on the apparent whim of the entrepreneurial founder — but at what cost? It was due to not 'minding the figures' sufficiently, from a risk perspective, that Larry Goodman lost control of his organisation to the banks for some years. The advice of his top managers was dismissed and there was little they could do about it, other than resign.

Mr Mooney of KPMG Stokes Kennedy Crowley told the Tribunal that the Iraqi deliveries amounted to £296 million out of a turnover of £2.3 billion for the three years to 1989.[41] At almost 13% of total turnover (and the greater part of the non-multiple business) and eighteen months' credit, it was a clear change in financial risk without the 80% export credit insurance cover. The Iraqi contracts offered attractive profit margins, and Larry Goodman as a dealer and risk-taker was tempted by the gamble. He also hoped to manage the risk by lobbying for improved export credit cover.

As it turned out, the large Iraqi contracts were an example of a salesman going after 'bad business' turnover and suffering an enormous bad debt which contributed to liquidity problems.

Business and politics: oil and water?

The nature of the Goodman organisation's business and its scale of operations in the agricultural industry in Ireland by 1980 inevitably meant that there was personal contact by its top management with state agencies, senior civil servants and politicians. Larry Goodman had access to successive governments at the highest levels.[42] He used government lobbying as part of his strategy to develop his company. The Tribunal Report cites export insurance cover, IDA grants and related financing support schemes (Section 84 loans). Financial contributions were made to the two largest political parties. The organisation seems to have regarded political lobbying as part of normal business activity.

Following a change of government in 1987, Larry Goodman made a request for increased export credit cover. In September 1987 the government increased the ceiling on insured exports to Iraq from £70 million to £150 million. Total liability on cover to Iraq at the time was about £25 million, thus the increase was effectively £125 million. The more supportive response of government in 1987 to the company's requests for increased insurance cover followed an extensively publicised press conference on 18 June 1987. The Goodman organisation, the Taoiseach and a number of government ministers announced a five-year development plan for beef processing. It was to involve the modernisation and expansion of the group's activities and the building of new plants to cater for increased capacity and added value through 'fifth quarter' processing. There were several discussions between Goodman representatives, government ministers and the IDA about the support package and its conditions. A difficult position was finally resolved[43] but the Goodman group did not proceed with the plan.

Subsequently the Insurance Corporation of Ireland (ICI), with its insurance expertise and market knowledge, raised questions. In addition, government departmental officials questioned the source of the beef exported to Iraq by the group. In October 1989 part of the insurance cover was withdrawn. Whether or not the group came to rely excessively on political intervention as an instrument to achieve its business objectives is problematical. It was paradoxical that it seems to have been a political intervention which helped exacerbate the group's problems.

The reasons for the financial collapse

The more immediate reason for the group's financial collapse was the loss of liquidity when a number of foreign banks withdrew or demanded repayment of their facilities in early August 1990. The banks became apprehensive about their level of exposure when Iraq invaded Kuwait on 2 August. The United Nations put in train a variety of economic sanctions which resulted in a drying up of Iraq's foreign exchange earnings and a freezing of overseas bank accounts. Almost immediately, the near £170 million owed to the group by Iraqi customers was no longer as valuable or as potentially liquid. Effectively, the group's primary source of working capital was cut off. It was unable to roll over the facilities or find adequate substitute loans on the financial markets. The banks appear to have been looking to their own position because most of the facilities were unsecured. Altogether, thirty-three banks were owed about £504 million.[44] The reasons advanced by Larry Goodman for the financial crisis in responses to Eoin McGonigal SC were revealing:

> *McGonigal:* I think then, as I was saying, the export credit was withdrawn in '89?
>
> *Goodman:* It was, yes.
>
> *McGonigal:* And the invasion of Kuwait and UN sanctions prevented payment?
>
> *Goodman:* Yes.
>
> *McGonigal:* And did that have an effect on the Company?
>
> *Goodman:* It had. We had a very valuable company at that point in time. At that particular point in time, 2 August 1990, there were a couple of things that happened, and we needn't be too long winded about it, but we had shares in Berisford, a company in England, that we were looking at for a particular reason in relation to Food Industries, those shares virtually collapsed because of a couple of happenings we can get into, if necessary, but, within a few days . . . Iraq invaded Kuwait and that resulted in, because of both of these exposures at the same time, in our discussions with the banks, we had too many lines of credit on call and they all called at the same time. All the banks, at that stage, that had any business in the Middle East, would see . . . what exposure do they have to companies doing business in the Middle East and they all clamoured, not just with our company but with every company, to have released their short term

finance. We had too much on short term and not enough on medium and long term, so that was the problem.[45]

Larry Goodman attributed the underlying causes to four elements: the Berisford share collapse; the Iraqi invasion of Kuwait; the short-term borrowing policy; and the attitudes and reactions of the banks. This writer's research evidence points to five reasons and some bad luck, only partially supporting these assertions:

1. the scale of the Iraqi contracts and debtor risk
2. investing heavily in Berisford International quoted shares
3. investing in Unigate quoted shares simultaneously
4. funding these volatile assets with short-term bank facilities
5. delaying or taking almost no defensive action until it was too late.

The negotiation of the first large Iraqi meat contract for $134 million in July 1987, followed by others of a similar magnitude, was the first mistake. This ill-advised contract imposed a huge degree of customer credit risk on the organisation before the expansion of the government's export credit scheme had been formally put before or approved by the Dáil. Up to then, contracts of the order of $25 million with Iraq were the norm. Once the export credit insurance cover was withdrawn in October 1989, and the Iraqi debt was over £100 million, the group was once again exposed to serious credit risk. The banks were informed and the credit facilities were sustained. According to Brian Britton, in evidence to the Tribunal, Iraqi debt was trading for about 55p in the pound.[46] After tax write-offs and certain other bank cover, Brian Britton estimated the net bad debt to the group might be only about £45 million. Clearly, there was an awareness of a high probability of non-payment of part or all of the debt. A number of other countries were unwilling to provide credit insurance for Iraq between 1987 and 1989.

The price and profit margin on the Iraqi contracts were higher than intervention or retail multiple sales. Vincent Browne claimed that the Goodman group was selling meat to Iraq at $3,500 per ton compared to a world price of $2,200 per ton.[47] Browne calculated that the 1987 and 1988 sales were 50,000 tons, which yielded an 'excess' profit of £40 million on the contracts. He noted that in the mid-1980s the Minister for Industry and Commerce had suspended all insurance for Iraq, and that other countries with export credit insurance schemes had done likewise.

The twin investments in Berisford International and Unigate, which commenced in September 1988, were a mistake. Through a series of separate deals, companies associated with the group (and with cross-company guarantees) had built up a 13% holding in Berisford. It was the second largest holding after Associated British Foods. The group's liquidity problems in the months before collapse were caused by margin calls by bankers as the Berisford share price fell on the market.[48] As the share price fell beyond a certain point, the bankers who had taken the shares as security sought additional cash injections in the form of margin calls to protect their exposure. Peter Fitzpatrick, the examiner, explained the procedure to Mr Byrne SC:

> *Fitzpatrick:* . . . at the banks' request I prepared a schedule of the sources of funds both for the initial investment in Berisford and Unigate and also for the margin calls which constituted additional security for the lending banks.
>
> *Byrne:* Can you just explain how the margin calls arrived. What are they?
>
> *Fitzpatrick:* Well essentially a syndicate of banks lent the original purchase consideration, for example, the Berisford transaction. It would have taken by way of security the share certificates in Berisford. If the share value fell then the value of the security would fall and there would be what they call the margin call, to top up the security.
>
> *Byrne:* That was a requirement then to put in place for the security to replace the drop in value of shares that had already been provided for security?
>
> *Fitzpatrick:* That's right.
>
> *Byrne:* And that was, what, how was it provided?
>
> *Fitzpatrick:* That was provided by way of a cash deposit . . .[49]

The initial acquisition price of the Berisford shares was Stg£98.7 million. Margin deposits cost an additional Stg£54 million and there were interest costs of Stg£21.7 million. The total 'carrying cost' of Berisford was Stg£174.4 million. This outlay was funded by a BNP syndicate loan of Stg£90 million, an Anglo-Irish Beef Processors advance of Stg£30.3 million and other group funds. The initial investment in Unigate amounted to Stg£62.2 million. By the time margin calls and interest costs were added the total carrying cost came to Stg£110.9 million. The initial purchase outlay was supported by Bank Paribas. Thus, a total of Stg£285 million was committed to the investments in Berisford and Unigate. By any standards, it was a heavy and risky outlay in comparison to existing group assets, working capital and net worth. Dividends received were insufficient to cover the interest costs on the loans and any fall in share values had direct implications for net worth and working capital.

In October 1988 Berisford's share price was Stg201p. By October 1989, it had fallen to 145p. The Goodman group bought more stock throughout this period. In March 1990 Berisford fell to 117p but recovered to 144p in April. The slide in the share price began gradually in June 1990, starting at 128p on Monday 4 June and finishing at 112p on Friday 29 June. During July the fall was more pronounced, with the price sliding to 100p on Monday 2 July and to 60p in the following two weeks. It steadied for a week and then drifted downwards to 45p by Wednesday 1 August — the day before Iraq invaded Kuwait. It was an unhappy coincidence. The combination of Berisford having its own trading and financial problems and the Goodman group being a weak investor with its holding overhanging the market contributed to a continuing slide in the quoted price. It eventually collapsed to 12p in September 1992. Ironically, after Berisford's disposal of British Sugar to Associated British Foods, repayment of bank debt and reorganisation of its management, Berisford's share price recovered, initially to 23p in January 1993 and then to 109p by November 1993. If we assume an average purchase cost to the Goodman group of Stg180p for the Berisford shares we can infer a near 75% capital loss on the investment. The loss on Unigate was quite small. On 1 August 1990, Unigate's quoted share price was 326p. It traded in the range 272p in October 1988 to a high of 418p in September 1989. It drifted downwards in late 1989 and through all 1990, reaching 276p in December 1990. It took until 1993 before the Unigate share price finally rose and stayed above the August 1990 level.

A total outlay of £452 million was committed to the combination of the Berisford and Unigate share investments and the Iraqi debt, as shown in Table 3.5. This can be compared to shareholders' funds of £192 million in 1989 which seems, in this writer's opinion, to have been an extraordinarily foolhardy gamble. The evidence suggests that the financial risk of the Goodman group was altered in quantum terms. The organisation moved from a policy of financial prudence and self-financing through retained earnings to one somewhere between serious financial exposure and speculation. The continuing commitment to such exposure, after the insurance cover was withdrawn in late 1989, right through to the collapse in

Table 3.5: Goodman International: the cost of the strategy (£m)

Berisford outlays	174
Unigate outlays	<u>111</u>
Carrying cost of investments	285*
Iraqi debt	<u>167</u>
Total combined outlays	452
less	
Write-offs — investments	162
— Iraqi debt	<u>158</u>
Total 'special' losses	320

*   The 'carrying cost' of the Berisford and Unigate investments includes rolled up interest.

Note: This summary does not include the £25 million Cyprus deposit.

Source: Tribunal evidence and financial statements.

the Berisford share price and the invasion of Kuwait by Iraq on 2 August 1990, suggests nothing less, in this writer's opinion, than an astonishingly high risk.

It is difficult to pinpoint the motivations which overrode rational actions to preserve the future of the group. It was exposed on two fronts and both were financed by debt. The company should have consolidated its position on one front. One could theorise that after the loss of export credit insurance, the high risk strategy was a rational one since there was nothing to lose and everything to gain if some form of joint venture and new borrowing facility encompassing both British Sugar and the group could be negotiated. The financial problem might have been 'leapfrogged' and future gains could have been a multiple of previous deals. Larry Goodman could argue that he might have pulled it off but for two 'bumps in the night' in relation to Iraq. Both could be viewed as bad luck and had political connections. The fundamental management issue was the extent of vulnerability to bad luck.

One might surmise that, to a degree, the organisation was seduced by the easy availability of bank loans and the encouraging advice of financial interests and brokers in London. It was a time of extensive 'deal-making' activity in many senses. It was also a period of greed and speculation in Wall Street and London which saw a frenzy of mergers and acquisitions, management buyouts, junk bonds and mezzanine financing, following deregulation.

A 'historical event' in the life of Larry Goodman

The trauma and tensions of the crisis days were more than hinted at by Larry Goodman in his Tribunal evidence:

> . . . the time we hit problems because of the Iraqi invasion of Kuwait. When that happened, we called a meeting with our banks and that meeting took place in London. It was on Wednesday. It was a historical event in my life. We were asked by the bankers to go back and see what the Irish government would do. I did not ask them to do anything. Our financial advisers put a proposal to them that did not encompass anything from government and they said agriculture was terribly important to Ireland, what are the Irish government going to do? And we were asked to put that and that was to be put by me and by our advisers which was IBI Investment Bank . . . and it is against that background that I spoke to Mr Haughey. I did not ask for any special financial package . . . I did not request any government money, not a penny. That would be alien to my thinking in terms of rescue. All I asked Mr Haughey to do was to reopen the Export Credit Insurance File, nothing more and nothing less . . .[50]

Mr Justice Hamilton then asked Larry Goodman, 'What exactly do you mean by asking Mr Haughey to reopen the Export Credit File?' Goodman replied:

> The file had been closed at that stage and void and just to really look at it . . .
> The banks had said to us that there were several other instances in similar situations where important industries would have a problem and government would support. We did not ask . . . I felt there was a stigma attached to it.
> We did not ask for examinership and when that came up with the banks I was quite annoyed. All I was asking for was the reopening of the file with the commitment so that we could go back. . . . We did not get it. We got something else . . .[51]

Had the Iraqi insurance cover been partially restored, the financial footing of the group might have been quite different. Further purchases of Berisford at the lower market price would have made an acquisition (or shared venture) much less expensive. Unlocking British Sugar might have covered the borrowings. What was really needed was time. We can speculate about the consequences of domestic and foreign political events on the eventual fate of the company.

When Larry Goodman said 'We got something else', he was not planning on examinership. Control over the organisation and related companies came under the supervision of the High Court, and extensive financial information was placed before the court and the banks through the examiner's reports. This was ironic, in view of the secrecy of the Goodman group. It was even more ironic that a political process facilitated the emergence of examinership and that Larry Goodman's firm should be the first to apply for the appointment of an examiner. It was a second historic day for Larry Goodman and a first for banks because examinership heralded a new era in corporate lending risk, relationships and practice.

The banks and the restructuring

The fact that thirty-three domestic and international banks advanced over £500 million on an unsecured basis, even 'short term', continues to be one of the riddles of the financial markets. It is partially explained by the relaxed credit policies of the time and the quest for market share. The credit analysis was slim. Certainly, if the banks analysed the audited financial statements (if they had sight of them), observed the debt/equity ratios, interest cover, liquidity and cash flow profile, and asked questions about the meaning of the 1989 'Notes' attached, it is difficult to see how such large advances could have been made.

After the collapse the banks had little choice but to support the restructuring proposals negotiated with the examiner. Because most loans were unsecured, they would have taken heavy bad debt losses anyway. The asset value of a meat-processing business would have been a fraction of the debt. It is doubtful that there would have been a buyer for the business as a whole, mainly because of its size, location, unique culture, history and characteristics. Though it may have been a bitter pill for some banks, the continuing involvement of Larry Goodman was intrinsic to recovering some value as a going concern because of his knowledge and expertise in a low-margin sector. The solution, therefore, revolved around the sustainable level of debt the business could service. Other issues were the governance, management and controls reorganisation, and the incentives to motivate Larry Goodman to achieve debt repayments to the banks. As noted earlier, Goodman continued as chief executive, but a new chairman and non-executive directors were appointed. Details of the financial restructuring are summarised in Table 3.6.

The banks appear to have received 60% of the equity of Goodman International (through a new ownership vehicle), with Larry Goodman

Table 3.6: Goodman International: the bank restructuring deal (£m)

Term loan	100	Seven-year loan; interest at DIBOR plus 2%.
Asset loan	<u>134</u>	Interest-bearing; DIBOR plus 2%; to be repaid out of proceeds of non-core assets.
Subtotal	234	Total of interest-bearing debt.
Iraqi debt	167	Non-interest-bearing.
Rump loan	<u>103</u>	Non-interest-bearing; to be repaid out of profits from 1997.
Subtotal	270	Total of non-interest-bearing debt.
Total debt	504	

Note: The above ignores normal and seasonal working capital. The linking of intercompany guarantees and assets was one of the primary reasons for the collapse of the meat-processing activity, despite the fact that it was reasonably viable. It might have survived the Iraqi 'bad' debt but not the burden of the Berisford investment losses with which it was entangled.

holding the remaining 40%. He seems to have had the opportunity of obtaining the return of most of the banks' holding if loan repayment targets were met. Of the £504 million bank debt, interest was payable on only £234 million. As a non-core asset, the valuable investment in Food Industries was sold off, as were the share investments and certain properties, to reduce the bank debt. As it turned out, the business climate in the industry proved difficult for such a level of debt 'workout' in relation to the profitability achieved (which seems to have been close to half the examiner's projections) and the value and timing of non-core asset sales. By 1995 the Iraqi debt had not been paid off nor had the £25 million Cyprus deposit been returned. The Berisford share disposal only recovered a fraction of the original investment outlay.

From a management perspective, the continuance of a profitable business was a remarkable achievement when account is taken of the publicity of the financial collapse, the examinership saga, the subsequent media allegations about industry irregularities and the establishment of an official Tribunal of Inquiry. It was evidence that there was a fundamentally sound business, with strong and supportive customer relationships. It also demonstrated that Larry Goodman and his team made the management transition from overzealous entrepreneur to a more formal and professional style with the governance changes.

In this writer's opinion the group's cash flow could never have paid off the banking consortium's loans. Continuing repayments of principal after servicing the interest-bearing loans would have left insufficient free cash flow available for reinvestment in the group's modernisation and continuing competitiveness. Perhaps the twenty-one banks who agreed to a 'buy-back' of equity and composition of loans had few viable alternatives by 1995. It was a costly 'bad debt' experience for them. Details are summarised in Table 3.7.

Table 3.7: Goodman International: estimate of how much the banks lost, 1990–95 (£m)

Non-interest-bearing debt	271
Interest foregone	130
	401
Unpaid portion of 'asset loan'	40
Total estimated losses	441
Deduct 'equity and debt buyout' payment	40
Losses (net) to banks	401*

*   These estimated losses are struck before taking account of any moneys which might be recovered from the Cyprus £25 million deposit, the Iraqi debt of £167 million or the claim against the Minister for Industry and Commerce.

Source: Estimates by author.

These bank debts were not the only losses. The Irish taxpayer, through the exchequer, appears to have lost about £8 million in unpaid PAYE and other taxes, following tax settlements.

Of course, by far the largest individual loser was Larry Goodman, because the write-offs were greater than the book value of shareholders' equity of £192 million. He was forced to relinquish equity majority and organisational dominance, and the culture of secrecy which pervaded the firm's affairs was to be no more. His personal fiefdom was part of his identity and yet in a surprisingly pragmatic and focused fashion he buckled down, first with bankers as partners and later with other business investors, in his quest to restore the company's fortunes.

Accounting and auditing issues

Evidence of a number of financial reporting issues emerged in the course of the research:

- debtors and bad and doubtful debt recognition
- contingent liabilities and off balance sheet financing commitments
- classification of employee payments and tax evasion.

In this writer's opinion the carrying value of 'debtors' was problematical in the case of the Iraqi debt owed on 31 December 1989. By letter dated 11 October 1989, the Minister for Industry and Commerce, Desmond O'Malley, through ICI, appears to have voided the export credit insurance policies because of alleged breaches of declarations in the policies. A departmental review indicated that 38% of the beef exported in 1987 and 1988 covered by the insurance was sourced outside the state.[52] There were a number of meetings between August and October 1989 between Goodman senior management and departmental officials. Clearly, in this writer's view, there was now a greater riskiness attaching to the value of this asset by the end of 1989, with implications for working capital (the level of net current assets had already fallen from £163 million to £95 million) and reported net worth of £192 million. The Iraqi debt at that time, which was of the order of £100 million, was material. Indeed, the matter was so grave it seems that the Goodman group's subsidiary, Anglo-Irish Beef Processors International Ltd, issued proceedings in the High Court against the Minister for Industry and Commerce and ICI on 12 October 1989, two and a half months before the year-end. The group informed bankers of this development and obtained their continuing support.

In these circumstances, this writer is of the view that the auditors would have been aware of the problems surrounding the Iraqi debt. The auditors' report on the 1989 financial statements, dated 30 March 1990, available to this author, did not appear to refer to any uncertainties. No Notes attached seem to have mentioned any uncertainty about the collectability of this debt, its value and the absence of insurance cover. Note 13, on debtors, in the 1989 financial statements, indicated £283 million due within one year and £25 million after one year. There was no specific mention of a provision for bad and doubtful debts or whether any balance was written off in 1989. There were media suggestions that a figure of the order of £15 million may have been provided. *Business & Finance* reported: 'It appears that some £30m was provided against Iraq in the 1989 accounts, leaving another £150m to be provided now.'[53]

Admittedly, circumstances changed between 1989 and 1990, following the Iraqi invasion of Kuwait and the consequent economic sanctions. Nevertheless, Iraq was viewed as a high credit risk in 1988 and 1989, long before the August 1990 invasion. As already noted, Brian Britton indicated that the market value of Iraqi debt was about 55% of face value. Because of this risk the company sought the increased level of export credit insurance from the government. After all, the Iraqi contracts now accounted for a much greater proportion of total turnover and debtors than heretofore.

Was there sufficient director and auditor objectivity in relation to the financial statements for 1989? The 1989 financial statements reported a paper 'return', but did they capture the 'risk' in the value and future liquidity of assets and liabilities in a 'true and fair view'?

There appear to have been many intercompany advances and bank guarantees across the group and related companies. Contingent liabilities are relevant to the debt/equity position,[54] possible liabilities and future liquidity. The obligations to bankers for Berisford's shares seem to have been an example of a contingent liability in 1989. They proved to be a catastrophic liquidity drain in the summer of 1990. How clearly did the bankers view the contingent liabilities? Note 22 'Contingencies' attached to the 1989 financial statements disclosed an amount of £306 million for 'Bonds and guarantees'. These were related to sales under intervention and exports abroad. An additional item under group obligations was £72 million for 'Guarantees in respect of financial obligations incurred by subsidiaries and related companies'. Of particular relevance, Note 12 'Financial Assets' showed a figure of £14.7 million according to the balance sheet of 1990. The Note records:

> The group's interest in quoted securities was acquired under a guarantee call whereby bank liabilities amounting to IR£41.6m of a fellow subsidiary which had purchased these securities were assumed. The quoted securities are mortgaged to a banking syndicate as security for its loans. The market value of the quoted securities at 31 December was £14.7m.

Related to this would have been the 1990 provision for £162 million against amounts receivable from fellow subsidiaries, shown under the 'Extraordinary Items' write-off of £370 million.

The issue of the taxation liabilities of the group also arose. Soon after the commencement of the Beef Tribunal and its liaison with the Revenue Commissioners, a representative of KPMG Stokes Kennedy Crowley visited the principal inspector of taxes on behalf of Goodman International. He disclosed that payments without deduction of taxes, and 'cloaked by fictitious invoices' (according to the Tribunal Report), had been made to employees in all plants over a number of years.[55] Following a number of meetings between the staff of KPMG Stokes Kennedy Crowley and the Revenue Commissioners, visits to plants and investigations by tax inspectors, the Revenue Commissioners were of the view that various sums totalling £8.6 million required to be included as untaxed remuneration. This amount was in respect of the 'tax evasion' activities and was in addition to executive remuneration 'tax avoidance' schemes. This part of the saga seems to have ended with the Goodman group making an offer of £4.1 million in January 1994 under the tax amnesty scheme. The revenue authorities advised the Tribunal that they were likely to accept the proposal.[56]

The Tribunal stated that during the course of the 1986 audit of the Cahir plant an audit team, supervised by a young articled clerk, John King, became concerned about cash payments to employees. The team also questioned £840,000 in payments to haulage contractors, on the basis of what appeared to be 'phoney invoices'.[57] Questioning the plant accountant or manager seemed to prove of little avail.[58] The Tribunal Report referred to 'various untruthful explanations'.[59] The audit team's findings were summarised in a memorandum to the audit manager and the audit partner and there followed discussions on the issue between senior representatives of the auditors and the Goodman group.

Soon afterwards, the auditors were advised by Goodman's financial executives that £1.9 million in this form of payment had been made in 1986 in four plants. These 'under the counter' payments were to employees generally on foot of bogus haulage invoices or to farmers in respect of livestock or otherwise. They were described as 'advances to employees' made by plant managers in anticipation of a new employees' bonus scheme without the approval of the board.

According to the Tribunal Report the audit team noted that some of the names of the bogus hauliers appeared on the previous year's, 1985, audit file. The Tribunal noted that the auditors 'accepted the representations made to them by the company'.[60] No further examination appears to have been made of the 1985 accounts. The 1986 'audit problem' was dealt with by seeking an understanding that the advances without deduction of PAYE would be repaid and that the repayment would be guaranteed by Goodman Holdings, the ultimate parent company of the group.[61] To facilitate the 'signing off' of the 1986 financial statements the amounts were deemed 'unauthorised advances taken by employees' by the auditors and were entered in a suspense account in debtors.[62]

KPMG Stokes Kennedy Crowley brought their findings to the top management of Goodman International in accordance with professional standards at the time. They were informed that this form of payment would cease immediately, 'pending implementation of a proper scheme'. According to the Tribunal, '[it] appears the practice did not cease but continued during the years 1987, 1988, 1989, and 1990 until the appointment of the Court Examiner in August that year'.⁶³ The Tribunal concluded:

> There is no reality in the representations made by Mr Britton to Mr O'Carroll of SKC that these payments made to employees without deduction of PAYE and PRSI contributions were either unauthorised or represented loans to those employees without the approval of the Board of the Goodman group of companies or they would ever have to be repaid to the companies by their employees and there is no evidence that they were ever repaid.
>
> These payments were and were intended to be payments to certain employees free of deduction of income tax and PRSI contributions and should have been declared as such and the appropriate tax paid and PRSI contributions in respect thereof made.⁶⁴

The Tribunal stated that the system of making such payments 'was widespread throughout the Goodman Group of Companies' and appeared in the weekly profit and loss accounts prepared by plant accountants and submitted to head office. These accounts were not disclosed to the auditors.⁶⁵

The Tribunal considered it appropriate to set out in detail both statutory and self-regulatory obligations relevant to professional accountants and auditors in respect of tax evasion activity. These codes included Section 94 'Revenue Offences' of the Finance Act 1983 and Part 5 of 'Miscellaneous Legal, Ethical and Practical Guidance' issued by the Institute of Chartered Accountants in Ireland. Section 9 of the institute's guidance states that if a member knows that his client intends to do an unlawful act, or his client has committed an unlawful act, and that such unlawful act would compromise the member, the member must cease to act. 'If the member had been communicating with a third party (for example, the revenue authorities) on the client's behalf and such third party is affected by the illegality, the third party should be notified of the withdrawal of the Member's services but should not be informed of the reason why.' Section 24 on 'Suspicion of a Client's Conduct' states that a member 'must not bury his head but must interrogate his client and make such appropriate inquiries and investigations as will either exonerate his client or confirm his suspicions'.

According to the Tribunal Report the Goodman International tax evasion and tax avoidance scandals continued for a number of years.⁶⁶ The amounts, in combination, seem to have been of the order of £16 million and several accountants, managers and employees appear to have been involved in the execution of certain of the 'schemes'. Thousands of crossed cheques were cashed in the bank on which they were drawn.

In the writer's opinion the accounting classification adopted to wage payments in the 'tax evasion' activity was a form of 'creative accounting' with the object of misleading the auditors and the tax authorities. The accounting literature tends to review 'creative accounting' in the context of valuation and credit decisions of the stockmarket and bankers.

The Tribunal reported that the claims of Revenue Commissioners' investigation officials that the reasons why tax inspectors, who had visited Goodman plants on a number of occasions, had failed to discover 'under the counter' payments to employees was established by the evidence.[67] According to the revenue authorities, the reason for their investigation failure was because of the system which 'was very well and professionally put together . . . had been organised by a large organisation . . . and it had been organised by professionals . . . chartered accountants were involved in this and they had put a lot of thought into it'.

In this writer's view the extent and continuance of the tax evasion behaviour raise questions about the role and effectiveness of financial control and integrity in the organisation and the weaknesses in internal control and internal audit.

The tax evasion activity of Goodman International was to have far-reaching regulatory consequences for companies and auditors in Ireland. The Tribunal noted that self-regulatory auditing guidelines of the time expected that auditors would bring illegal or questionable acts to 'the appropriate level of authority' in the company or to the shareholders. Of course, this could prove to be circular if the firm was owner managed and already had knowledge of the activity. The Tribunal recommended that auditors be obliged to report tax evasion to the Revenue Commissioners and that a provision to ensure this obligation be included in the next Finance Bill placed before the Oireachtas.[68] The draft bill included far-reaching provisions which led to an outcry from accountants, lawyers and other tax advisers. A revised version has left onerous obligations in place for auditors. Also, self-regulatory auditing rules were revised to include tax issues. In this writer's view the Goodman affair brought about a sea-change in the responsibilities of Irish auditors to the state, in comparison with their counterparts in Britain or Continental Europe.[69]

Reflections

It is revealing to examine Larry Goodman's explanations of the causes of the financial crisis (i.e. the Iraqi invasion, the Berisford share collapse, the short-term borrowing policy and the attitudes of the banks). The evidence available to this writer suggests different and more 'internal' reasons. The cash flow analysis suggests that the negative cash flows generated in 1988 and 1989 were due to the build-up of debtors (an additional £243 million), the largest proportion being the Iraqi contracts. The off balance sheet liabilities in respect of guarantees to banks and drawings from working capital to cover the margin calls for the associated group companies' commitments on the Berisford and Unigate shareholdings between 1989 and 1990 accounted for most of the net outflow of £281 million in 1990. Consequently there was a series of increasing 'financing shortfalls', starting at £108 million in 1988 and reaching £238 million in 1990. These financial deficits were continually financed by bank debt, which had swollen to £547 million by 1990.

In essence, Goodman International changed the operational and strategic risk profile of a successful business when it not only established Food Industries plc but proceeded in parallel to sell a much greater proportion of its output to a risky customer — Iraq — and took on excessive and hazardous short-term bank debt in the ill-fated Berisford/British Sugar project. The aggressive culture of the organisation and its need to achieve high productivity, sales and profits growth — underpinned by employee and management incentive payments — help explain the approach to business and the risks taken. This was displayed in the London speculations, the tax evasion schemes, the political lobbying, the administrative weaknesses, and the extent and uses of short-term debt. There are lessons also for auditors and the accounting profession about aggressive clients. In this writer's view the Goodman collapse and tax scandal could have been avoided. It damaged many reputations.

Fundamentally the organisation did not have the depth of top management or the financial control strengths to successfully cope with the two major strategic initiatives. This contributed to the escalation in short-term borrowing. Continuous injections of cash for the margin cover should have been a sufficient signal to cut losses. Goodman should have walked away from the Berisford adventure when the risk exposure became too hazardous. Admittedly, the opportunities for gain in British Sugar were attractive and would have transformed the group into a major European food company. Unfortunately, it did not have the equity base to move at that level of investment or risk. The financial crisis and subsequent write-off of its equity base was a self-inflicted injury. It was due in part to response delays, some bad luck, and a level of ambition and greed which overruled the relatively prudent and successful previous investment and financing policies.

The contrast with Kerry Group could not have been greater. It showed up in the governance structure, the management team and depth, the systematic planning and systems, and the financing of growth and a large takeover. By taking the stockmarket route, Kerry raised equity but also took on the formality of external regulation and disclosure, internal structures, and accountability to a sophisticated investor group. Almost fifteen months before collapse, Goodman International would have scored a minimum of 47 on Argenti's model — which would have put it in the 'watch' class, with some serious credit risk on an unsecured basis. By spring 1990, it would not have been difficult to arrive at a score in the range 64–69, which was well into the danger zone. Hindsight would deliver a score of not less than 71. Miller's 'Impulsive Syndrome' captured many of the interlocking corporate neuroses — though not completely, as the group was not altogether 'running blind'.

There were some similarities with GPA. In particular, the handling of public relations and media was a specific weakness which proved to be a serious problem. The views of Larry Goodman about risk, customers and markets, and the impotence of the accountant's view, illustrate the difficulty of controlling an ambitious and successful entrepreneur who has never previously experienced a severe setback.

The facts of the case supported the typology of causes of collapse suggested in Chapter 2: flaws at board and organisational level because of a dominant chief executive, insufficient management depth and weak financial control. These undoubtedly led to the unbalanced strategy of growth and the mistakes made in the Iraqi credit risk, the diversification 'big project' with Berisford and the excessive level of short-term debt — resulting in an unhealthy capital structure. Optimistic accounting in 1989 did not support a more cautious management strategy in 1990. This might be linked with multiple soft bankers who provided an excessive amount of unsecured credit — and paid the price.

The dominance of the entrepreneurial values of the 'trader and deal-maker' over the more cautious accountant's and professional management approach to risk management was dramatically illustrated. In an organisation of its size in the late adolescent stage, a hyperactive period emerged which led to near self-destruction.

Chapter 4

Kentz Corporation and the Failed Management Buyout

Growth is a goal as well as an obligation for all publicly held companies. But how to grow? What is healthy growth? It is clear that unrestrained growth for its own sake can cause serious problems. Thus it is management's obligation to ensure that a Company's viability is not jeopardised by indiscriminate expansion. It is an exciting experience for a Company to undergo exponential growth, but a wise management team understands that such growth places inordinate stress on the Company's people and systems.

We are clearly a growing Company, but more importantly, we are a Company that knows how to manage its expansion. . . . our management team is inherently conservative and deliberate and will not allow the Company's strength or purpose to be diluted. Also, I have observed that our Company's growth (like that of other successful companies) has been characterized by short periods of moderate growth and followed by periods of sustained faster growth. Such measured expansion is often optimal.

Joseph J. Jacobs, founder and chairman of the board,
Jacobs Engineering Group Inc., *Annual Report 1993*

Kentz Corporation: an unexpectedly sudden collapse?

Following an active international expansion programme in contracting, Kentz Corporation had, by 1993, transformed itself from a sizeable domestic enterprise into a large multinational group with a turnover of £325 million, offices in sixteen countries and contracts on five continents. Of the 4,200 people employed worldwide, 1,467 were Irish (with 936 based in Ireland). Of relevance to the town of Clonmel was the fact that over 100 skilled staff worked in the Kentz headquarters there and another 500 Clonmel people were employed on overseas contracts as engineers, apprentices and supervisors. Aileen O'Toole described it as a 'world class company' in her 1987 study of leading Irish firms.[1] Kentz was the largest electrical and mechanical engineering contractor in Ireland. In addition, the Kentz construction subsidiary, Mahon & McPhillips of Kilkenny, was one of the largest firms in its sector.[2] In 1988, the Kentz management team, led by Gus Kearney, had completed a buyout from Frank Kent, the son of the founder. An April 1993 interview with Gus Kearney, chairman and chief executive, and Michael Campbell, finance and managing director, claimed pre-tax profits of £9.4 million in 1991 and £8.5 million in 1992.[3] Profits for 1993 were projected to jump to £17 million, with a net worth at the year end of £41 million. With this performance the Kentz group's financial health seemed assured.

The appointment of receivers and a court examiner in January 1994 and extensive debt write-offs (estimated at £40 million) were evidence that the Kentz group was insolvent on both a 'going concern' and technical grounds for some time. The statements of affairs submitted to the High Court revealed an acute financial position and a net worth deficit by December 1993. By then it had become known in the trade that suppliers and contractors were complaining about slow payment. A UK creditor had presented a petition to a court in London for the winding-up of Kentz C&M (UK) Ltd. There were other legal initiatives by the British Inland Revenue for non-payment of taxes and by Barclays Bank in respect of loan facilities. Kentz employee morale was dwindling fast. Finally, on Wednesday, 19 January 1994, Barclays formally appointed Terry Carter and Maggie Mills of accountants Ernst & Young as receivers over Kentz C&M (UK).

The previous day, difficult talks had ensued through the night in the Kentz head office in Clonmel between its top management and senior executives from Allied Irish Banks. The Irish bankers were aware of the group's financial difficulties in its European, British and Irish operations. Kentz's Irish bank overdraft had been well in excess of approved facilities for some time, and some cheques had been returned 'unpaid'. On 19 January, the AIB/BNP consortium appointed Rory O'Ferrall and Patrick Butler of Deloitte & Touche, Dublin, as receivers over the Kentz group and a number of its Irish subsidiaries (including its holding company Holidair Ltd). An unparalleled period of acrimony publicised claims and counterclaims about behaviour and understandings between banks and a large commercial enterprise. In addition, the Revenue Commissioners revealed that they were unhappy about the absence of taxation returns and the non-payment of PAYE and VAT by the group's companies. In turn, the continuance and role of the examiner ended up before the Supreme Court for decision. The battle of wills between the banks and the Kentz management resulted in landmark legal decisions. These covered the role and authority of an examiner as compared to a receiver, and the examiner's ability to borrow money for working capital purposes while an evaluation of the affairs of the financially troubled company is being completed to check whether it can be restructured into a viable operation.

Perhaps because of its size, the *Irish Times* carried the headline on its front page on 20 January, 'Kentz directors believe that banks moved too quickly'. The Kentz application to the High Court to have an examiner appointed was resisted strenuously by the banks.[4] On 21 January, Mr Justice Costello agreed to the request to appoint Hugh Cooney as interim examiner. Subsequently, Hugh Cooney's position was confirmed and he was given time to carry out an evaluation and report back to the court. The degree of 'public concern' was evidenced by the fact that Ruairí Quinn, Minister for Enterprise and Employment, indicated the government's disappointment with the group's difficulties and that the state development agency, Forbairt, would be in close contact with the receiver to help solve the problems. The Kentz management sought government intervention through the Taoiseach and other ministers.

Finally, Mr Justice Costello, in the High Court on 1 May 1994, confirmed a rescue plan. This involved an extensive write-down of debts of the order of £20 million under seven schemes of arrangements supported by creditors of certain companies in the Kentz group, and the introduction of new capital of £6.75 million into a new holding company by Malaysian investors and £0.8 million by existing shareholders. Many other Kentz subsidiaries in Ireland, Britain, Belgium and Holland were put into receivership or liquidation — with most ceasing trading and laying off their employees.

It was a crisis not only for the organisation and its skilled employees, but also for the town of Clonmel and for the large number of subcontractors and trade creditors who were owed over £53 million. Apart from the media surprise at the apparent suddenness of the crisis, and the political concern about job losses and their impact on a particular region, the past public image of Kentz had been one of a progressive but relatively private organisation with a depth and breadth of engineering and contracting skills and outstanding project management expertise. Almost one year later, in January 1995, Kentz top management held a press conference to announce that, following the restructuring, they had achieved a break-even on £100 million turnover.[5] The Irish workforce had fallen from 972 to 460.

Three questions arise:

1. How could a management buyout of a long-established and successful firm go so terribly wrong?

2. How could a company with such projected levels of profitability and equity funds collapse within nine months with such a heavy deficit and write-offs by its creditors and bankers? Were there accounting, financial reporting and corporate regulatory issues?
3. Are there areas of difference and risk in connection with contracting firms as compared to manufacturing firms?

Background

M. F. Kent, the precursor of Kentz Corporation, was established in Clonmel in 1919 by Michael Kent, an electrical contractor. The company's life-cycle can be portrayed as growth between the 1920s and the 1940s, decline in the 1950s, recovery, renewal and extensive growth between the mid-1960s and the 1980s, followed by the major financial crisis in early 1994. M. F. Kent was a sizeable business by the 1920s, laying cables and installing street lighting, and later progressing to wiring large country houses and a variety of institutions such as colleges and hospitals. Peak employment reached almost 100 people. In 1949 its founder suffered a fatal heart condition and, under the direction of an accountant brother, the business continued on a much reduced scale.

Following the death of his uncle, the founder's son, Frank Kent, an engineer, joined the company in 1963 following some years with General Electric in the USA. There were just six employees. Soon afterwards, Gus Kearney joined as a young apprentice electrician. Kearney was to make rapid progress and become an integral part of the development and growth of M. F. Kent. By the early 1970s he had become general manager. Others who became senior management, such as Paul Lloyd and Sean White, also joined in this phase. They were to join with Gus Kearney and later recruits including Noel Kelly, on the Middle East activities, and Michael Campbell, an accountant, in organising a phased management buyout from Frank Kent between 1988 and 1990. A buyout price in excess of £5 million for the majority holding was suggested, indicating a profitable company. It seems prior to 1987, M. F. Kent was earning a reasonable 3% net profit margin on average on a turnover of the order of £50 million.

The following table summarises the key events in the life of Kentz Corporation from the time of the management buyout.

| **Key events in the life of Kentz Corporation** |

The seeds of crisis

1988		Frank Kent sells his 75% majority in management buyout led by Gus Kearney. Group subsequently reorganised with Kentz Corporation being formed as parent; M. F. Kent now a subsidiary.
		Gus Kearney assumes dual role of chairman and chief executive.
1989–90		Recession in developed world. Property markets, construction and capital spending adversely affected.
1990	August	Iraq invades Kuwait. Gulf war coincides with slackening off of new profitable Middle East projects for Kentz.
		Kentz looks to Europe, Britain, Africa, Malaysia and Singapore for major project work. Submits very competitive tenders.

The crisis develops: the big project

1991–92		Hotel des Arts project, Barcelona, involves heavy cost overruns. Delays in payments. Cash flow problems.
1992	January	Banks concerned. At meeting with Kentz senior management, banks suggest Kentz is overtrading and many queries to bank about creditworthiness. Banks point to need for stronger financial management. Banks noted that Campbell had dual role of managing director and financial director and Kearney, though chief executive, heavily occupied with supervision of contract work outside Ireland.
	February–March	AIB/BNP become aware of seriousness of Barcelona project problems. Banks travel to Barcelona.
	March	Banks become aware of problems with Morgan Bank project in Brussels.
	April	Banks write formal letters to Kentz about drawing cheques beyond the level of credit facility agreed. Further letters on same theme subsequently.
		Exchange of letters about Kentz's future plans; banks point out need for financial control and if Kentz wished it could seek new bankers.

cont.

Key events in the life of Kentz Corporation *cont.*

May	Banks propose independent consultants' report on Kentz. Initially to be KPMG Stokes Kennedy Crowley. Kentz eventually vetoes person proposed. Banks stipulate ongoing financial support only if consultants appointed. Eventually OC&C Strategy Consultants of London given assignment. Cost to be shared.
August	OC&C report submitted to Kentz and banks. Report critical of Kentz strategy, pricing policies, controls and risk management etc.
September	Meeting between Kentz and banks about OC&C findings and recommendations. Kentz accepts that group 'overheated' and management 'fire fighting'. New plans proposed by Kentz to correct problems.
Late September	Bank account running at £5 million in excess of agreed limit.
October	Banks express concern about adequacy of financial information received at meeting with Kentz. Banks write formally about financial information and more detailed cash flow statements.

Ineffective response to the crisis by the primary players

October	Banks point out that no audited financial statements received in respect of 1991. Banks told that internal management accounts show a profit of almost £8 million for 1991 and a tangible net worth of £19 million — which is in excess of covenant figure of £13 million. 1992 net profit projected at £10.5 million.
	Banks meet Industrial Development Authority (IDA), at its request, to discuss how Kentz could be supported and nature of problems.
November	IDA meets Kentz and discusses OC&C report.
	KPMG Stokes Kennedy Crowley write to Kentz about its situation and the need to review group operations, risk and management structures and group controls. Still no audited accounts for 1991. Banks told that 1992 profit projection reduced from £10.5 million to £8.6 million.

cont.

Key events in the life of Kentz Corporation *cont.*

1993	January	Banks and Kentz meet. Concern about financial information. No audited accounts for 1991 or 1992. Banks point out need for separate financial director. Campbell still combining roles.
	April	Two non-executive independent directors appointed to Kentz board with help of IDA. Kentz forecast 1993 profit at £20 million.
	May	Draft unaudited accounts provided for 1991 with profit of £4 million and net worth of £13.4 million. (Had projected £8 million and £19 million respectively.)

The position starts to unravel

	July	Banks commence returning cheques in excess of agreed limits.
	August	Kentz advise banks of £6 million loss provisions for European contracts.
	September	KPMG Stokes Kennedy Crowley issue draft accounts for board consideration. KPMG Stokes Kennedy Crowley draft letter to Kentz directors expresses concern about group financial situation, level of trading and financial risk. Accounting, internal and financial control issues and carrying values of assets together with 'uncertainties' and the possible qualification were noted.
	21 October	Revised draft financial statements for 1991 and 1992 issued. Lower profit and lower net worth (now £9.8 million compared with £13.6 million in September). KPMG Stokes Kennedy Crowley note that Kentz in breach of bank covenants. Cash flow projections for 1994 indicate need for £5 million additional bank facilities — which may not be forthcoming. 'Going concern' issue. KPMG Stokes Kennedy Crowley point out that Kentz group cannot prepare consolidated accounts on an ongoing basis. Meeting with banks with 1991 and 1992 draft accounts and cash flow projections to obtain support to enable accounts to be signed by auditors.

cont.

Key events in the life of Kentz Corporation *cont.*

	24 October	Kentz board meeting to consider draft accounts and financial position.
	29 October	Both 1991 and 1992 financial statements issued with extensive audit qualifications and notes on carrying values of assets and project claims. Any adjustment would reduce net worth — possibly to negative value.
	October–November	1993 forecast profit reduced to £10.9 million and subsequently to £5.4 million. (Had forecasted £20 million.)
	4 November	Meeting with banks. Issues relating to companies outside the group registered in Channel Islands which had been raised in management report of auditors.
	17 December	Senior bank delegation visits Kentz headquarters in Clonmel. Banks make a presentation to board on their view of strengths and weaknesses of Kentz group and matters needing urgent attention — specifically, a finance director. Banks agree to release £1 million of security over UK assets in favour of Barclays to facilitate payment of debts to UK Inland Revenue.

The group spins out of control: the final days

1994	13 January	Meetings of management and banks on Kentz UK project (Guy's Hospital) and finance problems following court actions of UK Inland Revenue authorities and other creditors.
	15 January	Kentz management spend weekend in discussions with Rory O'Ferrall and Patrick Butler of Deloitte & Touche assessing group position and options.
	17 January	Meeting between banks and Kentz about UK operations. Banks told of major cash problems and losses in other Belgian and Dutch projects apart from Morgan Bank contract. Kentz C&M (UK) ceases trading following the non-contested court action by the Inland Revenue and certain UK creditors.
	18 January	Banks meet Patrick Butler. Parties later travel to Clonmel. Meeting from 3 p.m. to 5.30 a.m. to discuss position and options. Kentz wants examiner; banks want receiver.

cont.

Key events in the life of Kentz Corporation *cont.*	
19 January	Barclays Bank appoints Terry Carter and Maggie Mills of Ernst & Young as receivers of Kentz C&M (UK) at request of Kentz board the previous day. Rory O'Ferrall and Patrick Butler appointed as receivers by Irish banking consortium.
21 January	High Court appoints Hugh Cooney as interim examiner.
22 January	Receivers 'cease to act'. Liquidator subsequently appointed to a number of loss-making subsidiaries.
1 May	Mr Justice Costello approves schemes of arrangement for write-down and schedule of settlement of debts with introduction of new equity by Malaysian investors.

Financial performance

The accounting figures for Kentz present a clear picture of a sales-oriented organisation which 'blew up' through overtrading. Turnover grew much too fast on falling (and insufficient) gross and net profit margins. In addition there was an unbalanced capital structure and insufficient working capital. There was a wholly insufficient equity capital base to act as a platform for the scale and riskiness of the new contracts taken on. Kentz was too dependent on debt supplied by its creditors and bankers to finance its rush for growth.

A summary of the key reported financial figures and ratios is shown in Tables 4.1 and 4.2.

Table 4.1: Kentz Corporation: key financial figures (£m)

	1988	1989	1990	1991	1992
Turnover	65	100	153	319	326
Gross profit	n/av.	15	20	32	37
Overheads	n/av.	10	14	31	29
Operating profit	n/av.	5	6	1	8
Bank interest	n/av.	1[e]	1	2	4
Associates (profit)	n/av.	–	–	–	1
Pre-tax profit/(loss)	1	4	5	(2)	3
Cash flow funding (deficit)	n/av.	n/av	n/av.	(15)	(5)
Total assets	n/av.	38	87	111	122

[e] Estimate

Source: Petition and affidavit materials to High Court by M. Campbell, January 1994.

Table 4.2: Kentz Corporation: key financial ratios

	1988	1989	1990	1991	1992
Profitability					
Gross profit margin	n/av.	14.6%	12.7%	9.9%	11.4%
Pre-tax profit margin*	1.70%	4.25%	3.39%	(0.63%)	0.64%
Pre-tax return/total assets	n/av.	n/av.	5.1%	(1.8%)	1.7%
Liquidity					
Current ratio	n/av.	n/av.	1.17:1	1:1	0.98:1
Quick ratio	n/av.	n/av.	0.91:1	0.81:1	0.73:1
Working capital/sales	n/av.	n/av.	5.4%	nil	neg.
Gearing/leverage					
Total debt/total assets	n/av.	n/av.	85.1%	92.2%	91.8%
Interest cover	n/av.	n/av.	5.8 times	0.7 times	2.2 times

* Excluding 'associates' profit contribution.
Source: Petition and affidavit materials to High Court by M. Campbell, January 1994.

The figures provide a classic illustration of overtrading. Gross profit margins were falling and overhead expenses showed no scale efficiencies, despite the increase in turnover. Bank interest charges were increasing sharply, reaching £4 million in 1992; this was much too heavy a burden for the underlying profitability on operations. Net profit margins were volatile and much lower in 1991 and 1992. Profit margins on sales and total assets of 0.6% and 1.7% respectively in 1992, following the previous year's losses, made the level of turnover and investment in assets unsustainable — particularly when combined with an unhealthy dependence on debt (85% of total assets in 1990 and 92% in 1992) and a low working capital level which became negative in 1992. These deficiencies left Kentz with high financial risk and insufficient financial resources and flexibility to absorb a setback. By most financing standards Kentz should have raised at least an additional £15 million in share capital in 1990 to support its expansion.

In this writer's view, following the management buyout Kentz pursued turnover and market share at the expense of economic profit margins and financial equilibrium. The group performance was particularly poor when the figures for Mahon & McPhillips were stripped out. According to the examiner's reports, the audited financial statements of Mahon & McPhillips reported a turnover of £41.3 million and £44.1 million and profits of £0.8 million and £1.3 million for 1991 and 1992 respectively.[6] This suggests a greater loss for the rest of the Kentz businesses in 1991 and very little profit at all in 1992 — even before adjustments for more prudent valuations and provisions for contracts and work-in-progress.

Comparing Kentz with Jacobs Engineering

Kentz and Jacobs Engineering were entrepreneurially driven organisations and both encountered a severe crisis some years earlier through overexpansion and inadequate cost and management control. In illustrating the problems encountered by M. F. Kent in the mid-1970s, O'Toole noted that scant attention was paid to management structures and controls, and that Frank Kent and Gus Kearney admitted:

> 'We were certainly over-trading, there was no doubt about that, and we hadn't the cost control systems we have now nor the tight management controls,' Kent recalls. 'My financial management was by the seat of my pants — I was owed this, I owed that and I had this amount in the bank. But we didn't know where we were going.' Kearney says the systems Kent had were unsuited to larger contracts: 'The bookkeeping on the £100,000 jobs was not good enough for the £1 million jobs.'[7]

Stokes Kennedy Crowley designed a revised organisational structure and management controls. A new financial controller, Michael McGarry, was recruited. The accounting firm found that M. F. Kent had delegated to people that were not ready, 'that we had over-promoted people'.[8] There was a lack of managerial and supervisory depth for the scale of its increased business and contracts at that time.

Jacobs Engineering Group, with a turnover of $1.14 billion in 1993 and 13,000 employees, was more than double the size of Kentz; nevertheless, it has many similar characteristics. Jacobs is an integrated engineering, construction and consultancy organisation operating in a wide variety of industries including pharmaceuticals, refining and petrochemicals, and biotechnology. It operates on a different level to Kentz on major projects in that it might award business to Kentz as a subcontractor. Jacobs has overseas offices in Dublin and London. Irish and UK turnover was $177 million in 1992 and $120 million in 1993. Operating profit on this Irish and UK turnover was $3.7 million and $2.2 million in 1992 and 1993 respectively. In contrast to Kentz, Jacobs was able to make a profit in both years in the UK and Ireland. Though not a perfect match, Jacobs is a useful benchmark because, like Kentz, it was international in its operations and it had the same general style of business activity and methodology. It also faced many of the same industry management processes, problems and decisions which would have confronted the Kentz group. Indeed, Noel Kelly, one of the long-standing executive directors of Kentz, claimed that 'the Kentz directors had considered a corporate restructuring and had contemplated trying to bring another major international contractor, such as Jacobs International, into Kentz as an equity investor'.[9] Jacobs Engineering had to surmount a difficult period in the early 1980s following the impact of the recession on capital investment in the USA and many overseas countries. Its response was much more hard-headed than Kentz's and it took heed of the lessons learned then when the 1989–93 recession occurred.

The turnover of Jacobs Engineering had grown from $186 million in 1976 to $323 million in 1982. However, pre-tax profits of $6.8 million in 1976 had declined to $4.2 million in 1982, having peaked at $20 million in 1981. New contracts and turnover fell dramatically — declining to $178 million in 1984. Net losses of $5 million and $9 million were sustained in 1983 and 1984 and a negative working capital position was experienced. Because Jacobs operated with a reasonably strong capital structure (equity was 33.3% of total assets in 1982) it was able to ride out the storm. Jacobs operated with conservative accounting principles in that it provided for project losses in their entirety in the period they became known. In neither of its two difficult years was its audit opinion qualified by its auditors. It sold off its head office on a leaseback arrangement and injected additional liquidity to support working capital. There were cutbacks on operating costs, personnel and overheads (by 35%) and capital spending. In 1984 dividend payments were stopped in order to conserve cash.

Over the next five years all long-term debt was paid off and Jacobs's financial position was so strengthened that by 1992 it had built up reserves of cash and marketable securities of $35 million. Perhaps the most significant strategic decision was to cut back on commitments to 'fixed-price' contracts. In 1981 fixed-price contracts represented 38% of revenues but by 1992 they had been reduced to 9% of total revenues. In contrast, 'cost-plus' contracts had risen from 53% to 87% of revenues in the same period. Dr Joseph J. Jacobs, its founder, had acknowledged in 1983 that 'The easy excuse for poor performance this year is the general economic condition and, in particular, the deep slump in process industry engineering construction that is being felt by all companies . . . At first our people, so used to an expansionist mode, did not in fact reduce overheads rapidly enough to fit our declining project awards.'[10]

Dr Jacobs's candid discussion of the management and people problems that had developed in the organisation are most revealing. In his autobiography he observed 'The real culprit was fixed-price bidding . . .'[11] Overheads had swollen and the productivity and performance of many of the senior executives had declined. Between 1984 and 1985 the organisation eliminated one whole layer of management. In addition, the external board members reviewed all aspects of Jacobs's business, management structure and project policies.

Jacobs went on to achieve consistently increasing profits between 1985 and 1993. Pre-tax profit margins increased from 2.1% in 1989 to 4.3% by 1993. Jacobs's pre-tax profit return on total assets was 14.5% in 1992 compared with a mere 1.7% for Kentz. The highest return on assets Kentz appears to have earned in recent years was 5.1%. Clearly, the profitability of Kentz had been uneconomic in relation to resources utilised for some years. More pointedly, the capital structure and working capital in relation to turnover and total assets of Kentz were much weaker than those of Jacobs as shown in Table 4.3.

Table 4.3: Capital structure and working capital comparisons for Kentz Corporation and Jacobs Engineering

	Kentz		Jacobs	
	1991	1992	1991	1992
Equity/total assets	8%	8%	41.1%	44.1%
Current ratio	1:1	1:1	1.4:1	1.6:1
Working capital/sales	nil	neg.	5.9%	8.4%

Source: Audited financial statements.

Product/market strategy

In the 1970s M. F. Kent moved from its traditional electrical engineering activity to larger and more sophisticated domestic industrial projects with Pfizer and with Merck, Sharpe and Dohme. From these it built up expertise in instrumentation and computerised technology. By the mid-1970s M. F. Kent had moved into mechanical engineering with the installation of piping and the erection of process and power plants. With a range of engineering expertise, Kent was able to quote for 'turnkey' projects. Large projects with NET and Irish Cement followed. However, a bitter strike for three weeks on the latter project brought all other Kent sites to a halt and this experience influenced Kent to look abroad more actively for business. First, like many other Irish companies in the industry, it was Saudi Arabia and the

Middle East that became the focus of its overseas activity. Kent's work stretched to Iraq and Libya. It was a subcontractor for leading groups such as Fluor, Bechtel, Jacobs and ABV. Being aware of its dependence on the Middle East and the declining rate of new project investment, Kent undertook work in South Africa and eventually Holland with a £20 million project on modernising the Esso refinery in Rotterdam through its good connections with Fluor. By the mid-1980s, Ireland accounted for only about 10% of the turnover of M. F. Kent.

In 1987 Kent entered the UK with the acquisition of Jefco, a small contracting company in Surrey. Later, there was an unsuccessful and expensive attempt to obtain work in the Ukraine. Finally, with the invasion of Kuwait by Iraq in August 1990, and the downturn of work in the Middle East, M. F. Kent (now Kentz) tendered for a number of large projects in Britain and Europe. The severe economic recession hit the engineering, construction and property sectors in the USA, Europe, Britain and Ireland between 1989 and 1993. The consequence was excess capacity and very competitive tenders chasing a shortage of work. The evidence suggests that Kentz seems to have tendered at an uneconomically low price and been awarded more contracts simultaneously than it ever undertook before. Part of the Kentz business philosophy appears to have been to bid very tight prices, coming in with the lowest tender for fixed-price contracts. With subsequent design changes and alterations to the work required, Kentz may have hoped to obtain a much higher profit margin on this new work. Apart from lower margins, the cash flow structure on European contracts was not as favourable as business in the Middle East.

The outcome to the hyperactive tendering period was a series of fixed-price contracts in Britain, Belgium, Holland, Germany and Spain which ended up as loss-makers and a drain on scarce cash flow and working capital. Examples were the giant £400 million Hotel des Arts project in Barcelona which appears to have been underbudgeted by the developer, American hotelier G. Ware Travelstead, with knock-on effects on contractors and subcontractors such as Kentz. It proved a difficult episode for Kentz from organisational, personnel morale and cash flow perspectives. Kentz's spending was considerably in excess of its estimates. We will never know whether it was a need for a short-term injection of cash flow to cover the Barcelona deficit, or the delusion that hyperactivity and low (or 'no') margin volume would bring benefits, that was the reason for the number of other contracts secured. Kentz appears to have had a further piece of 'bad luck' when it found itself with cost overruns on the Guy's Hospital extension in London in 1993 of the order of £4 million following cash flow shortfalls on the earlier Aldermaston Atomic Weapons Establishment project. To cap these overseas difficulties, Kentz also had problems on a Bord Gáis project in Ireland involving a compressor station for an interconnector with Scotland.

Whereas the Middle East and African activities seem to have been consistently profitable, the real difficulties emerged in Europe and Britain. There were reported losses of almost £4 million on the Morgan Bank contract in Brussels, and much heavier losses on other activities in Belgium, Holland and Germany appear to have totalled almost £19 million. Despite renegotiations, settlements and Kentz's claims to the contrary, it was suggested that it lost up to £6 million on the Barcelona contract alone.[12] Kentz seems to have been building up an extensive reputation for late payment to suppliers and subcontractors. An example in the UK was the Manchester firm Fluestox Engineering which was owed Stg£25,000; it only secured payment by petitioning the court to have Kentz C&M (UK) wound up.[13]

The tendering preparation and pricing policy for contracts was the crucial decision process in the organisation. Such an enormous increase in group turnover from close to £100 million in 1988 to £319 million in 1990, over so many large projects in different fields, put intense strains on the supervision and monitoring of performance, the technical and organisational knowledge base, and the information systems required because of the number of new personnel recruited. It is not surprising that OC&C consultants, in their 1992 review of the group (at the instigation of its bankers), stated:

> . . . in our and others' view, MF Kent has been 'an accident waiting to happen'. MF Kent has been a contractor prepared to take on more risk than competitors in pursuit of volume growth as a priority, potentially not fully evaluating the internal and external risks. This has not always been reflected in pricing. The consensus is that the theme of the next phase of development should be significant cultural change including a more vigorous approach to risk management.[14]

OC&C felt that Kentz management had 'bet the company' on a large project (i.e. Barcelona) and there was insufficient independent review, risk analysis and monitoring of all high value projects. Any argument about bad luck should be dispelled because the Kentz group certainly created its own vulnerability to any 'bumps in the night' which are part of the hazards of business — particularly in engineering contracting.

The Kentz group began to diversify away from its core strengths — its long-established electrical, mechanical and instrumentation contracting business — following the management buyout. In 1990 it acquired Mahon & McPhillips from the receiver. This was a long-established civil engineering contractor in Kilkenny with a sound reputation which had suffered financial difficulties arising out of cost and payment problems on a very large project. With a turnover of over £40 million it was a significant investment to finance apart from the management supervision considerations. In addition, there were a number of ill-advised smaller acquisitions, such as a shareholding in SMC software in Cork (which was loss-making), an equity stake in Countyglen plc (a small 'shell' company with a Stock Exchange listing), and a series of property developments in Dublin and Clonmel. These were a drain on scarce cash flow and liquidity, and on the focus of top management. They signify internal 'myths and delusions' about the competence of the organisation, as well as the absence of any coherent business strategy and plans which were grounded on a hard evaluation of internal resources and the state of the external environment.

Board and ownership structure

The board of directors up to 1988 comprised Frank Kent (a 75% shareholder) as chairman, and Gus Kearney (chief executive), and four other senior executives who held the balance of 25%, with Gus Kearney holding the largest portion. When Frank Kent sold his shares to the executive team in 1988 Gus Kearney ended up with the largest stake at almost 51%. On Frank Kent's resignation from the board Gus Kearney assumed the dual roles of chairman and chief executive. There was no outside independent non-executive director on the board.

Only after the recommendations of the OC&C consultants' report had been considered by the banks and the IDA and some pressure was brought to bear were two very experienced independent Irish directors appointed in April 1993 — Stephen O'Connor, chief executive of Waterford Foods plc, and Diarmuid Quirke, chairman of Irish Cement, Irish Steel and Heiton Holdings. Alfred Schaer, a US risk management specialist, was also appointed. Hiroshi Yumiketa from Japan, who had a business involvement with the Kentz group for some time (and who was a director of Kent Technologies), also joined the board. It was much too late for the independent directors to play an effective role. It gradually became clear that the group's operational and financial situation in Europe and Britain was approaching crisis.

Neither the 1991 nor 1992 audited financial statements were completed by spring 1993 and thus there was limited factual information. In this writer's opinion the basis of the 1993 and 1994 budgets and cash flow forecasts was flawed and this left the non-executive directors in a difficult position. They were dependent on the quality and timeliness of what internal management accounting information was available and the calibre of the financial controller. Obtaining useful information about the true state of affairs of the group was problematical. If they came up against the same attitudes as the banks experienced, it would have been almost impossible for them to act effectively — particularly because of the ownership and management structure.

What formality, structure and process attached to board meetings from late 1988 until spring 1993 when the non-executive directors were appointed? The absence of audited accounts for 1991 and 1992 until 29 October 1993 made it difficult for the board to carry out its statutory role very effectively. The information put before the board could not have been very accurate as it seems to have been based on 'estimates' and 'forecasts' for 1991, 1992 and 1993 which had a dubious foundation. The observations of the examiner about the deficiencies in management structure and operating systems suggest that the board was not doing its job adequately to ensure the organisation's survival. It is surprising that the banks, knowing the financial control and trading difficulties, did not insist that as a condition of continued financial support one of the non-executive directors be made chairman and that an experienced accountant be appointed to the board.

Management structure, style and culture

Up to 1988 Frank Kent was executive chairman, and Gus Kearney had been the chief executive for many years. Following the management buyout, Gus Kearney assumed the dual roles of chairman and chief executive and Michael Campbell held the dual positions of managing director and financial director. The other long-serving senior executives, who were also participants in the management buyout, were Noel Kelly (Middle East division director), Jim Finn (technical and engineering director), Sean White (group construction director) and Paul Lloyd (business development director). They were an active if unstructured team, as consortium bankers commented in their affidavit to the High Court in their justification for the appointment of a receiver rather than an examiner:

The senior management of the Group, in particular Mr Kearney, are people of energy and drive. Both the management and employees seemed to have a very high level of scientific and technical skill and they appear to be well able to attract business. That business has been greatly expanded since its acquisition by the present owners. The banks had reason to be very concerned however as to the financial control and management of the Group.[15]

Gus Kearney, with a strong personality, appears to have dominated many of the crucial strategic and policy decisions after the management buyout. The evidence suggests that the aggressive management style adopted in pursuing ambitious growth after 1989 appears to have been in contrast to the more deliberate management culture of the 1980s when Frank Kent, the controlling shareholder at the time, and Michael McGarry, the experienced financial director, were involved in top management prior to their resignations.

Apart from top management weaknesses, there was an insufficiently strong middle management layer. OC&C consultants observed that there was need for a review of management resources with a view to lengthening management in key areas. Serious weaknesses in the finance and treasury functions were noted, with a shortage of trained and experienced personnel. The examiner, Hugh Cooney, commented in his report to the court under the heading 'Management':

> . . . it is accepted that the management structure and operating systems within the Company and its related Companies, have been deficient and found wanting during the course of the last two years.[16]

Michael Campbell attributed much of the group's financial difficulties to the intense effort, at a cost to overall group management and other projects, which went into surmounting the Hotel des Arts debacle in Barcelona. In his petition to the High Court in January 1994 requesting an examiner to be appointed, Campbell admitted:

> Kent's original order was for US$28 million . . . Their ultimate turnover within the project was US$130 million or approximately one third of the Group's annual turnover. This required the application of a far greater proportion of the Group's resources to the project which caused an enormous strain on cash flow and personnel availability within the Group and corresponding difficulty in the application of these and other resources to other Group projects and the affairs of other Group companies . . .

Several directors had to apply themselves exclusively to the resolution of the Barcelona problem. Some of the Group managers became distracted and disillusioned by the debacle and it was difficult to motivate them to address the difficulties. Some in fact left the company.[17]

Undoubtedly, the Barcelona project affected the rest of the group. Many of the other large projects did not appear to receive the top-level monitoring and supervision which they needed. Group operating risk increased. Not only did the thin line of experienced project managers suffer attrition because of the organisational strains, tensions and disillusion caused by the 'Barcelona experience' but also the other large projects in Europe and Britain suffered because some of their personnel were sucked into the 'fire fighting' in Barcelona, leaving these projects dreadfully exposed. That Gus Kearney spent considerable time in the field with a 'hands-on' involvement with projects in the 1991–93 period indicates that the overall organisational chief executive and chairman roles may have suffered. There was insufficient time spent in standing back and reviewing the direction and resource structure of Kentz as a group.

In reviewing the conditions necessary for a successful rehabilitation of the group, Hugh Cooney made it clear that new equity and management changes would be necessary if the remaining elements of the group were to survive after a financial reconstruction:

> The success of the restructuring . . . is primarily based on the introduction of a substantial investment . . . and . . . that the Investor introduces and is a party to a re-organisation of the management structure.[18]

Under the subsequent reorganisation, with new Malaysian investors introducing capital, Kentz recruited a new financial controller. The main board was controlled by the new investors and they had representation on the management board. Gus Kearney was no longer chairman but retained the position of chief executive. At the press briefing in January 1995 Gus Kearney was reported to have explained 'The policy of the company is decided at board level and we are expected to implement it.'

Kentz needed a layer of management for operational direction and control so that the top management team could stand back more and manage the strategic direction and control. Instead, the top management team was doing both sets of tasks and, true to general corporate historical experience, the short-term and pressing issues took over from the longer term focus. There is support for this conclusion as regards Kentz in the OC&C report. Evidence is also provided by Gus Kearney's admission to the banks in September 1992 that the group was 'fire fighting' and had 'overheated' in the previous two years.

A number of symptoms lead to questioning the myth of the efficiency of management in Kentz from the late 1980s. There was the low level of profit margin over a period of years. Dealings with the consortium banks, subcontractors and trade unions seem to have been managed in a generally aggressive style — which, in the opinion of this writer, often appears to have resulted in poor relationships and unsustainable growth. The increase in complexity due to the diverse range of businesses and territories had made the top management task quite different. In the opinion of this writer, there had been an insufficient change in organisational structure or culture for its phase of growth.

Financial control

There is overwhelming evidence that financial control had broken down in the group some years prior to the collapse. The insufficiency and inaccuracy of financial information, the enormous differences between the 1991, 1992 and 1993 trading forecasts and the actual results, the constantly changing projections and estimates — all are a measure of the planning and control defects. It is an indictment of the competence of accounting and financial control that no audited accounts for 1991 were fully completed for twenty-one months, and that the auditors said the group was unable to prepare full consolidated accounts. The sharp jump in overheads from £14 million in 1990 to £29 million in 1992 suggests that cost control and financial disciplines were poor.

There was a clear absence of a sound financial policy as regards capital structure and working capital planning and control — as evidenced by the drawing of cheques in excess of the bank limits, the non-submission of taxation returns, and the non-payment of various taxes in a number of countries. Clearly, the defects which had been spotted by Frank Kent in the 1970s when M. F. Kent had been operating by 'seat of the pants' financial management systems had revisited the organisation. The departure of Michael McGarry, the experienced financial director, proved serious. The lethal twin failings of inadequate systems to meet the changing business needs and lack of top-calibre personnel resulted in insufficient restraint over an unbalanced corporate strategy. This is obvious from the level of commitments entered into on a large number of diverse engineering projects, combined with adventures into property and speculative stockmarket investment.

The serious weakness in controls, referred to by the auditors in a number of their management letters, is also evidence of the deficiencies in this functional area and in the accuracy of information. KPMG Stokes Kennedy Crowley were clearly concerned with the financial management of Kentz, and in their letter of 21 September 1993, they warned:

> . . . the group's financial position is currently not in balance with its trading position . . . this may require significant restructuring of the business and its finances as a matter of urgency. We consider this matter fundamental.
>
> Unless our recommendations . . . are implemented . . . the group will be in a very serious position and operating at an unacceptable level of risk.
>
> [The group] . . . has been somewhat slow historically to implement recommendations on internal and financial controls.[19]

In this writer's view, perhaps one explanation of the circumstances prevailing in the organisation was that the top management's delusion about performance was so deep that it began to believe its own forecasts and estimates as representing the economic reality. The management may have believed some of its forecasts initially, not realising the deficiencies in the accounting database and valuations. Another possible explanation, in the opinion of the writer, is that top management did not want to receive or hear adverse information on the overall performance of the organisation or the large projects. Often in such situations, perhaps due to delays and concealment and even a sense of fear, the full extent of a deteriorating performance may not filter upwards until the problem is so serious that disclosure is unavoidable.

It was remarkable that Michael Campbell continued to occupy the positions of managing director and financial controller — particularly after the banks pointed out the financial control weaknesses in January 1992. OC&C consultants were extremely critical of this function in their August 1992 report. No new senior appointment was made in 1992 or 1993. Perhaps it is not surprising that two of the finance staff left the group in October 1992 (according to the AIB affidavit). This would have made the functional weaknesses more acute. As Michael Campbell moved more into general management, the finance role seems to have suffered. An important theme to emerge was the increasingly symbiotic relationship between

Kearney and Campbell. Such a dependency, allied to a weak board and management structure, was fatal. It is strange that the Kentz bankers did not insist that an experienced accountant be seconded to the function until someone of adequate calibre was recruited. It seems that Kentz subsequently found it difficult to attract a suitably qualified accountant, in view of its difficulties and the nature of the managerial culture and structure.

Overtrading: capital structure and working capital

When one examines the scale of the increase in turnover in comparison to shareholders' funds, debt and working capital, it is clear that Kentz was overtrading for some years prior to its collapse. It had a very low profit margin on turnover, and its cash flow was totally insufficient to help sustain the pace of growth or attract external financial support. How could it stay 'financially alive' for so long?

Using a medical analogy, the 'prolonging of life' was due to a series of blood transfusions — both large and small — through the initial cash flow structure of new projects. The use of subcontractors and the delayed and non-payment of PAYE, other employment taxes and VAT helped finance the business for a period — at the expense of the exchequer and the taxpayer. Kentz was reported to owe almost £17 million to the taxation authorities, when its UK, Belgian and Spanish obligations were added to the Irish arrears.

Perhaps an important technical banking and financial control point to emerge was the extent of the interlocking company indebtedness and cross securities, guarantees and undertakings to banks between the various companies in the group and the parent. It appears not to have been appreciated by the Kentz management that if one leg of the group had a serious financial situation with its banks or other creditors which could end up in court, there were direct 'knock-on' consequences for operations in other territories. An example was the financial problem in Britain followed by the European operations. A point which should be emphasised was the extent of cash flow and intercompany debt moving between the various companies in the group. This would tend to conceal the impact of losses in various areas.

There were very serious financial consequences for the outside creditors of the various subsidiaries which were owed money by fellow subsidiaries. A case in point was Mahon & McPhillips. It appears to have been a profitable company according to its audited financial statements in 1991 and 1992. Its audited balance sheet showed 'cash' holdings of £11.3 million in

1991. Cash had fallen to £0.5 million by 1993; intercompany creditors had been paid off, but group intercompany obligations owing to Mahon & McPhillips had risen from £0.9 million in 1991 to £3.3 million in 1993. What was originally a positive net worth position was converted into a deficit when there was a write-down of work-in-progress and the intercompany debt. This reduced the resources available for creditors and the taxation authorities.

A further question from a financial control standpoint is: how could the Kentz group justify the payment of a dividend of £7.5 million in 1990 and another dividend of £4 million in 1992, when one takes account of the working capital and debt position? Cash flow projections, linked to the scale of new projects taken on, would have shown the equity capital needs of the group. These dividend payments appear to have been made for 'tax efficiency' purposes and the dividends were reintroduced as 'directors' advances'. Nevertheless, in this writer's view this transaction changed the riskiness of the director/shareholders' investment and had implications for the unsecured creditors. The 'accounting' basis of declaring a 1992 dividend seems questionable in view of the severity and nature of the auditors' qualifications and the nature of the information in the 'Notes' to the accounts on going concern and the carrying values of assets and liabilities. In this writer's opinion the low level of equity in relation to the debts of the group, combined with the state of the industry in the many economies in which it was operating, would have suggested greater concern for non-shareholder interests. The dividend policy of Kentz can be contrasted with Jacobs Engineering, where no dividends were paid for some years — despite its recovery in profits and its much stronger financial and equity capital position.

We get some idea of the conflicting views of Kentz and its bankers and ensuing tensions in the relationship from the assertions of a senior manager in AIB in his affidavit to the High Court:

> By September 1992 the excess over authorised limits on the Group's bank accounts was running at levels of up to £5.0 million. . . . The Group's senior management advised the Banks that matters were under control and order was being restored. The Banks continued to honour cheques presented for payment against the Group's accounts. At a further meeting on 1 October 1992 . . . my colleague —, on behalf of the Banks, said we were unhappy with the financial information we were obtaining . . . and that we feared that the Banks were not being made aware of further loss situations (which

— characterised as 'black holes') . . . Mr Kearney denied the existence of any 'black holes' and complained that the Banks were occupying too much of the Group's employees' time in dealing with the Banks' requests for information.[20]

Finally, in this writer's opinion, the bankers' covenant requirements of a net worth of not less than £13 million cannot be divorced from the problems of financial control, financial reporting and accounting measurement and valuation policies adopted.

Accounting issues

The delays in finalising audited financial statements, and the poor quality of accounting, internal control and financial reporting, have already been discussed. The examiner reported that the 'operating systems' had been 'deficient and found wanting' in the two years prior to the collapse.[21] The existing systems, procedures and personnel were overwhelmed by the hyperactive expansion of the group over such a diverse range of large projects in so many geographic regions. In September 1993, KPMG Stokes Kennedy Crowley, the group's auditors, wrote to the directors of Kentz expressing their concerns about a number of accountancy, internal and management control issues. They pointed to the financial position and the fact that the group was 'in a very serious position and operating at an unacceptable level of risk'.[22] The auditors had made recommendations on accounting and financial weaknesses before, but Kentz had not acted on them. In this writer's opinion it was a most extraordinary state of affairs — more reminiscent of a sole trader or start-up small business than a group with over 4,000 employees and a turnover of £319 million.

By September 1993, audited accounts for 1991 and 1992 had not been submitted to the group's bankers, and there were extensive payment delays in taxation. The Companies Acts require directors to have accounts prepared, audited and filed with the Companies Office within defined time limits. Group accounts are also required, where relevant. However, in their letter of 21 October 1993, KPMG Stokes Kennedy Crowley said the group 'cannot prepare proper consolidated accounts on an ongoing basis'. Obligations under the Companies Acts seem not to have been fulfilled.[23] In these circumstances, it seems most doubtful that the Kentz group could prepare budgets and cash flow forecasts with any degree of confidence in 1992 and 1993. In this writer's opinion any projections submitted to bankers could not carry much credibility.

Well-managed organisations of Kentz's size would certainly track their financial performance accurately, and the audit would have been completed in four to seven months at the latest. For example, CRH plc, the manufacturer and supplier of building materials, with a turnover of £1.1 billion and with activities in Ireland, Britain, mainland Europe and the USA, was able to have its audit opinion for the year ending 31 December 1992 'signed off' by its auditors on 2 March 1993. The Sisk group (Sicon), a large privately owned Irish building contractor, had its 1991 financial statements 'signed off' on 20 July 1992. More importantly, the fact that no audited accounts were finalised for 1991 and that the 1992 audited accounts were not 'signed off' until late October 1993 indicates that there was no independent confirmation to the directors of the accuracy of the figures or the true performance and financial position of the group. This is a remarkable situation for such a large organisation. In this writer's view it tells us something about its management culture. It raises questions about the role of the board and internal governance, and the basis of Kentz's trading policies and business strategy. One might ask what issues, responsibilities, actions and explanations might arise under the Companies Acts.

The 'accounting reality' proves very different when the audited figures are compared with earlier projections. It should be noted that the auditors expressed qualifications and reservations about the balance sheet valuations of a range of assets. Consequently any more prudent adjustments would result in significantly lower profits and higher losses in 1991 and 1992. A comparison between the 'estimates' and the audited figures (before adjustments for valuation uncertainties) is shown in Table 4.4.

Table 4.4:	Kentz profit projections and the subsequent reality (£m)	
	Projected profits	**Actual profits/(losses) per audited accounts**
1990	7.7	5.2
1991	9.4	(2.0)
1992	8.5	3.3*
1993	16.9	(40.0)[e]

*   Before adjustments. These financial statements were heavily qualified by auditors.
[e]   Estimate by author, based on the group deficit.
Source: *Business & Finance*, 8 April 1993 and 27 January 1994. Audited financial statements 1991 and 1992. Documents submitted to court by banks. Examiner's reports.

The board of directors of Kentz appears to have been unable to agree financial statements for 1991 with its auditors and consequently such audited accounts were not submitted to the shareholders or banks, nor filed in the Companies Office, during 1992.[24] The extraordinary delays in finalising the 1991 financial statements provide an insight into the differing views of auditors and clients on accounting matters. The auditors had written in explanation:

> At the request of management, we deferred completion of the 1991 financial statements because of the significant and material uncertainties existing at that time and our likely report on same.[25]

The auditors seemed to be indicating that they would have had no option but to 'qualify' their report because they could not accept crucial figures in the financial statements prepared by Kentz, due to the uncertainties surrounding costs, recoverable revenues and cash flows of some of the larger projects, such as Barcelona. In brief, in this writer's view in an attempt to avoid qualification, audited accounts were not finalised for 1991. There was also the £13 million net worth covenant to bankers. Indeed when the 1991 financial statements were eventually 'signed off' by the auditors on 29 October 1993, they revealed a net loss of £3.9 million for the year and shareholders' funds of £0.8 million — which could be augmented to £8.6 million if directors' advances of £7.4 million, being dividends reintroduced, and £0.4 million minority interests are added.

If such qualified accounts had been issued during the normal period, say in summer 1992, the extent of the audited 'true and fair' financial position of the group would have been obvious to the bankers. Kentz internal management figures for 1991, issued in October 1992, indicated a profit of £8 million and a net worth of £19 million. Then, in May 1993, revised draft unaudited accounts submitted to the banks indicated a profit of £4 million and a net worth of £13.4 million for 1991. Just five months later these figures had been transformed into an audited loss of £3.9 million. This loss would have been larger if any adjustments for more prudent carrying values of contract work-in-progress and debtors had been adopted.

Contract work-in-progress and debtors' amounts recoverable on contracts amounted to £70 million in both 1991 and 1992. Two points arise. First, any reduction in this asset's carrying value fed directly into the profit and loss account under revenue and profit recognition accounting principles. Profits would have been lower and losses would have been higher and consequently the net worth figure would not have met the covenant to bankers. Second, as these 'current asset' valuations represented 63% and 57% of total assets in the balance sheet in those years, any reductions in valuations also reduced the apparent strength of the working capital.

KPMG Stokes Kennedy Crowley also seem to have been unhappy with the draft 1992 financial statements submitted by the directors of Kentz on a number of occasions.[26] In September 1993 these draft statements reported a net worth of £13.6 million. One month later, Kentz revised the draft figures and reported a lower net profit and a reduced net worth of £9.8 million.[27] In this writer's opinion these financial statements had to be eventually recast on a more prudent basis of measurement and disclosure before the auditors would sign their opinion. The evidence indicates that in September and October 1993 Kentz top management appear to have been still seeking to avoid an audit qualification, but the auditors were taking a firm line on their independent position in expressing an opinion on the reliability of the figures. It is not often that evidence of such a series of altered financial data comes to light. From court documentation one media source thought the parties appeared to be trying to 'negotiate' a solution, though the auditors were making their stance clear:

> SKC did offer Kentz an 'out' by saying it would be possible 'not to qualify the audit report with respect to the uncertainties, once adequate provisions have been made and remaining uncertainties are disclosed in sufficient detail in the financial statements themselves'.
>
> But it cautioned that 'if we disagree with the final approach being adopted to a material extent in terms of provisions or disclosures, then there is a requirement that we qualify our audit report accordingly'.[28]

The auditors were correctly putting Kentz on notice that they wished to ensure adequate provisions for work-in-progress and debtors' balances for contract costs and disclosures on a number of issues. The tenor of this letter, and the fact that three letters were issued in September and October 1993, indicate some strain in the relationship. There were other audit 'loose ends' requiring further information or disclosure such as 'payments' of £2 million to secure contracts abroad during 1991 and 1992; contracts in non-group companies; details of non-group companies controlled by Kentz directors in the Channel Islands, West Africa and Malaysia; and whether the loans to directors totalling £920,000 were in breach of the limit permitted by the Companies Acts. These loans reached £1.5 million at one stage in 1992. Gus Kearney received loans totalling £888,000 during 1992 but these were reduced to £594,000 at the year end.[29] The 'Notes' to the 1992 financial statements subsequently disclosed that 'The loans are interest free and unsecured with no fixed term of repayment.' These advances represented a very material amount of the group's net worth and use of scarce resources at the year end.

Even though the draft financial statements dated 21 October 1993 were drawn up a little more prudently than the version considered by the Kentz board on 24 September (the 'amounts recoverable' from the Aldermaston and Morgan Bank contracts were reduced by £400,000 and £3.7 million respectively), the auditors seem to have remained unhappy about a number of issues. After all, the four fundamental concepts underlying accounting measurement involve prudence, continuity, consistency and matching if a 'true and fair' portrayal of an organisation's economic performance is to be presented. There was obvious uncertainty about the 'continuity' of Kentz and whether 'going concern' accounting principles could be adopted. In September and October 1993 the auditors had warned Kentz that the bankers might not be too happy with the financial picture of the group. In addition, the cash flow projections for 1994 indicated that the group needed £5 million more than the bank facilities currently available. Negotiations seem to have taken place to obtain the banks' approval to support a going concern assumption before the audit opinion was signed on 29 October 1993. In this writer's opinion the value of this approach was problematical, for we know, with hindsight, that the Kentz group only lasted another eleven weeks from the date of the audit 'signing off'. The separate financial statements of the loss-making Kentz UK company were heavily qualified because of its weak financial condition and dependence on the Irish group. The collapse of the UK company triggered a 'domino' effect because of intercompany debt and guarantees.

Despite the adjustments and disclosures incorporated by the Kentz directors, the auditors remained unhappy. The finally approved financial statements for 1991 and 1992 were qualified on the basis of a 'disagreement' on debtor and contract provisions. It should be noted that it is very rare for a large company to receive a qualified audit opinion — particularly for two years in succession.[30] It can be seen as a 'red flag' in the quality and credibility of the accounting policies in underpinning a true and fair view of performance and financial position. In this writer's view the nature of the qualification and the information therein, and the 'Notes', reveal a great deal about the organisation's management culture, and its policies and perceptions.

The Kentz audited accounts for 1992 reported a net profit of £2.4 million. If adjustments were made for the debtor valuation disagreements in the audit report, a net loss of £0.8 million would result. In effect, this writer concludes that such an adjustment would show losses for successive years rather than the illusory 'profit recovery' actually reported. Shareholders' funds were in deficit in 1992 and this negative measure of net worth could only be 'converted' into a positive position by the addition of the advances from directors — which were the dividends paid out in 1990 and 1992. Though these advances were subordinated to bank debt, there was no note of them being subordinated to the general group of creditors, to whom the Kentz group had obligations of £76 million. One might ask: how did the directors justify continuance of trading with a negative net worth, the position of creditors, the weaknesses in accounting, internal and financial controls, and the losses incurred?

The directors' opinion of what constituted 'a true and fair view' was clearly much more optimistic than the view of the auditors. In this writer's opinion the validity of the going concern basis of accounting might be raised, as it was noted that the financial statements were prepared on the assumption of a successful conclusion to the issues in Note 2, 'Financing Facilities'. The auditors warned that 'the financial statements do not include any adjustments that would result from a failure to obtain appropriate funding'. An examination of the 'Notes' attached to the financial statements reveals a discussion on the financial facilities position, and the fact that actual bank borrowings had been in excess of the committed facilities for some time, and that the borrowings were repayable at the discretion of the bankers. It was also pointed out that the net worth was less than the £13 million specified in covenants in bonding agreements. Despite all the foregoing uncertainties, Note 2 stated:

> Whilst the directors are presently uncertain as to the outcome of the matters mentioned above, they believe . . . it is appropriate for the financial statements to be prepared on the going concern basis.

In this writer's opinion, this statement by the auditors that they were not qualifying their report on the validity of applying the going concern convention — but directing the reader to Note 2 and the directors' assurances — is problematic. Bearing in mind the management style of the firm, and its earlier aggressive approach to financial statement preparation and submissions to the auditors, it would be surprising if the directors did not 'expect' a positive outcome to the range of problems being encountered which justified adopting the 'going concern' basis. The auditing practices adopted, partially arising out of weak regulatory standards, in effect passed over responsibility in the matter to the directors — with the reader having to read 'Notes' cast in a special language which did not provide much solid information for a judgment on the matter. In the writer's opinion it is unfortunate that the financial statements were not qualified on the 'going concern' concept with the evidence available on the group's affairs at the time, the cash flow forecasts and budgets, and their degree of reliability.

There was also the state of the UK company. After all, the auditors had written to Kentz about retaining the confidence and support of the banks. As the auditors can justifiably claim they acted in accordance with auditing standards in ensuring disclosure about the continuity issue, this suggests that revisions of auditing standards and auditor responsibilities be revisited. It was an example of where the external user was not in as strong a position as the auditor to make a judgment. After all, the auditor is required to offer an independent professional opinion on the accounting policies and judgments underlying the preparation of the financial statements. The Cadbury Report, which had been issued in December 1992, suggests that directors should have a 'reasonable expectation' that a company will continue for the 'foreseeable future'.[31] What constitutes 'foreseeable future' has not been clearly defined, but generally a period of the order of twelve months is understood to be appropriate.

In the audited financial statements for 1992, Note 3 pointed out that intangible fixed assets included £1.1 million of 'deferred expenditure' relating to business expenditure in the former USSR which had not proceeded for some years, and its recoverability was uncertain. The 'prudence' concept would expect this amount to be expensed rather than capitalised, particularly as it had been carried for some years. The treatment of this capitalised expenditure seems to be in conflict with the rulings and evidence as regards accounting treatment prescribed in Statement of Standard Accounting Practice (SSAP) No. 13. There was also reference to another questionable asset valuation — £0.9 million of unamortised goodwill on the acquisition of a software development company which was loss-making. Again, the carrying of this intangible asset by the directors, in the circumstances, appears to run counter to the prudence concept. In the writer's view the adoption of more prudent accounting policies would have resulted in reported net profits being converted into losses, and the net worth and working capital being materially reduced as shown in Table 4.5.

Table 4.5: Kentz Corporation: adjustments of accounting figures for 1992 on basis of more prudent accounting policies (£m)

	Net profit/ (loss)	Net worth	Net current liabilities
Per 1992 audited financial statements	2.4	10.0	(2.7)
Adjustments			
Morgan Bank contract	(2.7)	(2.7)	(2.7)
German Lander contract	(0.5)	(0.5)	(0.5)
Defence contract UK	(1.4)	(1.4)	(1.4)
Hospital contract UK	(1.0)	(1.0)	(1.0)
Deferred expenditure USSR	(1.1)	(1.1)	0
Goodwill	(0.9)	(0.9)	0
Subtotal	(7.6)	(7.6)	(5.6)
Adjusted 'more prudent' 1992 figures	(5.2)	2.4	(8.3)

Source: Audited financial statements and 'Notes' attached for Holidair Ltd for year ended December 1992 enclosed in petition to High Court by M. Campbell, January 1994. Adjustments by author based on 'fundamental uncertainties' qualification in auditors' report and information in 'Notes' to the financial statement for year ended December 1992.

These adjustments show that the net worth would have fallen to a mere £2.4 million in contrast to the minimum covenanted amount of £13 million — quite apart from a net loss of £5.2 million. The working capital position would have shown a much greater deterioration. One cannot avoid asking whether the accounting policies adopted in respect of revenue recognition on contracts (which dictates profit recognition) and the capitalisation of costs were driven by management imperatives rather than a neutral and 'true and fair' portrayal of the performance and position of the group.

Some of the responsibility for these accounting weaknesses rests not only with the directors but also with the regulatory framework of accounting and financial reporting in Ireland, rather than the auditors. In their survey of Irish practice based on 1990 published accounts, Brennan, O'Brien and Pierce found that disclosure in the area of 'long term contracts' was somewhat inadequate, and observed that 'None of the [six] companies disclosed the basis upon which turnover was ascertained, despite the explicit requirement of SSAP 9 to do so.'[32] The information in the Kentz case generally supports their criticisms, and suggests a need for a regulatory overhaul in accounting standards. The current accounting standard is weak in indicating a specific method for determining turnover (i.e. revenue recognition), and this is a major flaw. It uses the fuzzy language of ambiguity when it states 'turnover is ascertained in a manner appropriate to the stage of completion of the contract, the business, and the industry in which it operates'. Davies and his colleagues, having considered the standard, concluded that 'The issues of profit and loss recognition on contracts, and the position of variations in contracts and claims are not tightly framed nor is our knowledge about practice very clear.'[33]

This writer views such a degree of discretion and flexibility in the area of long-term contracts as providing opportunities for directors to adopt accounting valuation policies to suit the picture they wish to present from time to time, which may not portray a 'true and fair view' as was the evidence in the case of Kentz because of the auditors' audit qualification. The subsequent write-down of assets in the group (though it remained a going concern in examinership) and the extent of the write-down in asset values in the reorganisation figures put before the High Court suggest that the valuations of assets by Kentz were optimistic and that the auditors' concerns were justified.

External governance and regulatory issues

The degree to which external control can be exercised depends largely on the company's ownership structure, financing and relationships with outside bodies. Following the management buyout, the Kentz group remained a privately owned organisation with only its top management team as shareholders. There was no outside shareholder who could exercise some degree of accountability, restraint or caution. Most management buyouts involve a venture capital group or investment institution which supports the management and takes an equity stake or options. This investor usually would agree a business plan with the company and also put two experienced independent directors on the board. Financial information on performance would be monitored carefully, and for an organisation the size of Kentz the outside investor and directors would ensure there was a strong competence at the financial controller level.

The bankers represented an indirect control mechanism which failed. The banks might argue that they acted with the utmost forbearance. Unfortunately, the 'accommodating' policy facilitated a continuance of poor management control and structural weaknesses which seem to have been well known for at least eighteen months before collapse. Possibly, the political consequences of a very tough line by the banks outmatched their exposure when the scale of the group's operations and employment were considered. AIB and BNP lost almost £2 million each. The bank advances were shown in the 1992 balance sheet at £23.5 million — which the bank affidavit to the High Court in January 1994 indicated was in excess of agreed limits. From this writer's viewpoint it seems that the banks eventually adopted a policy of 'managing' the level of their risk exposure, rather than using intervention and change in the client's business to reduce its risk. If they were unable to extract audited accounts for 1991 by summer 1992 from a group the size of Kentz, then they should have drawn their own conclusions about the quality of the information received. ICC Bank seems to have adopted a passive stance in the whole affair. It had a relatively stronger security position because of its mortgages over certain properties — though it may also have had to make some provisions. It is unfortunate that the AIB/BNP consortium did not combine with ICC Bank. Such a move could have led to greater strength of 'persuasion', which might have resulted in corrective action before it was too late in 1993.

Though the level of total bank debt was high in comparison to the equity capital (even when we include directors' loans), it was relatively small in relation to the credit obtained from suppliers and the Revenue Commissioners. The large number of unsecured creditors (subcontractors) who were heavily dependent on Kentz also reduced the likelihood of actions which would have forced Kentz to reconsider its financing options. Certainly, a strong outside equity investor should have been brought in by 1991. Of course, this would have diluted the control of the management and impacted on the management structure, style and control process.

Group arrears of PAYE and VAT of over £11 million is surprising. With less than 1,000 employees in Ireland, the wage bill implies that adequate payments had not been made for a lengthy period. The schemes of arrangement showed that much of the debt due to the Revenue Commissioners was non-preferential, indicating that some PAYE and VAT was in arrears for more than a year.

An inspection of the Companies Office revealed that neither M. F. Kent nor M. F. Kent & Co. (International) filed 1991 and 1992 financial statements. The latter was the 'flagship' company of the group. There is no evidence of what actions, if any, were taken by the Registrar of Companies. More forthright pressure to file returns and financial statements could have had a beneficial effect on the affairs of the group. In this writer's view the threat of the sanctions on directors and the implications of the disclosure on credit and suppliers could have forced the management to act more prudently sooner. Would suppliers and subcontractors have provided such levels of credit if they were aware of the group's financial state as disclosed in the 1991 accounts?

The consequences

A report by the examiner indicated a deficit for M. F. Kent of £15 million. An estimated statement of affairs for the European operations (excluding Spain) showed a much reduced value for assets when compared to earlier management estimates. The estimated overall deficiency was £18.8 million. The European operations had group intercompany debt of £19.5 million, and the financial impact on Irish and other group companies' solvency, because of the large losses on European contracts, was very material.

The financial collapse led to heavy bad debt write-offs for most creditors, quite apart from many employees losing their jobs. For example, the AIB/BNP consortium, with £8.6 million in secured loans, agreed to accept £4 million in settlement. ICC Bank was owed £2.5 million by M. F. Kent, predominantly in relation to the Beech Hill property development in Dublin, but agreed that this debt be transferred directly to the weak property subsidiaries.

The Revenue Commissioners were owed at least £11.8 million, mainly on foot of employees' PAYE. Depending on the individual company and its particular asset/liability position, the revenue authorities accepted differing settlements. For example, in the case of M. F. Kent, where the obligations were £4.9 million, the Revenue Commissioners accepted 40p in the £1 for preferential debt of £2.3 million over twenty monthly instalments, and 20p in the £1 on the non-preferential arrears. In the case of Mahon & McPhillips the debt to the revenue authorities of £2.7 million was discharged by way of 60p in the £1 on preferential debt of £1.5 million in eighteen instalments, while 50p in the £1 was to be paid on the non-preferential arrears. No interest was to be paid on revenue arrears as part of the settlement. The unfortunate unsecured creditors received between 20p and 50p in the £1, depending on their status. The 'nominated' subcontractors were paid 100p in the £1. Some subcontractors suffered business difficulties as a result of the delayed payments and write-offs. The extent of cash flow and intercompany debt moving between the various companies in the group tended to conceal the impact of losses in various areas. There were very serious financial consequences for the outside creditors of the various subsidiaries which were owed money by fellow subsidiaries.

Reflections

The foregoing analysis disclosed elements of personality, strategy, managerial delusion, and organisational and management control weaknesses underlying the financial crisis in Kentz. A series of self-inflicted injuries undermined what had been a 'good business' within three years. The succession of 'big league' projects, and particularly the Hotel des Arts debacle, ravaged the health and resources of the group. Was this configuration of elements or themes unique to Kentz, or can some or all of them be considered to be generalisable to other organisations that have experienced a financial crisis?

On the surface, there appear to be some similarities in the themes emerging when we compare Kentz to Goodman International. Gus Kearney and Larry Goodman left school early and, through their force of character, energy and workrate, they were associated with the building up of the largest businesses in their respective sectors in Ireland. With an enthusiasm for sales and deal-making, both had expanded extensively abroad and had become 'international' organisations. Both were private and secretive organisations. Both had headquarters in relatively small towns — Clonmel and Ardee — and operated with a tightly knit top management team.

The 'number two' in each organisation was an accountant who seemed to move in close sympathy with the dominant figure in the organisation. This autocratic 'dominant figure' continued to have a personal involvement in all material decisions. Perhaps the most striking similarity was the radical shift in strategy which in both cases undermined a long-established sound business in a few short years. Bankers lost heavily in Goodman International whereas creditors absorbed most of the deficits in Kentz — with the exchequer losing in both.

Whereas Larry Goodman built his organisation almost single-handed, Frank Kent shaped M. F. Kent with Gus Kearney until the management buyout. After this buyout, the capital structure appears to have been weak, and within two years there was an insufficient equity and working capital base for the fast-growth strategy pursued. Both organisations operated in fiercely competitive, low-margin, mature industries. In contrast to Gus Kearney, Larry Goodman seems to have applied a calculative analytical precision to figures allied to the methodical measurement of productivity, costs and profit of activities against stringent targets. In this writer's opinion Kentz was turnover-addicted and exhibited all the 'growing pains' of transition.

In the main, it was a combination of some bad luck and an overambitious speculative investment adventure which led to the financial crisis at Goodman International. However, it was a much deeper management malaise at both operational and strategic levels which led to the crisis in the Kentz group. Weaknesses in financial control and governance issues were central to both cases. Their international success was testimony to product and service competence and competitiveness. The problem was the quality of the turnover and its pricing and profitability for the risks undertaken. Based on draft financial statements and the company's behaviour a year before collapse, a score of between 71 and 78 would have been merited on the Argenti model for Kentz — which was in the danger zone. The signals were there for those who could appreciate them. It was a classic example of Miller's 'Impulsive Syndrome: Running Blind'. Applying the Abidali and Harris Z score and A score failure predictive models for the construction industry would have marked Kentz out as high risk almost two years before actual collapse.[34]

The following themes emerge in the Kentz case. First, there was the combination of the dominant chief executive, a weak board structure, weak financial control and optimistic financial reporting at a crucial stage. Second, there was an excessive reliance on bank loans and other debt. Third, there was the 'big project' (financed by debt). Fourth, for an organisation of its size, there was insufficient depth of management, indicating the organisation's structural weaknesses and a dilution of its core competence and focus. The chief executive remained too involved with operational matters and did not give sufficient time to critical strategic issues. The consequence was 'overtrading'. The real profit performance had been uneconomic for years. This was due to weak pricing and a high cost structures, allied to poor management accounting systems and information. The emphasis was too much on turnover and not enough on profit.

The rapid change in expansion and debt policy in both Kentz and Goodman was almost a change of corporate personality within a very short period. Though difficult to explain, perhaps such sudden hyperactivity is a signal in itself that strategic controls are breaking down and corporate risk levels are rising. In the Kentz case the delay in audited accounts after the first year was a clear indication of defects in accounting and a management delusion syndrome where reality and ambition were divorced. The case brings out many accountancy, auditing and regulatory issues which require attention.

Because of the importance of estimating costs and monitoring performance over a potentially small portfolio of projects and customers, contracting can tend to be more risky than manufacturing at the adolescent stage. There seems to be less flexibility in product design, cost engineering and pricing. In particular an undue emphasis on fixed-price contracts can prove hazardous unless the operational planning and control systems are efficient and the organisation's growth is linked to a balanced resource strategy.

Chapter 5

Xtra-vision: A Stock Exchange Shooting Star

The desire to expand originates with the desire to succeed. Everyone who starts a small business envisions turning that enterprise into an established, profitable, large-volume operation in the future. That objective is entirely appropriate. It was the driving force that created the largest and most powerful organizations that operate today.

If you recognize the importance of expansion as part of owning and operating your own business, then you also understand the expansion ethic. It's often assumed that growth must continue indefinitely, that the faster the pace the better, and that growth means success. This ethic contains elements of truth. . . . But when growth becomes the purpose, actually it can ruin a business . . .

It's much less common to see an operation fail because growth has taken place too slowly, or because the owner cut back on expansion. The fact is, a company is at greater risk when growth comes about too quickly, since the owner often loses control over the business, stops contacting customers, and becomes a victim of the expansion ethic.

Michael C. Thomsett, *The Expansion Trap*[1]

Introduction

Xtra-vision was distinctly different from Goodman or Kentz. It was a young adolescent firm which became a 'public company' through a share quotation on the Unlisted Securities Market of the Dublin Stock Exchange. It was sponsored by a reputable bank/stockbroking house and a prospectus was issued. In theory, there were stronger governance and control mechanisms, through the board of directors, Stock Exchange regulations, statutory financial reporting and other disclosure requirements, which might have given it credibility for investors. There were two subsequent rights issues. Xtra-vision was a Stock Exchange 'shooting star' as its share prices rose and fell dramatically. Within two years, following a major financial crisis, a rescue had to be mounted. There were extensive investor losses. In this writer's view, it remains problematical that it achieved economic earnings from the time it was floated on the market. Applying the term 'bubble' might be too severe a description of the economic entity, but not of the share price movements.

Xtra-vision plc: a suitable firm for the Stock Exchange?

The rise and fall of Xtra-vision plc over a nineteen-month period, reflected in the volatility of its share price from a placing price of 48p in April 1989 to 107p within months and an eventual decline to under 6p, was one of the more colourful and questionable episodes on the Dublin Stock Exchange — particularly as the company was not a speculative mining or oil-prospecting share.

Xtra-vision was founded in 1982 by 21-year-old Richard Murphy when he started renting a small stock of videos from a rented premises in Ranelagh, Dublin. He subsequently leased another outlet in Stillorgan, Co. Dublin. By 1985, he had six outlets in Dublin's southside. Richard Murphy's business and bank overdraft problems were looked after by Herbert Boyle, a young chartered accountant, whom he had met in 1986. Boyle subsequently invested in the business and helped raise finance for expansion and working capital. Boyle is reported to have described himself as an entrepreneur first and an accountant second.[2] Initially Algemene Bank Nederland advanced a £500,000 loan. By 1987 Xtra-vision had expanded to Dublin's northside and it was running sixteen outlets.

In March 1988, Davy Corporate Finance, a member of the Davy Stockbrokers group, arranged a private placing of new shares, amounting to £610,000 (net), which represented 10% of the enlarged equity. In November 1988, Development Capital Corporation (DCC) subscribed £1.2 million for a further 10% of the equity. In addition, Mulroy Securities, as a nominee for private clients of Davy, invested £806,000 in new equity. This share subscription was at the equivalent of 28p per ordinary share, following the two for one bonus issue prior to flotation. DCC also exercised an option over 2% of the enlarged equity before flotation. By January 1989, with the additional capital, Xtra-vision had expanded to eighty-two outlets.

The company obtained a quotation on the Unlisted Securities Market in late April 1989 through a placing at 48p per share by DCC Corporate Finance through stockbrokers Davy and Panmure Gordon. By this time, following domestic and UK acquisitions, combined with the rapid development of new outlets across Ireland, the group had grown to a hundred outlets.

It was a spectacular debut and the share price reached 83p on the first day of trading. Xtra-vision's equity was valued at £42 million. Following the placing, Richard Murphy's shareholding fell to 52% (from 57.8%),

Herbert Boyle's was 9.6% and DCC held 10.2%. The chairman, Alex Spain, owned 507,000 shares, representing 1% of the equity. The placing valuation had made Richard Murphy, at twenty-eight, a paper multimillionaire. There was considerable publicity and euphoria surrounding Xtra-vision's market debut and initial share price movement. The share price quickly rose to a peak of 107p. Davy, in its research review of Xtra-vision of 15 November 1989, projected profits to increase to £4.5 million for 1989/90 and to grow dramatically to £11 million for 1990/91. Earnings per share were forecast at 5.8p and 11.8p respectively.

A rights issue in late October 1989, at 80p per share, raised £9.8 million to fund further expansion and acquisitions in the USA.[3] The preliminary statement of results for the year ended January 1990, dated 4 May 1990, announced a tripling of pre-tax profits to £4.5 million compared with £1.5 million the previous year. Earnings per share were 5.6p (double the previous year's). Alex Spain stated: 'The Directors anticipate further strong growth in sales and profits in the current financial year. At this early stage of the financial year the outlook is encouraging.'[4] This reported profit figure was in line with stockbrokers' published expectations and the share price remained unchanged at 70p. A second rights issue at 40p per share, for a further £10 million, was unveiled on 21 May 1990. The justification was to reduce bank borrowing, which had risen to £17.2 million at 18 May as a result of the group's expansion. The number of video stores had increased from 170 to 318 since the rights issue seven months earlier.

In an updated review of Xtra-vision, dated 22 May 1990, Davy now expected pre-tax profits of £7 million for the year to the end of January 1991. This was a sharp reduction on the earlier forecast of £11 million. The stockbrokers felt that following the rights issue Xtra-vision would be financially strong with a projected gearing ratio of 12%. Profit forecasts were thought to be conservative and the Xtra-vision shares were seen to have upside potential and were recommended.

At the annual general meeting on 22 August 1990, the chairman Alex Spain, to the surprise of investors and analysts, warned of current profit problems. He said a restructured board and management were reviewing Xtra-vision's affairs carefully. Within days, Davy revised its profit forecast for 1990/91 down from £7 million to £2.5 million. NCB Stockbrokers reviewed Xtra-vision's depreciation policy and restated their profit projection at £0.6 million.

On 6 December 1990, Alex Spain announced a net loss for the six months to the end of July 1990 of £20.6 million on a turnover of £15.8

million. The eventual outcome for the twelve months to end January 1991 was a net loss of £19.2 million. 'Prior year adjustments' of £4.8 million and a 'restatement' of the previous year's 1990 financial statements showed accumulated losses of £25.3 million and a negative net worth (at book value) of £2 million.

It was a most extraordinary reversal in the firm's reported trading pattern in such a short space of time. Davy's earlier profit forecasts seem to have raised many questions with investment institutions and smaller investors. The share price slumped. In late October Xtra-vision was unexpectedly reported by newspapers to be in financial restructuring talks with its bankers.[5] This was just seventeen weeks after the 'clean' audit opinion dated 29 June 1990 on its 1989/90 published financial statements. Between 1 June and 3 September 1990, Xtra-vision's share price had fallen from 55p to 16p. It had slumped to 7p by early November. In December NCB Stockbrokers announced that they had reached agreement on the terms of a recommended offer on behalf of Cambridge Group. In explaining the background to this offer to shareholders Alex Spain observed:

> The Board is currently forecasting a loss for the year to 31 January 1991. At 16 November 1990, the indebtedness of the Xtra-vision Group . . . was approximately IR£18.3 million. In view of this critical situation your Board sought to strengthen the group's financial position and examined all options in this regard, including the raising of additional funds through the stock market, and the possibility of attracting a trade investor into the group. Discussions with the group's bankers were also held with a view to negotiating a restructuring of the group's borrowings. While these options were being investigated, Cambridge approached the Board with the Offer and, having regard to the critical nature of the group's trading and financial position and to the lack of certainty in the other funding options, your Board decided to recommend acceptance of the Offer.[6]

The offer valued each Xtra-vision share at 5.2p and the entire equity at a mere £4.8 million. It was a far cry from Xtra-vision's market value of over £50 million soon after the shares were floated on the Stock Exchange, quite apart from the additional £20 million raised in two rights issues.

That a company so recently floated could launch two rights issues and then suffer such an extraordinary profits and financial setback in the space of two years instils some scepticism about its suitability for a public market. It seems to this writer that the debacle also raises questions about the role and credibility of the Stock Exchange, as well as of the company's sponsors and professional advisers. Nor does it inspire confidence in the regulatory mechanisms. Apart from the accounting and auditing issues, the questions about flotation price, sponsors' and brokers' involvement and recommendations, and the general 'hype' surrounding the shares in the writer's view invite discussion about potential conflicts of interest, objectivity and professionalism, as well as the effectiveness of self-regulation in capital markets. The case details put into question the corporate finance concept of an 'efficient market' in its information processing and equity valuation processes.

Background

A summarised historical review of critical events in the life of Xtra-vision is shown in the following table.

Key events in the life of Xtra-vision		
Start-up		
1982		Richard Murphy establishes Xtra-vision, with his first shop in Ranelagh, Dublin, followed by another in Stillorgan, Co. Dublin.
1985		Six shops in operation, all in Dublin.
Development stage		
1986		Ten shops. Herbert Boyle, chartered accountant, takes an equity stake and joins in the management of the company. Boyle negotiates £0.5 million loan from Algemene Bank Nederland, Dublin.
1987	End July	Sixteen shops, including new locations outside Dublin.
1988	End January	Twenty-five shops, concentrating on the domestic market. First moves into Cork, Galway, Limerick, Carlow and Mullingar.
Injections of new equity — fast growth		
1988	March	Davy Stockbrokers arrange private placing of (10% of enlarged) equity, raising £0.6 million.
	November	DCC invests £1.2 million in new equity and Mulroy Securities, as nominee for private clients of Davy, subscribes for additional equity of £0.8 million. This £2.0 million represents 16.5% of the enlarged equity base.

cont.

Key events in the life of Xtra-vision *cont.*		
	December	Acquires Avon Electrics — chain of six video rental stores in west London — at a cost of £0.6 million.
		Acquires four video rental stores from Infopress trading in the south of Ireland as 'Video City' for £0.4 million.
1989	End January	Eighty-two shops. New distribution centre, head office and large store in Tallaght, Dublin.
	End April	One hundred outlets: Republic of Ireland ninety-four, west London six.

Stockmarket flotation

	April	Public flotation on the Unlisted Securities Market by way of a placing by DCC Corporate Finance at 48p, market capitalisation £24.3 million.
	End May	Acquisitions and new stores in Northern Ireland, totalling sixty-nine.
	October	Rights issue at 80p per share, raising £9.8 million (net), one for four existing shares to help finance domestic expansion and acquisitions in the USA.
		Acquisition of two US organisations: Videosmith (eleven stores) in Boston and Video Library (twenty-seven stores) in New Hampshire. Initial consideration $7 million.
		Acquisition of Jack Beanstalk chain of fourteen stores in Britain. New stores opened brings total in Britain to fifty-four video stores.

Overexpansion/overtrading stage

1990		Additional eleven stores opened in USA.
	4 May	Preliminary announcement of 1989/90 profits of £4.5 million.
		£33 million invested in fixed assets and acquisitions in 1989/90.
	31 May	Rights issue raising £10 million at 40p per share.
	End June	325 video stores.

Financial crisis

	End August	Special business reviews being undertaken by restructured board and management. Profits warning.

cont.

Key events in the life of Xtra-vision *cont.*		
	6 December	Half year losses of £20.6 million. Problems in Northern Ireland, Britain and to some extent in the USA.
		Restructuring of business — concentrating on Republic of Ireland and Boston, USA. Write-offs of acquisitions and more prudent depreciation policy in respect of video tapes.
	December	Offer of 5.2p per Xtra-vision share by Cambridge Group.
1991	February	Rights issue of £3.4 million supported by Cambridge Group to correct negative equity position and working capital shortfall.
1991–93		Tight trading and liquidity position.
1993	September	Cambridge put into receivership by banking consortium.
1994	March	Xtra-vision enters examinership after difficult trading and stock write-downs.

Stockmarket flotation and rapid expansion

A near doubling of annual turnover in its early years is not unusual for a young organisation. For Xtra-vision, jumping from twenty-five to eighty-two stores in just over a year by early 1989 was remarkable. At the time of flotation, a few months later, the number had increased to a hundred, with ninety-four in the Republic of Ireland and six in the UK. When a rights issue was announced at 80p per share in late October 1989, six months after the flotation, it was intended to help finance the acquisition of two separate groups in the USA. A series of acquisitions and developments in Northern Ireland and Britain had raised the number of stores to over 320. Investment spending on acquisitions was £12.8 million, of which 62% represented 'goodwill'. This was in addition to £22.4 million on fixed asset expansion, which included the purchase of new video tapes, spending on leases and premises, and the transformation of new stores. New management structures were established for these two territories, with further group reorganisation and recruitment of senior personnel.

Turnover accelerated from £4.7 million in 1989 to £17.1 million in 1990 (a 264% increase). Total assets grew from £8.6 million to £36.5 million (a 324% increase). The balance sheet and cash flow statement showed a greater dependence on bank borrowing than expected by analysts at the time of the October 1989 rights issue. The rights issue document had indicated to shareholders that some of the funds raised would be used for working capital. It should be noted, too, that DCC Corporate Finance, as advisers to the board, had formally recommended to Xtra-vision shareholders that they approve the decision to make these acquisitions:

> The Board and its advisers, DCC Corporate Finance Limited, believe that the acquisitions are in the best interests of the Company and its shareholders and accordingly recommend that you vote in favour of the resolutions at the Extraordinary General Meeting.[7]

The Video Library acquisition in New Hampshire, USA, was to be a financial problem within a very short space of time, quite apart from the disasters in Northern Ireland and Britain, given the evidence of the speed of the retreat and the extent of the write-offs. It seems to this writer that the efficiency of the investment project research analysis and valuation in the USA and the UK was weak. Payment of 62% of the total outlay for goodwill without a subsequent economic cash flow return suggests that Xtra-vision paid too much for its acquisitions — particularly when most of the investment was soon written off. The background, experience and entrepreneurial orientation of Richard Murphy and Herbert Boyle, and the very youthful management team, made the role of the board and its advisers particularly critical.

Xtra-vision's strategy of opening new outlets and making domestic acquisitions to a large degree mirrored that of its counterpart in the UK, Cityvision plc, which had joined the Stock Exchange earlier. There were two crucial strategic differences. First, Cityvision focused on the UK solely and consolidated its operations under the 'Ritz' banner. Second, it operated with a very conservative capital structure policy. Its rights issue document of 20 February 1990 stated that the company had adopted 'a policy of minimal gearing, preferring to finance expansion from cash flow and from shareholders' funds rather than through bank borrowing'. This proved sound when the economic recession affected demand and profits.

Board and management structure

Apart from one member aged fifty-seven (his group in the UK was acquired), the average age of the nine Xtra-vision top managers was twenty-eight. Unfortunately, this spring of youthful energy and ideas operated within a weak organisational structure. There looks to have been insufficient business experience and internal checks and balances. The board of directors at the time of the flotation comprised the two 'founder' directors, Murphy and Boyle, and three non-executive directors — Alex Spain, chairman of DCC and a former managing partner of KPMG Stokes Kennedy Crowley, Gerard Whyte, an associate director of DCC (both were chartered accountants) and James Morris, managing director of Windmill Lane Studios.[8]

It would seem that the board was unwilling to take the necessary tough decisions until it was too late, partially due to inadequate information to control the company's growth and financial commitments. There would appear to have been insufficient challenge or confrontation in investigating and restraining the actions of the executive directors. It seems to this writer that Xtra-vision was often committed to expensive lease obligations in respect of sites for new stores without the board granting prior approval or the financial controller being sufficiently aware so that there would be ample time and resources to plan and manage cash flow. It looks as if the board was caught up in the excitement of the entrepreneurial exploits of the executive directors and DCC's encouragement for 'growth'. The evidence points to the sheer pace of the company's expansion overwhelming its managerial competence and its professional management abilities of direction, communication and co-ordination.

The accounting system was unable to keep up with the domestic and international expansion over such a short period. It is not surprising that the management information supplied to the board appears to have been incomplete. An organisation with such entrepreneurial actors requires a depth of experience and a strength of character to ensure effective managerial and financial control. The symptoms of mismanagement in the poor planning and financial and cost control were evident in the excessive rate of growth and overtrading. This led to an unsustainable level of overheads, stock losses (through weak stock control), low profit margins (on the revised accounting policies) and an unbalanced capital structure despite the equity raised through the public flotation and the two rights issues.

Business and marketing strategy

The barriers to entry into the video hire business were few. Essentially, it is a low-margin business operated with low overheads. The location of outlets and the product range are key elements in attracting demand. By 1990 this was no longer the strategy of Xtra-vision. Its urgency in expanding its chain of outlets together with quick completion of renovation seems to have proved extremely expensive. The domestic fast-growth strategy was partially a defensive one, designed to capture prime locations in order to achieve a dominant share in a fragmented market. The aim looks to have been to make it difficult for larger international competitors to enter the Irish market.

The ownership rate of video cassette recorders in Ireland in 1991 was estimated to be about 46%, compared with 71% in Britain and 76% in the USA. In theory, the prospects were good. The video rental market was young and had been growing at about 19% per annum, though the effect of the recession on demand, competition from movie channels on cable TV and the low barriers to entry were uncertain factors. Xtra-vision's expensive marketing and promotional activity in Ireland undoubtedly helped expand the overall market as well as assisting Xtra-vision in attaining a dominant market share at about 40%. It also attracted new domestic competition. Not surprisingly, by 1991 Xtra-vision found that some of its competitors were reducing prices by up to 20%.

Xtra-vision mainly promoted 'hit' videos (recent releases of popular films) rather than its library of a range of videos catering for all tastes. At one stage the group appears to have been spending over 75% of its outlays on 'big hits/recent releases', instead of a more usual 50:50 split in the product mix. The acquisition cost of recent releases was almost double the cost of standard videos. Though 'hit' videos could command a higher price for some months, their premium price life-cycle was short. Consequently, this writer concludes that the economic costs of depreciation, when added to marketing costs, did not allow the 'hit' videos to generate a sufficiently worthwhile profit margin when compared to the 'library' product. Management's understanding and application of basic cost analysis techniques, when formulating a product pricing and marketing strategy, seem to have been flawed. Management appears to have emphasised the less profitable product line. In this writer's view the depreciation policy adopted for financial accounting purposes may have contributed to managerial 'profit delusion'.

Financial performance

Xtra-vision's reported net margins, which peaked at 32.6% in 1989, were higher than those in most other industries. Details are shown in Table 5.1. The rate of profit growth was remarkable. Audited profits almost trebled for three years in succession, to peak at £4.5 million for the year ended January 1990. There then followed a loss of £19.2 million in 1991 and a subsequent return to profit in 1992, but a loss again (after further special write-offs) in

1993. Eventually, due to a difficult trading environment, the heavy burden of the debt and contingent lease liabilities taken on in the explosive growth phase up to 1990, examinership became the only option on 18 March 1994.

By any standards, Xtra-vision should have been a reasonably profitable firm; it was the market leader and had the strongest purchasing power. There was no international competition in Ireland during the trading periods reviewed. The figures on turnover and profitability up to 1990 suggested an extremely profitable operation earning a pre-tax profit margin of 26.4% on turnover. Real economic earnings turned out to be much weaker. In 1989 and 1990 the reported gross profit represented a margin of 41.4% and 41.6% respectively. In the 1991 annual report, the restated accounting policies resulted in the much lower gross profit margin of 11.2% in 1990 and 19.5% in 1991.

Table 5.1: Xtra-vision: financial performance

31 January	Turnover (£m)	Pre-tax profit/ (loss) (£ m)	Margin (%)	Number of stores
1986	0.4	0.1	26.8	10
1987	1.0	0.2	20.2	13
1988	2.1	0.6	26.5	25
1989	4.7	1.5	32.6	82
1990	17.1	4.5	26.4	282
1991	26.4	(19.2)	neg.	325
1992	22.9	1.1	4.8	139
1993	22.7	(4.6)	neg.	140

Note: The pre-tax profits/(losses) before 'extraordinary' items in 1991, 1992 and 1993 were £(2.3)m, £1.7m and £1.0m.

Source: Prospectus and audited annual reports.

Overheads, in the form of 'administrative expenses', increased as follows: 1989 £0.3 million, 1990 £2.2 million, 1991 £5.1 million, 1992 £3.0 million, 1993 £3.2 million. The rapid jump in these overheads can be traced to heavy outlays on television advertising and promotions, and, it seems, lavish 'lifestyle' spending by the executive directors and certain senior managers. Examples appear to have included fast trips by Concorde to New York, stretch limos and all the attendant expenses that can mushroom in a 'lifestyle' culture. Over ninety vehicles were acquired, many of them expensive four-wheel drive models with 'image' logo which provided a costly promotional and delivery service to the group's outlets. Under Sal Perisano's turnaround management this fleet was reduced to less than forty by early 1992. A new 'top heavy' management structure, with twenty-four area managers and increasing layers of management, combined with expensive office accommodation, particularly in the UK, added to the overheads.

Over the same period, the interest bill on bank loans increased from a mere £0.2 million in 1989 to £2.4 million in 1991. With an absolute gross profit earned (under the revised accounting policies) of £1.9 million in 1989 and £5.1 million in 1991, it was clear that Xtra-vision could not even achieve an operating profit before interest charges. The corrective action which produced an improvement in gross profit to £6.3 million in 1992 (a gross margin of 27.6%) was not sustained in 1993. The greater proportion of the operating profit of £2.7 million was absorbed by a bank interest bill of £1.7 million.

The first financial crisis

In April 1990 the board of Xtra-vision, seemingly with some pressure from DCC, tried to curtail the runaway spending. Independent accountants Simpson Xavier were brought in to review the group's financial affairs and prospects. Their findings appear to have indicated severe managerial problems linked to optimistic and inaccurate forecasts of profitability and cash flow. Basic business information seems to have been inaccurate. There were also suggestions of stock losses in some areas.

Some of the group's banks were threatening receivership as agreed facilities had been exceeded. Revised maximum facilities of £19 million were agreed in May 1990 with a consortium of seven banks.[9] This facility was linked to a reorganisation of the board and management and an immediate commitment to a rights issue of £10 million in new equity. Two very experienced chartered accountants were co-opted on to the board as non-executive directors: Eugene Greene, managing director of a leading food manufacturing company, and Anthuan Xavier, a partner in Simpson Xavier. James Morris and Gerard Whyte resigned. Another experienced chartered accountant, Liam Daniel, who was chief financial officer of An Post, was appointed to the new post of group financial director in July 1990.

Richard Murphy and Herbert Boyle initially agreed to have other responsibilities with the new board. Within months they were no longer directly involved in group management and they resigned from the board. Following urgent negotiations, Sal Perisano, the chief executive and a shareholder in the profitable Videosmith acquisition in Boston, agreed to move to Ireland in early September 1990 to take over as chief executive of the group. His incentive was a sizeable salary and share options, apart from the existing equity he held in the parent as a result of the Boston acquisition. His brief was to achieve a turnaround as quickly as possible.

The inadequate second rights issue and second financial crisis

Xtra-vision survived in late 1990 because rapid action was taken on three fronts. Cash losses were curtailed when the outlets in Northern Ireland, Britain and the poor quality stores in New Hampshire were closed. An intensive cost cutting programme saw 100 staff being laid off out of a total of 650. On the operations side, it was decided that the purchasing and inventory policy would maintain 'new releases' (hit videos) at 25% of total turnover with a widening of the 'library' of videos linked to more publicity.

In the subsequent turnaround effort from 1991, Sal Perisano emphasised in-store organisation, video display and classification with a wider 'library' focus.[10] The emphasis on 'recent releases' was reduced. A purchases to turnover target of 25% was set in order to balance activity with cash flow. Under the policies of Murphy and Boyle this ratio appears to have reached 50%. A new computerised stock and information management system categorised video products under seventeen headings, for example drama, adventure, comedy, sport and children, compared to four previously. The profitability of the business was very sensitive to volume because of the high level of fixed costs on retail outlets and the depreciation of video cassettes. The new information system helped plan and monitor a more efficient stock mix as well as support controls and customer service. With detailed budgets for individual stores, the uneconomic outlets were gradually identified. The new emphasis on individual store management involved more detailed attention to customer service, merchandising and layout. A more prudent depreciation policy was instituted. Finally, because of the management reorganisation and the more controlled and focused trading policies, a standstill was agreed with the banking institutions and Xtra-vision was given time to restructure its business and find new equity.

From the subsequent financial figures, it appears that Xtra-vision was unable to renew its video cassette stock at the target level of purchases of between 25% and 33% of turnover. This was partially due to the drain on cash flow by bank loan repayments as well as low operating profitability, as indicated in Table 5.2. To an extent, there was a circular cause and effect on volume turnover, profitability and cash flow because of the conflicts in investing in new stock and meeting the banks' debt reduction requirements.

Table 5.2: Xtra-vision: new video purchases to turnover

	Turnover (£m)	Video purchases (£m)	Purchases as % of turnover
1991	26.4	7.0	26.5
1992	22.9	4.6	20.1
1993	22.7	4.8	21.1

Source: Annual reports; computations by author.

In view of the second rights issue in May 1990, it is remarkable that Xtra-vision had run into a cash crisis with such large borrowings by November 1990. Rights issues usually help reduce borrowings and strengthen the financial position. Normally, in preparing for a rights issue, a board would review its future needs carefully. The auditors usually would be retained to investigate and report on the future cash flow and working capital adequacy so as to ensure that the financing arrangements were sufficient for the following twelve months or so. In this writer's opinion the extent of Xtra-vision's managerial and financial chaos can be gauged from the difference between its statements to shareholders of 31 May and 6 December 1990. In the former the chairman stated:

> The Group is budgeting for continued profit growth in the current financial year. At this early stage the directors consider the outlook to be encouraging . . .
>
> The net proceeds of the rights issue will be applied to reduce the borrowings of the Group which, at 18 May 1990, the indebtedness date, were IR£17.2 million, thereby providing the Group with flexibility to pursue opportunities for growth both through organic expansion and by acquisition.

At that stage the two acquisitions in the USA had been negotiated and further expansion in Britain and Northern Ireland had occurred. The statement also pointed out that the number of video stores operated by the group had increased from 170 to 318. Despite the injection of £10 million in new equity through the May rights issue Xtra-vision shareholders were advised in early December that bank indebtedness had reached £18.3 million[11] and that this represented a 'critical situation'.[12]

Based on this evidence, the trading and cash flow budgets prepared prior to the rights issue appear to have been grossly inaccurate. It is difficult to understand and explain such apparent incompetence, errors in information, or optimistic assumptions, bearing in mind the scale of the financing deficit and losses in relation to a total assets balance of £36.5 million in January 1990. In the writer's opinion, the quality of internal accounting information and investigation work undertaken, and the questions posed before the rights issue document was cleared, must be questioned. The issue was underwritten by DCC Corporate Finance and the brokers were Davy. The issue document stated that Richard Murphy held 40.38% of the existing equity, Herbert Boyle held 7.44%, the remainder of the board held only 0.92%, and DCC was the second largest shareholder with 9.93%. Under the heading 'Working Capital' the document stated:

> The directors consider that, having regard to the net proceeds of the rights issue and the bank and other facilities available, the Group has sufficient working capital for its present requirements.[13]

In view of the proximity of the financial crisis, it proved to be an unfortunate assurance.

Bailout by Cambridge

In February 1991 Cambridge Group plc acquired 48.2% of Xtra-vision and introduced new equity in supporting a 'rescue' rights issue of £3.4 million at a mere 6p per share. There were sweeping board changes. Colm Menton, chairman and chief executive of Cambridge, took over as chairman of Xtra-vision. He was joined on the board by his brother Liam and another Cambridge executive director. The recovery strategy, with Sal Perisano, was to downsize by selling off the loss-making activities abroad (except Boston), improve efficiencies, reduce overheads, and focus on greater customer service through better in-store display and organisation. The aim was to build up the strong brand name and focus as the market leader with 134 stores in Ireland.

The first year under Cambridge's supervision proved successful. There was a good turnaround to a pre-tax profit of £1.7 million for 1991/92 from a loss of £2.3 million (before write-offs) the previous year. This represented a profit margin of 7.3% on turnover, which was low in relation to capitalisation and assets. More specifically, the internal financial dynamics of Xtra-vision were a problem. Net cash flow to total debt, at 3.6% in 1991/92 and 15.5% in 1992/93, was insufficient to service the burden and provide some financial flexibility, as Table 5.3 shows.

Table 5.3: Xtra-vision: net cash flow to total debt

	1989/90	1990/91	1991/92	1992/93
Net cash flow (£m)	0	(0.5)	0.8	2.9
Total debt (£m)	21.2	23.6	18.1	18.7
Ratio (%)	0	(2.1)	3.6	15.5

Source: Audited financial statements; computations by author.

Following the rescue by Cambridge, almost all of the £3.4 million rights issue funds were used to reduce bank debt in 1991. In 1992/93, the greater part of the cash flow was used to bring down the bank debt by a further £2 million. Demand and margins remained tight in Ireland and the Boston subsidiary's profitability deteriorated. In addition, contingent lease liabilities on properties in Ireland and guarantees in respect of UK leases (when operations were sold off) became a cash drain when liquidity was tight.

This writer concludes that a number of lessons arise. First, the bank debt level at 61% of 1991/92 turnover was unsustainable in such a low margin and low cash flow business. Second, in this writer's opinion, Cambridge was bringing insufficient financial resources and industry technical expertise to the turnaround. Xtra-vision remained undercapitalised and no outsider could effectively intervene. The capital market was unhappy with what it saw as Cambridge's unattractive 'diversification' from financial services and took a more cautious view of Cambridge's prospects and risk through a lower share price.[14] Effectively, Cambridge was of a similar background and orientation to DCC, and therefore brought limited benefits, except to Xtra-vision's bankers who were repaid £5.6 million of their debt of £17.3 million together with interest during Cambridge's stewardship. Third, the trading environment at the time was difficult. Expected volume increases, which would have made a huge impact on profits and cash flow because of the degree of operational leverage, proved to be elusive.

The third financial crisis, examinership and reorganisation

After the disposals and a board and management restructuring, Xtra-vision returned to modest profitability and generated a positive cash flow which was primarily used to reduce the heavy bank debt burden. Lease payments on properties in excess of requirements (acquired during the rash 'growth' phase) continued to be a drain. Competition and weaker demand kept pressure on margins, since there was competitive price cutting in the industry for some time after the restructuring. In the year to January 1993 Xtra-vision reported a pre-tax profit of £1 million but a net loss of £4.6 million, primarily due to write-downs of its US assets and goodwill. Net worth in January 1993 had fallen to £0.8 million, compared to a bank debt of £12.5 million and increases in 'other creditors' to £6.2 million. There was a small decline in turnover and gross profit margins. By any measures, the financial health of Xtra-vision in 1993 was precarious. More importantly, the servicing of debt was a clear burden. Bank interest consumed most of the operating profit earned in the three years to 1993. Interest cover was very low. The majority of free cash flow was being absorbed by the repayments of the bank debt.

Cambridge went into receivership in September 1993. The continuance of difficult trading conditions and poor trading results in Xtra-vision brought further video stock valuation write-downs. There were also write-downs of goodwill and asset valuations of its remaining operations in the USA. The combination of these provisions resulted in a negative net worth and a very tight working capital position. Bank confidence eroded. Eventually, in late March 1994 Bernard Somers was appointed examiner.

The examinership proved successful because Xtra-vision as a strong brand name with 129 stores in Ireland was able to continue trading. The High Court approved a financial restructuring and the acquisition of the business by Maxwell Swain, a former regional manager of Xtra-vision's business in Northern Ireland.[15] The restructuring negotiated by the examiner involved a cash injection of £4 million, a write-down of bank debt from £11 million to £7 million (this was to be paid off over six years) and the payment of a range of 10p to 70p in the pound to unsecured and preferential creditors, with payments to be staggered. The Revenue Commissioners incurred losses on VAT and PAYE arrears. There were many similarities to the Kentz examinership financial restructuring.

Financial reporting issues

The rental of a video cassette for a night or two was the primary business transaction. Few videos were sold. The accounting concept of accruals, matching cost to revenue, through the depreciation policy adopted, was crucial to profit recognition in this business. This 'matching' concept is much more important in the leasing industry generally than in most others, because there is little else in outlays in the added value of the product, in profit recognition. Adopting a business perspective, it is plain that the revenue from a video (and particularly a 'new release') is not generated in a straight line fashion over thirty months. A new release, which may have cost Xtra-vision £65, will be very popular for perhaps six months, at which point it will be overtaken by other new releases. Thus it will have generated revenue of more than its cost in this period (at say £2 per unit of lease life). Once it is no longer 'new', subsequent lease activity will slow down and consequently by the second year the stream of revenue from that video will be greatly reduced. If we compare the stream of revenue and cost under a straight line depreciation policy to a residual value (believed to be £3 to £5 per cassette) it is evident that there is a mismatch which will lead to distortions in profit recognition — particularly in the first year, when the profit will be overstated. This delusion is magnified if the group is opening more outlets. It is a bubble-bursting recipe when growth slows down. Moreover, it should be noted that the purchasing and stocking policy of Xtra-vision, with its emphasis on new releases, was different from most other leading video rental groups. In consequence, in this writer's opinion the depreciation policy should have recognised the stock and product structure differences.

The 1990 published financial statements audited by KPMG Stokes Kennedy Crowley classified video cassettes under 'fixed assets'. The 1990 net book value was £13 million compared with £4 million in 1989. Depreciation of the video cassettes was on a straight line basis over thirty months to their estimated residual value. The basis of residual value was not disclosed. When Xtra-vision 'went public' in April 1989, its most recent balance sheet (to end January 1989) showed that video cassettes, at a cost of £5.1 million, made up 53% of its fixed assets of £9.6 million. Current assets were a very small element of its asset structure, as Table 5.4 reveals.

The rapid expansion of outlets fuelled a growth in turnover in 1989/90 from £4.7 million to £17.1 million. The rental income from this 'pool' of video cassettes was not homogeneous. It consisted of a narrow population of 'new releases' combined with a wider library of well-known films and 'classics/minority' and material for children. The purchase price varied from £65 for a new release to £30 for the majority of cassettes. Obviously, different usage activity and pricing structures applied to the different types of video cassettes as distinct product groups (particularly 'new releases' and 'library' videos). Video renting was a relatively new and growing service industry in the late 1980s. There appears to have been no industry depreciation standard. When discussing a variety of issues relating to video

Table 5.4: Xtra-vision: asset structure (£m)

	1989	1990
Fixed assets		
Video cassettes	5.1	17.1
Other fixed assets	4.5	20.1
	9.6	37.2
less depreciation	1.8	5.5
Net book value	7.8	31.7
Intangibles	–	0.2
Current assets		
Debtors	0.5	4.2
Cash	0.3	0.4
	0.8	4.6
Total assets (book value)	8.6	36.5

Source: Audited financial statements.

rental groups in the Britain, David Owen a leading London financial journalist commented:

> The art of accountancy pertaining to the video rental business does not have the ring of a box office smash. It has periodically acquired the status of a 'vexed issue' to its cult following of industry executives and sundry investors, however.[16]

Cityvision, the counterpart of Xtra-vision in the UK, had adopted a fifteen-month life on videos until 1988, when it doubled the life to thirty months. Of course, this change in policy helped treble reported profits. Smaller operators, such as Video Store and other independents, continued with a more conservative depreciation policy such as writing off two-thirds of the video cost in the first year followed by the balance in the second year, or writing off the total in one year.[17]

The concept of depreciation and underlying regulatory principles are pertinent. Depreciation of fixed assets (with a limited useful economic life) is required by the Companies Acts. The precise rules to be applied are less clear. The relevant accounting standard, SSAP 12, issued in January 1987, defines depreciation as 'the measure of wearing out, consumption, or other reduction in the useful life of a fixed asset, whether arising from use, effluxion of time or obsolescence through technological or market changes'.[18]

The useful economic life of an asset is the period over which the owner will derive economic benefits from its use. This writer believes that the

SSAP definition clearly views depreciation as a measure of consumption and not as a valuation basis. When we test the straight line policy adopted by Xtra-vision against the criterion of 'consumption', the result is curious. In this writer's opinion, attaching the fundamental concept of prudence leaves the outcome even more problematical as regards generally accepted accounting principles and the expression of a 'true and fair view' in the financial statements.

A doubling of depreciation (to something close to a fifteen-month life to residual value) suggests marginal profitability by Xtra-vision in the two years before the Stock Exchange launch. These adjusted profits would be lower if the basis of the restated 1990 accounts (issued with the 1991 accounts) had been adopted. Writing off depreciation at a rate of 80% of the cost of purchase in the first year would, it seems, have yielded losses. It looks unlikely that Xtra-vision would have issued a prospectus seeking 48p per share with a conservative depreciation policy. The reframing of performance on more conservative accounting measurement principles indicates that it was a low-margin business with low net cash flows. This required tight expense and stock controls. The high levels of overheads in Xtra-vision were beyond what the revenue/gross profit margin structure could bear. It seems to this writer that the earlier optimistic accounting policies had 'economic consequences' in influencing the decisions and actions of investors, bankers and Xtra-vision's board and management.

In this writer's opinion the depreciation policy adopted in the prospectus and the financial statements for the year ended January 1990 implies that the auditors approved the accounting policies used by the directors. The auditors provided a clean (unqualified) audit report. Following the rights issue in summer 1990, the reorganised board instituted a review of the business and the depreciation policy. It was agreed to adopt a more conservative approach. In the light of the above, the writer believes that three questions must be posed:

1. How could the auditors, as accountancy experts, sign an unqualified audit opinion for Xtra-vision for the year ended January 1990 which adopted a rate and level of depreciation which resulted in the reporting of 'a true and fair view . . . of the state of affairs of the Group . . . and of the profit and source and application of funds . . .' and subsequently give a similar opinion to the reporting of profit and loss under such a radically different depreciation basis (about three times the depreciation level) for the 1991 and restated 1990 figures?

2. To what extent did the growing level of profits reported, under the apparently optimistic depreciation policies adopted in the prospectus and the January 1990 financial statements, affect the share valuation of Xtra-vision and its ability to obtain credit from bankers and others?
3. Were the entrepreneurial founders, the senior management team and the board influenced by the reported profit performance of the organisation? Did the absence of more prudent accounting policies contribute to overexpansion? Did they fuel a 'self-delusion' about abilities and possibilities, and contribute to self-destruction? Richard Murphy was reported to have said 'I couldn't understand how we were making profits, but we never had any money.'[19]

The strategy underlying the phenomenal growth rate of sales proved unsustainable in net cash flows or returns on assets generated, particularly when bank loans had reached £17 million. Apart from the original management and board, the sponsoring groups, new investors and bankers appear not to have been efficient in linking business issues to financial analysis and future cash flow prospects.

When Xtra-vision abandoned its former depreciation policy on video cassettes they were reclassified as 'stock' and were valued 'at the lower of cost and average net realisable value'.[20] This change in accounting policy was justified on the grounds 'that it will give a fairer presentation of the results and the financial position of the business'.[21] Two points emerge. First, if the video cassettes were not all for sale, why were they classified as 'current assets'? The usual understanding of current assets is that the items included will be utilised in the short-term cycle of 'conversion' process from raw materials, services and added value into cash. If the video cassettes are acquired for their continuing use in business, are they not a fixed asset under the Companies Acts? Second, though Xtra-vision's accounting policies stated that 'net realisable value' was based on estimated normal selling price less further costs to be incurred to disposal, in this writer's view the readers of its financial statements could now be said to have less information on the 'basis' of valuation of the video cassettes, even though the 'Notes' to the financial statements did provide details of the purchases, sales and write-down to valuation. Subsequent reports indicated that before the collapse into examinership in March 1994, a further heavy write-down of video cassette stocks and property values became necessary.[22]

The validity of the 'going concern' concept faced the auditors between 1991 and 1993. In their audit report they indicated, under 'Fundamental

Uncertainties', that their opinion on the validity of the going concern basis was not qualified. Nevertheless, the auditors referred to the group's negotiations with its bankers and the critical assumption about budgeted video rental revenues in the context of generating sufficient cash flows. Under the statement of accounting policies, the directors stated that they were satisfied the group would have sufficient resources to meet projected requirements to 31 January 1994. The financial statements were signed on 23 June 1993; thus the expected future period of 'going concern' which was deemed the 'foreseeable future' looks to have been seven months. It was not very long. In fact, Xtra-vision lasted nine months; the court approved the appointment of an examiner on 18 March 1994.

The auditors, in accordance with practice of the time, dealt with the matter by way of a disclosure policy by the directors, and the apparent acceptance of the directors' assurances about adequacy of working capital, as stated in the 'Notes'. Similar to the Kentz case, there was no direct opinion by the auditors on the firm's ability to continue. In this writer's opinion they left the matter resting with management's assertions, who not unexpectedly felt satisfied about continuance prospects for seven months forward. This audit approach illustrated regulatory weaknesses in audit standards and practice. In the writer's opinion, the role, expertise and judgment expected of the independent professional were side-stepped by such regulatory standards.

Stockbroker analysts and their reviews

Within weeks of the placing price of 48p in April 1989 Xtra-vision's shares rose to 107p. Over the following twenty-one months the first rights issue was at 80p (October 1989), the second at 40p (May 1990) and the third at 6p (February 1991). Some of the stockbroker analysts' research reviews make strange reading. To this writer there appeared to be considerable 'hype' and bullishness about Xtra-vision's growth and profitability prospects.

Davy's review of 14 November 1989, when the share price was 86p, claimed that Xtra-vision had the potential to record earnings growth and that it was a buy at the current price level. At the time of the announcement of the second rights issue DCC Corporate Finance issued a press release dated 21 May 1990:

> In the seven months since October 1989, the date of the last rights issue, Xtra-vision has increased the number of video stores which it operates by 147 from 170 to a total of 317. The directors of Xtra-vision believe that, having regard to the continued expansion of the

Group, the capital base of Xtra-vision should be strengthened through the rights issue.

A day later, Davy forecast pre-tax profits of £7 million for the year to January 1991 and £9.6 million for 1992. Earnings per share were to rise to 5.1p and 6.5p respectively. Davy thought that the rights issue would make the group financially strong with a low gearing ratio of 12% on a pro forma basis and that the conservative nature of the forecasts did not reflect the upside potential in the shares; they recommended that shareholders take up their rights. Panmure Gordon of London were more cautious, observing that Xtra-vision's depreciation policy was the least conservative of its major competitors. Similar profit forecasts were offered for 1991 and 1992. At 36p on 17 July 1990 the shares were viewed as attractive.

After the traumas of the financial crisis and the Cambridge intervention in February 1991, Davy issued further reviews in May 1991[23] and December 1991.[24] In the May review pre-tax profits of £1.6 million and £2.6 million were forecast for the years ending January 1992 and January 1993, with earnings per share at 1.0p in each year (because of changing taxation rates) and a price/earnings ratio of 6.5 times at the current price. The review compared the adjusted (for depreciation policies) price/earnings of 9.1 for Cityvision in the UK with the lower 6.5 price/earnings for Xtra-vision. Davy felt that Xtra-vision had made progress by raising new equity, and by reorganising and selling off unprofitable overseas branches. With the share price at 6.5p in May 1991, they felt that in the short term investors might want to see signs of a recovery.

Davy's review of December 1991 reduced the 1993 forecast modestly to £2.4 million, but it now advanced a profit forecast of £3 million for 1994 (which proved a little optimistic). Davy reasoned, with the share price at 5p, financial risk remained high but the balance of rewards to risks was favourable. The shares were seen to represent good value. Davy, interestingly, highlighted a 'cash flow per share' and a price/cash flow multiple which was forecast at 3.2 for 1992 and 2.5 for 1993. The crucial question was how much was 'free cash flow' if the video cassette stock had to be renewed.

The strengths and weaknesses of Xtra-vision

There were a number of positive features to Xtra-vision before it lost its way:

- a clear product/service concept
- generally excellent store location

- superior store design and layout
- strong brand image
- good stock range and understanding of customer demand
- nationwide chain
- largest domestic market share (about 40%).

Xtra-vision's strengths were its entrepreneurial flair and market orientation within an Irish context. However, its weaknesses lay in its managerial organisation, administration and control. The Stock Exchange quotation and the rapid expansion through organic development and acquisitions in the UK and the USA were examples. In this writer's view the specific forms of mismanagement can be identified as:

- excessive growth in asset investment and turnover
- breakdown in planning and financial control disciplines
- breakdown in management accounting systems
- a weak board
- bad acquisitions
- excessive overheads and staffing
- tone from top inappropriate
- organisation too large and diverse for the experience and orientation of top management
- inappropriate financial reporting policies
- unbalanced product purchasing/marketing policy
- weak stock control.

The role of DCC

Davy Stockbrokers and DCC invested £2.6 million in Xtra-vision, which was a major part of the contributed capital and share premium. The DCC and Davy/Mulroy Securities investment was bought at an equivalent price of 28p per share. The placing price at 48p just six months later would have amounted to a potential capital gain of 72%. At 80p, the possible gain would amount to 320%.

In the writer's opinion DCC must take some responsibility for the Xtra-vision debacle for three reasons. First, DCC was experienced in venture capital. With its track record, this writer believes that it should have known what to look for and what type of strategy and controls were necessary in coping with the culture of a young entrepreneurial business. Second, DCC was the largest external shareholder. It sponsored the placing and underwrote the two rights issues at 80p and 40p before the takeover at less than 6p. This writer believes that DCC also gave Xtra-vision credibility by having its own chairman, Alex Spain, as chairman of Xtra-vision, and one of its senior executives as a board member. Thus it directly provided two of the three non-executive directors. Third, DCC was associated with the Xtra-vision rapid expansion and overseas acquisition strategy. These plans were clearly stated in the placing document[25] and the rights issue document.[26]

One can pose the question: would Xtra-vision have been able to raise equity on the capital market or run up a bank debt of £18 million without DCC's close involvement? In this writer's view, the strength of the board and the quality of management planning, information and control systems were also within DCC's realm of influence. Eventually, by May 1990 some Dublin investment institutions seem to have become unhappy about events in Xtra-vision — particularly following the second call for equity at half the price of the previous issue six months earlier. When confirming that DCC would be underwriting the issue, Jim Flavin, its chief executive, was reported to have remarked: 'We wouldn't be doing that if we weren't confident about the future . . . It is difficult . . . for the rest of the market to get a fix on such a rapidly-growing company'.[27] Institutions appear to have generally voted with their feet and walked away, viewing the prospects differently. They were proved right. It appears that there was considerable disquiet about profit forecasts and institutional briefings.[28] It will be recalled that Davy reduced its profit projections for 1990/91 from £11 million to £7 million, and that after the August profits warning Davy further revised its profit forecast to £2.5 million.

Reflections

Richard Murphy appears to have been a classic example of an entrepreneurial founder/manager driving an organisation to a size beyond his own managerial competence, aided and abetted by his accountant partner and financial advisers. Richard Murphy was sales and deal-making oriented. He did not have the managerial competence to make the transition from the entrepreneurial stage through adolescence. In this writer's opinion, the apparent defects at board level and deficient accounting policies and systems made overtrading and financial excesses possible. The organisation's crisis was self-inflicted. To an extent, the hyped-up publicity and euphoria of 'success' surrounding Murphy and Boyle may have 'gone to their heads'. Excessive prices seem to have been paid for some of the acquisitions and also there were doubts about the high outlays on leases for new stores.

The company overtraded and overexpanded in a similar fashion to Kentz Corporation. The evidence available to this writer points to accounting and information breakdowns, weak financial control and an apparent unwillingness to listen to or to face up to bad news. Thus, the theme of information suppression, at management levels, seems to appear again. The optimistic accounting policies may have fuelled performance 'self-delusion' in the executive directors' ambitions and actions. Surprisingly, the stockmarket and banks also appear to have been deluded for some time. They paid the price. Six months before collapse, Xtra-vision would have merited an Argenti score in the range 49 to 53, which was a red flag. The subsequent research evidence suggested a score of 69.

The cost to Richard Murphy was heavy. He had built up a valuable business with good locations. There were different managerial competencies required for twenty-five stores in 1988, compared to eighty-two in January 1989 or 325 in June 1990 — in Ireland, the UK and the USA. It seems that Richard Murphy lost everything. At the time of the flotation he had 26.3 million shares. It was 'paper' capital. He and Herbert Boyle agreed to support the second rights issue at 40p. Murphy's cash investment was £1 million for 2.5 million shares. Boyle had to find £250,000. Clearly, both suffered cash losses with the collapse in the share price. Seeking a flotation and pursuing an acquisitions strategy personally cost the entrepreneurial founders dearly, apart from losing the business. In this writer's opinion Xtra-vision was not suited to the stockmarket and Murphy and Boyle would have been better off staying private and domestic.

Despite being a public company with non-executive directors on the board, the familiar themes of founder dominance, weak management and poor financial control appeared. In this writer's view the board does not appear to have had a sufficient number of independent directors who were willing to confront and challenge the founders. Once again the theme of the 'big project' emerged. Similar to the Goodman and Kentz cases, aggressive accounting and self-delusion, in a material way, seem to have blinded the primary actors to economic reality. There was also an accountant partner/associate who generally supported the managing director's strategy and policies, instead of acting as a brake. However, in Xtra-vision the founder had to depart, unlike in the cases of Goodman and Kentz. Finally, this writer believes that the sponsors could have exercised more restraint on the rash of big project strategies. Xtra-vision need not have failed, as the core business concept was sound — given tighter controls on overheads and investment.

Chapter 6

GPA: A Case Study in Market Share Fixation

> ... I have no spur
> To prick the sides of my intent, but only
> Vaunting ambition, which o'erleaps itself,
> And falls on th' other.
> William Shakespeare, *Macbeth,* Act 1, Scene 7

What was different about GPA?

The rise and fall of GPA will remain a corporate enigma in Irish business history. It is an important business case, not because it was the largest failure in Ireland, the UK or the Continent, but because there are many generalisable lessons.[1] These concern business strategy, governance, personality, culture and organisational issues, and how they can link with accounting, finance and dividend policies in a capital-intensive industry.

In 1992 GPA owned 315 aircraft and operated 409 (when leased-in equipment was included). It managed a larger fleet than British Airways, Lufthansa or Air France. A year later the group fleet had grown to 457 aircraft.[2] Total assets were $7.5 billion and total liabilities were $7.3 billion.[3] It was the largest lessor of modern aircraft in the world.

GPA's turnover of $2 billion in 1991/92 was greater than that of any other Irish business firm, such as Smurfit, CRH, Dunnes Stores or Telecom Éireann. For 1991/92, GPA reported pre-tax profits at $278 million, total assets of $6.5 billion and shareholders' equity of $1.2 billion. The board's proposal on 29 June 1992 to pay a similar dividend as the previous year, after the failed flotation, and the clear audit opinion, suggested the group was financially healthy.[4] Yet it was in financial distress within five months. Its arch rival, International Lease Finance Corporation (ILFC) of California, continued to maintain its steady profit and turnover growth in the same period.

GPA was different from the adolescent firms studied earlier, inasmuch as it was larger and more profitable, and adapted its equity base, board of directors, organisational structure, and management planning and control systems. It also developed extremely effective market intelligence information systems. The external picture portrayed in early 1992 was that of an organisation which successfully 'managed' fast growth, complexity and change in its industry and product range. It seemed to have coped with the growing pains and the organisational change through the professionalism and depth of its senior personnel. There were some strong non-executive directors and a very experienced and stable top management group. Domestic and international financial institutions privately invested over £500 million in share capital in GPA, over 100 international banks advanced almost $5 billion in loans, and $500 million in quoted unsecured debt had been raised on the New York public debt market in December 1991. The 'inner reality' was that fundamental flaws in organisational power and decision-making resulted in an overriding deal-making and 'sales mania' culture. A marketing emphasis dominated all other objectives to the detriment of financial equilibrium. This marketing success was founded on a self-confidence in GPA staff instilled by Tony Ryan and Maurice Foley. The triumphs of the aircraft purchase strategy in the late 1980s and the penetration in the world operating lease markets and aircraft remarketing with financial products bred an organisational culture and style which moved from self-belief to arrogance.

Of the 317 employees at March 1992, nearly 40% lost their jobs directly with GPA. These included Tony Ryan, the founder, and most of the long-standing top management team such as Jim King and Colm Barrington and the well-known non-executive directors. The board was totally restructured. Only Maurice Foley remained as a non-executive director, apart from John Tierney and Patrick Blaney who were also retained as senior executives.

Though many of the insiders differed in their views on aspects of GPA's governance, management, strategy, financing and accounting,[5] all advanced the same view as Sir John Harvey-Jones that the failure of the Stock Exchange flotation was the ultimate cause of its financial collapse.[6] This debacle led to a crucial loss of confidence in GPA by product, credit and capital markets. First, potential customers for its financially engineered aircraft sales activity wanted to be sure that GPA would remain in existence to remarket aircraft when the current operating leases completed their cycle. This concern and weak markets dramatically reduced a primary source of cash flow — sales of assets. After all, aircraft sales amounted to $1.1 billion in 1991/92 compared to $0.8 billion in leasing revenue. Second, bankers were reluctant to offer new lines of credit and, eventually, existing lines were frozen because GPA was having difficulty in complying with its covenants. They were concerned about the high level of debt and the impact on GPA's balance sheet and cash flows of the future financial commitments for the purchase of new aircraft for $2.3 billion to March 1993 and $1.8 billion to March 1994. GPA was suddenly seen to be a risky creditor by October 1992. Third, the small number of existing shareholders who already had a large investment in GPA were unwilling to subscribe to a private rights issue of either equity or preference stock after the failed flotation. They also saw GPA as becoming high risk, particularly as leading institutional investors shunned the public issue. Most of the larger institutional shareholders who wished to dispose of equity through the public offer were weak shareholders; even the two Japanese banking groups were experiencing their own problems with the downturn in property and share values in Japan.

This writer does not agree that the failure of the international public offer (IPO) was the primary cause of GPA's collapse. GPA's problems were much more fundamental and internal. The failed IPO reflected these underlying flaws in governance structures, culture, strategy, decision-making and financing. After all, the IPO was sponsored by leading investment bankers and stockbrokers in Dublin, London, New York and Tokyo. In theory, it should not have failed. In practice, a sophisticated capital market expressed its doubts about GPA's equity risk and return. It is a very rare phenomenon for a flotation raising over $800 million to actually fail. If there had been any doubts or perceived problems in advance, the flotation would have been withdrawn.

The culture of GPA was an aggressive one. This characteristic was reflected in its share pricing expectations and the structuring of the public offer. A more modest approach, in this writer's opinion, would have accepted a lower share price and less complexity, which would have overcome the perceived risk and timing problems, and protected most of the shareholder value.

The fundamental cause of GPA's financial collapse was the enormous scale of new aircraft purchases. In effect, GPA overtraded just like the entrepreneurial fast-growth firms studied earlier. Contracted commitments to purchase almost 300 new aircraft from manufacturers amounted to $9.4 billion at March 1992.[7] The greater proportion of this obligation was payable in the four years ending March 1996. A minimum of $2.2 billion was contracted for payment during the nine months ended December 1992, $2.6 billion for 1993 and $2.4 billion for 1994.[8] Deposits and progress payments of $780 million were a material non-earning investment to carry on the balance sheet (it was 63% of shareholders' funds). These advances to the manufacturers had balance sheet 'carrying value' as long as GPA could finance the aircraft purchases. If it could not, then a difficult stance by the manufacturers could cause large write-offs.[9] Such a heavy equity reduction would have dangerous implications for GPA's debt/equity covenant agreed under its secured corporate credit facility of $2.4 billion. This massive capacity expansion was aimed at underpinning a single-minded strategic marketing objective of absolute dominance in all aspects of the world operating lease market in modern aircraft.

Background

Key events in the life of GPA	
1975	Guinness Peat Aviation (GPA) founded by Tony Ryan (10%), Aer Lingus (45%) and Guinness Peat (45%).
	Tony Ryan appointed chief executive.
	Company initially engages in aircraft brokerage and wet leasing.
1978	Net profit recorded of $1.1 million.
1979	First aircraft purchased – a second-hand Boeing 737-200.
	Air Canada joins as equal equity partner (33.3%).
	GPA concentrates on operating leasing from own portfolio of aircraft.
1982	Maurice Foley joins as 'No. 2' with the title of president.
1983	GPA records a turnover of $70 million and net profit of $8 million.
	General Electric Capital Corporation (GECC) of USA invests $18 million in new equity at $27 per share for a 22.5% holding.
1985	Tony Ryan becomes chairman and continues as chief executive.
	Bank of America leads an 'evergreen' syndicated loan agreement of $135 million.
	Combined fleet of GPA and its affiliates now forty-four aircraft.
1986	Turnover of $155 million and net profit of $25.1 million.
	GPA acquires its first new aircraft, a Boeing 737–300, directly from a manufacturer.
	GECC sells majority of equity holding at $87 per share to Mitsubishi group of Japan.
	Private placement of $125 million in convertible preferred securities with Japanese and US investment institutions.
	Aer Lingus sells some of its holding to Air Canada, and the Long-Term Credit Bank of Japan acquires GPA equity.
	Tony Ryan awarded honorary doctorates by the University of Dublin (Trinity College) and the National University of

cont.

Key events in the life of GPA *cont.*

	Ireland. Ryan also made an honorary fellow of the Irish Management Institute.
1987	$1.5 billion seven-year revolving corporate debt facility secured on pool of aircraft negotiated with international banking syndicate led by Citibank. Lead manager roles assigned to Mitsubishi and the Long-Term Credit Bank of Japan.
	Equity rights issue of $100 million at $200 per share.
1988	Private placing of $83 million equity subscription at $250 per share.
	GPA announces new aircraft purchase orders of $3.2 billion.
	Combined fleet of GPA and its affiliates reaches 104 aircraft.
1989	Turnover $1.04 billion and net profits of $152 million.
	GPA sells thirty-four aircraft and leases back eighteen.
	GPA announces future purchase commitments of $10.2 billion (the majority to be delivered within five years). Additional purchase options of almost $7 billion envisaged investments of almost $17 billion on new aircraft within a decade.
	GPA raises $192 million in new equity through private placements with Irish and foreign investment institutions in June at $425 per share.
	Yen20 billion ($143 million) quoted Euroyen note issued in September.
	Share transfers in December at $650 per share: GPA equity capitalisation valued at $3.9 billion.
1990	Corporate credit facility increased by $900 million to $2.4 billion. Syndication underwritten by seventy-six banks. A new associates credit facility for $1.25 billion, on similar lines, arranged for principal leasing joint ventures.
	In spring, the GPA board decides against the proposal for a stockmarket quotation in 1990.
	Turnover $1.96 billion and net profit of $242 million.
	GPA sells sixty-six aircraft and leases back thirty-two.
	Iraq invades Kuwait in August.
1991	Turnover $1.9 billion and net profit $262 million.
	Takes delivery of eighty-two new aircraft and sells thirty-nine aircraft.
	GPA group's portfolio reaches 219 aircraft. Fleet managed now 307 aircraft.
	General economic and airline industry cyclical recession evident.
	Unsecured debt issue of $500 million with quotation on New York stockmarket placed with financial institutions.

cont.

Key events in the life of GPA *cont.*

1992	Private placement of $100 million in preference shares with US pension fund.
	GPA successfully designs and achieves aircraft lease portfolio securitisation issue (ALPS 1); raises $521 million on fourteen of GPA's aircraft.
	Turnover of $2.0 billion and $265 million net profit announced.
	GPA and affiliates take delivery of 102 new aircraft directly from manufacturers and acquire twenty-five aircraft from airlines. Sell thirty-six. Company and affiliates now own 315 aircraft, valued at $6.5 billion, and manage 409.
	GPA announces it will proceed with an international public offer in June to raise additional equity in the USA, the UK, Continental Europe, Japan and Ireland. Quotations planned for New York, London, Tokyo and Dublin.
	Flotation fails.
	ALPS 2 (securitisation issue) plans abandoned.
	Private equity and preference share placement plans abandoned.
	GPA admits it is in discussion with its bankers (over 100).
1993	GPA records net loss of $1.0 billion on turnover of $1.7 billion for 1992/93.
	Total assets $7.5 billion and total liabilities and provisions $7.3 billion.
	Financial, organisational, board and management restructuring agreed with bankers, shareholders and aircraft suppliers.
	Tony Ryan and others resign as executives and directors.
	GECC to purchase forty-four aircraft at a price lower than book value to provide net liquidity of $465 million, after secured bank debt. GPA enters management contract with GECC through which a new management company manages primary business activity. GECC receives options to acquire majority of equity voting rights.
1994	GPA records net loss of $68 million on turnover of $1.8 billion (including approximately $1 billion GECC transaction).
1995	GPA records a net loss of $26 million on a turnover of $1.6 billion. Equity only $111 million, total debt $5.9 billion and total assets $6 billion.
1996	GPA successfully negotiates sophisticated financial restructuring involving the disposal of majority of aircraft in fleet to related newly formed companies with a linked underwriting of the placement of certificates and notes as financial securities which raises $4 billion. Proceeds used to pay off secured and other bank debt. GPA's total debt now reduced to $1.5 billion.

A history of GPA, primarily from an internal perspective, has been colourfully recounted by O'Toole.[10] Clearly, the idea and the firm's early formation from 1975 to 1982 were almost synonymous with the vision and energy of Tony Ryan. The decade of evolution and extraordinary growth from 1983 to 1992 was built on the professional management skills of Maurice Foley, and a bright and young executive team which was driven with a fearsome intensity for the sales deal by an opportunistic Tony Ryan — who seems to have been no easy taskmaster. The early Monday morning 'seagull' reviews of performance, market information from staff in the field, and pressure to 'do business' are legendary.[11] The drive for performance and innovation, allied to the intelligence on markets, customers and competitors, was renowned.[12]

Of the organisations investigated in this study, GPA and Waterford Crystal stood head and shoulders above all others in achieving 'world class' status for professionalism of product concept, quality and innovation. In turn, this was translated into a dominant share in their target market segments on a worldwide basis. A very strong group culture and identity was fundamental to the success of both organisations. Driven by Tony Ryan, GPA was sales and marketing focused and the 'deal' producers in GPA were rewarded with ample financial incentives.

Most GPA executives did not stay in their offices. They spent up to half the year flying from Shannon to existing and potential customers around the world in a relentless pursuit of business. The second in command, Maurice Foley, brought a critical conceptual and formal organisational perspective to activity. GPA's 'products', such as the operating lease or the securitisation of aircraft with leases in place, were financially engineered. Their conception and execution required financial, legal and administrative expertise. Many of its staff were among the outstanding professionals in their discipline.[13]

By 1990, GPA was among the most innovative firms in its industry worldwide. It was a creative deal-maker which constantly broke new ground. Many of its product concepts were ahead of large US, Japanese, British and European banks. For example, *Aerfinance Journal,* when announcing its 1991 'Deals of the Year' based on subscribers' votes, only made two awards out of four categories as the deals had to be deemed 'outstanding'. Morgan Stanley bank and GPA were voted the American and European winners.[14] GPA created a 'ground breaking $428m export credit facility' to finance fifteen Airbus A320s. The real proof of the consistently high level of organisational expertise was the fact that GPA won the award again the following year for successfully introducing a first ever aircraft lease portfolio securitisation (ALPS 1) sale, which involved $521 million and fourteen aircraft in late June 1992. The receipt of the award in New York in April 1993 for this achievement must have been a bitter-sweet moment for GPA's executives. It was overshadowed by the depth of the financial crisis, and the tensions and sensitivities of the rescue negotiations with its bankers and GE Capital.

In 1984 GPA's total revenues were $89 million; by 1992 they reached $2 billion. Audited pre-tax profits rose to $279 million compared to just $13 million a decade earlier. Initially, the backbone of the 1980s growth was selling the concept of the 'operating lease' to airlines. There was also the trading of aircraft between airlines. Much of the expansion of turnover in the late 1980s and early 1990s was due to the sale and leaseback of aircraft to Scandinavian and Japanese investment groups. GPA had now become a trader and a financial intermediary between aircraft manufacturers, airlines and various investors who wished to have a diversified portfolio of assets. Modern aircraft, with values ranging between $30 million and $125 million on six-year operating leases, could be compared to office blocks or shopping malls in asset risk and return criteria. Indeed, much of GPA's business concept could be likened to a property investor and developer. There was a rental stream on a long-life asset and added value could be created (though somewhat differently) by selling on an asset with an income stream to a financial institution for investment purposes.

In May 1990 in a research review, US investment bank Salomon Brothers described GPA as 'The World's Leading Aircraft Lessor'.[15] Internally and in presentations to institutional investment groups, GPA expounded its fourth rolling five-year plan which aimed at net profits of over $500 million by 1994. In the shorter term it planned to attain a dominant market share worldwide in Stage 3 modern aircraft. Its strategic vision, in the medium term, was to widen its activities to become a leading financial services group on a wordwide basis. Its financial objectives included a 25% compound growth rate in earnings and a 30% return on equity up to the mid-1990s.

To obtain such a high return on equity requires a balancing of the accounting and financial dynamics of the business. Like property, an aircraft is a long-life asset, often with low initial returns on assets. GPA was a financial intermediary between investors, banking institutions, manufacturers and airlines. It made a margin in the middle by buying as cheap as possible in bulk (it is reputed to have obtained discounts of 17% to 20% on 'list price') and renting out the asset, generally to customers with a weak credit rating — particularly when it was hell-bent on capturing a dominant market share. The stronger airlines could buy directly from the manufacturers and obtain long-term finance. GPA's competitors were not only other leasing organisations but also banks[16] and the aircraft manufacturers themselves, where margin and risk were acceptable. To generate economic returns, GPA borrowed extensive levels of cheap debt and produced transaction margins higher than the cost of funds. The surplus became the return on equity. Thus, the maximisation of equity returns and dividend payouts depended on a narrow intermediary's margin, a tightly managed operating cost structure and a high debt/equity ratio at the lowest cost of funds. For example, GPA achieved a net profit margin of a mere 4.78% on average total assets in 1991/92. This was converted into an apparently buoyant return on average equity of 23.3% because assets were 4.8 times the shareholders' funds — debt being the crucial leveraging mechanism. The higher the return on assets, or the debt level, the higher the return on equity. In the previous year the net profit to assets was higher at 6.85% and the net return on average equity was 27%.

Accounting figures could portray a profit figure in the short run, as the total assets grew depending on accounting principles and policies adopted. Sustainable growth was quite a different matter. It required balancing cash flows. The dynamics of cash flows in the case of GPA showed them to be consistently in a spiral of larger deficits and greater volatility. It was an extraordinarily cash-hungry business and thus the interaction of its growth rate and capital structure decisions was more fundamental to its continuance than it was to most others. The same business principles applied to property investment and development companies.[17]

The rise and fall of GPA will be examined through several interconnected elements which contributed to its problems. The product/market strategy and the aircraft purchasing programme will be looked at in conjunction with that of its main competitor, ILFC. Financial performance, growth rates, profitability and financial health will be benchmarked against ILFC. Changes in ownership and power, and their implications for board structure and governance, will be analysed. The management structure and culture will be considered as an underlying explanatory element. The evidence for overtrading as a direct cause of distress will be presented. The aggressive nature of GPA's accounting policies and their connection to capital structure, covenants and dividends will be analysed. Stockbroker analysts' views of GPA will be questioned. Finally, the reasons for the failed flotation will be examined and discussed.

Product/market strategy and competitive position

The core activity for both GPA and ILFC was the 'operating lease' of aircraft. They effectively created and built this growing market from the early 1980s. Though the demand for new aircraft was primarily underpinned by the growth in air travel, the industry was not yet at the mature stage. It had grown at about 14% per annum in the 1960s and 9% per annum in the 1970s. The fuel shock of 1979 and the subsequent economic recession reduced growth to about 2.5% per annum to 1983. World traffic growth subsequently rebounded to about 8% per annum and was expected to continue growing at around 6% per annum in the late 1980s to 2000. It had an elasticity of about 2.0 to GDP growth. Faster growth rates were predicted in Asia/Pacific Rim because of its economic expansion and Japanese outward tourism.

There were specific aspects of the market in the 1980s that had a pronounced impact on aircraft demand. First, there was deregulation in the USA and many other developed countries which led to the birth of new carriers, lower fares and increases in traffic. Air travel became a mass-market activity. Second, the Aloha 'open top' Boeing 737 incident in April 1988 convinced the general public and the major airlines that many commercial fleets were reaching mechanical and structural obsolescence. It was estimated that about 37% of all aircraft were over fifteen years old.[18] Third, several cities introduced new noise legislation which required expensive adaptation of older aircraft. New Stage 3 aircraft (post-1985) were quieter and more fuel efficient.

Many established airlines suffered losses in the early 1980s and their balance sheets had weakened. Because of new technology and design changes, the cost of the new Stage 3 aircraft was much higher than earlier models. This increased opportunities for financial intermediaries because many carriers were insufficiently healthy financially to buy direct from the manufacturers. Also, carriers wanted flexibility in the new era of deregulation and competition. Demand for operating leases grew rapidly. It was estimated that in 1981 the proportion of jet aircraft on operating lease was about 6%. By 1989 the proportion had risen to 16%. Many leading international carriers were acquiring portion of their fleet requirements on operating leases. Examples in Europe were KLM and British Airways. The latter had 72 aircraft on operating lease out of a total fleet of 224 at March 1990.[19]

Like ILFC, GPA commenced business as a broker/dealer in second-hand aircraft. Within two years it reported net profits of $1.1 million. Activities widened from aircraft brokerage between airlines to the lucrative but risky 'wet leasing' of aircraft to Nigeria and subsequently Sri Lanka. In the early 1980s GPA started offering operating leases of second-hand aircraft to smaller airlines. Both GPA and ILFC were hard-working sales-oriented innovators who expanded the concept and market for the operating lease. By the early 1990s they dominated their niche market worldwide in modern Stage 3 aircraft.

Founded in 1973, just two years earlier than GPA, ILFC was very different in management style and strategy.[20] Though ILFC raised capital on NASDAQ, New York in 1983, a 'family' ethos continued, with the founding Hungarian immigrant families making up a tightly knit top management team. They adopted imaginative but cautious business policies based on a very professional analysis and understanding of the industry and its cycles. The contrasts in growth rates, product profitability, customer profile and cash flow between the two companies could hardly have been much greater. There were also differences in cost structure, financial strategy and capacity planning.

ILFC made a major strategic decision in March 1984 when it negotiated an order for ten 'new generation' Stage 3 Boeing 737–300 aircraft direct from the manufacturer. It was an investment of almost $250 million, which was sizeable in comparison to its total assets of $352 million at the time. Six aircraft were already signed up for leases with domestic and international airlines. It was a deliberate change in strategy to substitute new aircraft for old, despite the fact that there was a profitable demand for older and cheaper aircraft. By the end of 1985 54% of ILFC's fleet of thirty-nine aircraft were new.[21] In May 1985, ILFC agreed with Boeing conditions and terms for thirty-two new aircraft. The deal included major volume price concessions.[22] The order was extended to fifty-four new aircraft, with the spacing of deliveries up to 1991.[23] ILFC was underpinning its future growth and market share plans. With its quotation on NASDAQ, it raised capital through further equity and convertible preference stock issues.

In strategic thinking and action, ILFC had stolen a march on GPA from a competitive market position. It had also become larger and financially stronger. GPA acquired its first new aircraft from a manufacturer, a Boeing 737–300, in 1986. In a rapid response, GPA initially ordered six new Boeing aircraft but this was later extended to seventeen in 1986. GPA's financial commitments for aircraft purchases jumped from $35 million in 1985 to $210 million in 1986. Both firms increased their order commitments further in 1987. In what might be described as a bidding competition, GPA increased its purchase commitments to $3.2 billion by the end of March 1988. However, in May 1988, ILFC leapfrogged into a more aggressive competitive stance with the largest order ever for commercial jet aircraft — $5 billion for 130 aircraft.[24] From this perspective, the gigantic $17 billion combination of firm orders and options for 308 aircraft announced by Tony Ryan in April 1989 might be seen as a 'close out' gamble to ensure a dominant market share. Between them, GPA and ILFC captured a strategic proportion of manufacturers' output which placed them in a commanding position to supply many airlines. GPA obtained a median discount of about 17% on the list price. Tony Ryan commented:

> This commitment enables GPA to retain in the 1990s its 40% to 50% market share of the new aircraft operating lease business, which continues to grow rapidly. This market share will sustain our industry leadership and help us to develop other profitable services around the core business. The wisdom of GPA's decision to make substantial commitments to new aircraft is now widely recognised.[25]

The scale of the firm orders can be gauged by the fact that by April 1989 GPA had taken delivery of 111 new aircraft from manufacturers. Under the new schedule, 66 were to be delivered in 1989 and 83 in 1990. GPA's ambitious five-year plan, 1989–94, envisaged a near trebling of the leasing fleet and an extensive aircraft sales programme. Net profits were planned to jump from $152 million in 1989 to $521 million in 1994 — delivering a compound earnings per share growth rate of 27% per annum.

The growth and decline of GPA can be illustrated in the curve of its annual capital investment outlays on aircraft in comparison with ILFC's. ILFC was the larger of the two and spent more on investment until 1986. Between 1987 and 1991, GPA's annual capital outlays were almost consistently double those of ILFC. For example, it spent $1.9 billion and $2.5 billion in 1990 and 1991 compared with $1.0 billion and $1.1 billion respectively for ILFC. Following its collapse, GPA's investment outlays dwindled dramatically. In 1993 and 1994 ILFC spent $5.4 billion compared with outlays of less than $1 billion for GPA. Clearly, with larger capacity expansion, ILFC achieved greater market share at the expense of a weakened GPA. By 1995 ILFC had total assets with a balance sheet value of $10.4 billion compared to GPA's $6.1 billion. More importantly, from a future competitive position, ILFC agreed commitments with manufacturers to purchase 236 new aircraft, deliverable between 1995 and 2000 at an expected investment outlay of $13.4 billion. GPA reduced its purchase commitments to $2.8 billion — most of which was deferred to 1997/98 and beyond. GPA won a short-term market share battle but it lost the war through lack of strategic control.

A formidable marketing, promotion and overall managerial achievement resulted in GPA becoming the world's largest aircraft lessor by 1991, with 19.7% of the total jet aircraft lease market and 36.5% of the world Stage 3 aircraft market. A market share analysis is shown in Table 6.1.

Table 6.1: Estimated market shares of aircraft operating lessors (post-1985 Stage 3 aircraft) (%)		
	1991	**On order**
GPA	36.5	49.4
ILFC	17.4	29.8
ANSETT	10.8	4.0
GE Capital	5.4	–
Polaris	5.2	–
Subtotal	75.3	83.2
Others	24.7	16.8
Total	100.0	100.0

Source: Hoare Govett, UK Investment Research, *GPA Group plc: The World's Leading Aircraft Lessor*, London, 1 June 1992, pp. 15 and 22.

GPA not only achieved a world market share that was double its nearest rival. Its massive forward purchase order programme with aircraft manufacturers, which was almost half of all aircraft lessor orders, was designed to enable it to dominate leasing and aircraft financial products markets and, to a degree, aircraft availability to financially weaker or fast-expanding airlines. In effect, these large orders were not only interlinked with a dominant market strategy but extensive sales of aircraft products which would deliver not only liquidity but 'front-loaded' profits on leases.

From a sales and marketing perspective, the achievements of GPA up to 1991 were outstanding. There were some differences in product type. ILFC concentrated more on wide-bodied larger aircraft. ILFC was more aggressive and pioneering until the mid-1980s. It was then overtaken by GPA in sales techniques, innovativeness and the remarketing and securitisation of aircraft and related financial products. A major difference in policy was that ILFC was more conservative in linking aircraft orders to agreed leases with airlines long before the delivery took place. Its strategy was to order between 60% and 80% of its forecasted demand, depending on the point in the industry cycle.

This cautious culture pervaded all aspects of ILFC's business. It tended to work closely with high-quality smaller airlines as well as with the large international groups, offering very competitive lease rates. The aim was to reduce credit risk as much as possible. In contrast, GPA claimed that its expertise in managing credit risk provided the basis for greater growth and profits. For example, Colm Barrington declared:

> The way we see it, we'd rather lease a plane to a shaky credit for $300,000 a month for 3 years than lease one to American Airlines for $200,000 a month for 20 years. . . . We believe the short-term deal at the higher margin is a better credit, as long as we can redeploy the plane if the carrier defaults.[26]

ILFC stuck to its core business of marketing 'operating leases'. It sold small numbers of aircraft in straight airline transactions. It did not engage in the packaging of aircraft and leases or the securitisation initiatives of GPA. From ILFC's Californian perspective, GPA was perceived to be driven by British and Irish accountancy and tax regulations which were much less stringent than those operating in the USA. For example, unlike GPA, ILFC could not complete a sale and leaseback on a new aircraft and recognise an upfront profit directly.[27] Also, ILFC did not operate through joint ventures.

GPA's elegant but risky remarketing strategy[28] helped engineer earnings per share growth and reduce external equity capital requirements for a period. It fitted well with management's share ownership structure and dividend policies as well as the incentive culture of the organisation. It depended on the willingness of more and more international bankers to advance larger amounts of credit, most of which was secured on aircraft. Because of the increasing scale of debt ($5 billion in 1992, compared with just $2.1 billion in 1990), GPA's financial flexibility and ability to comply with financial covenants were diminishing. The organisation became much riskier because its fast growth was based on a strategy which assumed no demand discontinuities. It depended on the financial markets being favourably disposed to the organisation's financing needs as well as investors' interest in its remarketing packages.

Because it did not expect the severity of the fall in demand and margins, GPA had not curtailed any planned purchases. The downturn in the cycle in the airline industry from 1991 reduced the demand for aircraft by most major carriers, paralleling the cyclical slumps experienced by capital equipment manufacturers.

Financial performance

The financial summary set out in Table 6.2 shows that the most dramatic period of growth in sales and pre-tax profit in the life-cycle of GPA was between 1985 and 1990. After that it reached a plateau. An analysis reveals four dominant characteristics: the changing rate of gross profit, the escalating levels of overheads and of bank interest, and the high dividend payout policy. Consequently, profit retentions were remarkably small for a fast-growth adolescent firm.

Table 6.2: GPA: early and late adolescent trading performance ($m)

31 March	Turnover	Gross profit	Overheads	Interest	Pre-tax profit/(loss)	Dividends
1983	70	n/av.	4	n/av.	9	3
1984	90	25	5	7	13	9
1985	202	33	7	17	17	7
1986	155	45	9	20	25	11
1987	360	105	16	23	72	36
1988	650	168	19	52	107	49
1989	1,042	244	18	88	158	68
1990	1,962	350	17	128	247	100
1991	1,889	446	63	138	281	96
1992	2,010	490	44	184	279	98
1993	1,742	68	52	255	(1,022)*	9
1994	1,841	330	53	315	(71)**	1
1995	1,617	449	86	379	(32)***	–

*   After charging restructuring costs and provisions of $783 million.
** After further restructuring costs and provisions of $33 million.
*** After net charge of $16 million for restructuring credits and other affiliated company losses.
Note: Gross profit reconstructed by author to identify the profitability of operations. The cost of bank loan and bond interest has been separated.
Source: Audited financial statements from 1986. Form 20-F filed with SEC, Washington DC. Stockbroker and other documentation for 1983–85.

The gross profit margin peaked in 1987 at 29.2%. It then fell to 23.4% in 1989 and weakened to 17.8% in 1990. This change coincided with a doubling of turnover and a marked change in the mix of 'products'. The remarketing of aircraft with leases to investors and financial institutions dominated activity. Despite the recovery in margins to 24.4% in 1992, it was a long way off the high range of 1986–89. The precipitous decline in 1990 was history repeating itself; the gross profit margin had fallen from 27.8% in 1984 to 16.3% in 1985. The evidence suggests that more volume at lesser margins produced the strong profits growth of 55% to $247 million in 1990. It should be noted that, like Goodman International, the gross margin was minimal (at 3.9%) in its crisis year 1993. The added burden of restructuring costs of $783 million contributed to the loss of $1 billion, which almost wiped out shareholders' funds.

The decline in gross profit margin was particularly due to the impact of reducing leasing margins as detailed in Table 6.3. Higher aircraft remarketing margins might have been expected, in view of the supposed 'added value' created by the leasing and tax packages, and the volume discount obtained from manufacturers. No depreciation appears to have been charged in the year of sale against this activity. Depreciation charged to book value may not have matched declines in aircraft market value. Sales of aircraft assets jumped from $422 million in 1987/88 to a peak of $1.48 billion in 1989/90 and fell for two years in a row to $1.1 billion in 1991/92.[29]

Table 6.3: GPA: gross profit margins (%)

31 March	Leasing	Aircraft remarketing
1988	47.2	10.2
1989	38.0	13.6
1990	44.3	8.4
1991	39.7	14.3
1992	32.6	15.5

Source: IPO Prospectus, June 1992, p. 21 and annual reports. Data reconstructed by author; bank interest extracted from leasing.

GPA had the strategic option of holding all aircraft as assets, and growing in relation to the income stream from the leases and its capital structure decision. The consequences would have been very different for market share growth and equity dilution, because the asset base would have expanded even more rapidly than it did, in view of the purchase commitments from 1989.

The marked increase in overheads from $17 million in 1989/90 to $63 million in 1990/91 remains difficult to understand from a productivity standpoint. It was partially due to special payments to executives under an incentive scheme. Also there was a heavy investment in information systems software and hardware, and in personnel in worldwide marketing and the creation and process execution of lease structures and aircraft remarketing. Changes in the arrangements with associated companies had some impact. As part of its expensive marketing approach, GPA opened an office in Dublin and overseas offices in London, Stamford, New York, Los Angeles and Tokyo. Though overheads fell to $44 million in 1991/92, they increased subsequently. In contrast, ILFC's overheads were much lower. In 1992, with overheads of $21 million, ILFC generated profits of $246 million, which testified to more careful cost control and productivity of operations than GPA.

The burden of interest costs became more demanding from 1988. In 1991/92 total interest charged was $184 million; in the next three years it rose to $379 million. But for the increase in the bank interest bill, GPA would have reported a modest net profit in 1994/95, instead of a loss. Up to the time of the financial crisis, GPA was able to borrow at rates equivalent to LIBOR + 0.75%. After appearing to be close to 'events of default' under its banking contracts, GPA seems to have agreed to harsher interest terms with the banks in the restructuring agreement.[30]

Earnings per share growth was strong. Between 1984 and 1988, earnings per share achieved a compound growth rate of 49% per annum. The period 1988 to 1992, during a recession, was somewhat slower but very impressive, with earnings per share growing annually by almost 21%. Maurice Foley, vice-chairman and president, mentioned in the 1990 annual report that 'the return on average equity was 32%'.[31] These high returns were attained mainly on the basis of a high debt/equity ratio. In these circumstances, the extraordinarily high dividend payouts are difficult to understand.

The dividend policy for a fast-growth company with a consistently high return on capital and capital needs generally runs counter to finance theories where there are institutional shareholders with risk diversification through a structured portfolio. In the three years to March 1992 the equity dividends amounted to $219 million, which was 31% of net profits after the high preference dividends. One explanation is that the distribution policy was driven by the non-diversified shareholders — the management team. An alternative explanation is that shareholders wanted a high dividend because GPA was perceived as a risky investment. This latter argument is difficult to sustain as ILFC, despite having a stockmarket quotation for some years, did not pay an equity dividend until 1988. It was in the same risk class but its payout ratio was extremely modest — leaving it with a much higher retention ratio. In comparison to ILFC, this heavy dividend policy weakened GPA's equity base.

Table 6.4: Financial performance analysis: GPA and ILFC

Measure	GPA	ILFC
Growth		
Turnover growth rates (compound p.a.)		
1983–87	64%	33%
1987–91	33%	31%
Total asset growth rates		
1983–87	82%	39%
1987–91	51%	41%
Earnings per share growth rates (compound p.a.)		
1983–87	49%	36%
1987–91	21%	14%
Profitability and financial health		
Pre-tax profit margin on turnover		
1985	16.4%	28.6%
1986	19.9%	40.4%
1987	16.5%	39.0%
1988	15.2%	31.8%
1989	12.6%	28.4%
1990	14.9%	24.9%
1991	13.8%	26.5%
Return on equity		
1989	27.4%	19.0%
1990	26.4% (24.1%)*	18.3%
1991	21.5% (24.7%)*	17.1%
Cash flow/total debt		
1989	8.5%*	8.3%
1990	5.8%*	8.3%
1991	6.1%*	8.4%
Total debt/equity		
1989	2.4:1 (3.0:1)*	3.4:1
1990	3.4:1 (4.5:1)*	3.7:1
1991	4.3:1 (6.2:1)*	3.6:1
Interest cover		
1989	2.6 times	1.7 times
1990	2.8 times	1.7 times
1991	2.4 times	1.7 times

cont.

Table 6.4: Financial performance analysis: GPA and ILFC *cont.*

Measure	GPA	ILFC
Cash flow/interest		
1989	2.0 times	2.2 times
1990	2.1 times	2.3 times
1991	1.9 times	2.6 times

*   Recomputation per US GAAP, otherwise information taken as reported in financial statements. GPA reported according to Irish GAAP, ILFC operated on US GAAP.

Source: Audited financial statements; ILFC, Form 10-K, filed with SEC, Washington DC; computations by author.

A benchmarking analysis against its primary competitor ILFC helps support a judgement on GPA's financial performance. An evaluation of the evidence as disclosed in Table 6.4 reveals very different profiles.

On the surface, GPA seems to have had a good track record on earnings per share and expansion criteria — ahead of ILFC's performance. Turnover and earnings lagged behind the growth in assets from 1987 because of the heavy upfront investment in new aircraft. Despite this, GPA recorded a stronger return on equity, even after adjusting its figures to US GAAP.[32] Superficially, GPA appeared a more energetic and efficient organisation in marketing and capital returns.

The real area of difference was in net cash flows and capital structure, where GPA was weaker and more volatile. GPA's debt/equity ratio, though rising, appeared a little stronger than ILFC's in 1990, but it weakened to 4.3:1 versus 3.6:1 in 1991. If GPA's figures are converted to US GAAP, the debt/equity ratio of 6.2:1 was of considerable concern: it was almost double that of ILFC and indicated a very different order of financial risk. GPA's financial health was weaker from income and capital gearing measures. More significantly, it was the stability of ILFC's figures compared to the volatility of GPA's that distinguished the two firms. The cash flow to total debt profile was an example: GPA was not only weaker but it was also more volatile.

In this writer's opinion GPA pursued growth at the expense of trading margins. After 1987, GPA operated a dual product portfolio with different margins and operational costs compared to ILFC's focus on the operating lease product. ILFC consistently earned a profit margin on revenue which was double that of GPA. In 1991 it achieved 26.5%, compared to 13.8% for GPA. This was a testament to ILFC's superior management competence in strategic thinking, operational efficiencies and control of costs. There appears to have been also much more risk in GPA's operations (sales and leaseback commitments, customer bad debts and aircraft downtime). The research evidence suggests that in its quest for volume, GPA created an expensive marketing and administrative structure to achieve its (temporary) dominant market share and short-term profit objectives. GPA employed 304 people[33] compared to less than forty in ILFC. GPA's wage and salary bill was $31.4 million in 1991/92. There were 119 staff in GPA Leasing — more than one for each of its 101 airline customers. Staff numbers in GPA Capital escalated. There were just nine in this aircraft remarketing and financial products side of the business in 1989. By early 1992 it had jumped to forty-one staff, which was more than one for each of the thirty-six aircraft sold in the year.

Finally, the differences in dividend cover underline ILFC's prudent financial control policies which reflected its more conservative corporate culture. GPA's more aggressive corporate culture was translated into higher levels of financial risk. In this writer's opinion the dynamics of the GPA financial profile are evidence of the dominance of entrepreneurial risk-taking and 'sales mania' at the expense of a more balanced set of business objectives. Financial equilibrium was being tested constantly.

In 1983, ILFC's total assets of $302 million were almost treble those of GPA, but its pre-tax profits of $14.8 million were only marginally ahead of GPA's $13.4 million. By 1986 GPA had overtaken ILFC in assets and profits and by 1988 GPA's reported profits soared to $159 million compared to just $66 million for ILFC. There was a modest fall in ILFC's profits in 1988 due to competition and tighter leasing margins in contrast to GPA's 49% increase in profits from $107 million the previous year.

Perhaps the greatest difference between the two organisations' policies was the increased emphasis from 1986 on aircraft sales (i.e. 'remarketing') by GPA. Up to then both had broadly similar turnover figures. In 1987 GPA's revenues soared to $650 million compared to ILFC's $180 million. The difference in revenues (but not total assets) became much more marked by 1990, when GPA's total revenues amounted to $1.9 billion compared to just $466 million for ILFC. Aircraft sales contributed almost $1.3 billion (68%) of GPA's revenues. GPA committed itself to a heavy investment programme but aircraft sales not only were delivering liquidity to finance these continuing forward commitments but also underpinned most of the big jump in profitability. The profit stream was now of a different risk class because of GPA's greater dependence on asset sales rather than just leasing revenues. The calculation of such 'profits' also rested on depreciation policies and residual values, together with any contingent risks on future commitments. GPA's equity (under US GAAP) was just 17% of total debt, but it fell to 14.5% in 1991 compared to a consistent 17.8% for ILFC. These were competitive issues in a capital-intensive industry.

Shareholders and board: the changing power structure

To understand GPA, it is necessary to review its changing power structure through the composition of its share ownership. These changes facilitated the apparent dominance of Tony Ryan over the board and management, which arose not only from his dual role as chairman and chief executive from 1985 to 1992, but also because of his 8% shareholding and the continually changing shareholder and board composition.

The GPA power structure can be categorised into four periods. At the 'birth' in 1975, with a total start-up equity capital of $50,000, Aer Lingus and the Guinness Peat Group each owned 45% of the issued equity, with Tony Ryan holding the balance of 10%. The board representatives of these controlling shareholders had direct power to exercise control and discipline over the company. By 1979 it purchased its first (second-hand) aircraft, a Boeing 737-200. Increasing capital needs were met by an equity injection by Air Canada on an equal shareholder basis with Aer Lingus and Guinness Peat. The issue price valued GPA's equity at $26 million — considerably in excess of book value. By 1983 annual turnover had risen rapidly to $70 million and net profit was $8 million. With total assets of $101 million and shareholders' funds of a mere $13 million, GPA seems to have been overtrading and heavily in debt. Maurice Foley, who was a senior executive of Aer Lingus and one of its representatives on GPA's board, joined as number two to Tony Ryan in 1982 with the title of president.

This was the start of the second stage in the evolution of GPA when a greater emphasis was placed on planning and organisation. Ryan and Foley had different but complementary strengths which proved to be a formidable combination. A fourth shareholder, General Electric Capital Corporation, was introduced in August 1983 with a new equity subscription at $27 a share; this was an injection of $18 million for a 22.5% stake. GPA was now valued at $80 million — 2.6 times the book value. With its investment and two strong board representatives, General Electric played a positive role in a new period of healthy growth in turnover and profitability in GPA's early adolescence stage up to the mid-1980s.

Tony Ryan, who was chief executive, assumed the additional position of chairman in 1985. Up to then the position rotated between representatives of the two original sponsoring shareholders and it is surprising that they acquiesced in this dual appointment. The move, in the opinion of this writer, effectively redefined the fundamental power structure, organisational culture and objectives of GPA. The third and most decisive stage in GPA's history began in April 1986 when General Electric disposed of the majority of its equity holding to a combination of the Mitsubishi Corporation and the Mitsubishi Trust and Banking Corporation of Japan at a share price of $87 per share. In the same month, Ray Lindsay of Air Canada, Gary Wendt of General Electric, and the resourceful and experienced Gerard Dempsey of Aer Lingus resigned from GPA's board. Two new non-executive directors from Mitsubishi and the Long-Term Credit Bank of Japan took their places.

The exit of General Electric as a shareholder and the loss of its forceful representative on the board should not be underestimated. It was surprising that it disposed of a shareholding in such a profitable organisation. In the same year General Electric bought into Polaris, a very large lessor of second-hand aircraft. This did not prove a particularly good investment. It was certainly ironic that General Electric's finance subsidiary GECAS and Gary Wendt returned in 1993 to rescue GPA for the banks, almost on their own terms.

A $100 million rights issue in September 1987 at $200 per share followed by a private placing of $83 million in new equity with institutional and corporate investors in April 1988 at $250 per share strengthened the capital base to $454 million and widened the shareholder group. At $250 per share GPA equity was valued at $1.4 billion in 1988. By 1990 GPA was approaching late adolescence. At this fourth stage, with diverse shareholder interests, the end of an era was reached: Aer Lingus and Air Canada, with stakes below 10%, were no longer dominant shareholders; Mitsubishi Trust and Banking Corporation held 12%. GPA now had six institutional/corporate shareholders with a stake of 5% or more who controlled almost 48% of the total equity. The balance of much smaller stakes was spread over a wide range of financial institutions. Tony Ryan's 8% and the management team's 8%, when combined, made them the largest shareholder group and a defining force. Details of shareholdings are set out in Table 6.5.

The years 1988 and 1989 were the two most critical years in GPA's realignment of shareholder power, board influence, and strategic investment and financing decisions. Firm orders for new Stage 3 aircraft from

Table 6.5: GPA: shareholding structure, May 1990 (%)

Tony Ryan and GPA employees	16*
Mitsubishi Trust and Banking	12
Aer Lingus	10
Air Canada	9
Long-Term Credit Bank of Japan	6
Prudential Insurance (USA)	6
Irish Life	5
Japan Leasing	3
General Electric	3
Irish financial institutions	11
Japanese institutions	7
North American institutions	6
Other	6
	100

* Tony Ryan and the GPA executive and employee group each held approximately 8% of GPA's equity.

Source: Davy Equity Research, Guinness Peat Aviation — Leaders in a $500m Market, Dublin, 15 June 1990, p. 27.

manufacturers increased from $3.3 billion to $10.2 billion in April 1989, most of which were to be delivered within five years. This excluded additional options and associated companies' commitments. Despite the obvious financing requirement, apart from servicing a variety of debt facilities, no further equity share capital (apart from options and conversions) was subscribed after 1989.

The board power vacuum can be gauged from its size and composition and the number of changes made. Between 1986 and 1992 there were twenty-one retirements and twenty appointments. Between 1989 and 1992, out of the thirteen board members, the number of executive directors increased from three to six. The basis of non-executive directorship seems to have been dominant shareholder driven until 1986, with senior executives from these shareholders playing an active role. The sale of most of General Electric's shareholding to the Japanese institutions and the private placements of equity changed everything. The non-executive group was now splintered. It appears to have been less able to challenge the power of the chairman/chief executive and the top management.

A number of substitutions among the three Japanese directors until July 1991 left only Shinroku Morohashi, president of Mitsubishi Corporation, with a span of experience of GPA. Remarkably, there were no Aer Lingus executives on the board of GPA after the 1991 departure of Denis Hanrahan, even though it remained one of the largest shareholders with almost 9% of the equity worth about £199 million. None of the new group of non-executive directors appointed in 1986 were on the board in 1992 at the time of the ill-fated flotation, apart from Geoffrey Knight, who had been a director since 1976. Tony Ryan appears to have been in a pivotal position to influence the board membership, which it seems he did. Sir John Harvey-Jones admitted 'Until I joined the board the selection of directors was decided by Tony on his own.'[34]

In this writer's opinion, a flaw in the board composition was the absence of an outsider from the industry after Claude Taylor of Air Canada resigned in 1990.[35] The input of a formidable chartered accountant was also missed when Gerard Dempsey of Aer Lingus resigned.[36] Peter Ledbetter's resignation in March 1990 left no qualified accountant on the board until John Tierney, the long-standing chief financial officer, was finally co-opted in February 1992 in preparation for the IPO. In the opinion of this writer it was remarkable that such a large, fast-growth organisation with extensive bank debt could be permitted by the non-executive directors to operate without a financial director who was a qualified accountant. All the statutory financial statements between 1986 and 1992 were signed by Tony Ryan and Maurice Foley. The institutional shareholders seem to have remained strangely passive.

This writer believes that the various departures of non-executive directors in the 1986–92 period created discontinuities in relationships, information flows, knowledge base and influence. The power vacuum was magnified by the increased number of executive directors. A greater responsibility for governance and strategic control fell on Geoffrey Knight and four other non-executive directors in particular. These were Sir John Harvey-Jones and Dr Garret FitzGerald, who were appointed to the board in 1987; Peter Sutherland, who joined in January 1989; and Nigel Lawson, who was co-opted in March 1990. Gerald Greenwald, a partner in Dillon Read of New York, joined in July 1991.

It is difficult to see how the non-executive directors could operate cohesively as a check and balance to such an extremely powerful and ambitious top and middle management team from 1987 onwards — particularly when they were demonstrating a very successful track record. By 1990 the large talented top management group appear to have dominated almost all strategic thinking. The non-executive directors seemed to have some difficulty in restraining management's expansionist and risky strategies. Sir John Harvey-Jones appears to have admitted as much when talking about the responsibility of the board: 'The non execs had [a] significant impact on the decisions of the executives but obviously not significant enough.'[37]

By the late 1980s full board meetings would appear to have become less frequent. They seem to have been held four times a year. Distance and cultural issues had a bearing. It should also be noted that the Japanese non-executive directors made up a sizeable board constituency during a crucial phase in the late 1980s to early 1990s. In Japan the role of non-executive directors vis-à-vis executive directors, their attitudes and the nature of corporate governance are different from the tradition in the UK and Ireland.[38] It is surprising that the Irish investing institutions, in view of their level of investment, were not actively involved in board nominations.

By 1989 GPA had established an audit committee and a compensation committee. Nigel Lawson was appointed to chair the audit committee in 1991, following the resignation of Denis Hanrahan. In this writer's opinion a weakness was that this committee did not include a qualified accountant non-executive director. Sir John Harvey-Jones chaired the compensation committee. A third committee, officially called the 'Executive Committee', also operated for some time.[39] It comprised Tony Ryan, Maurice Foley, Colm Barrington, James King, Sir John Harvey-Jones and Nigel Lawson.[40] Unlike the partially collegiate format which had been the organisational model, a revised corporate structure was introduced. Tony Ryan chaired GPA Leasing and Nigel Lawson chaired GPA Capital, the asset sales and securitisation business unit. (A 1990 Salomon Brothers research report stated that Nigel Lawson was retained as a consultant and main board director with the aim of developing its financial services division.[41]) Peter Sutherland chaired GPA Technologies and Sir John Harvey-Jones was associated with GPA Group Corporate, which co-ordinated the overall strategic direction of the group.[42]

This raises an issue on which there are competing views. If non-executive directors become closely involved in strategic and policy analysis, decision-making and recommendations to the full board, is overall board objectivity compromised? Will the checks and balances role of the non-executive directors in challenging top management proposals and performance be as active? Admittedly, these non-executive directors are less remote from the company's affairs and they should have a greater understanding of strategy and policy.

Management, organisation and culture

The development of GPA was built around Tony Ryan and a small top management team up to the late 1980s. Ryan as the co-founder had a personal investment of $5,000 for 10% of the equity. The fledgling operation was joined by Graham Boyd in market intelligence and Peter Ledbetter, a young chartered accountant. The growing business led to the recruitment in 1981 of Colm Barrington (35), initially on joint ventures, and John Tierney (36) as chief financial officer. Barrington had worked for a leading US hotel chain on property acquisitions and financing, and Tierney was financial controller of an Irish manufacturing firm. The group was augmented in 1982 with James King (43), Maurice Foley (42) and Juan O'Callaghan (early 50s) joining it.

At the time, expansion and change in operations were rapid and the youthful GPA seems to have been experiencing 'growing pains' — particularly in the area of management systems and planning. Barrington and King headed up the two early joint ventures, GPA Midland and Irish Aerospace. Before joining the staff of GPA Foley had been a non-executive director of GPA and general manager of ancillary activities with Aer Lingus. With an MBA and solid professional management experience, he brought a new sense of professional planning, organisation and order to GPA's affairs. O'Callaghan had previously worked in sales with Boeing and in aviation consulting in the USA. He brought a hard-headed focus and structure to corporate planning and industry strategic analysis until he left in 1989. His critical and independent contribution to top level decision-making appears to have been subsequently missed. Brian McLoghlin, the chief legal officer, and Liam Barrett, the company secretary, also joined in the early 1980s. It was to be a settled and relatively cohesive top group for seven vital years of growth and a successful implementation of a radically new strategy: buying Stage 3 aircraft from manufacturers for both operating lease and remarketing to investors and institutions. There was a balance to this group which proved effective in coping with the tensions and complex problems of a hypergrowth organisation.

The organisation was structured on a functional basis until March 1990. The 'Office of the Chairman' as a form of executive committee comprised Ryan, Foley and Ledbetter. Ryan not only concentrated on commercial and corporate strategies but also, with a heavy travelling schedule, adopted a 'hands-on' approach to specific marketing initiatives in building up relationships. Marketing and customer service were decentralised to the overseas offices, the Shannon head office retaining very tight control over credit assessment, pricing and contract structures. Aircraft acquisition and financing were head office functions. This structure also included a number of aircraft specialist groups focusing on Boeing, Airbus and Fokker.

The 'Office of the Chairman' group was the top management team. They focused on strategy and its implementation. By the late 1980s day-to-day management of operations and senior executive reporting relationships were with Maurice Foley. Sir John Harvey-Jones' wide experience with Imperial Chemical Industries proved useful in a review of the organisation structure. The financial services (aircraft remarketing) group developed by Colm Barrington was expanded. A second group of very able younger executives, such as Philip Bolger, Patrick Blaney and Michael Dolan, emerged in leasing and financial services. In addition, Sean Donlon and Richard O'Toole were recruited from the diplomatic corps.

The first significant change in the management structure occurred when Colm Barrington, who was the group's chief marketing officer, joined the top group in the 'Office of the Chairman' in 1989. In 1990, both he and James King joined Ryan and Foley as executive directors and the long-serving Peter Ledbetter resigned. Then, in March 1990 the group was restructured into three business units — GPA Leasing, GPA Capital and GPA Technologies. This underpinned the strengthened position of Barrington. The emphasis was now on asset sales and securitisation as the major source of revenue, rather than just leasing. GPA, in effect, confirmed its deal-making culture. This increased emphasis on asset sales appeared to represent a change in strategy. The five-year plan commencing April 1989, presented to investment institutions and indicating that leasing profits would remain ahead of asset sales profits, was undergoing revision.

GPA saw itself as a 'quality people organisation' with the 'premier people' in marketing. It had a closely knit group culture that expected peak performance from above average people. The money incentives, in the form of a base salary top-up and dividends, were seen as sharing the wealth created. The culture revolved around taking and managing risks. According to one interviewee:

> ... we were aggressively competitive and maybe we were too self-confident ... we created some hostility outside ... we were in a hurry and we were here to make profits ... some people outside were pleased to see us have problems.[43]

Outsider interviewees referred to arrogance and a certain disdain in GPA dealings with some investment institutions and others.[44] It appears that a similar attitude was experienced in media relations, as suggested by material in Brenda Cullen's case study.[45]

The announcement by Tony Ryan on 7 November 1991 that Maurice Foley 'wished to relinquish his executive role in the company at the end of October 1992' surprised and concerned investors and others — particularly when GPA indicated that it was planning a public flotation.[46] (It was just seven months before the eventual flotation date.) It represented the first sign of a break-up of the successful management duo and possible changes in power structure and strategy. The capital market reaction was such that a change of heart took place, and by the time the details of the flotation were announced some months later Maurice Foley had signed a new service contract as group chief executive until March 1994. The incident provided an insight into the entrepreneurial organisation. It seems to have disturbed potential investors, as management stability was seen as essential, particularly in view of the conditions in the industry and the changing responsibilities of the group.

Growth, cash flow and financing shortfalls
Growth

Interview sources pointed to excessive growth and overtrading as a cause of GPA's distress. Dublin and London investment managers highlighted their concern with GPA's existing debt levels and future funding gaps.[47] The documentary evidence corroborates this criticism. As an illustration, a comparison of asset growth rates between GPA and its direct competitor ILFC over the eleven-year period 1983–93 is summarised in Table 6.6. GPA's asset growth between 1983 and 1987, the first stage of its adolescent cycle, was a phenomenal 84% per annum compound compared with 39% per annum for ILFC. In the second stage of this cycle, from 1987 to 1991, GPA's expansion rate continued at 51% per annum compound compared with 41% for ILFC. These were extraordinary rates of expansion for both organisations in relation to fleet capacity growth and replacement in the airline industry. They signify the extent of their successful worldwide marketing penetration.

It is revealing to compare GPA's growth in assets with Ireland's largest industrial leasing firm, Woodchester Investments plc. GPA was just two years older. Woodchester made staggering surges in size in its early years. Unlike GPA, Woodchester achieved a large part of its expansion through a series of acquisitions in Ireland and the UK. Up to 1989 Woodchester seemed to double in total assets each year. The three years to December 1992 saw very

Table 6.6: Total asset and profit growth: GPA and ILFC ($m)

	GPA		ILFC	
	Total assets	Pre-tax profits	Total assets	Pre-tax profits
1983	111	13	302	15
1984	279	17	352	17
1985	438	25	561	23
1986	730	72	805	49
1987	1,263	107	1,138	70
1988	2,019	158	1,765	66
1989	3,065	247	2,580	95
1990	4,591	281	3,524	123
1991	6,500	279	4,564	140
1992	7,524	(1,022)	6,087	246
1993	7,129	(71)	8,140	279

Note: Financial data as reported in financial statements. GPA per Irish GAAP, ILFC per US GAAP. GPA year end 31 March 1993 and ILFC year end 31 December 1992 taken as comparable for 1992.

Source: GPA annual reports from 1986 and Form 20-F filed with SEC, Washington DC, James C. Halstead and Julius Maldutis, *GPA Group Ltd: A Leader in Worldwide Aircraft Leasing*, Salomon Brothers, New York, 1989. ILFC, Form 10-K from 1984, SEC, Washington DC.

limited expansion, with total assets growing from £1.1 billion in 1990 to £1.4 billion in 1992. Unlike GPA, which kept expanding, Woodchester had a consolidation phase. The major injection of new share capital by Credit Lyonnais helped double shareholder funds and strengthened liquidity immeasurably, at a critical time in the economic cycle. Conversely, GPA never pulled back or consolidated financially after 1989.

A cash flow profile of GPA

An examination of GPA's cash flow profile over the seven-year period to March 1993 reveals much about the organisation's business and financing policies and the weaknesses in strategic financial control. It is summarised in Table 6.7. Two features stand out: first, the small proportion of earned cash flow and its volatility (when interest and dividends are deducted); second, the unbroken series of annual financing shortfalls, which peaked in 1991/92 at $2.3 billion, because of the aggressive growth strategy. In the five years to March 1992, total investments in new aircraft and related items amounted to $9 billion. The financing shortfall was $8.3 billion. Apart from 1986, when new equity raised exceeded incremental debt, the ambitious aircraft ordering programme clearly created a huge demand for financing and liquidity. As the analysis shows, this financing shortfall was primarily supported from two risky sources — incremental debt and asset sales. Asset sales were not the real source of funds as was thought. The revenue figure represented the gross position. In each instance, because of their secured position, a certain amount of bank debt was repaid but new advances were provided against purchases. Consequently, the purchase and sale of aircraft was linked with new bank credit and rollover facilities.

Asset sales generated $4.8 billion in the five-year period to March 1992. Proceeds peaked in 1989/1990 at $1.3 billion. The additional share capital raised of $421 million (net) over five years seems pitiful in comparison with the $380 million paid out in dividends in the same period. In contrast, additional debt aggregated to $3.5 billion. GPA may have reported increasing profit and earnings per share figures up to 1992, but the 'cash reality' was very different. The excessive and continuous dependence on asset sales and bank debt over a long period in an economic cycle is clearly evident. GPA left itself extraordinarily vulnerable to timing and market issues outside its control.

Capital structure and gearing
Capital structure strategy

Though ILFC was only two years older than GPA, its early NASDAQ equity quotation bound it to the strict disclosure, accounting and corporate regulatory requirements of the Securities and Exchange Commission. ILFC operated for many years with joint founders Steven Udwar-Hazy, president, Leslie Gonda, chairman and chief executive officer, and Louis Gonda, executive vice-president, occupying the top positions. They functioned as a relatively cautious three-man executive team. ILFC's chairman was aged seventy-one. The board comprised just five people — the three executive directors who controlled over 60% of the equity and two non-executive directors from financial institutions. In August 1990 AIG, the leading US insurance group, made an agreed takeover bid for ILFC. The founders traded ownership and control for personal wealth and secure financial backing for a capital-intensive organisation. They also read the stockmarket cycle well, selling out at close to the top.

Woodchester Investments followed a similar pattern to ILFC. It can be compared with GPA as its founder, Craig McKinney, also held the dual positions of chairman and chief executive. Nevertheless, there was a very

Table 6.7: GPA: summarised cash flow analysis ($m)

	1987	1988	1989	1990	1991	1992	1993
Net cash flow*	19	65	219	107	54	243	178
Investments	544	842	1,379	2,111	2,111	2,558	1,971
Financing gap	525	777	1,160	2,004	2,057	2,315	1,793
Aircraft sales	225	413	637	1,305	1,217	1,185	701
Bank debt repaid	n/av.	n/av.	626	2,862	3,831	3,124	1,759
New financing required	300	364	1,149	3,561	4,671	4,254	2,851
New share capital	10	102	90	206	0	24**	0
New debt	210	320	1,004	3,378	4,907	4,342	3,016
Increase in net cash	(80)	58	(55)	23	236	112	165

*   After working capital changes, taxation and dividends.
** Net increase after redemption.
Source: IPO Prospectus, June 1992, annual reports and Form 20-F filed with SEC, Washington DC; computations by author.

definite difference in policy on shareholding control, financing, publicity and regulatory scrutiny. Woodchester was founded in 1977 but in 1982 it obtained additional equity capital through a placing on the Unlisted Securities Market. Further capital was raised in 1986 through a 29% share placing with British and Commonwealth Holdings, which was subsequently sold on to the large French banking group, Credit Lyonnais in December 1989. In June 1990, Credit Lyonnais agreed to inject £100 million additional equity into Woodchester to support its expansion in return for 45% of the equity and greater board representation and business influence.

The founders of both ILFC and Woodchester raised equity capital on the Stock Exchange much earlier in their cycle than GPA, and they subsequently permitted another larger and financially stronger group to acquire equity control, with cohesive board representation. These were significant strategic moves by two capital-intensive businesses which grew rapidly but whose founder/managers were willing to dilute control for greater financial backing as the economic cycle was starting to turn.

GPA considered a public flotation in 1986. Professional advice appears to have pointed to uncertainties, partially because of how various matters might be perceived by the market, and the board did not proceed.[48] In June and December 1989, GPA raised $209 million in equity through a successful private placement with Irish and foreign institutional and corporate investors. The $650 share price in the December 1989 placing implied an equity market value of $3.9 billion compared to a book value of $893 million. In March 1990, there was little doubt that GPA would have obtained a Stock Exchange listing, but the board decided against proceeding. In retrospect, this turned out to be a fundamental mistake bearing in mind the volatile nature of capital markets. The clear need for equity was apparent when the level of capital commitments in its forward plans was considered. Some existing institutional shareholders had expectations of a quotation. Stockmarkets were very buoyant at that time and GPA was favourably viewed. The 'airline recession' had not surfaced and the Gulf war had yet to occur.

No further equity was raised in 1991 and apart from a $100 million private placement of preference shares in early 1992 there had been no material share capital injection since the December 1989 placing. It was a fatal strategic mistake reflecting the underlying internal weaknesses that stemmed from a reluctance by senior management to dilute control and their unrealistic expectations about share values. Fuelling the foregoing was an unduly optimistic marketing view of the demand for the two primary products, the credit outlook for the industry and the impact of the recession on the industry cycle.

The increasing interest burden

GPA did not explicitly show its interest charge on the face of its consolidated profit and loss account. Details of interest payments, charges and amounts capitalised were included in 'Notes' attached to the financial statements. By any standard, the actual amount of interest charged each year was a heavy burden. The interest bill for 1991/92 was $221 million, which was almost 83% of the year's reported net profit of $268 million; this compared with the interest cost two years earlier of $146 million, which was 60% of the $242 million net profit.

The actual cash outflows in respect of annual interest payments were materially greater than the figure charged against profit. The 1990 charge was 91% of the real figure but the 1991 and 1992 charges were lower — 81% and 83% respectively. Not all the interest paid from 1988 was booked directly through the profit and loss account. Increasingly larger amounts were capitalised and added to the 'aircraft deposits and predelivery payments' item in the balance sheet. The interest capitalised rose from $5 million in 1988 to $13 million in 1990 and $37 million in 1992.

Two classic measures of capital structure and debt servicing capability — interest cover and cash flow to interest — suggest GPA was adequate but not strong. On the surface, GPA's interest cover appeared healthier than ILFC's, at 2.4 times compared with 1.7 times. Converting the data into cash flow presents a very different picture. ILFC emerges in a more comfortable position, as shown in the comparative analysis in Table 6.4. The reason for the very different signal under the cash flow analysis is explained by GPA's less conservative depreciation and dividend policies. It is also arguable that there was greater stability and quality in ILFC's interest and cash flow cover, because the source of the earnings was based on a higher proportion of leasing income. GPA's profitability was much more dependent on aircraft sales, which was volatile in volume and profit margin.

Balance sheet gearing

An examination of GPA's debt/equity ratio points to a continually deteriorating capital structure from 1989/90, as shown in Table 6.4. ILFC had a consistently stronger capital structure. Moreover, ILFC was generating a healthier cash flow stream to the level of debt owed. GPA's debt/equity ratio for bank covenant purposes reached 3.3:1 by March 1992. This was the highest since 1985 — which was the era before the extensive expansion and new aircraft purchase programme. If we bear in mind GPA's financial commitments of $2.4 billion in 1992/93 and $2 billion in 1993/94 and further obligations to the aircraft manufacturers, the urgent need for GPA to raise equity is apparent. Because of its scale and dominant market share in world markets it lost its financial flexibility and was now vulnerable to being 'stretched' on the rack of debt and loan covenants unless both the capital and aircraft markets improved dramatically.

Even the term structure of GPA's debt and its policy in bank borrowing must be questioned. The $2.4 billion corporate credit facility (CCF) was being repaid at the rate of 1% per quarter of the principal from December 1990 until September 1992, when the repayments of principal were to increase to 2% per quarter. Finally, a 61% 'balloon' payment of the expected balance of the facility was scheduled for September 1996. The associates credit facility (ACF) of $1.25 billion had broadly similar repayment arrangements, lagging one year behind the CCF. Its final 61% 'balloon' repayment was scheduled for September 1997. Both facilities were secured on GPA's aircraft assets. Bearing in mind the life of the majority of aircraft assets as indicated by the depreciation policy adopted (i.e. twenty-five years with a residual value of 15%) it is remarkable that there was such a mismatch between the duration of the loan facility and the asset life-cycle and earning rate.

ILFC had a different financing strategy. It borrowed very little from banks. By raising equity on the stockmarket in New York in 1983 ILFC built up recognition and a profile with New York institutions.[49] Through its cautious image and stable financial ratios it raised unsecured debt on the public market through issues of public bonds, medium-term notes and commercial paper. It relied on four leading US investment houses — Merrill Lynch, Morgan Stanley, Salomon Brothers and Goldman Sachs — to organise, underwrite and place its offerings. This policy facilitated strong credit ratings (usually A+ by Standard and Poor's and A2 by Moody's)[50] — particularly after its acquisition in 1990 by AIG.[51] The resulting low cost of capital was a competitive weapon for a financial intermediary in a capital-intensive industry. In 1992 ILFC issued $1.2 billion in new public debt and $100 million in preferred stock.

Fixed charges coverage
A more probing analysis of financial gearing is revealed by comparing the aggregate of GPA's payments of interest to banks plus leases-in (on the sale and leaseback aircraft) with the leasing revenue from customers. Because GPA adopted a policy of purchasing and doing sales and leaseback deals on aircraft, it was both leasing-in and leasing-out. In 1987 GPA paid out a total of $38.1 million in lease rentals and loan interest compared with a leasing revenue of $102 million. By March 1992 the outflows grew to $631 million compared to revenues of $975 million. This reflected the effects of the very active sale and leaseback strategy of aircraft and increasing dependence on bank debt.

The deteriorating trend in coverage is illustrated in Table 6.8. Annual outflows as a percentage of inflows rose from 37.4% in 1987 to 62.5% by March 1992. This indicates that the cash inflow 'cover' for contractual financial commitments (quite apart from the amortisation required under the CCF and ACF loan facilities) had weakened dramatically.

Did GPA overtrade?
The financial evidence indicates that despite its size, apparent financial sophistication and supposed 'heavyweight' board, GPA exhibited all the signs of 'overtrading'. In common with many entrepreneurially dominated businesses it failed to complete the transition through the 'adolescent' stage. GPA was experiencing a material fall in profit margins on assets for some years. It was 11.8% in 1985 and fell to 10.2% in 1988. In 1990 it declined to 9.5% and then 6.9% in 1991. In the two years to March 1992, prior to the IPO, the margin halved to 4.8%.

Table 6.8: GPA: fixed financial charges to leasing revenue (%)

1987	37.4
1988	42.9
1989	40.1
1990	52.8
1991	59.6
1992	62.5
1993	64.7

Definition: Aggregate of annual lease rental and loan interest payments as a proportion of annual aircraft leasing revenue.
Source: Annual reports.

The symptoms of an overtrading condition identified in GPA are summarised in Table 6.9 in the form of a 'configuration index'. This cluster of critical ratios clearly indicates that investment in assets was expanding at a much faster rate than profits, cash flow or shareholders' equity. The really critical cross-over point occurred in 1991. The asset investment index reached 629, whereas the equity and pre-tax profit indices at 463 and 426 had not kept pace. The further expansion in the asset index to 890 by March 1992 clearly worsened an already weakened condition. Revenue growth fell seriously behind the asset expansion for the two years prior to the crisis. Cash flow levels also lagged behind and consequently the debt index grew to 997. GPA exhibited all the classic symptoms of overtrading by 1992 in growth, profit margins, equity capital base and excessive reliance on debt.

Table 6.9: GPA: the overtrading configuration index

	1987	1988	1989	1990	1991	1992
Total assets	100	173	277	420	629	890
Revenue	100	181	289	545	525	559
Equity	100	164	241	395	463	544
Pre-tax profit	100	162	239	374	426	423
Retained profit	100	159	263	444	519	531
Cash flow	100	138	214	395	449	532
Total debt	100	174	284	413	679	997
Liquidity	100	466	0	(184)	288	316

Note: All figures indexed with base year 31 March 1987.
Source: Annual reports.

Liquidity never seems to have been particularly strong. The real meaning of liquidity and medium-term debt structure alters radically when covenants and 'events of default' come into play. Some pointers to financial pressures and implications for future liquidity, in the absence of a significant injection of new equity, emerged when GPA stated in the IPO prospectus in June 1992: 'At present, the Directors believe that there is limited scope for the Company to arrange additional syndicated credit facilities with commercial banks.'[52] The implication was that sufficient further secured loans would not be available to meet the projected cash flow deficits. This tells us something about the banks' views of financial risk and/or the difficulties GPA had in negotiating changes in debt covenants. It suggests, not surprisingly, that the banks wished to see a stronger equity base when GPA's total assets expanded rapidly from $1.26 billion at the end of March 1988 to $6.5 billion at the end of March 1992. It was an exceptional rate of expansion with such a large level of assets.

In this writer's opinion the overtrading index inevitably leads to the conclusion that financial control was inadequate. Thus there was disequilibrium in balancing the growth rate with capital structure and liquidity policy. The growth rate and profit margins did not match. In view of the level of future financial commitments and the cycle in the industry, the capital structure and liquidity situation were imprudent. Like Goodman International, Kentz Corporation and Xtra-vision, the culture and objectives of the entrepreneurial founder and deal-making marketing executive team overwhelmed the accountants and financial equilibrium.

Bank covenants

The terms of bankers' covenants and consequential financial risk became a crucial element in GPA's spiral into financial distress. Under the secured corporate credit facility and other facilities, the covenant requirements included:

- a maximum debt to equity ratio of 4.25:1
- total ordinary share dividends of not more than 35% of net profits available for the ordinary and A ordinary shareholders in the year
- interest and debt service cover by profit and cash flow.[53]

These covenants represented constraints on investment, financing and dividend policies. The debt/equity and dividend restrictions became tight by 1992. The dividend payout ratio of 32% did not leave much scope for an increase. This was material, because the ordinary share dividend was static for three successive years. The debt/equity ratio had reached 3.3:1, the highest for six years. The level of shareholders' funds fell to just 19% of total assets in 1992, compared with 29% in 1990. Converting these figures to US GAAP would leave GPA's 1992 equity base significantly below the 21.7% equity/assets ratio of ILFC. In addition there were contingent liabilities under some of the sale and leaseback deals.

A financial projection for 1993–94, assuming a similar cash flow pattern as the previous year (which was optimistic), indicated a prospective debt/equity ratio for covenant purposes of 4.0:1.[54] In this writer's opinion this left insufficient headroom for contingencies and depended on a steady state outcome for 1993/94. The evidence indicates that GPA had few options in the short term. It appears to have had no alternative but to try to raise new equity or preference share capital, despite conditions in the capital market.

Internal plans and profit expectations

GPA prepared numerous forward plans on a rolling basis. There was also some corporate modelling of the impact of changing demand and margin variables. Unfortunately, the 'worst case' scenario seems to have been insufficiently cautious. The effect of the industry cycle downturn on margins and remarketing was underestimated. The extent of the tightening of financial and capital markets and their changing views on the industry proved unexpected.

Between 1977 and 1990 GPA worked through three basic five-year plans. A presentation to fund managers and analysts in spring 1989 claimed that 'GPA has in the past exceeded its planned profit target by significant margins'. Initially, the profit targets were quite modest. In the first five-year plan covering 1977 to 1981, the start-up stage, profitability was not expected to be strong. In its first full year's trading GPA reported a profit of $495,000. A figure of $1.1 million was attained in 1978 — which was in excess of the projected target at the end of five years. By 1981 profits had risen to over $4 million. Over the period, aggregate profits of $9.7 million were earned, compared to an initial target of $1.8 million. It was an excellent achievement by any standards.

The second five-year plan, from 1981 to 1985, envisaged profits growing more gradually from $4 million to $10 million. Actual performance was much better in the latter years, with pre-tax profits of $13 million and $17 million in 1984 and 1985 respectively. Aggregate profits for the five years reached $49 million compared to the target of $32 million.

The third more formal GPA five-year plan from 1986 was more ambitious. Profits were planned to pass $100 million in 1989. Maurice Foley pointed to corporate objectives which included:

- to maintain our profit, productivity and earnings per share growth and our return on assets
- to put together the equity base needed to support substantial further growth
- to expand the company's ownership group
- to build up our management and human resources to support our growth.[55]

Actual profit performance continued to outpace, modestly at first, the demanding targets. Net profits of $152 million in 1989 and $242 million in 1990 were quite extraordinary in comparison with targets and previous performance. They represented not only the initial payoff of the new aircraft purchasing strategy and strong marketing, but also the change in product and profitability mix with more aircraft sales (i.e. 'remarketing'). These aircraft sales brought in a gross profit of $43 million in 1988, which was almost 46% of the $93 million gross profit achieved by aircraft leasing.

Within two years aircraft sales had more than trebled to $1.48 billion. They generated a gross profit of $125 million, which was now 60% of the leasing contribution. Tony Ryan opened his 1990 chairman's statement by proclaiming:

> For the fourteenth consecutive year, GPA Group's profit, earnings per share, dividend and shareholder's funds have all increased significantly. The consolidated net profit of GPA Group increased 59% to $242.3 million and earnings per Ordinary share increased 49% to $41.93. The proposed total dividend is $12.00 per share, up 37%.[56]

It seemed a dazzling performance. The results of 1988/89 led to a revision of the five-year plan in early 1989. Consequently, net profit was forecast to grow from $210 million in 1990 to $375 million by 1992 and to $521 million by 1994. The exceptional profit buoyancy of 1989 was one element which may have helped stimulate a more optimistic view of future expected performance. This was the picture GPA portrayed in briefing sessions to fund managers and stockbroker analysts. The optimism was reflected in the 1990 stockbroker research reports of Davy and NCB. The similarity of both sets of profit and earnings per share forecasts and their relatively close alignment with GPA's presentations were striking.

Dividend policy

GPA paid out almost as much in dividends as it raised in additional new share capital in the five-year period to March 1992. Dividends declared amounted to $380 million whereas net new share capital introduced was $420 million. An examination of the details of the dividends paid reveals some interesting issues. Not only was the dividend payout high for a young fast-growth company, but continuous financing shortfalls were financed by an increasing debt burden. In contrast the total dividends paid by ILFC were minuscule and an equity dividend did not commence until 1988. As can be seen from Table 6.10, GPA paid dividends of $68 million out of a net profit of $152 million in 1988/89 and $100 million out of profits of $242 million in 1989/90. In this writer's opinion these overall payout ratios of 45% and 42% respectively were very high in the company's financial circumstances. In both 1990/91 and 1991/92 the overall payout ratio amounted to 37%.

Table 6.10: Total amount of dividends paid by GPA and ILFC ($m)

GPA		ILFC	
1987/88	49	1987	2
1988/89	68	1988	8
1989/90	100	1989	11
1990/91	96	1990	7
1991/92	98	1991	10

Source: Annual reports.

Tony Ryan and the GPA management and staff held almost 16% of its equity through general purchases and share option schemes. In addition, the top management group were holders of A preference shares, which entitled them to a dividend based on a profit participation formula. Similarly, the dividend on the A ordinary shares held by Tony Ryan based on a profit participation formula provided a remarkably high return by capital market criteria.[57] For the three years ending March 1992, dividends of $2.32, $2.34 and $2.38 were paid on these A ordinary shares compared with $0.60 each year on the other ordinary shares. These A ordinary shares, which represented just under 9% of the issued equity capital, absorbed 29% of the total ordinary dividend paid. The A ordinary dividends paid from 1985 to 1992 are set out in Table 6.11. Effectively, these shares were entitled to a dividend equivalent to the earnings per share for the year.[58] This superior rate of dividend on the A ordinary shares was based on an arrangement

Table 6.11: Dividends paid on GPA's A ordinary shares ($m)	
1985	1.8
1986	2.0
1987	4.6
1988	6.7
1989	10.0
1990	14.9
1991	21.9
1992	22.3

Source: Annual reports.

approved by shareholders. This special dividend entitlement appears to have been extended from 1990 to 1994.[59]

The A preference shares were a particularly valuable investment incentive for the executive directors and certain senior executives. Up to 1986 the dividend on these shares was based on the following formula: 10% of the excess of net profits over $1 million after other preference dividends.[60] The dividend entitlement from 1987 to 1991 was altered to participation in the net profit in excess of $22 million until 1991, when it was adjusted (from 1991 to 2000) to 7.5% of net profits in excess of $100 million.[61] The motivation for the executives to pursue higher profits seems obvious. In this writer's opinion when this was combined with the executive payment incentive scheme, which incorporated return on equity as a key element, the balancing of growth in activity and reported profit against the increased risk profile became problematical. In turn, the role of accounting policies in profit and liability recognition became more crucial. The pressures on management for earnings cannot be ignored. The role of independent directors, the audit committee, the senior financial staff and the auditors became more important as a controlling mechanism

Was it coincidental that sales of aircraft, many on a sale and leaseback arrangement, jumped from $68 million in 1986 to $235 million in 1987 and rapidly to $1.48 billion in 1990? The ability to recognise an upfront profit under Irish GAAP was a major contributor to the net profit growth to $242 million in 1989/90. The profit participating A preference dividend jumped to $24.2 million.[62] The issued A preference capital grew gradually from a mere $85,000 in 1986 to $102,000 in 1990 with a very modest premium over the nominal value. The dividend gave a huge rate of return as the summary in Table 6.12 shows.

Table 6.12: Dividends declared on GPA's A preference shares ($m)

Year	Amount
1986	2.3
1987	4.9
1988	8.7
1989	14.3
1990	24.2
1991	11.3
1992	12.2

Source: Annual reports.

GPA employees, other than Tony Ryan, held equity which may have been valued at $160–240 million. Many drew down bank borrowings to support their investment. One example came to public light in a court action by a branch of the Bank of Ireland against Colm Barrington for a loan secured against GPA shares, which the bank claimed were unsaleable and of no value in January 1993.[63] Tony Ryan entered into a loan agreement in 1988 with a commercial banking associate of Merrill Lynch of the USA. A balance of $35 million was owed in 1992 on the security of certain of his GPA shares.[64] High dividends would have helped employees service any borrowing, apart from the implications for share price.

Aggressive accounting policies

GPA's accounting policies were consistently raised by institutional investment/portfolio managers in the research interviews.[65] They were viewed as aggressive. This allegation was forcefully refuted by some (but not all) GPA personnel. It was pointed out that these policies had the approval of the GPA audit committee as well as a Big 6 auditing firm, and that they were within accounting regulations.

An analysis of GPA's financial reporting practices does indicate that they appear to have been materially less conservative than those of ILFC. Indeed, if GPA was operating in the USA with exactly similar accounting policies to ILFC, its reported net profit would have been almost one-third less than the figure reported in Ireland in the five years prior to the flotation. The different regulatory framework of accounting in the USA relating to the timing of profit recognition, and company specific practices in depreciation and the capitalisation of certain expense items, would explain the difference.

The area of leasing and financial reporting has been controversial for the accounting profession and standards setting bodies in the UK and Ireland

and in the USA for some time.⁶⁶ Wolk, Francis and Tearney note that the area of leases has generated more accounting standards than any other single topic in the USA.⁶⁷ They counted ten standards by the Financial Accounting Standards Board and six by the earlier professional standards bodies culminating in Statement of Financial Accounting Standard (SFAS) 13 in 1977.⁶⁸ In the UK, the length of time and controversy involved in the gestation of Statement of Standard Accounting Practice 21 are outlined by Davies, Paterson and Wilson.⁶⁹ After five years of debate it was finalised in 1984. Revised regulations were outlined in Financial Reporting Standard (FRS) 5, which was issued by the Accounting Standards Board in 1994. The accounting policies of GPA can, therefore, be examined through the regulatory framework and specific company accounting policy choices.

The different regulatory frameworks

Lessor accounting has been governed by SSAP 21 'Accounting for Leases and Hire Purchase Contracts' since July 1984.⁷⁰ The emphasis of the standard is much more on lessee than on lessor accounting and disclosure. There is very little difference between Irish and US GAAP as regards lessees.⁷¹ It is in the area of sale and leaseback of assets with operating leases that a fundamentally opposing view on profit recognition by lessors is adopted by SSAP 21. It will be recalled that GPA not only leased-out aircraft which it owned but also it engaged in a large number of sale and leaseback transactions. The latter aircraft were thus leased-in and leased-out.

Briefly, the recognition of a (capital) profit on a sale and leaseback transaction for accounting purposes in Ireland was based on the classification of the lease. If it was a finance lease, the profit or loss arising was deferred and recognised and spread over the shorter of the lease term or the useful life of the asset. If it was an operating lease the full gain was recognised immediately (i.e. an 'upfront' profit) provided the sale was recorded at fair value. In contrast, under US GAAP, any gain arising from the sale and leaseback of an operating lease has usually to be deferred and recognised by way of amortisation over the period of the leaseback. The critical element, therefore, was the classification of the lease.

The failure of Atlantic Computers, the largest computer leasing group in the UK in 1990 (which triggered the collapse of British & Commonwealth, the quoted financial services group), raised questions about leasing companies, accounting and the issue of residual values of assets. The subsequent Department of Trade and Industry report of the inspectors' investigation confirmed that there was faulty accounting and auditing.[72] In autumn 1991, the new Accounting Standards Board invited the Institute of Chartered Accountants in England and Wales to review SSAP 21. The subsequent report discussed a number of practical difficulties experienced with SSAP 21, such as the reality of distinctions between finance and operating leases, accounting for sale and leaseback transactions and accounting for residual values.[73] The apportionment of ownership risks and rewards of the asset was seen as a fundamental criterion.

The report pinpointed the situation where a firm as the owner of an asset could realise a profit on sale and continue to use the asset without retaining it on the balance sheet.[74] Under the accounting standards of the time, the criteria for removal (derecognition) of a currently owned asset were different from those applying to capitalisation (recognition) of an asset not previously owned. These contrary principles were felt to be wrong. Six qualitative tests were suggested to help in determining substance over form. The whole debate about whether a distributable profit had really been earned was prompted by various financially and legally engineered sale and leaseback deals by hotel and store groups — quite apart from lessors such as GPA. The implementation of FRS 5, 'Reporting the Substance of Transactions', by the Accounting Standards Board in 1994 can be viewed as corrective action in an area where the accounting standard (SSAP 21) was ambivalent. It adopted the overriding principle that transactions should be accounted for according to their economic substance rather than their legal form.

In this writer's opinion considering the convenience of Irish accounting standards, the structure of executive incentive schemes and the profit participation dividend basis of the A ordinary and preference shares, it is not surprising that GPA completed so many sale and leaseback transactions in the period 1988–91. In March 1992, eighty-six aircraft (being 37% of GPA's owned fleet) were leased-in. Over 40% of all aircraft sale revenues between 1985/86 and 1991/92 were through sale and leaseback deals. The differences (which were very material) in reported net profit as computed under Irish and US GAAP for the four years 1988/89 to 1991/92 are set out in Table 6.13.

Table 6.13: Comparison of GPA net profit under Irish and US GAAP

	1988/89	1989/90	1990/91	1991/92
Irish GAAP ($m)	126	206	242	249
USA GAAP ($m)	84	121	152	202
Difference %	33	41	37	19

Source: Annual reports; computations by author.

GPA acted legally under prevailing company law and accounting standards. Its management availed of financial reporting regulatory and business opportunities to manage earnings performance. The fuelling of the growth in earnings by the sale and leaseback profits facilitated high incentive compensation payments and the high dividend payout policy. The lower profits under US GAAP and bank covenant constraint would have resulted in materially lower dividends. Net worth would also have been considerably lower, with diminished opportunities for growth financed by debt because of the maximum debt/equity ratio permitted by the covenants. Greater injections of share capital would have been necessary earlier or the investment programme would have had to have been curtailed. More conservative accounting standards might have saved GPA from self-destruction.

It is clear from Table 6.14 that Irish accounting standards and practices were much less conservative in lessor profit and net worth recognition than were US standards. The question is whether they had economic consequences for the fate of GPA and other lessors as well as their investors, bankers and creditors.

Table 6.14: Comparison of GPA shareholders' funds under Irish and US GAAP

	1989/90	1990/91	1991/92
Irish GAAP ($m)	893	1,047	1,230
USA GAAP ($m)	646	781	848
Difference (%)	28	25	31

Source: IPO Prospectus, June 1992; SEC Public Debt Registration Document, December 1991

Company specific accounting practices

The audit opinion in both 1986 and 1987, which referred to GPA's accounting policies, contained identical wording:

> We have examined the financial statements set out on pages . . . in accordance with approved auditing standards. These financial statements have been prepared on the same basis as the statutory financial statements of GPA Group Limited, on which we have reported as auditors, and in accordance with the accounting policies set out on pages . . .
>
> In our opinion, these statements give, on the basis of such accounting policies, a true and fair view of the state of affairs of the

company and of the group at 31 March 1986 and of the profit and source and application of funds of the group for the year then ended.[75]

In the opinion of this writer this was not a common type of audit report in that it referred directly to the accounting policies in those specific years.

GPA's calculation of net profit was determined by the nature of revenue recognition with regard to aircraft sales and cost recognition in three areas — depreciation and residual values, capitalisation of interest ($37 million, $26 million and $13 million in the three years to 1991/92) and other outlays. ILFC charged a higher rate of depreciation and did not capitalise 'costs incurred in respect of aircraft leases'. However ILFC, like GPA, did capitalise some debt interest and debt issue costs. If we recompute GPA's profitability according to ILFC's accounting policies in two steps — company specific and regulatory framework — materially lower levels of profit emerge for GPA as summarised in Table 6.15.

Table 6.15: Comparison of GPA net profits under alternative accounting policies and regulatory standards ($m)

	1989/90	1990/91	1991/92
GPA reported net profit	242	262	265
Deduct			
Expenses deferred	8	1	20
Additional depreciation	0	20	33
	8	21	53
Adjusted profit at company specific policies	234	241	212
Sale and leaseback adjustments (US GAAP)	79	93	44
Revised profit per US GAAP and ILFC policies	155	148	168
Difference from reported profit	36%	44%	36%

Source: Annual reports; Form 20-F filed with SEC, Washington DC; IPO Prospectus, June 1992. Certain data computed by author.

Before taking account of the regulatory effect, the impact of adopting the more conservative accounting policies of ILFC is particularly evident in 1991/92. In that year GPA's net profit would have been $212 million rather than the reported $265 million if computed on the basis of ILFC's accounting policies. The trend before the flotation would have been downward — $241 million and $234 million in the two previous years.

When the adjustment for the regulatory difference in the treatment of sale and leaseback profits is factored in, the net profit at $168 million in 1991/92 is 64% of the reported GPA profit. In this writer's opinion it is difficult to avoid the view that GPA adopted more aggressive accounting policies than ILFC — quite apart from the regulatory standards in the two domains.

An example of this approach to profit recognition was the rate of depreciation on aircraft. GPA's depreciation charge was a function of the asset life-cycle and the residual value adopted. As far back as 1986, GPA was calculating depreciation on a straight line basis to residual values, over twenty-five years with a 15% residual value for all aircraft on an operating lease. In contrast, Aer Lingus, who was a major shareholder, was depreciating its aircraft fleet over a range of life years varying from twelve to eighteen years with a residual value varying between 10% and 15% of cost. In 1986, ILFC was depreciating its fleet on an estimated useful life of aircraft of ten to twenty years with residual values of 10% to 15%. What is particularly noticeable is that ILFC and a number of airlines were depreciating the older technology (Stage 2) aircraft over much shorter life-cycles than GPA. For example, in 1986 and 1987 when GPA was using a life-cycle of twenty-five years on all its aircraft on operating lease, ILFC was adopting ten to sixteen years on its Boeing 737–200s and 727–200s, and sixteen years on its DC 10s. However, GPA was using a shorter life-cycle of sixteen years for some of its refurbished fleet. British Airways adopted a life-cycle of twelve to sixteen years for its aircraft fleet for depreciation at that time.[76] This was later extended to a range of fourteen to twenty years with 0% to 10% residual value. KLM used fifteen to eighteen years with a 10% residual value and SAS used nineteen years. In summary, all these companies adopted more conservative depreciation policies than GPA.

The depreciation expense charged as a percentage of the carrying value[77] of aircraft assets was lower in GPA than in ILFC — 4.6% and 4.3% compared with 5.6% and 5.3% in the late 1980s and early 1990s. With aircraft assets in billions of dollars a 1% difference had a major impact on the profit and loss account. In the USA, the estimation and disclosure of residual values were controversial and one of the greatest problems was auditing lessors' financial statements.[78] The economics of leasing often revolve around residual values, which according to US writers Kay and Searfoss 'are probably the most significant real asset of the leasing company'.[79] Some research interviews with this author argued that the market value of the GPA fleet was in excess of the book value. For example in the IPO prospectus, BK Associates in their letter of 9 June 1992 considered $4.568

billion to be a 'Current Fair Market Value' of GPA and its subsidiaries on 31 March 1992, which was 7.7% higher than the book value.[80] The operative word is 'current' as the historical experience was for aircraft values to decline in periods of lower demand, as the industry was cyclical.

After the financial crisis, GPA's March 1993 financial statements contained a provision for 'exceptional depreciation' of $128 million. This was additional to the normal charge for 1993 of $198 million. Its scale is significant and, perhaps, tells its own story. When considering depreciation, not only is there the allocation issue in matching benefits with use of an asset, but there is also the policy of the organisation in its self-financing ability to replace its assets — particularly when the cost appears to be increasing. There is evidence of price inflation in aircraft costs (in US dollars).[81] It is debatable as to what extent GPA's depreciation policy was a creature of its marketing strategy in pricing and market share — quite apart from its favourable impact on reported profit. In this writer's opinion, a more conservative depreciation policy would have served GPA better in the long run. The interaction between profit and pricing might have depressed volume and the unduly optimistic management view of market demand. The aggressive aircraft ordering and drawdown strategy might also have been tempered.

Deferred expenditure accumulated to $54 million as an intangible asset on GPA's balance sheet in March 1992, but portion was included in the accounting 'big bath' after the crisis; $20 million of this intangible asset was written off as an exceptional item in the 1993 financial statements.

The efficiency of stockbroker analysts

For several years, two Irish stockbroking houses, Davy and NCB, issued extensive research reports on GPA.[82] Both emphasised past and expected future earnings per share performance and used it as a basis for an opinion on GPA's share valuation. In their report dated 10 March 1989, Davy pointed to the strengthening of demand for new aircraft and the buoyant conditions in the operating lease market. Both were consistently bullish about prospects for the industry and GPA. In their 1990 reports, both projected very similar earnings per share growth. In the five-year period to 1995 Davy expected earnings per share growth of 20% per annum, and stated that growth could be as high as 25% if the world economy expanded at more than 3%. A two-year recession might reduce earnings growth to between 10% and 15%. In discussing investors' concerns about the impact of 'cyclical factors' on the industry, Davy accepted that GPA was in a capital-intensive business but pointed out that, unlike other capital-intensive industries, the aircraft leasing business was less prone to cyclical influences. This, they argued, was due to the mobility of aircraft as an asset, because of regional economic variations.

In 1990 NCB projected a 20% compound growth in earnings per share to 1994 and felt that GPA shares should be valued at a premium of 10% over ILFC shares although ILFC had a public quotation. A price/earnings ratio of 13.5 times and a valuation of $650 (equivalent to $16 at the time of the flotation in June 1992) were deemed justifiable. In 1991 NCB thought the adverse market conditions would slow down GPA's short-term growth, but earnings per share were forecasted to increase by 10% in 1992 and 15% in 1993 and 1994. In 1991, Davy projected GPA's balance sheets for both 1992 and 1993. They concluded the debt/equity ratio would rise from 2.33 in 1991 to 2.67 in 1993, and it would remain easily within its bank covenant limits, even without an equity injection. NCB also thought GPA's debt/equity ratio would not rise above 2.7:1 over the two years to 1993.

In their 1992 reports, before the flotation, Davy and NCB forecast broadly similar pre-tax profits for the three years to 1995 as well as similar earnings per share and dividends for 1993, as summarised in Table 6.16.

Table 6.16: Davy and NCB 1992 forecasts for GPA

	Davy	NCB
Pre-tax profit ($m)		
1992 Actual	279	279
1993 Forecast	375	370
1994 Forecast	457	474
1995 Forecast	580	565
Earnings per share ($)		
1992 Actual	2.30	2.30
1993 Forecast	2.41	2.40
Dividend ($)		
1992 Actual	0.60	0.60
1993 Forecast	0.65	0.66

Source: *Guinness Peat Aviation: Cleared for Take-off*, Davy Equity Research, Dublin, 26 March 1992; *GPA Group plc: Issues for Discussion*, NCB Stockbrokers, Dublin, June 1992.

Davy's reports failed to identify any concerns with GPA's accounting policies. In their lengthy company analysis in June 1990, Davy covered accounting matters in one paragraph. GPA was described as being relatively conservative in its treatment of lease income and profits. Davy's report of March 1992 briefly mentioned accounting matters. Under 'valuation issues' there was a short reference to adjusting GPA's earnings to US GAAP.

In contrast, both NCB and Riada Stockbrokers included a section on GPA's accounting policies in their 1992 reports. NCB noted that US GAAP did not permit the immediate and full profit recognition of gains on sale and leaseback transactions and that GPA's earnings per share under US GAAP would have been materially lower. They pointed out that ILFC followed a more conservative depreciation policy, and they calculated the impact on GPA's profits of using ILFC's policy — but offered no views otherwise. They also commented on the fact that GPA had stated that there could be no justifiable reason for changing its depreciation policy and that no change was intended. Riada noted that leasing companies in general had considerable scope to bring forward income and defer costs, and that the adoption of conservative accounting policies was vital to the fair representation of performance. Riada mentioned the difference between US and Irish GAAP as regards sale and leaseback gains and the fact that initial costs attributable to aircraft leases were written off over the life of the lease. Surprisingly, Riada seemed to suggest that GPA's accounting policies were conservative.

Stockbroker analysts' reviews in advance of the IPO

Though there was no profit or dividend forecast by the GPA directors in the IPO prospectus (as is usual in Dublin and London, but not in New York under Securities and Exchange Commission regulations), there were a number of 'favourable' stockbroker reports with forecasts of increasing profits. Many of these lengthy reviews were issued by brokers who seemed to have been associated directly or indirectly with the offer or advisers to the offer. Examples were Nomura Research Institute, Goldman Sachs, Yamaichi, Swiss Bank Corporation, Barclays de Zoete Wedd, and Hoare Govett. All were bullish about its prospects. They saw GPA's equity as an attractive investment being offered at an undemanding price/earnings rating which could yield useful capital growth within three years.

In Dublin, detailed reports by Davy and NCB were equally favourably disposed to GPA's prospects. The cover of Davy's March 1992 research report *Guinness Peat Aviation: Cleared for Take-off* featured a jet aircraft soaring through clouds to a blue sky.[83] The imagery, in retrospect, could have reflected the Icarus tale. The report was buoyant on GPA's prospects. Pre-tax profits were expected to increase by 36% in 1992/93, 22% in

1993/94 and 27% in 1994/95. Growth in earnings per share and dividends was also forecast. At $12, GPA's shares were viewed as somewhat undervalued and offering opportunities for capital gain. Riada were more cautious in their analysis and review of the risk elements, but predicted growth in earnings for 1993. They indicated their difficulty in determining an appropriate valuation framework for GPA and noted that, when quoted, GPA would be the largest stock in the Irish equity index with a weighting of almost 20% — which was important to the attitude of Irish investment institutions. NCB, like Davy, forecast sizeable profit growth in 1993, 1994 and 1995. Nevertheless, they concluded that GPA benefited from 'supernormal' profits in the late 1980s and early 1990s. This they credited to good industry analysis and timing in its Stage 3 ordering strategy, the special position of the industry, and an imbalance between the supply and demand of aircraft which inflated margins. NCB felt that market conditions would be less buoyant for the remainder of the 1990s and that GPA's profit growth would be less rapid. Like Riada, NCB found it difficult to identify comparative stocks as reference points for a valuation. ILFC, as a subsidiary of AIG, was no longer quoted. Having reviewed various US stockmarket ratings, NCB concluded that, on balance, $11 per share was appropriate.[84]

Goodbody issued a commissioned general review of the airline industry, which expressed concern about the short to medium term because of excess capacity. Taking a very definite view, Bloxham Stockbrokers expected the issue to be successful at $11 a share but they felt that it was 'not an investment for the risk averse' and 'investors might be better off waiting until after the IPO, when a true market for the shares can be established'. Bloxham noted that the world credit and airline industries were in a 'poor state' and that GPA would do well to maintain its profitability during the industry's cyclical downturn.[85]

In London, Kleinwort Benson issued a cautionary holding report in April 1992, following their analyst's briefing visit to Shannon. Kleinwort's June report on the flotation was quite negative. Kleinwort stated that they had followed and met with GPA over a number of years and concluded that neither the price/earnings ratio nor the yield indicated for the price took sufficient account of the near-term risk and uncertainties. The timing of the offer was viewed as less than ideal.[86]

Reasons for the flotation failure

It will be recalled that GPA successfully raised $500 million by way of an issue of unsecured medium-term bonds on the US public debt market in December 1991. A prospectus giving more details on its affairs than was previously available was registered with the Securities and Exchange Commission.[87] Demand for the issue was so strong that the planned $250 million was doubled and it was oversubscribed.[88] How then could an equity flotation encounter such an absence of demand just six months later?

There were several newspaper[89] and investment journal[90] articles on the flotation collapse. On separate occasions, Tony Ryan and Maurice Foley aired their views.[91] This writer would have certain reservations about the Ryan/Foley conclusions. They appear to have omitted to mention the share price, the selection of advisers, the weak conditions of the airline industry, the fact that GPA's underlying profitability and financial position had weakened since March 1992, and that there were very real risks in the short-term outlook. After all, in August 1992, GPA reported a net profit of $49 million for the first quarter to end June 1992 of the 1992/93 financial year. This was materially down on the $69 million net profit for the same quarter of the previous year.

Based on the research evidence this writer believes that there were essentially five reasons for the IPO collapse:

- share price
- timing
- organisational structure of the offer
- the shares' technical circumstances
- public relations.

Share price
The key financial measures on the share price range of $10.00–12.50 are set out in Table 6.17.

On the face of it, the offer's financial statistics looked reasonable. The price/earnings ratio in the range 9.8 to 11.8 was not demanding for a supposed 'growth' stock. In the Irish market, AIB at 175p and Woodchester at 170p were on price/earnings ratios of 9.7 times and 9.4 times respectively. AIB was yielding 6.3% and Woodchester 3.6%. Similar financial stocks were available in London. As an 'unseasoned' share it would be usual for GPA's offer price to be pitched at a discount to existing securities, except for better expectations about earnings and risk. GPA did not issue a profit forecast, nor was its offer underwritten — as is the normal practice in Dublin and London. This was due to GPA's targeting of four markets and the 'book-building' approach adopted for New York and Tokyo.

Table 6.17: GPA's IPO share price financial statistics

	At $10 per share	At $12.50 per share
Market capitalisation	$2.9bn	$3.6bn
New equity introduced	$554m	$696m
Net tangible assets per share	$6.10	$6.60
Pro-forma earnings per share, based on previous year (1991/92)	$1.02	$1.06
Price/earnings ratio, based on previous year (1991/92)	9.8 times	11.8 times
Gross dividend yield	3.2%	2.5%
Dividend cover	3.4 times	3.5 times
Market to book values	1.63 times	1.9 times

Source: IPO Prospectus, June 1992; certain data calculated by author.

Unless it could definitely deliver some capital gains with stronger earnings and dividends in the near term, GPA's minimum bid price of $10 was at the high end of any investment institution's valuation range. In this writer's opinion an $8 price tag would have made the risk/return relationship more attractive and may have attracted sufficient demand.[92] Many Dublin and London analysts had noted the fall in leasing margins and the decline in the second-hand values of aircraft. They also mentioned the softening in demand because of the recession and the oversupply from manufacturers, who had increased production output in 1989. The internal validity of several of the analysts' reports was questionable, because, in this writer's opinion, many appeared to fail to link their analysis and findings to eventual profit forecasts and conclusions.

At March 1992 GPA operated a fleet of 409 aircraft. It had already captured a dominant world market share of 20%. Firm orders were committed for 146 new aircraft in the twenty-one months to December 1993, at a cost of $4.7 billion.[93] The capital market saw the placing of these aircraft with customers as a daunting marketing task, particularly as GPA admitted that thirty-two aircraft were then not in revenue service with lessees.[94] In addition, existing aircraft coming off lease had to be placed. There was not only a placement risk at lower margins, but also a credit risk. The prospectus pointed to debtor provisions and rescheduling because of the difficulties facing the airline industry in some countries. The market could see that revenue from aircraft sales (remarketing) peaked in 1990 and fell subsequently. GPA acknowledged that due to 'the difficult trading conditions prevailing in the aircraft industry which were exacerbated by the relative lack of finance available for purchasers in such transactions' margins and demand were weaker.[95]

Pulling together these elements — weak demand, lower margins, tighter liquidity in aircraft asset markets, a financial commitment to purchasing six aircraft per month at a cost of $200 million and existing borrowings of $4.2 billion — left sophisticated investors with little doubt as to the increased business and financial risk of GPA. The prospective position for profits and financing, even if a net $554 million in additional equity was raised, was problematical. The question of bank covenants constraining dividends and debt/equity under the corporate credit facility[96] was of concern to new investors. If profits fell, or at best were maintained, the dividend could fall or remain stagnant. It seems there were doubts about whether the equity being raised was sufficient. A rights issue within two years could not be ruled out. The market felt the balance of probabilities was that GPA's share price, even at $10, could fall in the short to medium term. The expected return did not compensate for the perceived risk in the stock, particularly when the technical implications of share 'overhang' were added to the equation.

The quality of GPA's profit stream, particularly in its stability, was of concern to investors. Aircraft remarketing was viewed as a volatile 'deal-making' activity, and had not the same credibility as leasing revenue. In addition, there appear to have been questions about accounting matters. GPA executives were undoubtedly innovative in creating financial products from leases. The forthcoming securitisation issue (ALPS 1) was a testament to their talent. It was the 'dependence' on this volatile and lumpy activity for profit and liquidity which worried institutional investors.

How could GPA justify a flotation price in the range $10.00–12.50? In brief, its board and top management seem to have been fixated by the secondary transaction at $16.25 price, in a private sale, for less than 5% of the equity almost two years earlier. Almost all staff and directors were investors, with an estimated 16% holding worth about $370 million at $10 per share. There were the share option schemes in 1986 and 1990. Depending on when the options were awarded the prices varied from $1.75 to $11.75. In 1991 options on 1.3 million shares were granted at $11.75. At the time of the public offer there were options to purchase 4.8 million shares at a weighted average price of $9.11. Many staff purchases appear to have been with the help of bank borrowing. There would have been 'wealth' deficits for many at an offer price of, say, $8 per share. The motivation and the value of the share option incentive schemes may have had a bearing.

In this writer's opinion, the evidence suggests that the board did not fully appreciate the changes in the market realities in view of the poor timing of the offer. In this writer's view the IPO price might have been seen as a gamble for existing investors but, more seriously, it was in effect putting the organisation at risk. There were many reports of a disagreement between GPA and Goldman Sachs about the IPO price. It would seem that the $16.25 (i.e. $32.50 pre-split) secondary transaction price in 1990 was used by GPA as an anchor price. Despite the changes in the general level of stockmarket prices and industry sentiment between 1990 and 1992, it looks to have taken extensive persuasion by the investment banks to bring the price range down to $10.00–12.50. There were also the losses of the order of $4 billion in the world airline industry between 1990 and 1991, and the bankruptcy and financial distress of some airlines.

In April 1992, the influential S. G. Warburg Securities of London released a research report on the aerospace industries which was negative about prospects for two to three years.[97] It cited overordering in the 1980s, overcapacity, weak airline returns and a contraction of bank credit. Warburg noted that, because of changes in tax legislation in the USA and particularly Japan, the extensive demand for finance leases by investors to shelter profits from tax would reduce sharply.

A related issue was that the share prices of most financial institutions had fallen since 1990 because of weak credits, bad debts and lower growth expectations. The share price of Allied Irish Banks fell on average by 23% between May–June 1991 and May–June 1992. Citicorp shares traded at $24 on 1 June 1990, then halved in price in 1991 and only recovered to $16 in April 1992. Mitsubishi's share price was in the range Yen2250–2280 in April–May 1990 but declined to Yen1860–1750 by April–May 1992. In Ireland, the share prices of two leading industrial stocks, Smurfit and CRH, fell on average by 7% and 13% between May–June 1991 and May–June 1992. GPA's board and management appeared to think its share price could run counter to other broadly comparable stocks from an investor risk/return value perspective.

Timing

Timing was a contributory factor. Markets were not as confident in 1992 as in 1990. They had recovered from setbacks in late 1990 and early 1991, the exception being Tokyo. The combined effects of the recession and the Gulf war in August–September 1990 weakened confidence. The old adage of 'raising money when the market is strong, not when you need it' was certainly applicable in the case of GPA. The major stockmarkets all suffered a very sharp setback in November 1987 (Black Friday) but recovered. A decline occurred again in October 1989, though it was not as serious.

Share prices on all the leading stockmarkets had strengthened in 1990. For example, in London the FT 100 Index moved from a range of 1712–1862 in 1988 to 1793–2407 in 1989. Weakening a little in early 1990, it recovered to 2371 by June 1990. There was a definite deterioration in prices in autumn 1990 and it was not until April 1991 that the index improved to 2400 again. It continued to be reasonably steady for the rest of 1991 and into spring 1992. London improved from 2660 to 2697 in May 1992 but it weakened in June to 2493.

New York moved on similar lines to London in 1990 and 1991 but in 1992 it was slightly stronger and steadier than London. The airline sector had gone against the market in 1992 with the Standard and Poor's Airlines Index falling from 304 in January to 272 in April and 260 in May. The Standard and Poor's Composite, Industrials and Airlines Indices showed small weaknesses in June 1992 but recovered modestly in July. This decline was also reflected in the Dow Jones Industrials Index which fell from 3397 in early May 1992 to 3319 in early June.

The Dublin ISEQ Index showed a broadly similar pattern, declining heavily in the latter part of 1990 from 1704 in May to 1201 in December. There was a modest recovery to 1444 in August 1991, and it remained in that range until early 1992 when it once again fell from 1437 in April to 1379 in May and to 1311 in June. Dublin continued to decline moderately for the rest of 1992, reaching 1227 in December.

By far the greatest structural weaknesses in share prices and market confidence were in Tokyo.[98] The Nikkei 500 Index opened in 1990 at 2320, which was close to its high for some time. By March 1990 it fell to 1919 and to 1456 in December 1990. Unlike the other stockmarkets, prices in Tokyo did not recover. Indeed 1992 proved to be a particularly bad year, with the Tokyo market opening at 1409 but falling to 1169 in April and weakening further to 1110 in June. This was particularly serious for GPA because of the extensive Japanese shareholding, the pattern of Mitsubishi Bank's share price, and the fact that Nomura, a Japanese financial services institution, was the global co-ordinator for the public offer.

During the same period, a number of planned offers, which were viewed as doubtful, were withdrawn in good time. An example was 3i, a well-known venture capital and investment institution in the UK. The New

York and London markets were reasonably strong in a general sense in 1992. The Wellcome plc public offer, which was managed by Morgan Stanley and raised $4.25 billion, was successful some weeks later. In brief, institutional investors had money to invest but they were selective and conscious of stock specific risk.

The GPA IPO was sizeable by Dublin and London experiences but not in New York. US institutions were central to the success of the offer because of their long investment experience and their knowledge of the airline industry. The weak trend of the specific airline index was detrimental to the US investment institutions' confidence. The GPA offer price should have compensated for the perceived risk and poor prospects for the industry. It didn't.

Structure and organisation of the offer

Generally, the Dublin and London approach is to underwrite flotations so that the equity funding is guaranteed. The fact that the GPA offer was not underwritten contributed to its riskiness. The 'book-building' exercise adopted by the advisers was so structured that it effectively precluded underwriting. Of course underwriting would have resulted in hard negotiations and compromises on a definite share price. In this writer's opinion GPA took the high risk route in an attempt to secure the highest share price. It seems to have hoped that interaction and competition between the larger markets would help demand for the stock in the expected bidding process within the $10.00–12.50 range. Instead, the poor response in New York rebounded in London and dampened interest there. Outside Dublin, there was hardly any serious institutional interest at all.

GPA chose a Japanese house which appears to have had little previous global offer experience as lead manager. The combination of Japanese, US, UK and Continental investment banks was complex and risky. In view of the competition between US and Japanese houses in global markets, the flotation arrangements may not have been enthusiastically supported by some. In December 1991, GPA had successfully raised $500 million in quoted debt securities in New York through Merrill Lynch, Goldman Sachs and Salomon Brothers. It is strange that a leading US bank was not appointed as lead manager and that GPA did not choose New York as the primary market for the equity flotation. It seems that GPA's approach to business led to the structure of the offer and share price. The international public offer without underwriting seems to have been the outcome of many conflicting objectives.

Technical issues

The amount of existing equity being disposed of by the Japanese banks and the long-standing shareholders, Aer Lingus and Air Canada, and the fact that GPA required a 'lock-in' period against the selling of shares by other institutional investors, did not help the flotation. From a technical supply/demand influence on the future share price, there was concern about a share supply overhang. After all, fifteen existing shareholders planned to dispose of 25.5 million shares in the IPO at a minimum of $10 per share, which meant that other investors in the market had to produce at least $255 million. At 43% of the new equity being raised for the organisation itself, this sale by existing shareholders was a very sizeable requirement from the market, apart from the psychological impact.

In this writer's view, because of the structure of the flotation offer, these existing shareholders were not selling on the usual arm's length basis, with the price being determined by the market. Buyers could not make an offer on the basis of what they thought the shares were worth, except within the $10.00–12.50 price range. The four largest selling shareholders — Mitsubishi Trust and Banking, Air Canada, Aer Lingus and the Long-Term Credit Bank of Japan — were offloading shares valued at about $181 million. Whereas it might have been accepted that long-standing shareholders Aer Lingus and Air Canada might need funds for fleet replacement, there may have been other reasons why US or Japanese institutions were not disposed to buying shares being offloaded by the Japanese banks. Kawasaki, Mitsubishi Corporation and Nippon Total Finance were also selling shareholders.

At GPA's insistence, 81% of existing equity shareholders signed a controversial 'lock-in' agreement not to dispose of any further shares, without the prior written consent of GPA, until after the financial results to end March 1993 were officially released.[99] This writer believes that planned sales by some existing shareholders and this 'lock-in' created a perception of weak shareholder backing and the potential for market oversupply. Adding the possibility of a rights issue in 1993 or 1994, experienced institutional investors judged that the market price for GPA shares could remain depressed for some time.

Tony Ryan blamed the unwillingness of the London Stock Exchange to include GPA in its index as a serious blow, because it could affect portfolio selection in London institutions. It is difficult to accept this assertion as no other large Irish-based company (such as Smurfit or CRH) was included in the London index. The argument could also apply to the New York or

Tokyo exchanges and, to a degree, it suggests misconceptions of capital market indexes, structures and sectoral cultures.

Public relations

The term 'hostile' was used in relation to some UK journalists in their coverage of GPA's performance and other matters surrounding the planned public flotation.[100] This media 'Paddy bashing' was believed to have contributed to the IPO failure. It is an important issue of public and private concern, in view of the small size of the Irish capital market and the capital needs of larger Irish firms with extensive international business. Whether the media comment was balanced and fair, or whether GPA executives were unduly sensitive to any critical comments on the business, or whether their attitudes and actions with the media contributed to the problem is a subject for debate.

Brenda Cullen has examined the problem from a strategic management of public relations and corporate communications perspective.[101] Her case material suggests that it was primarily an internal management weakness. This author would partially agree. Some authoritative elements of the British press, such as the *Financial Times*, appeared generally consistently negative — for some years before the public flotation.[102] In this writer's opinion, some US articles, particularly in *Forbes*, seemed very critical.[103] The Cullen analysis primarily concentrates on a relatively short period prior to the flotation and provides some examples. This writer could add more.[104] In this writer's opinion, the extensive leading article in the *Financial Times* on the Saturday before the flotation was particularly bearish on risk and prospects:

> Tony Ryan and his team deserve all credit for their past achievements. But this is a high-risk share issue that private investors would do well to shun, even on a maximum price-earnings ratio of 11.8. Many British institutions, meantime, will be happy to give it a wide berth and leave the Japanese to make the running.[105]

A different choice of advisers, with more depth of experience, might have been more politically suitable from an institutional perspective. It could have ensured a more positive media and public relations outcome.

Though GPA had been a relatively secretive organisation, it held briefings for bankers and selected investor groups for some years prior to the flotation in its widening search for capital.[106] This writer believes that gaps in understanding the dynamics of GPA's business continued, because there were misgivings about how GPA could both increase its existing high market share, maintain its margins and expand profits, and also compete with the fundamental suppliers — aircraft manufacturers and banks. As one adviser who had attended a number of briefing sessions put it:

> The answers given by GPA executives were inevitably imprecise. . . . In response to critical comments about the effects of deregulation and competition in international aviation, most briefings were told that the GPA 'quality assessment of customers' would avoid the bad operators or riskier markets. This seemed illogical as GPA was constantly promoting its overall share of world leasing as in the top three in the world and accounting for a bigger market share each year.[107]

Damaging press comment in spring 1992 suggesting acrimonious exchanges between the financial advisers (particularly Goldman Sachs) and GPA's top management about the proposed flotation price, with several references to Tony Ryan's views, seem to have affected earlier timing options and some market sentiment. Somewhat late in the day, P. J. Mara, a former government press secretary, was retained as a public relations consultant in March 1992. It was seen as an unusual choice by the media and financial community.[108] The *Financial Times* commented:

> Mara played a key role in Haughey's surprisingly long existence as Ireland's prime minister.
>
> PJ, as he likes to be known, is the consummate spin-doctor. He manages to keep his boss one step ahead of the baying hounds of the press corps, putting them off the scent with humorous, in-depth, off-the-record briefings . . .
>
> Nevertheless, it's a strange appointment. A bit like putting Sir Bernard Ingram, Mrs Thatcher's old mouthpiece, in charge of British Airways' public relations.[109]

Though a new advertising and active promotional policy followed, there was insufficient time to recover the lost ground. GPA executives spent endless hours on briefings to investment institutions in eight countries. It seems that this exercise started too late and was less extensive than the subsequent Wellcome Trust issue — which succeeded some weeks later.

Who lost money in GPA?

The $1 billion loss in the 1993 accounts and the terms of the financial restructuring agreed with the bankers resulted in a zero valuation being put on GPA's shares by Irish institutions. The investment write-offs affected their Irish equity portfolio performance. As a crude guide to their investment losses, Table 6.18 sets out the valuations of holdings at $10 per share. The Japanese banks along with Air Canada, Aer Lingus and the Prudential Insurance Company of America stood out as the largest investors — apart from Tony Ryan and the GPA staff. Most of the larger Irish investment institutions were shareholders. Most of the Irish, UK and Continental advisers and regional managers for the offer had acquired equity holdings. Nomura Securities and Yamaichi Securities, who were looking after Japan, were sizeable holders, as were Salomon Brothers in the USA. Surprisingly, the names of Goldman Sachs, the lead manager in the USA, or Merrill Lynch did not appear to be on the share register.[110]

Table 6.18: GPA: larger equity and preference shareholders

	Number of shares (m)*	% of total equity	Value at $10 per share ($m)
Institutions			
Mitsubishi Trust and Banking Corporation	25.60	11.3	256.00
Air Canada	21.70	9.6	217.00
Aer Lingus	19.90	8.8	199.00
Prudential Insurance Company of America	15.40	6.8	154.00
Long-Term Credit Bank of Japan	13.80	6.1	138.00
Investment Bank of Ireland	7.60	3.2	76.00
Irish Life Assurance	5.40	2.4	54.00
Citicorp	4.80	2.2	48.00
Kawasaki Enterprises	4.20	1.9	42.00
Northwestern Mutual Life Assurance	3.70	1.5	37.00
AIB Investments	3.70	1.5	37.00
Bank of Nova Scotia	3.50	1.5	35.00
NCB Trust	3.00	1.3	30.00
Ulster Investment Bank	2.90	1.3	29.00
Mitsubishi Corporation	2.90	1.3	29.00
Nippon Total Finance	2.80	1.2	28.00
Ulster Bank Nominees	2.70	1.2	27.00
Nomura International	2.70	1.2	27.00
Swiss Bank Group	2.60	1.2	26.00
			cont.

Table 6.18: GPA: larger equity and preference shareholders cont.

	Number of shares (m)*	% of total equity	Value at $10 per share ($m)
Dai-Ichi Corporation	2.40	1.1	24.00
Deutsche Bank Group	2.40	1.1	24.00
Tokio Marine & Fire Insurance	2.40	1.1	24.00
Whirlpool Financial Corporation	1.90	0.9	19.00
General Electric Credit Corporation	1.90^e	0.9	19.00
Norwich Union	1.30	0.6	13.00
Salomon Brothers (affiliate)	0.90	0.4	9.00
Foreign & Colonial	0.80	0.4	8.00
Yamaichi Securities	0.80	0.4	8.00
Public School Employees Retirement System (2nd Preference)	100.00	Pref.	100.00
Directors			
Tony Ryan	18.70	8.0	187.00
Maurice Foley	1.50		15.00
Colm Barrington	1.10		11.00
James King	0.60		6.00
Patrick Blaney	0.20		2.00
John Tierney	0.10		1.00
Sir John Harvey-Jones	0.08		0.80
Dr Garret FitzGerald	0.04		0.45
Geoffrey Knight	0.04		0.44
Peter Sutherland	0.03		0.34

* Holding based on proposed one-for-one share split if IPO had been successful.

e Estimate.

Source: IPO Prospectus, June 1992. *Annual Report 1993*. Register of Shareholders in the Companies Office, Dublin.

Reflections

This writer believes that examinership might have been the better option for the restructuring and rehabilitation of GPA as an organisation. The equivalent asset class collapse of Olympia & York in May 1992, the largest property developer in the world, went that route and recovered some shareholder value. Examinership also benefited Goodman International,

Kentz Corporation and Xtra-vision. Bankers compromised in the restructuring. In GPA the international bankers appear to have earned more money — through fees and a higher interest rate basis. In this writer's opinion the question of conflict of interest arises when one considers the players in the restructuring and rescue. Examinership might not have suited the international banks. The apparent passiveness of the Irish institutions, particularly as shareholders, in these circumstances was remarkable.

Examinership would have resulted in a different form of negotiations because of altered power structures. The international banks had the most to lose as they could not easily liquefy their security because of the impact of a 'fire-sale' of GPA aircraft on worldwide asset values. Like property, the value of security for other aircraft-related bank loans and the domino effect had to be considered. GPA's bankers and other holders of unsecured debt and commercial paper were heavily exposed in the short term. GPA borrowings were $5.6 billion at March 1993[111] and the quoted medium-term notes in New York fell in price from 99/45 in the quarter ended December 1992 to the range 67/35 three months later.[112] A debt write-down and debt-for-equity swap with bankers for part of their loans, and with aircraft manufacturers for predelivery payments, could have recapitalised GPA without such enormous fees and write-offs. The alternative option of receivership would not have suited the bankers at all.

In this writer's opinion the so-called rescue of GPA can be viewed variously as a technical bank work-out or an international financial and industrial power-play in exploiting opportunities around assets and markets, depending on the lens adopted. Not only did it leave little in shareholder value, but it reduced the original GPA organisation to a shadow of its former self. Effectively, it became a treasury and accounting mechanism. The management contract with GE Capital Aviation Services (GECAS) under the restructuring appears to have taken much of the core activity into foreign control, with perhaps different strategic objectives — though much of the operational expertise remained under GECAS in Shannon. The collapse and rescue, in essence, look to have wiped out the further possibilities for strategic development in a broad range of financial services and greater added value under GPA and Irish control. Decision-making power went elsewhere, and thus there were also public interest consequences.

This writer believes that GPA's market share fixation and self-inflicted capacity problems led to weaker quality business. The result was higher bad debts and provisions and a lower capacity utilisation experience in 1992 and

1993 as the industry cycle turned. The $10 billion aircraft purchase commitment, with $815 million deposits and predelivery advance payments, was the equivalent of the 'big project', which, combined with debt, sank a worthwhile firm. The causes of GPA's downfall are myriad and intertwined. In this writer's opinion, apart from overtrading, there was the strategic 'quantum leap' in the scale of orders for new aircraft for some years into the future, an excessive reliance on debt financing, aggressive accounting policies in profit recognition, insufficiently cautious cost analysis and pricing policies on leasing and related transactions, and a high level of overheads and staffing in an industry where margins were tight. The emphasis on market share domination was at the expense of margins, overheads and a sustainable capital structure. It conflicted with the apparent attempt to avoid dilution of control by top management. We should not forget the stress on profit growth, which seemed to be driven by the executive compensation and dividend incentive schemes, at the expense of the organisation's risk profile. There were reminders of Slater Walker Securities.

This writer believes GPA paid out excessive levels of dividends for a growth company — leading to a thinner net cash flow (before aircraft disposals) than ILFC in relation to investment growth and bank debt. After all, aircraft leasing is a capital-intensive business. These dividends could not have been paid if more conservative accounting standards had prevailed in Ireland at the time. In this writer's opinion, there were 'economic consequences' to accounting regulations in an imprudent dividend policy and a risky investment strategy. It is debatable whether GPA would have made such purchase commitments and attempted to use aircraft sales as a dual profit and financing mechanism.

The institutional investors in New York, London and Tokyo recognised the entrepreneurial and risky corporate profile and uncertain short-term outlook for GPA. The evidence suggests they concluded that the share price sought did not compensate for the risk/return profile.

The importance of timing in a public flotation clearly emerges. To a degree, GPA was unlucky. Nevertheless, the board's judgment in selecting advisers and agreeing a share price seems to have been suspect. Careful planning and well-executed public relations play a role. Doubtless, it is easy to use hindsight to say that the deferment of the flotation in spring 1990 was a fundamental mistake. Stockmarkets go through cycles, but it was clear that in early 1990 they had strengthened compared with previous years.

In this writer's opinion, the effectiveness of the board in decision-making and strategic control must be questioned in view of GPA's overtrading and weakening risk profile — particularly as regards the mismatch between future commitments, capital structure and the industry downturn. GPA seemed to have all the trappings of good governance, but in reality the dominance of Tony Ryan and the power of the top management team appear to have held sway, from this writer's viewpoint. Eventually, governance flaws, through the weak board structure and a small number the non-executive directors, were critical. Miller's 'Impulsive Syndrome' captures many of the elements.

In retrospect, it seems that, just like Xtra-vision, GPA was not suited to be a quoted public company because of its management style and culture at the time. Up to that point, in this writer's opinion GPA had controlled almost every aspect of its business in a manner which seemed to benefit management. The share prices struck for the Irish 'grey market' and the small number of trades look to have been an inadequate barometer to share value for a sale of $800 million on an open public market. Obtaining finance through secured bank debt or unsecured medium-term debt on the New York market was quite a different matter from raising equity — which is a much riskier security. It seems that the GPA team thought they could also 'manage' the critical elements of the IPO. In the stand-off of 'let's see who needs who', when it came to price, New York voted with its feet; London followed the cue and so did Tokyo. Ireland was destined to play a minor role because of the scale of the issue in relation to the domestic financial institutions and their existing holdings in GPA.

Could GPA's collapse have been predicted? One cannot ignore the six years of consistent cash flow/funding gap which was plugged by increasing amounts of bank debt. GPA followed the pattern of the earlier fast-growth entrepreneurial adolescent firms. Sixteen months before it was in discussions with its bankers, it would have scored a minimum 61, a danger sign, on Argenti's model. It would have risen to 76 before the flotation. Perhaps many of the financial institutions fully appreciated the danger zone GPA was in — before it did itself. Sir Lewis Robertson's views on executive structure, financial control, multiple banks and covenants were borne out — as was his conclusion about the feebleness of institutional investors.[113]

The cluster of themes leading to distress in GPA was closer to that in Goodman International than in most of the other cases already examined. Both were profitable organisations, but the difference was that Larry Goodman understood profits, productivity and risk — apart from the London adventure. Both had an insufficient understanding of public relations and the importance of attention to the media — until it was too late. GPA's own attitude may have angered the British media. Nevertheless, there were some worrying jingoistic and discriminatory attitudes, in turn, which suggest that the London market may not always be the optimum arena for certain types of Irish companies to raise equity. Going directly to New York may have proved more efficient.

The failed flotation was the third crucial turning point, the others being the large aircraft order in 1989 and the decision not to seek a quotation in 1990. It led to an evaporation of confidence, which is such a critical ingredient in a capital-intensive business, particularly one with such financial commitments. Within two months a downward spiral of decline commenced and GPA could not escape the outcome. Arrogance was its Achilles' heel. In this writer's opinion its management was so overtly confident of the success of the IPO that no 'fallback' or contingency plan seems to have been in place to maintain at least $1 billion in shareholder value.

An aggressive attitude and excessive self-confidence were part of GPA's style. These characteristics look to have blinded its top management and the next tier of senior executives to the realities of the conflict between their aircraft purchasing strategy and the changing market conditions of the economic recession and the Gulf war. In this writer's opinion GPA's culture led to an attempt to impose its view on the capital market. It lost heavily, because management seems to have been blinkered to the economics and psychology of that market. GPA's weakness was that it had insufficient experience of a recession in its business and this was reflected in its naive modelling of a cyclical downturn. Houston's stress on the timing of expansion and the stage in the economic cycle was well illustrated.[115] Greed and bad luck played their role.

Chapter 7

Arthur Guinness and P. J. Carroll: Diversification and Decline of a Core Business

I'm the chief executive and intend to remain here as long as God will permit me.
Armand Hammer, chairman of Occidental Petroleum, on the occasion of his eighty-second birthday when he refused to name a successor.[1]

Introduction

What have Arthur Guinness, P. J. Carroll, Irish Press and Waterford Wedgwood in common? All were extremely successful 'family' companies which encountered a crisis, the roots of which can be traced to some aspect of ineffectual family influence. In each case the organisation's decline was evident for some time and it was, or should have been, realised internally. The scale of the financial crisis and the period of turnaround, and its degree of success, varied enormously.

Guinness and Carroll are taken together as they offer similar lessons regarding diversification losses and marketing management deterioration leading to a blindness to customer and market changes in their core business. Both were able to trade out of their setbacks without any financial reorganisation or special support, though in Guinness many employees were laid off. P. J. Carroll stopped paying dividends for some years. Arising out of various crises, the 'family' chairmen had to step down, thus ending continuity at the helm which had lasted for 227 and 136 years respectively.

Arthur Guinness Son and Company Limited[2]
Background

Technically or financially speaking, it could be argued that Guinness is no longer an Irish company but one of the UK's larger multinational drinks exporters, with a turnover of over Stg£4 billion. Its takeover of Bell's and Distillers, a major section of the Scottish whiskey industry, in 1985 and 1986 utterly changed its character. Nevertheless, Guinness was founded in Ireland, and for almost two hundred years its head office was in the St

James's Gate brewery in Dublin. The very essence of Guinness as a drink is synonymous with Dublin and Irishness.

Founded in Dublin by Arthur Guinness in 1759, it initially concentrated on brewing ale. It was not until 1796 that 'porter' was produced. The term 'stout' seems to have emerged from a heavier form of dark porter, known as 'stout porter'. By 1799 Arthur Guinness had abandoned brewing other beers and specialised in porter.

There would be no shortage of heirs as Arthur fathered twenty-one children by his wife Olivia, of whom ten survived. Upon his death in 1803, aged seventy-eight, following a life of energy and business ambition, Arthur Guinness left valuable personal estate, a thriving brewery and his name on the product that was to become internationally famous — Guinness stout.[3]

The brewery continued under direct family management into the twentieth century, despite a Stock Exchange quotation in London in 1886, with the help of Barings, the leading merchant bank. This event was evidence of the company's success — the issue was heavily oversubscribed though there was controversy about the allocation of shares to Dublin. The Guinness family retained one-third of the shares, but continued to dominate the board with six seats.[4] If the Dublin stockbroking and investor community felt aggrieved by the flotation, the same could not be said of the Guinness employees — everyone received a bonus of between one and three months' wages. This was testament to the company's culture of benevolent and enlightened policies towards its employees, apart from the extensive civic works in Dublin and London in housing and other social facilities.

By 1906 St James's Gate had become the largest brewery in the world, and was earning annual profits of over £1 million.[5] An internal management and supervisory ladder, leading to the top position of brewer, became the basis of the organisation structure. The brewery building programme was so extensive, from giant copper tanks to internal railways, that a brewing equipment modernisation and replacement programme did not have to be initiated until the 1970s. Edward Guinness, the younger son of Benjamin (who was the grandson of the founder, Arthur), was in charge from 1876 until just before his eightieth birthday in 1927. It must be a record in family business that the Guinness brewery in Dublin had been in the hands of just four family members, in direct lineage, for 168 years. Rupert, the second Earl of Iveagh, took the helm, aged fifty-three, and was soon to make his distinctive and positive contribution by introducing advertising — thus breaking with family tradition. Rupert's only surviving son, Arthur, was killed in action in World War II but the extraordinary

Guinness longevity ensured that, before he died aged ninety-three, he had passed the chairmanship over to his grandson, Benjamin, in 1961.

Key events in the life of Guinness	
1759	Arthur Guinness acquires St James's Gate brewery in Dublin. Initially brews ales.
1796	Commences brewing 'porter'.
1799	'Stout' (also known as 'dark porter') brewed.
1803	Arthur Guinness dies aged seventy-eight. Second son, named Arthur also, takes over.
1822	Brewery concentrates on high-quality 'porter'.
1824	Exports to Britain commence.
1855	Benjamin (aged fifty-seven) succeeds Arthur (aged eighty-seven).
1868	Arthur and Edward, Benjamin's oldest and youngest sons, take over.
1876	Edward buys out Arthur.
1885	Edward becomes the first Lord Iveagh.
1886	Guinness obtains share quotation on the London Stock Exchange. Company now largest enterprise in Ireland.
1906	Company net profit over £1 million.
1910–18	Extensive investment in St James's Gate brewery modernisation and expansion.
1919	Company net profit over £2 million.
1927	Edward (aged eighty) passes over the chairmanship to his son Rupert (aged fifty-three).
1929	Company commences advertising – 'Guinness is good for you'.
1932	Guinness employs approximately 4,500 in Ireland.
1934–35	New brewery built at Park Royal, London.
1945	Rupert's only surviving son, Arthur, killed in action in Second World War.
1960–65	New breweries built in Nigeria, Ghana, Malaysia and Jamaica. Draught stout sales volume expands as a result of new keg and dispenser system technology and improvement to quality. Guinness joins other brewery groups in developing Harp lager in Britain and Ireland.
1961	Rupert (aged eighty-eight) passes over the chairmanship to his grandson, Benjamin (aged twenty-five).
1973	Group turnover £223 million and net profit £14 million.
1974–80	Guinness makes large number of acquisitions and investments in non-brewing sectors.

cont.

Key events in the life of Guinness *cont.*	
1976	Group turnover £499 million and net profit £20 million.
1979	Group turnover £687 million and net profit £32 million.
1981	Group turnover £906 million and net profit £7 million.
	Between 1973 and 1981, Guinness's market share falls from 10.5% to 6.2% in Britain and approximately from 90% to 80% in Ireland.
	Share price falls heavily to 51p.
	Ernest Saunders recruited as new chief executive.
1982	Group turnover £1.0 billion and a net loss of £26 million recorded.
	Saunders initiates massive group restructuring, involving disposals of most of non-brewing interests and brewery cost-cutting, efficiency and modernisation programmes.
1983	Turnover reduced to £872 million but profit recovery to £23 million.
	Extensive market research, marketing and advertising investment.
1985	Volume growth in stout. Turnover £1.2 billion and net profit of £51 million.
	Acquisition of Bell's (quoted medium-sized Scottish whiskey group).
1986	Controversial acquisition of Distillers (quoted giant Scottish whiskey group).
	Lord Iveagh (Benjamin Guinness) becomes president and Ernest Saunders assumes chairmanship with role of chief executive also.
1987	Department of Trade and Industry appoints inspectors to conduct an inquiry into circumstances of Distillers takeover.
	Ernest Saunders dismissed. New outside chairman; board and top management reorganised.
1990	Saunders, merchant banker, stockbroker and other businessmen brought to court by Serious Fraud Office, London.
	Saunders and others jailed.

Product, market and competitive position

Because the drink's consistency is heavier than ale, Guinness charged more for its product. An added advantage was that its longer life enabled it to be exported, particularly to the former British colonies, much more easily than ales. Though sales of Guinness stout dominated the Irish beer market, the greater proportion of the firm's output was sold in the UK. Guinness had been shipping its stout to England through Liverpool and Bristol since 1824 and a combination of superior brewing techniques and consistently high quality, which was the cornerstone of the business, helped make inroads into the English market.

Guinness was thought to have medicinal qualities. It was seen as an ingredient in the therapeutic process in recovery from illness or as a restorative after a day's work. Officers and soldiers were first reported to have called for it during the Peninsular and other colonial wars. This was probably the start of the 'health' properties folklore. The slogan 'Guinness is good for you' was launched in England in 1929, leading to a modest expansion of sales. Bensons produced a series of imaginative and entertaining (but not hard-selling) advertising ideas, which did not upset the Guinness family business concept. That firm held the advertising account for forty years until J. Walter Thompson took over in 1968.

Between 1934 and 1936 a second brewery was built in Park Royal, London. This project was a milestone. The Guinness brewery in Dublin was not only the largest enterprise in the country; its needs as a modern brewery required that it provide many of its own supplies, partially because of the weak economic and business infrastructure in the country at the time. Part of the reason for setting up the London brewery was concern over the outcome of the 'economic war' between Britain and Ireland and how the firm's exports to Britain might be affected. The more modern Park Royal brewery led to a major reduction in the role of the management of St James's Gate brewery in the overall strategic direction of the Guinness group. Separate subsidiary companies were established and the group head office moved to London in the 1950s. Under clearly defined trading responsibilities between the two breweries, St James's Gate was allocated the north of England from Liverpool.

In 1981 the UK accounted for about two-thirds of Guinness's stout sales in the UK and Ireland. Almost half the output of the Irish brewery supported this market. Guinness stout was positioned at premium beer prices in the UK to provide an attractive gross profit margin. This was designed as an incentive to the tied houses (which were usually owned by British breweries) to carry it as a product which was not in competition with their group's house ales. A decline in beer consumption in the UK between 1979 and 1982 led to a fall in production from 41.2 million barrels to 36.5 million barrels. Major changes in taste had occurred. Lager beer had grown rapidly from 15% of the market in 1973 to 33% by 1981. It grew further in the mid-1980s, with Continental products such as Carlsberg making inroads. This was stimulated by the demands of the younger drinking population — those aged under thirty-four were estimated to account for 64% of the consumption of draught lager. Consequently, the 'pub' and 'take-home' markets had become extremely competitive.

A feature of the UK beer market was the 'tied house' nature of its distribution system, which was dominated by the 'big six' breweries that controlled about 76% of the market. Bass held about 20% of the UK market, with a pub estate of almost 7,500 houses. Allied-Lyons held about 13%, followed by Whitbread with about 12%; Grand Metropolitan, and Scottish and Newcastle both held about 11%. Courage held about 9%. In addition, there were a large number of small but very active regional brewers. In contrast, Guinness owned no 'tied houses' and was stocked in about half of them.[6] In brief, Guinness was becoming a marginal player in the UK market, offering an expensive niche product (to older traditional drinkers) with a declining demand. Its stout sales had fallen from a 10.5% market share in 1973 to about 6.2% in 1981.[7] Guinness also participated in a consortium brewing Harp lager in the UK, but its earlier good performance had weakened.

In Ireland, Guinness's dominant market share of the beer market in the early 1980s was under threat. Stout and ale were losing market share to lager, similar to the UK experience. Though Guinness controlled Harp lager production and marketing in Ireland, it was losing market share to Heineken, which had bought Murphy's brewery in Cork. Foster's and Carlsberg were being brewed under licence and marketed actively by another Cork brewery, Beamish & Crawford. This significantly greater competition by multinational lager brands was a threat to the group's major source of profit, in view of the very weak profit performance in the UK. Clearly Guinness had both product and marketing problems. The primary product, Guinness stout, appeared to have passed through a plateau in demand and to have entered the decline stage of the product life-cycle though it had created a strong quality image — improved draught stout technology had led to a growth in demand in the 1970s. During the 1970s marketing of Harp lager in the UK and Ireland had been successful, but later it lost market share to the fashionable Continental lagers.[8]

In the 1960s and 1970s, the group's expansion arose from the successful promotion of draught as distinct from bottled Guinness, and the building of new Guinness breweries in Nigeria, Cameroon, Ghana, Malaysia and Jamaica. Guinness was also brewed under licence in fifteen other countries. In Ireland, having spotted the trend towards lighter drinks, the group had redeveloped the old Great Northern Brewery in Dundalk to produce Harp lager. In 1962 Guinness also linked up with Ind Coope, a leading UK brewery, bringing together Macardle Moore and Cherry's under the banner of Allied Irish Breweries. Two years later Guinness acquired the long-established Smithwick's brewery of Kilkenny, which commanded a strong position in the ale market. The quality and life-cycle of draught stout were improved through new technology in dispensing, storage and distribution systems. These improvements, together with the advent of metal kegs, meant that draught stout volumes increased so much that production capacity problems emerged.

The Dublin efficiency and capacity dilemma

Due to capacity constraints in the Park Royal brewery the question arose as to whether it would be feasible to build a new third brewery in the north of England or expand one or both of the existing breweries to meet demand. There were now separate managing directors in Dublin and London, both reporting to a group managing director in the London head office. Eventually, the board decided in favour of a Dublin capacity expansion — provided it achieved a much lower operating cost structure. Dublin was overmanned in comparison with most of its competitors. This became the stimulant to the first development plan 1971–76, when a reduction of 1,100 employees was attained compared to the target of 1,400.

Paddy Galvin, a Catholic, was the first 'outsider', in terms of religion and work experience, to be promoted to personnel director and appointed to the Dublin board in the mid-1970s. By 1984 he had been put in charge of all the group's breweries in Ireland. Galvin was the agent of sweeping changes in attitudes, structural and managerial reorganisation, facilities modernisation, rationalisation and work practices. A combination of sensitive negotiations with trade unions, widespread communication and consultation with employees, and an investment programme of £140 million in new technology and redundancy helped underpin the brewery's competitiveness at the time. The establishment of a Brewery Council in St James's Gate, with representatives of all disciplines and crafts, was a vital ingredient in the process of spreading understanding of the need for change in order to remain competitive. The council improved communications and information flows, ensuring greater employee discussion of decisions and feedback to management. Employment was reduced from 3,600 to 2,500. The 'continuous competitiveness plan', initiated in the mid-1980s, combined with the complete rebuilding of the brewery, with state of the art technology, reduced employment to 1,600 in 1987 and 900 in 1992. The productivity and profitability gains were immense. By 1992 the group's Irish operations earned profits of £123 million and paid a dividend of £98 million to its parent in London.

The Guinness culture

The Guinness family was a benevolent employer. There was a wide range of medical and sporting facilities for its employees, as compared to other large firms. Generations of Dublin families worked at St James's Gate.

A bureaucratic and old-fashioned hierarchical management style and organisation had operated. Ferry claimed:

> The company could not understand change, only preservation. It could not understand growth, only moderating the decline. Inside the breweries, highly trained chemists still bore job titles with the word 'Brewer', as if PhD chemists were meant to be flattered by the Victorian-style craftsman title. The anachronism extended to many areas of management . . . Ian Cheshire, a young management consultant brought in by Saunders, saw the old management as symptomatic of Britain's paternalistic management culture of the 1970s. 'They were gents, well bred, chummy, all with nice houses. They saw themselves as neo-aristocrats, behaving decently and selling beer to a decent public'.[9]

There was a dominance of brewer/management recruitment from Oxford and Cambridge.[10] Guinness was the first brewery to recruit first-class chemists and other scientists. The aim was to adopt a scientific approach to brewing and consistent quality. This scientific culture eventually expanded beyond the brewing process as use was made of statistical analysis in the management of operations. Thus the 'brewer system' (as it was known) became the foundation for a new cadre of top and middle management. Bobby Howick, a former sales director, claimed 'there was still a strong element of the old school tie. A chap who went to Trinity College (Dublin) would not be considered good enough. You had to come from Cambridge or Oxford to be considered a brewer.'[11] Nevertheless, this Oxbridge recruitment system must surely be seen as part of the success of Guinness and the quality of the product for over sixty years, until it had outlived its usefulness. It was not until the 1960s that changes in recruitment and management promotion policies began to infiltrate the Dublin brewery. These followed initiatives promoted by General Sir Charles Harvey who had a strong interest in modern management principles.[12] Harvey was an assistant managing director with responsibility for personnel matters. His more enlightened approach broke the ground for changes in recruitment and promotion. The increase in sales volumes of draught stout and the impact of other brewery changes forced Guinness to change its own approach to management structure. By the mid-1960s the 'brewer system' as the foundation stone of the company's strong development in the twentieth century had outlived its usefulness. New types of expertise and a wider source of graduate intake and internal promotion, particularly in marketing and personnel management, were urgently needed.

John Lynch, later director general of FÁS who began his career as a 'boy' with Guinness, likened the hierarchy of the company to the British army — a paternalistic but benevolent place to work, where only Protestants could aspire to the higher salaried positions. This can be seen more as a reflection of the dominant management culture and values of Guinness rather than as religious discrimination. Lynch recalled:

> You had the chief executive General Sir Charles Harvey. Underneath him were a whole series of brewers. Those would be the colonels. Beneath them were the departmental managers, the majors. Below them were the number one clerks . . .
>
> Then there was the labouring class as it was known. It was highly structured. The supervisors would be the sergeant majors and the rest were foot soldiers.[13]

F. W. Peard, deputy managing director of Guinness in the 1970s, who had started in St James's Gate in 1939, observed: 'In those days Guinness was a production-dominated company, dedicated to making good beer, and more and more of it. The black stuff sold itself. The profits rolled in and accountants were required only to measure the dimension!'[14] Demand was so strong that the important criterion was the quality of the stout. This underpinned the dominant brewer group's extensive role in the organisation's affairs for generations. The brewer group produced all the top management internally and became the 'professional' managers as the Guinness family handed over power. The London and Dublin managing directors were always brewers. They met the demands of the various stakeholders in Guinness up to the 1960s. The narrowness of their focus was exposed by a series of changes — in the market, in the industry structure and competition, and in the industrial relations climate.

When the elderly Rupert Guinness handed over the reins of power to his young grandson Benjamin in 1961, it was a fateful decision. At the time

Benjamin was twenty-five years old, having just finished his studies at Oxford. It seems that his business experience was negligible. By all accounts, he had little liking or aptitude for commercial management. A combination of living in Ireland (for tax reasons) and poor health appears to have had implications for his board effectiveness, leaving a vacuum in the supervision of the group's top management who were based in London. Benjamin's principal interests were horses and literature. He was considered to be shy and retiring.[15] It was, perhaps, an unavoidable but untimely responsibility to thrust on Benjamin, even allowing for family exigencies and tradition. What was now a much more complex group, with two bureaucratic management structures spanning two separate 'kingdoms', was about to face a new competitive climate in Ireland and the UK. Guinness, as a mature organisation, was compelled to urgently develop a new corporate strategy. Like P. J. Carroll, Guinness had to cope with the impact on volume demand of changing government budgetary policies from the mid-1960s with a greater reliance on excise duties.

An insight into the interweaving of the Guinness family identity with the values of the business is provided by Benjamin's comments in 1979, on the retirement of his relations Lord Moyne and Lady Dufferin after forty-five and thirty years on the main board:

> I believe that we have derived considerable strength from the fact that members of the Guinness family have been close and active in their participation in the business since the start at the St James's Gate Brewery in 1759. By this link through 220 years, we have built on the traditions which characterise your Company, based as they are on a high standard of integrity and quality of the products and services we offer to our customers.[16]

Financial performance

By 1973 the group's total turnover had reached £232 million and pre-tax profits were £24 million. In the early 1970s, Guinness was one of the UK's top 100 companies in terms of market capitalisation on the London Stock Exchange. By 1981, its share price (having adjusted for the one-for-one scrip issue in 1980) had fallen to a mere 51p and its market capitalisation was less than half the value of some years earlier.

As summarised in Table 7.1, pre-tax profits peaked at £53 million in 1979 and declined to £43 million in 1980. Thus earnings per share fell by 23% in 1980 and by a further 27.7% in 1981. The reported earnings per share as shown on the face of the accounts appeared to be ample for a dividend payment.[17] Dividend cover was shown at 2.7 times and 1.9 times in 1980 and 1981 respectively.[18] At the net profit level, after extraordinary charges 'below the line' the picture was very different. Despite a near quadrupling of turnover to £906 million in the decade to 1981 (representing a near 18% compound growth rate), net profits had slumped to just £7 million and did not cover the dividend of almost £9 million in 1981. The net loss of £26 million in 1982 was due to extensive write-offs and provisions in extraordinary items of £49 million — following disposals and closures and the withdrawal from film financing and distribution. The dividend, which had been static for three years to 1981, now appeared to be under threat because it was paid out of reserves.

The decline in Guinness's performance was such that by 1981 it no longer qualified for inclusion on the UK top 100 companies, yet it employed 21,900 people worldwide (of whom 11,600 were in the UK). With the divestment of non-brewing activities and the forceful drive for

Table 7.1: Guinness: financial performance (£m)

	Turnover	Trading profit	Interest charges	Pre-tax profit*	Extra-ordinary items	Net profit/(loss)**	Dividend
1973	232	22	3	24	(2)	14	4
1974	272	23	4	23	1	10	4
1975	339	29	6	29	2	17	5
1976	414	36	6	39	3	20	5
1977	499	39	6	40	2	22	6
1978	643	44	7	45	2	23	7
1979	687	53	11	53	(2)	32	9
1980	784	47	13	43	1	22	9
1981	906	42	14	42	10	7	9
1982	1,043	54	16	51	49	(26)	9
1983	872	51	8	59	7	23	10
1984	924	61	7	70	10	28	12
1985	1,188	81	13	86	3	51	21

*   Pre-tax profit has been arrived at by adding share of profits of associated companies.

** After deducting taxation, extraordinary charges and minority interests. The basis of the taxation charge was altered in 1978. Data not adjusted retrospectively beyond 1975 — no data available.

Source: Annual reports.

greater brewing productivity and modernisation, the total number employed worldwide had fallen to 12,600 by 1983.

The evidence of the decline in the company's performance had been obvious for some years. Its trading margins on turnover had halved between 1973 and 1981, falling on a consistent basis from 9.5% to 4.6%. The reasons for this were a decline in brewing margins from 9.8% in 1976 to 7.7% in 1981 and low margins culminating in net losses in 1981 on diversified activities, which accounted for almost one-third of total turnover. Guinness's profit margins were consistently lower than those of its main competitors in the UK, such as Bass and Whitbread, as demonstrated by the figures in Table 7.2.

Table 7.2: A comparison of brewers' profit margins (%)

	Guinness	Whitbread	Bass
1977	9.6	10.6	n/av.
1978	8.3	9.7	10.8
1979	9.6	10.3	10.4
1980	7.7	10.4	10.0
1981	6.6	11.0	8.7

Definition: Profit before interest and tax in relation to turnover. Profit includes 'associates' contribution.

Source: Based on *Investor's Chronicle* materials.

Though there were underlying differences in business structure (Guinness did not have 'tied houses'), nevertheless, the Guinness profit margin had dropped significantly below those of Whitbread and Bass. It is the trend in the relative decline which signals deteriorating operating efficiency allied to weak top management and board control. Return on shareholders' funds (book value) was poor for some years. At 8.5% in 1981 it was clearly uneconomic when compared with interest rates and inflation at the time.[19]

The stockmarket viewed Guinness as a declining company with poor prospects.[20] Its share price recovered from 51p to 70p following the news in October 1981 that Ernest Saunders had joined Guinness as the new managing director and that two other senior executives had been recruited as part of a top management shake-up. An additional consideration was that Guinness had announced that it was maintaining its dividend. The market had been predicting a fall in profits and there was a very real worry that the dividend would have to be reduced. The *Investor's Chronicle* commented:

Shareholders in Arthur Guinness should be pleased on two main counts with the group's results . . . First, the final dividend has been maintained, which looked unlikely at one stage. Secondly, Guinness is reaffirming its intention to crack down harder on its motley collection of non-brewing interests, which have been a persistent drain in recent years.[21]

Though its market capitalisation had increased from £89 million to £123 million, it was almost exactly half the 'book value' of the 1981 shareholders' funds of £243 million. The gap between market and book values suggested that Guinness was a potential takeover target. At 70p Guinness shares traded on a price/earnings ratio of 9 times compared to 10.6 times for Bass. One indicator of the stockmarket analysts' concerns was the fact that Guinness shares were on a dividend yield of 10% compared with a much lower 6.8% yield for Bass. In a direct indication of a rerating of Guinness by analysts, between early 1979 and mid-1981 the Guinness share price fell by 45% in comparison with the FT Actuaries Brewers and Distillers Index.

Guinness's strategic weaknesses in the UK

As a measure of its decline, by 1981 Guinness reported a UK turnover of £405 million but trading profits of a mere £6 million. In contrast, the Republic of Ireland operations generated a trading profit of £28 million on a turnover of £282 million. Non-brewing activities, which were primarily in the UK, accounted for almost one-third of the group's turnover but produced a trading loss of £3 million in 1981, compared to a modest profit of £6 million in the previous year. In summary, the Irish operations were providing most of the group's profit. This raised questions about the effectiveness of the London management, and the group acquisition and diversification strategy in the UK.[22]

The Bass and Whitbread dividends had increased annually in contrast to the static dividend in Guinness. By 1981 the Guinness dividend was not sustainable without a major improvement in profitability. In particular, if the profit contribution from 'associates' was stripped out (it was £13.5 million in 1981, compared with £8.5 million in 1980), there would have been a loss in 1981. From a financial gearing perspective, the profit cover for bank interest charges was falling sharply. If the contribution from associates (it appears that about half was received in dividends) and the extraordinary items charged 'below the line' were deducted from the profit reported, the interest cover in 1981 would have been very weak at one and a half times.

Table 7.3: Guinness: trading profits (£m)

	Brewing	Other activities	Total
1976	31	5	36
1977	29	10	39
1978	31	14	45
1979	40	15	55
1980	44	6	50
1981	48	(3)	45

Note: 'Trading profit' is calculated before charging bank interest, central management costs, taxation and 'extraordinary items' (which amounted to £10 million in 1981).
Source: Annual reports.

The combination of weakening market position, productivity, profitability and financial status indicated that Guinness was in decidedly weak circumstances by early 1982 and seemed to be in a downward spiral. In pressing for security, it was not surprising that the banks looked to their own interests.

In retrospect, in this writer's opinion it seems that Guinness suffered from a combination of benign deterioration of its core brewing business and a series of problematic diversification investments for perhaps a decade prior to its near precipitation into financial disaster in 1982.

Cash flow profile

The extent of the Guinness group's financial vulnerability can be gauged from the fact that between 1981 and 1983 its bankers moved from a long-standing position where almost all facilities were unsecured to one where almost half were secured by charges on its assets. For a number of years up to 1982 Guinness had not earned sufficient cash flow to cover its fixed asset investment. This was surprising for a profitable mature organisation, particularly when there had been limited investment in brewing production modernisation and technology. As a consequence of the weak levels of cash flow, financing shortfalls had been funded by increasing amounts of bank borrowing. A summary of its cash flow profile is shown in Table 7.4.

The failed diversification strategy

Acquisitions in the 1960s and 1970s helped non-brewing activities account for 27% of total turnover by 1977. In that year the proportion of the group's

Table 7.4: Guinness: cash flow profile (£m)

	1979	1980	1981	1982
Cash flow from operations	66	53	56	26
less				
Taxes	16	14	19	23
Dividends	9	9	9	9
	25	23	28	32
Working capital	(16)	(8)	(4)	24
Net cash generated	25	22	24	18
Fixed asset and other investments	40	45	39	25
Financing shortfall	(15)	(23)	(15)	(7)
Funded by:				
Sale of assets	8	5	4	38
Bank loans	24	4	36	(25)
Change in cash position	17	(14)	25	6

Source: Annual reports; computations by author.

£39 million trading profit (mainly from 'general trading') which was accounted for by non-brewing activities jumped to £9.8 million from £4.9 million the previous year. This had resulted from a deliberate diversification strategy.[23] Lord Iveagh explained that to achieve a growth objective and to be less vulnerable to government actions in the major drinks markets, the strategy was to widen the earnings base. He provided an insight into top management thinking:

> This policy has taken us into a wide number of business areas . . . but in almost all cases you will notice that the activities have the common theme that we are trying to get closer to the ultimate customer. We aim to use our experience in marketing and branding these products or services to supply both the industrial and the individual consumer.
>
> We have chosen to follow this policy over the past years by developing relatively small units in each field rather than by the acquisition of large companies.[24]

The diversification investments in the 1970s fell under the following headings:

- confectionery
- general trading
- plastics and materials handling
- leisure
- meat and fish processing
- film financing and distribution.

It was an extraordinarily diverse range of interests with a very problematic thread between internal organisational competencies and customers. Confectionery included Nuttalls sweets and Callard & Bowser, the manufacturer of world-famous toffees. General trading included Drummonds chain of chemist shops, Crookes Laboratories (pharmaceuticals), Lavells newsagents, photographic distribution, engineering, biotechnology, baby toiletries and children's clothes. By 1980 the Guinness group controlled 306 shops. Plastics and materials handling investments had evolved out of the usage of plastic in the distribution of beer. GPG International of that division was the largest injection moulder of plastics in the UK. In 1977, Guinness acquired a controlling interest in White Child & Beney, which operated in the related field of containers and shop equipment supplies. In 1980 Li-Lo was bought, bringing the group into plastic products for houseware, gardening, sports and leisure. The primary investments in the leisure industry were the cruiser hire interests on the Canal du Midi, the Loire Line operating on the Canal Lateral à la Loire, the Norfolk Broads in the UK and the Emerald Star Line on the Shannon. In addition, Guinness acquired extensive sailing and holiday interests in the Aegean and the Caribbean. It was suggested that Guinness controlled the largest leisure fleet in western Europe.[25]

This scatter-gun range of investments immediately provokes questions about focus of competence, and coping with diversity. The diversification strategy did not link in with any existing expertise or distribution system, other than the claimed expertise in marketing and branding. This is questionable considering the poor marketing and market share performance in the UK, its largest market, before the arrival of Ernest Saunders. One wonders how blinkered Guinness was to its own weaknesses and to the need for comprehensive and timely management information and control systems.

By 1980 Guinness publicly acknowledged that, in comparison with other brewing companies,

> . . . most of our other businesses have been much harder hit by the recession. Volumes and margins have suffered, causing a serious drop in profits. . . . The speed at which the recession developed caught some managements less well prepared than we had hoped, but the experience has taught us some lessons.[26]

Trading profits in the non-brewing activities slumped from £15.2 million in 1979 to £5.4 million in 1980. It was an expensive learning exercise for management, the board and the suffering shareholders. In 1981, Lord Iveagh, in his first admission of a retreat from the disastrous diversification strategy so recently justified, viewed the year as a watershed one.[27] There was a reference to a need for improved profitability and the strengthening of planning and management. There was no mention of the role and structure of the board. The single most important decision taken that year was to recruit a firm of head-hunters, who introduced Ernest Saunders to Guinness. He joined as the new group managing director from October 1981.

The fundamental causes of Guinness's problems

How did Guinness deteriorate into such a weak commercial and financial position? What did it do to recover so strongly and so quickly? What prompted the board to take remedial action before it was too late?

In this writer's opinion the fundamental causes of Guinness's problems were its weak board, the organisational structure, an absence of clearly defined strategic objectives linked to strict planning and control, and an unduly paternalistic and inbred culture. In 1981 the parent board consisted of seventeen directors, of whom eight represented some branch of the Guinness family. Remarkably, the apparent expectation of the Guinness 'birthright' to board membership was continued in October 1979 with the co-option of the Marquess of Dufferin and Ava, the Hon. Finn Guinness and the Hon. Simon Lennox-Boyd. Lord Iveagh enlightened his shareholders by informing them: 'These younger members of the Guinness family had spent a substantial part of this year visiting many parts of our Group in order to familiarise themselves with our business'.[28] Peter Guinness worked in an executive capacity in looking after the overseas activities. Six non-family executive directors sat on the board: A. J. Purssell, the group managing director (who had joined the organisation in 1948 and came up through the brewing side in London and Dublin); M. R. Hatfield and

M. Hely Huchinson, the managing directors of the London and Dublin brewing subsidiaries; M. B. Ogle who headed the general trading activities; S. E. Darmon who looked after the plastics and materials handling business; and W. A. Spicer, the group financial director. Robert McNeile, former managing director of the Guinness parent company who had been recruited as a brewer in 1936, was deputy chairman. There were just two non-executive non-family directors: A. C. Parsons, the senior partner of the firm of lawyers who advised Guinness, and Dr T. K. Whitaker, a former leading Irish civil servant.

The board's composition looks to have been weak in a number of respects. In the opinion of the writer, it was unwieldy: there were too many 'family' members with insufficient business expertise to contribute, while the large number of powerful executive directors helped them dominate the accountability process and policy formation. The opportunity for the two non-executive directors to play an effective role within such a board structure was limited, and they also appeared to have little direct business expertise.

The power of the executive directors looks to have been reinforced by the composition of the 'Managing Director's Committee' which was chaired by A. J. Purssell. The 1979 and 1980 annual reports stated that the committee 'advises and makes recommendations to the Board'. The Guinness organisation could be viewed as a series of 'baronies' or independent fiefdoms. This was partially due to history — the founding role of the Dublin brewery in markets and expertise, the transfer of parentage to London in the 1950s and the subsequent creation of two separate brewing subsidiaries with their own top management groups.[29] Some directors took a personal interest in the diversified activities. Ogle was a forceful character. It seems that an unspoken policy of not questioning one another's responsibilities may have tended to prevail.

Much of what was suggested by other writers about the absence of management accounting information or the weakness of planning and control systems seems exaggerated.[30] Several months before each year end, the larger companies had a formal objectives and strategic review with the subsequent preparation of detailed annual budgets and three-year plans. In turn, there was systematic monitoring of actual against budget. In some of the diversified overseas activities, controls were weaker. Information on the weakening performance trends, particularly in the UK, was available to the group managing director and the board. The management defect suggests an absence of strong group leadership and a reluctance to take tough decisions. Both Purssell and the board should have demanded better performance from management. Essentially the board was a passive forum on strategic and operational control. Almost a decade earlier, Channon, when discussing family business, noted that Guinness 'did not impose great pressure on its management'.[31] This relaxed attitude appears to have contributed to the organisation's decline.

Ernest Saunders was highly critical of the board processes he encountered on joining Guinness:

> What struck me most forcefully when I went through that first meeting was the absence of any facts and any sense of urgency, despite the picture painted by the brokers' reports. There was lots of chat and many opinions on all sorts of subjects from a group of what seemed to be very pleasant people talking as if they were in a private club.[32]

Though this description may have been coloured by subsequent events, it comes close to this writer's research evidence. Not only had Guinness drifted into being a sleepy organisation, but this decline had been enabled by docile London investment institutions. The Guinness board (primarily seven of the eight family members) controlled directly only 3.6 million ordinary shares. When family beneficial and other interests are added the amount totalled 18.6 million — which was 10.6% of the issued equity. Even when the Iveagh Trustees' holding of an additional 6.25%, allied to other associated holdings, are included the board's influential voting power was probably less than 20%. Institutions and, to a lesser extent, small shareholders controlled almost 80% of the voting equity, yet their representation on the board seemed minimal.

The Saunders turnaround and transformation of Guinness

Lord Iveagh's resolve to strengthen management and improve profitability appears to have come from two sources: pressure from the London institutions and his concern that the dividend would have to be reduced in 1982. Iveagh head-hunted Ernest Saunders from Nestlé in Switzerland. Saunders insisted on the title of managing director, thus forcing A. J. Purssell to become deputy chairman.

Saunders had a set of solid marketing achievements behind him. He gained his initial experience with J. Walter Thompson, the large advertising agency. He moved to Beechams and was responsible for reinvigorating

Lucozade as a brand. He repeated the exercise with Horlicks for Nestlé, where he had an established reputation. The Saunders plan for the turnaround of Guinness was not confined to strengthening marketing. It proved to be a whirlwind of change which went far beyond what was initially expected internally or by the stockmarket. It involved:

- changes in the top management, the organisation structure and the board of directors
- reducing the overall cost base and improving productivity in Park Royal and St James's Gate
- bringing in Bain as management consultants to help analyse activities and policy options, and then help implement and monitor decisions
- disposing of 140 subsidiaries in non-core and loss-making activities
- investing in marketing and repositioning the brands
- improving product quality and delivery systems
- introducing tighter cost and capital expenditure control systems allied to a new financial control unit.

Saunders was not called 'Deadly Ernest' for nothing. His ruthless determination and pressure on management to perform made it clear that he wanted costs reduced. The 'efficiency programme' in Park Royal and the 'future competitiveness plan' in St James's Gate were implemented with reduced employee numbers and a variety of other cost savings. There was the potential threat of a 'greenfield' brewery in the north of England with all the benefits of modern technology and low operating costs if Dublin resisted radical change. The combination of skills and organisational and political wiles brought about by Brian Slowey and Paddy Galvin and their team in St James's Gate (and the other Irish operations) helped achieve a transformation. The elimination of the loss-making diversifications and the benefit of the new marketing strategy saw Guinness achieve increased volumes (in draught rather than bottled beer) and improved market share. The production cost savings over 1982 and 1983 supported a larger spend on marketing, product quality and dispensing technology improvements.

The recovery plan established strict targets across all activities and the evidence of a turnaround was visible within a year. The 1982 net loss of £26 million was converted into a net profit of £23 million in 1983. By 1985, before the acquisition of Bell's or Distillers, the profit had more than doubled to £51 million. The 1985 dividend of 7.2p represented a 47% increase on the 1981 dividend which had been under threat. Not surprisingly, the Guinness share price jumped to 280p and the company had a stockmarket valuation of £880 million by January 1986.[33] The value of the Guinness family and trust shareholdings had almost quintupled since the darker days of the early 1980s.

Saunders drew heavily on the Bain consultancy team for his first two years. He particularly relied on Olivier Roux, a senior member of the Bain group, in financial matters and eventually had him appointed to the board as financial director in 1985. The board had been slimmed down to twelve by 1983, of whom seven were drawn from the Guinness family. A most significant change was the co-option of Dr Arthur Furer, chairman of Nestlé, as a non-executive director. Saunders's board associates had increased further by 1985, with the appointment of Thomas Ward and Victor Steel as well as Roux. Ward was a US attorney who had worked with Saunders when he was with Nestlé, and Steel, who was appointed managing director of Guinness Brewing Worldwide, had been a director of the Beecham group.

Ernest Saunders, now chief executive, had achieved a reputation as a manager and marketing genius.[34] This enabled him to influence the Guinness board to make acquisitions in the Scottish whiskey industry with a view to improving profit performance by more imaginative brand management. The first acquisition was Bell's and later, more controversially, Distillers.[35] In this writer's view the structure of the Guinness board with an absence of sufficient 'outsiders' led to an extraordinary acquiescence by Lord Iveagh when he relinquished the chairmanship to Saunders in July 1986 and accepted the honorary position of president.

Saunders now held the dual roles of chief executive and chairman and his apparent self-delusion resulted in activities which ended in conflict with Olivier Roux and a Department of Trade and Industry inspection. Saunders was eventually dismissed and a number of new directors, including Sir Norman Macfarlane as chairman, were appointed. It was remarkable that the investment institutions had not played a more positive role in the appointment of directors earlier. The scandal involving the circumstances of the Distillers takeover and the apparent use of company funds could have been avoided. The financier Boesky's revelations to the Securities and Exchange Commission in the USA appear to have revealed the Guinness share support activities in the takeover of Distillers.[36] The 'Notes' to the Guinness 1986 financial statements referred to 'Unusual Transactions' which mentioned a $100 million investment in a US partnership and various payments amounting to £25 million for which 'adequate reasons for payment have not been established'.[37] The auditors' report stated that 'in respect of these transactions and arrangements, proper accounting records were not kept throughout the period by the company'.[38] Clearly, there were breakdowns in financial control and the board seems not to have been aware of the nature of these payments. There followed the extensively publicised appointment of inspectors by the Department of Industry and Trade to investigate the affairs of Guinness, and subsequent court trials of Ernest Saunders, a merchant banking adviser and a variety of other City and business associates. Saunders and others were jailed — though they argued that they did nothing very different from what was common practice in London.

When Benjamin, the third Earl of Iveagh, at forty-nine, surrendered the chairmanship in July 1986 to the chief executive, Ernest Saunders, it was the end of a proud tradition. This unique family reign directly from the founder though six generations for 227 years had come to an end in distinctly ignominious circumstances. This affair was all the more unfortunate for Benjamin Guinness, in view of the magnificent recovery of the brewing business, in productivity, draught quality, marketing and product delivery systems, and advertising effectiveness. These resulted in an increased market share in Ireland and Britain with higher profits, dividends and share price.

Despite the scandal, the doubling of Guinness's earnings per share, dividends and share price between 1986 and 1990 was a testament to the vision and foundation laid down by Ernest Saunders, with admittedly excellent follow-on strategic marketing and brand management supervised by Anthony Tennant. Guinness had been transformed into a world-class organisation, a major player in the world's drinks industry, and one of the UK's largest exporters.

Ernest Saunders undermined the academic concept of the product life-cycle in the mature stage by investing in Guinness stout (rather than treating it as a 'cash cow'), with a systematic approach to market research, product repositioning — by moving to under thirty-five year olds and crossing social sectors — and imaginative and targeted advertising. He emphatically reversed the decline of Guinness as a product. Perhaps his managerial epitaph is fittingly summed up by Ferry:

> 'People used to say he was the "axeman" or the "iceman". But that wasn't Ernest. What Ernest loved most of all was the Guinness brand' said former Bain consultant David Hoare.
> 'If Ernest died and you cut him open, you'd see brands'.[39]

Saunders arrested the decline of a mature company by an icy determination to rein in two separate managerial kingdoms where the board had lost control of operational performance and strategy. Through discipline, systematic analysis, scientific marketing, imaginative brand identity and positioning, a focus on quality, greater technology across production and distribution, his legacy was above all else a cultural transformation.

P. J. Carroll
Background

The new 'high' of P. J. Carroll's share price at 200p in the late 1980s was evidence of the stockmarket's belief in the group's favourable future prospects. This share price was a considerable achievement, bearing in mind the doubtful prospects of the tobacco industry in the domestic market. In three successive five-year periods from 1974 ordinary dividends had doubled, and it looked as if this performance would be achieved again by 1990. However, owing to heavy losses and the group's slow recovery, no final dividend on the ordinary shares was paid for 1990 and no dividends were subsequently paid up to 1994. Reminiscent of the pattern of entrepreneurial firms such as Goodman and GPA, it was a remarkably sudden and steep downturn in fortunes after a lengthy period of outstanding success.

The announcement on 26 June 1990 of the results for the eighteen-month period to March 1990 confirmed the unexpected profits warning of the second interim statement issued in December 1989. The net loss of £21 million (after write-offs of £25 million) was much larger than market forecasts. It was announced that Laurence Crowley, a leading accountant with extensive experience as a corporate receiver/liquidator in KPMG Stokes Kennedy Crowley, was to be appointed chairman. The ordinary share price fell to 129p on 29 June compared with 150p in early May. By September it declined further to 105p. Subsequently there was a modest recovery in the share price, on the basis of a possible takeover bid.

The resignation of Don Carroll as chairman of P. J. Carroll in February 1990 was unexpected. He had been a director of P. J. Carroll for thirty-five years and its chairman for thirty years. It was a sad, but honourable, end to an illustrious business and public service career. P. J. Carroll had been an Irish barometer of best practices in all its management functions for decades; its crisis in the early 1990s was a personal and corporate tragedy of heroic proportions in Irish life.

Founded in Dundalk in 1824 by Patrick James Carroll, P. J. Carroll & Co. flourished in the tobacco business to become the largest employer in the town. A widening of its domestic market as a manufacturer of cigarettes led to a stockmarket quotation in 1934. Less than twenty years later it was in serious decline with a market share of just 9% and a dependence primarily on one product — the plain cigarette Sweet Afton. The competition being offered by two local manufacturing subsidiaries of cigarette multinationals — John Player and W. H. Wills (who were later to merge) — was proving too much. A grim picture was later painted by Don Carroll, a great-grandson of the company's founder, about his first impressions on joining in 1952, having qualified as a chartered accountant. The quoted share price was below its par value. He recounted:

> This was in 1952 and there had been a very severe budget. There was hardly any work in the factory — stocks had been sold to the retail trade before the budget. The dividend that year cost £12,000 and it was not covered by the profits. The employees were all kept on, dusting the walls and cleaning the machines . . .
>
> Carrolls was not going well. The product was bad: shopkeepers would say, 'Sorry, we've only Afton'.[40]

The business was managed and controlled by his two uncles but he soon persuaded them to engage management consultants A.I.C. to work on production and quality improvements. Working with A.I.C. gave Don Carroll his first experience of managing change; employees were initially reluctant to accept the new methods, practices and measurement schemes. By 1955 sales volume and production efficiency had improved and profitability had been restored. In particular the product quality was much better. Market share increased to 18%. Don Carroll was made factory superintendent and in 1955 he was appointed to the board. In 1957 he joined his uncle Walter Carroll as joint managing director.

In 1958 P. J. Carroll successfully launched Carrolls No. 1, a filter-tipped cigarette which was to take 60% of a small but fast-growing niche market. A further new product, Major Extra Size, was successfully launched and this led to other market successes with a brand management and target marketing strategy supported by very precise advertising, packaging and promotion policies. Rapid expansion took place and a state of the art manufacturing and distribution facility was built in Dundalk. A strong management team was recruited in the late 1950s. First came Derrik Corbett as the chief accountant, followed by Des Ryan from A.I.C. who took over Don Carroll's production position. Aidan Manahan and John Lepere were recruited to develop sales and marketing. Further deepening of this team was achieved with the recruitment of additional production and marketing expertise. P. J. Carroll became a paragon of modern management systems and market research techniques. It also built up quite advanced skills in tobacco leaf buying and treatment.

In a significant strategic shareholding initiative in 1960, Don Carroll negotiated with the Rothmans group (formerly Carreras) to invest new equity in P. J. Carroll for modernisation and development. Rothmans acquired the Carroll family shareholdings, giving it negative control with a holding of 40% of the equity. For Rothmans, P. J. Carroll was a minor national cigarette manufacturer in an oligopoly dominated by a few multinational groups. For P. J. Carroll, Rothmans provided a strong platform for development with access to world-famous cigarette brands, technology and marketing systems.

Don Carroll was elevated to the positions of chairman (taking over from his uncle Jim) and chief executive. On moving to an executive position in banking in the UK for a period in the 1970s, he assigned the chief executive role to Des Ryan, but he continued as chairman.

Key events in the life of P. J. Carroll	
1824	Tobacco manufacturing and distribution company founded in Dundalk by Patrick James Carroll.
	Eventually moves from local business to national distribution.
1934	Company attains a share quotation on the Dublin Stock Exchange.
	Primary cigarette brand Sweet Afton.
1952	Market share in Ireland has dwindled to 9%. Marginal profitability.
	Having recently qualified as a chartered accountant, Don Carroll (aged twenty-four) joins company. He initially works in production function.
1955	Market share recovers to 18%. Product quality, production efficiencies and profitability improved.
1956–58	Recruitment of strong management team across all functional areas — Des Ryan, Derrik Corbett, Aidan Manahan and John Lepere.
1958	Carrolls No. 1, a filter-tipped cigarette, launched successfully.
1960	Rothmans (formerly Carreras) acquires a 40% equity holding through injection of cash for new equity and purchase of majority of Carroll family holding.
	Extensive investment in plant modernisation and development.
	Don Carroll becomes chairman and chief executive.

cont.

Key events in the life of P. J. Carroll *cont.*	
1970	Don Carroll resigns as chief executive to take up a senior role in a leading London financial institution. He continues as chairman.
1972–73	Dakota (packaging) and Cahill May Roberts (pharmaceutical distribution) acquired.
1974	Share price 18p (April). Net profit £2 million.
1977	Market share reaches 48% with the success of Carrolls No. 1, and subsequent launch of Major Extra Size and Rothmans King Size across various market segments. Net profit £3 million. P. J. Carroll wins first ever 'Published Accounts Award' established by the Leinster Society of Chartered Accountants. (Carrolls went on to win this award more times than any other organisation.)
1977–82	Joint venture with Bank of Ireland and Fieldcrest Inc. to establish Fieldcrest Ireland (a high-quality towelling plant) in Kilkenny. Heavy losses incurred and the project ends in receivership, with the sponsors writing off investments.
1980	Market share 52%. Group turnover £70 million and net profit £6 million.
1983	Market share 56%. Group turnover £105 million and net profit £8 million.
1984	Market share 55%. Group turnover £147 million and net profit £8 million.
1985	Don Carroll takes over the role of chief executive (and continues as chairman) on the retirement of Des Ryan.
1986	Company announces its planned diversification strategy into aquaculture and mail order. Share price falls from 190p in May to 155p in June. Acquisition of firms in the USA and salmon farming interests in the west of Ireland. Turnover £128 million and net profit £11 million.
1987	Disposal of packaging and pharmaceutical distribution businesses. Investment on salmon farming and US mail order activities proceeds.
1988	Market share falls to 50%. Group turnover £78 million and net profit £10 million. Extensive further investment in salmon farming in Ireland and mail order catalogue and mail order clothing firms in the USA.

cont.

Key events in the life of P. J. Carroll *cont.*	
1990	Market share falls to 44%. Group turnover £147 million and net loss £21 million.
	Don Carroll resigns and board restructured.
	Rothmans makes successful offer for full equity control.
1991	Disposal of salmon farming and some of US mail order investments.
1992	Market share 40%. Turnover £52 million and net profit £5 million.
	Disposal of balance of US mail order investments.
1994	Market share 35%. Turnover £50 million and net profit £3 million.

Marketing and financial performance

The successful recovery from the late 1950s through to the 1980s was an extraordinary management achievement as evidenced by market share captured and consistent increases in profitability and dividends. Details of this financial performance are summarised in Table 7.5. This was achieved in a competitive and hostile environment. Its growth in turnover and dividends is all the more commendable when it is noted that it was all self-financed. From 1960 P. J. Carroll never made a rights issue. In 1974 the company earned a pre-tax profit of £3.4 million and paid a net dividend of 1.2p per share. The share price (having adjusted for subsequent scrip issues) at 6 April 1974 was 18p. By December 1984 the share price had grown to 123p. In 1986 Carrolls reported a peak pre-tax profit of £13 million (a modest improvement on the previous year). Not only was Carrolls debt free, but it had built up a cash surplus of £14 million. The share price reached 212p early in 1986 but by June it had slipped to 155p, primarily as a result of the market's reaction to the first initiatives in the new diversification strategy into aquaculture and mail order. By 1986 P. J. Carroll had become the third largest industrial firm quoted on the Irish Stock Exchange

Market share increased from 9% in 1952 to 18% in 1955 and with the successful launch of the new brands on the Irish market it reached 48% in 1977 and 52% by 1980. This dominant market position, achieved at the expense of subsidiaries of US and UK tobacco multinationals, reached a peak of 56% in 1983. Its three brands, Major Extra Size, Rothmans King Size and Carrolls No. 1, continued to hold their position as the three largest selling brands in the mid-1980s.

Table 7.5: P. J. Carroll: financial performance

	Turnover (£m)	Net profit/(loss) (£m)	Dividend (pence)
1974	n/av.	2	1.2
1975	n/av.	2	1.4
1976	n/av.	4	2.0
1977	n/av.	3	2.0
1978	54	3	2.4
1979	61	5	2.8
1980	70	6	3.6
1981	86	4	4.2
1982	97	8	4.9
1983	105	8	4.9
1984	147	8	5.5
1985	123	10	7.0
1986	128	11	7.5
1987	129	6	7.8
1988	78	10	8.2
1990*	147	(21)	8.2
1991	109	(1)	–
1992	52	5	–
1993	57	8	–
1994	50	3	–

* 18 months because year end extended to March 1990.

Note: Turnover is net of excise duty. Net profit is the profit attributable to shareholders after taxation, and exceptional and extraordinary items. Dividends have been recomputed by the author to adjust for scrip issues.

Source: Annual reports.

By any standards, the market share and profit growth were formidable achievements for P. J. Carroll's management team against two competitors who were backed by the resources of leading tobacco multinationals. P. J. Carroll had been managed efficiently on a number of fronts; not only had it developed and marketed new products well, but it had also introduced plant and production modernisation and productivity rationalisations (reducing the production workforce, and encountering the occasional strike in Dundalk). It had performed in a market which had experienced annual declines in volume demand of between 2% and 6%, which had accumulated to a real volume reduction in demand of almost 25% between 1980 and 1987.[41]

By 1988 there had been a divestment of two divisions and partial entry into new ventures. Group turnover declined from £123 million in 1985 to £80 million in 1988. An operating profit of £8 million was reported in 1988 compared with £12 million in 1985. The reduction in profits was attributed to the start-up losses of £5.4 million on the new ventures. The tobacco division's operating profit rose from £10 million in 1985 to £14.1 million in 1988. Over these years, group central management costs increased from £0.2 million to £1.6 million; these expenses were to jump to £3.1 million for the eighteen-month period to end March 1990. Up to 1988 the conventional ratios, as shown in Table 7.6, would have looked very stable and would not have signalled an impending crisis.

Table 7.6: P. J. Carroll: some conventional financial ratios

	1985	1986	1987	1988
Operating profit margin	9.8%	9.5%	7.6%	9.9%
Equity/total assets	61%	61%	57%	53%
Current ratio	1.9:1	1.9:1	1.6:1	1.8:1
Interest cover	No net interest. Surplus cash balance.			
Stock/turnover*	21%	19%	19%	31%

* Stock/turnover = year-end stock as a percentage of sales.
Source: Annual reports.

Profitability, gearing and liquidity all appear healthy. Cash flow to debt has not been evaluated, as there was no bank debt. The one figure which does stand out is the extent of the change in stock levels in relation to turnover in 1988 — partially due to the disposal of the pharmaceutical distribution business, but also due to the growing investment in working capital in the new ventures. The detailed movement in the funds flow statement reveals that there was an additional investment of £4 million in stocks, which was material when compared to previous experience. Stocks can be the 'graveyard' of companies and perhaps this build-up was a warning sign. P. J. Carroll did not collapse and one of the reasons for its survival was the absence of debt at the time of the new diversification strategy. What are not revealed in the figures are the advertising and promotion cutbacks which improved short-term profitability but weakened the future market position of the brands and future tobacco profitability. The scale of the two new venture commitments in resource consumption — managerial and financial — was to have a heavy adverse impact on the 1990 figures.

The continuing poor performance of P. J. Carroll's share price in relation to the market index in the late 1980s (there was no comparable quoted company) and the first negative net cash flow of £8 million in 1988 were more realistic pointers to the troubled future position. P. J. Carroll's share price fell behind the stockmarket index in 1983, matched it in 1984 and 1985, and consistently fell behind from then on — at 60% over four years. In summary, the 'configuration' of known organisational and strategic information would probably have been a stronger predictor of a marked change in the risk class of the organisation and its vulnerability to a crisis.

Performance of the core tobacco division

P. J. Carroll became increasingly efficient in its tobacco operations. This was indicated by the improved trading margins which peaked at an extraordinarily high 23.1% in 1988, as shown in Table 7.7. Evidence subsequently indicated that a substantial part of the profit gains in 1987 and 1988 was due to sharp cutbacks in its annual advertising and promotion budget which had been running at the order of £4 million per annum. It is surprising that analysts did not question how tobacco profit margins had risen so quickly when domestic market demand was declining.

Table 7.7: P. J. Carroll: tobacco division performance

	Turnover (£m)	Operating profit (£m)	Profit margin (%)
1982	48.2	5.9	12.2
1983	52.3	6.6	12.6
1984	52.6	5.9	11.2
1985	60.3	9.2	15.3
1986	60.8	10.9	17.9
1987	56.6	11.9	21.0
1988	55.5	12.8	23.1
1990*	77.0	15.0	19.0
1991	51.3	10.2	19.9
1992	51.6	8.9	17.3
1993	57.1	8.4	14.7

* 18 months because year end extended to March 1990.

Source: Riada & Co. 1988 review; annual reports with adjustments by author to achieve comparability.

The near doubling in tobacco profit margins from 12.2% in 1982 to 23.1% in 1988 through a combination of efficiencies and 'income smoothing' devices — both real and artificial — is striking. It was followed by continually falling profit margins, with just 14.7% being earned in 1993. This reduction was predominantly due to the sharp fall in market share (to below 40%), leading to low production capacity utilisation. Tobacco turnover peaked at £60.8 million in 1986, compared with £57.1 million in 1993. Taking price increases into account, the real reduction in value equivalent was £10 million. The gross profit contribution on lost turnover was almost £5 million.

The strategic dilemma

Having reached a peak market share of 56% in 1983, it was clear to Carrolls that growth in the domestic tobacco sector was over — particularly with the new competitive response from Gallaher and John Player & Sons. Both of these had restructured their operations and management. Domestic market demand had been falling annually since 1980. A primary reason was the sharp increase in government taxation on cigarettes, at more than twice the rate of inflation for the four-year period ending in 1982 (value added tax and excise duty had reached 74% of the selling price in 1984 compared to 62% in 1978). Greater health awareness and government anti-smoking campaigns also played their part. Government restrictions on the forms of cigarette promotion and advertising also contributed to the fall in demand and difficulties in launching new products.

Tobacco division profits fell in 1984 and more drastic internal rationalisation became necessary. Numbers employed were reduced, primarily by voluntary redundancy. P. J. Carroll was unable to make up for the loss of domestic market volume with increased export sales. Exports were never more than 6% to 8% of turnover — it was one of the constraints of being associated with Rothmans. The long-term outlook for the tobacco division was not favourable.

P. J. Carroll was different from its two domestic competitors in that it was not a wholly owned subsidiary where strategic decisions on future investment plans were made by the parent top management overseas. It had a stockmarket quotation, a Carroll at the helm and an independent board. It seemed to operate with operational and strategic autonomy from Rothmans. The reality was that with just over 39% of the equity Rothmans had effective control — it was by far the largest shareholder and had representatives on the board. It would have been most difficult for another firm to make a hostile takeover bid. In 1983, Irish Life Assurance held about 7%. The board and the Carroll's family interests controlled just 5%. Rothmans was in a position to stop any diversification initiatives if it so wished. The explanation of P. J. Carroll's freedom of strategic initiative lay in Don Carroll's vice-chairmanship of the Rothmans London board and his long-standing relationship with Anton Rupert, a controlling shareholder in the parent. In contrast, Gallaher was operating as a 'cash cow' through the harvesting policy of its parent in taking out most of its profits as dividends. P. J. Carroll had the freedom to look on itself from a 'national' and independent perspective and consider corporate strategy objectives which did not necessarily maximise short-run cash flows and profit.

Diversification initiatives started as early as 1964 with the abandoned proposal to merge P. J. Carroll with Waterford Glass and Irish Distillers in order to exploit export opportunities. In 1972 P. J. Carroll acquired Dakota, a print and packaging firm which was one of its principal suppliers of high-quality packaging — P. J. Carroll accounted for over 40% of its output. This was followed by the acquisition of Cahill May Roberts, the largest pharmaceutical wholesaler and distributor in Ireland. A joint venture in Fieldcrest Ireland in the late 1970s — involving P. J. Carroll and the Bank of Ireland (where Don Carroll was a board member), each holding 25% equity, and the American parent, Fieldcrest Inc. — proved disappointing. It was a high-quality terry-towelling plant established as a greenfield operation in Kilkenny. To the embarrassment of the Irish partners, it went into receivership in 1982 with P. J. Carroll writing off £3 million. The Dakota and Cahill May Roberts[42] profits remained disappointingly low, in comparison to the tobacco business, as they only contributed between one-sixth and one-seventh of group profit, as summarised in Table 7.8.

Table 7.8: P. J. Carroll: operating profits (£m)

	1980	1986
Tobacco division	5.9	12.8
Pharmaceutical division	0.8	1.2
Print and packaging division	0.3	0.5
Total	7.0	14.5

Source: Annual reports.

In this writer's view P. J. Carroll had two choices. It could manage a declining business through a series of operational downsizings and pay its shareholders dividends from surplus cash flow. Alternatively, it could attempt to diversify into divergent business interests around its existing management skills and customer and technological knowledge base. Taking account of its independence, its past success in building brands and its dominant and profitable market share in its cigarette business, it is not surprising that Carrolls felt it could diversify successfully into a new business. Discussions with the McGrath family about a merger with Waterford Glass in 1984 came to nothing.

There seem to have been three other stimulants to a new venture. First, there were no more challenges in the tobacco business; it could be said to have become 'boring'. Second, there was the need to exorcise the ghost of Fieldcrest. Third, there was the issue of the personality and changing role of Don Carroll in the organisation at a crucial time in its history. We gain some insight into his drive and zest for a challenge at the end of a long interview with Ivor Kenny:

> Personally, I have never wanted power. I want to bring about constructive change . . . Change has always fascinated me. It's an extremely challenging and stimulating thing. But power is a very worrying thing and not something which I greatly enjoy.[43]

It wasn't just Don Carroll. More or less the same management team had been doing more or less the same job for over twenty years. Attempting to create a new core business certainly posed a radical and exciting challenge for everyone. Don Carroll returned to the position of chief executive (and retained the position of chairman) on the retirement of Des Ryan in August 1985. This preceded the critical two-and-a-half-year period when the two new venture investment decisions were being implemented.

Despite good profitability and a strong dividend yield, the share price began to drift continuously downwards from 1986. Some stockbroker analysts doubted the diversification strategy. John Brindle, investment manager of Standard Life, publicly criticised the plan in late 1986. Nevertheless, Standard Life seems to have had a change of mind, for it joined Irish Life with a holding of over 5% of the equity in 1987[44] followed by IBI Nominees and Norwich Union who took large holdings.[45]

Davy, P. J. Carroll's stockbrokers, seem to have been disenchanted with the diversification strategy for some time. Davy had commented in their report dated 20 June 1988 that both salmon farming and direct marketing were high risk. They noted that at a price of 154p Carrolls was on a price/earnings ratio of 12.4 compared to much lower equivalent ratios for comparable companies in the UK and USA. P. J. Carroll's share price had performed poorly against the Dublin stockmarket index: the share price had been 51% behind the market over three years and 26% behind in the twelve months to June 1988.

The 'marketing driven' diversification strategy

On 16 June 1986, P. J. Carroll announced its 1985/86 interim results and the initial details of its diversification plans.[46] P. J. Carroll's share price was 155p, having been 190p in early May before analysts reduced their profit expectations. Whereas analysts have suggested that some of P. J. Carroll's diversification activities mirrored the personal pursuits of Don Carroll, they were grounded in a certain rationale. In 1986 the cigarette business was achieving a gross profit margin of over 50% and a net margin of almost 18%. By divesting itself of its pharmaceutical distribution and printing activities, the group was moving out of low-margin, low-growth, competitive businesses. The underpinning philosophy was that P. J. Carroll had a competitive competence in marketing and brand management — somewhat similar to the ideas enunciated by Ernest Saunders in Guinness. Don Carroll stated:

> Previously, we had tended to think of the development of the new core businesses in terms of investment strategy rather than of marketing strategy. This time we have addressed the question in quite a different way. We have asked ourselves what we are best at . . .
>
> We have concluded that the skills we have accumulated in developing and launching over the past twenty-five years Ireland's three most popular cigarette brands could be applied with equally good effect in direct marketing of consumer products.[47]

Aquaculture was felt to offer substantial export opportunities. Salmon farming was initially capital intensive since it had a three-year operational cycle while the fish reached maturity. Though it was seen as a risky process, it was thought to be very profitable. Davy Stockbrokers suggested an average net margin of between 25% and 30% on turnover.[48] The aquaculture venture was making an economic and social contribution to an underdeveloped area (the west of Ireland) through direct employment and other spending. It was a high added value activity, making an economic contribution to the nation — a theme which had been associated with Don Carroll and some of his managers.

Direct marketing was much less capital intensive and it offered a net margin of the order of 10% on turnover. It opened up growth opportunities in a much larger market and was not dependent on the performance of the Irish economy or fiscal policy, with its consequences for Irish industrial competitiveness, wage rates or the value of the Irish currency. Thus there was a balancing of capital outlays and a separation of industries and markets. Several internal project analyses and commissioned reports from McKinsey and other consulting groups followed. Management justified the proposals by linking them to the group's perceived marketing strengths — the 'distinctive competence' and the 'common thread' in strategic terms.[49] Despite the management's positive recommendation, the board was divided on the decision.

This marketing-led project philosophy is difficult to reconcile with the analytical frameworks suggested by writers on corporate strategy such as Ansoff and Porter.[50] Ansoff would argue that the essential relationships with customers or technology were absent. From a structural industry analysis, Porter's competitive advantage framework would advocate either cost leadership, differentiation or focus. The last two approaches would tenuously fit P. J. Carroll's strategic behaviour. The company was trying to make inroads into two specialist but difficult markets — a branded premium salmon product in Europe and the USA, and a niche mail order market in quality and well-designed apparel and other leisure items in the USA.

The twin new ventures: aquaculture and direct marketing

The first step in the execution of the new diversification strategy was the purchase in February 1986 of Thomas & Thomas Rodmakers in Massachusetts. It was a small manufacturer of quality fishing rods, which it sold through mail order in the USA. It subsequently incurred losses. This was followed by the investment of £2.5 million in July 1986 into recapitalising (and taking a 75% interest) and expanding Bradán Mara Teo. It was one of the oldest salmon-farming companies in Ireland, established by Údarás na Gaeltachta in 1976, with farms in Carna, Lettermore and Lettermullen in the west of Ireland. At the time Bradán, with an output of seventy tons, was loss-making and close to liquidation.[51] Carrolls subsequently bought two lakes in the west of Ireland and built a land-based hatchery for the production of salmon smolt in Lough Derryclare. The project plan aimed to build an integrated facility for all salmon-farming processes. The 'production' process involved a long lead time — between three and four years. In the early years, in an attempt to accelerate production, smolts were brought in from Iceland.

Though salmon farming is an established industry in Norway and Scotland, it is viewed as risky. Internally, there is the long lead time, the susceptibility to disease, quality control and stock loss rates and the impact of the weather. Expertise in hatchery management, disease monitoring and stock husbandry are critical. Efficiency, accuracy and productivity in the diet structure, feed conversion ratio and the numbers employed are central to profitability because of the high cost of fish food and labour inputs. For example, Bradán was reported to have lost 60% of its stock in the dry hot summer of 1984 partially due to sun rays and sea lice infestation.[52] The ESB and Guinness stocks were also badly affected. A second hatchery was purchased in Bunclody, Co. Wexford, primarily to reduce the risk of disease. The external element of business risk was the volatility of demand for and price of fresh salmon. There was oversupply and dumping in Europe by Norwegian producers. Norway produced 38,000 tons and Scotland 10,000 tons of 'Atlantic' salmon. Market price varied between £3,500 and £5,000 per ton between 1986 and 1987 and fell to £4,300 in 1988. It had become a commodity product in a competitive market dominated by the powerful Norwegian producers. The US market offered better prices and Carrolls hoped to sell some output of smoked salmon, at good margins, through its new mail order arm.

The objective was to expand aquaculture capacity to 2,000 tons. This compared with a total Irish production of 1,250 tons from about twenty fish farms in 1986. Domestic salmon consumption, at 978 tons, was growing at less than 10% a year. In contrast, European and US markets were expected to grow at not less than 25% a year. The marketing plan was to double Ireland's 3% market share with a product concept built around branded high-quality fresh and smoked salmon which would command a premium price, particularly in France and the USA. The salmon-farming venture was effectively a greenfield one because of the scale of the expansion of the relatively simple Bradán operation which, with allied integration of processes and facilities, was planned to double the whole country's existing capacity. It demanded not only fixed asset investment, but further injections of working capital to cover the cost of smolts, feed, labour and other resources over the minimum three-year egg to fish cycle as 'work-in-progress' stocks built up.

With the new capacity, production increased to 400 tons in 1987. The plan was to produce 800 tons in 1988 and 1,600 tons in 1989. It was an ambitious project of which marketing was only one ingredient. Hatchery and husbandry expertise, good luck, and a more stable market price structure were also essential. Had it succeeded it would have been a high added value activity which would have contributed to national objectives in developing indigenous industry, regional employment and exports as well as an operating profit of the order of £5 million by the early 1990s.

The second diversification initiative was a direct marketing business in the USA. The Thomas & Thomas Rodmakers acquisition was followed by a £3 million investment in the creation of *Carroll Journals*, its own direct marketing catalogue. This proved more difficult to get off the ground than expected, and it was supported by two 'bolt-on' acquisitions with direct marketing expertise and customer lists. Initially, £4 million was spent in buying an 80% stake in G. H. Cotton Company of Tennessee in November 1987. Set up in 1984, it marketed women's quality apparel through its own catalogue, and also provided an order acceptance and fulfilment service for other mail order firms. The following year Bedford Fair, of Mount Kisco, New York, was acquired. It marketed two catalogues specialising in women's apparel. By 1988 the first edition of the *Carroll Journals* was test-marketed in the USA. It offered a range of 260 leisure-related, household and clothing products — of which thirty-eight were sourced in Ireland. Though the mail order industry was a mature one in the USA, P. J. Carroll's business concept was to capture a niche of the upmarket demand for well-designed and fashionable women's merchandise. The target market was the urban, professional and managerial group with sufficient disposable income to identify with a country lifestyle rooted in a traditional and classical taste. It was visual merchandising with each page representing a shop window. By all accounts, the *Carroll Journals* was very well produced, but expensive to mount.

Much of the investment in the restructuring of the business of P. J. Carroll had been completed by September 1988, as summarised in Table 7.9. The scale of the financial commitment to the two new divisions, at £42 million, exceeded the investment of £38 million in the existing core tobacco business. Some £14 million of these new investments was reflected in 'goodwill' written off. Of the £22 million capital spending in direct marketing, just over 50% was in goodwill. It was a sizeable premium, which was not to be recovered. Cash balances had increased to more than £14 million in 1987. The riskiness of the diversification policy was wisely counterbalanced by a low financial risk, because these initiatives were predominantly financed by cash balances and the core tobacco activity cash flow.

Table 7.9: P. J. Carroll: the changing investment profile, 1988 (£m)

	Investment in divisions	Sales
Tobacco/corporate	38	55
Aquaculture	20	7
Direct marketing — USA	_22_	_40_
	80	102

Source: Annual Report 1988.

The disastrous outcome to the diversification strategy

The group was profit-making in all its activities until it entered aquaculture — which never made money in five years, as shown in Table 7.10. After three years' losses, direct marketing achieved a £4 million operating profit on a turnover of £51 million in 1991. This was close to the target margin of 10% assumed in the initial plans. The reported losses on the new activities at operating level tend to understate the full extent of their drain on group resources. 'Exceptional' or 'extraordinary' items in the profit and loss accounts aggregated to £42.3 million in the period 1990–93, being £25.2 million in 1990, £12.7 million in 1991, £5.1 million in 1992 and a net gain of £0.7 million in 1993.

Had a longer time horizon been accepted by the board on the new ventures (if cash haemorrhaging had ceased) then heavy write-offs may not have been necessary. Apart from markets and operations proving much more complex than envisaged in both project plans, it seems the unreliability of internal management accounting information in both aquaculture and direct marketing added to the uncertainties and a critical loss of board confidence in their future. The aquaculture division was sold in September 1991 as a going concern to Gaelic Seafoods, a leading Scottish fish-farming group, for a reported £5 million — compared to a total original investment of the order of £25 million.[53] Stuart Baillie, managing director of Gaelic, felt that Carrolls had resolved most of the fish-farming problems and that 'a hell of a lot of money has been invested and it's difficult to make a return, but we feel we got it at the right price'.[54]

Cash flow profile

The cash flow profile illustrates starkly the impact of the change in strategic direction on liquidity, as summarised in Table 7.11. As would be expected in a well-managed mature business, a surplus cash flow and an increasing cash balance were being achieved annually between 1983 and 1987. Annual

Table 7.10: P. J. Carroll: divisional analysis of financial performance (£m)

	1986	1987	1988	1990*	1991	1992	1993
Turnover							
Tobacco	61	57	56	77	51	52	57
Pharmaceutical	61	62	–	–	–	–	–
Print and packaging	9	9	9	–	–	–	–
Aquaculture	–	–	3	9	7	–	–
Direct marketing	–	1	12	60	51	–	–
Total	131	129	80	146	109	52	57
Gross profit	n/av.	42	42	77	56	30	30
Overheads							
Distribution	n/av.	3	5	8	6	2	2
Marketing and administration	n/av.	29	29	64	36	19	19
Rationalisation provisions	n/av.	4	–	–	–	–	–
Total	n/av.	36	34	72	42	21	21
Operating profit	12	6	8	5	14	9	9
Divisional profitability							
Tobacco	11	8**	14	18	12	9	9
Pharmaceutical	1	2	–	–	–	–	–
Print and packaging	1	1	1	–	–	–	–
Aquaculture	(1)	(1)	(1)	(3)	(1)	–	–
Direct marketing	–	(3)	(5)	(7)	4	–	–
Central management charge	–	(1)	(1)	(3)	(1)	–	–
Total operating profit	12	6	8	5	14	9	9

*   18 months because year end extended to March 1990.
** After charging rationalisation provisions of £4 million.

investment outflows on the core business ranged between £2 million and £3 million. The first heavy outflow was £8 million in 1987. The additional investment on new fixed assets and acquisitions in the next two accounting periods, of £20 million and £16 million respectively, were of a new order of magnitude. In addition, there was the large outlay of £13 million on the increased working capital needs of the new ventures.

When the negative cash flows and drain on liquidity from diversifications became clear, it is not surprising that a new chairman was

Table 7.11: P. J. Carroll: cash flow profile (£m)

	1983	1984	1985	1986	1987	1988	1990*
Cash inflows							
Operations	11	11	15	15	12	11	11
Taxation	(1)	(1)	(1)	(3)	(2)	(1)	(1)
Dividends	(4)	(4)	(5)	(5)	(5)	(6)	(10)
Bank interest	1	–	1	1	2	1	(1)
Exceptional	–	–	–	–	–	–	(7)
Working capital	–	–	(2)	3	1	(13)	1
Net cash flow from operations	7	6	8	11	8	(8)	(7)
Investments							
Fixed assets	3	2	2	4	8	8	13
Acquisitions	–	–	–	–	–	12	3
Total investment outflows	3	2	2	4	8	20	16
Cash flow surplus/(deficit)	4	4	6	7	–	(28)	(23)
Funding							
New equity/grants	–	–	–	1	1	2	3
Sale of assets	–	–	–	–	–	14	–
Change in net cash/bank loans	4	4	6	8	1	(12)	(20)

* 18 months because year end extended to March 1990.

Source: Annual reports; certain data restructured by author for comparative purposes.

appointed to review management and strategy. The £23 million cash deficit in 1989/90 following a £28 million deficit the previous year was a catharsis. What the cash flow analysis reveals is that the company made too heavy a level of diversification investment over too short a time span. The crisis in 1990 was severe. It inflicted a serious injury to the group's business confidence, in loss of market share and the launch of new products; to a lesser extent the financial health of its core tobacco activity was weaker. Net working capital had fallen to £7 million in 1991 — in contrast to £33 million in 1988. There was also the bank debt of £23 million.

Diversification has always been a problem for the major tobacco companies. For example, Philip Morris of the USA, the world's largest cigarette manufacturer, though it had acquired large multinational food companies such as Kraft Industries and General Foods as well as Miller's Breweries, was still earning the majority of its profits from its tobacco division ($5 billion out of a total of $7 billion in 1989). The cigarette business continues to be one of the most profitable around the world.[55]

Scapegoats and responsibilities

Many media commentators and analysts found reasons for criticism after the unexpected February 1990 announcement of Don Carroll's retirement as chairman of P. J. Carroll. Not all stakeholders in Carrolls shared such critical views. Indeed there were many who complained to RTE about the nature of an insensitive interview (described as an 'ill-tempered harangue' by one newspaper[56]) with Don Carroll on the *Today Tonight* current affairs programme.[57] It did not give sufficient weight to earlier management achievements and his contributions to public service.

The resignation of Don Carroll was associated with the release of subsequent financial results by the group which were much worse than envisaged by earlier interim statements. Don Carroll was very honest when he replied to an interview question about the future profitability of aquaculture and direct marketing, stating that he had learnt a lot in the previous six months:

> . . . specifically that I was quite wrong to have forecasted then, given the basis of the quality of knowledge which management had in the company and I fell into that trap of too great optimism. I feel very badly about having made a public expression of expectation which was so grievously wrong and I don't want to put myself in that position again. I just want to live up to performance rather than making forecasts.[58]

Whereas Don Carroll appears to have been the public scapegoat for the £21 million net loss for the eighteen months to March 1990, one must also question the role of others. The dynamics of power in P. J. Carroll were complex. In theory the board had ultimate power and responsibility for the organisation's direction and performance. Leaving aside the diversification, how did the board, or Rothmans, justify the heavy cutback of spending on advertising and promotion for some years? Interview and other sources[59] corroborated the view that there appeared to be proportionately greater reductions in the advertising spend, compared to its competitors, in the late 1980s. In 1993, Richard Kelly, marketing manager of P. J. Carroll, concluded 'The brands were not supported for three years in the late 1980s and market share declined in direct correlation.'[60] He noted that the launches of new products called Mascot and Compass in 1989 and 1990 had not been successful and these products had to be withdrawn primarily because P. J. Carroll had misjudged the market. He stated that they 'were launched outside of an overall clear strategy over a three to five year period. We hadn't launched a brand for seven or eight years before Mascot. The company had taken its eye off the ball.' What were the top marketing management doing and what type of business plans and market analysis were being presented to the board of directors over these years? What questions were the board asking about the tobacco division's product/market performance and its future competitive position?

In this writer's opinion Rothmans was in a uniquely powerful position with its 39% shareholding. Admittedly, Don Carroll had had a long-standing relationship with Anton Rupert, which may have had its own implications for the supporting role played by Rothmans' representative directors over the years — until a change of mind in early 1990. Rothmans had effectively mirrored the paternalistic attitudes of Don Carroll by its acquiescent 'hands-off' policy for many years. Rothmans did not object to the Fieldcrest investment or the plans to tie into other joint ventures before the aquaculture and direct marketing forays. Rothmans had done very well on their Irish investment, in financial and marketing terms. One can pose the question: what were Rothmans and its representatives doing about new product and marketing initiatives in P. J. Carroll in the mid to late 1980s, when, with its multinational marketing research information, it would have been aware of changing trends to low-tar product demand and the new product launches of competitors? In practice, it can be argued that Rothmans held the real power behind the scene. Admittedly, P. J. Carroll was one of the 'jewels in the crown' of the Rothman empire. It seems to have had a much better track record and a higher market share than any other associate in the UK or Continental Europe, which gave Don Carroll and the management considerable credibility.

The fact that Irish investment institutions held some 30% of P. J. Carroll's equity is also relevant to its performance and governance. By all accounts, they were very acquiescent until the appearance of the disappointing second interim report in December 1989. The circumstances of P. J. Carroll in the mid to late 1980s, to a degree, reflect the pusillanimity of Irish stockbroking and fund management senior personnel as well as an absence of operational business expertise which could have mounted an adequate challenge to the company's performance and strategy. The adoption of a more vigorous questioning policy earlier might have brought pressures which could have strengthened the hand of a dissident minority on the board.

Comparing P. J. Carroll with Gallaher (Dublin)

In the late 1980s and early 1990s, P. J. Carroll lost market share to Gallaher (Dublin), its primary rival who manufactured the Benson and Hedges and Silk Cut brands. Estimates for 1989 suggested P. J. Carroll's market share had fallen to 48% and Gallaher's had grown to 30%.[61] By 1991 Gallaher claimed 36.5% and that it was close to rivalling P. J. Carroll's 40% market share. Finally, it was estimated that by 1993 Gallaher had overtaken P. J. Carroll at 38% to 36%.

Gallaher (Dublin) had taken a different strategic view of its development. It remained solely in its core tobacco business, acting as a 'cash cow' for its US parent, American Brands Inc., as evidenced by its investment and dividend policy summarised in Table 7.12. The increase in dividend paid from £5 million in 1988 to £19 million in 1994 indicates the degree of profitability and cash 'harvesting'. Gallaher's successful new brand launches in the low-tar segment of the market (which proved to be a rapidly growing sector), before government restrictions on advertising were implemented, resulted in greater capacity utilisation and a sharp increase in profits. In contrast, the impact of a shrinking overall market combined with a sharp loss of market share (down from 50% in 1988 to 40% in 1992) left P. J. Carroll with excess manufacturing capacity and lower profitability in its core tobacco business. According to the 1992 annual report of Gallaher, the overall market declined by 3% in that year.

Trends in gross profit margin provide a stark illustration of the differences between the two competitors' core tobacco business as shown in Table 7.13. Gallaher's gross tobacco turnover (including excise duty) increased from £120 million in 1988 to £198 million in 1992. In contrast, in the same period, P. J. Carroll's tobacco activity turnover declined from £205 million to £203 million. P. J. Carroll's low gross profit margin of 33% in 1987 in the 'old' business portfolio represented the impact of the lower profit margins (less than a quarter of the tobacco activity) in the wholesale pharmaceutical distribution activities, whose turnover equalled that of the tobacco division. Following the divestment of the pharmaceutical and printing divisions in 1987 and 1988 the gross profit margin increased dramatically to 54.5%, because it now primarily related to the high-margin tobacco activities. A clear picture of tobacco gross profits emerged in 1992 — with a margin of 57.6%. A combination of loss of market share, loss of

Table 7.12: A Comparison of the profitability and dividend policy of P. J. Carroll and Gallaher

	P. J. Carroll		Gallaher	
	Profit/(loss)	Dividend	Profit	Dividend
1988	10	6	6	5
1990	(21)*	6*	10	9
1991	(1)	–	11	10
1992	5	–	13	12
1993	8	–	16	15
1994	3	–	19	19

* 18 months because year end extended to March 1990
Note: Profit is defined as net profit after charging all expenses, interest, taxation, and exceptional and extraordinary items.
Source: Annual reports.

product competitiveness and underutilisation of capacity resulted in the fall in margins in 1993. The comparison of gross profit margin trends in Gallaher and P. J. Carroll, as direct competitors, reveals broadly similar margins and trends, though account should be taken of P. J. Carroll's product mix at the higher margin end of the market. Consequently, gross margins at 51.6% in 1993 were due to continuing competitiveness problems. In 1992, Gallaher increased its turnover by 22.6% which was more than double the 10.7% gain for P. J. Carroll.

Table 7.13: The changing gross profit margin profile of P. J. Carroll and Gallaher (%)

	P. J. Carroll		Gallagher
1987	33.0	(Old business mix)	n/av.
1988	54.5	(New business mix)	49.4
1990	52.9*	(New business mix)	51.0
1991	51.2	(New business mix)	55.1
1992	57.6	(Tobacco business)	58.3
1993	51.6	(Tobacco business)	51.6

* 18 months because year end extended to March 1990.
Note: Before charging exceptional and extraordinary items including stock write-offs. Gross profit margins are calculated before deducting distribution, marketing and administration expenses as reported in the financial statements.
Source: Annual reports.

The strategic and tactical errors

P. J. Carroll's crucial errors, which can be classified as strategic and tactical, are summarised in Table 7.14. Carrolls was somewhat unlucky in both the Fieldcrest and direct marketing ventures. Having to cope with a recession in the early stages of market entry was unfortunate timing. P. J. Carroll's strategic mistakes were in formulation and execution. The new twin-pronged strategy left top management doing battle on three fronts over diverse businesses and geographical areas (and also separate locations in the USA); this made it difficult not only for management but also for the board. In this writer's view more than ever the board, because of its knowledge base, was separated from the new business activities and was more dependent on the top management. It appears it was also forced to rely on management accounting information on the new ventures, but Derrik Corbett, the experienced financial director, had taken early retirement in 1988. His successor stayed only six months. Much 'soft' data appeared to confirm that progress was being made. It proved to be flawed, and board monitoring and control appear to have been undermined. In this writer's opinion not only was there an inadequate internal expertise in top management in the business of the two new projects, there was also nobody on the board who had direct experience in the areas either.

This writer concludes that P. J. Carroll's errors can be categorised as ones of commission (the aquaculture and direct marketing diversification) and omission (failing to cater for changing market taste — the need for new products in the low-tar category). How could Carrolls, with its successful track record, deteriorate from successful management to mismanagement over such a short space of time? The full answer is elusive because it encompasses so many elements including personality, power, culture, organisation structure and strategy.

The lack of response to changing market taste and demand for low-tar cigarettes can be ascribed partly to marketing management complacency. In 1983 Carrolls controlled a commanding 56% of its domestic market and still retained 55% in 1986. It produced the three largest selling brands on the Irish market — Major Extra Size, Rothmans King Size and Carrolls No. 1. To consider launching a competitive cigarette in the lighter low-tar category in the early 1980s when this was a relatively small niche in the total market did not seem attractive and apparently went against the product philosophy of the organisation. Carrolls perceived the intrinsic characteristic of its cigarettes as offering a heavier and 'real' smoking experience. The lighter, and more ambiguous, smoking experience being offered by the new low-tar

Table 7.14: P. J. Carroll's mistakes

Strategic

Investment
- The Fieldcrest project in 1978
- The aquaculture project in 1986
- The direct marketing project in 1986
- The rapid expansion of the aquaculture and direct marketing projects in 1987–89

Product innovation
- The lengthy delay in introducing low-tar cigarettes

Organisation structure and board of directors
- Creeping bureaucracy in the 1980s
- The retirement of the long-established senior management team between 1982 and 1988 with inadequate succession planning
- Don Carroll taking over the combined roles of chief executive and chairman from August 1985 until December 1987
- The resignation of Sean Dior, financial director, in August 1988 after only six months' service followed by weaknesses in financial control in the late 1980s
- The appointment of David Fish as chief executive in January 1988 and his resignation in March 1990
- The dominance of Don Carroll in the mid to late 1980s
- The absence of sufficient counterweight directors or critical comment and control on the board in the mid to late 1980s

Tactical

Short-termism
- The sharp cutback on advertising spending in 1987

Systems
- The inadequate information and management control systems in the new aquaculture and direct marketing divisions
- Inadequate financial control over spending on new projects which was in excess of plans

cigarettes went against the product culture of Carrolls. There was also the concern that the existing successful portfolio of products' high market share should not be disturbed.

It is surprising, with its scientific approach to consumer market research, that Carrolls seems to have failed to detect the changing taste among young people and the faster growth of the low-tar niche market. One answer was the increasing bureaucracy of the organisation. Another was retirement among, and the changing preoccupation with the new ventures of, the senior marketing management. The diversification strategy was certainly an ingredient in its losing sight of the core tobacco business. This blindness to changing consumer taste provided the two competitors, Gallaher and John Player & Sons, with the opportunity they needed. Both developed better quality and improved taste brands for the low-tar and milder and longer cigarette niches. With attractive packaging and more effective marketing John Player Blue and Silk Cut made inroads into the fastest growing sector — resulting in claims that John Player Blue had overtaken Major Extra Size as the best selling brand.[62] Between 1989 and 1994, P. J. Carroll belatedly launched seven new brands in the low-tar lighter cigarette sector to arrest its market decline without any marked success.[63]

Of more fundamental importance was the structure of the board and senior management team. In this writer's opinion top management succession was faulty. The break-up of a long-standing management team began with the retirements in 1982 of Aidan Manahan, sales and subsequently marketing director, and Joe McKinley in tobacco operations. Charles Carroll, an uncle of Don Carroll, who specialised in tobacco purchasing, took his leave in 1984. Some younger senior managers also left for other positions. The retirement of Des Ryan in 1985 was a special loss. He had been group chief executive and a balancing influence on the organisation's affairs for fourteen years. A crucial weakness was Don Carroll's assumption of the dual roles of chief executive and chairman from August 1985 until December 1987. In addition, decentralised authority and responsibility were introduced with the diversification policy. The new management structure was explained by Don Carroll:

> In the past responsibility for strategic initiative as well as overall strategic control was held at the centre. In the future we want as far as possible to see strategic initiative originating in each operating activity. We shall be engaged in continuing dialogue with individual managing directors concerning their objectives and priorities, where they believe they ought to go and the means by which they think they should get there.[64]

The planning and management accounting information and control systems now assumed greater importance with this autonomy. David Fish, who had previously been chief executive of Cadbury in Ireland following international marketing experience in the USA, was recruited as general manager in July 1986. He was appointed a director in January 1987 and chief executive officer from January 1988. Derrik Corbett, the long-standing finance director, took early retirement in February 1988 followed in December by John Lepere, the marketing 'guru' of the organisation since 1962.

It was a demanding brief for David Fish in view of the management and board structure and the strategic hyperactivity. He had resigned by mid-March 1990, a month after Don Carroll. Apart from mistakes and weaknesses at senior management, there were shortcomings at an operational management level in the three divisions. In tobacco there were marketing weaknesses. In the aquaculture and direct marketing ventures there was clearly an insufficient strength and depth of management in technical expertise and management accounting. Don Carroll perceptively acknowledged this after the crisis:

> I think the challenge of what we are trying to do is spread on much too thin a management base and a serious problem which flows from that is that the multiplicity of things which need urgent decisions really preclude the opportunity to consider anything sufficiently deeply to make absolutely certain the decision is right. And that takes a lot more time in new situations in which there isn't a track record and past experience to work on. So it's the narrow base of management in my view rather than the quality of management. We made wrong decisions because we didn't know enough about specific operational detail to make the right decisions.[65]

Direct marketing seems to have been heavily dependent on consultants to help it create and test-market *Carroll Journals*. In his first chairman's statement, in summer 1990, Laurence Crowley noted that the various parts of the direct marketing division had been closed down because profitability 'could not be achieved within the requisite time scale'. The Bedford Fair acquisition was to be the sole focus of direct marketing investment in the USA and its management capability was 'being broadened and deepened'. Carrolls had entered a very different business culture when it invested in the USA. A possible explanation for the direct marketing debacle was that Carrolls moved too quickly, acquiring three companies in very different locations within a short time and making changes in its operations before it adequately experienced the American business culture and understood the market.

When discussing aquaculture Laurence Crowley pointed to the increase in production capacity from 100 tonnes in 1986 to 2,500 tonnes in 1990:

> The very rapid pace of development placed enormous strains on the management of the Division. Significant losses have been incurred

throughout this period, partly of a developmental kind to be expected in the initial phases of a new business venture, but clearly exacerbated by the speed with which the business was built from small beginnings.[66]

The aquaculture and direct marketing 'mismanagement' can be viewed as partly strategic, because of the headlong speed of expansion in each activity and the decision to invest in two new risky ventures that were so different and so geographically distant. This was a mistake of both top management and the board. This writer found it remarkable that the board permitted the organisation to invest at such a scale and move into such a degree of business risk exposure on two separate ventures at the same time, particularly when there seems to have been no experienced head office expertise in the areas.

Board structure

In the opinion of this writer, the fundamental weakness in P. J. Carroll, as in Guinness, was the board structure and its consequences for the distribution of influence and power in decision-making, management structure, authority, responsibility and corporate direction. Like Guinness's board, P. J. Carroll's board was large, with a membership ranging between twelve and fourteen. Six (including Don Carroll) were executives. Another two directors were former executives and four were 'independent' non-executive board members. At the time, there was just one representative from Rothmans. The significant change was when Don Carroll assumed the combined role of chairman and chief executive in August 1985. This crucial event occurred when there was a change in the composition of the 'independents' with two long-established directors retiring and two new younger directors — James Osborne and Charles Carroll (a cousin of Don Carroll) — being appointed from January 1986. He had held the dual positions of chairman and chief executive of P. J. Carroll before — from 1960 to 1970. In that period under his very effective leadership, not only did the organisation appreciably strengthen in its market position, product portfolio and profitability, but also he brought together a balanced and strong top management team. As one interviewee put it to this author:

> In those years Don Carroll resuscitated the company with incredible energy, drive, vision and command. He was a statesmanlike, patrician figure with so many abilities. He saw ahead and negotiated the non-threatening partnership with Carreras, the international cigarette group.

It was then a company focused on one industry in one country. In the mid-1980s P. J. Carroll was attempting to radically transform its business interests. The risk profile was much greater. The power and influence of Don Carroll, in board dynamics and over the executive management team, were crucial at the time of the decisions to invest in aquaculture and direct marketing. In the vital period 1984 to 1988 there were major changes in top management and in the composition of the board. In the view of this writer, this lack of continuity and weakness in management succession plans made the organisation unduly dependent on Don Carroll — and increased his power. Also the board was dominated by current and former executives.

The board seemed to offer a weak challenge to Don Carroll in the vital period of the aquaculture and direct marketing projects. Some of the executive and non-executive directors did advocate alternative views, but they were in the minority. He was a formidable adversary, competitively, intellectually and in character, quite apart from the fact that many on the board had an allegiance to him. But there was another side to such a gifted leader. It seems that different views on strategy and policy were apparently not always appreciated.

It appears that the new younger independent directors, James Osborne and Charles Carroll, attempted to influence events and question information, policies and the unfolding strategy. They had arrived after the diversification projects had been approved. It was the first time that real boardroom conflict became apparent. One business weekly, which corroborates this author's evidence, reported in February 1990:

> Nor did Rothmans support dissidents in the Carroll boardroom where Dublin solicitor James Osborne challenged Don Carroll two years ago but got little support.
>
> Those who questioned the wisdom of Carroll's strategy inside its boardroom were largely left to fight alone. Irish institutional investors were in no hurry to question what was going wrong.[67]

By early 1988 there was some concern about the nature and scale of the diversification commitments, not only by equity market analysts but also at board level. The internal board challenge to Don Carroll, by a minority, continued for two years before certain new Rothmans directors seemed to take notice — due to changes in personnel and power in the parent. In 1988 Rothmans had increased its direct representation to three members.

Accounting and financial policies and management information breakdowns

The fact that P. J. Carroll won the first ever Leinster Society of Chartered Accountants Published Accounts Award for 1977 and many times subsequently is an indication of the high quality of its financial reporting and disclosure policies. The group was one of the pioneers in Britain and Ireland in studying the effects of inflation and accounting for performance on the enthusiastic initiative of Don Carroll. It acted as a field tester of the new concepts being developed by the Morpeth Committee in the UK.[68] There was also a heavy commitment in the design and early computerisation of management accounting and information systems.

Not only did P. J. Carroll pursue prudent accounting policies, but its financial policies and dividend payout ratios were most conservative. A self-imposed restriction on borrowing was emphasised by Don Carroll when he asserted 'prudent management of the resources within our control has ensured that we retain our financial vigour'.[69] Don Carroll's chairman's statements for thirty consecutive years were a model of clarity and pertinent information on the policies and issues touching on business performance, objectives and future strategic direction.

Because of its enlightened financial reporting policies, Carrolls was regarded as having a strong accounting and financial control function. This had evolved under the careful direction of Derrik Corbett. His successor, Sean Dior, resigned in August 1988, after only six months' service. This created a serious vacuum in this function at a time of great organisational complexity. In this writer's view it was a fatal defect. It was not until June 1990, after the appointment of Laurence Crowley as chairman, that Cecil Hayes was recruited as group finance director.

The fact that there were new ventures, with fixed asset and working capital commitments, made financial controls more important in 1988 than at any time in the previous decade. Top management and the board also needed reliable information on actual performance, to enable them to meet their monitoring role. It is strange that the board appeared to allow such a financial control gap to develop and continue for so long over such a critical period. It is no coincidence that there would appear to have been accounting and management control deficiencies in the aquaculture and direct marketing divisions for some time up to 1990. The new organisational structure had given the three divisions considerable autonomy in their operations, with their own support and accounting personnel. The corporate plan envisaged a four-year timeframe to 1989 to achieve the transition from a development stage to initial commercial success and break-even. Economic profitability was expected to emerge in the early 1990s.

As envisaged, start-up losses were reported in aquaculture and direct marketing in 1987. Encouraging progress in their development was announced by the company in 1988.[70] Aquaculture was expected to contribute to profits in 1989 and further investment was expected to be minimal. Direct marketing had annualised sales of £40 million; the objective was to increase volume 'substantially' by the beginning of the 1990s and to achieve a target 10% net profit margin. The 'above the line' development expenses were planned to decline and it was intended that in 1990 direct marketing would be at or above break-even point. It had been an intensive exercise according to Don Carroll:

> Looking back over the past three years one cannot but feel a sense of satisfaction as to what has been achieved; I have said earlier that it is momentous. Much still remains to be done, in particular further strengthening of management and developing processes and systems which will enable us to exploit the potential which we have acquired. The very substantial progress made already gives grounds for confidence that our expectations can be realised.[71]

Some months later, at the annual general meeting on 13 February 1989, shareholders were informed that the financial year end was to be changed to end March 1990 rather than 30 September 1989. Once again the chairman indicated continued progress when he commented that the 'experience in the year thus far confirms our belief that the transition phase will be completed within this accounting period'. Group trading profit for the twelve months was projected to be of a similar order to the previous year. Aquaculture was expected to show profits for the first time and direct marketing was expecting to move from the weaker performance of the previous year.

On 15 June 1989, P. J. Carroll released its interim report for the first six months to end March 1989. The trading profits in respect of the three divisions at £4.0 million were slightly ahead of those of the two previous six-month periods. The review of performance was encouraging and the board continued to indicate that the twelve-month figures would be much in line with those of the previous year. Looking forward, it stated for 1990: 'the end can be seen of the transition phase as the contribution from sales begins to cover the heavy development outlays'.

Unfortunately it was not to be. The board released its second interim report on 8 December 1989, disclosing a sharp fall in group trading profit for the twelve months to end September 1989 — £1.7 million compared with £7 million for the same divisions in 1988. This implied a trading loss of £2.3 million in the second six-month period, in contrast to the expectations of a stable performance. The reasons were increased deficits in both the aquaculture and direct marketing divisions and a profit decline in the tobacco division. The statement commented: 'The Board is particularly disappointed with these results which fall so significantly short of the indications given in the first interim statement published in June.'

The earlier representations about progress and expected performance were made in good faith, based on the internal divisional information, budgets and management estimates. Unfortunately, this internal management information either was not up to date or not wholly based on fact, or was unreasonably optimistic in its estimates of performance. The fact that P. J. Carroll announced a loss of £12 million (which became £21 million after charging 'extraordinary items') for the eighteen months to March 1990 (and had further provisions and write-offs in subsequent years) was further evidence that all had not been as well as indicated in its new ventures and that quite a different accounting representation was now being adopted.

In its audited financial statements to end March 1990, P. J. Carroll charged £16 million as 'exceptional items'. The largest individual element of this figure was the item defined as 'Aquaculture division: stock losses and provisions — £5.6 million'. This suggests that the valuation of stocks and work-in-progress in internal management accounts may have been flawed. It suffered heavy stock write-offs during a period of change. In this writer's view, perhaps the critical issue is not the amount of write-off (which itself was material) but the possible 'information distortion' effect on the earlier measurement of the division's profitability and performance. Overvaluation of stocks and work-in-progress can lead to overstated gross profit margins and camouflages poor operational management performance. In the aquaculture division, when the more realistic measure of performance emerged, the board seem to have become aware of major weaknesses in the division's cost controls and its cost structures, as well as very heavy capital outlays, which were considerably in excess of norms expected for the industry.

In a perceptive research report for Davy Stockbrokers of 8 May 1990, six weeks before P. J. Carroll's preliminary announcement of its disastrous results, analyst John O'Reilly commented that there were others who had made money out of aquaculture and direct marketing and he asked why had

Carrolls experienced such problems. He suggested that though there was no simple answer it seemed that Carrolls went into these operations too deeply and too fast. Objectives were blurred, costs were excessive and the operational controls, systems and management expertise were inadequate for these new activities.[72] It would seem that Carrolls had excellent management information systems for its tobacco activity, but it was unable to transfer this expertise to the different technology and processes of the new ventures — which had a different culture. It also raises questions about internal controls and internal audit.

Reflections on Guinness and P. J. Carroll

The circumstances of P. J. Carroll in the early 1950s and Guinness in the UK in the early 1980s were very similar in their core business. Though they were in decline they were renewed by strong new leadership through a combination of better marketing, product positioning and more efficient production methods. In each case a new management team was moulded.

Following its great success for almost three decades P. J. Carroll became complacent in the tobacco business. There was a 'delusion syndrome' about the transferability of its management and marketing expertise and the apparent success of the new ventures based on estimates and future projections rather than tested factual data. One must wonder whether the board also was contaminated by such an illusion for a vital three years before the crisis broke. P. J. Carroll's assumption that cigarette marketing expertise was transferable to other businesses in different geographic locations with different customers, cultures, distribution channels and promotional processes proved flawed. The fact that the tobacco division failed to launch new low-tar brands in the mid to late 1980s and started to lose market share raises questions about whether the marketing expertise had weakened or whether it had not been really matched competitively until marketing management changes were made in Gallaher.

Testing the Guinness and P. J. Carroll cases against the elements of the downward spiral model of decline advocated by Hambrick and D'Aveni provides some insights into their earlier organisational weaknesses.[73] The 'early impairment' stage was evident in Guinness as margins in brewing and market share (particularly in the UK) were weakening some years before the crisis but the underlying problems were not addressed because of a bureaucratic management structure operating as two independent empires in Dublin and London. Market scanning information was inadequate. Guinness had spotted the trend towards lager and had moved early. It had not reacted sufficiently in its core product — stout — in modernisation investment or marketing. P. J. Carroll committed a similar mistake in not adapting its product range early enough to changes in a growing niche market. Its blindness and failure to act were fostered by culture and belief in its own 'strong taste' well-established products which were at the upper end of the market with higher margins. Thus both organisations declined to the 'inaction stage' in their core business. Both adopted diversification strategies as a response to their perceived problems. Both lost money and let their core business weaken, though much more so in P. J. Carroll. In Guinness the problem was accumulated slack in production costs and productivity, whereas Carrolls had always kept its production facilities modern and productivity was good — there it was a marketing fault.

The reduction in costs and improved efficiency in Guinness were an indication of the scale of accretion of slack and inefficiency which is often endemic in a mature organisation. The attention to resolving the problems in each case was delayed by the financial slack available to absorb the cash flow deficits. Both were financially strong organisations and thus had sufficient resources, despite the losses and balance sheet write-offs in asset values on the disposal of the diversification investments, to survive the crisis and provide time for a turnaround attempt. The outcomes and approaches were different — even though both were 'brand' businesses. With financial back-up, Guinness's marketing expert was able to restore the core business with an imaginative and methodical approach to product and brand reinvigoration, a ruthlessness on cost efficiencies and achieving performance targets, and a change in culture allied to improved communications.

There was less slack in P. J. Carroll's system to enable cost savings to be achieved and the environment was much more hostile in trying to hold market share and launch new brands. Carrolls could not advertise like Guinness because of government restrictions and the market was declining. Whereas Guinness represented a successful turnaround within three years, Carrolls remained problematical after five years with a steadily declining market share and indifferent profitability. The issue of earnings management emerged in P. J. Carroll but not in Guinness. Some interviewees felt that the Guinness loss of £26 million had been created by overstating the extraordinary items write-offs of £49 million. In fact, Guinness appears to have had further material charges under this heading for some years subsequently, raising the question as to how a charge can be 'extraordinary' every year for a decade.

Both had weaknesses at board level. In this writer's opinion Guinness had a number of family members with little to contribute and P. J. Carroll had a surfeit of executives and retired executives on the board. Governance was weak at board and shareholder levels until the crisis was obvious. In both it needed sweeping changes in board and senior management to institute correctional action. At top management level it was a case of near complacency in Guinness in contrast to the hyperactivity of Carrolls. This writer believes that both also had weak financial control — at a strategic level in Guinness and at both strategic and operational levels in its later years at P. J. Carroll. New financial directors were recruited at the turnaround stage in both cases. The findings from the two cases suggest that there is a connection between efficient governance, strong financial control and information allied to an independent power at board level which is a counter to the chief executive's influence. Prior to the crisis, the selection of board members seems to have been decided by the Guinness family and Don Carroll respectively. Were the investment institutions and Rothmans so disenfranchised that they seemed to be unable to take more positive action in advance? The evidence from the two cases demonstrates the extraordinary position and power of the family and the family name. In this writer's opinion the Guinness family saw it as their right and inheritance to dominate the board and feebly let the senior management control their separate empires as the organisation's performance declined. A combination of name and ability led to Don Carroll dominating his board and management. In both instances, there was an extraordinary acquiescence by others who had much greater voting power.

In Miller's syndrome typology, Guinness was a good example of the 'Headless Firm' which was drifting aimlessly. In contrast, P. J. Carroll captured most of the characteristics of the 'Impulsive Syndrome' and it did 'run blind' at a critical period, when there was, apparently, information systems failure in the new ventures. Perhaps the old adage to take caution when organisations extend their accounting year or delay the submission of their results was a cue to problems in P. J. Carroll — though admittedly the board provided twelve-month unaudited figures, these proved ineffective. Carrolls effectively imploded. The scale of the diversifications and the range of associated business problems appear to have overwhelmed the accounting information systems.

Chapter 8

Irish Press and Waterford Wedgwood: The Clash Between Culture, Craft and Change

So these princes of ours, who had been for many years entrenched in their states, have no cause to complain of fortune because they have lost them; the fault lies rather in their own ineptitude, for, as in tranquil times they had given no thought to the possibility of change (a common failing of men, who rarely think of storms to come while the sun yet shines), adversity caught them unprepared.

Niccolò Machiavelli, *The Prince*

Introduction

Printing and publishing newspapers for the domestic market and the manufacture and marketing of quality crystal products aimed at export markets may not seem to have much in common. Yet many similar themes influenced the crisis in the Irish Press group and Waterford Wedgwood. Both were primarily production-oriented enterprises which were very labour intensive. The craft and skill of employees were dominant in the creation and identity of the product. Underlying each organisation was a complex mixture of an internal culture, a relatively short history, a link to a founding family and a long-established personalised and paternalistic management style, revolving around a few people. By the third generation of family, both organisations were in a downward spiral of decline.

Waterford's core crystal business was eventually saved by a very large equity injection and sweeping board and management changes. The three newspapers of the Irish Press group ceased publication, in controversial circumstances, in June 1995. The appointment of an examiner, at the request of employees, was followed by a receiver and a liquidator to the publishing subsidiary on the initiative of the directors. The loss of a long-established trio of daily, evening and Sunday newspapers had more than just creditor and employment consequences. There was the loss of a voice representing a particular group which had consequences for the public interest, the quality of democracy and a healthy competitiveness and diversity in the media in Ireland.

Both organisations were 'national institutions' with well-established brand names. Interestingly, their creation sprang from very different patriotic and nationalistic motives. The founding families were heavily involved in the struggle for Irish independence. Each ended up on opposite sides of the civil war of 1922–23. Eamon de Valera's name is synonymous with Irish republicanism, the *Irish Press*, Irish politics and the development of the state for almost forty years.[1] The *Irish Press* was the brainchild of Eamon de Valera. The aim was to provide support for Fianna Fáil and communicate an alternative view to that of the two major newspapers — the *Irish Independent*, which was anti-Fianna Fáil and supportive of the Free State government, and the *Irish Times*, which then had a unionist perspective.[2]

Perhaps the 'practical' political background and business contribution of the McGraths, the 'sponsors' and builders of Waterford Glass with Joe Griffin, are less well known. Both Joe McGrath and Michael Collins resigned from their positions in Craig Gardner, the public accounting firm, on Good Friday 1916 to fight in the Easter Rising. McGrath was the Minister for Industry in the first Free State government.[3] He left politics in 1924 to establish himself as an accounting and business adviser. Subsequent joint venture business interests included the lucrative Irish Sweepstakes and Irish Glass Bottle. Waterford Glass was established with very noble motives at a time of high emigration. A primary objective was to create employment and show that Irish skills and management could match the world.

The two enterprises arose out of a profoundly committed sense of nationalism by both families. Practical patriotism in action in one contrasted with political patriotism in the other. The *Irish Press* was founded in 1931 and Waterford Glass in 1947, though the McGrath and other sponsoring families did not become involved until three years later when they helped the company avoid collapse.

After their earlier struggle to survive, both organisations grew as a result of the expansion of consumer spending in the USA and Ireland in the 1960s and 1970s. Each was extraordinarily innovative in its product/market strategies in the growth and adolescent stages. Waterford created a brand name, and with a variety of designs, good product positioning and supportive marketing distribution arrangements, it became the market leader in its niche market for leaded crystal glass in the USA. The Irish Press group successfully launched evening and Sunday papers in the late 1940s and early 1950s, after twenty years of publishing a daily paper.

Both were 'family' dominated and were affected by the untimely death of a 'family' chief executive at a critical time in their history. The external environment, which was buoyant in the 1970s, was less benign in the 1980s in consumer spending, advertising revenues, volume demand, price, and changes in consumers' tastes and competition. The impact of new technology also became an important strategic issue. In both organisations serious industrial relations problems emerged, resulting in strikes over pay, conditions and outmoded work practices. The strategic and operational managerial roles became more complex. The internal and external organisational environments required change and adaptation at a level of managerial competence which was beyond the family interests. In this writer's view mismanagement operated for years.

Irish Press
Background

The idea of a republican newspaper took root following the release of Eamon de Valera from detention in 1924, after the civil war.[4] The debacle of the 1925 by-elections, when Seán Lemass pointed to the hostility of the existing press and the church to de Valera's political aims, provided further stimulation. The founding of the Fianna Fáil political party in 1926 underlined the imperative to counter the political stance being taken by the other national papers if it was to win an election. Publishing the *Nation*, on a weekly basis from 1927, was a step on the road to offering an alternative vision for a new Ireland.

Apart from active fund-raising in Ireland, de Valera spent three periods fund-raising in the USA in 1927, 1928 and 1929, on the last occasion spending some time studying newspaper technology and management.[5] This US capital was invested through the Irish Press Corporation in the USA. Eamon de Valera was appointed a trustee and representative of the US shareholders, and, combined with his own shareholding, this endowed him with almost personal control over the new organisation. In addition, the articles of association included a clause which stated there would be a controlling director who 'shall have sole and absolute control of the public and political policy of the Company and of the editorial management thereof'.[6] It was to prove to be a powerful platform for dominating what was to become, effectively, a family company.

The Irish Independent group of newspapers, which actively supported Free State government policies, was founded by the self-made wealthy businessman, William Martin Murphy, in 1905 through a merger of his other publishing interests and the purchase of the bankrupt *Irish Daily Independent*. Murphy was a nationalist with conservative middle-class views.[7]

He was elected to the Westminster parliament as a nationalist in 1885. He is probably best remembered for his leading role in the 1913 lock-out by employers against recognition of the trade union movement led by Jim Larkin and James Connolly, though it seems he was a more progressive employer and businessman than most of his counterparts.[8] As president of the Dublin Chamber of Commerce at the time, he was the public expression of the hated employers in a bitter dispute. It should also be recalled that the *Irish Independent* condemned the 1916 Easter Rising and the links with left-wing elements who were seen as 'Larkinism' and the citizen army.[9]

Key events in the life of Irish Press	
Birth	
1931	*Irish Press* launched on 5 September.
	Founded by Eamon de Valera, who becomes first controlling director and editor-in-chief.
	Major Vivion de Valera (his son) assists in operations.
	Frank Gallagher appointed editor. Resigns five years later.
1942	Jack Dempsey appointed general manager.
Adolescence	
1949	Seán Lemass appointed managing director.
	Sunday Press launched.
1951	Major Vivion de Valera appointed managing director and takes over as controlling director and editor-in-chief.
1954	*Evening Press* launched.
Maturity	
1977	Jack Dempsey retires as general manager.
1981	First trading loss in decades.
1982	Death of Major Vivion de Valera.
	Dr Eamon de Valera (grandson of Eamon de Valera) appointed controlling director, editor-in-chief and chairman.
1983	Donal Flinn appointed non-executive chairman. A. G. Galligan and Seán McHale, businessmen, appointed to board in non-executive capacities.
1984	Flinn and McHale resign from board. Dr Eamon de Valera reassumes chairmanship.
	Elio Malocco (brother-in-law of Dr Eamon de Valera) co-opted to board.

cont.

Key events in the life of Irish Press *cont.*

1985	Acquisition of Southside Newspapers.
1986	Plans to introduce new technology and implement redundancy, changes in work practices and rationalisation lead to bitter disputes with employees and trade unions. Twelve-week work stoppage (lock-out) at *Irish Press*. Six-week stoppage at *Sunday Press* and *Evening Press*.
1987	Closure of Southside Newspapers.
1988	Conversion of *Irish Press* from broadsheet to tabloid format.
1989	Creation of two subsidiaries to operate newspaper publishing and hold ownership of titles.
	Announcement of partnership with Ingersoll Publications of USA with new investment in subsidiaries.
1992	Court case instigated by Irish Press parent against Ingersoll Publications interests.
1993	Irish Press interests successful in court case.
1994	Independent Newspapers acquires 25% equity stake in publishing subsidiaries and advances secured loans.
1995	Industrial relations dispute in May. Publication suspended.
	In June, three journalists successfully petition the High Court to appoint an examiner to two Irish Press publishing subsidiaries.
	Attempts at agreeing scheme of arrangement and acceptable conditions for purchase and relaunch of titles fail.
	In September, receiver and liquidator appointed to publishing subsidiary.
	In November M. Walsh, director and B. Ryan, secretary of parent, resign. Board reduced to three people.
	Resolution that Dr Eamon de Valera and Vincent Jennings be removed as directors of Irish Press plc fails at annual general meeting.

The legacy of the Irish Press group's political origins

In a comparative study of organisational mortality in the Irish and Argentinean newspaper industries between 1800 and 1975, Carroll and Delacroix[10] found that many failed in their early years because of the phenomenon of the 'liability of newness' identified by Stinchcombe.[11] Their study is relevant to this research because it examined the relationship of organisational age and the probability of death. They found that in Ireland the survival probabilities of new newspapers were higher than those in Argentina, and that they had a 50% chance of surviving five years. Similar to other types of firm mortality studies, age was a critical variable in the early years. Newspapers which survived twenty years had a very high probability of survival. The Irish Press group celebrated its fiftieth anniversary in 1981 and, based on these findings, its newspapers would not have been expected to collapse. Carroll and Delacroix offered one caveat to their hypothesis:

> We expect newspapers born in politically turbulent years to be short-lived. This expectation is based on two possibly additive but distinct theoretical ideas. First, newspapers founded during political crises are likely to be established for an explicit political purpose and, consequently, to become obsolete once the crisis is resolved. Second, political turbulence disrupts, or is a sign of disruption of, the previous social alignments; it often alters the ties between social groups and societal resources. When such realignment proceeds, resources are free for a short period. As ecologists have pointed out, the first group to exploit these resources are those with the most flexible structures. . . . These first movers thrive in irregular resource spaces.[12]

This view reflects much of the experience of the Irish Press group. It was prophetic because the Press's main rival, Independent Newspapers, was the first to move into the 'irregular resource spaces' when it recognised past political influences and social attitudes were breaking down in the late 1970s. Ireland began to change much more rapidly. Membership of the European Economic Community raised living standards and influenced expectations, social attitudes and legislation. The defeat of Fianna Fáil in the June 1981 election, the formation of the short-lived Fine Gael/Labour coalition, and that government's budget defeat but early return to power in December 1982 were evidence of a watershed in the underlying social and political processes in the country.[13] The fact that referenda on abortion and divorce could even be mounted in 1983 and 1986 was evidence of some stirring in the conservative social attitudes and mores of Irish society.[14] Additionally, there was a serious attempt at dialogue between the British and Irish governments which resulted in the Anglo-Irish Agreement in November 1985.[15]

In 1981 the Irish Press group dominated Irish newspaper sales, but within five years its decline was such that it was overtaken by the three matching titles of Independent Newspapers. The passing of control from the Murphy family to Dr A. J. F. O'Reilly in 1973 was to lead to a new strategic vision and culture for the Independent group. New professional management was recruited, there was a greater emphasis on marketing and new editors were appointed with a brief to modernise the papers and meet the needs of the new younger Irish consumer as indicated by market research.

The Irish Press group, unlike the Independent, was unable to shake off the combination of traits it acquired at birth — the nationalistic and conservative tinge of the morning paper which also touched the Sunday title, and the continuing power and influence of the de Valera family interest — which Stinchcombe hypothesised as special features of an imprinting.[16] There was very little effort by management to change the outmoded editorial approach to the three papers. As a result the content and layout were dictated almost exclusively by the editors, unaided by modern management training or up-to-date information on their consumers, present or future.

The influence of history and culture on the 'product'

The forces that shape a product create their own culture and a relationship with a particular consumer group. This culture and a continuity of management style may support stability in a particular product identity, though the nature of the consumer and the market may change. The political and social forces which gave birth to the *Irish Press* and the strong personalities who initially crafted its form and content in order to communicate a particular message also defined the product and its target consumer group. The *Irish Press* was launched on 5 September 1931. The circulation success of the young newspaper, particularly in western and rural areas, was immediate. A leading modern historian, Joe Lee, observed:

> The *Press* quickly proved itself a brilliant journalistic venture, comparable in its immediate impact to William O'Brien's *United Ireland* of 1882. Indeed, the *Press* recalled much of the style and substance of the early William O'Brien. Its ebullient free-wheeling polemical style outraged genteel spirits, but for a stridently popular paper, it descended to the gutter level remarkably rarely.[17]

Circulation of the *Irish Press* moved from 78,000 copies in the first three months of 1932 to 91,000 copies in the fourth quarter. In the election month of January 1933 a daily average of 115,000 copies were sold compared with the *Irish Times* and the *Cork Examiner* which sold a daily average of about 50,000 copies each in the same period. Lee saw the *Irish Press* playing a vital propaganda role in helping Fianna Fáil win election victories 'not only by confirming the convictions of the faithful, but also by converting previous non-voters or even unbelievers'.[18]

Frank Gallagher, the first 'chief editor', had a profound influence in shaping the style and focus of the paper. Like most of its employees, particularly the journalists, he had strong republican sympathies, having been interned during the civil war and involved in an anti-Treatyite publication. He was one of the very few to have a professional journalist background, and had considerable flair and an enormous capacity for work. He instructed staff to find Irish angles for their stories, reflect these in the headlines and be wary of the imperialist tone of British and foreign news agencies. He was also aware of the need to attract female readers and ensure the *Irish Press* was not solely a Dublin newspaper.[19] Journalistically it was innovative, carrying out major investigations into such relevant issues as the poor housing conditions nationwide. It presented itself as the voice of the small person, being unafraid to rail against the establishment. In its time it was a modern newspaper and its general layout, especially its front page, contributed towards its success.

The financial difficulties of the early years resulted in considerable strain between editorial demands for resources to support the quality and reputation of the 'product', and the board's (mainly de Valera's) concern about possible bankruptcy because of the insufficiency of start-up capital. De Valera had not met his fund-raising targets in the USA, primarily because of the recession. The competitive reaction of the established rival papers was intense. The big difference was in the amount of advertising secured from business and professional interests — which had serious financial consequences for the *Irish Press*. Michael O'Toole vividly illustrated the straitened circumstances of the young organisation:

> Penury soon became a fact of life at Burgh Quay. Frank Ridgeway, the cashier, would frequently have to empty the cash register at the front counter in order to pay an impatient creditor waiting in his office upstairs . . . he often had to leave by the works entrance so as to avoid those demanding payment in the front office.[20]

An American efficiency expert, Jack Harrington, was recruited by the nervous American shareholders to help stave off possible bankruptcy. He involved himself in all aspects of the paper's affairs, including the reorganisation and redesign of the newsroom.[21] Harrington's efforts helped to cut costs and improve distribution efficiency, saving the *Irish Press* from closure. However the journalists and eventually Gallagher took exception to Harrington's interventions and a directive from the National Union of Journalists forbade co-operation with him. According to O'Toole:

Gallagher never succeeded in grasping one of the most basic facts of newspaper publishing — that in a financial crisis the accountant will supersede even the most brilliant editor.[22]

Gallagher was revered by his staff and he trained most of them, so pressure on him from Harrington and the board, together with his eventual resignation, caused an upheaval that contributed to the long-standing division between management and editorial staff that lasted into the 1980s. The episode illustrates how a combination of personalities, circumstances and events tend to shape attitudes, culture and tradition.

Another key element in the newspaper's production was the role of the typesetters and the printers who exercised a lot of restrictions.[23] Printing methods had changed little over hundreds of years for 'these kings of old style craftsmen' who, according to Oram, 'lived in an enclosed social order amid the heat, dirt, and noise'.[24] But all was to change utterly in the 1980s, with the coming of computers, desk top publishing — and silence. The wide range of expertise, craft skills and traditions encompassing editors, journalists, printing, production, advertising, and distribution staff, apart from the administrators, that makes up the complex organisational configuration behind a newspaper was about to be challenged by the age of technology and more discerning consumers.

Product/market and competitive position

Improved economic conditions and the benefit of the circulation success and increases in advertising revenue helped the Irish Press group become much more profitable in the 1970s. In 1979 the *Sunday Press* achieved weekly sales of almost 391,000 copies, the *Evening Press* had daily sales of 171,000 copies, and the *Irish Press* sold almost 101,000 copies daily. The Sunday and evening papers became the largest selling newspapers in their markets, while only the *Irish Independent* outsold the *Irish Press* in its market with daily sales of 186,000 copies. The *Irish Press* and the *Evening Press* won the United Newspaper Award and the Westminster Press Trophy in 1979 for the highest percentage increase in sales and the highest absolute sales increase respectively.

Nineteen eighty-one was a proud year for the group. It celebrated its fiftieth anniversary with the *Irish Press* and *Evening Press* increasing their daily circulation to 105,000 and 178,000 copies respectively. Despite these market improvements, the financial performance was poor with a net loss of £1.6 million because of 'profitless volume'. This paradox was the first signal of a downward spiral to financial deterioration. There were weaknesses in cost and financial control, reflecting the lack of management depth and systems, as the 'old guard' management were handing over the reins. There had been a number of problematical wage increases under the guise of productivity negotiations, which were common to all the daily newspapers at that time, but which in the Press's competitors bought the kind of change needed to meet the new needs of the consumer. While the circulation of the Irish Press titles continued to look healthy in the late 1970s, the seeds of the group's decline had been sewn. The Independent group had laid the foundation for its competitiveness which eventually undermined an ailing Irish Press group.

As illustrated in Table 8.1, the fall in circulation for the three Irish Press newspapers between 1980 and 1994 was much greater than that experienced by their rivals. The Irish Press group's daily, evening and Sunday paper circulation declined by 62.2%, 68.6% and 58.9% respectively — consistently losing market share to Independent Newspapers. In contrast, the *Irish Times* increased its circulation and the *Cork Examiner* suffered a much smaller decline. This clearly indicates the problem was internal. In 1980 the *Irish Press* had 22.5% of the domestic market, which was just over half that of the *Irish Independent* (43.2%). By 1987, it declined to 20.6% compared to 40.3% for its rival. The inexorable slide began in the late 1980s. The *Irish Press*'s market share had dropped to a marginal 9.7% in 1994 compared to 36.2% for the *Irish Independent*. Independent Newspapers and the British Express group together controlled the *Star*, a tabloid newspaper which was launched in 1990 with some success, accounting for 17.8% of the market by 1994. The *Star* also represented the introduction to Ireland of the almost printerless newspaper, with a sizeable proportion of journalists working on contract and a heavy dependence on casuals. Many believed it would be the future blueprint for the Independent group newspapers, especially the *Evening Herald*.

Competition for consumers and advertising grew especially strongly in the 1990s, not just from national television and radio, but also local radio. British daily papers, which accounted for 16.5% of the Irish market in 1977, grew to 21.1% in 1990 and jumped to 26.2% in 1994.[25] UK Sunday newspapers' penetration declined for a period in the mid-1980s to 31.5% in 1990, but expanded to 36.4% in 1994.

Though the market environment for the Irish Press group was more difficult in the 1980s and 1990s, its poor financial performance contrasts with the profitability of the Irish Times and Independent Newspapers as shown in Table 8.2. The Cork Examiner also reported stronger financial returns than the Irish Press group.

Table 8.1: Circulation of Irish Press and domestic competitors' newspapers

	1980	1991	1993	1994	% change
Morning					
Irish Press	100,000	59,000	45,400	38,800	(62.2)
Irish Independent	191,000	151,000	143,800	144,700	(24.2)
Irish Times	83,000	94,000	91,500	93,400	12.1
Cork Examiner	70,000	57,000	53,000	52,100	(25.7)
Evening					
Evening Press	172,000	81,000	60,000	54,100	(68.6)
Evening Herald	127,000	98,000	93,000	92,000	(27.6)
Sunday					
Sunday Press	381,000	201,000	171,000	156,500	(58.9)
Sunday Independent	281,000	237,000	251,000	255,800	(9.0)
Sunday Tribune	87,000	90,000	88,000	79,400	(8.7)
Sunday World	347,000	241,000	269,000	205,400	(40.8)

Source: Annual reports; *Irish Times*, 30 May 1981; *Irish Times*, 15 March 1994; Competition Authority, *Report of Investigation of the Proposal whereby Independent Newspapers plc would increase its shareholding in the Tribune Group from 29.99% to a possible 53.09%*, Dublin 1992; Competition Authority, *Interim Report of Study on the Newspaper Industry*, Dublin, 1995.

One can pose the question: how could such a level of decline continue over such a lengthy period and what aspects of mismanagement were its causes? After all, its domestic competitors, Independent Newspapers and the Irish Times (after a reorganisation), achieved a higher circulation and a better financial performance despite the many changes in the market.

Financial performance

After the launch of both the *Sunday Press* and the *Evening Press*, the profitability and financial health of the Irish Press group improved immeasurably. By the mid-1970s the directors recommended, for the first time, the payment of a dividend on the ordinary shares. In 1979 Irish Press reported excellent results. Turnover grew by 15.4% to £15.7 million and the pre-tax profit improved by 51% to £1.2 million. The dividend was increased by 50% to 21p per £1 share. Despite the purchase of some nearby properties for almost £1 million, mainly for investment purposes, the

Table 8.2: Profit/(loss) performance of Irish Press and its main domestic competitors (£m)

	Irish Press	Irish Times	Independent Newspapers
1987	0.1	1.3	8.0
1988	(1.5)	1.7	11.0
1989	(1.7)	6.0	16.0
1990	(2.8)	3.8	10.0
1991	(0.8)	1.0	8.0
1992	0.4	(0.1)	13.0
1993	(1.2)	0.4	24.9

Note: Owing to the accounting policies adopted, the group results from 1989 to 1993 did not fully consolidate the figures of Irish Press Newspapers which reported consistent losses as follows: 1989 £1.2m, 1990 £6.0m, 1991 £2.6m, 1992 £0.5m, 1993 £2.7m.

Source: Annual reports for Irish Press and Independent Newspapers; *Irish Times* reports for Irish Times figures.

balance sheet remained strong from gearing and liquidity perspectives. Bank borrowing at £338,000 was a mere 7% of shareholders' funds.

In his chairman's statement for 1979, Major Vivion de Valera prophetically warned that newsprint and labour costs 'represent an overall cost increase which remain unacceptable so long as the business expands at a slower rate'. He expressed concern about falling net profit margins: though the 1979 figure was 7.7% compared with an average of about 5.7% for some years, it had been 10% in 1973. In 1979 Independent Newspapers reported a further improvement of its fortunes with a profit of £4.2 million on a turnover of £37.2 million. Its profit margin at 11.3% was well ahead of Irish Press and was evidence of stronger commercial management.

However, 1981 proved to be a year of serious setbacks, with a net loss of £1.6 million compared to a profit of £0.7 million the previous year. More importantly there was the retirement of Jack Dempsey from the board, followed, in 1892, by the death of Major Vivion de Valera. Both had been intimately involved with the spirit and management of the organisation for fifty years. It was to prove to be the group's death-knell. There were net losses in six of the eight years up to 1989, as summarised in Table 8.3.

The losses from 1981 were financed initially by a tightening in working capital and additional bank debt. Up to 1980 the Irish Press group was almost debt-free. This reflected a conservative financial policy arising from a

Table 8.3: Irish Press: financial performance (£m)

	Turnover	Pre-tax profit/(loss)
1972	5.6	0.5
1973	6.1	0.6
1974	7.1	0.1
1975	8.6	0.1
1976	10.4	0.4
1977	12.6	0.7
1978	13.6	0.8
1979	15.7	1.2
1980	17.8	0.7
1981	20.4	(1.6)
1982	23.2	(0.1)
1983	23.0	(1.5)
1984	24.4	(3.4)
1985	23.0	(2.8)
1986	30.3	0.5
1987	31.8	0.1
1988	31.7	(1.5)
1989	28.7	(1.7)
1990	n/av.	(2.8)
1991	n/av.	(0.8)
1992	n/av.	0.4
1993	n/av.	(1.2)
1995*	n/av.	(0.8)

* 15 months to end March 1995.

Note: Owing to the accounting policies adopted, the group results from 1989 to 1993 did not fully consolidate the figures of Irish Press Newspapers which reported consistent losses as follows: 1989 £1.2m, 1990 £6.0m, 1991 £2.6m, 1992 £0.5m, 1993 £2.7m.

Source: Annual reports; figures as reported in financial statements.

cautious attitude to debt, and a will to avoid dependence on any outside interest which might attempt to influence policy.

The three-year period 1983–85 accounted for combined losses of £7.7 million as the result of lengthy strikes and the cost of redundancy and rationalisation schemes; also at this time the morning title began to materially lose market share. In this writer's view, the weak board and management capacity, allied to a combative industrial relations climate, seemed to trigger an erosion of critical personnel and financial resources.

Despite the injection of new equity by Ingersoll Publications, and the management agreement between it and Irish Press, losses continued in the 1990s. How did the group manage to survive for so long, in view of the cash haemorrhage? It would seem to be a classic illustration of the 'permanently failing organisation'.[26]

The windfall sales of the Irish Press holding of Reuters shares for £5 million following its flotation and of the O'Connell Street premises during the mid-1980s helped finance most of the £6 million funding gap arising from negative operating cash flows and annual capital expenditures on new technology and equipment. For four years in succession, current liabilities exceeded current assets and by 1988 the net current liabilities reached £2.3 million. The bank debt, which grew to almost £1.5 million, was secured by a fixed charge on certain properties from 1985. The debt/equity ratio was unsustainable, particularly in a negative cash flow and loss-making condition, with total debt at £8.7 million and the book equity at £1.6 million. The first reprieve of the organisation in the 1980s was supported internally by an erosion of its asset base — which had been accumulated by good husbandry and financial thrift over the previous fifty years.

Corporate reorganisation: ring-fencing the newspapers

The second reprieve of the group was attained by way of a reorganisation of its operational activities and a financial injection by a partner. In 1989 two separate subsidiaries were established, one (Irish Press Publications) to hold the three titles, and the other (Irish Press Newspapers) to operate and publish the three papers in partnership with Ingersoll Publications, which was to hold 50% of the equity in both. The Ingersoll investment and managerial involvement, announced on 7 July 1989, amounted to acceptance by the Irish Press board that the group had insufficient internal management and financial capability. As part of the capitalisation of the new subsidiary companies, Ingersoll invested £6 million through equity and loans to these companies, using Irish Press Publications as the primary funnel for the funds to the newspaper publishing company. The equity capitalisation of £2 million (only £1 million was cash) was much too low for a firm which had a £28 million turnover and required a turnaround.

The Ingersoll investment was the primary source of funding of the redundancy and reorganisation costs of almost £5 million incurred in 1990. The outcome proved disastrous, though the loss of just £0.5 million in 1992 did represent a partial recovery until 1993 when a loss of £2.7 million was incurred. Loans of £5 million were advanced by the partners in 1990 and a further £5 million in loans was advanced through its sister company Irish Press Publications in 1991. By the end of 1992 the three newspapers had incurred accumulated losses of £10.3 million in three and a half years. Despite this outlay and a capital investment of £3 million there was no recovery to a positive cash flow position in 1993 or 1994 and losses continued. This publishing activity had operated on a negative equity position from 1990 but by 1992 the balance sheet reached a most remarkable state. Shareholders' funds and subordinated loans were vastly exceeded by the accumulated losses. Total assets of £9.3 million were financed by creditors and other related party loans — some of which were secured. The Irish Press parent advanced loans also. Details of the trading performance of Irish Press Newspapers (the operating subsidiary) are shown in Table 8.4.

Table 8.4: Trading performance of Irish Press Newspapers (£m)					
	1989	1990	1991	1992	1993
Turnover	16.4	29.0	29.0	28.8	26.8
Gross profit	5.9	10.4	12.0	12.0	9.9
Distribution expenses	2.7	4.8	5.5	5.1	4.8
Administrative expenses	4.3	7.0	9.0	8.0	7.7
Total operating overheads	7.0	11.8	14.5	13.1	12.5
Operating loss	(1.1)	(1.4)	(2.5)	(1.1)	(2.6)
Exceptional and other overheads	(0.1)	(4.6)	(0.1)	0.6	(0.1)
Net loss for year	(1.2)	(6.0)	(2.6)	(0.5)	(2.7)
Total staff costs	8.8	16.3	14.8	14.8	14.8

Source: Audited financial statements and annual report of Irish Press plc 1993.

The gross profit margin of 36% in 1990 was no improvement on the two previous years, and it fell well behind the 39.4% achieved in 1987 when the last net profit was recorded. This low margin was due to a combination of poor labour productivity, falling capacity utilisation as circulation declined, and insufficient advertising revenue. The improved margin of 41.4% in 1991 reflected the impact of the redundancy programme. However, the recovery in gross profit was absorbed by a sharp jump in administrative costs. This was attributed to increased expenditure on promotion, mainly in an effort to redesign and relaunch the *Evening Press* in two sections in April 1991 and subsequently to minimise the extent of what proved to be a mistake. The daily circulation of this title was ahead of its competitor, the *Evening Herald*, until 1988 and was still very close to it until 1990, but fell to 86,000 copies in 1991 and 72,000 in 1992. By 1994 its daily circulation had fallen to 54,000 copies, compared with 92,000 copies for the *Evening Herald*.

There was clearly a mismatch between gross profit generated from direct operations and the size of the overheads required to run the business. This was a repeat of what occurred earlier when the staff costs were reduced, indicating a downward productivity spiral linked to ineffective strategic marketing management. In 1993, the gross profit margin fell to 36.9%. An indicator of relative productivity was that turnover per person employed in Irish Press Newspapers was £45,000 compared to £58,000 in the Cork Examiner group or almost £70,000 in the Irish Times.[27] Unaudited information suggested the decline went into 'freefall' in 1994, as a net loss of £4.5 million was incurred for the fifteen months to end March 1995, bringing the shareholders' funds deficit to £15 million.[28]

The newspaper publishing arm ran up accumulated losses of £13 million by the end of 1993. The cash for the additional loans provided by the Irish Press parent came from the sale of a further tranche of Reuters shares. Advances of £2 million were written off, and the balance sheet of the parent was decidedly thin. Coopers & Lybrand, who had been the group's auditors for decades, resigned. The new auditors, Deloitte & Touche, drew attention to the going concern basis of the financial statements.

In the meantime the partnership between Ingersoll Publications and the Irish Press parent company broke down following serious disputes over many matters including management arrangements, strategy, new financing and decision-making powers. The clash became so bitter that the parties engaged in a long court case which ended with a judgment in December 1993 in favour of Irish Press plc. There were further hearings on valuation and damages in 1994 and the amounts awarded to Irish Press and Irish Press Publications were appealed by Ingersoll, which also was ordered by the High Court to sell its shareholdings in the subsidiary companies to Irish Press plc.

The final, shorter reprieve from a complete cash shortage arrived with the advance of modest funds by the Irish Press parent and by the acquisition of a 24.9% interest in both subsidiaries by Independent Newspapers in December 1994, accompanied by loans of £2 million, of which £1 million was secured on the newspaper publishing assets and the other £1 million was secured on the assets of Irish Press Publications, which had ownership of the three titles.[29] This followed an invitation to certain groups to invest. The decline continued, and since no significant financial or management reorganisation materialised, the end finally arrived amidst another industrial dispute on 26 June 1995 with the appointment of Hugh Cooney as examiner by the High Court.

The financial position of Irish Press Publications deteriorated to the extent that the examiner's report to the court indicated a total deficiency of £18.9 million compared with total assets of about £5.5 million.[30] Employees were shown to be owed £3.6 million. Unsecured creditors (other than related group companies) were owed £4 million, of which £1.9 million was owed to the Revenue Commissioners. The collapse involved a cost to the state as well as to employees.

Reasons for the collapse of the Irish Press group

News International, the leading UK group which publishes the *Times*, the *Sunday Times*, the *Sun* and the *News of the World*, made a submission to the Irish Competition Authority on the Irish Press group.[31] At the invitation of the Ingersoll interests, it reviewed the affairs of Irish Press, but declined to get involved because of its 'fundamental problems'. News International concluded:

> ... the Irish Press Group had poor production facilities with a large underemployed workforce. Rationalisation was required. The internal strife in the Irish Press Group had been simmering for a long time. The continuing high cost base had never been addressed. Certain fundamental changes in business practices should have been introduced. The Press Group had been mismanaged for the past 15 years, contributing to low morale. It also had a rural and older person profile and emigration would have contributed to the decline of the paper.[32]

Many commentators have pointed to the circulation decline and financial losses,[33] but few isolate the interconnecting causes. Perhaps the questions to be answered are:

- What seemed to be the nature of the apparent 'mismanagement' of the Irish Press group?
- How could the poor performance of such a national institution continue for so long without corrective action?

- Why did the various attempts at a turnaround fail?

In the opinion of the writer, the following framework of defects and mistakes provides some insights into the variety of problems of the organisation.

Defects
1. Unbalanced weak board structure from the mid-1980s.
2. Absence of top management succession arrangements in the late 1970s, resulting in weak leadership and the lack of a coherent new strategic vision from the mid-1980s — when it became vital. Little new blood.
3. Insufficient depth of middle management and lack of support.
4. Nature and delivery of product dominated by outmoded editorial, design and content, despite the change in market and competition. Production-oriented. Apparently blind to market change until too late.
5. Political heritage traditionally seemed to drive objectives and culture. New people in the 1970s diluted spirit. The vacuum (or change) in ideals was insufficiently checked by a commercial profit-making orientation. Control partially lost by top management to employees and trade unions, who seemed to operate for their self-interest.
6. Very poor industrial relations climate. Trade unions seemed unwilling to negotiate sufficient work practice changes and rationalisation of print workforce — despite financial problems and external changes in technology, market and competition in domestic and international industry.
7. Weak operational cost control, specifically in labour productivity. Even after the first redundancy programme, the number employed in 1988 was 794 and the staff costs were 55% of turnover.
8. Printing equipment dated. Some machines almost forty years old.

Mistakes
1. Title and power attached to 'controlling director and editor-in-chief' passing to third generation apparently without appropriate training or experience. The third-generation syndrome.
2. Management seemed to buy industrial relations peace in late 1970s and early 1980s but bad habits in work practices and poor productivity continued because, unlike competitors, changes were not insisted on. Example: four-day working week for journalists and printers; refused to revert to a five-day week later after years of losses.

3. An editor appointed managing director in 1987 instead of bringing in an outside, commercially experienced person, and new blood.
4. Management appears not to have held out for full implementation of new technology and work practices in 1985 after long work stoppage.
5. Asset base (and reserves) diminished twice in shoring up losses rather than devoting a greater proportion to 'investment' in production process modernisation and marketing.
6. Appears not to have undertaken market research until it was too late when circulation decline became systematic. Looks to have underestimated the management change and culture of Independent Newspapers in its marketing focus and the extent of the challenge to the evening and Sunday titles.
7. Management seems to have permitted too much independence to editors; did not insist on a changed product or change the editor when market share deteriorated.
8. Acquisition of Southside Newspapers in 1985. Diverted scarce management time and focus. Loss-making.

The lack of management succession and management depth

Apart from Eamon de Valera and the short contribution of Frank Gallagher (and the strong editors, such as Douglas Gageby, of the two new titles in their early days), the two people who managerially built up the daily title, and successfully launched the Sunday and evening titles in 1949 and 1954, were Major Vivion de Valera and Jack Dempsey. Both were with the *Irish Press* from its establishment in 1931. Major Vivion took over from his father as controlling director and editor-in-chief in 1951. In the early days Seán Lemass, de Valera's trusted assistant and superb organiser,[34] was managing director for a period. Jack Dempsey had been general manager for thirty-five years when he retired as an executive in 1977. He continued as chairman until 1981.

Major Vivion died in early 1982 and Jack Dempsey a year later. With their background and involvement in the three papers, they had power and commanded respect. Major Vivion, who was authoritarian and paternalistic, primarily focused on the editorial side. Dempsey, who was shrewd in business and organisational matters, looked after the commercial side and built up very good relationships with the leading advertising agencies. Although both were in ill-health for some years before their withdrawal from executive duties, Major Vivion was not expected to die in his late sixties. It was an extraordinary record that both were associated with the group for fifty years. In addition, C. J. Furlong, the long-retired advertising manager, resigned from the board at the end of 1982.

Management and editorial succession arrangements seemed not to have been adequately planned. The grandson of the founder, Dr Eamon de Valera, who was in his late twenties, was brought in immediately as controlling director and editor-in-chief. In this writer's opinion his disciplinary background and work with a subsidiary of Cement Roadstone had provided insufficient business or managerial experience for his new role. It can be viewed as an example of duty and responsibility being thrust on a male family member to continue the tradition. There was also the personal relationship between grandson and grandfather.[35] Colm Traynor, the long-serving personnel manager, took over from Dempsey. There was continuity at senior editor level with Tim Pat Coogan in the *Irish Press*, Vincent Jennings in the *Sunday Press* and Sean Ward in the *Evening Press*.

With an apparent absence of management depth at senior or middle management level (though there were a number of good people at the latter level who seem not to have been delegated appropriate authority and responsibility), much of the tone and direction of the three titles fell to their editors, who were not properly trained for a wider role. There was no formal management development programme in the company. In this writer's opinion the sway of the editors in the Irish Press group was almost unique in Ireland by the 1980s. In describing their autonomy and near absolute power, one interviewee explained: 'They were like bishops who could, and did, run their dioceses as they so wished.' In the formulation of the structure and themes as well as when the papers went to press, the editors called 'the time' and, it seems, generally dominated the limited commercial managerial input. Hitting the streets at the earliest time with the first editions to ensure circulation seems to have become a casualty to outmoded editorial and journalistic attitudes on occasions.

The change of ownership in its competitor

Developments in its main competitor, Independent Newspapers, could not have been much greater. It is in this light that the weaknesses in the board and management structure of Irish Press must be viewed. The changes in organisational structure and business focus of the Independent titles from the late 1970s to mid-1980s contrast greatly with the appearance of complacency and time-warp in the inbred culture of the Irish Press group.

Tony O'Reilly had a successful marketing background, having been primarily responsible for the development of the 'Kerrygold' brand for Irish dairy produce internationally before moving on to Heinz in the UK and the USA.[36] By then chief executive of Heinz in the USA, he acquired a dominant shareholding in Independent Newspapers from the Murphy family in 1973. His investment of £2 million was primarily financed by personal borrowings.[37] His stated objective was to turn Independent into an international media publications group. Part of the purchase arrangements involved share conversions based on earnings per share growth over a period of years. Following the acquisition, the profitability of Independent Newspapers fell for some years and then recovered dramatically to a pre-tax profit of £1.4 million in 1976, growing to £4.1 million in 1979. Dividends increased from 1.7p in 1973 to 10.0p in 1979. O'Reilly had debt to service and therefore growth in dividends was a fundamental objective of Independent Newspapers. By 1985 the annual dividend had increased to 15p. Achieving adequate profitability to service capital was essential.

By 1978 the management of Independent Newspapers had been restructured. Joe Hayes, recruited from the cigarette manufacturers, Gallaher, was initially marketing director and eventually became managing director with responsibility for the three primary titles and the provincial operations. The top three executives — Bartle Pitcher, Liam Healy and Joe Hayes — were co-opted to the board, which was also strengthened with the co-option of O'Reilly's business colleagues, Vincent Ferguson and Nicholas Leonard (who some years earlier was associated with *Business & Finance*). Rodney Murphy continued as chairman until his death in 1980, when Tony O'Reilly moved from vice-chairman to chairman. The debt and liquidity problems of Fitzwilton, which had previously absorbed his attention as a leading shareholder and director, were overcome[38] and O'Reilly was now in a position to focus on the accelerated development of Independent Newspapers.

With O'Reilly's strong background in brand management, it is perhaps not surprising that a greater emphasis in marketing was soon evident. John Meagher of Irish Marketing Surveys was appointed deputy chairman in 1982 and was given a partial executive role later. The Independent group's management reshuffles underpinned the power of the marketing people to influence the 'product formulation' of the daily, evening and Sunday titles so as to improve market shares in circulation and advertising revenue.

The management competence and cultural differences between the competitors

By 1985 the difference in board structure and 'management capacity' of the two groups could not have been greater. Following the loss of Jack

Dempsey and Major Vivion de Valera in 1981, the depleted and internally based Irish Press board co-opted A. G. Galligan, a successful businessman. Dr Eamon de Valera became chairman of the group as well as editor-in-chief. The board was further strengthened in May 1983 with the appointment of Donal P. Flinn, a former managing partner of Coopers & Lybrand in Dublin (who became chairman), and Sean McHale, a management consultant with extensive top management experience. The new directors' first year was to be a baptism of fire. There was a strike and losses of £1.5 million were incurred. Flinn pointed to the fact that staff costs rose from 56.6% of turnover in 1982 to 61.4% in 1983 and stated that 'a meaningful increase in productivity' could be achieved through the introduction of new technology linked to savings in employee costs.[39] He noted that there were 'indigenous weaknesses in the operation, structure and organisation' of the company. This was a cue to change and strengthen the management and editorial arrangements which had been inherited from another generation and were suited to very different circumstances.

In April 1984 both Flinn and McHale resigned — the former over 'differences with the Controlling Director on Company policy', and the latter over 'a disagreement . . . concerning the Board's business strategy in relation to the Company's problems'.[40] In the opinion of this writer the 'traditionalists' seemed unwilling and unable to change, or to relinquish the near suffocating control they exercised over all aspects of the group. Dr Eamon de Valera reassumed the chairmanship and Elio Malocco, his brother-in-law, a young solicitor, was co-opted in the same month. Once again, the board comprised a small group of four, with de Valera and Malocco representing the family, the others being Colm Traynor, the general manager (who was to retire in 1987 after thirty-seven years' service), and the one 'outsider', A. G. Galligan.

The top management team looked to be thin, and for a period in 1986 some senior management expertise was apparently provided by a partner in Coopers & Lybrand, the group's auditors. The departure of its able personnel manager, Pat Lunny, who was with the group for five years, was a further blow to its top management resource. It seems that Irish Press tried unsuccessfully to recruit a new managing director with commercial experience outside the group. This was not surprising, in view of the extent of the control over policy, the organisation's culture and its lack of sufficient management depth, quite apart from the business problems it faced. The top management gap was filled by the appointment of Vincent Jennings as general manager and a director in early 1987. His previous experience had been as editor of the *Sunday Press* for nineteen years.

With Galligan as the one outsider, the small Irish Press board continued to wrestle with commercial matters. It was remarkable that over the years so few executives were appointed to the board. The contrast between the governance and management cultures of Irish Press and Independent Newspapers could not have been greater — with all the implications for strategic marketing, quality of decision-making, status and credibility of senior executives and power of implementation. It was also the difference between an internal and an external focus. In the writer's opinion, Irish Press appears not to have responded adequately to the competitive challenge or the change in the market.

Poor management of industrial relations: trade union and employee resistance to change

Because of craft traditions, the difficulty in negotiating change with employees and trade unions to improve productivity through the use of new technology was common to all the leading newspaper groups. However, the extent of the bitterness and intransigence in industrial relations appears to have been exceptional in the Irish Press group. It experienced far more work stoppages and strikes than its competitors. There was a three-and-a-half-week strike in 1983 involving the National Union of Journalists. The 'lock-out' in 1985, when the *Irish Press* was off the streets for twelve weeks and the other two titles were unavailable for six weeks, was symptomatic of the unhealthy industrial relations climate. The causes, to an extent, are interconnected.

The tradition of division and suspicions between the editor/journalist and management groups, which continued from the Gallagher days, was counteracted by Major Vivion de Valera and Jack Dempsey because of their authority. Their loss left a managerial vacuum. Labour costs were higher than necessary, judging by allegations about the sick roster, bogus illnesses and the basis of certain overtime shifts.[41] In this writer's opinion a combination of the rigidity of craft traditions, poor trade union leadership and, above all, a degree of management feebleness from the late 1970s resulted in avoiding strategic and hard negotiations with a definite will to implement the necessary changes for survival over time. Petty decisions by management caused staff resentment. In this writer's opinion the apparent mismanagement of trade unions and employees was such that it has been suggested that trade union power and intransigence came close to anarchy:

> The printers were frequently on go-slows which ensured that the *Evening Press* was constantly late in the marketplace. This kind of

industrial action made proof-reading virtually impossible and the papers were filled with misprints. The motto seemed to be: 'It'll do' . . .

During this period some trade union officers had worked themselves into positions of such power that even the most senior editorial executives feared them.[42]

Undoubtedly this also contributed to the drop in circulation. The absence of sufficient management depth left a vacuum, with many journalists and editorial staff working hard to bring out a paper in weak organisational circumstances without clear objectives or policies.[43] A militant minority had considerable influence. Poor internal communication was addressed by management in the late 1980s. This initiative was resented by many trade union officials, because it was seen to dilute their influence.[44]

In the writer's opinion there were several management decisions which added to the industrial relations problems. A four-day week was granted to journalists and printers in the late 1970s. The fact that staff costs had reached 61% of turnover in 1983 suggests that employees had 'captured' an unjustifiable and unsustainable proportion of the organisation's operating resources at the expense of generating sufficient funds to support marketing and new investment. Rather than exercise cost control and attain improved productivity, Irish newspapers increased their prices at an average of more than double the rate of inflation in order to meet their cost increases.[45] The Irish dailies became much more expensive than their UK competitors. It is not surprising that they lost market share and the total demand for domestic newspapers weakened. For example, the price of the *Irish Press* increased from 35p in 1984 to 70p in 1995 (the *Irish Independent* was 80p), whereas the *Times* and *Guardian* increased from 40p and 30p to 45p and 50p respectively in the same period.[46] In 1995, UK tabloids, the *Daily Mail*, the *Mirror* and the *Sun*, were priced at 47p, 45p and 40p in Ireland.

When management produced its corporate plan for 1988–93 as a blueprint for the group's recovery, it aimed to return to a five-day working week.[47] The Labour Court and Professor Basil Chubb, as mediator, came down on the side of management. It was to no avail in negotiating real productivity gains. On the other side, management had not paid agreed national pay increases for some years, as recommended by the Labour Court. The employees' pay fell materially behind that of their counterparts in the other newspaper groups. This was resented and nourished an entrenched form of organisational civil war.

The decline in innovation and remaining a prisoner to history

Following its pioneering spirit in journalism in the 1930s, the Irish Press group continued to introduce innovations up to the 1980s. The group had a long tradition of excellence in sports reporting in all three of its titles. It introduced women's features, new Irish writing and book reviews under Louis Marcus, and was first to break many important political stories, where Michael Mills established an outstanding reputation as a political reporter. It developed many fine journalists and was a training ground for a new group in the 1970s and early 1980s, such as Mary Kenny and Vincent Browne, who went on to establish their reputations elsewhere. The *Evening Press* created the concept of the 'small ad' for personal advertisers which was hugely successful, leading to the demise of the long-established *Evening Mail*. Terry O'Sullivan's colourful social column known as 'Dubliner's Diary' proved very popular. The *Evening Press* displayed a flair which also captured many women readers.

However, the *Irish Press* appears to have changed little by the 1980s, remaining conservative with a Catholic and republican tinge. It was as if it was in a time-warp, and lost its sense of flair and innovation in journalism and liveliness of product. Similarly, in this writer's view, the evening and Sunday titles did not change sufficiently in response to the altered demographic structure, consumer attitudes and buying power. Some of the group's earlier political influence remained. The initial bedrock readers of Irish Press newspapers were an unusual combination of the Dublin working class, and small farmers and people in rural areas and on the western seaboard generally. By the 1980s, its rural readers were dying off and reading habits were changing in Dublin with the penetration of the much cheaper UK tabloids. Half the population of the country was under twenty-five, and the migration from rural to urban centres was well established.

The Irish Press design and 'product formulation' culture was production oriented and was not sufficiently reshaped to appeal to a younger population. It remained within a structure determined by its editors, based on history, rather than changing to appeal to new potential readers. It was seen to be insufficiently lively. The Independent Newspapers approach became consumer driven as a result of extensive market research. The aim was to target its titles primarily at the under thirty-fives and adopt a 'lighter' approach. The woman reader was also targeted. Acquiring the *Sunday World*, which was a tabloid, gave the Independent group a portfolio of titles which reached a wider market population. This policy was reinforced with the successful launch in 1987 of the *Star* as a daily tabloid.

Through its research the Independent group discovered what appealed to ABC1 social class readers and what was a draw for advertisers. It identified themes and issues which attracted readers. It focused on developing journalists' understanding of the need for a balance which would integrate editorial policy and also sell newspapers and advertising. An example was the much greater emphasis on the 'gossip' and 'political backchat' columns of the *Sunday Independent*. In contrast, the Irish Press group did not appear to undertake any material market research until the late 1980s. It was then too late. The *Sunday Independent* overtook the *Sunday Press* in circulation in 1988 because the latter seemed to have no clearly defined target market, and generally had an unattractive layout and balance of features. Only the sports section remained top class.[48]

The Irish Press titles lost their way in a changing Ireland. In this writer's opinion there was an imbalance in the formulation of the 'product' on the basis of a marriage between editorial policy and marketing — the latter was neither really understood nor apparently held in esteem. Thus marketing remained sidelined at a critical period. The daily and Sunday titles remained dependent on rural and older readers. The sharper commercial focus of the Independent group resulted in it capturing 33% of ABC1 social class readers for the *Irish Independent* compared to only 8% for the *Irish Press*. It was also slightly ahead in the evening sector. The *Sunday Independent* achieved a penetration of 48% in 1990–91 compared to 26% for the *Sunday Press*.[49] Another fatal blow was the loss of many senior journalists and editors (often to its competitor), as this weakened morale.

The loss of advertising

Advertising is a major revenue source for newspapers. In the 1980s, the newspaper industry lost market share to television and radio, and this affected the revenue of all the newspapers, forcing tougher competition for circulation and press advertising. Tony O'Reilly railed against

> . . . the uncommercial nature of the competition which the print media face from the four State-owned television and radio channels . . . there is an unacceptable level of distortion in the market for advertising revenue, which has resulted in Ireland reflecting the highest television and radio market shares and the lowest newspaper market share to be found in any European country.[50]

O'Reilly claimed that the newspaper share of total advertising expenditure fell from 54% in 1975 to 40% in 1985. By 1991 the total advertising outlay was estimated to be £202 million, of which 37% went to national newspapers.⁵¹ With its focus on a target market which was more appealing to the advertising agencies, the Independent group consistently captured increasing market share in newspaper advertising spend. It reached a 49% market share, compared to 13% for the Irish Press group, by 1994.⁵² The Cork Examiner group, operating on a relatively narrow provincial base and with two titles, attracted almost the same advertising spend as the Irish Press group.

The consequences for total revenue were fatal for the Irish Press group. Irish newspapers averaged a 43%/57% split between advertising and sales revenue, with a greater proportion of advertising achieved by the quality newspapers because of the higher ABC1 social class disposable income and the jobs/appointments pages. The Irish Press group, because of its readership profile and weak commercial management, was unable to achieve more than 30% of total revenue from advertising in the late 1980s, having been at 36% in 1983. It should have been at minimum 50% more, and this would have delivered an additional £5 million in revenue per annum.

The Irish Press group made a number of useful innovations in response to the flagging circulation figures. It was the first to introduce colour pages in its Sunday paper, followed by its other two titles, through a preprinting contract with Smurfit Ireland. However, in this writer's view there were a number of design and marketing mistakes. In 1988 the *Irish Press* was relaunched in tabloid form. This was an attempt to reposition it as a popular paper aimed at the middle market. The outcome was unsuccessful, partially because of price and an apparent conflict in focus and content for a tabloid. In 1990 the *Irish Press* was priced at 50p compared with 40p for the *Star* and 35p for the *Daily Mirror*, the *Sun* or the *Daily Mail*. A redesign of its masthead proved unattractive. A reformatting of the evening paper was also unsuccessful as the restructuring into two sections appeared to confuse readers.

The research evidence suggests that vital management time and competitive focus were absorbed by the industrial relations strife — quite apart from the operational efficiency of the group. It was split between two locations with expensive computer-based production equipment lying idle for some years. It seems that management was also diverted by the acquisition of Southside Newspapers in 1985. It distributed seven freesheets and the aim was to improve the group's attraction to advertisers. Heavy losses in Southside forced the group to put it into liquidation in early 1987. An example of the difference in commercial acumen between the Press and

Independent groups was when Irish Press management looked to be caught off-guard in 1988 by the introduction of a form of lotto game called 'Fortuna' by the *Irish Independent*, which proved very popular. Circulation of the *Irish Press* slumped by a reported 20,000 copies for some time.[53] Having failed to overcome the threat by court action, the Irish Press group seems to have been forced to respond with 'Bonanza', its own game, at considerable expense. It subsequently dropped the game and tried to compete on cost with a promotional campaign which emphasised the 10 pence price differential. Previously the difference had been 5 pence.

In the writer's opinion the lock-out and work stoppages from the mid-1980s were not only evidence of serious industrial relations problems and poor management, but were also symptomatic of poor communications and a worsening in morale because of the losses. Staff knew of the management defects and that much of the production machinery was old. It seems that because of the uncertainty about the future many able journalists and editors left. It was a sea-change from the liveliness and crusading spirit of the 1960s and 1970s. Hugh Oram captured the feeling of the 1980s well with a quote from one journalist:

> It was like living over the San Andreas fault in California. But people get used to it. We've had difficult times here . . . but it hasn't always been like that. I would hope and believe that we will come out of it and go back to that period between the 1960s and 1980s, when it was a very, very happy ship indeed and we were leading the pack.[54]

Unfortunately, it was not to be.

Endgame and the wrong partner?

The poor performance of the Irish Press group and the key to its persistence lay in the fact that a small set of shares, the B shares (controlled by members of the de Valera family and a trust), had voting rights and the majority, the A shares representing many small subscribers and the money raised in America, did not.[55] The writer concludes that, because of the structure between the American and Irish shareholdings, the de Valera family interests commanded voting control of Irish Press with the inherited family title of controlling director and editor-in-chief (even though they did not contribute the main share capital). They had effective control of the group. In this writer's opinion it seems to have been almost impossible for anyone to challenge this power or change the main board of directors and top management responsibilities.

It might be argued that Irish Press was unlucky in its choice of partner in 1989 in an attempt to infuse fresh capital and management into its newspaper publishing. Alternatively, it could be argued that stronger investors would not have become involved on the terms agreed to by Ingersoll Publications. Power to make management and editorial changes would have been fundamental — in view of past performance and market share. It has been suggested that the Smurfit Group, having some experience of the Irish Press through its colour page printing contract, considered an involvement, but preliminary negotiations came to nought.

The Irish Press board settled for a partner who proved unable to effect a turnaround, partly, it seems, because of insufficient expertise and partly because of the conflicts which emerged between the two interests. Ingersoll Publications grew rapidly in the 1980s under Ralph Ingersoll, the son of the founder. At the time of its investment in Irish Press it was reputed to be the twentieth largest news media group in the USA with 200 suburban newspapers. It had moved into the UK with the purchase of newspapers in Birmingham and Coventry as part of a European expansion strategy. Many of the acquisitions appear to have been funded by debt and within a year of the Irish Press involvement, Ingersoll Publications was experiencing financial problems. In a restructuring, it was left with its two provincial newspaper investments in Britain, apart from Irish Press.

In an effort to strengthen the parent board, Dan McGing, a former partner in Coopers & Lybrand with considerable business experience, was co-opted in April 1991 and appointed chairman. He lasted just over a year and resigned following differences with Dr Eamon de Valera. The following day, A. G. Galligan, who was a stalwart supporter of the tradition and history of the Irish Press group, resigned in sympathy with McGing. In this writer's opinion this was a landmark point in the collapse of confidence.

The boardroom and managerial conflict between the two partners ended up in a lengthy High Court action during 1993[56] and a Supreme Court action in 1994, which was generally decided in favour of Irish Press interests. Ingersoll had to sell back the shareholdings in the publishing subsidiaries. One can only speculate on the effect of this lengthy court action on the focus of the board and senior management.

The acceptance of an investment for 25% of the equity in the publishing subsidiaries and a £2 million secured loan from a subsidiary of Independent Newspapers (when up to £15 million was needed to restructure properly) was contrary to the very purpose and history of the Irish Press group. In this writer's opinion it was a final desperate act to avoid any other form of solution which might have led to loss of control of the titles. It could be seen as a final abandonment of idealism and innocence by the controllers — following the footsteps of the trade unions and certain employees some years earlier.

Appointment of examiner and the failed rescue

The appointment of an examiner was made under very different circumstances from those in the Goodman International and Kentz Corporation cases. The request was from three journalists, in their capacity as creditors, with the support of the National Union of Journalists. It was opposed by the board. A train of interconnecting events followed. An editor was dismissed after he wrote an article in another newspaper which was critical of Irish Press management. There was a stoppage of work by journalists and the three titles were absent from the streets once again. The response by the board was to liquidate the newspaper publishing company.[57] It was as if there was an inevitability on the road to self-destruction.

Hugh Cooney, who had successfully negotiated a reconstruction and scheme of arrangement in the complex Kentz case, was appointed examiner — but with very tight terms of reference — by the High Court. In his first report, Cooney concluded that, subject to certain conditions, 'the company and at least part of its undertaking, is capable of survival as a going concern'.[58] The conditions included new investment and technology, redundancies and changes in work practices and, more significantly,

> ... management and board changes may be required in order to facilitate the introduction of new investment. If necessary, the existing board members must be prepared to resign.

Hugh Cooney identified Irish and American investment interests with expertise who were willing to attempt a turnaround. He also drafted a scheme of arrangement involving both the newspaper-publishing and the title-holding subsidiaries of the Irish Press group.

The examiner's second report and attaching documentation make most interesting reading.[59] Much constructive work was completed within a very tight time scale. Access to the titles by the new investors and the publishing enterprise underpinned the reorganisation plan. The board of Irish Press had different views. There appears to have been a difference of opinion between the examiner and the directors on whether Irish Press Publications was insolvent. It had £6 million in liabilities and its primary asset was ownership of the three titles, which had their value revised upwards to £10 million by four directors (a fifth thought they were worth £100,000). It seems that, having already agreed terms and conditions of an involvement with the examiner, the Irish-American group who expressed serious commitment through their adviser, John McStay, withdrew on 18 August 1995. McStay wrote to Hugh Cooney saying his clients were concerned about the lease/option of the titles and a 'sustained legal challenge to the proposed scheme' which apparently could prevent the relaunch of the Sunday paper before Christmas (which was deemed essential).[60]

With no new investment, the prospects of survival collapsed and the examinership was immediately ceased. On the nomination of directors, Tom Grace of Price Waterhouse was appointed liquidator of Irish Press Newspapers on 8 September 1995, and was followed by Ray Jackson of KPMG as receiver. This closed an era of newspaper publishing which had been closely interwoven with Irish history and the pioneering of an innovative and radical product. In this writer's opinion the third generation of the family presided over its decline. It was surprising that Fianna Fáil, either as a political party or through its senior members, appeared to stand by when it may have had some possibility of influence. After all, one could not expect an intervention by any other party in view of the historical context.

A managerial explanation might be *folie a deu*. Two years after the liquidation, despite announcements through its new subsidiary, Solange Ltd,[61] Irish Press had not relaunched any of the titles.

Waterford Wedgwood
The rebirth of a tradition

The history of fine cut glassware in Ireland has a long association with County Waterford. During the reign of Elizabeth I glass was first blown near Dungarvan in the parish of Mogeely. The extensive adjacent forests which provided ample supplies of firewood were a primary determinant of location. Government restrictions on the felling of timber led to the cessation of glassmaking in 1641. Italian innovations in the refinement of the manufacture of 'flint glass' through the production of lead glass yielded a glass of more durability which, when cut, reflected great prismatic brilliance. A number of 'flint glass' houses were operating in Ireland in the eighteenth century and, following the repeal of restrictions on Irish commerce by Grattan's Parliament in 1779–80, the Irish glassmaking industry began to flourish.

The Waterford Glasshouse was established in 1783 by the Penrose brothers. Glassmaking craft workers were imported to help develop native skills. The country as a whole, and Waterford in particular, built a reputation for fine cut glassware. In 1799 the Penrose house was sold to the Gatchell family. A large export trade flourished to France, Spain, Portugal and North America. The imposition of high excise duties by the government and a recession resulted in financial problems and, one by one, the Irish glasshouses began to close down. The Waterford Glasshouse was practically the sole survivor until it too finally ceased trading in 1851.[62] With its demise the skills and tradition of glassmaking died.

Almost a century later, in 1947, Bernard Fitzpatrick, a jeweller in Dublin, and Charles Bacik, who had been one of Fitzpatrick's suppliers up to 1939 and was looking for a new location to establish a business, agreed to revive the dormant industry in Waterford. Bacik, a Czech nationalist, had survived a very difficult period; he was incarcerated by the Germans and soon after the end of World War II found his glass factory in Czechoslovakia nationalised by the new government. With the help of Miroshov Havel, an artist from Prague, a study of old Waterford crystal pieces in the National Museum helped produce a set of designs.[63]

Start-up losses mounted and finance was running out. Bernard Fitzpatrick convinced Joe McGrath and Joe Griffin, two wealthy self-made businessmen in Dublin, to invest in the project in 1950. For primarily patriotic motives — to help employment — Joe McGrath and Joe Griffin made an extensive investment of finance and management time in helping to get the faltering business off the ground. It was eight years before it made a profit. Indeed, Waterford accumulated losses of over £100,000 before it reported its first profit of £7,665 in 1955. In today's terms the losses would be the equivalent of about £2 million. It was a courageous investment by the McGrath family and other interests.

Paddy McGrath, the youngest son of Joe McGrath, who worked in the Hospitals Sweepstakes and for a few years in the Irish Glass Bottle Company and who succeeded his father as chairman of Waterford Glass in 1966, recalled:

> We didn't start Waterford Glass. A group of men had got together and came to us to ask if we would have an interest in it. We had been in the glass business since 1932 and knew that it was the greatest way of burning money that you ever came across. Anyway, Waterford got into some trouble and we took it over completely: half IGB, half McGrath interests. That was in 1950. My father was chairman of Waterford Glass — though I used to take meetings for him — and we had no chief executive for a while until we appointed Noel Griffin.[64]

A relationship with the Belgian group, Glaceries de Saint Roch, followed by the Société de Participations Verrieres SA, who took an equity stake, provided Waterford with technical assistance. Eighty Czechs, Belgians and Italians, both cutters and blowers, were recruited. With the expertise of the Winkelman father and son team, they helped nurture the industry and train Irish apprentices. Many teething problems in mastering the art of melting and blowing crystal persisted up to 1954, after which volume and sales began to grow steadily.[65] The objective was to produce the highest quality lead crystal glass — but this required very high employee skills as it was a craft industry. Like printing, the technology of glass-blowing changed little over centuries. Waterford's glass-blowing teams used the traditional tools such as hollow irons and wooden templates. Apprenticeship for glass-blowers was for five years and an intensive apprenticeship training programme (involving blowing, cutting and engraving) was developed which created a cadre of highly skilled Irish craftsmen, who in turn passed on their skills to others.

The recruitment of Noel Griffin in 1950 as a young accountant and general manager to look after the commercial side, and subsequently Con Dooley from the Department of Foreign Affairs to develop outlets and sales in the USA, helped create a viable business after a few years.

The skilled craftsmen and training practices were Waterford's primary asset in maintaining its product reputation and turnover. Early output was based on old Irish and Huguenot designs. As Waterford achieved penetration in the leading department stores in the USA in the late 1950s and early 1960s, over 70% of its output went to that market. Waterford crystal was at the top end of the US market in price and quality. A combination of American postwar buoyancy in demand for high-quality luxury products, and the fact that old Waterford glass retained a prestige image in America, particularly among Irish-Americans as family heirlooms (which became treasured possessions), helped create a substantial market niche for the new Waterford Glass products.[66]

Paddy McGrath maintained that Waterford's products were consistently near the top of brides' lists in America for thirty years.[67] Demand exceeded supply, and the latter could only be expanded as new craftsmen and teams were trained. From 1952 craftsmen worked in teams on piece-rates. Because of the buoyant demand and the ability to command a high price for the product, there was little restraint on production spoilage/yield rates and craft wage rates. Undoubtedly, the craftsmen evolved into an elite and powerful group; they were on first-name terms with the managing director, Noel Griffin, because of his style and the fact that he joined at the same time as many of the early apprentices, who were now the senior craftsmen.

Key events in the life of Waterford Wedgwood

Birth

1947	Waterford Glass established by Charles Bacik and Bernard Fitzpatrick in Ballytruckle, Waterford with the objective of reviving a hand-craft crystal industry. Foreign craftsmen recruited and local apprentices taken on.
1950	Joe McGrath, Joe Griffin and Irish Glass Bottle Company provide funding and management, and acquire controlling interest. Belgian glass firm Glaceries de Saint Roch provides technical assistance and takes 9% equity stake. Noel Griffin joins as accountant and general manager.
1951	Johnstown factory starts production.
1954	Accumulated losses of almost £100,000.
1955	First profit — £7,665.
1958	Expansion funding provided by loans of £200,000 from Irish Glass Bottle.
1961	Establishes US marketing and distribution subsidiaries.

Adolescence

1966	Irish Stock Exchange quotation raises £300,000 in new equity. Finances rapid growth and working capital. Paddy McGrath takes over from his father, Joe, as chairman.
1969	Rights issue raises £400,000 equity. Capacity expansion.
1970	Acquires John Aynsley & Son, fine bone china manufacturers in UK.
1971–74	Acquires 60% Switzers (department stores), 100% John Hinde (postcard manufacturer) 100% Smith Group (garages, motor distributors, etc.).
1972	Group turnover £18 million. London Stock Exchange quotation.
1975	Group turnover £60 million. Rights issue of 10% convertible preference shares raises £5.2 million. Convertible to equity between 1978 and 1987.
1977	McGrath family investment company, Avenue Investment Company, reduces Waterford equity stake from 41% to 32%.
1979	Group turnover £136 million. Pre-tax profit £11.6 million. Butlerstown factory commences production. McGrath family investment company reduces Waterford holding to 25%.

Maturity

1980	First profits fall in twenty-six years. Pre-tax profits £8.1 million. Patrick McGrath Jr (third generation) co-opted to board.

cont.

	Key events in the life of Waterford Wedgwood *cont.*
	McGrath companies, Avenue Investment Company and Crest Holdings, reduce Waterford equity stake to 20%.
1981	Noel Griffin, managing director, dies unexpectedly.
	Owen Kealy, financial director, promoted to top position.
1982	Waterford Crystal established as a subsidiary of Waterford Glass Group.
1983	Five-day strike over PAYE deductions in crystal factories.
	'Waterford' registration as a trade mark approved by Supreme Court.
1984	Following market rumours, in May board admits discussions in progress about a possible offer for Waterford.
	Sale of McGrath family interests (20% of Waterford equity) by Avenue Investment Company and Crest Holdings at 40p per share (£17 million) to Globe Investment Trust, London, in August.
	David Hardy and Quentin Morris, directors of Globe, co-opted to Waterford board.
	Paddy Hayes, formerly chairman/chief executive of Ford Ireland, co-opted and appointed deputy chairman.
	Charles Bacik, Bernard Fitzpatrick, Con Dooley, Seamus McGrath and Alan Jeffers (Avenue Investments) resign as directors.
1985	Three-year wage agreement signed with trade unions in March. Includes favourable wage rate increases and employee profit/share participation scheme.
	Paddy McGrath steps down as chairman in May. Paddy Hayes appointed executive chairman.
	Owen Kealy, managing director, and Tom Aspel, sales director, retire and resign from board. Patrick McGrath Jr also resigns as a director.
	Sweeping changes in top management. Hayes starts recruiting some ex-Ford people.
	New strategic objectives established, focusing on core business, level of debt, new marketing initiatives and new crystal designs.
	Divestment of non-core businesses: sells Switzers (1985), Smith Group (1986) and John Hinde (1988).
	Share price hits a high of 86p.
1986	Record pre-tax profits of £18.5 million announced for 1985. Dividend up 20% to 2.40p.
	Initial public offering through American depository receipts (ADRs) listed on NASDAQ yields £29.2 million (at the equivalent of 136p).

cont.

	Key events in the life of Waterford Wedgwood *cont.*
	Share price at 118p (ex dividend) on 7 October, the day before the offer to acquire Wedgwood group for £255 million.
	Globe Investment Trust holding halved to 10.25% on 31 October. Wedgwood shareholders accept offer in November.
1987	Waterford Glass Group name changed to Waterford Wedgwood
	Record pre-tax profits of £23.7 million announced for 1986.
	In August, board announces redundancy, cost reduction, new work practices and new equipment programme to improve competitiveness. 750 jobs to go.
1988	Board announces net loss of £47.8 million for 1987, after costs of redundancy and rationalisation programme.
	In September, board announces pre-tax profits of £2.5 million for six months and 'a notable turnaround'. Profits to 'bounce back' in the second half of 1988.
1989	On 24 January, board announces 'accounting errors overstating the valuation of finished stocks and work in progress during 1988' in Waterford Crystal. Performance to be lower than previous expectations. Managing director (crystal division) and group finance director resign.
	Quoted share price falls from 89p to 78p. Declines to 47p by December.
	Net loss of £5.2 million for 1988 in April. Interim figures incorrect. No final dividend. Paddy Hayes resigns as executive chairman. Howard Kilroy becomes non-executive chairman. Board appoints Paddy Byrne as group chief executive. Paddy Galvin recruited from Guinness as a group director and head of the crystal division.
	Total debt £290 million and interest bill £11 million becoming a burden.
1990	Net loss of £29 million announced for 1989. Interest bill now £18 million. Debt/equity ratio unsustainable.
	£96 million in new equity in April. Shuttleway Holdings invests in 29.9% of the equity at 37.5p per share.
	Fourteen-week strike. New labour agreement subsequently.
	In December ceramics and crystal businesses separated financially to protect ceramics from crystal's losses.
1991	Net loss of £28.2 million reported for 1990 in May.
	New £105 million bank refinancing facility for three and a half years. Tight covenants.
	cont.

	Key events in the life of Waterford Wedgwood *cont.*
1993	Donald Brennan, a managing director of Morgan Stanley, New York, appointed non-executive chairman in June.
	Net loss of £19 million for 1992 announced in April.
	Share price falls to 18p but recovers to 41p by December.
1994	Tony O'Reilly takes over as non-executive chairman in January.
	Net profit of £9 million for 1993 announced in April — first profit since 1986
	Share price improves to 58p by December.
1995	Net profit increases to £20.6 million for 1994. Dividend declared for first time since 1988.

Adolescence and maturity

Noel Griffin operated with almost complete authority. Under his leadership there was a massive growth in output, sales, profits and employment, almost continuously from the mid-1960s into the late 1970s. With his energetic and earthy management style he received unwavering loyalty from the craftsmen — who benefited from the success in terms of very high earnings. Griffin described the glass-cutters as 'kings' of the industry. A craft culture was encouraged. We can only speculate that considerable bonding took place in these production teams because of the interdependence of craft skills in fashioning the finished cut glass. It was almost a 'one man show', more reminiscent of small business than a major company, that continued for thirty years until Noel Griffin's illness and tragic death in his late fifties in 1981.

The fast-growth early adolescent period of the 1960s was initially financed by internal profits — net profit margins were of the order of 15%. A Dublin stockmarket quotation in 1966 raised equity. A rights issue followed in 1969 to support investment in additional capacity to meet the buoyant demand. By 1972, turnover had reached £18 million and pre-tax profits £2.4 million. In 1970 Waterford acquired Aynsley China, a manufacturer of high-quality fine bone china tableware and figurines with a near 200-year-old tradition in the UK. Aynsley was a good fit.

A diversification strategy started with the acquisition of a 60% interest in Switzers, one of Ireland's leading department store groups, with Harrods of London as the minority partner. This was followed by a number of investments; the purchase of the Smith Group, a large garage and motor services group with the Renault distribution franchise for Ireland, in 1974 was the largest. In its core business, Waterford widened its product range from stemware to lightingware and later giftware. Waterford's reputation was such that in the US it sold more high-quality hand-made crystal than the combined sales of all its competitors from Europe. Its chandeliers illuminated the nave of Westminster Abbey, the President Kennedy Centre in Washington and the President's room in the London Stock Exchange.

With close to 2,700 people employed in crystal production in the Waterford and Dungarvan factories, Joe McGrath and his sons certainly achieved their aims in self-help economic regeneration. The McGrath family and related interests, through the Dodder Investment Company, held a dominant 41% of Waterford's equity, and continued to control its affairs. Paddy McGrath, as chairman, his brother Seamus, Noel Griffin, Charles Bacik and Bernard Fitzpatrick, with four executive directors from the crystal activity, dominated the board.

Profits trebled between 1974 and 1978. The financial success of the group was such that Paddy McGrath was able to introduce his 1979 chairman's statement by noting it was the twenty-fifth year of successive profit growth. Turnover jumped to £136 million and pre-tax profit reached a peak of £11.6 million. In his chairman's statement of May 1980, Paddy McGrath stated he was 'very confident of sales and profits for the Group as a whole during the coming year . . . The Waterford Glass Group continues to be as strong as ever.'[68]

In fact, contrary to this optimistic expectation, net profit fell by 32% in 1980. It was the first fall in profit in twenty-six years. As shown in Table 8.5, there was a profit decline again in 1982 and it was not until 1984 that the profit at £14.6 million surpassed the 1979 figure. Despite the good profits in 1979, there was an operational cash flow deficit because of a large jump in working capital. A further four years' cash flow deficits were funded by bank debt and by 1983 Waterford's debt/equity and interest cover ratios were weak. There were further good profit results in 1985 at £18.5 million and 1986 at £23.7 million. There followed slumps to £10.3 million and £2.7 million in 1987 and 1988. The loss of £20.6 million in 1989 heralded a period of four years of deficits. It was not until 1993 that the group returned to profitability. No dividend was paid between 1989 and 1993. The 1994 payment was less than one-third (in real terms) the 1987 dividend.

Key financial ratios also indicated a solvency deterioration. As shown in Table 8.6, the cash flow/debt, debt/turnover, debt/equity, interest cover and liquidity ratios all signalled weaknesses in performance and financial health. The improved 1986 profits were achieved on earlier forward hedging

Table 8.5: Waterford Wedgwood: trading performance

	Turnover (£m)	Pre-tax profit/(loss) (£m)	Dividend (pence per share)
1974	45	3.5	0.5
1975	60	4.7	0.6
1976	80	6.8	0.6
1977	101	9.0	0.9
1978	117	10.6	1.3
1979	136	11.6	1.5
1980	154	8.1	1.5
1981	190	10.4	1.5
1982	204	8.5	1.5
1983	213	10.2	1.7
1984	245	14.6	2.0
1985	255	18.5	2.4
1986	131	23.7	2.9
1987	282	10.3	2.9
1988	304	2.7	1.2
1989	349	(20.6)	–
1990	308	(21.4)	–
1991	292	(2.6)	–
1992	274	(17.0)	–
1993	319	10.1	–
1994	325	22.6	0.8

Note: Profits and losses are as reported before charging 'extraordinary items' (i.e. expenses) of £2m in 1984, £8m in 1985, £3m in 1986, £30m in 1987, a gain of £10m in 1988 and an expense of £1m in 1990.

Source: Annual reports.

positions at an exchange rate which was no longer available. Hedging could not save the crystal division in subsequent years until the dollar strengthened again. Thus the fall in profitability could be predicted within a range. Remarkably, this underlying trend did not show through in the share price in 1986, at the time of the Wedgwood acquisition, or again in 1987.

Labour costs, competitiveness and the dollar

Waterford's quoted share price began to fall in reaction to the declining profits. By January 1983 it had declined to a level not far off its book value at 18p compared to 28p two years earlier. The same dividend of 1.5p per share was paid for four years in succession. The chairman tended to blame

Table 8.6: Waterford Wedgwood: some critical financial ratios

	1984	1985	1986	1987	1988	1989	1990	1991	1992	1993	1994
Cash flow/debt*	9.2%	20.9%	5.1%	1.3%	(14.4%)	(3.2%)	7.1%	(4.2%)	4.2%	14.9%	18.8%
Debt*/total assets	52.4%	49.8%	68.0%	71.7%	72.0%	74.7%	51.9%	50.8%	58.6%	56.0%	53.7%
Debt*/turnover	57.8%	42.9%	60.2%	82.5%	95.6%	71.1%	50.4%	49.0%	52.3%	48.5%	47.6%
Interest cover	2.4 times	2.6 times	5.4 times	0.3 times	1.1 times	neg.	neg.	0.7 times	neg.	2.4 times	4.4 times
Net profit margin	6.0%	7.2%	17.8%	(3.6%)	0.1%	(5.9%)	(7.0%)	(0.1%)	(6.2%)	3.2%	7.0%
Working capital/turnover	29.3%	24.7%	48.4%	25.8%	32.8%	16.1%	26.6%	38.6%	36.0%	37.7%	37.0%
Current ratio	1.7:1	1.8:1	1.4:1	1.6:1	1.6:1	1.4:1	1.8:1	2.9:1	2.8:1	2.9:1	2.8:1

* All liabilities

Source: Annual reports; data computed by author.

the world recession for the weak results, though there was a brief mention of 'the loss of productivity'.[69] Paddy McGrath also mentioned that 'Severe price increases over a number of years . . . were not sufficient to maintain healthy margins and we are examining our costs with the aim of improving competitiveness so as to avoid the danger of over-pricing our products.'[70]

In fact, management's full capacity output/full employment policy for its skilled workforce was the dominant reason for the falling margins, higher working capital and increasing debt. The latter led to a jump in interest costs — £6 million in 1982, compared to £2.2 million in 1979 and £1 million in 1978 — which was a burden on weaker operating profits. By 1983, profit margins fell to 4.8%, which was half the level of five years earlier and less than one-third the margin of 14.7% in 1972.

Waterford Crystal, like the Irish Press group, was extremely labour intensive. Staff costs amounted to 70% of total costs[71] and about 55% of selling price. Employees were very well paid. Most demands by the trade unions were acceded to by management over the years so that there would be neither confrontation nor loss of output. Almost half the workforce were 'skilled' and by 1987 each of these earned almost £21,000 per annum through the team piece-rate payments system (a smaller group of elite craftsmen earned over £34,000 each). The average employee wage was £14,000 per annum. Anderson noted that by the mid-1980s, Waterford's labour rates were 77% above the industrial average for Ireland.[72] For the first time over such a lengthy period, production exceeded demand and stock levels increased sharply between 1979 and 1983. Because wages constituted a high proportion of stock values, there was a high cash requirement for working capital. The company's stock levels were also affected by a tighter stocking policy by the leading US department stores due to the 1980–81 recession spending cutbacks.

To compensate for increased labour rate concessions, management resorted to price increases which generally exceeded inflation in the company's main markets. Irish and UK prices were increased progressively so that there was little difference in price in its three primary markets by 1987.[73] By the early 1980s, apart from the original stemware range which was the backbone of development, the two newer product ranges, lightingware and giftware, were contributing to capacity expansion and increases in jobs and output. However, the past experience of consistent volume growth came to a near halt, primarily because of price resistance. For example, a traditional stemware product, such as a 'Lismore Goblet', which would have carried a retail price of $20 in the USA in 1978 jumped to $33 by 1982. Other factors were changing consumer tastes and the absence of sufficient new designs in the Waterford stemware range in particular.

Three markets, the US, Ireland and the UK, accounted for 86% of Waterford's crystal turnover. US and Irish sales accounted for 60% and 17% respectively. Because US tourists made up the greater proportion of Irish sales, almost 70% of turnover was US dollar related. The trend in the US dollar/Irish pound exchange rate, which was crucial to Waterford, is shown in Table 8.7. It shows that there was a currency gain of 21.6% in 1981 followed by three successive years of just over 12% per annum. Thus it can be seen that most of the growth in turnover between 1982 and 1985, as shown in Table 8.5, was due to a hardening of the dollar and aggressive price increases in every year (except 1984 in the USA). When the US dollar/Irish pound relationship changed sharply to a reversal of 25.9% in 1986 and a further decline of 10.9% in 1987, this showed through in reduced crystal division turnover in 1986 and 1987 (see Table 8.8). Waterford operated a sophisticated treasury function (by Irish standards) and it was policy to hedge the dollar forward by at least one year; this provided some short-term protection. Currency volatility continued into the 1990s.

Table 8.7: US dollar/Irish pound exchange rates*

	Dollars to pound	Rate of change (%)
1979	2.047	–
1980	2.061	−0.7
1981	1.616	+21.6
1982	1.421	+12.1
1983	1.247	+12.3
1984	1.087	+12.8
1985	1.066	+1.9
1986	1.342	−25.9
1987	1.488	−10.9
1988	1.525	−2.5
1989	1.418	+0.7
1990	1.659	−17.0
1991	1.614	+2.7
1992	1.707	−5.8
1993	1.467	+14.8

*   Exchange rates in Dublin market, period averages.
Source: *Quarterly Bulletin of Central Bank of Ireland*, Spring 1994, Table B6, p. 24.

By the mid-1980s, almost 3,100 people were employed in two factories in Waterford and a third in Dungarvan, contributing £50 million to the local economy. Waterford crystal was recognised, particularly in America, as the best quality product in the upper end of the market. It was a magnificent business achievement, brought about in just thirty years. The parallels with the Irish Press group were in the focus on an internal culture because of the production process and craftsmen's identity with product and the management arrangements centring on a small number of long-standing key authority figures.

In the opinion of the writer, by 1982 Waterford faced a series of interconnecting dilemmas:

External

- Evidence after the recession that price increases could no longer be used to cover wage increases and maintain profit margins; volume growth hard to achieve and price resistance being met
- New technology being used by competitors, who had much lower costs
- Market demand changing — beginning to suit new technology rather than expensive craft skills
- Distribution channels changing; department stores adopting new (less favourable) policies

Internal

- The death of Noel Griffin and the inadequate management structure
- Almost the same inbred board structure for generations
- The loss of competitiveness due to high labour costs and poor productivity
- The decline in profit margins reducing cash flow support for the high working capital levels
- High debt levels
- Smith and Switzer acquisitions performing poorly
- Negotiations for changes in production and work practices proving difficult with trade unions
- McGrath family commitment weakening — shareholding reduced from 41% to 20%; other family company problems

Waterford management consistently seemed to buy industrial relations peace up to the late 1970s because it could afford to do so. Demand exceeded supply and annual price increases did not seem to lessen buyer enthusiasm until the recession in 1980. The very material improvement in the US dollar/Irish pound exchange rate for four successive years to 1984 facilitated further labour wage 'buyoffs' and, to an extent, alleviated pressure to face the underlying weaknesses in competitiveness and pricing policy. Contrary to previous practice, very modest price increases were implemented in 1983 and 1985 (below the US inflation rate), and there was no increase in 1984.

The death of Noel Griffin created a vacuum in authority. The lack of development and depth in the management structure for an organisation of its size and complexity was exposed by this tragedy. Brophy concluded that its culture and management style flowed from the idealistic principles of the founder/sponsors, Joe McGrath and Joe Griffin, i.e. that Irish people, given the finance and leadership, could produce goods of the highest quality and sell them competitively in world markets.[74] The management style was both entrepreneurial and paternalistic, with strategic decision-making centred around the two long-standing dominant figures — the chairman, Paddy McGrath and managing director, Noel Griffin. This was very similar to the experience of Irish Press. Brophy commented:

> The founding families were people of action, not words and this has been translated into a style of management where results would normally be considered more favourably than effort. Waterford Glass managers tend as a consequence to get things done and be less concerned with analysis and rhetoric.[75]

The founding set of values encompassed a concern for the individual employee, good working conditions and attractive benefits, which forged great loyalty and stability. Very few employees in operations or management left Waterford Crystal; indeed they were a closely knit group, most of whom grew up together, with sons following fathers into well-paid jobs in the crystal factories. Unfortunately the management structure remained underdeveloped for such a large and increasingly complex organisation.

Much was centred around Noel Griffin and a functional hybrid structure with the acquired companies operating as semi-autonomous divisions. Such centralisation of authority was undoubtedly creating problems. Brophy cited pressures building up 'with respect to allocation of time and availability of information for rational investment decision-making'.[76] When Owen Kealy, the financial director, was appointed to take over as managing director on the death of Noel Griffin, he changed the organisation structure to a multidivisional form, with the group holding company separated from the crystal activity. Waterford Glass Group plc was now the parent and Waterford Crystal Ltd became the operating division in a corporate reorganisation which was somewhat similar to that undertaken by the Irish Press group some years later.

By the early 1980s many work practice changes in demarcation between different craft groups, attendance levels and product quality (there was a high reject rate, which was costly to productivity) were sought by management. Few were agreed to by the trade unions. According to McSweeney, the unions' position was that there would be no compulsory or voluntary redundancies, no loss of earnings and the employees involved would participate in any savings resulting from a change in work practices.[77] Management also wanted to substitute technology for labour and introduce cheaper labour to reduce costs. Productivity was now emerging as an issue. However, both management and unions believed that the hand-made craft tradition was intrinsic to the quality and desirability of the Waterford product, and was central to the advertising theme. This gave the unions considerable power of veto, and management seemed reluctant to take a firmer line on productivity. Supreme Court approval of Waterford as a trade mark in 1983 was a precursor to alternative manufacturing options and helped change the balance of power between unions and management. From the writer's perspective the attitudes of many Waterford Crystal employees and trade union officials, particularly from the late 1970s, seemed to contrast with the early idealism and practical patriotism of the McGrath and Griffin families.[78]

Weaknesses in financial policy and financial control were evident in Waterford as far back as 1980, with the build-up of stock, increasing leverage and the series of negative cash flows until 1984. The group operated with a high level of bank debt from 1980. The interest cover weakened (but became more volatile with the changes in the yearly profits) to just under four times (it was over six times up to 1980). The near doubling in turnover from £136 million in 1979 to £245 million in 1984 put pressure on financing needs. A rights issue would have been appropriate from a prudent financing perspective but it would have posed problems for the McGrath family.

The sale of the McGrath family equity to Globe: a new management and a new strategic plan

The progressive reductions in the McGrath equity interest from 41% to 20% partially reflected the family views of uses of the resources and the financing demands of a portfolio of businesses controlled by Avenue Investments, the family investment holding company. The announcement in May 1984 that Waterford was in discussions about being taken over came as a surprise internally and caused some uncertainty. A few weeks later the *Economist* commented:

> Strategic mistakes have driven Waterford to seek a partner . . . Diversification from top-of-the-range operations has not repaid the group's investment . . .
>
> Waterford is also top heavy. Since the founding of the company in the 1940s, the three families involved . . . have swelled the board . . . The board also spends a lot of time wrangling with the third generation McGraths, who want to cash in their grandparent's effort.[79]

Negotiations with P. J. Carroll and others came to nothing. The nature of the eventual disposal of the McGrath 20% shareholding to Globe Investment Trust in August 1984 was remarkable. It seems that Avenue was under some pressure to sell as it built up heavy bank debt through difficulties experienced in a number of its business interests with two, Avair and Waltham Holdings, going into receivership.[80] London bankers Morgan Stanley and stockbrokers Panmure Gordon were urgently looking for a buyer. Globe, one of London's larger investment trusts with assets of over Stg£500 million, had a policy of taking strategic stakes in a small number of companies as part of its equity portfolio. It paid 40p per share — yielding Avenue £17 million. In this writer's view it was surprising that the McGraths, of all people, sold their interest to a UK investment group with little industry-specific management expertise to inject. As a financial investor, Globe would not normally be seen as a long-term shareholder. Leading Irish industrial firms could certainly have found £17 million — but seem to have decided otherwise.[81]

Two directors of Globe, David Hardy (its chairman) and Quentin Morris, were co-opted to the board of Waterford. Soon afterwards, the whole of the 'old guard' founder group resigned, followed by Paddy McGrath in May 1985. Globe arranged for Paddy Hayes, a former chairman and chief executive of Ford Ireland, to join the Waterford board as deputy chairman and he succeeded Paddy McGrath as executive chairman. Within six months more than half of the board resigned. Only one non-executive director, Patrick Kilroy a solicitor in Dublin who was associated with the Smith Group, continued. The manner of the McGrath and founding interests' rapid departure left few overlaps and, in effect, represented a discontinuity. Admittedly, it paved the way for new blood.

The first major decision of the depleted board, in March 1985, was to agree a three-year wage deal with the trade unions which guaranteed a minimum 7% wage increase per annum and a level of profit participation. It was expensive, as the base payment was almost double current and projected rates of inflation in the USA and Ireland. The total cost was subsequently estimated at between 44% and 62%. The Irish inflation rate for the three-year period accumulated to just 18%.[82]

The co-option of Howard Kilroy of the Smurfit Group, Gerard Dempsey of Aer Lingus and David Dand, managing director of Gilbeys Ireland (whose reputation was associated with 'Baileys Cream' as a brand), as non-executive directors brought broad business, industrial accounting and strategic marketing expertise to the company. Waterford undoubtedly needed new leadership and a new vision. Appointing Paddy Hayes as executive chairman with the backing of a 20% shareholder and a major strengthening of the board seemed a correct first step. At the executive level, Owen Kealy, the managing director, and Tom Aspel, the former sales director, resigned. Hayes recruited three ex-Ford senior staff, first Redmond O'Donoghue for sales and marketing and later Paddy Byrne and Richard Barnes, whose initial assignments were in Wedgwood as chief executive and finance director, respectively. O'Donoghue and Byrne were co-opted to the parent board in 1986 and 1987.

Hayes had a reputation as a demanding but fair manager who was not afraid to take tough decisions. Sometimes he could be confrontational. He believed in the Ford way of professional management through teamwork, systematic analysis, market research, strong marketing, planning and the setting of ambitious targets. The first major outcome was a five-year corporate plan for 1986–90. It established the key objective of increasing annual earnings by 20% per annum. The strategy to achieve this included:

- reducing debt to a 50% debt/equity ratio and achieving an interest cover of four times
- disposing of non-core businesses
- reorganising marketing organisational structures and practices; introducing new patterns in stemware and new lines in lightingware and giftware; increasing the advertising budget; reducing sales dependence on the USA

- improving productivity, reducing production costs per unit and increasing production output through new payments scheme, new furnace and greater mechanisation investment
- improving stock control and order/delivery service response
- exploring acquisitions or associations which complement the core business
- exploring the possibility of production capacity outside Ireland.

The 1985 and 1986 financial statements reported an improvement in the crystal division's profits. The forward hedging of the dollar at much more favourable exchange rates in 1983 and 1984, allied to some price increases, protected turnover values and profit margins because of the dollar fall of almost 26% in 1986. Hayes and his team achieved the divestment, debt and marketing targets, apart from crystal dependence on the USA. The Smith Group was loss-making from 1982, as a result of Renault's declining market share. Between 1985 and 1986 Waterford had to make write-downs and provisions of £11.7 million to enable it to dispose of the Smith Group at a nominal consideration.

US market share in 1986 increased from 23% to 28% in the full lead crystal stemware, which was the top end of the market. A restructuring of management responsibilities created a four-person team in group headquarters which was chaired by Paddy Hayes and included Brian Patterson, formerly of Guinness and the Irish Management Institute who had been recently recruited (management and corporate development), Redmond O'Donoghue (sales and marketing) and Anthony Brophy (finance). C. O'Connell and W. Power were managing director and general manager of the crystal division. It was a combination of three new and three old.

Following its acquisition, a separate team was established for Wedgwood, which involved three of its previous senior executive directors and was headed up by Paddy Byrne as managing director since his predecessor retired soon after the acquisition. In addition, Bob Davies was recruited as Wedgwood's finance director in May 1987.

The Wedgwood acquisition

In October 1986, the Waterford board made an 'agreed' bid of £255 million for the Wedgwood group. The 220-year-old Wedgwood company was a leading brand identified with fine bone English china and earthenware. Its primary markets were the UK (43%) and the USA and Canada (32%), with more recent penetration in Japan. With a share exchange or cash offer, at Waterford's share price of 127p, Wedgwood's shares were valued at 555p — a 46% increase over the 380p market price before the offer. Wedgwood had made a rights issue at 187p in December 1985. The dramatic rise in its share price was triggered by the purchase of 10% of its equity by London International Group (which owned Durex contraceptives, Royal Doulton and Worcestershire Spode) and a hostile takeover bid which valued Wedgwood at £106 million less than Waterford's offer. The Waterford offer price put Wedgwood on a historic exit price/earnings ratio of 16.5 times (before adjusting for a £1 million pension contribution holiday). It was heavily dilutive of Waterford's earnings capacity for some time. The goodwill element, at £146 million, was 57% of the purchase price. Wedgwood's most recently reported pre-tax profits of £20.7 million and margins at 13.6% were at a peak. It would need to earn a pre-tax profit of £51 million to earn a return of 20% on Waterford's investment outlay. In brief, Wedgwood would have to almost treble its turnover. A free cash flow analysis made no difference because of Wedgwood's low depreciation charge of £3 million and its working capital needs. In this writer's opinion, taking the additional capacity investment required to generate such a profit level, Waterford overpaid, if the cost is linked to the valuation — irrespective of how it was financed. However, given that the greater part of the consideration was Waterford equity, it was predominantly a paper purchase and might be viewed as good value. After all, for the next four years Wedgwood profits helped to cover the crystal division's losses.

It was an opportunistic move with Waterford acting as a benevolent 'white knight'. Though the combination of Waterford and Wedgwood's products and markets was held out as the perfect match, it was a very large acquisition for Waterford to digest. Wedgwood had almost double Waterford's turnover; it was spread over eighteen factories and employed 7,600 people.[83] Wedgwood was going through a rationalisation stage and the goodwill element of the acquisition cost covered reorganisation provisions of £23.7 million[84] (of which £18.6 million was drawn on for Wedgwood's 1987 results). Wedgwood was to become the 'milch-cow' in saving Waterford.[85] As shown in Table 8.8, Wedgwood remained profitable when Waterford Crystal incurred heavy losses. An analysis of the post-acquisition figures between 1987 and 1994 does not point to a material rise in Wedgwood's turnover and profitability because of marketing and brand synergies — even when taking account of the 1990–93 recession. In 1994 its operating profit was £17 million compared to £13 million for Waterford Crystal.

Table 8.8: Comparison of the financial performance of Waterford Crystal and Wedgwood (£m)

	Waterford		Wedgwood	
	Turnover	Profit/(loss)	Turnover	Profit
1982	60[e]	6[e]	117	8
1983	73	7	121	6
1984	98	11	138	13
1985	106	15	146	16
1986	94	17	152	21
1987	76	(19)	170	25
1988	94	(21)	190	22
1989	112	(21)	165	16
1990	87	(5)	156	18
1991	73	(1)	193	13
1992	76	1	175	11
1993	102	8	193	9
1994	109	13	193	15

[e] Estimate

Note: Profit is the 'operating profit' before charging bank interest or any exceptional or extraordinary items.

Source: Annual reports of Waterford Glass Group plc, Waterford Wedgwood plc, Wedgwood plc; Wedgwood takeover listing document 1986.

Evaluating Wedgwood's post-acquisition performance, it is difficult to conclude that the investment met economic criteria from a cost of capital perspective. The acquisition of such a blue-blood British company with a brand name might be seen as more managerialist than shareholder-value driven. The irony is that the Wedgwood shareholders, who accepted Waterford shares in exchange, lost out badly. Over half the group's new shareholding was in the UK.

The scale of Wedgwood's business and its location led to a serious diversion of group management and the board's time during the period in 1987 and 1988 when the crucial productivity and cost reduction programme was being implemented in Waterford. The group was implementing production rationalisation in Wedgwood in 1987 with a workforce reduction of 968 people. There was considerable new investment, restructuring and disposal of unprofitable subsidiaries and surplus assets. Reorganisation costs of £13.1 million were incurred in 1987 alone. Added to the Waterford senior management's 'learning curve' was the time invested in understanding Wedgwood's products, markets and marketing approach, and how the brands might operate together. In addition, the Waterford board took on additional bank debt of £63 million to fund the acquisition — at a time when it knew it was facing an expensive redundancy programme in the crystal factories. The strategy of reducing debt was, in effect, abandoned. The debt/equity ratio rose to 66%, despite the equity placing of $29 million in American depository receipts in New York, and it could hardly avoid a material increase with the investment programme envisaged for both operations.

The crystal division's redundancy and accounting disasters

The steep decline in the US dollar/Irish pound relationship in 1986, which would eventually affect the profitability of 75% of output, allied to changes in stocking policy by US department stores and the use of new technology by competitors put pressure on the new management team to seek work practice changes and a lower cost structure. Many competitors were using cheaper machine-blown blanks and machine cutting was becoming so sophisticated that 'blind' tests found it difficult to distinguish between hand-cut and machine-cut stemware products. Management also regarded machines as offering better capability for consistency, product control, design changes and small batch production.[86] Waterford's own market research indicated that demand was moving from the heavier and traditional deep-cut and complex designs to shallow-cut and simpler designs. Such a change in the product range drew 'intense workplace hostility' according to McSweeney, because it could result in less cuts and a reduction in cutters' pay.[87] The willingness of the unions to demand additional pay with any excuse was illustrated when a section of the main crystal factory was asked by management to use red rather than green product markers. The request was refused without extra payments. A trade union official explained their action: 'It makes no difference what colour it is. It's a chance to get some more money back from them.'[88] During the course of initial negotiations with management, the unions sought external advice on the management information provided and the business options from an academic team from Warwick University. It seems that the conclusions of the academics generally supported the management initiative.[89]

In August 1987 the board reported a 73% decline in operating profits in the crystal division for the first six months of 1987. It simultaneously announced its objective of reducing manufacturing costs 'as an essential measure' and that a plan was under negotiation with the trade unions. The plan involved job reductions of 750 through a voluntary redundancy programme, a capital investment of £18 million in new technology (including diamond cutting wheels and melting tank furnaces in the Dungarvan factory in 1988 and the Kilbarry factory in 1989), revised work practices which would incorporate the use of the new equipment, and flexibility and mobility within the craft sections. The expectation was that there would be a 20% decrease in unit production costs. In light of the earlier business and competitiveness assessment underlying the strategy of the five-year corporate plan for 1986–90, it took a year-and-a-half's fall in the dollar by over 30% to bring about some urgency in taking action.

Employees received official details of the redundancy plan in September. It was most attractive by Irish standards: a skilled blower or cutter, aged forty-nine, who was earning £23,000 a year would receive a lump sum of £40,860 and a pension and social welfare supplement of £237 per week.[90] In fact more employees than were required — 1,005 in all — opted for the redundancy package as it seems that there were no material restraints in ensuring balance across sections and skills at the option of management. Some of the senior craftsmen were reputed to have received amounts varying between £60,000 and £80,000, depending on service. Some moved on to found Tipperary Crystal. The total cost of this programme in 1987 amounted to £49.8 million.[91]

Despite the group net loss of £47.8 million, which was held out as a 'one-off' cost, good progress was reported in the 1987 annual report, where the chairman concluded that the group 'is emerging as a leaner, fitter and more competitive organisation'. The results for the first six months of 1988 appeared to confirm the cost and profit improvement with interim pre-tax profits of £2.5 million. The board stated that the first continuous tank furnace, costing £9 million, had become fully operational in July and was consistently meeting its production targets. The old carborundum cutting wheels were replaced by 300 diamond wheels and management was confident 'that reduced unit production costs will continue'. The interim statement asserted that the group 'has achieved a notable turnaround in the first half of the year and is now well placed for profitable growth'. The chairman concluded:

> At the Annual General Meeting in May I said I believed that Group profits would 'bounce back' in the second half of 1988. The continuing strength of Wedgwood, the record crystal orders . . . and, particularly, the major reduction in crystal unit production costs, support this belief.[92]

Unfortunately, it appears that this optimistic expectation was based on inaccurate internal production efficiency and management accounting information. To the shock of the capital markets, the Waterford board issued a press release on 24 January 1989 announcing that an internal review it initiated in December 'indicated accounting errors overstating the valuation of finished stocks and work in progress during 1988'. Colm O'Connell, the Waterford Crystal chief executive, and Anthony Brophy, the group finance director, resigned. Peat Marwick McLintock (and not the auditors Price Waterhouse) were asked to conduct an independent review. The stockmarket price fell from 89p to 78p and stockbroker analysts drastically revised their profit forecasts. Davy Stockbrokers had issued a report dated 17 January 1989, indicating that they were cautious about the extent of the productivity progress, and that consequently their current forecast was being reduced to a pre-tax profit £17.5 million for 1988. Immediately after the 'accounting errors' announcement, Davy's profit forecast was reduced to £10 million for 1988 — which, through no fault of theirs, proved optimistic.

The board issued a press release on 10 April admitting that the financial performance was poor with a pre-tax profit for 1988 of only £2.7 million. No final dividend was to be paid. It was worse than the analysts' revised forecasts. The investigating accountants had reported that:

- the restructuring of Waterford Crystal was necessary, but it was 'inadequately planned and there were significant shortcomings in its subsequent management and control'
- 'when progress fell short of the budgeted level, stocks were over-valued and costs deferred with the result that misleading information was presented to the Board' and corrective action was delayed
- 'management's ability to reach realistic long-term agreements with the workforce will . . . be critical to Waterford's future . . . [and] a key factor in the . . . return to profitability'.[93]

Internal management accounts for 1988 overstated profits by £15 million, of which £8 million was in stock valuation and £7 million was mainly in cost deferrals. More detailed explanations were never revealed by the board, other than stating that a loss of £12.3 million was incurred by the crystal division in the first half-year, instead of the reported profit of £1.2 million.[94] A loss of £8.2 million was incurred in the second six months. The media offered various explanations.[95] It seems that some internal staff may have suspected there were production problems and costs were in excess of plan. Teething troubles with the new furnace were a factor as well as the higher costs of regrouping of teams. The mismatch between blower and cutter capacity and production flows was solved by the temporary contracting of many recently retired craftsmen. Perhaps it was thought that the planned productivity improvements would smooth the problem costs over a longer period.

In this writer's opinion it is surprising that senior financial executives could miss accounting errors of such a magnitude in a division with a turnover of £94 million and inventory of the order of £40 million. The board and the audit committee, who would have been dependent on the internal personnel, systems and controls together with any other reviews of the interim published figures, would not have found it easy to detect such errors. The operation of internal control and internal audit must have been problematical. The outcome was that corporate credibility seems to have been undermined in the capital markets.

The incident was reminiscent of the P. J. Carroll debacle where there were information breakdowns internally and externally surrounding the costs and performance of a new investment. Paddy Hayes, with some dignity, took responsibility and resigned. Howard Kilroy became non-executive chairman. Paddy Hayes was somewhat unlucky. In this writer's opinion he took too much on, given the management teams available in both Wedgwood and Waterford Crystal. While he appears to have been taking a strategic view of future direction, there seems to have been insufficient attention to detail. The £50 million cost reduction programme needed a much more 'hands-on' involvement to ensure it was planned and implemented efficiently. Wedgwood's management accounting information on performance and profitability after its acquisition was nailed down by recruiting Bob Davies from Coopers & Lybrand as finance director from May 1987. Ironically, it was when Davies subsequently raised questions about Waterford's internal figures that Paddy Hayes initiated an internal review. This writer concludes that the scale of the 'accounting errors', the duration of their concealment and the fact that misleading information was presented to the board and shareholders indicate that there was a serious breakdown in accounting competence, professionalism, and financial control and systems.

Paddy Hayes and his team tried to bring a new professional management culture to Waterford. It was not an easy task, in view of the paternalistic family background allied to the role of the craftsmen and the power and policies of the trade unions. Hayes's managerial career with a multinational car firm, allied to a less familiar management style, may not have been the best preparation for an organisation characterised by its deep craft traditions, pride and close employee identity with the product. The misleading production and accounting information suggests that there were tensions about reactions to the performance reality. From this writer's perspective, the nature of the affair suggests that there were insiders and outsiders, and that the new management team and board members were among the latter.

Many of the problems of Waterford's production cost structure were blamed on the three-year wage agreement negotiated with the trade unions in March 1985. Globe Investment Trust had taken a 20% stake six months earlier. With its two board members and the retirement of most of the old guard, Globe was the strategic and dominant shareholder who initiated the top management change. It commanded pivotal power on strategy approval, the five-year corporate plan, investment decisions and the monitoring of performance. Globe must take a primary responsibility for the subsequent weak position of Waterford Crystal following its failed turnaround. Globe had sold 18.6 million shares for about £23.5 million by 31 October 1986 — just before the Wedgwood acquisition. Its 20% holding fell to just 10.25% of the issued equity (before the acquisition enlargement).[96] It realised a capital profit of over 300% on that proportion of its investment in just over two years. The balance of 24.3 million shares was, effectively, a free investment in Waterford. To this writer it was an interesting London interpretation of what had seemed to be a long-term investment. Irish Life, IBI, AIB and Standard Life were also to become sizeable investors, but none were in the same position as Globe — apart from being somewhat passive. In two and a half years, Waterford lost the continuity and authority of an authoritative shareholding.

The failed turnaround

The board instituted a further management restructuring following the resignation of Paddy Hayes and the earlier departures of O'Connell and Brophy. Paddy Byrne moved from Wedgwood to become group chief executive, Bob Davies became group financial officer and Paddy Galvin was recruited from Guinness in May 1989 as chief executive of the crystal division. Despite the commencement of a new set of negotiations with the trade unions and new design and marketing initiatives, the overall gross profit margin for 1989 declined by 3.8 points to 42.1% and a net loss of

£29 million was incurred — despite the profitability of Wedgwood. This was primarily due to a loss of £21.2 million in the crystal division and an interest bill of £18.8 million. Total debt reached £248 million in comparison with shareholders' funds of £74 million.

Bank debt, at £167 million at the end of 1989, became unsustainable. The group's weak financial position was corrected by an injection of £96 million (net) of new equity on 29 April 1990. This was achieved through a placing (at 37.5p) with a consortium of a Morgan Stanley (New York) investment fund and Fitzwilton, the Irish quoted firm associated with Tony O'Reilly. The consortium, known as Shuttleway, would hold 29.9% of the enlarged equity. A general shareholders' rights issue was mainly supported by institutional investors at 27.5p — compared with 127p in late 1986. Waterford now had a new strong investor with a major stake in the company. The consortium appointed four directors to the board. These included Tony O'Reilly representing Fitzwilton and Don Brennan, a managing director (with previous US industrial experience) from Morgan Stanley. By any criterion, the restructured board was extremely strong.

Some weeks earlier, on 5 April, following the breakdown of negotiations with management about further rationalisation, cost reductions and productivity changes, the crystal staff commenced a fourteen-week strike. A net loss of £28.2 million was incurred in 1990. The loss in the crystal division was reduced to £5 million before an attributed £10 million in 'strike costs'. An entrenched position was taken up by the trade unions, despite the difficult competitive environment — somewhat similar to the Irish Press experience. At this time Waterford was increasing spending on advertising under new marketing initiatives. The advertising copy emphasised the unique, personal and highly skilled craft creation and 'brilliance' of a typical glass, and linked the originality and uniqueness of the product to the senior craftsmen with such phrases as 'From the white-hot ovens of Waterford Crystal, formed by the mouths of skilled blowers and the hands of master cutters . . .' Perhaps the advertising claims affected the attitudes of the craftsmen as well as the consumers. Behind this exterior it was known that technology had now advanced to the extent that it could be introduced without risk to product excellence — but the craftsmen harboured other perceptions.

In 1991 overall losses were reduced to £5.2 million, with the crystal division reporting a loss of £1.2 million despite some rationalisation. Waterford Crystal turnover fell to £73 million compared to £112 million in 1989. Despite the introduction of several new designs, the high price of the crystal products was affecting demand. There was a small improvement in 1992 turnover, mainly due to the launch of a new mid-price range under the title 'Marquis brand', which was outsourced from glass manufacturers in Slovakia and Germany. Waterford Crystal reported a £0.5 million operating profit but the costs of further rationalisation in Waterford Crystal (£9 million) and Wedgwood (£8 million) left a net loss of £19 million in 1992. There was a fall of almost 30% in volumes in both Waterford Crystal and Wedgwood because of the recession.

In 1984 Waterford achieved a cash surplus for the first time in many years. However, by 1986, with the acquisition of Wedgwood, there was a large cash need as the acquisition was on the basis of a share exchange or cash alternative offer. There was an eventual cash need of £59 million on the £255 million Wedgwood acquisition, as £196 million in new equity was issued (including £29 million in US ADRs). With the heavy cash outlays on redundancy, restructuring and new technology, and the five years of trading losses at Waterford Crystal, the group returned to its former experience of cash deficits for seven consecutive years from 1986 to 1992.

As shown in the cash flow analysis in Table 8.9, without the equity injection of £96 million in 1990 by the Shuttleway consortium it is difficult to see how Waterford Wedgwood would have survived. The interest bill reached £19 million by 1989 and the group incurred an 'operating' loss *before* any finance charges. Net bank debt jumped to £125 million (compared to shareholders' funds of £84 million at book value). It was a grim financial position by the end of 1989. By 1990 the group breached certain financial covenants in its banking agreements and the auditors, Price Waterhouse, drew attention to the financial position of the group in their audit opinion.

The Waterford board and the consortium investors were distinctly unhappy with progress. The prospect of a dividend remained remote and the debt/equity position was deteriorating once again. By spring 1993 three years would have passed without turnaround reaching economic levels. This was due to the difficult external environment and the continuing high cost structure. The employees also suffered. Apart from the loss of good wages in 1990, because of the strike, there was almost three months of short-time working in 1991.

The second turnaround

In late 1992 the Waterford board sought wage reductions and redundancies in the crystal division. The successful experience of outsourcing the Marquis range combined with the fact that market research findings

Table 8.9: Waterford Wedgwood: cash flow profile (£m)

	1986	1987	1988	1989	1990	1991	1992	1993
Trading cash flow	14	(24)	(26)	(7)	(15)	0	0	11
Working capital	(3)	27	(16)	(1)	26	(6)	6	12
Operating cash flow	11	3	(42)	(8)	11	(6)	6	23
Investments								
Capital expenditure	17	70	47	17	8	8	7	11
Acquisitions	255	–	–	–	10	–	–	–
Total investment	272	70	47	17	18	8	7	11
Cash surplus/ (shortfall)	(261)	(67)	(89)	(25)	(7)	(14)	(1)	12
Financed by:								
Sale of assets	9	49	46	7	1	2	–	–
New equity	196	–	10	1	96	–	–	–
Change in cash	(2)	(9)	(36)	46	7	9	–	6
Change in bank debt	58	27	69	(29)	(97)	3	1	(6)

Source: Annual reports; cash flows computed by author.

revealed that 'Waterford' as a brand name was not identified with the city of Waterford provided some flexibility in manufacturing outside Ireland. Gross profit margins remained low and they had not improved by 1992, as shown in Table 8.10.

Management released its cost improvement plan in late August 1992. It required 500 redundancies, wage cuts of up to 25% and radical changes in work practices. An extensive series of in-house seminars on the plan was conducted for employees. The negotiations with the trade unions proved difficult. The Waterford Crystal and parent boards stood firm on the plan, which was turned down twice by the workforce in November. By December the crystal division management was instructed to prepare an alternative manufacturing plan with up to half the existing crystal production being outsourced. Less severe proposals put forward by the Amalgamated Transport and General Workers Union (ATGWU) were, in turn, rejected by management. Difficult and tense negotiations, conciliation

Table 8.10: Waterford Wedgwood: gross profit margins (%)

Year	%
1986	50.4
1987	42.6
1988	45.9
1989	42.1
1990	45.2
1991	43.7
1992	42.5
1993	41.5
1994	46.6

Source: Annual reports; data computed by author.

and Labour Court intervention in late December, which generally supported the management proposals, finally resulted in the trade unions recommending the package in early January 1993.

The cost improvement agreement was a radical change in pay policy and conditions for the craft workers in particular, as it involved pay cuts of 25%. Other workers faced pay cuts of between 7% and 15%, and management salaries were to be reduced by 15%. There was to be a pay freeze and an industrial peace clause for three years and major changes in work practices and payment systems. After the vote Walter Cullen, the ATGWU district organiser, was reported as saying that the decision was not an easy one for the union's members.[97] The company's board made it clear that it would stand firm and take drastic action on outsourcing to achieve lower costs and profitability. It set target margins of 50% for gross profit and 15% for operating profit on sales, if the crystal division was to be economic and satisfactorily service its cost of capital. Employees realised that the financial separation of the crystal division from Wedgwood was a reality.

Directors' freedom is often constrained by technical legal and financial issues. In May 1991 a refinancing agreement was signed with a syndicate of banks to provide £105 million for three and a half years to support the turnaround. It was conditional on the separation of the two businesses, together with financial covenants which imposed specific performance targets.[98] At the time, the auditors, Price Waterhouse, in their 1990 audit report referred to a 'Note' attached to the financial statements which drew on the bank refinancing agreement in justifying the adoption of the going concern basis by the directors. The borrowings and interest costs were separated out for servicing by each entity; Wedgwood had provided certain guarantees. The 1991 audit report contained a similar caveat and a similar

'Note' to the accounts, which referred to 'modest headroom' in complying with the financial covenants. However, a projected heavy loss for the group for 1992, which turned out to be £19 million, and an increase in the bank debt were evidence of a disappointing rate of recovery in the crystal division. This financial performance and a difficult environment stiffened the resolve of the directors to grasp the productivity and cost reduction nettle.

The group's share price fell to a low of 14p during 1992 but recovered to 19p by December. However, the Shuttleway consortium which invested at 37.5p in April 1990 was suffering heavy losses. The prospect of an economic return on investment was distinctly doubtful without extensive changes in manufacturing competitiveness. Much was already done on the marketing and new product side with larger marketing outlays. The crystal division was now close to its financial covenants and there was pressure on its board.

In 1993 and 1994 the crystal division reported operating profits of £8 million and £13 million, representing margins of 7.6% and 12%; this was moving towards the objective laid down by the board. Wedgwood's profits recovered from £9 million to £15 million, which was a long way off the performance at the time of the acquisition, despite much new investment and rationalisation. The impact of the cost improvement agreement was such that the total group staff costs fell to 40.5% of turnover in 1993 and 1994 compared with 48% in 1991. The group's gross profit margin improved to 46.6% in 1994, its highest since 1986. The net profit of £20.6 million in 1994 enabled the board to recommend a dividend of 0.8p per share — the first dividend since 1988. The share price reached 58p in December 1994, indicating that the market believed that a reasonable business turnaround had finally been achieved. Though there was still £86 million in long-term bank debt to be repaid, the financial position improved and for two years in a row there were surplus net cash flows, which marked a change from the deficits of many years.

Reflections on Irish Press and Waterford Wedgwood

There were many similarities between Irish Press and Waterford Wedgwood apart from being long-established organisations with more than one 'family' member on the board. There were board and governance weaknesses at a vital time in their cycle of change. The environment in terms of competition became more difficult. The evidence points to ineffective strategic management control over cost structures, profit margins, performance against objectives, and loss of market share. Much of Waterford's diversification investment did not provide an economic return.

Similarly, the Irish Press group incurred losses on its acquisition of Southside Newspapers. In both cases, the second generation of the family did not seem to make adequate provision for succession. In this writer's view, transition to the mature stage was flawed because of poor organisation structures and insufficient senior, non-family, professional management. The management style appears to have remained too personalised and the structure of both boards was too inbred.

Central to the Irish Press and Waterford problems was the fact that staff costs were too high a proportion of total costs. Both experienced serious labour relations disputes and lengthy strikes over new productivity proposals. In this writer's opinion a combination of short-sighted trade union policy, an active and militant element in the workforce, and feeble management policies contributed to the overall corporate crisis. The turnaround period in Waterford was lengthy and failed twice. Similar to P. J. Carroll's experience, the Irish Press group found it difficult to arrest a slide in market share, and the attempted turnaround with a partner failed. The sweeping management and board changes in Waterford can be contrasted with the very limited mutation in the Irish Press group.

Irish Press and Waterford seem to have entered a downward spiral before losses were reported. In this writer's view, an initial blindness to market changes by the Irish Press group and the weak productivity and competitiveness of Waterford Crystal represented the first stage of decline. Each organisation's problems appear to have been compounded by subsequent mistakes or omissions in adaptation, for example converting the *Irish Press* to a tabloid format or the botched and costly redundancy and rationalisation programme in Waterford which did not deliver the productivity required.

Both organisations also suffered from marketing weaknesses (as did P. J. Carroll, though in that case it was after a long period of success). Marketing was a primary defect in the Irish Press group until the late 1980s — when it was almost too late. In this writer's opinion, to a degree, this reflected the 'family' dominance and their paternalistic approach in contrast to the more commercial approach required for the changing internal and external environment of the 1980s. Each organisation seems to have been dominated by a crucial group who were part of the founding ethos — the senior editorial staff and journalists in Irish Press and the skilled teams of blowers and cutters in Waterford. Meanwhile the nature of consumer demand changed, competition became more intense and new more cost-effective and sophisticated technology was adopted by competitors. Because both

Irish Press and (to a slightly lesser extent) Waterford were production-oriented organisations, they did not adapt sufficiently. In the former, the family dominance continued and perhaps that represented part of the cause of its continuing crisis, in this writer's view.

From this writer's perspective, the problem in each case was caused by the inability of the family successors to 'manage' change, difficult industrial relations issues and a weak top management team. They were unwilling to take tough decisions. Instead they rested on their success — just when it was starting to crumble. The market and competition changed and heavy price increases affected demand. Difficulties in negotiating change with the trade unions and the craft traditions contributed to the financial crisis. The poor health and loss of key management figures in the early 1980s in both companies exposed flaws in the top management structure and organisation as underlying internal weaknesses grew. Miller's typology suggests Irish Press fulfilled the criteria of the 'Stagnant Bureaucracy' syndrome, whereas Waterford was closer to the syndrome of the 'Headless Firm'.

Similar to the Guinness experience, new management had a relatively short life in Waterford and Irish Press. Conflict, controversy and struggles over power tended to intermingle with the turnaround process. There were collisions between a variety of coalitions and interests reflecting different traditions, cultures and styles. Examples were the departure of Ernest Saunders in Guinness, Paddy Hayes in Waterford and Ralph Ingersoll in Irish Press. In this writer's opinion crises in organisations appear to have implications not only for the reputations of the long-serving executives but also for the 'new brooms' if they have insufficient power and backing from the board, controlling shareholders and bankers, or if they are insufficiently skilled and sensitive to organisational politics and undercurrents.

Chapter 9

Irish Shipping: A Vessel Without a Chart or Compass

Numbers are symbols, very much like words, with their own intrinsic simple meanings, when they stand alone, and far more complex and meaningful when in the context of pertinent other numbers. A child learns the alphabet, and then how to put letters together to spell words, and words together to make sentences, until he or she grows up to read or write a book where the real meaning will often be found between the lines. 'Cat' can mean a kitten to a child, a Siamese or Persian to a pet owner, or a tiger to a hunter. If I tell you there are five apples in the basket on the table, what does that tell you? That there are five apples in the basket. Or, if you knew there should be six, that someone had eaten one of your apples.

In business, numbers are the symbols by which you measure the various activities. . . . When you add and subtract all the numbers, you come up with the well known 'bottom line' on your profit and loss statement. That's very simple, like spelling 'cat' . . .

Harold S. Geneen, *Managing*[1]

The collapse of Irish Shipping: a national scandal

The collapse of Irish Shipping is taken on its own, because it was a unique event in Irish corporate history. It has implications and lessons for the state sector in terms of its governance, competence in monitoring, decision-making processes and public policy.

On 14 November 1984 an extraordinary general meeting of the shareholders of Irish Shipping, being the Minister for Finance or his representatives, unanimously resolved this special resolution:

> . . . that it has been proved to the satisfaction of this meeting that the company cannot by reason of its liabilities continue its business and that the company be wound up by the court and that the directors be authorised and instructed to petition the court for the winding up of the company and to apply to the court for the appointment of a provisional liquidator.[2]

Events moved quickly. The shareholders' meeting immediately followed an earlier board meeting. The directors were required to apply to the court for the appointment of a provisional liquidator. That afternoon, the chairman, Frank Belton, in an affidavit to the High Court, explained that he and his fellow directors felt that, as further government finance had been refused, Irish Shipping would be unable to meet its debts as they fell due. Certain suppliers were already withdrawing credit facilities and were insisting on dealing on a cash basis. It was in the best interest of creditors and the company that a provisional liquidator be appointed.[3] Maurice Tempany was appointed as provisional liquidator, and took control of the company later the same day.

When word of the appointment of the liquidator reached the Dáil, there was consternation. An immediate request to debate a motion that the liquidation decision be reversed was tabled by the opposition, Fianna Fáil. Eventually a four-hour period from 6.30 p.m. was agreed. It was a highly charged and acrimonious debate. Apart from the policy and financial issues, there were other agendas. After all, Irish Shipping had been established by Seán Lemass under instructions from Eamon de Valera in 1941. It was central to Irish neutrality during World War II.

Jim Mitchell, Minister for Communications in the Fine Gael/Labour coalition, justified the government's decision on the basis that it would require £108 million in advances (growing to £144 million to cover interest costs) to keep Irish Shipping operational for the following five years.[4] This level of funding could not be defended in view of the commitments given by Irish Shipping management to foreign charters without government approval, and the government's tight budgetary position.[5] The government would meet any commitments it had made under explicit guarantees. Charles Haughey, leader of the opposition, replied:

> . . . as far as all other creditors of the company are concerned they will have to take their place in the queue. The Government will not accept responsibility for discharging these liabilities in full. This is the sort of thing which is unworthy of a shyster company director, to distinguish between liabilities specifically guaranteed by the Minister for Finance and other liabilities. They are all liabilities of this company.
>
> This is a State company. Nobody would ever have any impression other than that the State was ultimately responsible and liable for every debt incurred by Irish Shipping. That is why we have State companies. They command the credit-worthiness of the Government. . . . A State company must honour its obligations and the Government must stand behind all State companies. . . . That is what the public . . . have been led to expect.[6]

Charles Haughey was actively supported by John Wilson and Albert Reynolds (former ministers whose portfolios had included Irish Shipping), Pádraig Flynn and Seamus Brennan, who was vice-chairman of the joint Oireachtas committee which was reviewing the affairs of Irish Shipping at the time. Seamus Brennan disagreed with the financing figures advanced by Jim Mitchell. He suggested that the total cash requirement was closer to £76 million, particularly if the government was to be directly associated with the renegotiation of the charter terms at more favourable rates. He also called for an inquiry into the collapse.[7]

Senior members of the cabinet, including Taoiseach Garret FitzGerald, Minister for Finance Alan Dukes, and Minister for Labour Ruairí Quinn, supported the liquidation decision and noted that Irish Shipping had received a positive response to its request for help in spring 1984. Another £144 million was seen as a waste of taxpayers' money at a time when the country's borrowing and budgetary positions were under pressure and needed correction to ensure international credit confidence. The Dáil was reminded that the company's ill-fated management decision to engage in extensive long-term financial commitments on charters had been taken without advising government or obtaining its approval.

The government defeated the Fianna Fáil motion by seventy-five votes to sixty-seven. The fate of Irish Shipping and its employees was sealed. The cabinet had been aware of the possibility of liquidation eleven months earlier, as the following extracts from Gemma Hussey's cabinet diary[8] suggest:

> Thursday 15th December 1983. We had a preliminary discussion about the awful decision on Irish Shipping which is before us.[9]

> Friday 16th December 1983. The Cabinet today decided on the fate of Irish Shipping. There really was no alternative to liquidation unless they could miraculously re-negotiate in Hong Kong. Ruairí Quinn was articulate and good on the subject — I believe he will be more constructive than Frank Cluskey.[10]

How a state company could collapse with such enormous losses to stakeholders has never been publicly explained. There was no public inquiry. The outcome was that the various processes subsequent to the collapse had the consequence of suppressing much of the information about blame, responsibilities and lessons. Employees, banks, preferential and unsecured creditors all suffered severely — despite Irish Shipping being owned and controlled 100% by the state.

Four questions arise:

- How could a large company, described as 'the jewel in the crown of the state sector', be liquidated within two and a half years of announcing record profits?
- How could a state-sponsored body run up such extensive debts and leave its employees and creditors with such losses?
- What was the role and responsibility of the board, management, ministers and civil servants? Are there lessons for the efficient supervision and management of state sector companies?
- Could the collapse have been prevented?

The speed of the collapse of Irish Shipping surprised everyone. The board of the company and the officials of the Department of Communications had been aware for more than two years of the tightening cash flow position, its future capital needs, and its inability to continue with existing bank facilities without further government support. A report by new chairman Frank Belton on 24 September 1984 presented sombre cash flow projections and led to the Department of Communications requesting a decision from government. Losses were now running at a higher level than those envisaged in an earlier submission of 31 January 1984. Additional support of £12 million was necessary to continue through 1985. A number of its charter commitments would then terminate — the first in September 1985, another in March 1986 and two larger Panamex vessels in May and November 1987, followed by two in early 1988. The board of Irish Shipping put two options to government:

- the immediate winding-up of the company, or
- a final attempt at renegotiations, with government support, with the foreign shipowners.

The board unanimously supported the second option.[11] It had made it clear in its report and subsequent discussions that, because of the financial and legal position and the responsibility of the directors, continuance of trading would not be possible without a revised financing plan. The group balance sheet at March 1984 had recorded shareholders' funds of £2.7 million compared to loans of £73.6 million.[12] Clearly, the group was moving towards a negative equity position and further cash losses would erode the creditors' position. Also, banks and certain creditors were taking a tougher line on credit availability. The government's negative response left the board with few options to liquidation — other than to resign *en bloc* immediately.

Very little information has been made available on the affairs of Irish Shipping.[13] When confirming the official liquidator's appointment on 17 December 1984, the High Court requested that the liquidator provide a report to the court by June 1985 on the causes of the failure of the company, whether any fraud had been committed and certain other issues. This unusual step by the High Court indicated the serious public concern issues, as it was aware that no public inquiry or inspectors' investigation had been initiated. Unfortunately, the liquidator's report was never published, though some extracts found their way to the media.[14] Of course, a liquidator's report, bearing in mind the narrow powers of investigation, could only provide a primarily internal view of events. The role and actions of civil servants and ministers, on behalf of the state as owner and ultimate controller of Irish Shipping, could not be adequately examined. A joint Oireachtas committee had been reviewing the affairs of Irish Shipping when liquidation intervened. The committee's requests for civil servants from the Department of Finance and the Department of Communications to appear before it were refused. All the company's board members (except one) and management also found excuses for their non-appearance.

The failure of Irish Shipping was more than an embarrassment: in this writer's opinion it was a scandal, which was compounded by the fact that there was no published inquiry into its affairs to provide lessons to avoid the further costs to taxpayers of public sector inefficiencies.

Background

Key events in the life of Irish Shipping	
1941	Irish Shipping established in March to provide shipping capacity to transport scarce food and supplies because of World War II.
	Representatives of Wexford Steamship Company and Limerick Steamship Company appointed to the board with civil servants.
	Purchases and charters-in ships.
	Reardon Smith & Sons appointed company's agents and brokers.
	Captain John O'Neill, formerly of Reardon Smith, appointed company's representative in USA and Canada.
1945	L. S. Furlong, a civil servant, appointed secretary.
	cont.

Key events in the life of Irish Shipping *cont.*

1946	Transfers marine underwriting business to Insurance Corporation of Ireland (ICI) in return for 48% of its equity.
	Strategic fleet, for national purposes, set at 250,000 tons.
1948	Captain John O'Neill and L. S. Furlong promoted to position of joint general managers.
1961	Captain John O'Neill retires and L. S. Furlong continues as sole general manager.
1963	Second Programme for Economic Expansion reduces strategic fleet capacity to 155,000 tons.
	Company loss-making for some years.
1965	P. H. (Percy) Greer appointed chairman.
1966	W. A. (Willie) O'Neill recruited to position of assistant general manager and commercial manager.
	Operations restructured, costs reduced and profitability restored.
1971	A. McElhatton promoted to financial controller.
1973	Celtic Bulk Carriers established as joint venture with Reardon Smith to operate ship capacity pooling arrangement.
	Irish Continental Line established as joint venture with Scandinavian shipping firms to operate a car ferry (*St Patrick*) between Ireland and France.
	W. A. O'Neill promoted to general manager on retirement of L. S. Furlong.
1975	W. A. O'Neill appointed to board.
1977	Irish Shipping acquires 100% of Irish Continental Line.
	Celtic Bulk Carriers arrangement altered to a 50:50 pooling basis with four ships from each company.
1978	Second car ferry *(St Killian)* acquired for Irish Continental Line.
1979–81	Nine long-term charters signed.
1980	Total capacity of owned and chartered ships shown at 392,000 tons.
	First Oireachtas committee report compliments Irish Shipping on its performance.
1981	Company contract with Verolme Dockyard in Cork to build *Irish Spruce* on government's instructions.
	Total capacity of owned and chartered ships shown at 407,000 tons.
	Pre-tax profit of £4.2 million reported.
1982	Record pre-tax profit of £5.5 million reported.
	W. A. O'Neill (general manager and director) appointed executive chairman on retirement of P. H. Greer.
	W. A. O'Neill advises government department of chartering problems. Report submitted on deficits and financing needs.

cont.

	Key events in the life of Irish Shipping *cont.*
1983	Accumulated long-term charter capacity 395,000 tons.
Irish Spruce delivered by Verolme. Total capacity of owned and chartered ships now 491,000 tons.
Sale of ICI shares to Allied Irish Banks.
Report submitted to government department in October with detailed cash flow projections to 1986, requesting £16 million in new equity in the next six months and a total of £39 million over three years.
Cabinet decides in December to advance no further funds but to provide guarantees for additional bank borrowings.
1984	Negotiations in March with owners of ships in Hong Kong and Tokyo lead to a modest reduction in charter rates.
Bill amending borrowing limits and government policy approved in Dáil in April.
W. A. O'Neill resigns as executive chairman in August following request from minister. Frank Belton appointed non-executive chairman.
Maurice Tempany appointed provisional liquidator by High Court on 14 November.
Acrimonious Dáil debate on government policy.
High Court confirms Maurice Tempany as official liquidator and orders him to submit a report on the causes of failure and other matters.
1994	Liquidation still continuing. Employees given *ex gratia* payment by government. Unsecured creditors had received no payment from liquidator.

The necessity and urgency behind the establishment of Irish Shipping are colourfully demonstrated by Ronan Fanning.[15] Within a year of the outset of the war in Europe in 1939, Ireland was virtually blockaded — primarily by German U-boat activity in the west. Britain withdrew all its shipping tonnage for its own pressing needs and the small Irish fleet's small vessels traded on the Irish Sea or to the Continent. Nine had been sunk and vital supplies were running dangerously low. John Leydon, secretary of the Department of Supplies, submitted a memorandum to government on the formation of a shipping company coupled with a request for an allocation of $2 million to buy ships. The secretary of the Department of Finance, J. J. McElligott, responded favourably, but he ruefully pointed out that 'two millions represents all the dollars we have or are likely to have for a long time to come and so must cover not only the purchase of ships but of stores, cargo, crew, commissions, insurance etc.'

Fifteen ships, amounting to 78,000 dead-weight tons, were acquired, of which nine were purchased and six were on long-term charter. Several were over forty years old. The management of this 'rustbucket' fleet was contracted out to Wexford Steamship Company, Limerick Steamship Company and Palgrave Murphy. Over 1.1 million tons of essential commodities consisting mainly of wheat, fertilisers and foodstuffs was brought into the country in the five years to 1946. Unfortunately, two ships were sunk and Irish lives were lost in this hazardous activity.

In 1946, the government decided that Irish Shipping should continue under direct company management and that a modern strategic fleet of 250,000 dead-weight tons should be created. Meanwhile, the company had passed over its valuable insurance business to Insurance Corporation of Ireland, in return for 48% of that company's quoted equity.[16] It was to prove a lucrative investment. Nineteen new ships brought the aggregate capacity to 195,000 tons by 1963. North Atlantic and Baltic liner trades were terminated because of heavy losses and the fleet concentrated on the international tramp market. Market conditions proved extremely competitive and the shipping industry worldwide went into recession with excess capacity and low rates. The break-even position of the postwar years turned into recurring annual losses, reaching a peak of £1.4 million in 1965/66. Accumulated losses were £4.5 million and Irish Shipping's share capital and reserves had been eroded.

A board and departmental review led to a complete corporate reorganisation, with changes in top management, reductions in staffing, revised objectives and commercial policies. The Second Programme for Economic Expansion reduced the strategic fleet mandate to 155,000 dead-weight tons. Changes in management and negotiations with unions led to reductions in staff and overhead costs and changes in the composition and operation of the fleet — with a smaller number of larger ships. A recovery followed, and consistently better levels of profits were reported from 1968/69 at £0.3 million to £3.3 million in 1981/82.

Irish Shipping helped establish the first car ferry direct to the Continent in 1968 with French and other partners.[17] The withdrawal of its ships, at short notice, by Normandy Ferries left no service in 1972. The government was concerned about the tourist industry, and in response Irish Shipping re-established the service on its own. It formed Irish Continental Line in 1973, operating the newly acquired *St Patrick*. In 1978 a second car ferry, the

St Killian, was acquired. Both vessels were financed from Irish Shipping's own resources and bank borrowings.

In 1973, Irish Shipping formed a joint venture with the Reardon Smith Line of Cardiff, under the title of Celtic Bulk Carriers. It started initially as a pooling of seven Reardon Smith ships with four from Irish Shipping. Later it became a 50:50 venture on a joint and several liability basis, with each group contributing four ships. This pooling enabled the partners to quote contract rates to shippers of large quantities of bulk cargo, such as steel and timber, and achieve higher value earnings through term contracts rather than operate on the spot market. Irish Shipping management claimed the pool was so successful that Celtic Bulk Carriers augmented its capacity by operating as a time charterer of other people's ships. In 1980 management claimed it 'now is probably the biggest shipper of steel from Europe to the United States, and of timber from the United States to Europe'.[18]

Trading and financial performance

A summary of Irish Shipping's trading performance is shown in Table 9.1. The rapid growth in turnover from 1980 was attributable to the second ferry (*St Killian*) and the additional capacity of the chartered-in activity of Celtic Bulk Carriers. Time charter hire revenues had increased from £8 million in 1978 to £14 million in 1984. Passenger revenues increased from £5 million to £15 million, and freight from £8 million to £18 million. However, the augmented tramp capacity (the nine charters and *Irish Spruce*) between 1981 and 1983 did not yield sufficient revenues as rates collapsed. Profitability margins from tramping — quoting for the transport of cargo from port to port — had always been poor, and it seems most of the volatile and modest operating profits were earned by Irish Continental Line. Indeed, much of the group's reported profit was generated by surpluses on the sale of ships (which cost much more to replace) and various other investments. By 1983 the cupboard was bare, and there was little else to sell to raise cash outside the core business, once the ICI shares were disposed of to Allied Irish Banks.

Because of the way the data was structured in the published profit and loss account, the 1982 trading decline was not immediately obvious from the financial statements. The recorded operating surplus of £3.2 million allied to the £3.6 million share of profits from associates (mainly ICI) less interest was transformed into an audited pre-tax profit of £5.5 million. P. H. Greer, at the start of his chairman's statement, extolled it as 'the highest

Table 9.1: Irish Shipping: trading performance (£m)

	1975	1976	1977	1978	1979	1980	1981	1982	1983	1984
Turnover	n/av.	n/av.	n/av.	21.4	24.1	31.4	36.7	40.0	38.5	47.5
Operating profit/ (loss)	2.2	0.3	1.5	1.4	1.8	2.4	2.3	(0.1)	(10.7)	(18.2)
Bank interest	0.7	0.6	0.8	1.4	1.8	1.3	1.1	1.4	2.6	4.7
Profit/(loss)	1.5	(0.3)	0.7	0	0	1.1	1.2	(1.5)	(13.3)	(22.9)
Associates	0.5	0.8	1.0	1.3	1.7	2.4	3.0	3.6	3.0	0.1
Provisions	–	–	–	–	–	–	–	–	5.7	9.5
Surplus/(loss) on sale of assets	–	0.5	0.8	–	1.3	–	–	3.3	3.8	(1.8)
Taxation	0.3	0.3	0.4	0.6	0.6	0.8	1.1	1.1	1.0	0.2
Net profit/(loss)	1.7	0.7	2.1	0.7	2.4	2.7	3.1	4.3	(13.2)	(34.3)

Source: Audited financial statements; data restructured by author.

the Company has achieved since it was incorporated forty-one years ago'. He pointed out that it was the fifteenth consecutive year in which he had had the pleasure in announcing a profit. It was also to be the last. The economic reality was quite different. But for a 'one-off' capital gain on the sale of a ship, yielding a surplus of £3.3 million, which had been included in operating profits, there would have been a small operating loss, as shown in Table 9.1, because of the decline in tramp and charter rates. The cash flow position was very different: the profits of associates, at £3.6 million in the group accounts, only yielded £382,000 in dividends to Irish Shipping.

The revised structuring of the profit and loss account in Table 9.1 shows that the improvement in Irish Shipping's reported pre-tax profit performance between 1978 and 1982 was really created by the growth in ICI's profits. For example, ICI's pre-tax profits for the year ending December 1980 were reported at £6.9 million. Irish Shipping held 41% of ICI's equity which implies a 'share' amounting to £2.8 million under equity accounting procedures. The amount for 'associates' profits' shown in Irish Shipping's profit and loss account came to £3.0 million for 1980/81. Clearly, ICI was the dominant element.

The decline in revenue rates from 1981 in relation to fixed costs is reflected initially in the level of losses in the smaller directly owned fleet, and later in the larger chartered fleet. Losses, which had been minimal in 1981/82, rose dramatically to 17.9% of turnover in 1983 and 38.3% in 1984. The tramp shipping activity was losing money. Servicing the extra

Table 9.2: Irish Shipping: financial analysis

	1978	1979	1980	1981	1982	1983	1984
Net profit/(loss)*/ turnover margin	6.1%	12.4%	11.2%	11.1%	13.7%	(31.7%)	(67.2%)
Interest cover	1.0 times	1.7 times	1.9 times	2.1 times	neg.	neg.	neg.
Cash flow/debt**	10.0%	16.9%	23.2%	11.1%	(9.0%)	(15.5%)	(20.0%)
Debt**/total assets	58.5%	49.3%	42.8%	64.3%	52.0%	60.2%	92.2%
Working capital/ sales	(3.7%)	5.3%	(1.0%)	5.3%	20.2%	(1.4%)	(31.7%)

*   As reported in the profit and loss account.
** All liabilities.
Source: Audited financial statements; ratios computed by author.

debt from 1978 to finance the second Irish Continental Line ferry was a drain on the operating profitability and the modest cash flows of the parent. Debt/equity, interest cover and return on capital were consistently weak, as evidenced by the financial analysis in Table 9.2, which highlights weak trends by 1982. In view of past profitability and the low margins in the business, the payment of the additional bank interest on the increased borrowings in 1983 and 1984 could not have been sustainable. In the circumstances, an interest bill of £4.7 million in 1984 would have been a material depletion of working capital.

The company's financial reality was much less impressive from a cash flow perspective, as summarised in Table 9.3. In 1982, the net cash flow from operations was a negative £7 million after a long period of volatile and very modest positive flows. Indeed, in eight of the nine years to 1984, due to investment requirements and shipping loan repayments, there was a 'financing gap' which was primarily bridged by additional debt — somewhat similar to GPA, but for different reasons. Despite its growth in assets and the Irish Continental Line new venture, no new equity was introduced by the government (except for the very modest amounts under the special *Irish Spruce* deal in the early 1980s).

Organisation and management

The turnaround from losses to profitability from the late 1960s must be seen against the backdrop of changes in the board and management at that time. The board had changed little in the previous decade until Liam St John Devlin, Dermot Barnes, Noel Griffin and P. H. Greer joined between 1959

Table 9.3: Irish Shipping: cash flow profile (£m)

	1976	1977	1978	1979	1980	1981	1982	1983	1984
Cash flow from operations	1	3	3	1	4	2	(7)	(20)	(7)
Acquisition of fixed assets	2	17	7	0	0	2	25	24	46
Repayment of loans	2	2	4	4	5	4	4	4	8
Total outflows	3	16	8	3	1	4	36	48	61
Sale of assets	1	3	0	4	0	1	18	10	19
Financing gap	2	13	8	(1)	1	3	18	38	42
Funded by:									
New equity	0	0	0	0	0	1	0	2	1
New loans	0	14	6	0	0	2	32	23	42
Cash change	(2)	1	(2)	1	(1)	0	14	(13)	1

Note: Cash flow from operations after adjusting for working capital changes.
Source: Audited financial statements; computations by author.

and 1962. Devlin and Barnes had a family business background whereas Griffin and Greer were respectively managing directors of Waterford Glass and Unidare, successful companies with quotations on the Dublin Stock Exchange. All four were to remain with the company into the 1970s. Greer became chairman in March 1965 and continued in this position for seventeen years until June 1982 when he had reached his seventieth birthday.

From 1948 to 1961, Captain John O'Neill (who had provided the vital expertise and connections in the war years) and a former civil servant, L. S. Furlong, were joint general managers. When Captain John O'Neill retired in 1961, L. S. Furlong continued as sole general manager. W. A. O'Neill, a chartered accountant with management experience in CIE and Gilbeys, was recruited as commercial manager and assistant general manager in early 1966. Another outside appointment was that of Aubrey McElhatton as accountant. He was promoted to the post of financial controller in 1971, and W. A. O'Neill took over as general manager from L. S. Furlong in 1973. In a departure from tradition, W. A. O'Neill was appointed to the board in 1975. He built up a close working relationship with P. H. Greer and was seen as the driving force behind the recovery in Irish Shipping's fortunes. Derry O'Neill, a son of Captain O'Neill, was promoted to chartering and operations manager in 1973. He reported directly to W. A. O'Neill.[19]

In addition to his position as financial controller of Irish Shipping, Aubrey McElhatton was appointed director and general manager of Irish Continental Line in the late 1970s and continued in that capacity until 1983. Captain Coleman Raftery moved from Irish Shipping to become Irish Continental Line's well-respected operations manager and director. J. N. McGovern, who had been with Irish Shipping since 1949, was appointed company secretary in 1971 and held that post until 1982. He was also secretary of Irish Continental Line.

It was a narrowly based management team with a concentration of functional duties and responsibilities. Together with P. H. Greer, they directed the group's activities and strategic actions. The concentration was further narrowed when W. A. O'Neill was appointed executive chairman by the Minister for Finance from July 1982. Aubrey McElhatton succeeded him as general manager until August 1983, when he resigned to become general manager of Oceanbank Developments, the joint venture with Allied Irish Banks which controlled Irish Continental Line and the property investments. J. N. McGovern, who had been deputy general manager since July 1982, took over as general manager in August 1983 and remained there until the liquidation.

The absence of any outside appointments to key management positions and the duplication of positions as the group expanded were remarkable. It was not until late August 1984, just two and a half months before the collapse, that Frank Belton was appointed non-executive chairman and a pivotal outside influence was instituted. There seems to have been no financial controller of the company from July 1982 to liquidation.[20] Haughey Boland, the auditors, seconded a member of staff in a consultative capacity. Bearing in mind the size of the group, with a number of diverse activities as well as over 900 employees, the organisational and management structure was inappropriate, as noted, after the collapse, by the second Oireachtas committee report in 1985.[21]

The Tempany report on the causes of failure

The report of the liquidator Maurice Tempany to the High Court was not made public.[22] Creditors could obtain it, under certain terms. It appears that few received copies, and only a small number of short selective extracts found their way to the media.[23] To date, the Tempany report on the causes of the failure of Irish Shipping has not been analysed or reviewed publicly in any detail. The report can be considered authoritative and reasonably comprehensive, within the framework adopted by Tempany and his team in acting on the instructions of the High Court.[24] As liquidator, Tempany had access to considerable internal company documentation, such as minutes of board meetings, correspondence, memoranda and company records and accounts, as well as the five Irish Shipping reports submitted by the board to government between October 1982 and September 1984 on its financial problems. In addition, Tempany and his team analysed responses to questionnaires submitted by twenty-nine people drawn from former directors, advisers and senior executives.

Maurice Tempany attributed the failure of Irish Shipping to the 'contributory factors' summarised in Table 9.4.[25]

Table 9.4: The Tempany 'causes of failure' of Irish Shipping

1.	Commitment to enter into large chartering-in contracts during the period 1979–81
2.	The financial position of the company at the time of the charter commitments
3.	Adverse market conditions
4.	Nature of control by the board of directors
5.	Nature of government control and involvement
6.	Policy of diversification — cash flow versus profitability
7.	Internal and financial control
8.	Inability of Reardon Smith Line to meet their obligations to Celtic Bulk Carriers
9.	Market conditions during the time of asset disposals
10.	Losses incurred during 1984 and projections for 1985 more adverse than those submitted to government in February 1984
11.	Decision by government not to provide any further finance

Source: Report of the Official Liquidator to the High Court, June 1985.

Five additional points could be added to Tempany's findings.[26] These focus on three internal and two external issues:

1. strategic direction and corporate planning
2. organisation and management
3. the political and economic agendas of the government
4. the competence and expertise of civil servants in monitoring and problem analysis
5. the financial reporting and disclosure of performance and financial capacity.

This writer offers the following views on the elements contributing to financial collapse. First, there was no evidence of comprehensive planning, for example three- or five-year corporate plans which would have been a standard part of the process of setting objectives and plotting a unified strategy. Ideally, these would have been approved by the board, but the apparent flaws in the board's structure, involvement and control, allied to the weaknesses in information flows and financial control, were such that effective planning was not possible. Second, the narrow management group and the internal dynamics of relationships between the chairman and the chief executive, and between the latter and the chartering and operations manager, had the effect of hoarding power and information over crucial decisions, activities and direction. The Celtic Bulk Carriers and long-term charter decisions suggest a splintering of the company into separate fiefdoms, with the board having little knowledge of the real position until late 1982. Third, the wider political and economic context of its shareholder environment proved unforgiving at a vital stage. The government had an economic agenda to cut borrowing and improve state sector efficiency. Irish Shipping became an example. Fourth, the ability of the state to monitor the stewardship and efficiency of its investment, because of deficiencies in specialist accountancy expertise in the civil service and other inefficiencies, seems to have been fatally flawed. Fifth, the formal reporting and disclosure of financial performance and commitments, according to the audited financial statements from 1981 onwards, was problematical in this writer's opinion.

The big project and a weak partner

Despite the mandate to operate a strategic fleet of 155,000 dead-weight tons, the company's eight bulk carriers amounted to 228,000 tons in 1977. The sale of two ships reduced capacity to 159,000 tons by 1979. In addition, through Celtic Bulk Carriers as a separate joint venture division, the company chartered-in ships, generally for a fixed period of six months or a year. However, there is evidence of some contracts in the 1970s for five years.[27]

In its 1979 annual report, Irish Shipping revealed for the first time that it had chartered seven ships with a capacity of 201,000 tons — bringing its total deep-sea tonnage to 360,000 tons. Details of the charter periods were not disclosed. The additional capacity was justified as a commercial operation.[28] Management claimed that the joint venture with the Reardon Smith Line since 1973 had been very successful.[29] Though a profit of £18 million was mentioned, it is difficult to reconcile the group's share of earnings with a subsequent divisional analysis of profitability over a decade to 1982, as shown in Table 9.5. Accumulated chartering profits for ten years were just £1.7 million. The deep-sea tramping of the strategic fleet had incurred losses of £10.3 million over the decade, confirming that it was a difficult and competitive business.

Table 9.5: Irish Shipping: divisional analysis of profitability, 1973–82 (£m)

Strategic fleet losses	(10.3)
Chartering profits	1.7
Ferry profits	7.6
Profit on sale of deep-sea ships	3.9
Profit on sale of ferry vessel	3.5
Loss on sale of rig	(0.4)
Stevedoring profits	1.4
Agency profits	0.5
Other activities losses	(0.2)
Investment income	2.2
Associated companies (ICI etc.)	14.7
Net profits reported 1973–82	24.6

Source: Joint Oireachtas Committee on Commercial State-Sponsored Bodies, *Second Report on Irish Shipping Ltd*, Dublin: Stationery Office 1985, p. 69.

The core business of tramping had effectively been restructured with the pooling arrangement with Reardon Smith, using Celtic Bulk Carriers as the administrative mechanism.[30] Through the operation of nine additional chartered-in ships, secured on medium- and long-term contracts, the partners through Celtic Bulk Carriers had materially augmented their capacity on a quasi-permanent basis. Management thought these ships, with Far Eastern management and crews, would provide a low-cost competitive trading position. An equity participation option of 50% was agreed on two of the ships and 25% on three, at the end of the charter period, for an additional 10% rate.[31]

These long-term charters were signed between 20 September 1979 and 22 July 1981 (by Celtic Bulk Carriers for seven, and Irish Shipping for two) with a number of Hong Kong shipowning companies, who in turn agreed contracts with Japanese shipbuilders and financial institutions. The shipowning companies and the signed charters provided the financial security for the shipbuilding debts. Four charters were for eight years, four for five years and one was for four years.[32] These contracts were not hedged with back-to-back charter-out contracts, as was generally Irish Shipping and Celtic Bulk Carriers' previous policy, nor did they contain any provision for early termination.[33] The seven Celtic Bulk Carriers contracts had aggregate fixed commitments of $156 million and the two directly chartered by Irish Shipping had a total forward obligation of $71 million. With its joint and several liability with Reardon Smith, Irish Shipping was dependent on two sets of risks — the outlook for capacity demand and rates in the deep-sea tramp market, and the financial strength of its joint venture partner. The nine chartered ships' aggregate capacity was 400,000 tons. When *Irish Spruce* (72,000 tons) and the existing owned ships were added, the total fleet capacity had risen to an extraordinary 553,462 tons by 1984.[34]

As there were long lead times, the first three ships were delivered between July and November 1980, one was delivered in 1981, four in 1982 and the ninth in April 1983. Four were large 60,000-ton Panamex vessels and the remaining five were 30,000-ton Handysize vessels. The Panamex and Handysize vessels were chartered-in at an average rate of $15,000 and $6,500 per day.[35] These chartering commitments amounted to a total annual payment of $34 million to the shipowners.[36]

Tramp rates had been very volatile for the three decades from 1946. Taking the 1976 index rate as a base, rates had been 50% below it for almost two-thirds of the time. In 1977 P. H. Greer remarked:

> This market is so volatile, consisting as it does of booms and depressions, with more depressions than booms that it would be impossible consistently to generate profits sufficient to ensure the constant renewal of the fleet in this way.[37]

In 1978 there was a recovery and a further hardening in 1979. Rates peaked in 1980 and early 1981 but then, between late 1981 and 1984, they fell more heavily than any recent experience. Remarkably, in 1980, before many of the charter contracts were signed, P. H. Greer was reiterating a cautious view:

> While the market is better now than it has been for many years it would be foolish to anticipate that it will continue at its present level for a long period. Past experience counsels caution.[38]

In March 1981 it was possible to earn $20,000 a day (a $5,000 daily surplus over the charter-in rate) on a Panamex vessel. By December 1982, this rate had fallen to $3,000 a day, with no escape from the cash loss of $12,000 per day per large ship.[39] The smaller vessels were similarly affected, and were only earning $1,500 per day.[40] By 1984, rates had only modestly improved, with the Panamex daily rate reaching $5,000. In brief, the joint venture's newly committed capacity was earning about 30% of its fixed outgoings — suggesting possible cash losses of the order of £15–20 million per annum. The irony was that six of the nine ships were delivered after rates had materially weakened. The delivery of a Panamex and a Handysize in November 1982 and April 1983, when rates had plummeted, was particularly incongruous. Like GPA, the timing of Irish Shipping's capacity expansion could not have been any worse in a notoriously cyclical industry.

In December 1982, Reardon Smith advised Irish Shipping that it could no longer meet its obligations under the Celtic Bulk Carriers joint venture. It was seeking an arrangement with creditors to avoid liquidation. For a payment of just £2 million, Irish Shipping agreed to accept total liability for all nine charters for the following few years. Though Reardon Smith had had an association with Irish Shipping since its foundation, it was a financially weak and unsuitable partner for a joint venture on a joint and several basis in 1973. The risk exposure in the seven years to 1980 was quite minimal when the activity mainly involved short-term charters — particularly when they were arranged on a back-to-back basis with outward contracts at reasonably modest profits. Signing nine medium- to long-term charters on an open basis changed the risk dimension totally. Reardon Smith, because of its frail financial condition, had more to gain. In three of the seven years to 1979, Reardon Smith incurred losses, and in 1978 and 1979 losses amounted to £14.4 million. At 227%, its debt/equity level had disimproved seriously by 1979. Borrowings jumped from £10.1 million in 1973 to £45.3 million in 1977; only with the sale of assets did they contract to £23.3 million in 1979 — which was still high. Reardon Smith subsequently went into liquidation in June 1985. Irish Shipping's liquidator furnished a claim for £12 million, but because of the large deficit, it remained unpaid.

In this writer's opinion, the unhedged charter contracts were effectively a gamble. How can they be explained? First, it was thought in some shipping circles that, with the second oil crisis and increase in price in 1979, the general demand for coal would increase and that this would absorb excess tramping capacity. In Ireland, the Electricity Supply Board was building a coal-burning generation station at Moneypoint, Co. Clare. Irish Shipping was in discussions with the ESB and it indicated to the first Oireachtas committee review, in 1980, that it hoped to get part or all of the contract to ship coal to Moneypoint — which was expected to start in late 1984 at an annual rate of 300,000 tons, rising to 750,000 tons in 1990.[41]

A summary of Irish Shipping's increasing capacity is shown in Table 9.6. In this writer's opinion it is remarkable that the extent of the chartering-in commitments and the Celtic Bulk Carriers joint venture with Reardon Smith did not provoke some searching questions from the relevant government departments. After all, there were references to the venture in the company's 1980 submission to the first Oireachtas committee as well as in the committee's report.

Table 9.6: Irish Shipping: increasing deep-sea tonnage capacity (thousand tons dead-weight)

	Chartered	Owned	Total
1979	201	159	360
1980	233	159	392
1981	176	159	335
1982	247	159	406
1983	337	154*	491
1984	307	246**	553

*   Includes *Irish Spruce*, 72,000 tons.
** Two chartered-in ships acquired.
Source: Annual reports.

Charters and leases can assume similar characteristics. Because the nine new charters were medium to long term, and five had an equity interest, they could be viewed as the equivalent of finance leases, from an economic and usage standpoint. Thus Irish Shipping was taking on not only additional capacity but also additional financial gearing. The excess capacity and gearing position was further exacerbated by the acquisition of *Irish Spruce* from Verolme Dockyard in Cork on the specific instructions of the government[42] — though it seems neither the government nor civil servants were aware of the growing charter commitments, nor do they appear to have been informed at the time. The minister advised the Dáil in 1980 that *Irish Spruce* would enable Irish Shipping to quote for the transport of coal to Moneypoint.[43]

Defects in internal governance and control

The liquidator Maurice Tempany highlighted the 'nature of control by the board of directors' and 'internal and financial control' as two of the causes of the failure.[44] This author would agree.

Board structure defects

The articles of association limited the board to seven members. In this writer's view two directors, the chairman P. H. Greer and the general manager W. A. O'Neill, were in a powerful position to influence board processes, decisions and policies in the critical 1979–82 period because of their roles, lengthy service and strong personal relationship. The lack of continuity and expertise among certain other board members in that period added to their hegemony. Greer had been appointed to the board in July 1962 and subsequently was chairman for seventeen years from 1965. W. A. O'Neill joined the company as a 'new broom' in 1966 and was appointed general manager in 1973. His elevation to the board in 1975 was evidence of his standing. When he was appointed to the new role of executive chairman in July 1982, apparently at the instigation of P. H. Greer, this strengthened his power.

From the time of the company's formation the board had considerable business competence, related shipping industry expertise and stability, arising from the company's historical association with the Limerick and Wexford steamship companies. The first break in this essential knowledge base and stability was the last-minute nomination of two new board members by the Fine Gael/Labour coalition government in its dying days in June 1977. Two businessmen with shipping knowledge, Hugh McMahon from Limerick and Frank Reihill from Dublin, were not reappointed at short notice. The following year, Edward Keegan, a partner in KPMG Stokes Kennedy Crowley who had not been on the board for long, was not reappointed. A form of 'musical chairs' ensued with Reihill, McMahon and Keegan returning between 1979 and 1981. Denis Murphy, a Cork businessman, and Liam McGonagle, a Dublin solicitor, joined in 1981 and 1982 respectively. Subsequently, Reihill and McMahon departed and five other changes occurred — the most important being the appointment of Frank Belton as non-executive chairman on 29 August 1984. He was a senior partner in Craig Gardner/Price Waterhouse. Maurice Tempany commented on these governance flaws:

> There were a number of areas where there were conflicts between a private limited company competing in a commercial world on the one hand and a company owned by the Minister for Finance on the other.[45]

He cited the 'removal of directors with short or no notice . . . by the Minister for Finance' and 'changes in the board . . . brought about by changes in the Government' as examples.

Alternating governments between 1977 and 1982 were similar in their attitudes. Apart from P. H. Greer and W. A. O'Neill, only one director, T. A. Finucane, held his position between 1978 and 1982. This extraordinary instability in composition undoubtedly affected the board's knowledge and authority over the group's affairs. It left the new or returning member dependent on the O'Neill–Greer axis. The dominating character of P. H. Greer was, apparently, reflected in his style of chairing board meetings. Thus, in this writer's opinion, the combination of the foregoing elements would not have been a strong basis for much interrogation of executives on strategy or policies. Unlike the state's other transport companies, such as B&I or Aer Lingus, there were no worker directors on the Irish Shipping board. If there had been this could have led to a strengthening of information flows as undoubtedly a number of administration employees would have been aware of Celtic Bulk Carriers' activities.

It was inevitable that linkages between the subsidiaries and the main board were broken by the discontinuity of membership. For example, Hugh McMahon was appointed as a non-executive representative to attend the quarterly meetings of Celtic Bulk Carriers. A similar arrangement operated for Irish Continental Lines. When McMahon was not reappointed to the Irish Shipping board in 1977, no other Irish Shipping non-executive director took over this role at Celtic Bulk Carriers. Irish Shipping directors did not receive copies of the minutes of the meetings of Celtic Bulk Carriers. Consequently, in this writer's view it effectively became an independent fiefdom, with no proper supervision or accountability. Maurice Tempany noted that the three Irish Shipping representatives on Celtic Bulk Carriers were its three senior executives, the general manager W. A. O'Neill, the chartering and operations manager Derry O'Neill and the financial controller Aubrey McElhatton.[46] Absence of interlocking board involvement facilitated a breakdown in information flows.

The first reference to the ill-fated chartering-in contracts appears to have been in the June 1981 board minutes. The issue was taken a step further at the August meeting when W. A. O'Neill discussed the Celtic Bulk Carriers operation and explained that international tramp rates had slumped. The board was warned that cash losses could occur. Directors began to express concern at the losses on the charter-in activities at the November and December meetings. Only two of the nine new vessels were in operation at that time. It seems that the overall total group profit (with the benefit of asset disposals and the share of ICI's profits) camouflaged the true economic reality, and assuaged the need for urgent action. As the minutes for December 1981 recorded:

> . . . the board expressed some concern about the loss (£384,000) sustained on chartered-in tonnage in the eight months to the end of November, while noting with satisfaction the projected overall profit (£5,329,000) for the year ended 31 March 1982.[47]

Finally, in late February 1982, the board agreed that a projected cash flow statement for 1982 should be put before it. It seems from the minutes that it was not until late May that the board requested Derry O'Neill, the chartering manager, to submit a detailed report on the activities of Celtic Bulk Carriers and the chartering — in and out — projections. In June 1982 the reality of Irish Shipping's risk exposure became clear, when Derry O'Neill informed the board that Irish Shipping's name was on most of the contracts because of constraints placed on Reardon Smith by its bankers. The June 1982 minutes recorded the board's belated policy that no vessel be chartered-in for a period in excess of six months without its approval. Hugh McMahon suggested that 'Reardon Smith should be asked to give Irish Shipping some collateral for its exposure . . . for the benefit of the pool'.[48]

In July 1982 the board was advised by W. A. O'Neill that cash flow projections indicated that the company would need an additional £18 million funding by early 1983. He was hopeful of an improvement in the monthly loss rate. Following further discussions in September, the board decided to immediately advise the government. A draft of a submission on the problem with projections of losses, cash flows and capital need was approved in early October and forwarded to government, dated 14 October 1982. From the onset of the problem, it seems to have taken a year for the board to fully appraise the government of the serious situation facing the company. The evidence suggests that the civil servants and government took a further fifteen months to take a decision, as the position spiralled out of control. It was even longer before any serious corrective action was attempted.

This knowledge vacuum among non-executive directors placed greater stress on the effectiveness of the formal management information, planning, control and feedback. In Irish Shipping's particular circumstances, the role and responsibility of the financial controller were crucial. By 1978 the business portfolio had become more complex. The mid-1970s to early 1980s had been a time of change in the group's business portfolio. Irish Continental Line had been launched and expanded. There were a variety of initiatives in stevedoring, agency services and property development in a joint venture with ICI. In addition the level of financial gearing, from interest cover and debt/equity standpoints, had become risky, with the latter reaching 113% in 1978. The company had agreed with the Oireachtas committee in 1980 that its debt/equity level needed to be reduced, as a matter of policy, to between 50% and 60%.[49] The committee had been told that it was planned to curtail fleet expansion until borrowings had been reduced to more sustainable levels.

Financial control defects

In this writer's opinion there is evidence that there were serious weaknesses in financial control for some years. There were structural defects, with Aubrey McElhatton operating in a number of roles. According to Tempany's report, McElhatton, who had succeeded W. A. O'Neill as general manager in July 1982, continued to be responsible for the financial control function until August 1983, when he resigned to become general manager of Oceanbank Developments.[50] The fact that Ronan Nolan, a partner with the auditors, Haughey Boland, was seconded earlier as financial adviser to the company in a consultative capacity points to the lack of a sufficient internal resource in the accounting/finance function. It is remarkable that the board permitted such an organisational defect to continue, given the group's circumstances.

Judging by the liquidator's report, a very weak internal control environment appears to have operated:

- The liquidator was of the opinion that there were no internal control procedures for chartering commitments by the company during the period 1970 to September 1984, when Frank Belton instituted changes.[51] He expressed a similar conclusion about Celtic Bulk Carriers.[52]
- The auditors did not submit a memorandum on internal control in 1981 and 1982. A memorandum was prepared after the 1983 audit, and it concentrated on recommendations to improve internal control in the agency division. Though this report was discussed with W. A. O'Neill, there was no evidence that it was brought to the notice of the other directors. The memorandum on internal control after the 1984 audit, dated 10 July 1984, was discussed at the board meeting of 25 July.[53]
- All bank accounts were operated by one signatory. On becoming chairman just ten weeks before collapse, Frank Belton instructed that two authorised signatures should apply.

- Expense returns for departmental heads were not signed as evidence of approval, according to the auditors' memorandum of July 1984.[54]
- There were no formal internal control procedures for capital expenditure. Board minutes showed that the board did authorise the purchase of ships and premises, but there was no mention of the chartering commitments.[55]
- There was no internal auditor.

Apart from these defects in internal control, there were other specific issues which reflected weak financial control.

- Overall control of chartering was seen as being so weak by Frank Belton that he stated at a board meeting on 24 September 1984 that he wished to ensure the board retained control of this activity, and that new controls were to be instituted.[56]
- The pension fund for senior management was substantially underfunded.[57]
- The minutes of Celtic Bulk Carriers 'show that decisions were nearly always made outside the meetings on chartering-in tonnage'. No minutes were kept of the subcommittee.[58] Important decisions on major financial commitments were, in effect, being taken at management level without detailed proposals and evaluations being made with any degree of formality. The board was not being advised nor was its approval sought.
- The April 1984 board minutes record that a number of directors felt that Irish Continental Line was 'far too remote from the Irish Shipping board'. One director requested that quarterly reports be made available on its affairs.

The absence of information on future chartering commitments and the other information weaknesses indicate the inadequacy of management and board planning and control processes for a group of its size and complexity.

Financial reporting and finance issues

Maurice Tempany drew the attention of the court to three matters on the accounting policies of Irish Shipping:

- the distortion of the debt/equity position
- the valuation of assets
- the information provided under contingent liabilities.[59]

The liquidator's report also pointed to issues about representations between the board and the auditors in the matter of a 'going concern' qualification.[60] These accounting and auditing issues were particularly relevant. Apart from an illusion of financial stability, in this writer's opinion they may have contributed to misunderstandings about the company's ability to continue trading, its backing by the government, and its perceived riskiness and capacity to discharge all its financial obligations. There was also the question of stewardship and accountability to government.

Distortion of the debt/equity position

In 1983 Irish Shipping changed the basis of measurement and presentation of its assets and liabilities. Lease and hire-purchase debt of £21.3 million was netted against fixed assets in the group balance sheet. Fixed assets and long-term debt were correspondingly reduced. On the face of the balance sheet, debt was shown at £25.9 million whereas under previous accounting policies it would have been reported at £47.2 million. There was reference to netting in the statement of accounting policies on fixed assets but there was no reference to this as a material change in policy.

Maurice Tempany stated that 'This netting of assets and liabilities is not considered to be good accounting practice.'[61] He noted the effect was to improve the reported debt/equity ratio for 1983. In the 'Five Year Comparative Statement' the debt/equity ratio was shown at 65.6% compared with 46% for 1982, 65% for 1980 and 94.3% for 1979. If the previous year's accounting policy had been adopted, the debt/equity ratio would have been 104%, i.e. high financial risk and in excess of the 50–60% range proposed to the first Oireachtas committee.[62]

Valuation of assets

This debt/equity distortion was made greater by a revaluation surplus in the financial statements in respect of the *Irish Spruce*. This vessel was booked in as an asset at £10 million. A revaluation 'by the Company's chief engineer' according to the 'Notes' to the financial statements[63] indicated a surplus of £4.1 million which was added to value of assets and, correspondingly, the reserves. This piece of 'window-dressing' improved the debt/equity ratio which otherwise would have exceeded 110% on long-term debt alone. Maurice Tempany said that he 'had been unable either to obtain a copy of the valuation report or identify the engineer involved'.[64] In this writer's opinion it is surprising that fuller disclosure on this revaluation was not made in view of the materiality of the figure. If it had been an investment property, under SSAP 19 the basis of the valuation and the qualifications of the valuer would have been expected to be detailed. In this writer's view the issue points to weaknesses in financial reporting regulatory standards at the time.

The financial statements of a company are the product of top management and board of directors. Possible concerns about perceived riskiness in 1983, having reported a net loss of £13.2 million, could be softened if the debt/equity ratio was not too high. Irish Shipping was not quoted on the Stock Exchange, and thus its financial statements were not subjected to the scrutiny of stockbroker analysts. The media's analysis was superficial and it did not take a critical view until very late in the day. In the main, the company's bank debt was secured on ships and guaranteed by the government. The unsecured creditors, such as the Chinese shipping companies, were much more vulnerable.

Contingent liabilities/future charter obligations

It is surprising that there was no reference to the nine charter contracts in the accounts — particularly when it appears that five were associated with the purchase of an option to exercise an equity interest in ships.[65] These vessels were an operational resource of the company to attain turnover and profit. It can be argued that the longer term charter arrangements were the equivalent of use of a fixed asset. Under the 1963 Companies Act all capital commitments are required to be disclosed and it was a thin line as to their definition. In this writer's opinion it is remarkable that the directors, management and auditors did not see it as appropriate to record certain of these obligations under 'capital commitments' or elsewhere in the 'Notes' to the accounts in view of their status and scale for future cash flows.

Going concern uncertainties

The financial statements for the year ended March 1984 were approved by Irish Shipping's directors at the board meeting on 7 June 1984. They were signed by the chairman W. A. O'Neill and Edward Keegan, both chartered accountants. A net loss of £34.3 million was reported, compared to a loss of £13.2 million the previous year. Shareholders' funds in the group balance sheet were shown at £3 million, compared with loans of £74 million and current liabilities of £24 million. The parent company balance sheet disclosed a £4 million negative equity position. The auditors' report made no reference to any reservations or uncertainties. Five months later a provisional liquidator was appointed.

In the Dáil Minister for Communications Jim Mitchell referred to an estimated statement of affairs at 31 August 1984 from the company, which showed assets of £23 million and total liabilities of £117 million.[66] According to the liquidator's report to the High Court, the book value of assets was £21 million and total liabilities amounted to £108 million. It is difficult to reconcile the financial position portrayed in the audited accounts, the subsequent events and the extent of the deterioration in the financial position, as subsequently measured.

In their report dated 7 June 1984, the auditors stated that they had 'obtained all the information and explanations we considered necessary' and that in their opinion the financial statements gave 'a true and fair view of the state of affairs of the company and the group at 31st March 1984'. There was no reference to any going concern uncertainty or to the 'Note', 'Basis of Accounting', attached to the financial statements.[67] This 'Note' stated:

> Projections for the calendar years 1984 and 1985 show a continuation of trading losses and cash deficits. The Government response to the projections has been to provide guarantees in respect of additional finance required to fund the projected cash deficits for the years in question.
>
> The directors are satisfied that the company and its subsidiaries will continue their operations for the foreseeable future and accordingly the group financial statements have been prepared on a going concern basis.[68]

The minutes of the Irish Shipping board meeting of 30 May 1984 record that the draft financial statements for the year ended March 1984 were circulated, and a number of adjustments were agreed. A representative from the auditors' firm appears to have been in attendance. The minutes also record the apparent concerns of certain directors to avoid a qualified audit report, which would be damaging to the company.[69] One director argued that 'the credibility of the board would be damaged by the qualification'. The representative from the auditing firm explained that the government 'had gone out of its way to make it clear that its support only extended to the end of 1985'. This is what caused concern.[70]

This writer has formed the view that a solution to the auditors' apparent concerns was achieved by the issue of a 'letter of representation' of 7 June 1984, signed by W. A. O'Neill as chairman on behalf of the board. It stated that the board was satisfied that adequate cash resources were available to meet working capital and capital expenditure needs to end December 1985, and that if any further financial support was required thereafter, it would be forthcoming following discussions with the owners of the chartered-in vessels and the government. The letter to the auditors concluded, 'Accordingly, we are satisfied that the Company and its subsidiaries will continue its operations for the foreseeable future.'[71]

In this writer's opinion best practice in auditing would be to seek independent corroboration and evidence of such an assurance of support towards continuity of operations. Detailed cash flows to 1986 appear to have been available and their sensitivity to any deterioration in trading was relevant in making a judgment. According to Maurice Tempany's report trading results presented to the board in April and May had shown that earnings were falling behind projections and that there had been an additional drawdown of £4 million from Allied Irish Investment Bank, reflecting a tightening cash flow position.[72] In this writer's opinion, in view of the circumstances of the company and the explicit policy of the government, it was heroic acceptance of faith by the auditors to appear to accept the letter of representation by the board.

These financial statements were submitted to the department and the minister and would have been laid before the Dáil. The annual general meeting was held on 27 June 1984. At this meeting, the shareholders, being the Minister for Finance or his representatives, adopted the accounts, implying they were considered and approved.[73] In light of this, in this writer's view it would not have been unreasonable for employees and creditors to assume that the basis and principles of accounting were well grounded and that the adoption of the continuity principle was justified. It seems that there is no evidence that the government departments objected to the statement by the directors in 'Note 1 Basis of Accounting' attached to the financial statement about the government's response to the projected cash deficits — with all the implications it might have for a user.

The treatment of capital profits on ships as operating profit

The occasional capital profits on the sale of ships and other assets were included in the operating profit and not shown separately on face of the profit and loss account — even as an exceptional or extraordinary item, as might have been an interpretation under SSAP 6.[74] Admittedly, brief information was disclosed in the 'Notes' attached to the financial statements. The amounts were material in the years they occurred (as shown in Table 9.1) and the treatment masked the poor trading performance of the deep-sea tramping and chartering activities. After all, in 1982, when supposed record profits were achieved, the reported operating surplus of £3.2 million would have been a small loss if the capital gain of £3.3 million on the disposal of a ship had not been included.

External governance defects

The shareholder of a state-sponsored body is the Minister for Finance, who appoints the directors in consultation with the minister of the government department responsible for the organisation's direct supervision and overall policy.[75] The Minister for Finance also had extensive rights to information under the articles of association of Irish Shipping:

> The Directors shall, whenever and so often as the Minister for Finance may require, furnish to the said Minister such particulars (being particulars within the power, possession or procurement of the Company) as he may require in relation to any undertaking in which the Company may hold an interest.[76]

The articles included the usual requirement that the directors ensure 'full and true accounts . . . be kept'[77] and that they furnish a profit and loss account and balance sheet which 'shall be drawn up in such manner as may be directed by the Minister for Finance';[78] 'such balance sheet shall contain . . . a summary of the capital, assets and liabilities of the Company, together with such particulars as will disclose the nature of such assets and liabilities'.[79] The Minister for Finance could also request the directors to provide 'all such information and explanations as he may require in connection with any matter arising upon any profit account or balance sheet of the Company or upon any report of the directors'.[80]

Clearly, government departments were not solely dependent on the audited financial statements for information on the affairs of the company. They had the authority to ask probing questions and to review any aspect of the organisation's performance. Civil servants from the Department of Communications claimed that they first learned of the company's serious financial position at a meeting in July 1982 requested by W. A. O'Neill. In October a written report from Irish Shipping confirmed the situation and detailed the extent of the chartering commitments and projected financial deficits. The civil servants and the minister were reported to have been 'shocked by the report'.[81] Second and third written reports appear to have been submitted to government in January and October 1983. The department received fourth and fifth reports in February and September

1984. This writer views it as surprising that, when the first written report was received, no independent assessment by a firm of accountants or consultants was ordered by the department. Equally surprising was the fact that no changes in top management or the chairmanship were sought.

The delays in decision-making and in taking action were extraordinary. The dismal projections in the 1982 report were confirmed by the loss of £13.2 million in 1983. It took three further reports and the confirmation in the 1983/84 financial statements of a £34.3 million loss together with the erosion of almost all the shareholder funds before Frank Belton was eventually appointed as chairman in late August 1984. It seems that the civil servants and government remained dependent on the information and projections prepared by the company's management — in which there were obvious deficiencies. W. A. O'Neill maintained some optimism about the recovery of future tramp market rates, which was not borne out. No material injection of equity was advanced. Instead, the government's guarantees increased the debt level; the relatively high interest rates of the time added to the burden. Surprisingly, after the December 1983 cabinet decision to guarantee additional bank borrowings, when the possibility of liquidation was acknowledged, no civil servant seems to have joined the Irish Shipping negotiating team that travelled to Hong Kong and Tokyo in January 1984 to renegotiate the charter terms. The shipowners, apparently, never believed liquidation was a possibility, nor do they appear to have been fully aware of government policy limits in supporting the company. The shipowners' offer of much reduced charter rates in November 1984, on liquidation, was too late.

In most private sector organisations, where the dominant shareholder is external to the board, and a level of losses is revealed which is primarily due to management decisions, that shareholder would usually insist on a change of chief executive and chairman. Examples occurred in Xtra-vision, GPA, Guinness, P. J. Carroll and Waterford Glass. Inaction and a lack of purposeful intervention to allay losses and prevent collapse characterised the stance adopted by the government. In this writer's opinion the efficiency, expertise, management and organisational structure of the civil service in relation to the Irish Shipping debacle have to be questioned. It is astonishing that the Department of Communications, with a staff of thirty-six,[82] did not employ a qualified accountant.[83] Who had the competence to review the financial statements, reports and financial projections of Irish Shipping and pose suitable questions on its performance, policies and prospects, when the problems were out in the open from autumn 1982?

The apparent delays in putting a paper before the cabinet for decision in December 1983 suggest that the Department of Finance's monitoring and involvement did not compensate for the inefficiencies in supervision and control by the Department of Communications. These weaknesses by both government departments are all the more remarkable in view of the number of reports submitted by Irish Shipping on its financial needs and the fact that there was an extensive involvement by the Department of Finance on the funding arrangements for the *Irish Spruce* and capitalisation of Irish Shipping in this period.

All the directors were appointed by the Minister for Finance and the articles of association stated that 'The business of the Company shall be managed by the Directors in such manner as they may think most expedient.'[84] There is a direct link between the ownership of Irish Shipping, the wide authority and powers of the minister in appointing directors and in obtaining such additional information as may be required, and the conferred power on the directors to manage the company. In discussing state-sponsored bodies,[85] Dooney and O'Toole express the view:

> Each body operates under the general control of a minister, who is responsible for ensuring that the body carries out the tasks for which it is set up but who does not intervene in the day-to-day carrying out of these tasks.
>
> State-sponsored bodies are therefore part of the system of government, and the government is ultimately responsible for their performance. This situation underlines the fundamental difference between private sector companies, who are responsible to shareholders, and state-sponsored bodies, whose shareholder is ultimately the Minister for Finance.[86]

Unlike companies in the private sector, the board of a state-sponsored body cannot co-opt directors of suitable calibre for a particular role and mix, nor can they appoint or sack their chairman. Only the Minister for Finance can take such actions. The continuance of P. H. Greer as chairman for seventeen years, and the appointment of W. A. O'Neill as executive chairman in succession in 1982, were crucial decisions. The many other board changes in the late 1970s and early 1980s also affected the effectiveness of the governance structure of the company, as found by the liquidator.

To a degree, a combination of a difficult and charged Northern Ireland political situation, domestic politics and changes in government and ministers in the vital period 1980–82[87] may have contributed to weaknesses in overall supervision at that time. However, once the Fine Gael/Labour coalition government assumed office on 14 December 1982, the Minister for Communications, Jim Mitchell, was responsible for its affairs from then until its liquidation two years later. The government through the Minister for Finance appointed the directors and auditors, thus determining much of the internal and external governance framework, together with the meanings and expectations they shaped. A number of reports were received over two years. In this writer's opinion the subsequent statement by the Minister for Communications is certainly difficult to reconcile with the preceding events and inaction.

> Ten days after the liquidation of Irish Shipping the lessons and implications for the state sector in particular and the economy in general are, I hope, beginning to seep in.
>
> The message is not, as some commentators seem to think, a singular message for the state sector. No, much more than that, it is a message which should be clearly understood by all and sundry at home and abroad.
>
> The message is simply this: the messing is over. The Government means business and toughness and courage will not be lacking in order to restore control of public expenditure . . .
>
> Irish Shipping was for many years the jewel in the crown of the state sector. It was up to recently proof positive that state enterprise could work. That it should be scuttled by a series of unauthorised decisions in no way diminished its earlier testimony to the efficacy of state enterprise.[88]

Another external governance flaw was the process of inquiry and the report on Irish Shipping of the Joint Oireachtas Committee on State-Sponsored Bodies in 1980–81. This eleven-member committee comprised TDs and senators from the three largest political parties. As part of its process, the committee would have sought submissions from the company and relevant government departments. Oral hearings also took place. The 1980 inquiry seemed comprehensive when the report, published in March 1981, reviewed Irish Shipping's objectives, operational and financial performance, board and management, capital structure, future plans and relationships with government departments.[89] It noted that a fleet of 150,000 tons capacity was considered adequate to meet basic strategic needs in times of emergency and that Irish Shipping was expanding its fleet tonnage when it could be justified on purely commercial grounds. The Oireachtas committee concluded the report by congratulating the board, management, staff, masters and crews of Irish Shipping 'for the highly efficient manner in which they have discharged their responsibilities'.[90] In light of the subsequent revelations, this is embarrassing to have on the public record. After all, between September 1979 and November 1980, six of the nine long- and medium-term charters had been signed and this unknown strategic decision had circumvented the agreed debt/equity ratio and capital spending objectives — and sealed the fate of the company.

The liquidation and some consequences

The liquidation has proved a lengthy and costly affair. The preponderance of debt was in the form of unsecured creditors, who submitted claims for £213 million.[91] Of this amount, £27 million was owed to Allied Irish Bank and Citibank. The original unsecured claims included future charter amounts under contract, but through adjudication the liquidation admitted £75 million.

Following liquidation, the assets realisations were limited. The two wholly owned ships of the fleet, the *Irish Rowan* and the *Irish Cedar*, were sold by public tender in Hong Kong and in Mombasa, Keyna, and fetched just £2.5 million and £2 million respectively. By May 1989, the total liquidation inflows were £12.8 million and outflows were £7.5 million.[92] The £1.4 million liquidator's fees and £800,000 legal fees were the largest element in the liquidation costs, followed by employee costs. With accumulated interest, the balance available for the unsecured creditors amounted to £7.9 million at December 1992.[93] Ironically in view of their job losses, one of the larger sources of cash, for the benefit of the liquidation, appears to have been the surplus of £1.1 million realised on the winding-up of the ships masters and officers' pension scheme, based on actuarial reports. Irish Continental Line continued operations and was sold to a financial consortium. The remaining 300 Irish Shipping employees in the deep-sea tramping activities suffered badly, as they received their statutory rights at the time and no more. Despite a strike-free record and the fact that they had no role in the cause of the decline of the company, they lost their jobs — which they thought were secure. They filed claims with the liquidator for redundancy, minimum notice, wages and holiday pay. Most received just two and a half days' pay for each year of service. Typically, many in their forties and fifties received between £3,500 and £4,500, and because of their specialised field, their job prospects were poor. Moreover, with the freezing of the pension schemes, their future pensions would be modest. It was an extraordinary stand by the government in relation to employees of a state-sponsored body — when compared to public sector policies in respect of redundancy in other state bodies and the special early-retirement schemes for civil servants or teachers, or when compared to redundancy schemes in leading private sector companies at the time. The excuse that it would open the floodgates to claims for equal treatment by the unsecured creditors is difficult to sustain. It was, in this writer's view, a miserly and cold-hearted attitude.

Despite subsequent political promises of six weeks' pay for every year of service, no such payment was made. It took the filing of a £13 million claim in the High Court by employees for loss of earnings arising out of government negligence in its supervision and control of the affairs of Irish Shipping before a realistic government response emerged. Finally, in 1994, ten years after liquidation, the government agreed an amount of three weeks for every year worked, up to a maximum of £50,000 per person. The process and outcome were shabby in the extreme.

By far the largest losses were experienced by the Chao family of Hong Kong who were the main shareholders in the Wah Kwong Shipping Company which had provided six of the chartered ships.[94] It was a medium-sized firm with a quotation on the Hong Kong stockmarket. Following the Irish Shipping liquidation, its shares collapsed and a restructuring became necessary because of bad debts (it also suffered smaller losses with two other shipping companies). Some of the ships were legally seized by Japanese banks and sold on the open market — with claims on Wah Kwong also. It was a traumatic period for the two Chao brothers and their father as they struggled to save their family company through intense negotiations with financial institutions, the introduction of external family resources and a dilution of equity control. It was only in 1992 that the financial restructuring was completed and the share price had recovered. In this writer's opinion it is unlikely that six ships would have been made available on long-term charter by a company the size of Wah Kwong, on the basis of the financial risks it took, if Irish Shipping had not been a state-sponsored body, 100% owned by the Minister for Finance.

The cash cost to the state in guarantees and other payments up to 1988 was £89 million,[95] and may have since reached £103 million (before any implicit interest costs). Indeed, the special financing package for *Irish Spruce* with a Japanese banking house approved by the Department of Finance has been the largest element of cost. The cost, in terms of honour and responsibility, has been inestimable.

Government responsibility

The Minister for Communications Jim Mitchell argued that Irish Shipping was 'scuttled by a series of unauthorised decisions'.[96] In the Dáil he stated that the charter agreements were entered into 'without the knowledge or consent of either the then Minister for Transport or the then Minister for Finance'[97] and that any agreement by the government to make finance available to meet such liabilities 'would be a complete abdication of expenditure control' as indicated in the national plan *Building on Reality*.[98] In essence, he was saying the responsibility lay with the company — which was, in effect, its management and board of directors. Thus the government's justification for liquidation was the absence of its approval for the financial commitments and its economic policy of fiscal rectitude.

This author is of the opinion that the government remains responsible for all the debts of a commercial state-sponsored body. After all, such a body reports to the minister of a designated government department who has authority over its affairs. The one shareholder is the Minister for Finance, who appoints all the directors. The minister, through the civil servants, has the authority to ask probing questions and to review any aspect of the organisation's performance.

As stated earlier, there is a direct link between the ownership of Irish Shipping, the wide authority and powers of the minister in appointing directors, and the conferred power on the directors to manage the company. From 1979, the company's annual reports provided summaries of the growing chartered-in tonnage. This expansion might have provoked some questioning by competent officials. The relevance of the strategic tonnage was accepted by the Oireachtas committee in 1981 and there is no evidence that any change in policy was recommended by civil servants or decided by government — until it became convenient in 1984.

The breakdown in processes of external governance by the various ministers and their officials has already been analysed. The department was verbally advised of the problems in July 1982 and then in writing in a report in October 1982 — it certainly cannot have been unaware of the seriousness of Irish Shipping's future prospects. Detailed cash flow projections, profit and loss accounts and balance sheets for the three years to March 1986 were again provided in other reports. Losses of £22 million, £24 million and £19 million were projected, with interest costs becoming a heavy burden (a figure of £9.7 million was shown in the 1985/86 projections). Irish Shipping argued that:

... these prudent projections which may well represent the reality of the situation, serve to highlight the impracticality of continuing to meet the cash deficits with government guaranteed short term borrowings.[99]

Irish Shipping's board pointed out that the addition of future borrowings contributed to the company's problems and that a point would be reached, if it had not already been reached, when the company would have no prospect of ever being able to repay these borrowings from its own resources, even if an early return to profitability was achieved. Equity injections were sought as part of a package which included renegotiation of rates and refinancing — but the request for equity was refused. The questions of honour and ultimate responsibility appear not to have been criteria in the decision-making framework.

Reflections

Irish Shipping did not have the managerial or financial resource to take on the risk and financial commitments of the long-term charters. The investment in Irish Continental Line and the small number of larger replacement vessels had already left its debt/equity position vulnerable. Real profitability was marginal. With no home base for the fleet, unless the ESB contract became a reality some years down the line at a profitable margin, the tramping activity had little business logic — other than the country's strategic needs. In this writer's view the governance and organisational structure weaknesses compounded the problem and gave free rein to management to take enormous risks. The absence of employee representatives on the board was a further information and control weakness which facilitated management domination of strategy. Many of the characteristics fitted Miller's syndrome of 'Swimming Upstream'.

The liquidation of Irish Shipping and the treatment of its employees and creditors (and bankers to an extent) were a national scandal. Even with liquidation, Irish taxpayers suffered heavily. In light of the actual costs, it must be questioned if the collapse and loss of credibility in certain circles were justified. The treatment of B&I, which had a poor financial performance for many years and was a drain of almost £120 million on the exchequer, was in marked contrast. Sins of commission seem to be penalised much more heavily than sins of omission.

Given that Irish Shipping was the first Irish or indeed European state-owned company to collapse and fail to pay its unsecured creditors, it was strange that no official inquiry or investigation was ordered (other than the

High Court order for a liquidator's report). In this writer's opinion it was a most extraordinarily irresponsible way for the government of the day to deal with the problem and avoid facing up to public findings about possible negligence and responsibility. There were lessons to be learned by government, civil servants, directors, managers and auditors of state-sponsored organisations. The appointment of experienced and competent directors, rotation of the chairmanship, financial control, and comprehensive information on decisions and future financial commitments were internal issues. Externally, the ineffectual monitoring by the civil servants and the government's slow response — apart from the fact that no outside assessment was sought — were highlighted. The absence of suitable accountancy expertise was a serious weakness in the relevant government department. No other European country would sweep such a serious scandal quietly 'under the carpet'.

Chapter 10

Conclusions

With this manufactured mystique about leadership, we simply pander to our leaders' desire for power, which is intoxicating enough in itself. This is exactly the wrong approach. We must see our leaders, not as superior beings, but simply as fallible individuals in positions of power and responsibility. The false distinction between 'leader' and 'manager' contributes to false or lowered expectations about what either can do for the group.

C. M. Kelly, *The Destructive Achiever*[1]

Introduction

Though the primary themes leading to distress in adolescent and mature firms were multifarious, some surprisingly common patterns of behaviour and characteristics emerged, though often for differing reasons. Clear and common patterns could be identified for the adolescent firms, but there was a greater variety and complexity in the distress syndromes of mature firms. These findings derive from a small sample, the nine detailed cases presented in this study, but they are not rejected by the characteristics of the other nine cases investigated (see Appendix 1).

This chapter will first discuss age patterns and the surprising extent of profit reversals. Then the causes of mismanagement will be examined separately for adolescent and mature firms. The author's own framework, arising out of this exploratory study, will be presented as a basis for classifying the themes in the distress and failure process. The roles of bankers and stockbroker analysts will be discussed. Accounting, auditing and the system of corporate regulation will be reviewed in the light of the study's findings, and recommendations for change will be made. Issues of public concern, such as losses of taxation, will be raised, and proposals will be made to help detect and prevent financial crisis, distress and, above all else, failure. After all, in the nine cases studied, all but Irish Press seemed to have a successful track record. The evidence suggests that with the exception of Kentz and Irish Press the crises could have been avoided. Self-inflicted injuries, delusion and blindness were the order of the day.

Age patterns

The age patterns of the adolescents point to two identifiable crisis periods — very early on entry to adolescence and late in this stage, when maturity is beckoning. The Kentz management buyout and Xtra-vision, at the age of six and eight years respectively, were examples of the difficult crossover from 'youth', which showed up an apparent inability to change to a professional managerial style, with stronger systems and new structures, from the dominant 'deal-making' entrepreneurial style which entailed little delegation from the top. GPA and Goodman, aged seventeen and thirty-six years respectively, were in the late period of adolescence when they abruptly moved from a reasonably balanced growth strategy to hypergrowth, fuelled by excessive debt.

No identifiable age patterns emerged among the mature firms — with two being over a hundred years old and three being between forty-two and sixty-four years old. Guinness and P. J. Carroll had sixth and fourth generation family members at the helm, while the dominant families at Waterford and Irish Press were in their second and third generations when the problems emerged.

The extent and speed of the profit reversals

Three of the four adolescents reported consistently excellent growth in annual profits and earnings per share prior to the crisis. Kentz was the exception, where some volatility was exhibited. In the five years before the crash, good growth in profits was reported (though margins were low) for the first three years, followed by a loss and then a recovery (based on optimistic accounting). All four adolescent firms experienced extensive losses and write-offs in the post-crisis financial statements. In the mature company group, prior to the financial crisis, Waterford and Irish Shipping had been reporting profit growth, Irish Press had a variable record, P. J. Carroll was relatively static and Guinness had been reporting a decline for some years. Certainly, the reversal of fortunes in P. J. Carroll, Waterford Wedgwood and Irish Shipping was unexpected. A summary is shown in Table 10.1.

The extent and speed of the collapse from profit to loss in both groups were remarkable. In three of the four adolescent firms (GPA being the exception) the post-crisis loss wiped out all shareholder capital — leaving them in a negative equity situation. GPA, Goodman and Xtra-vision were illustrations of the phenomenon of fast-growth profit plunging into dramatic losses. Return to profitability in GPA and Xtra-vision was not

Table 10.1: The extent of the profit/reversals in the crisis firms (£m)

Firm	Profit in year preceding crisis	Post-crisis loss
Adolescent		
Goodman International	29	(417)
GPA	$268m	($1bn)
Kentz Corporation	2	(20)*
Xtra-vision	3	(19)
Mature		
P. J. Carroll	10	(21)
Guinness	7	(26)
Irish Press	1	(2)
Irish Shipping	5	(12)
Waterford Wedgwood	18	(48)

* Based on company's High Court affidavit and material in the reports of the examiner.

Source. Annual reports of firms except for Kentz Corporation.

achieved for some years. In the mature firms, P. J. Carroll, Waterford Wedgwood and Irish Shipping exhibited surprisingly similar patterns.

How can such huge reversals be explained? The greater part of these post-crisis losses was caused by more prudent values being placed on assets (leading to large asset write-downs), the recognition of certain liabilities and a variety of 'bankruptcy costs' — heavy legal, accountancy and bankers' fees in the restructuring. Some of these accounting adjustments raise serious regulatory questions. This writer is of the opinion that on more than a few occasions 'red flags' failed to appear in the auditors' reports prior to liquidation/examinership. The suddenness and depth of the financial crisis in the four adolescent firms were such that three had a financial crisis within six months of a clean audit report (Xtra-vision was the exception). Moreover, three of the adolescents (Kentz being the exception) had previously reported continuous profits growth. This coincidence was an unexpected finding of the research. The benchmark companies did not have quite the same profits patterns nor did they encounter such profit setbacks.

Three of the four adolescent firms were in good financial health up to a year or two before they collapsed. Kentz was the exception. It was able to continue trading despite its weaknesses in capitalisation for some years because of contract payments and delays in paying suppliers and payroll taxes. Apart from Irish Shipping and Irish Press, the three other mature firms were in a reasonable financial position up to a year before crisis — though Guinness was exhibiting income gearing weakness. Comparisons with benchmark organisations in the same industry pointed to very different patterns in strategic decisions, governance and management structures — with more consistent performance. To some degree, this neutralises the impact of the external environment in markets, competition and economic cycles, and points to the characteristics of the firms themselves as the primary cause of financial distress.

Themes and patterns of adolescent firm distress and failure

The four adolescents can be described as fast-growth entrepreneurial firms. All were innovative and energetic in their activities. Indeed, it could be said that some were more progressive than the benchmark firms. They successfully adapted and changed from their initial product/market position at their birth/youth stage. On reaching adolescence, they had successfully moved into new products and markets. Indeed GPA, Goodman and Kentz were able to operate on an international stage, and were described as 'world class' enterprises in their field.

In the opinion of this writer the primary elements of and reasons for mismanagement that were identified among the adolescent firms are as set out in Table 10.2.

Excessive growth

The theme which stood out above all others was the unsustainable rate of growth of the adolescent firms. Their rate of expansion exceeded that of the benchmark firms, who were also leaders in their industry. The rush for supernormal growth, within a short time span, was clearly evident. This overexpansion can be classified as either overtrading or overinvestment.

Kentz, Xtra-vision and GPA were extremely successful within a defined product/market strategy, but in a rush of uncontrolled hyperexpansion, funded by excessive debt, they overtraded and triggered a liquidity crisis with cash flow shortfalls. In Xtra-vision and GPA a culture of 'sales mania' and the bid to achieve a dominant market share were driving forces. Goodman International was most successful in its sector but it overinvested by attempting a large acquisition through purchase of an asset of volatile value — quoted shares — financed by short-term bank borrowing. In all four instances the firms, through their aggressive expansion which was

Table 10.2: Elements of mismanagement: adolescent firms

Mismanagement themes

1. Overtrading	Kentz, Xtra-vision, GPA
2. Overinvestment/acquisitions	Goodman
3. Big project — betting the business	Goodman, Kentz, GPA
4. Unbalanced capital structure	Goodman, Kentz, Xtra-vision, GPA
5. Major change in risk profile	Goodman, Kentz, Xtra-vision, GPA
6. Action/bad timing — economic/industry cycle	Goodman, Kentz, GPA
7. Weak management accounting information systems	Kentz, Xtra-vision
8. Aggressive accounting — delusion	Goodman, Kentz, Xtra-vision, GPA
9. Overhead cost control	Kentz, Xtra-vision, GPA

Reasons for mismanagement

1. Domineering chief executive/dual role	Goodman, Kentz, GPA
2. Aggressive/deal-making culture	Goodman, Kentz, Xtra-vision, GPA
3. Growing pains — transition management skills, systems and culture	Kentz, Xtra-vision
4. Weak board/internal governance structures	Goodman, Kentz, Xtra-vision, GPA
5. Weak financial control	Goodman, Kentz, Xtra-vision, GPA
6. Poor strategic planning/control	Goodman, Kentz, Xtra-vision, GPA
7. Management balance/depth	Goodman, Kentz, Xtra-vision
8. Executive/staff incentives/pressure	Goodman, GPA
9. 'Soft touch' banks	Goodman, Xtra-vision
10. Passive shareholders	Xtra-vision, GPA
11. Problematic auditing/accounting/regulations	Goodman, Xtra-vision, GPA

funded by debt, left themselves vulnerable to bank pressures and illiquidity. In the case of Kentz and GPA, problems also occurred through covenant compliance and financial matters.

How might the symptoms of 'overtrading' be recognised? After years of fast but reasonably steady growth in assets and turnover, each organisation proceeded to move sharply from its previous pattern by making a quantum leap (or a series of such leaps) in asset investment, mainly financed by debt. All the 'overtraders' suddenly expanded at a much more rapid rate than other equivalent-sized leading companies in their industry. Examples are the contrast between Goodman International and Kerry Group, or between GPA and ILFC (or Woodchester). Most of these benchmark organisations also had periods of rapid growth, but there followed a period of consolidation for a year or two. Kerry Group, like Goodman International, made a large acquisition (Beatreme). However, it had already raised new equity on the stockmarket and was able to make a subsequent rights issue to keep the proportion and term structure of debt and interest costs at a sustainable level in relation to profits and cash flow. Many writers and bankers focus on too rapid a rate of expansion of 'turnover' in relation to 'capital' and 'profitability' when discussing symptoms of 'overtrading'. The evidence from this study indicates that growth of asset investment precedes turnover by a much faster rate and is generally not matched.

The phenomenon of 'betting the business' on the big project appeared in three of the four companies (Xtra-vision being the exception). The amount of Goodman International's investment in the Berisford and Unigate shares was greater than its net worth (quite apart from the Iraqi debtors). In Kentz, the Barcelona project was almost equal to all other business on hand at one period — despite the weak equity and working capital base. The scale of GPA's $10 billion financial commitments for new aircraft purchases, at the rate of over $200 million a month in 1992 and 1993 alone, was breathtaking in its audacity in comparison to financial capacity, structure and covenants. There was also the challenge of finding customers with a reasonable credit risk, at profitable margins, for this enormous expansion of capacity.

The large scale of the new project investments unbalanced the firms in financial and managerial resource depth, and the management accounting and control systems were unable to keep up with the new scale. There was also increased business risk. In most instances the big project involved new markets, new customers, a new product or new technology. The evidence also suggests that the existing business suffered as an overstretched management team tried to grapple with the new project problems. Time and competence became scarce resources. Examples abound in Kentz in particular. The big project also created a new level of financial risk. The burden of the big project going wrong was the final straw that effectively pushed the firms into crisis. The exception, in its management and systems, was GPA: there it was a combination of two strategic errors in timing of capacity investment and capital structure.

Capital structure and financial control
All the adolescent cases exhibited an excessive dependence on bank debt to finance growth and expansion. There were distinguishing financing patterns between Kentz and Goodman and their benchmark firms. Xtra-vision can be set against its counterpart in the UK, which had a policy of no bank borrowing; thus, when there was a cutback in consumer spending, it was able to ride out the recession since it was not burdened by debt, as was Xtra-vision. GPA and Goodman had by far the largest amounts of bank borrowing at $6 billion and £507 million respectively. Another noticeable feature was the number of banks involved in most of the cases. GPA and Goodman obtained facilities from 103 and 33 banks respectively. Consequently, no single bank could have a deep relationship which would prompt it to fully appreciate the firm's business and management, and the issues in its industry. Nor would it be able to influence the entrepreneur on policy and structure. Moreover, in the case of Goodman International, the multi-bank involvement seems to have resulted in few of the banks knowing the full state of affairs about new facilities, spending commitments and off balance sheet obligations that were being undertaken. The issue of intercompany cross-guarantees and commitments (off balance sheet) was a problem feature for banks and creditors in Goodman International and Kentz. These off balance sheet commitments, when they crystallised in 1990, totally altered the debt/equity relationships in Goodman International's case.

The excessive level of debt taken on by the adolescent firms was a defective capital structure decision. This fundamental mistake can be linked to ineffective financial control, weak strategic control by the board in financial strategy, and the influence of the founder/entrepreneur. Raising additional equity capital always has implications for dilution of ownership and control. In most cases the banks' facilities were secured on the firm's assets (except for Goodman International). Thus, the banks' view of financial risk must have been different from the firm's. The adolescent's collapse resulted in total loss of equity investment, whereas the banks recovered some of their loans — though there were heavy bad debt write-offs in three instances. The exception was GPA, where the banks made money. In Goodman International the banks 'took a bath', as almost £400 million of the £500 million in unsecured facilities proved worthless.

The income and balance sheet leverage and cash flow ratios of the benchmark firms differed from the distress firms studied. There were signals in respect of debt servicing problems well in advance. Though the adolescent firms were reporting profits, their cash flow statements —

without exception — told a very different story. Their cash flows were in deficit for more than three consecutive years and the net cash flow from operations was more volatile than that of the benchmark firms — as also were many of the critical financial ratios. This points to weaker financial planning and control.

It was remarkable that the banks advanced such levels of facilities, despite the evidence of overtrading and capital structure imbalance. What criteria did they use to justify their decisions? In a sense, soft bank lending, fuzzy criteria and poor monitoring of the adolescent firms contributed to the financial crisis and the banks' bad debts. The banks seem to have been a 'soft touch' in the cases of Goodman International and Xtra-vision — and they paid the price.

In all the adolescent cases, there was weak financial control. Part of the responsibility for overtrading and excessive debt rests with this function. Indeed, there were management accounting breakdowns in both Kentz and Xtra-vision, which resulted in inaccurate profit and cash flow projections. Thus the board and top management were 'driving blind'. In both these companies, there was poor cost analysis and cost control of unsustainable overheads. In both Goodman International and Kentz there was the surprising situation where the company was left without a financial controller for a critical period, as the accountant was given a general management role or was 'captured' by the aggressive entrepreneurial culture of the firm.

Responsibility for management accounting information and cash flow projections, as well as accounting policies adopted and the quality of external financial reporting, rests with the financial controller and the board of directors. In all the companies, critical accounting policies appeared optimistic, and to an extent this can be linked to the need for improving profits, covenants and the high levels of debt. The evidence indicates that the will of the founder/entrepreneur tended to hold sway over the financial controller in such matters as capital structure and other critical accounting policies. Though there were questions regarding technical competence in some cases, the real issue centred around the strength of character and calibre of role played by the top financial executive in attempting to influence financial policy and in ensuring adequate management accounting and control systems — together with the presentation and interpretation of effective control information to top management and the board.

Board defects in active pursuit of responsibilities contributed to financial control weaknesses. Remarkably, GPA did not have a financial director until four months before the flotation. It is also worth noting that the board in GPA did not appear to address the financial control function by appointing a qualified accountant with this responsibility to the board earlier. The investment institutions and banks appear to have done little in this regard either.

The importance of timing and fundamental changes in equity capital ownership structure were illustrated in the differences between GPA and its benchmarks, ILFC and Woodchester. They provide important lessons in financial strategy. These organisations had many similarities in terms of a dominant personality who had 'driven' the firm's strategy and growth. However, both ILFC and Woodchester made the decision to raise additional equity capital through a stockmarket quotation much earlier in their growth cycle than did GPA. Then the astute timing, in 1990, of ILFC and Woodchester's willingness to dilute key shareholders' control by being involved with a financially stronger organisation made an enormous difference to financial market credibility. It helped them ride out the recession. GPA paid the price of holding on.

Dominant chief executives, weak board governance and management culture

In this writer's opinion in all four adolescent firms there were internal governance weaknesses due to either a weak board structure or ineffective board participation and role. Goodman International and Kentz were private companies and had no outsiders on the board — at least not until the latter was teetering at the edge, and it was obviously too late. Larry Goodman and Gus Kearney, apart from being dominant shareholders, held the dual positions of chairman and chief executive, which was a platform for almost total power over organisational decisions and actions. In the other two firms there were, in theory, stronger boards because they included non-executive directors. In practice their composition was flawed. In GPA for many years Tony Ryan held the dual role. When this situation is combined with a high number of executive directors and the absence of stability and cultural cohesion in non-executive appointments, then the chairman/chief executive is in a powerful position to dominate the board and the organisation. In summary, the corporate governance framework was not sufficiently strong or structured to challenge the management on strategy, management structure, performance and the changing risk profile. There were no effective countervailing forces to make the chief executive and the symbiotic management team accountable for their stewardship.

The life-cycle model indicates that different competencies require emphasis in the transition from the entrepreneurial start-up stage to the adolescent stage. Clearly, in all the adolescents, the passage to the next stage of the life-cycle was not successfully achieved — hence the crisis. Centralised power and decision-making was the order of the day in Goodman International, Kentz and Xtra-vision. In these three — and, to an extent, even in GPA — the founders were unable to sufficiently adapt the culture despite outward appearances. Interestingly, in three of the four adolescent cases some form of 'partnership' (in a managerial and collegiate sense) of two people helped develop the organisation through to its early adolescent stage. For over twenty years, the expansion and success of M. F. Kent (the precursor to Kentz) was due to the talents and energies of Frank Kent and Gus Kearney. Similarly, there was the combination of Maurice Foley and Tony Ryan in GPA. Xtra-vision took off when Herbert Boyle joined Richard Murphy. Two founding executives, when they work together, can be a powerful combination in driving an organisation's culture and can hold particular sway on a board. Quasi-symbiotic relationships between an 'entrepreneurially captured accountant' and the dominant personality in the firm seemed to emerge in Goodman International and Kentz.

The evidence shows how difficult it is to 'control' the entrepreneur — particularly an expansionist-oriented one with a forceful character. In most firms the financial director could not overrule or argue strenuously with the founder. In a private company there is a real problem because the entrepreneur owns the company. In a public company, with a weak or badly structured board, there is the problem that the directors are often dominated by the founder/entrepreneur. Where the dual roles of chairman and chief executive are held by one person, the position of the financial controller/director is particularly difficult because there is no independent chairman to act as a restraining influence, take certain initiatives or raise items for the board's consideration. To a degree, an audit committee would counterbalance this problem — if experienced and independent directors were members of it.

Themes and patterns of mature firm distress and failure

The evidence points to a different emphasis in the primary themes associated with crisis and distress in the mature firms, as compared to the adolescents. In particular, the fundamental themes revolve around market and competitive change, and the firm's response to this, rather than overtrading. In this

Table 10.3: Elements of mismanagement: mature firms

Mismanagement themes

1. Response to change — market/customers, competition/technology	Guinness, P. J. Carroll, Irish Press, Waterford
2. Marketing ineffectiveness	Guinness, P. J. Carroll, Irish Press
3. Big project/hyperactive	P. J. Carroll, Waterford, Irish Shipping
4. Diversification/acquisitions	Guinness, P. J. Carroll, Irish Press
5. Capital structure	Waterford, Irish Shipping
6. Investment timing	Guinness, P. J. Carroll, Irish Shipping
7. Cost and overhead productivity	Guinness, Irish Press, Waterford
8. Weak management accounting information systems	P. J. Carroll, Waterford, Irish Shipping
9. Change in risk profile	P. J. Carroll, Waterford, Irish Shipping
10. Aggressive accounting — delusion	Irish Shipping

Reasons for mismanagement

1. Domineering chief executive/dual role	P. J. Carroll, Irish Press, Waterford, Irish Shipping
2. Weak governance/board structure	Guinness, P. J. Carroll, Irish Press, Irish Shipping
3. Management kingdoms	Guinness, Irish Press, Irish Shipping
4. Bureaucracy	Guinness, P. J. Carroll, Irish Press
5. Weak financial control	P. J. Carroll, Waterford, Irish Shipping
6. Management depth/structure	P. J. Carroll, Irish Press, Irish Shipping
7. Poor strategic planning/control	Guinness, P. J. Carroll, Irish Press, Irish Shipping
8. Passive shareholders	Guinness, P. J. Carroll, Irish Press, Irish Shipping

writer's view the primary elements of and reasons for mismanagement that were identified among mature firms are as set out in Table 10.3.

Poor adaptation to market and technology changes was responsible for the decline of four of the five mature companies, the exception being Irish Shipping. Despite the fact that their products were in the mature stage of their life-cycle, with the benefit of market research, Guinness and Waterford were able to make marketing, product design and distribution changes which reinvogorated their appeal to customers. Marketing was strengthened. There were improvements in quality and an investment in new technology. Lighter designs in the traditional Waterford Crystal range and the successful launch of the 'Marquis' range for a different less expensive segment of the market improved turnover. Both organisations had extensive 'slack' in direct production costs and overheads. Cost reductions improved competitiveness and released resources for reallocation to marketing and design — apart from improving profits and supporting badly needed new plant investment. In contrast, Irish Press and P. J. Carroll were too slow in their response to changes in consumer tastes. They lost market share quickly and failed to recover it. Irish Press could be viewed as a 'permanently failing organisation' which remained trading despite a near decade of losses through squandering its financial reserves while failing to adapt both managerially and in product design, until it was too late. Defects in governance and ownership control were fundamental to its problems, arising out of its 'family' heritage and the absence of management succession and a depth of professional management. Waterford and Irish Press failed to address their staff productivity and trade union problems adequately until very late in the day. This is an issue that family firms seem to find difficult to face. Trade union policies contributed to the financial crisis of Irish Press and Waterford. Indecisive industrial relations/human resource management also played a role. Guinness and P. J. Carroll successfully negotiated staff reductions and changes in work practices.

To differing degrees, the decline of Guinness, P. J. Carroll and Waterford was stimulated by their diversification strategies. Not only did they deplete their financial resource base, as a result of losses and investment write-offs, but there was the diversion of management time and lack of focus on the core business at a critical juncture in the marketplace. In all three, there was an inappropriate organisational structure and depth to manage the diversified activities. The timing of the Wedgwood and Southside Newspapers acquisitions by Waterford and Irish Press respectively was questionable, when urgent attention was needed in the core business.

Four of the five mature firms might be described as 'family' dominated because of the actual influence of family members on their boards and management. In the writer's opinion these organisations were partially treated as managerial fiefdoms. The issue of management succession planning was an important element, particularly in the 'family' firms. Also, the ingredients of family identity and heritage together with the influence of the organisation's history and culture were powerful elements in strategy. Guinness and P. J. Carroll made the transition to professional management. Theirs was a governance weakness in the structure and operation of the board. In Guinness there were too few experienced non-executive directors and a plethora of ineffective family members. This left a vacuum in which top management fiefdoms could flourish — with consequent weakening in competitive performance — particularly in the UK. In P. J. Carroll, the family chairman and the executives dominated the board despite their small shareholding. In both Guinness and P. J. Carroll, the investment institutions were feeble in their intervention as joint owners until very late in the day. In Waterford and the Irish Press group the dominant family shareholdings were the key to the weak board structure and the ineffective management responses to the declining performance.

The five-stage life-cycle of birth, growth, maturity, revival and decline proved a useful framework in attempting to distinguish the characteristics of the sample of organisations in the study. The attempt at diversification or risky growth strategies illustrated a managerial intervention aimed at achieving a 'revival' stage in a number of the mature organisations. Unfortunately, because the strategy combined an unrealistic degree of risk and too large a commitment of resources, in some cases (P. J. Carroll and Irish Shipping) the actions accelerated the decline stage.

Whereas the Argenti model signalled that all the adolescent firms were 'at risk' some time in advance of the crisis, it proved a less effective predictor for the mature firms. The ratio models would not have helped in the cases of P. J. Carroll, Waterford and, to a degree, Guinness. Ratios would have signalled (weakly) Irish Shipping because of its debt/equity situation. Irish Press carried limited debt but the continuing loss-making situation, allied to loss of market share, was its own signal. The experience of applying the 'downward spiral' model in helping to understand and predict the problems of the mature companies was mixed. Some certainly fitted into the stages of blindness, inaction and faulty action. In this writer's view these included Guinness, Irish Press and Waterford. However, P. J. Carroll and Irish Shipping took off in an explosion of hypergrowth and investment, and much higher risk levels, after a period of modest growth. In both P. J. Carroll, with its diversification strategy, and Guinness, with its diverse interests from retailing to film finance, the core business lost market share as management 'took its eye off the ball'.

The collapse of Irish Shipping resulted in a heavy cost to the taxpayer. Its problems were due to poor internal and external governance, linked to the power and responsibility of the Minister for Finance and the Minister for Communications. The debacle raises questions about the effectiveness of civil servants' supervision and about policies of overall control and efficiency in the state sector. The absence of suitably qualified accounting expertise in the civil service was revealed. The delays at board level in detecting the charter commitments and the further delays and indecision at civil service and government level in taking corrective action were astounding. The treatment of the employees and distancing of itself from responsibility by government were unforgivable. Failure to cover all debts of a state company was dishonourable. At the end of the day the eventual cash cost to the state was not materially different from what it would have been if Irish Shipping had continued in existence. The docility of the greater trade union movement, and particularly those in the state sector, was remarkable.

In state companies the Minister for Finance appoints all board members and nominates the chairman. The lack of continuity in board composition certainly contributed to Irish Shipping's problems. How searching the board was in its supervision of management — given the serious weaknesses in financial control organisation and systems — we will never know. The role and competence of the chairman are perhaps even more crucial in a state-sponsored body than in the private sector. Apart from determining the nature of board input, there is the relationship with the government minister and the civil servants. Perhaps one lesson is that all board appointments should not be made by the Minister for Finance. Outside bodies such as chambers of commerce and the Irish Congress of Trade Unions should be able to nominate board members.

An analytical framework of mismanagement

From the findings on the nature and causes of mismanagement, and drawing on other models, this writer has constructed the following elements of an analytical framework in an attempt to explain the spiral of adolescent and mature firms into corporate financial distress and collapse. The framework starts with the fundamental assumption that if there is a serious defect in the primary structure and competence of the organisation (such as a dominant chief executive, a weak board or an inadequate financial controller) this becomes the springboard for serious mistakes in decision-making. These mistakes can be classified as those of 'omission' and those of 'commission'. The former refer to a state where there is insufficient decision-making (or procrastination) about critical internal and external issues facing the organisation, whereas the latter are those decisions reflecting definite strategies and policies about products, markets, organisation structure, growth rate, investment projects and capital structure. Mistakes of omission are less discernible but more insidious because they take time to show adverse consequences — depending on the organisation's rate of growth and changes in its environment. The outcome to these managerial mistakes will eventually show up in a variety of 'symptoms', such as loss of market share, a succession of negative cash flows, loss of some executives, financial reporting issues and financial ratios.

An illustration is provided by the circumstances of GPA, in the opinion of this writer. The governance and financial control weaknesses highlighted in the case analysis facilitated two critical mistakes of commission — overambitious growth (including the 'big project' in the form of the huge level of financial commitments in aircraft orders) and an unbalanced capital structure. There was insufficient equity and too much secured bank borrowing with onerous repayment terms. There were also mistakes of omission. GPA did not adequately respond to a definite downturn in its industry cycle. Optimism was eventually close to self-delusion. The outcome was that GPA overtraded and left itself vulnerable. The symptoms of these organisational defects were reflected in its growth rate, cash flow profile, multiple bankers, board changes, financial ratios and financial reporting policies. Benchmarking GPA against its primary competitor, ILFC of California, sharpened the analysis of its self-inflicted problems.

Details of this proposed analytical framework of mismanagement are set out in Table 10.4. The analytical framework identifies which elements of mismanagement are critical, important and less common. Not surprisingly, issues such as financial control, systems, reaction to industry changes, overtrading and capital structure are prominent. In summary, the biggest contributors to financial crisis emerge from two ends of the activity spectrum — hyperactivity and near inertia.

Financial reporting issues

The extent of the 'profit reversals' with such heavy losses reported after the financial crisis challenges the trustworthiness of the financial reporting process in many of the companies investigated. The 'big bath' losses included accounting adjustments in respect of assets and liabilities carried in the balance sheet at values which did not reflect an economic reality or prudent accounting policies for some years. Consequently it can be argued that earlier levels of profits had been overstated for some years in some cases. The post-crisis accounting adjustments certainly indicate problematic financial reporting policies in the cases of Kentz and Xtra-vision. The position is arguable but less clear-cut in GPA. The comparison with the benchmark companies pointed to aggressive or optimistic accounting in the four adolescents' crises. In some, the objective was to secure bank facilities. In others, it seemed to be earnings per share with considerations for incentives, dividends and share values.

Table 10.4: Analytical framework of mismanagement

Characteristic	Adolescent	Mature
1. Defects in governance, management structure and competencies		
Board structure	critical	critical
Style of chief executive; chairman and chief executive roles combined	important	important
Top management balance	important	important
Middle management depth	critical	less common
Financial controller who can control	critical	important
Recognition of internal and external pressures and signals	important	critical
Internal understanding of corporate risk profile and decision-making style	important	important
2. Managerial decision mistakes		
Mistakes of omission		
Management accounting and cost analysis systems	critical	less common
Financial control of cash flow and future commitments	critical	important
Management planning, control and information systems	critical	important
Slow or non-response to demand, competition and technology changes	less common	critical
Slow or non-response to economic/ business cycle changes — investment/ capacity timing	less common	critical
Absence of a coherent and balanced strategy	important	important
Mistakes of commission		
Overaggressive business strategy	critical	less common
Growth rate — overtrading	critical	less common
Acquisitions	less common	critical
Diversification	less common	critical
Capital structure	critical	less common
Pricing	critical	less common
Unwarranted optimism — self-delusion	critical	less common

cont.

Table 10.4: Analytical framework of mismanagement *cont.*		
Characteristic	**Adolescent**	**Mature**
3. Symptoms		
Loss of market share	less common	common
Growth rate in relation to return on investment	common	less common
Increasingly risky capital structure	common	less common
Three consecutive years of negative net cash flows	common	less common
Aggressive accounting policies in comparison with industry peers	common	less common
Multiple bankers in comparison with industry peers	common	less common
Loss of financial controller	sometimes	less common
Delays in finalisation/submission of financial statements	common	less common
Deterioration in profitability, debt and cash flow ratios in comparison with industry peers	common	common
Auditors' report and notes — any red flags?	sometimes	less common
Management attributing problems to external events	sometimes	common
Inertia or hyperactivity in response to clear signals of problems	sometimes	common

In this writer's view the role of the auditors can be questioned. In some cases, the auditors took an independent stance and stood up to management in advance of the crisis — Kentz is an example. It can be argued that ineffective internal management accounting and poor external financial reporting and disclosure were causal factors in the financial crisis. They also contributed to the critical delay in recognising and correcting deep problems in some organisations. Optimistic accounting policies masked the underlying financial performance and position, and often helped disguise the increased riskiness of the firm. Poor accounting fed a managerial and board self-delusion about performance and the dubious business strategy being followed. More prudent financial reporting policies would have saved some of the companies from the serious crisis encountered. The more realistic and sobering information thus provided would have assisted the chief executive (if he were willing to accept the information) and the board in strategic decision-making, and would have triggered a more cautious and critical reaction from both bankers and investors. Some financial controllers/directors were in a difficult position between the chief executive and the board. In some instances, they moved to another organisation or took early retirement.

A common problem in the adolescent firms was the unwarranted business optimism which seems to have also infected the trading and cash flow projections and the accounting policies adopted. The high level of 'reported' profitability reinforced a degree of optimism which made it more difficult for the management of these organisations to face economic reality. There is also the question of the competency of stockmarket analysts in understanding the companies, their prospects, and their accounting policies. A similar doubt emerges in respect of the bankers, considering they were still advancing loans when some companies were in an 'at risk' zone.

In this writer's opinion, seven of the nine cases presented, there was clear evidence of material accounting/financial reporting inaccuracies which could affect investor/banker decision-making, and the board supervision/management control of the organisation. These are set out in Table 10.5.

Table 10.5: Financial reporting matters

1.	Goodman International	Off balance sheet commitments; bad/doubtful debt provisions
2.	Kentz Corporation	Valuation of contracts and work in progress/debtors; intangible assets; financial reporting delays; going concern
3.	Xtra-vision	Depreciation policy and restated accounts
4.	GPA	Sale and leaseback profit recognition; depreciation; capitalisation of expenses
5.	P. J. Carroll	Valuation of work in progress; misleading interim accounts; income smoothing; advertising outlays
6.	Waterford Wedgwood	Valuation of work in progress; capitalisation of production expenses; misleading interim accounts
7.	Irish Shipping	Netting loans against assets; disclosure of long-term charters and future obligations/contingencies; going concern concept

Though in recent times there have been inspectors' investigations and reports into alleged corporate irregularities in Ireland, such as in Telecom Éireann, Greencore and Countyglen, none have examined accounting and auditing principles in instances where larger firms have collapsed. This is in contrast to the investigations and commissions established in many other countries when there is a major corporate collapse involving allegations of mismanagement and financial reporting inefficiencies. The only equivalent insight we have is the liquidator's report on Irish Shipping, which contains definite findings and views on the effectiveness of the board, financial control, internal controls and certain financial reporting issues. Revelations about tax evasion and the conduct of auditors were brought out by the Tribunal of Inquiry into the beef-processing industry. This affected the revision of an auditing standard and led to changes in the law under the Finance Act 1995 for auditors and tax advisers.

Inquiries abroad have led to revisions of the regulatory system in company law and accounting and auditing standards, and to self-regulatory codes and their enforcement. There has been the unwelcome publicity for the parties involved and evidence for disciplinary proceedings against accountants, together with sanctions and fines by accountancy bodies.[2] The Ryan Commission's January 1992 findings and recommendations on financial reporting in Ireland,[3] together with the response by the accountancy bodies and government, are inadequate in the light of the findings of this study. It will take a particularly large corporate debacle coinciding with an interested government department before we see illustrations of optimistic or incompetent accounting and auditing exposed.

The rotation of audits every five years and the publication of details and payments for all consultancy work undertaken by the practice associated with the auditors would provide stronger incentives for independence in respect of larger/public concern organisations. The differing interpretations of 'true and fair', between directors and auditors, raise doubts as to whether this term has a useful meaning and role in framing financial statements. The study brought out the ambiguities in certain accounting standards. Examples were the valuation of long-term contracts and work in progress in the engineering/construction industries, the basis of depreciation, recognition of profit in the leasing industry and the 'economic consequences' of poorly framed accounting standards.

Public interest issues

The cases of Kentz and Goodman International highlighted the non-payment of substantial amounts of payroll taxes to state authorities. It was the court action by the Inland Revenue authorities in the UK that proved the 'final straw' in the collapse of the Kentz group. In Goodman International the Beef Tribunal Report illuminated the accounting classification of certain costs as 'haulage' rather than 'wages'; at least £4 million had been paid to employees 'under the counter'. In addition, substantial amounts were paid to employees and management by way of dividends without appropriate deduction of tax. The state only recovered portion of each of these taxation debts. The apparently cavalier approach to honouring statutory obligations in passing over payroll and certain other taxes to the revenue authorities has moral and ethical ramifications — quite apart from the legality issue. There is the position of the corporation and its obligations to the state as a 'corporate' citizen. Payroll taxes, such as PAYE, are deducted on a form of trusteeship basis on behalf of the employees to be passed over to the state.

Unfortunately, in a number of the cases where collapse or financial distress occurred, there were direct, indirect and opportunity costs to the wider public interest. The collapse of GPA resulted in Aer Lingus writing off over £100 million of its balance sheet assets. The liquidation of Irish Shipping by the government was supposed to save the exchequer money — yet post-liquidation payments through guarantees to financial institutions and related matters appear to have cost about £103 million.

The financial distress of both Goodman International and GPA may have resulted in medium- to long-term costs to general economic development. In both cases a large number of international banks were involved. In the GPA debacle there were Irish investor losses of almost $1 billion. With GPA over $6 billion in debt at the end of March 1993 and bank advances to Goodman International of over £500 million, the credit rating of and credit availability to 'international' Irish companies may have suffered for a period. Had GPA successfully completed the share flotation, it would have had the foundation and credibility to support its ambition to become a more widely based global financial services organisation. With the special expertise and institutional contacts developed in its capital markets unit, harnessed to its marketing strengths, GPA had the potential to advance into related activities in securitisation in asset and risk transformation. GPA's collapse had wider economic opportunity costs.

The recommendations of the UK Cadbury Committee's report on corporate governance would be of some benefit in terms of board structure.[4] From the information available, it appears that only Waterford Wedgwood and GPA had an audit committee at the time of the financial crisis. It should be noted that the existence of an audit committee did not prevent the issuance of a misleading interim statement to shareholders or a breakdown in management accounting systems in Waterford Wedgwood.

The business cycle

The twenty-five-year period 1970–94 illustrated the reality of recurring business cycles of varying intensities. GPA and Xtra-vision had not managed the business through a serious recession before. Unbounded optimism continued until the reality of a cash crisis loomed up. Larry Goodman had a long and successful track record. He created his own vulnerability by the Berisford speculation. The Kentz top management also should have been able to cope — most of its management team had plenty of experience in a notoriously cyclical industry. Irish companies with investments abroad automatically become prone to the vagaries of economic movements, interest rates, credit confidence and currency values elsewhere. It can be argued that the real tests of successful entrepreneurs and business managers are their abilities to predict, be prepared for and ride out economic and industry downturns. It is much easier to grow during an economic upturn. Capital investment timing and more prudent financing policies, such as raising additional equity through rights issues allied to a reduction in borrowing and stronger liquidity in the upward time of the economic cycle, paid off.

GPA and Goodman are classic examples of misfortune through mistiming. In GPA's case it missed the market by not seeking a quotation in 1990 when prices and asset values were still buoyant. Goodman misread the effect of the downturn in the US property market on the value of Berisford's equity shares. The extensive property adventures in the USA outweighed the good performance of its sugar-processing activities. The solid and consistently profitable core business of meat processing in Goodman International was almost undermined by the sharp drop in Berisford's share price.

The study provided ample evidence of the difficulties and losses (or twilight zones) of acquisitions. Examples were:

- Goodman's involvement in Berisford
- Xtra-vision's purchases in the UK and USA
- Guinness's many and varied diversifications
- P. J. Carroll's acquisitions in the USA

- Waterford's earlier acquisitions, for example the Smith Group; Wedgwood was worthwhile
- Irish Press's purchase of Southside Newspapers.

A number of the acquisitions not only were loss-making but also absorbed excessive management time and contributed to the weakening of the core business — acquisitions by P. J. Carroll, Guinness and Waterford would be examples.

Recognising and preventing possible financial distress and failure

Society will never completely eliminate corporate financial crisis, distress and failure, because of human folly, greed and managerial weaknesses — allied to the impact of bad luck when an organisation has left itself vulnerable to cyclical downturns and other external environmental influences. However, it is certainly possible to reduce the incidence of financial distress and failure through avoiding the common defects and mistakes which can emerge in adolescent and mature firms or through detecting and understanding the symptoms of the underlying destructive phenomena and taking firm corrective action in time.

Internally, there are the growth, organisational change, financial control, capital structure and optimistic accounting issues which dominate the entrepreneurial adolescent organisation. The banks and investment institutions, as external providers of finance (a critical scarce resource of the growth firm), are generally in a position to play an influencing role in the areas of financial control and capital structure. These institutions depend on reliable information flows, and could in turn ensure, through their covenants, the strengthening of internal planning and control systems. This could curb the entrepreneur's excessive growth ambitions and the resulting risk profile. Indirectly, these financial institutions can play a role in the firm's governance through the board and management structures, particularly if the firm is raising equity. The continuance of the 'entrepreneurial personality' in the dual roles of chairman and chief executive in three of the four adolescent firms studied was a particular signal in such larger organisations — whereas it would be more acceptable in smaller ones. The combination of the foregoing characteristics is also a cue to the culture of the organisation.

If the financial controller and the auditor played more forceful roles in the adoption of conservative accounting policies and of suitable internal and management accounting and control systems, they would provide a partial balance to the optimism and risk-taking propensity of the entrepreneur. They would also support the availability of more dependable performance information and cash flow projections to board members and bankers. Consecutive annual cash flow deficits and volatility or comparative weaknesses in financial ratios are clear signals of a potential crisis. When the adolescent firm's growth rates are moving towards an overtrading profile, and this phenomenon is combined with governance, organisational, capital structure, financial control and accounting information systems weaknesses, then financial crisis is nearly inevitable. The growth rate has become unsustainable for the managerial and financial resources. As this study has shown, the entrepreneurs were unable to manage the transition through adolescence. In particular, the evidence pointed to two periods of risk — early and late adolescence. The former seems to emerge towards the end of the first decade, when the firm achieves some degree of institutional acceptance. This financial and capital market 'benediction' can stimulate unbalanced growth ambitions — as exemplified by Xtra-vision — which can sow the seeds of self-destruction. The period of risk in late adolescence is less definite — from late teens to early thirties, as suggested by GPA and Goodman International. In each organisation, there was an escalation in growth well beyond the previous fast-track record, which, in the absence of an adequate equity base, stretched the financial capacity to breaking point.

In some mature organisations the warning signs are clearly evident for some years, either through either through a declining financial performance when compared with competitors or through losses; this was the case in Guinness, Irish Press and Waterford. The possibility of a crisis in P. J. Carroll was less obvious externally, other than the knowledge that it was diversifying to an enormous extent in relation to the size of the existing core business. The weak board structure, with few independent non-executive directors, was a pointer to the potential for weak strategic control in Guinness, Irish Press and Waterford. The degree of change in board membership was a signal to possible governance defects in Irish Press and Irish Shipping — as it was in GPA also. The 'big project' was apparent externally in P. J. Carroll and Waterford well before the crisis. It did not emerge until quite late in the day in Irish Shipping. In each case the board should have been more alert to the risks. Also, it is perhaps more than coincidental that there was a breakdown in internal management accounting systems in each of these organisations. The relationship between dysfunctional information systems and major new investment projects which are not performing to expectations is an important theme for boards to monitor.

The relevance of the corporate regulatory system

The evidence from some of the case material suggests that a strengthening of the Irish corporate regulatory system is desirable. It could help prevent governance defects, information distortions and breakdowns. Consequently, some of the instances of distress and failure could have been avoided. For example, if Kentz had been forced to file financial statements within the prescribed time limits, its executive directors would have been forced to sign off the financial statements for 1992 a year earlier. This could have forced them to face up to the difficult financial and managerial realities of the organisation's position. Publicity on the filing of the accounts would have alerted the extensive group of unsecured creditors, and possibly the Revenue Commissioners, to the degree of insolvency risk. Earlier action could have lessened the financial losses suffered by creditors. At the time, because of loopholes in the relevant legislation, Goodman International also was able to avoid the filing of financial statements. Again, one might speculate on whether such high levels of borrowings would have been undertaken if financial disclosure, through filing of accounts in the Companies Office, had been a statutory requirement at the time.

The Tribunal of Inquiry into the beef-processing industry and the liquidator's special report for the High Court into Irish Shipping indicated managerial and accounting defects, with questions raised about the role of the auditors. Both of these reports emanated from outside the corporate regulatory system. It is remarkable that there were no official inquiries or inspections, under the Companies Acts, into the reasons for the collapse of any of the other larger public interest organisations, as has taken place in many other countries in similar circumstances. The small number of departmental reports on inspections to date, such as those into Greencore, Telecom Éireann and Countyglen, have tended to focus on specific managerial and board issues and decisions — not accounting and auditing behaviour. It is surprising that the circumstances surrounding the collapse of Kentz, Xtra-vision or GPA, with such losses to stakeholders, did not prompt an investigation. Nor indeed was there any evidence of special regulatory action by the Stock Exchange or the professional accountancy bodies in relation to germane issues in certain of the cases studied. The specific responsibilities and performance obligations of directors, internal accountants and auditors have not been examined.

In view of the foregoing, we must question the overall surveillance and effectiveness of the corporate regulatory system. There has been inadequate review and feedback on its operation and efficiency. The limited evidence available suggests that there are serious flaws in the quality of corporate governance and financial reporting in Ireland. This influences the characteristics of accountability and the efficiency of the financial and capital markets. In the field of financial reporting, Ireland is unique in not having an enforcement agency, such as the Review Board in the UK or the Securities and Exchange Commission in New Zealand. The recommendations of the Ryan Commission or the subsequent Company Law Review Group in this regard[5] have not yet been fully implemented. It is a serious gap in the regulatory framework, particularly in respect of quoted companies on the Stock Exchange and larger private and state sector organisations.

It would be sobering for company directors and the firm's accountant if the financial statements were required to be signed by the chief financial officer for larger and public interest companies and the directors took personal responsibility for all debts if audited financial statements were not filed by the required dates. The evidence suggests that the auditors' responsibility should be widened beyond an independent opinion on the reliability of the financial statements. Auditors should state, in the case of larger organisations, not only whether in their opinion the organisation is operating with efficient internal control systems but also whether its management accounting information and planning systems are appropriate and operating adequately to meet the needs of efficient corporate governance. After all, many audit methodologies include a review of these activities. The cases of Kentz and Irish Shipping provided evidence that the auditors had sounded an internal warning in their written advice to the directors of certain deficiencies in the organisation's control systems.

Bankers, analysts and investment institutions

The efficiency of bankers, stockbroker analysts and institutional investors is critical in avoiding and preventing corporate financial crisis. The evidence suggests that in the entrepreneurial adolescent cases the banks seemed to prove a 'soft touch'. They often made available loans which fed an unsustainable growth rate and greatly increased these organisations' financial risk through an unbalanced capital structure. Also, the banks appeared to monitor and control their advances in a surprisingly relaxed manner — when they became active it was too late in most instances. The cash flow and other information that they already had (or should have had) available raises questions concerning rigour of analysis and decision-making. The scale of lending (in relation to turnover, assets or cash flow) to Goodman

International and Xtra-vision are examples. The evidence from the cases suggests that banks cannot be considered very effective control agents by way of intervention in firms' affairs.

In this writer's opinion the research evidence raises questions about the efficiency of stockbroker analysts, particularly in the entrepreneurial adolescent cases. Apart from apparent weaknesses in appreciating the firms' underlying business dynamics and accounting policies, there seemed to be a surprising degree of optimism, particularly about adolescent firms' prospects and profit forecasts. From time to time, differences in expectations emerged between a company's brokers and others. The institutional shareholders have the expertise and variety of research support to make informed judgments. It is less easy for private investors.

The case material suggests that the institutional equity shareholders seemed to be weak control agents despite their powers in relation to the appointment of directors and the approval of financial statements. There was little evidence of their intervention in matters of board structure, competence and balance, quite apart from other governance issues relating to the strategy and direction of the firm. In this writer's opinion, GPA and P. J. Carroll can be cited as examples. A more active and interventionist role by the fund managers of Irish investment institutions could certainly help prevent instances of self-inflicted corporate financial crisis in the future.

Appendix 1

The Research Sample

Firm	Activity	Age (years)	Turnover/ total assets (£m)	Crisis date
Eleven entrepreneurial adolescent firms				
Bailieboro Co-operative*	Dairy processing	19	75	February 1986
Cambridge Group	Lease and confirming finance	7	93	September 1993
Goodman International	Meat and dairy processing	36	926	August 1990
GPA	Aircraft leasing	17	$6.5bn	June 1992
Kentz Corporation*	Engineering contractors	6(32)	326	January 1994
Memory Computers	Hardware and software developers	14	13	November 1989
PMPA	Motor insurance	17	159	October 1983
Power Corporation	Property developer	19	420	June 1992
Tribune Group	Newspaper publisher	9	9	February 1992
Xtra-vision	Video rental	8	17	December 1990
Yeoman International	Leasing finance	8	330	December 1990
Seven mature firms				
P. J. Carroll	Cigarette manufacturer	166	147	February 1990
Guinness	Brewer	222	906	September 1981
Insurance Corporation of Ireland	General insurance	47[e]	210	April 1985
Irish Press	Newspaper publisher	64	27	June 1995
Irish Shipping	Deep-sea tramping	43	48	November 1984
Merchant Banking	Private bank	20[e]	n/av.	March 1982
Waterford Wedgwood	Crystal glass	42	349	April 1989

* Bailieboro Co-operative and the predecessor to Kentz Corporation — M. F. Kent — were founded much earlier but had been almost dormant until the arrival of Paddy O'Brien (at Bailieboro) and Frank Kent and Gus Kearney (at M. F. Kent) as new young blood.

[e] author's estimate

The above table summarises details of the original eighteen cases investigated. Nine of these were presented in the study while the other nine were omitted because of space constraints.

The research evidence was based on approximately 170 interviews by the author with members of the board and management of the firms investigated and certain benchmark firms. Interviews were also held with some competitors, stockmarket analysts, fund managers with large investment institutions and a small number of bankers (on general distress issues rather than specific cases because of client confidentiality). Most accountants who acted as liquidators and receivers were unwilling to speak about specific companies. Audited financial statements were analysed in all cases. The extent and research quality of the material varied widely from case to case. In some instances internal management reports and board minutes were made available. There was useful and authoritative court or tribunal documentation in the cases of Irish Shipping, Irish Press, Kentz and Goodman International.

In two of the nine cases presented, the chief executive at the time of the crisis was deceased by the time the research was conducted. Of the seven remaining, four were interviewed — which is a tribute to their courage. In all nine cases, board members were interviewed and in six instances, financial controllers were interviewed.

Qualitative methodology underpinned the research.[1] The approach adopted was to test the validity of the information received. The analytical methodology involved the comparison of a distress/failure organisation with a competitor or a broadly similar type of firm. This was not always possible in a small country such as Ireland. Nevertheless, GPA could be compared with ILFC in the USA, Goodman International with Kerry Group, Kentz with Jacobs International, P. J. Carroll with Gallaher, and Irish Press with Independent Newspapers. Apart from matching organisations in order to pinpoint any differences, a comparative analysis of characteristics, themes and patterns within the research sample was undertaken. This 'rolling comparison' generated insights, particularly for the entrepreneurial group.

Many of the issues that featured in the cases presented in this study were repeated in the other organisations that were studied. This was so particularly in the entrepreneurial adolescent cases. For example, in this writer's opinion Cambridge, Yeoman, Power, Bailieboro and PMPA expanded too rapidly, with an insufficient equity base, and overtraded. Cambridge, Yeoman and PMPA made unfortunate acquisitions which depleted their resources — particularly in Yeoman's case. Memory Computers and the Tribune Group were somewhat different. Both started well as young organisations with a narrow product base. They appeared unable to adapt to the next stage to meet customers' needs. Worldwide changes and competition in computer software and technology overtook Memory as it tried to go it alone against the giants in the industry. The Tribune Group, like Irish Press, seemed insufficiently commercial (such as advertising revenue) and marketing orientated. Its circulation declined quite rapidly, but it always seemed to be able to find sponsors (eventually Independent Newspapers) to keep it financially afloat. In this writer's view, it was an example of the 'permanently failing organisation'. In this writer's opinion, the themes of dominant chief executives, ineffective boards of directors, insufficient management depth and organisation structure, weak financial control and deficient management accounting information systems appeared in most of these cases also. Accounting policy issues emerged in Memory Computers, Bailieboro Co-operative, Cambridge, Power and PMPA. In this writer's view, the question of property revaluations, capitalisation of interest and non-consolidation of subsidiaries (with a heavy debt burden) were accounting matters in Power Corporation which reflected weaknesses in financial reporting regulatory standards pertaining to property investment and development companies at the time.

In the mature group sample Insurance Corporation was a significant case because of the public interest issues. Its near £300 million deficit cost the Irish exchequer and Allied Irish Banks (who made the acquisition) heavily. A case against its auditors was settled 'on the steps' for a reported £77 million and was shared between the government and AIB. Like PMPA, the accounting issue was the recognition of liabilities and prudent provisions. Merchant Banking, a small private bank, was of public concern, because depositors lost money. Similar to PMPA and Insurance Corporation there were questions about external regulatory efficiency — quite apart from internal governance and accounting weaknesses. A considerable proportion of its resources appeared to be linked to companies in the property and building activities associated with its dominant shareholder. Thus there was inadequate portfolio diversification for a bank — leaving it with a risky asset base. When the building and property companies collapsed, in this writer's opinion they effectively brought down Merchant Banking with them.

Appendix 2

Outcome to the Financial Crises in the Eighteen Cases

Receiver/liquidator appointed
Cambridge Group
Memory Computers
Irish Press
Irish Shipping
Merchant Banking

Examiner/administrator appointed
Goodman International (partial takeover)
Kentz Corporation (takeover)
Xtra-vision (takeover)
PMPA (takeover)
Insurance Corporation of Ireland (takeover)

Non-statutory financial restructuring
Yeoman International
Power Corporation
Bailieboro Co-operative (takeover)
Tribune Group (partial takeover)
GPA (partial takeover)
Waterford Wedgwood

Other
Guinness (management/board changes, rationalisation)
P. J. Carroll (takeover)

Notes

Chapter 1: Introduction (pp. 1–18)

1. E. J. Webb, D. T. Campbell, R. D. Schwartz and C. Sechrest, *Unobtrusive Measures*, Chicago: Rand McNally 1976, p. 185.
2. *Business & Finance*, 20 April 1989. $10 billion in firm orders and $7 billion in options.
3. See Table 6.18, p. 00.
4. The June 1989 private placing was at $425 a share. The price peaked at $650 in July 1990 (the equivalent of $16.25 if compared to the 1992 IPO prospectus price range of $10.00–12.50).
5. 'Larger institutions to sell GPA as others buy', Market Commentary, *Sunday Business Post*, 14 June 1992.
6. 'GPA may pitch new shares at $25, Directors own £170m shares', *Irish Times*, 17 March 1992, p. 12.
7. 'Ryan misunderstood but bullish, GPA braves sentiment on share price', *Sunday Tribune*, 26 April 1992.
8. 'Market takes the cancellation in its stride', *Financial Times*, 19 June 1992.
9. *Sunday Tribune*, 28 June 1992, p. C8.
10. David Nally, 'GPA shares for sale at $8 each', *Sunday Tribune*, 6 September 1992.
11. Matt Cooper, 'GPA too big to be allowed fail', *Sunday Business Post*, 15 November 1992.
12. A. L. Stinchcombe, 'Social Structure and Organizations', in J. G. March (ed.), *Handbook on Organizations*, Chicago: Rand McNally 1965, pp. 153–93.
13. William Weitzel and Ellen Jonsson, 'Decline in Organizations: A Literature Integration and Extension', *Administrative Science Quarterly* 34 (1989), pp. 91–109.
14. Edward I. Altman, *Corporate Financial Distress*, New York: John Wiley 1983; Donald B. Bibeault, *Corporate Turnaround*, New York: McGraw Hill 1982.
15. James Bettman and Barton Weitz, 'Attributions in the Board Room: Causal Reasoning in Corporate Annual Reports', *Administrative Science Quarterly* 28 (1983), pp. 165–83; Barry Staw, Pamela McKechnie and Sheila Puffer, 'The Justification of Organizational Performance', *Administrative Science Quarterly* 28 (1983), pp. 582–600; Richard D'Aveni and Ian MacMillan, 'Crisis and Content of Managerial Communications: A Study of the Focus of Attention of Top Managers in Surviving and Failing Firms', *Administrative Science Quarterly* 35 (1990), pp. 634–57.
16. Stuart Slatter, *Corporate Recovery*, Harmondsworth: Penguin 1984, pp. 61–76.
17. Data kindly provided to the author by Dun & Bradstreet, Dublin.
18. Ibid.
19. Ibid.

20. This strike-off rate suggests these companies were not trading nor were they births in the corporate activity sense. The number of company 'deaths' primarily through strike-offs from the companies register were: 8,975 in 1990, 6,127 in 1992 and 13,815 in 1993.
21. Data kindly provided to the author by Dun & Bradstreet, Dublin.
22. Altman, *Corporate Financial Distress*, pp. 40–41.
23. P. Colbert and C. McCarthy, 'The Irish Stock Exchange: Company Quotations During the Period 1950–1979', *Irish Business and Administrative Research* 2, 2 (October 1980), pp. 3–9.
24. Frank Fitzgibbon, *Sunday Tribune*, 13 March 1994, p. C6.
25. Neil Fligstein, *The Transformation of Corporate Control*, Cambridge, Mass.: Harvard University Press 1990, pp. 226–58.
26. R. A. Brealey and S. C. Myers, *Principles of Corporate Finance*, 3rd edn, New York: McGraw Hill 1981, Chapter 33.
27. See for example, John Stanley, 'The rise and fall of Barrow Milling', *Irish Times*, 4 August 1984, p. 20.
28. Frank Fitzgibbon, *Sunday Tribune*, 13 March 1994, p. C6.
29. Ivan Fallon, *The Player*, London: Hodder & Stoughton 1994.
30. Kieran Kennedy, Thomas Giblin and Deirdre McHugh, *The Economic Development of Ireland in the Twentieth Century*, London: Science Paperbacks 1988, p. 252.
31. Lars Mjøset, *The Irish Economy in a Comparative Institutional Perspective*, Dublin: National Economic and Social Council 1992.
32. R. Kinsella, W. Clarke, D. J. Storey, D. Mulvenna and D. Coyne, *Fast-growth Small Firms: An Irish Perspective*, Dublin: Irish Management Institute 1994.
33. *Survey of Corporate Insolvencies*, Dublin: Institute of Chartered Accountants in Ireland 1996.
34. Edward I. Altman, 'The Success of Business Failure Prediction Models: An International Survey', *Journal of Banking and Finance* 8 (1984), p. 175.
35. Aileen O'Toole, *The Pacesetters*, Dublin: Gill & Macmillan 1987.
36. Thomas Peters and Robert Waterman, *In Search of Excellence: Lessons from America's Best-Run Companies*, New York: Harper and Row 1982.
37. See Philip Beresford and Chris Blackhurst, 'Fallen Idols', *Sunday Times*, 4 March 1990.
38. Tom Bower, *The Final Verdict*, London: HarperCollins 1995.
39. Atlantic Computers plc, Atlantic Computer Systems plc, *Report of the Inspectors appointed by the Department of Trade and Industry*, London: HMSO 1994.
40. 'Not enough fingers to plug the dyke', *Financial Times*, 15 May 1992, p. 22.
41. Joni J. Young, 'Getting the Accounting "Right": Accounting and the Savings and Loan Crisis', *Accounting Organisations and Society* 1, 1 (1995), pp. 55–80.
42. B. D. Merino and S. Y. Kenny, 'Auditor Liability and Culpability in the Savings and Loan Industry', *Critical Perspectives in Accounting* 5, 2 (1994), pp. 179–94.
43. Paul Barry, *The Rise and Fall of Alan Bond*, London: Doubleday 1990.
44. Alfred D. Chandler, *Strategy and Structure: Chapters in the History of the American Industrial Enterprise*, Cambridge, Mass.: The MIT Press 1962.

45. Ibid., pp. 52, 373.
46. AIB had bad debt provisions of £174 million, £188 million and £154 million in the three years to end 1993. Bank of Ireland had a similar experience: its 1993 provision was £153 million. The bad debts were significantly larger than the net profits for several years.
47. Ivan Fallon, 'Smith takes City conflicts above the line', and Kirstie Hamilton and Jeff Randall, 'Swiss Bank rattled by its outspoken analyst', *Sunday Times*, 16 August 1992, Business, pp. 2–3; J. Cassidy, J. Randall and K. Hamilton, 'Revealed: how the top firms massage their profits', *Sunday Times*, 16 August 1992, Business, pp. 1–3; see also Terry Smith, *Accounting for Growth*, London: Century Business 1992.
48. J. F. Weston and T. E. Copeland, *Managerial Finance*, 8th edn, New York: CBS Publishing 1986.
49. Donald C. Hambrick and Richard A. D'Aveni, 'Large Corporate Failures as Downward Spirals', *Administrative Science Quarterly* 33 (1988), pp. 1–23; Weitzel and Jonsson, 'Decline in Organizations', pp. 91–109; Kevin Keasey and Robert Watson, 'Financial Distress Prediction Models: A Review of their Usefulness', *British Journal of Management* 2 (1991), pp. 89–102.
50. Weitzel and Jonsson, 'Decline in Organisations', p. 91.
51. Richard A. Smith, *Corporations in Crisis*, New York: Anchor Books, Doubleday 1966, Preface.

Chapter 2: Causes of Corporate Financial Distress and Failure (pp. 19–48)

1. Sir Kenneth Cork, *Cork on Cork*, London: Macmillan 1988, pp. 37–8.
2. J. E. Walter, 'The Determination of Technical Solvency', *Journal of Business*, January 1957, pp. 30–43; W. H. Beaver, 'Financial Ratios as Predictors of Failure', *Journal of Accounting Research. Empirical Research in Accounting: Selected Studies* 4 (1966), pp. 71–111.
3. Donald C. Hambrick and Richard A. D'Aveni, 'Large Corporate Failures as Downward Spirals', *Administrative Science Quarterly* 33 (1988), pp. 1–23.
4. William Weitzel and Ellen Jonsson, 'Decline in Organizations: A Literature Integration and Extension', *Administrative Science Quarterly* 34 (1989), pp. 91–109.
5. Kevin Keasey and Robert Watson, 'Non-financial Symptoms and the Prediction of Small Company Failure: A Test of Argenti's Hypothesis', *Journal of Business Finance and Accounting* 14, 3 (1987), pp. 335–54.
6. Michael T. Hannan and John Freeman, *Organizational Ecology*, Cambridge, Mass.: Harvard University Press 1989.
7. J. Bruderl and R. Schussler, 'Organizational Mortality: The Liabilities of Newness and Adolescence', *Administrative Science Quarterly* 35 (1990), pp. 530–47; A. L. Stinchcombe, 'Social Structure and Organizations', in J. G. March (ed.), *Handbook on Organizations*, Chicago: Rand McNally 1965, pp. 153–93; H. Aldrich and E. R. Auster, 'Even Dwarfs Started Small: Liabilities of Age and Size and their Strategic Implications', *Research in Organizational Behaviour* 8 (1986), pp. 165–98.

8. Richard A. Smith, *Corporations in Crisis*, New York: Anchor Books, Doubleday 1966.
9. Joel E. Ross and Michael J. Kami, *Corporate Management in Crisis: Why the Mighty Fall*, New Jersey: Prentice Hall 1973.
10. John Argenti, *Corporate Collapse*, Maidenhead: McGraw Hill 1976; John Argenti, 'Company Failure — Long Range Prediction Not Enough', *Accountancy*, August 1977, pp. 46–52; John Argenti, 'Predicting Corporate Failure', *Accountants' Digest* No. 138, London: ICAEW Summer 1983.
11. Argenti, 'Predicting Corporate Failure', p. 18.
12. Ibid.
13. Hambrick and D'Aveni, 'Large Corporate Failures as Downward Spirals', pp. 1–23.
14. Richard A. D'Aveni, 'The Aftermath of Organizational Decline: A Longitudinal Study of the Strategic and Managerial Characteristics of Declining Firms', *Academy of Management Journal* 32, 3 (1989), pp. 577–605.
15. Peter McKiernan, *Strategies of Growth: Maturity, Recovery and Internationalisation*, London: Routledge 1992, p. 73.
16. Stuart Slatter, *Corporate Recovery*, Harmondsworth: Penguin 1984.
17. Stuart Slatter, *Gambling on Growth*, London: John Wiley & Sons 1992, pp. 237–70.
18. When giving a lecture in Glasgow in 1991 on the subject, Robertson was engaged on his seventh corporate rescue in a decade.
19. Sir Lewis Robertson, 'Company doctor offers prescription', *Financial Times*, 18 December 1991, p. 12.
20. Bill Houston, *Avoiding Adversity*, London: David & Charles 1989.
21. Early in the research the author interviewed a number of Irish bankers and accountants.
22. Ray Jackson and John Crawford, *Why Businesses Fail*, Dublin: KPMG Stokes Kennedy Crowley 1992.
23. Geoffrey Mills, *On the Board*, London: George Allen & Unwin 1985.
24. The leading English economist Alfred Marshall compared a firm to a tree in the forest.
25. K. E. Boulding, *The Reconstruction of Economics*, New York: Wiley 1950.
26. E. T. Penrose, 'Biological Analogies in the Theory of the Firm', *American Economic Review* 42 (1952), pp. 804–19.
27. John R. Kimberly and Robert H. Miles, *The Organizational Life Cycle*, San Francisco: Jossey-Bass 1980; John Freeman, 'Organizational Life Cycles and Natural Selection Processes', *Research in Organizational Behaviour* 4 (1982), pp. 1–32.
28. Robert E. Quinn and Kim Cameron, 'Organizational Life Cycles and Shifting Criteria of Effectiveness: Some Preliminary Evidence', *Management Science* 29, 1 (1983), pp. 35–51.
29. Danny Miller and Peter Friesen, 'Successful and Unsuccessful Phases of the Corporate Life Cycle', *Organization Studies* 4, 4 (1983), pp. 339–56, and also

'A Longitudinal Study of the Corporate Life Cycle', *Management Science*, 30, 10 (1984), pp. 1161–83.
30. Gordon L. Lippitt and Warren H. Schmidt, 'Crises in a Developing Organization', *Harvard Business Review*, November–December 1967, pp. 48–58; Larry E. Greiner, 'Evolution and Revolution as Organizations Grow', *Harvard Business Review*, July–August 1972, pp. 37–46.
31. Eric G. Flamholtz, *Growing Pains*, San Francisco: Jossey-Bass 1990.
32. Ibid., pp. 13–14.
33. A. M. Pettigrew, 'On Studying Organizational Cultures', *Administrative Science Quarterly* 24 (1979), pp. 570–81.
34. Linda Smircich, 'Concepts of Culture and Organizational Analysis', *Administrative Science Quarterly* 28 (1983), pp. 339–58.
35. John P. Kotter and James L. Heskett, *Corporate Culture and Performance*, New York: The Free Press, Macmillan 1992.
36. Ibid., p. 8.
37. Greiner, 'Evolution and Revolution', p. 42.
38. Ichak Adizes, 'Organizational Passages — Diagnosing and Treating Lifecycle Problems of Organizations', *Organizational Dynamics*, Summer 1979, pp. 3–25; Ichak Adizes, 'Mismanagement Styles', *California Management Review*, 19, 2 (1976), pp. 5–20.
39. Robert F. Hartley, *Management Mistakes and Successes*, 3rd edn, New York: John Wiley & Sons 1991, pp. 298–311.
40. David Thomas, *Alan Sugar: The Amstrad Story*, London: Century 1990.
41. Charles Raw, *Slater Walker: An Investigation of a Financial Phenomenon*, London: Andre Deutsch 1977.
42. Jim Slater, *Return to Go: My Autobiography*, London: Weidenfeld & Nicholson 1977.
43. Ibid., pp. 256–7.
44. Ibid., p. 260.
45. Peter Drucker, *Management*, New York: Harper and Row 1973, p. 772.
46. J. Weston and E. Brigham, *Managerial Finance*, London: Holt Rinehart and Winston 1979.
47. Donald K. Clifford, 'Growth Pains of the Threshold Company', *Harvard Business Review*, September–October 1973, pp. 143–54.
48. Ibid., pp. 153–4.
49. Flamholtz, *Growing Pains*, pp. 67–8.
50. Peter Lorange and Robert T. Nelson, 'How to Recognize — and Avoid — Organizational Decline', *Sloan Management Review*, Spring 1987, pp. 41–7.
51. Ibid.
52. Robert Heller, *The Fate of IBM*, London: Little, Brown & Co. 1994.
53. Thomas J. Watson Jr and Peter Petre, *Father, Son & Co.: My Life at IBM and Beyond*, New York: Bantam Press 1990.
54. Ibid.
55. Michael Edwardes, *Back from the Brink*, London: Pan Books 1984.
56. Lee Iacocca with William Novak, *Iacocca: An Autobiography*, New York: Bantam Books 1986.

57. Watson and Petre, *Father, Son & Co.*, p. 342.
58. Derek F. Channon, *The Strategy and Structure of British Enterprise*, London: Macmillan 1973.
59. Ibid.; Alfred D. Chandler, *Strategy and Structure: Chapters in the History of the American Industrial Enterprise*, Cambridge, Mass.: The MIT Press 1962.
60. Sean Brophy, *The Strategic Management of Irish Enterprise 1934–1984*, Dublin: Smurfit Publications 1985.
61. R. Belfield, C. Hird and S. Kelly, *Murdoch: The Decline of an Empire*, London: Macdonald 1992.
62. 'Rupert Murdoch: down and up in Beverly Hills', *Financial Times*, 27 August 1992, p. 23.
63. Ibid.
64. Ibid.
65. Hambrick and D'Aveni, 'Large Corporate Failures as Downward Spirals', pp. 13–14.
66. Ibid.
67. Weitzel and Jonsson, 'Decline in Organizations', p. 97.
68. Paul McGrath, 'Organisational Decline in the Public Service', *Administration* 41, 4, (1993/94), pp. 362–84.
69. Danny Miller, 'Common Syndromes of Business Failure', *Business Horizons*, November 1977, pp. 43–53.
70. Danny Miller, *The Icarus Paradox*, New York: Harper Business 1990.
71. J. Cassidy, J. Randall and K. Hamilton, 'Revealed: how the top firms massage their profits', *Sunday Times*, 16 August 1992, Business, pp. 1–3.
72. R. A. Brealey and S. C. Myers, *Principles of Corporate Finance*, 3rd edn, New York: McGraw Hill 1981.
73. D. Gwilliam and T. Russell, 'Polly Peck: Where Were The Analysts?', *Accountancy*, January 1992, pp. 25–6.
74. T. Pijper, *Creative Accounting*, London: Macmillan 1993, Chapter 8.
75. See for example ibid.; K. M. Naser, *Creative Financial Accounting*, Hemel Hempstead: Prentice Hall 1993; Katherine Schipper, 'Earnings Management', *Accounting Horizons*, December 1989, pp. 91–102; O. D. Moses, 'Income Smoothing and Incentives', *The Accounting Review*, April 1987, pp. 358–77; M. Pincus and C. Wasley, 'The Incidence of Accounting Changes and Characteristics of Firms Making Accounting Changes', *Accounting Horizons*, June 1994, pp. 1–24.
76. See George Foster, *Financial Statement Analysis*, 2nd edn, New Jersey: Prentice Hall 1986, Chapters 3 and 4.
77. See ibid. and also Bill Rees, *Financial Analysis*, 2nd edn, Hemel Hempstead: Prentice Hall 1995, Chapters 3 and 4.
78. Much of the research has been excellently summarised by Foster, *Financial Statement Analysis*, Chapters 15 and 16; Edward I. Altman, *Corporate Financial Distress*, New York: John Wiley 1983; *Journal of Banking and Finance* 8, 2 (1984), special issue on company and country risk models, edited by Edward I. Altman, especially Edward I. Altman, 'The Success of Business Failure

Prediction Models: An International Survey', pp. 171–98; Rees, *Financial Analysis*, pp. 291–325.
79. James A. Ohlson, 'Financial Ratios and the Probabilistic Prediction of Bankruptcy', in Ray Ball and S. P. Kothari (eds.), *Financial Statement Analysis*, New York: McGraw Hill 1994, pp. 512–34.
80. Richard Taffler, 'Empirical Models for the Monitoring of UK Corporations', *Journal of Banking and Finance* 8 (1984), pp. 199–228.
81. D. A. J. Marais, *A Method of Quantifying Companies' Relative Financial Strength*, Bank of England Discussion Paper No. 4, 1979.
82. John Robertson, 'Company Failure', *Management Accounting*, November 1983, pp. 24–8; John Robertson, 'Laker Airways: Could the Collapse Have Been Foreseen?', *Management Accounting*, June 1984, pp. 28–31.
83. Edward Cahill, 'Irish Listed Company Failure, Financial Ratios, Accounts and Auditors' Opinions', *Irish Business and Administrative Research* 3, 1 (1981), pp. 19–31; Edward Cahill, 'Corporate Financial Distress: A Problem of Our Times', *Accountancy Ireland* 14, 1 (February 1982).
84. Peter Clarke, 'An Empirical Analysis of Useful Financial Ratios: An Explanatory Study of Irish Public Quoted Companies', *Irish Business and Administrative Research* 11 (1990), pp. 40–52.
85. M. E. Zmijewski, 'Methodological Issues Related to the Estimation of Financial Distress Prediction Models', *Journal of Accounting Research. Supplement: Studies on Current Econometric Issues in Accounting Research*, 1984, pp. 59–82.
86. See F. L. Jones, 'Current Techniques in Bankruptcy Prediction', *Journal of Accounting Literature* 6 (1987), pp. 131–64; Kevin Keasey and Robert Watson, 'Financial Distress Prediction Models: A Review of their Usefulness', *British Journal of Management* 2 (1991), pp. 89–102.
87. H. Koh and L. N. Killough, 'The Use of Multiple Discriminant Analysis in the Assessment of the Going Concern Status of an Audit Client', *Journal of Business Finance and Accounting* 17, 2 (1990), pp. 179–92.
88. *Journal of Banking and Finance* 8, 2 (1984), special issue.
89. Keasey and Watson, 'Non-financial Symptoms', pp. 335–54; Kevin Keasey and Robert Watson, 'The Non-submission of Accounts and Small Company Failure Prediction', *Accounting and Business Research* 73 (1988), pp. 47–54.
90. J. H. von Stein and W. Ziegler, 'The Prognosis and Surveillance of Risks from Commercial Credit Borrowers', *Journal of Banking and Finance* 8, 2 (1984), pp. 249–68.
91. A. F. Abidali and F. Harris, 'A Methodology for Predicting Company Failure in the Construction Industry', *Construction Management and Economics* 13 (1995), pp. 189–96; K. C. Chen and C. J. Lee, 'Financial Ratios and Corporate Endurance: A Case Study of the Oil and Gas Industry', *Contemporary Accounting Research* 9, 2 (1993), pp. 667–94.
92. J. A. Gentry, P. N. Newbould and D. Whitford, 'Funds Flow Components, Financial Ratios, and Bankruptcy', *Journal of Business Finance and Accounting* 14, 2 (1987), pp. 595–606; A. Aziz and G. H. Lawson, 'Cash Flow Reporting and

Financial Distress Models: Testing of Hypotheses', *Financial Management* 18 (1989), pp. 55–66.
93. Keasey and Watson, 'Financial Distress Prediction Models', pp. 89–102.

Chapter 3: Goodman International: Overambitious Expansion (pp. 48–93)

1. Jeff Randall, 'Goodman turns up the heat', *Sunday Times*, 27 May 1990.
2. Ibid.
3. Ibid.
4. Ibid.
5. *Irish Times*, 18 August 1990.
6. Ibid.
7. Ibid., 20 August 1990.
8. *Irish Independent*, 24 August 1990.
9. Ibid.
10. Beef Tribunal evidence, L. Goodman, Transcript Book 180A, 10 March 1993, pp. 86–7.
11. Ibid.
12. Fintan O'Toole, *Meanwhile Back at the Ranch: The Politics of Irish Beef*, London: Vintage Books 1995, p. 27.
13. Fintan O'Toole (ibid., p. 25) described the production side of the industry as follows: 'It is a rough, frantic and sometimes brutal business, a world of blood and bone and knives and stench. In the words of one contractor who worked exclusively for Goodman: "You need to be a half-savage to do it. It's not women's knickers we're making or ladies' perfume."'
14. Beef Tribunal evidence, L. Goodman, Transcript Book 179A, 9 March 1993, pp. 64–5.
15. Ibid.
16. Ibid., pp. 71–3.
17. Examples were Denny's (pork), Duffy's (convenience meats), the activities of the Cork Marts/IMP Group (beef) and the Ballyfree and Grove Farm poultry/white meat operations in Ireland. There were a number of other acquisitions of dairies and smaller meat activities in Ireland and the UK.
18. Chairman's statement, Kerry Co-operative Creameries, *Annual Report 1985*, p. 3.
19. 'Business Review', Kerry Group plc, *Annual Report 1986*, p. 4.
20. Clover's annual operating profit margin, before interest charges, ranged between 1.2% and 1.6%, which was about one-third of the margin being achieved by the Goodman organisation.
21. Making deductions from Beef Tribunal data, it seems that Goodman International's pre-tax profits were about £6 million in 1983, £20 million in 1986 and £24 million in 1987. They jumped to £33 million in 1988, partially on the basis of the high-margin Iraqi contracts.
22. According to the annual reports of 1989 and 1990.
23. Beef Tribunal evidence, B. Britton, Transcript Book 176B, 4 March 1993, p. 88.

24. Beef Tribunal evidence, L. Goodman, Transcript Book 179A, 9 March 1993, p. 67.
25. Ibid.
26. Beef Tribunal evidence, B. Britton, Transcript Book 178B, 8 March 1993, p. 80.
27. Beef Tribunal evidence, L. Goodman, Transcript Book 179B, 9 March 1993, p. 117.
28. Ibid., pp. 125–6.
29. Veronica Guerin, 'The farmer, the baron, the broker and the priest', *Sunday Business Post*, 26 July 1992.
30. Beef Tribunal evidence, B. Britton, Transcript Book 176B, 4 March 1993, p. 92.
31. Ibid., pp. 88–9.
32. Ibid., p. 94.
33. Niall O'Carroll was also president of the Institute of Chartered Accountants in Ireland.
34. Beef Tribunal evidence, N. O'Carroll, Transcript Book 116B, 15 September 1992, p. 64.
35. Ibid.
36. Beef Tribunal evidence, B. Britton, Transcript Book 176B, 4 March 1993, p. 104.
37. Ibid.
38. Ibid.
39. Beef Tribunal evidence, L. Goodman, Transcript Book 179A, 9 March 1993, p. 73.
40. Beef Tribunal evidence, L. Goodman, Transcript Book 181A, 11 March 1993, pp. 71–2.
41. Beef Tribunal evidence, Mr Mooney, Transcript Book, 20 January 1993.
42. *Report of the Tribunal of Inquiry into the Beef Processing Industry*, Dublin: Stationery Office 1994, p. 231.
43. Ibid., Chapter 7.
44. Ten banks were owed £255 million. Commerzbank, London; Credit Agricole; AMRO, London; and Lloyds, London were owed £35 million, £33 million, £31 million and £28 million. Bank of Ireland and Ulster Bank were reported to have advances of £21 million and £18 million according to *Business & Finance*, 13 September 1990.
45. Beef Tribunal evidence, L. Goodman, Transcript Book 179B, 9 March 1993, pp. 105–6.
46. Beef Tribunal evidence, B. Britton, Transcript Book 178A, 8 March 1993, p. 24.
47. Vincent Browne, *Magill,* June 1989, p. 4.
48. Beef Tribunal evidence, 20 January 1993.
49. Beef Tribunal evidence, P. Fitzpatrick, Transcript Book 156B, 20 January 1993, pp. 58–9.
50. Beef Tribunal evidence, L. Goodman, Transcript Book 181A, 11 March 1993, pp. 66–7.

51. Ibid., p. 67.
52. *Report of the Tribunal of Inquiry into the Beef Processing Industry*, pp. 185–7.
53. *Business & Finance*, 30 August 1990.
54. Ken Peasnell and R. A. Yaansah, *Off Balance Sheet Financing*, London: ACCA Research Report 1988.
55. *Report of the Tribunal of Inquiry into the Beef Processing Industry*, p. 332.
56. Ibid., pp. 334–5.
57. Ibid., p. 315.
58. Ibid., p. 316.
59. Ibid.
60. Ibid., p. 327.
61. The Tribunal Report states that Niall O'Carroll did not receive a written reply to his letters of May and September 1987 to the company seeking confirmation to this outlining of the position. Ibid., p. 325.
62. Ibid., p. 327.
63. Ibid., p. 330.
64. Ibid., p. 329.
65. Ibid., p. 330.
66. Ibid., pp. 330–46.
67. Ibid., pp. 330–31.
68. Ibid., p. 336.
69. See P. Bougen, E. Cahill and J. Young, 'What the Papers Said: The Irish Accountant and Tax Evasion' (forthcoming).

Chapter 4: Kentz Corporation and the Failed Management Buyout (pp. 94–130)

1. Aileen O'Toole, *The Pacesetters*, Dublin: Gill & Macmillan 1987.
2. It was also leading a flagship £8 million urban renewal scheme in Clonmel.
3. *Business & Finance*, 8 April 1993.
4. The court action by the Inland Revenue authorities in the UK and certain creditors left the Irish group no alternative but to seek the appointment of a receiver there and a receiver or an examiner in Ireland. Also, the fact that some of its European activities went into liquidation before and after Christmas heralded a deeper financial crisis because of the extensive intercompany debt and guarantees in the group.
5. Excluding 'one-off' £1.5 million legal and other fees associated with the restructuring. *Irish Times*, 11 January 1995.
6. Report to High Court under Section 18 of the Companies (Amendment) Act 1990 by Hugh Cooney, Examiner, February 1994.
7. O'Toole, *The Pacesetters*, p. 83.
8. Ibid.
9. *Irish Times*, 21 January 1994.
10. Chairman's statement, Jacobs Engineering Inc., *Annual Report 1983*.
11. Joseph J. Jacobs, *The Anatomy of an Entrepreneur*, London: MacDonald 1991.

12. 'Kentz chased losses from one contract to another', *Sunday Business Post*, 23 January 1994.
13. According to the *Irish Times*, 21 January 1994.
14. AIB Affidavit to High Court objecting to Kentz board request for an examiner, January 1994.
15. Ibid.
16. Report to High Court under Section 18 of the Companies (Amendment) Act 1990 by Hugh Cooney, Examiner, February 1994.
17. Affidavit to High Court by Michael Campbell requesting the appointment of an examiner on behalf of the board, January 1994.
18. Report to High Court under Section 18 of the Companies (Amendment) Act 1990 by Hugh Cooney, Examiner, February 1994.
19. *Irish Independent*, 27 January 1994.
20. AIB Affidavit to High Court objecting to Kentz board request for an examiner, January 1994.
21. Report to High Court under Section 18 of the Companies (Amendment) Act 1990 by Hugh Cooney, Examiner, February 1994.
22. *Irish Independent*, 27 January 1994.
23. See Edward Cahill, 'Corporate Governance and Accountability: The Information Gap in Ireland', *Ireland: A Journal of History and Society*, pp. 91–102 1, 1 (1995).
24. Ibid.
25. Letter of 21 September 1993 from KPMG Stokes Kennedy Crowley to Kentz according to *Irish Independent*, 27 January 1994: 'SKC warned Kentz about "unacceptable level of risk"'.
26. Ibid.
27. 'Evidence reveals prior warnings to Kentz', *Sunday Independent*, 23 January 1994.
28. *Irish Independent*, 27 January 1994.
29. According to information in the 'Notes' to the audited financial statements included in Michael Campbell's January 1994 petition to the High Court.
30. In their survey of 142 sets of financial statements of Irish listed public companies and commercial state-sponsored bodies, Brennan, O'Brien and Pierce found only one audit opinion which was qualified due to a 'fundamental uncertainty'. See Niamh Brennan, Frank O'Brien and Aileen Pierce, *A Survey of Irish Published Accounts*, 2nd edn, Dublin: Oak Tree Press 1992.
31. *Report of the (Cadbury) Committee on the Financial Aspects of Corporate Governance*, London: Gee December 1992, p. 42.
32. Brennan, O'Brien and Pierce, *A Survey of Irish Published Accounts*, pp. 64–8.
33. M. Davies, R. Paterson and A. Wilson, *UK GAAP*, 4th edn, London: Macmillan and Ernst & Young 1994, p. 734.
34. A. F. Abidali and F. Harris, 'A Methodology for Predicting Failure in the Construction Industry', *Construction Management and Economics* 13 (1995), pp. 189–96.

Chapter 5: Xtra-vision: A Stock Exchange Shooting Star (pp. 131–56)

1. Michael C. Thomsett, *The Expansion Trap*, New York: American Management Association 1990, pp. 27–8.
2. Jim Cashman, 'Battle of the videos', *Irish Independent*, 14 June 1990.
3. Xtra-vision plc, Rights Issue (at 80p per share), Underwritten by DCC Corporate Finance, 25 October 1989.
4. 'Prospects', Xtra-vision, Preliminary Statement for year ended 30 January 1990, 4 May 1990.
5. *Irish Independent*, 31 October 1990.
6. Letter dated 6 December 1990 to Xtra-vision shareholders from Xtra-vision board in connection with Cambridge offer.
7. Xtra-vision plc, Rights Issue Document, 25 October 1989, p. 8.
8. Unfortunately Windmill Lane Studios entered examinership almost a year later but subsequently was successfully restructured.
9. These were Allied Irish Banks, Bank of Ireland, Algemene Bank Nederland (Ireland), Irish Intercontinental Bank, Woodchester Investment Bank, Bank of Nova Scotia and National Westminster Bank.
10. Matt Cooper, 'Xtra-vision boss goes "for the kill"', *Sunday Business Post*, 30 June 1991.
11. This was the level of bank debt at 16 November 1990 according to the documentation.
12. Recommended Offer by NCB Stockbrokers on behalf of Cambridge Group plc for Xtra-vision plc, 6 December 1990, p. 5.
13. Xtra-vision plc, Rights Issue Document, 31 May 1990, p. 11.
14. Bill Murdoch, 'Cambridge expects to double profits over three years', *Irish Times*, 9 July 1991.
15. *Irish Independent*, 23 June 1994, Business, p. 1.
16. David Owen, 'Video hire group's depreciation puzzle', *Financial Times*, 11 October 1990.
17. *Investor's Chronicle*, 30 November 1990.
18. Statement of Standard Accounting Practice No. 12, *Accounting for Depreciation*, London: Accounting Standards Committee, 1987.
19. *Sunday Tribune*, 27 March 1994, C7.
20. Davy Stockbrokers indicated in a research note of 7 May 1991 that Xtra-vision was now writing off 80% of the cost of tapes in Ireland and the UK in the year of purchase. (Tapes in the USA were to be written down over thirty months to their residual value.)
21. Xtra-vision, *Annual Report 1991*, p. 17.
22. *Irish Independent*, 19 March 1994, p. 15.
23. Davy Equity Research, Xtra-vision, 7 May 1991.
24. Davy Equity Research, Xtra-vision, 6 December 1991.
25. Xtra-vision plc, Placing Document, 28 April 1989, pp. 5 and 11.
26. Xtra-vision plc, Rights Issue Document, 25 October 1989, p. 8.
27. *Irish Times*, 25 May 1990.

28. Damien Kiberd, 'Xtra-vision profit forecast to investors over twice likely level', *Sunday Business Post*, 5 August 1990.

Chapter 6: GPA: A Case Study in Market Share Fixation (pp. 157–221)

1. In the banking sector, BCCI in the UK and Credit Lyonnais in France may have been larger.
2. GPA Group plc, Irish and International Offer Document (restructuring), 22 September 1993, p. 37.
3. Ibid., p. 105.
4. Report of directors and financial statements 31 March 1992, GPA, *Annual Report and Accounts 1992*.
5. During the course of the research interviews with this author.
6. 'Troubleshooter under fire', *Sunday Tribune*, 14 November 1993, C2; 'Mr Troubleshooter', *Business & Finance*, 18 November 1993, pp. 27–8.
7. GPA, *Annual Report and Accounts 1992*, Note 23, p. 52. This commitment was based on 1992 prices. Adjusting for price escalation would bring it to about $10.3 billion. In addition, at March 1992 GPA had options to purchase aircraft valued at over $8 billion between 1992 and 2000.
8. IPO Prospectus, 9 June 1992, p. 37.
9. GPA charged $391 million to its 'restructuring costs' of $652 million in 1993. Of this sum, $231 million was for the write-off of 'predelivery payments' and $160 million was for 'manufacturer credits and other costs'.
10. Aileen O'Toole, *The Pacesetters*, Dublin: Gill & Macmillan 1987, pp. 34–55.
11. Ibid. pp. 51–2.
12. Ibid.
13. As part of the research process, this writer interviewed a number of directors and senior management. As a group they were much more impressive than those in most other entrepreneurial firms studied. Some were almost zealous in their belief in GPA strategy and policies, and would argue vigorously against views expressed by this writer in earlier drafts. Of all the firms studied they generally seemed to be a closely knit group.
14. *Airfinance Journal*, May 1992, p. 12.
15. *GPA Group plc — The World's Leading Aircraft Lessor*, James C. Halstead, European Equity Research, Salomon Brothers, London, 2 May 1990.
16. Mark Snelling, 'Will the banks remain faithful?', *Airfinance Journal*, November 1993, pp. 42–6.
17. Alastair Ross Goobey, *Bricks and Mortals*, London: Century Business, Random House 1992.
18. *GPA Group Ltd: A Leader in Worldwide Aircraft Leasing*, James C. Halstead and Julius Maldutis, Salomon Brothers, New York, February 1989.
19. British Airways plc, *Annual Report and Accounts 1989/90*, p. 60.
20. See John Bailey and David Learmount, 'The West Coast lessors', *Flight International*, 3 September 1988, pp. 95–8; Jacqueline Gallagher, 'Off balance sheet risks', *Airline Business*, June 1988, pp. 36–7; 'ILFC scoops

up Dragonair A320 deal', *Aerfinance Journal*, January 1992, p. 12; Chris Kjelgaard, 'ILFC: where next?', *Aerfinance Journal*, February 1993, pp. 4–8.
21. *International Lease Finance Corporation (ILFC) — An Extraordinary Company*, Salomon Brothers Inc. Stock Research, New York, 11 March 1986.
22. Ibid., p. 5.
23. Form 10-K, ILFC, 1986 and 1987, Securities and Exchange Commission, Washington DC.
24. Bailey and Learmount, 'The West Coast lessors', *Flight International*, 3 September 1988, p. 95.
25. Chairman's statement, GPA, *Annual Report and Accounts 1989*, p. 9.
26. John H. Taylor, 'Fasten seat belts please', *Forbes*, 2 April 1990, p. 84.
27. Bailey and Learmount, 'The West Coast lessors', *Flight International*, 3 September 1988, p. 96.
28. Selling aircraft outright or through a 'sale and leaseback deal', where it was leased in as well as leased out.
29. IPO Prospectus, 9 June 1992, p. 45.
30. GPA, Restructuring Document, 22 September 1993, Note 10, p. 119.
31. GPA, *Annual Report and Accounts 1990*, p. 11.
32. Generally Accepted Accounting Principles.
33. GPA, *Annual Report and Accounts 1992*, Note 31, p. 60.
34. 'Troubleshooter under fire', *Sunday Tribune*, 14 November 1993, C2.
35. Dr Garret FitzGerald could not be said to have filled this role as he had not worked in Aer Lingus for almost thirty years. Since then he had pursued a successful economic consulting and writing career before rising to the highest levels in politics as leader of the Fine Gael party and Taoiseach.
36. Gerry Dempsey was the first non-practising chartered accountant working in industry to become president of the Institute of Chartered Accountants in Ireland.
37. 'Troubleshooter under fire', *Sunday Tribune*, 14 November 1993, C2.
38. Jonathan Charkham, *Keeping Good Company: A Study of Corporate Governance in Five Countries*, Oxford: Clarendon Press 1994, Chapter 3. See also, R. A. G. Monks and Nell Minow, *Corporate Governance*, Oxford: Basil Blackwell 1995, pp. 271–87.
39. According to the *Annual Report and Accounts 1991*, p. 4, the 'Executive Committee' operated during 1990/91 and it was intended to continue unaltered up to 1992.
40. Ibid., p. 4.
41. *GPA Group plc — The World's Leading Aircraft Lessor*, James C. Halstead, European Equity Research, Salomon Brothers, London, 2 May 1990, p. 15.
42. *Guinness Peat Aviation — Leaders in a $500m Market*, Davy Equity Research, Dublin, 15 June 1990.
43. GPA director interview with author.
44. GPA released quarterly reports to the media on its financial performance from the late 1980s. This author was refused a copy of its annual report in 1989.

When a large Irish investment fund, with which this author was an analyst and adviser, was offered the opportunity to invest in GPA, the annual report was sought. It took some time to arrive.

45. Brenda Cullen, 'GPA: The Global Flotation that Failed', Case Study, ECCH, Cranfield, 1994.
46. GPA press release, 'GPA names Maurice Foley Deputy Chairman', 7 November 1991.
47. In interviews with the author.
48. There was a somewhat unusual caveat in the auditors' reports for 1986 and 1987 which is dealt with later in the discussion of accounting policies.
49. *International Lease Finance Corporation (ILFC) — An Extraordinary Company*, Salomon Brothers Inc. Stock Research, New York, 11 March 1986.
50. 'ILFC: where next?', *Aerfinance Journal*, February 1993, pp. 4–8.
51. Corporate Credit Report, ILFC, *Aerfinance Journal*, May 1993, p. 22.
52. IPO Prospectus, 9 June 1992, p. 54.
53. See GPA, *Annual Report and Accounts 1988*, p. 13; also *Annual Report and Accounts 1992*, Note 22, p. 50 and IPO Prospectus, 9 June 1992, p. 79.
54. As calculated by this author. Market demand and leasing margins had weakened.
55. GPA, *Annual Report and Accounts 1986*.
56. GPA, *Annual Report and Accounts 1990*.
57. GPA, *Annual Report and Accounts 1986* and *Annual Report and Accounts 1990*.
58. GPA, *Annual Report and Accounts 1986*, Note 14, p. 40.
59. GPA, *Annual Report and Accounts 1990*, Note 14, p. 34.
60. GPA, *Annual Report and Accounts 1986*, p. 41.
61. GPA, *Annual Report and Accounts 1990*, p. 35.
62. Based on 11% of $220 million.
63. *Irish Times*, 26 January 1993.
64. IPO Prospectus, 9 June 1992, p. 110.
65. This author spoke with senior managers in six investment institutions.
66. H. Wolk, J. Francis and M. Tearney, *Accounting Theory*, Cincinnatti: South-Western Publishing Co. 1992, Chapter 17 'Leases'; M. Davies, R. Paterson and A. Wilson, *UK GAAP*, 4th edn, London: Macmillan and Ernst & Young 1994, Chapter 17 'Leases and Hire Purchase Contracts'.
67. Wolk et al., *Accounting Theory*, p. 510.
68. Ibid.
69. Davies et al., *UK GAAP*, p. 864.
70. SSAP 21, London: Accounting Standards Committee, 1984.
71. V. Pereira, R. Paterson and A. Wilson, *UK/US GAAP Comparison*, London: Ernst & Young and Kogan Page 1992.
72. E. W. Hamilton and J. R. Scott, *Report of Investigation into the Affairs of Atlantic Computers plc*, London: HMSO 1994.
73. Technical Release of Institute of Chartered Accountants in England and Wales Financial Reporting and Auditing Group (FRAG 9/92), 'Review for Major Practical Problems of SSAP 21', London.
74. Ibid.

75. The 1986 report was signed by Peat Marwick Mitchell & Co. and the 1987 report was signed by KPMG Peat Marwick.
76. British Airways plc, Prospectus for public flotation on the London Stock Exchange, February 1987.
77. The average book value of aircraft.
78. Kay and Searfoss, USA, 1989.
79. James J. Johnson, Richard J. Dowen and Curtis L. Norton, 'An Assessment of Lessor Accounting for Residual Values', *Accounting Horizons* 7, 3 (September 1993), pp. 55–65.
80. IPO Prospectus, 9 June 1992, pp. 83–4.
81. Notes to financial statements, GPA, *Annual Report and Accounts 1992*.
82. For example, Davy issued an equity research note dated 10 March 1989, a lengthy and detailed research report *Guinness Peat Aviation — Leaders in a $500m Market*, 15 June 1990, a research note dated 11 June 1991, and a detailed research report *Guinness Peat Aviation: Cleared for Take-off*, March 1992. NCB issued detailed research reports dated February 1990 and June 1991, and *GPA Group plc: Issues for Discussion*, June 1992.
83. *Guinness Peat Aviation: Cleared for Take-off*, Davy Equity Research, Dublin, March 1992.
84. *GPA Group plc: Investment Report*, Riada & Co., Dublin, March 1992; *GPA Group plc: Issues for Discussion*, NCB Stockbrokers, Dublin, June 1992.
85. *GPA Group plc:* Bloxham Stockbrokers, Dublin, 1 June 1992.
86. Kleinwort Benson Research Report, *GPA Flotation*, June 1992.
87. 'GPA's $500m bonanza', *Aerfinance Journal*, January 1992, pp. 24–5.
88. Ibid.
89. See for example, 'Ryan says GPA not threatened', *Irish Times*, 20 June 1992, p. 16; John Plender and Roland Rudd, 'The deal that did not fly', *Financial Times*, 19 June 1992, p. 16 and also p. 20 special full page headed 'GPA group's aborted global issue'; Rory Godson and David Nally, 'GPA — what went wrong, where to now', *Sunday Tribune*, 21 June 1992, Business Section, C1 and C7; Matt Cooper, 'What went wrong', *Sunday Business Post*, 21 June 1992; Kirstie Hamilton, 'Crash landing', *Sunday Times*, Business Section, 21 June 1992, p. 8.
90. Richard House, 'GPA's crash landing', *Institutional Investor*, pp. 36–41; Simon Brady, 'How Ryan got it wrong', *Euromoney*, July 1992, pp. 26–31; Aline Sullivan, 'The need for GPA to cut spending and raise new funds', *Airfinance Journal*, August 1992, pp. 12–13.
91. See Chairman's statement, GPA, *Annual Report and Accounts 1992*, p. 15 and 'Foley fights back', *Airfinance Journal*, July 1992, pp. 2–4.
92. According to portfolio managers interviewed by the author.
93. IPO Prospectus, 9 June 1992, p. 37.
94. Ibid., p. 26. Twenty-two of these non-earning aircraft were owned by GPA, eight by joint venture companies and two were leased in.
95. Ibid., p. 51.
96. Ibid., p. 79.

97. S. G. Warburg Securities, *Aerospace Review*, April 1992.
98. 'Back in the sick-bay', *The Economist,* 14 November 1992, p. 85.
99. Matt Cooper, 'Bluff and counter-bluff as GPA seeks "lock-in"', *Sunday Business Post*, 26 April 1992, p. 13.
100. Matt Cooper, 'Media blitz keeps GPA grounded', *Sunday Business Post*, 13 September 1992, p. 32.
101. Cullen, 'GPA: The Global Flotation that Failed'.
102. See Ron Cooper, 'Is Ryan flying too high?', *Euromoney*, April 1989, pp. 35–40; Lex Column in *Financial Times*, 7 June 1990; John Plender, 'A business comes back to earth', *Financial Times*, 7 January 1991 (long article beside the 'editorial/leader column' p. 10); Nigel Cope, 'GPA comes down to earth', *Business*, May 1991, pp. 59–61.
103. See John H. Taylor, 'Fasten seat belts please', *Forbes*, 2 April 1990, pp. 84–8 and Rita Koselka, 'See-through airplanes', *Forbes*, 22 June 1992, pp. 43–4.
104. Richard Thomson, 'Problems in Japan dog GPA flotation', *Independent on Sunday*, 10 May 1992.
105. John Plender, 'Full throttle for a turbulent take-off', *Financial Times*, 13 June 1992, p. 6.
106. 'GPA's $500m bonanza', *Airfinance Journal*, January 1992, pp. 24–5.
107. Interview and personal communication to the author by a leading Irish investment adviser.
108. See Cullen, 'GPA: The Global Flotation that Failed', p. 10.
109. *Financial Times*, 1 April 1992.
110. The author examined the share register for the two years before the flotation and the year after it at the Companies Office, Dublin.
111. GPA, Restructuring Document, 22 September 1993, p. 121.
112. GPA Form 20-F, 31 March 1994, p. 38 registered with the Securities and Exchange Commission, Washington DC.
113. Sir Lewis Robertson, 'Company doctor offers prescription', *Financial Times*, 18 December 1991, p. 12.
114. Bill Houston, *Avoiding Adversity*, London: David and Charles 1989.

Chapter 7: Arthur Guinness and P. J. Carroll: Diversification and Decline of a Core Business (pp. 222–77)

1. J. Vitello-Martin and J. Moskin, *Executives' Book of Quotations*, New York: Oxford University Press 1994.
2. This was the title of the parent company in 1981 at the time of its crisis; some years later it was changed to Guinness plc.
3. Peter Pugh, *Is Guinness Good For You?*, London: Financial Training 1987, p. 2.
4. Nick Kochan and Hugh Pym, *The Guinness Affair*, London: Christopher Helm 1987, p. 3.
5. Pugh, *Guinness*, p. 9.
6. *Financial Times*, 17 April 1984, pp. 33–7.
7. Jeffrey Ferry, *The British Renaissance*, London: Heinemann 1993, p. 54.
8. Ibid., p. 66.

9. Ibid., p. 49.
10. Guinness may have been no different from other leading firms in the industry. Indeed, many long-established British industries that required some technical/scientific expertise had similar attitudes and cultures.
11. *Sunday Press,* 8 August 1993.
12. Sir Charles Harvey was one of the founders of the Irish Management Institute.
13. 'The pint of plain is your only man', *Sunday Press,* 8 August 1993, p. 27.
14. F. W. Peard, in *CIMA 75th Anniversary Membership Directory*, Dublin 1994, p. 113.
15. Kochan and Pym, *Guinness Affair*, p. 6.
16. Chairman's statement, *Annual Report 1979*, p. 12.
17. See Consolidated Profit and Loss Account, *Annual Report 1981*, p. 16 and Five Year Financial Survey, *Annual Report 1981*, p. 29.
18. Ibid., p. 29.
19. Co-incidentally, in 1981, the Guinness annual report stopped showing a five-year graph of pre-interest profit to net assets employed; the trend was downwards.
20. *Investor's Chronicle,* 22 January 1982.
21. *Investor's Chronicle,* 18 December 1981.
22. It was not surprising that the London management subsequently came under the 'Saunders' axe much more so than the Dublin structure.
23. See Lord Iveagh's Chairman's statement, *Annual Report 1977*.
24. Chairman's statement, *Annual Report 1978*.
25. Ferry, *British Renaissance*, p. 53.
26. *Annual Report 1980*, p. 15.
27. Chairman's statement, *Annual Report 1981*.
28. Chairman's statement, *Annual Report 1979*, p. 18.
29. F. W. Peard, in *CIMA 75th Anniversary Membership Directory*, Dublin 1994.
30. See Ferry, *British Renaissance*, and James Saunders, *Nightmare*, London: Arrow Books 1988, p. 59.
31. D. F. Channon, *The Strategy and Structure of British Enterprise*, London: Macmillan 1973.
32. Saunders, *Nightmare*, p. 59.
33. 'Saunders turns Guinness from victim into predator', *Financial Weekly*, 30 January 1986, pp. 50–55.
34. Ibid.
35. Kochan and Pym, *Guinness Affair*.
36. Ibid.
37. *Annual Report 1986*, p. 33.
38. Ibid., p. 56.
39. Ferry, *British Renaissance*, p. 83.
40. In a conversation with Ivor Kenny in May 1987. Ivor Kenny, *In Good Company*, Dublin: Gill & Macmillan 1987.
41. Davy Stockbrokers, 'P. J. Carroll and Company plc: Company Analysis', 20 June 1988, p. 5.
42. The Cahill May Roberts profitability improved remarkably after management buyout.

43. Kenny, *In Good Company*, p. 330.
44. *Annual Report 1987*, p. 36.
45. *Annual Report 1990*, p. 33.
46. *Irish Times*, 17 June 1986.
47. Chairman's statement, *Annual Report 1985*.
48. Davy Stockbrokers, 'P. J. Carroll and Company plc: Company Analysis', 20 June 1988.
49. H. Igor Ansoff, *Corporate Strategy*, New York: McGraw Hill 1965.
50. Ibid.; Michael E. Porter, *Competitive Strategy: Techniques for Analyzing Industries and Competitors*, New York: The Free Press 1980; Michael E. Porter, *Competitive Advantage: Creating and Sustaining Superior Performance*, New York: The Free Press 1985.
51. *Irish Times*, 24 June 1986.
52. Davy Stockbrokers, 'P. J. Carroll and Company plc: Company Analysis', 20 June 1988 p. 22.
53. 'Carrolls £20m fishfarm bath', *Business & Finance*, 26 September 1991.
54. Ibid.
55. David Nally, *Sunday Tribune*, 23 September 1994, p. C5.
56. 'How the Don packed it in', *Sunday Independent*, 11 February 1990.
57. 'RTE interview criticised', *Irish Times*, 10 February 1990.
58. Alan Ruddock, 'Carroll says depth of management was to blame', *Sunday Tribune*, 17 February 1990.
59. Goodbody Stockbrokers Equity Report, 'P. J. Carroll and Company plc', September 1990, p. 11.
60. S. O'Connell, 'Carrolls seeks major reversal of fortune', *Sunday Business Post*, 30 May 1993.
61. *Irish Times*, 5 October 1990, p. 13.
62. Brian Carey, 'Cigarette sales dip 9%, but "Blue" does best', *Sunday Business Post*, 1993.
63. 'Carrolls takes a swipe at Silk Cut', *Sunday Business Post*, 12 June 1994.
64. Chairman's statement, *Annual Report 1985*, p. 7.
65. Alan Ruddock, 'Carroll says depth of management was to blame', *Sunday Tribune*, 17 February 1990.
66. Chairman's statement, *Annual Report 1990*.
67. *Business & Finance*, 15 February 1990, p. 6.
68. Kenny, *In Good Company*, p. 324.
69. Chairman's statement, *Annual Report 1983*.
70. In his letter to shareholders dated 1 December 1988.
71. Chairman's statement, *Annual Report 1988*, p. 11.
72. Davy Equity Research, 'P. J. Carroll: Substantial Provisions Likely in Accounts to March 1990', 8 May 1990; 'Carroll's own broker is very critical', *Irish Times*, 11 May 1990.
73. Donald C. Hambrick and Richard A. D'Aveni, 'Large Corporate Failures as Downward Spirals', *Administrative Science Quarterly* 33 (1988), pp. 1–23.

Chapter 8: Irish Press and Waterford Wedgwood: The Clash Between Culture, Craft and Change (pp. 278–339)

1. J. J. Lee, *Ireland 1912–1985*, Cambridge: Cambridge University Press 1989.
2. Ibid., p. 29.
3. Ivor Kenny, *In Good Company*, Dublin: Gill & Macmillan 1987, p. 79.
4. Lord Longford and Thomas P. O'Neill, *Éamon de Valera*, London: Arrow Books 1970.
5. Michael O'Toole, *More Kicks than Pence*, Dublin: Poolbeg Press 1992.
6. Ibid., pp. 57–8.
7. Dermot Keogh, 'William Martin Murphy: Dublin Financier (1844–1919)', in *Dictionary of Business Biography*, London 1986, pp. 389–94.
8. Ibid.
9. Lee, *Ireland*, p. 30.
10. G. R. Carroll and Jacques Delacroix, 'Organizational Mortality in the Newspaper Industries of Argentina and Ireland: An Ecological Approach', *Administrative Science Quarterly* 27 (1982), pp. 169–98.
11. A. L. Stinchcombe, 'Social Structure and Organizations', in J. G. March (ed.), *Handbook on Organizations*, Chicago: Rand McNally 1965, pp. 153–93.
12. Carroll and Delacroix, 'Organizational Mortality', pp. 187–8.
13. Dermot Keogh, *Twentieth-Century Ireland: Nation and State*, Dublin: Gill & Macmillan 1994, pp. 354–74.
14. Ibid., pp. 370–73.
15. Ibid., p. 368.
16. Stinchcombe, 'Social Structure and Organizations'.
17. Lee, *Ireland*, p. 168.
18. Ibid., pp. 168 and 176.
19. Ibid., p. 218.
20. O'Toole, *More Kicks than Pence*, pp. 69–71.
21. '. . . to prevent the congregating of sports casuals and to eliminate the smell of drink . . .' Ibid., p. 71.
22. Ibid., p. 73.
23. Hugh Oram, *Paper Tigers*, Belfast: Appletree Press/Dublin: RTE 1993, p. 64.
24. Ibid., p. 60.
25. Competition Authority, *Interim Report of Study on the Newspaper Industry*, Dublin, 1995, Table 5.
26. Marshall Meyer and Lynne Zucker, *Permanently Failing Organizations*, California: Sage 1989.
27. Turnover per employee computed by the author based on data in Competition Authority, *Interim Report*, Chapter 2.
28. Irish Press plc, *Annual Report 15 Months to March 1995*, Note 1, p. 14.
29. Reports of the Examiner Hugh Cooney to the High Court; Statements of Affairs and notes attached.
30. Report of the Examiner of Irish Press Newspapers Ltd pursuant to Section 15 of the Companies (Amendment) Act 1990, July 1995.
31. Competition Authority, *Interim Report*, para. 4.139.

32. Ibid., para. 4.140.
33. See Matt Cooper, 'Crisis Hits the Irish Press', *Business & Finance*, 11 May 1989; Frank Fitzgibbon, 'The New Press Gang', *Irish Business*, August 1989; Frank Fitzgibbon, 'Reuters to the Rescue', *Irish Business*, May 1989.
34. Lee, *Ireland*, p. 152.
35. Young Eamon was reared for a period by his grandparents as his mother died when he was a child.
36. Ivan Fallon, *The Player*, London: Hodder & Stoughton 1994, Chapters 8, 10 and 11.
37. Kenny, *In Good Company*, p. 168.
38. Fallon, *The Player*, Chapter 12.
39. Chairman's statement, *Annual Report for 52 weeks ended 1 January 1984*.
40. Ibid.
41. O'Toole, *More Kicks than Pence*, p. 139.
42. Ibid., p. 139.
43. Ibid., p. 140.
44. Ibid., p. 141.
45. Competition Authority, *Interim Report*, paras 4.232–40 and Table 15.
46. Ibid., Table 17.
47. Frank Fitzgibbon, 'Reuters to the Rescue', *Irish Business*, May 1989.
48. Frank Fitzgibbon, 'The New Press Gang', *Irish Business*, August 1989.
49. Competition Authority, *Report of Investigation of the Proposal whereby Independent Newspapers plc would increase its shareholding in the Tribune Group from 29.99% to a possible 53.09%*, Dublin, 1992, Table 9, p. 29.
50. Chairman's statement, Independent Newspapers, *Annual Report 1985*, p. 3.
51. Competition Authority, *Report of Investigation*, Table 6, p. 24.
52. Competition Authority, *Interim Report*, Table 25.
53. *Business & Finance*, 11 May 1989.
54. Oram, *Paper Tigers*, p. 129.
55. Gerard Flynn, 'Irish Press Struggle Intensifies', *Business & Finance*, 11 June 1992, pp. 8–10; and 'Press poised on the brink', *Sunday Tribune*, 4 June 1995, p. 3.
56. Brian Carey, 'For the glory of God and the honour of Ireland', *Sunday Business Post*, 20 June 1993; Christopher McKevitt, 'A marriage made in hell', *Sunday Tribune*, 20 June 1993.
57. 'Press management firm on Rapple sacking', *Irish Times*, 29 May 1995, p. 5; 'Liquidation of company can still be halted before meeting of creditors', *Irish Times*, 7 June 1995, p. 7.
58. Report of the Examiner of Irish Press Newspapers Ltd pursuant to Section 15 of the Companies (Amendment) Act 1990, July 1995.
59. Affidavit of Hugh Cooney to the High Court of 21 August 1995 in the matters of Irish Press Newspapers and Irish Press Publications.
60. Section 11. Letter of 18 August 1995 from McStay to Cooney. Affidavit and Report of the Examiner Hugh Cooney to the High Court of 21 August 1995.
61. Chairman's statement, Irish Press plc, *Annual Report 1995*, p. 4.

62. Sean Brophy, *The Strategic Management of Irish Enterprise 1934–1984*, Dublin: Smurfit Publications 1985, pp. 167–8.
63. Philip Anderson, *Waterford Crystal Case Study*, European Case Clearing House 1994 (Case No. 393-101-1).
64. Kenny, *In Good Company*, p. 84.
65. Brophy, *Strategic Management*, p. 169.
66. Ibid., p. 173.
67. Kenny, *In Good Company*, p. 84.
68. Waterford Glass Ltd, *Annual Report 1979*, p. 8.
69. *Annual Report 1980*, p. 6.
70. *Annual Report 1982*, p. 5.
71. Chairman's statement, *Annual Report 1984*, p. 5.
72. Anderson, *Waterford Crystal*, p. 5.
73. *Securing the Future — The Business Plan for Waterford Crystal: An Information Booklet for Employees*, Waterford Crystal 1987, p. 12.
74. Brophy, *Strategic Management*, p. 191.
75. Ibid.
76. Ibid., p. 182.
77. Brendan McSweeney, 'Accounting in Organizational Action: A Subsuming Explanation or Situated Explanations?', *Accounting, Auditing and Information Technologies* (forthcoming).
78. The militancy of the trade union leadership was reflected in the tax protest strikes over PAYE deduction in 1983. *Business & Finance* suggested that 'Waterford Glass is in the grip of the Left' and that much of the industrial action at the time was politically motivated. 'Waterford Glass, Victims of the New Left', *Business & Finance*, 19 May 1983, p. 8.
79. *The Economist*, 9 June 1984.
80. 'Debt crisis forces sell-off', *Irish Times*, 15 August 1984, p. 12.
81. One interviewee from another large Irish organisation told the author that they were concerned that the industrial relations climate (which was an open secret) might adversely affect their other industrial interests. They perceived a massive managerial and organisational cultural change allied to additional investment to achieve a reasonable financial return. It was decided it was not worth the risk and the drain on management resource.
82. 'Clawing Our Way Back to Profit', *Accountancy Ireland* 25, 6 (December 1993), p. 35.
83. 'Waterford and Wedgwood — A New Partnership in Excellence', document sent to Wedgwood shareholders from Sir Arthur Bryan, Chairman, 4 November 1986.
84. Waterford, *Annual Report 1986*, Note 27, p. 43.
85. 'A white knight with slightly tarnished armour', *Financial Times*, 21 March 1989, p. 20.
86. McSweeney, 'Accounting in Organizational Action'.
87. Ibid.
88. Ibid.

89. *The Economist*, 1988
90. *Voluntary Parting and Early Retirement Scheme 1987: An Information Booklet for Employees,* Waterford Crystal 1987, p. 13.
91. It comprised exceptional 'excess production costs . . . and stock provisions' of £14.8 million and extraordinary redundancy, early retirement and productivity payments of £35 million.
92. Waterford Glass Group plc, *Results for the Half Year Ended 30 June 1988,* September 1988.
93. Dennehy Associates, Dublin, News release, Waterford Glass Group, 10 April 1989.
94. Edward Cahill, 'Some Prudent Advice for Waterford Glass', *Business & Finance,* 20 April 1989.
95. Aileen O'Toole and Dan White, 'What Went Wrong at Waterford Glass', *Business & Finance,* 13 April 1989; Rory Godson, 'The breaking of Waterford Glass', *Sunday Tribune,* 9 April 1989.
96. Recommended offer by S. G. Warburg, letter of 4 November 1986 to Wedgwood shareholders, Appendix 4, p. 27.
97. Brian Carey, 'Waterford Crystal had plan to move 50% production abroad', *Sunday Business Post,* 10 January 1995, p. 3.
98. Waterford Wedgwood plc, *Annual Report 1990,* Note 1, p. 16.

Chapter 9: Irish Shipping: A Vessel Without a Chart or Compass (pp. 340–76)

1. Harold S. Geneen, *Managing,* London: Grafton Books 1985, p. 139.
2. Report of the Official Liquidator to the High Court on Irish Shipping Ltd, June 1985, p. 37.
3. *Irish Times,* 15 November 1984.
4. *Dáil Reports,* 14 November 1984, vol. 353, cols 2077–9.
5. Ibid.
6. Ibid., col. 2110.
7. Ibid., cols 2135–6.
8. Gemma Hussey, *At the Cutting Edge: Cabinet Diaries 1982–87,* Dublin: Gill & Macmillan 1990.
9. Ibid., p. 75.
10. Ibid., p. 76.
11. Joint Oireachtas Committee on Commercial State-Sponsored Bodies, *Second Report on Irish Shipping Ltd,* Dublin: Stationery Office 1985, p. 46.
12. In fact the loan position was much higher because £16.9 million in leasing and hire purchase debt had been netted against fixed assets.
13. Paul McGrath, 'Organisational Decline in the Public Service', *Administration* 41, 4 (Winter 1993/94), pp. 362–84.
14. Ibid., p. 378.
15. Ronan Fanning, *The Irish Department of Finance 1922–58,* Dublin: Institute of Public Administration 1978, pp. 349–50.
16. Irish Shipping built up an expertise in shipping insurance during the war, as insurance was either unavailable or very costly.

17. There are suggestions that B&I was reluctant to take on this role and/or become involved.
18. Submission of Irish Shipping to Joint Oireachtas Committee, 1980, Appendix to Joint Oireachtas Committee on Commercial State-Sponsored Bodies, *First Report on Irish Shipping Ltd*, Dublin: Stationery Office 1981.
19. W. A. O'Neill and Derry O'Neill were not related.
20. Report of the Official Liquidator, p. 27.
21. Joint Oireachtas Committee, *Second Report*.
22. Ibid., p. 378. I obtained a copy of the liquidator's special report to the High Court from a creditor.
23. See Frank Fitzgibbon, 'Tempany's investigation uncovers a web of mismanagement and bad judgment at Irish Shipping', *Irish Business,* October 1985, pp. 12–17; *Irish Times*, 7 October 1985.
24. Maurice Tempany was president of the Institute of Chartered Accountants in Ireland and senior partner in Ernst & Whinney.
25. Report of the Official Liquidator, Section 2, p. 1.
26. I interviewed members of the board, members of management and George Chao of Wah Kwong Shipping, Hong Kong, the largest unsecured creditor. Similar to McGrath ('Organisational Decline in the Public Service') this author found access to people and documentation most difficult. It proved to be one of the most demanding cases to research. Unfortunately, with the passage of time, some members of the board and management had died or were ill.
27. Report of the Official Liquidator, Section 2, p. 3. The minutes of the meeting of 2 May 1974 of Celtic Bulk Carriers indicate that two vessels, *Uni Hong Kong* and *Uni Africa*, had been rechartered 'for a whole of the five year chartered periods showing a daily profit per vessel of £536'.
28. See Joint Oireachtas Committee, *First Report*, p. 1.
29. Ibid., p. 37.
30. P. H. Greer gave some details of the joint venture in his chairman's statement, *Annual Report 1973*.
31. Joint Oireachtas Committee, *Second Report*, p. 16.
32. Report of the Official Liquidator, Section 2, p. 12.
33. Ibid., Section 2, p. 4.
34. *Annual Report 1984*, p. 9.
35. Joint Oireachtas Committee, *Second Report*, p. 16.
36. Ibid., p. 22. However, Irish Shipping's 'Report on Position as at 30 September 1983 and Review of Alternative Future Courses of Action', October 1983, p. 7 (internal company document submitted to government) indicates a figure of £32.8 million.
37. Chairman's statement, *Annual Report 1977*.
38. Chairman's statement, *Annual Report 1980*.
39. Joint Oireachtas Committee, *Second Report*, p. 20.
40. Report of the Official Liquidator, Section 2, p. 13.

41. It seems that the contract was to be shared between Irish Shipping and a Japanese group at a competitive rate. Joint Oireachtas Committee, *Second Report*, p. 30.
42. Verolme went into liquidation in 1985.
43. *Dáil Reports,* 9 December 1980, vol. 325, cols. 706–18.
44. Report of the Official Liquidator, Section 2, p. 1.
45. Ibid., Section 2.5 'Nature of Government Control and Involvement', pp. 19–20.
46. Ibid., Section 6.3, p. 5.
47. Ibid., Section 6.3, p. 6.
48. Ibid., Section 6.3, p. 8.
49. Ibid., Section 6.3, p. 10.
50. Ibid., Section 2.7, p. 27.
51. Ibid., Section 2.7, p. 26.
52. Ibid., Section 2.7, p. 27.
53. Ibid., Section 2.7, p. 26.
54. Paul Sweeney claims that one manager ran up expenses of £55,000 in two years prior to liquidation. Paul Sweeney, *The Politics of Public Enterprise and Privatisation*, Dublin: Tomar Publishing 1990, p. 81.
55. Report of the Official Liquidator, Section 2.7, p. 27.
56. Ibid., Section 2.4, p. 16.
57. Ibid., Section 2.7, p. 27.
58. Ibid., Section 2.4, p. 16.
59. Ibid., Section 6, pp. 1–2.
60. Ibid., Section 3, pp. 9–11.
61. Ibid., Section 6.1, p. 1.
62. Joint Oireachtas Committee, *First Report*, p. 10.
63. *Annual Report 1983*, Note 7(b), p. 23.
64. Report of the Official Liquidator, Section 6, p. 2.
65. Chairman's statement, *Annual Report 1983*.
66. *Dáil Reports,* 14 November 1984, vol. 353, col. 2081.
67. *Annual Report 1984*, p. 17.
68. Ibid.
69. Report of the Official Liquidator, Section 3.3, pp. 9–10.
70. Ibid., Section 3.3, p. 10.
71. Ibid.
72. Ibid., Section 2.10, p. 35.
73. Memorandum and Articles of Association of Irish Shipping Ltd, p. 27. According to the Articles of Association (Article 57) this meeting 'shall . . . receive and consider the accounts and balance sheet and the reports of the directors and auditors'.
74. Statement of Standard Accounting Practice 6, 'Extraordinary Items and Prior Year Adjustments'.
75. It was the Department of Transport and subsequently the Department of Communications in the relevant period for Irish Shipping.

76. Memorandum and Articles of Association of Irish Shipping Ltd, Article 88, p. 34.
77. Ibid., Article 121.
78. Ibid., Article 123.
79. Ibid., Article 124.
80. Ibid., Article 126.
81. Joint Oireachtas Committee, *Second Report*, p. 21.
82. Sweeney, *Politics of Public Enterprise*, p. 83.
83. Speech of Jim Mitchell, Minister for Communications, at the annual dinner dance of the Institute of Certified Public Accountants in Ireland, Dublin, 24 November 1984. Official press release, Government Information Services.
84. Memorandum and Articles of Association of Irish Shipping Ltd, Article 83.
85. Sean Dooney and John O'Toole, *Irish Government Today*, Dublin: Gill & Macmillan 1992, pp. 152–4.
86. Ibid., p. 152.
87. Dermot Keogh, *Twentieth-Century Ireland: Nation and State*, Dublin: Gill & Macmillan 1994, pp. 350–68.
88. Speech of Jim Mitchell, Minister for Communications, at the annual dinner dance of the Institute of Certified Public Accountants in Ireland, Dublin, 24 November 1984. Official press release, Government Information Services.
89. Joint Oireachtas Committee, *First Report*.
90. Ibid., p. 26.
91. Report of the Official Liquidator to the High Court, 24 February 1993.
92. Report of the Official Liquidator to the High Court, May 1989.
93. Report of the Official Liquidator, 24 February 1993, Appendix 7.
94. It was surprising that Wah Kwong did not take legal action against the government. The Chao family had to focus on saving their company.
95. *Annual Report of Committee of Public Accounts*, Dublin Stationery Office: 1989, p. 47.
96. Speech of Jim Mitchell, Minister for Communications, at the annual dinner dance of the Institute of Certified Public Accountants in Ireland, Dublin, 24 November 1984. Official press release, Government Information Services.
97. *Dáil Reports*, 14 November 1984, vol. 353, col. 2080.
98. Ibid., cols 2080–81.
99. Irish Shipping, 'Report on Position as at 30 September 1983 and Review of Alternative Future Courses of Action', October 1983, p. 10.

Chapter 10: Conclusions (pp. 377–402)

1. C. M. Kelly, *The Destructive Achiever*, Reading, Mass.: Addison Wesley 1988, p. 10.
2. Edward Cahill, 'Audit Failure', in G. McHugh and D. Rowe (eds.), *Financial Reporting and Auditing*, Dublin: Oak Tree Press 1995; Edward Cahill, 'The Regulation of Financial Reporting in Ireland', in S. McLeay (ed.), *The Regulation of Financial Reporting in the European Union*, London: Macmillan 1997 (forthcoming).

3. *The Report of the Commission of Enquiry into the Expectations of Users of Published Financial Statements* (Ryan Report), Dublin: Institute of Chartered Accountants in Ireland 1992.
4. *The Report of the Committee on the Financial Aspects of Corporate Governance* (Cadbury Report), London: Gee December 1992.
5. *First Report of the Company Law Review Group*, Dublin: Stationery Office 1994.

Appendix 1 (pp. 403–05)

1. W. J. Bruns and R. S. Kaplan, *Accounting and Management: Field Study Perspectives,* Cambridge, Mass.: Harvard Business School 1987; E. Gummesson, *Qualitative Methods in Management Research*, California: Sage 1991; R. Ryan, R. Scapens and M. Theobald, *Research Method and Methodology in Finance and Accounting,* London: Academic Press 1992; Robert K. Yin, *Case Study Research: Design and Method,* Thousand Oaks, California: Sage 1994; Charles C. Ragin, *The Comparative Method,* Berkeley and Los Angeles: University of California Press 1987.

Index

Abidali, A.F. and Harris, F., 129
accounting, 15–16
    aggressive, 42, 197–203
    cosmetic, 42
accounting issues
    Goodman, 86–91
    Irish Shipping, 363–8
    Kentz, 117–25
    P.J. Carroll, 272–5
accounting standards, 42
    leasing, 197–203
Accounting Standards Board, 13, 198, 199
adolescent organisations, 4
    patterns of, 380–86
    problems of, 29–34, 35
advertising, 303–5
Aer Lingus, 160, 177, 178, 182, 324, 360
    depreciation, 202
    and GPA collapse, 1, 3, 180, 213, 396
    GPA losses, 216
Aerfinance Journal, 163
aggressive accounting, 42, 197–203
AIB/BNP consortium, 95, 98, 126, 127
A.I.C., 244
AIG, 186, 206
Air Canada, 1, 160, 177, 178, 180, 213, 216
Air France, 157
air travel, 166
Aldermaston, 121
Algemene Bank Nederland, 132, 135
Allied Irish Banks, 1, 207, 210, 332, 346, 348, 352, 372
    and Kentz, 95, 114, 116–17
    problems, 8

Allied Irish Breweries, 228
Allied Irish Investment Bank, 367
Allied-Lyons, 227
Altman, E.I., 11
Altman, E., Haldeman, R.G. and Narayanan, P., 43
Amalgamated Transport and General Workers Union, 335–6
American Brands Inc., 264
Amstrad, 32–3
analysis, financial, 20–21, 42
Anderson, 318
Anglo-Irish Beef Processors International Ltd, 80, 87
Anglo-Irish Meat Company, 53
Ansoff, H.I., 256
Apple Computer, 32
aquaculture, 256–8, 269–70
Argenti, John, 26
Argenti model, 22–4
    Goodman, 93
    GPA, 220
    Kentz, 129
    and mature firms, 389
    Xtra-vision, 156
Argentina, 282–3
Arklow Pottery, 9
Arthur Guinness Son and Co Ltd, 4, 18, 222–44, 255, 270, 313, 325, 332, 339, 369
    age pattern, 378
    background, 222–5
    business cycle, 397, 398
    cash flow profile, 235
    Dublin dilemma, 228–9
    failed diversification, 235–8
    financial performance, 231–4
    fundamental problems, 238–40

Index

Guinness culture, 229–31
patterns of mature failure, 387–90
product, market, competitive position, 225–8
reflections, 275–7
Saunders transformation, 240–44
speed of profit reversal, 378, 380
strategic weaknesses in UK, 234–5
warning signs, 399
Asda, 48
Aspel, Tom, 312, 324
Associated British Foods, 80, 81
Atlantic Computers, 198
Atlantic Computers plc, 13
auditors
  legal responsibilities, 91
  role of, 395, 398–9, 401
auditors' reports
  Goodman, 86–91, 394
  GPA, 391, 394
  Irish Shipping, 363–8
  Kentz Corporation, 117–25
  P.J. Carroll, 272–5
  Xtra-vision, 148–52
Australia, 13, 14, 38, 44, 47
Avair, 323
Avenue Investment Company, 312, 323
Avon Electrics, 136
Aynsley China, 311, 314

Bacik, Charles, 309, 311, 312, 315
Bailieboro Co-operative, 57, 68
Baillie, Stuart, 259
Bain, 241, 242
Bank of America, 160
Bank of Credit and Commercial International (BCCI), 13
Bank of England, 33
Bank of Ireland, 8, 197, 247, 253
Bank Paribas, 80
bankers, 15, 25
  analysis by, 42
  and Goodman, 75, 84–6
  and GPA, 158–9, 192–3
  and Kentz, 125–6
  role of, 383–4, 398, 401–2

bankruptcy, 6
Barclays Bank, 95, 101, 102
Barclays de Zoete Wedd, 205
Barings Bank, 13, 223
Barnes, Dermot, 350–51
Barnes, Richard, 324
Barrett, Liam, 182
Barrington, Colm, 2, 158, 170, 181–3, 197
Barrow Milling, 10
Bass, 227, 233, 234
Beamish & Crawford, 4, 227
Beatreme Foods Inc., 58, 62, 382
Beaver, W. and Altman, E., 43
Bedford Fair, 258, 269
Beech Hill, Dublin, 127
Beecham group, 240–41, 242
beef industry, 54–5
Beef Tribunal, 88, 395, 396, 400
  bogus payments, 89–91
  Britton evidence, 68, 69, 71, 73–4, 79
  Fitzpatrick evidence, 80
  Goodman evidence, 53, 54, 56–7, 69–70, 76, 78–9, 83–4
  Mooney evidence, 76
  O'Carroll evidence, 71–2
beer market, 226–8
Bell Group, 14
Bell's, 222, 225, 241, 242
Belton, Frank, 341, 343, 346, 352, 359, 361–2, 369
Bensons, 226
Berisford International, 48–9, 67, 83, 92, 382, 397
  and auditors, 88
  disposal, 85
  investment risk, 65, 72, 79–82, 93
  secret moves, 58, 63
  shares collapse, 78–80
B&I, 360, 375
'big project', 37
  Goodman, 93
  Irish Shipping, 354–8
  Kentz, 108, 129
  Xtra-vision, 156

436

BK Associates, 202–3
Black Friday, 211
Blaney, Patrick, 158, 183
BNP, 80
board of directors
   Goodman, 67
   GPA, 177–81, 219–20
   Guinness, 238–40, 277
   importance of, 25
   Irish Press, 295–7, 299–300, 305–7
   Irish Shipping, 354, 359–62
   Kentz, 109–10
   P.J. Carroll, 262–3, 268–71, 277
   Waterford Wedgwood, 320, 322–5, 332
   Xtra-vision, 138–9
Boesky, 242
Boland's Bakery, 9
Bolger, Philip, 183
Bond, Alan, 14
Bond Corporation, 14
Bord Gais, 108
Boulding, K.E., 27
Bower, Tom, 13
Boyd, Graham, 182
Boyle, Herbert, 132–3, 135, 138, 143, 155, 386
   flotation, 139, 145
   losses, 156
   resignation, 142
Bradan Mara Teo, 256–8
Brazil, 57
Brealey, R.A. and Myers, S.C., 42
Brennan, Donald, 314, 333
Brennan, N., O'Brien, F. and Pierce, A., 124–5
Brennan, Seamus, 342
Brent Walker, 13
Brindle, John, 254
British Airways, 157, 166, 202
British and Commonwealth Holdings, 13, 187, 198
British Leyland, 37
British Sugar, 58, 63, 81, 82, 83, 92
Brittain Group, 10
Britton, Brian, 67–75, 79, 87

and Iraqi debt, 75–6
Brophy, Anthony, 321, 325, 330, 332
Brosnan, Denis, 70
Browne, Vincent, 79, 302
BSE restrictions, 55, 63
Business & Finance, 1, 87, 298
business cycles, 25–6, 397
Butler, Patrick, 95, 101, 102
Byrne, Mr, SC, 80
Byrne, Paddy, 313, 324, 332

Cadbury Report, 123, 268, 396–7
Cahill, Edward, 43, 44
Cahill May Roberts, 247, 253
Cahir Meat Packers, 56, 89
Callard & Bowser, 237
Cambridge Group plc, 10, 134, 137, 145–7
Campbell, Michael, 95, 97, 98, 100, 111–12, 124
   dual role, 110, 114–15
Canada, 13
Canal du Midi, 237
Canary Wharf project, 13
Carlsberg, 226–7
Carroll, Charles, 268, 270, 271
Carroll, Don, 244, 245–8, 253, 272, 273, 277
   diversification, 255
   dominance, 267, 270–71
   on management, 268, 269
   personality, 254
   scapegoat, 262–3
Carroll, Jim, 246
Carroll, Patrick James, 244, 246
Carroll, P.J. *see* P.J. Carroll
Carroll, Walter, 244
Carroll, G.R. and Delacroix, J., 282–3
Carroll Journals, 258, 269
Carter, Terry, 95, 102
causes of failure
   accounting views, 26–7
   aggressive and cosmetic accounting, 42
   analytical perspectives, 20–21
   downward spirals, 39–41

financial problems of growth, 34–5
financial ratio predictive models, 43–7
life-cycle theory, 27–9
management perspective, 21–6
problems of adolescence, 29–34
problems of maturity, 35–9
syndromes of failure patterns, 41
Celtic Bulk Carriers, 345, 348, 353, 354–8, 360–61, 361–2
Cement Roadstone, 297
Central Bank, 10
Chandler, A.D., 14
Channon, D.F., 37–8, 240
Chao family, 373
Cherry's, 228
Cheshire, Ian, 229
Chrysler, 37
Chubb, Professor Basil, 301
CIE, 351
Citibank (Citicorp), 161, 210, 372
Cityvision plc, 138, 149
Clarke, P., 43
Clifford, D.K., 35
Clover Meats Co-operative, 59
Cluskey, Frank, 342
Colbert, P. and McCarthy, C., 8
Collins, Michael, 279
Colorall, 13
Common Agricultural Policies (CAP), 57–8
Communications, Department of, 343, 344, 366, 368–71, 374, 389–90
Companies Acts, 117, 118, 120, 149, 151, 365
Companies Office, 117, 119, 400
Company Law Review Group, 401
conglomerates, 9–10
Connolly, James, 281
Connor, Aidan, 69, 72, 75–6
Continental Illinois Bank, 13–14
Coogan, Tim Pat, 297
Cooney, Hugh, 96, 102, 111, 112, 294, 307, 308
Coopers & Lybrand, 50, 75, 293, 299, 306, 331

Corbett, Derrik, 244, 246, 266, 269, 272
Cork Examiner, 5, 284, 287, 293, 304
corporate culture, 30–2
corporations. *see also* causes of failure
  accounting, 15–16
  adolescent failures, 380–86
  age patterns, 378
  analytical framework of mismanagement, 390–91
  business cycle, 397–8
  causes of failure, 19–47
  corporate regulatory system, 400–401
  decline and crisis, 5–6
  economic context and performance, 9–11
  extent and speed of profit reversals, 378–80
  failure prevention, 398–9
  financial reporting issues, 391–5
  health and pathology, 1–5
  international collapses, 12–15
  management problems, 11–12
  'organisational disease', 3–5
  patterns of mature failure, 386–90
  public interest issues, 396–7
  rates of failure, 6–9
  recognition of crisis, 16–17
cosmetic accounting, 42
Costello, Mr Justice D., 96, 102
Countyglen plc, 109, 395, 400
Courage, 227
Craig Gardner, 279, 359
Crawford, John, 26–7
creative accounting, 22, 40, 42, 91
Credit Lyonnais, 13, 185, 187
Cregan, Denis, 70
Crest Holdings, 312
CRH plc, 8, 118, 157, 210, 213
Crookes Laboratories, 237
Crowley, Laurence, 244, 269–70, 272
Cullen, Brenda, 184, 214
Cullen, Walter, 336
Cyprus, 85, 86

Daily Mail, 301, 304
Daily Mirror, 301, 304
Dakota, 247
Dand, David, 324
Daniel, Liam, 142
Darmon, S.E., 239
D'Aveni, R.A., 275
Davies, Bob, 325, 331, 332
Davies, M., Paterson, R. and Wilson, A., 198
Davy Corporate Finance, 132–4
Davy Stockbrokers, 135, 145, 153, 154, 155
   on GPA, 1, 194, 203–6
   on P.J. Carroll, 254–5, 274–5
   on Waterford Wedgwood, 330
DCC Corporate Finance, 135–6, 138–9, 142, 145–6
   role in Xtra-vision, 154–5
   on Xtra-vision, 152–3
de Valera, Dr Eamon, 281, 282, 297, 299, 306
de Valera, Eamon, 279, 280, 281, 285, 296, 341
de Valera, Major Vivion, 281, 289, 296–7, 298–9, 300
debt servicing
   GPA, 188–92
Deloitte & Touche, 95, 101, 293
Dempsey, Gerard, 178, 180, 324
Dempsey, Jack, 281, 289, 296–300
Denmark, 11
depreciation, 149–51, 153
   GPA, 202–3, 205
   Xtra-vision, 147–52
Development Capital Corporation (DCC), 132–3
Devlin, Liam St John, 350–51
Dillon Read, 180
Dior, Sean, 267, 272
direct marketing, 258, 259, 269–70
Distillers, 222, 225, 241, 242
diversification
   Guinness, 235–8
   P.J. Carroll, 253–9
Dodder Investment Company, 315

Dolan, Michael, 183
Dome Petroleum, 13
Donlon, Sean, 183
Dooley, Con, 310, 312
Dooney, S. and O'Toole, J., 370
Dow Jones Industrials Index, 211
downward spirals, 39≠41, 338
Drucker, Peter, 34
Drummonds, 237
Du Pont family, 14–15
Dublin Stock Exchange, 10, 59, 211
   Goodman crisis, 48–9, 69
   GPA failure, 1, 2, 158–9, 187–8
   numbers listed, 8
   regulatory system failure, 400–401
   Xtra-vision, 131, 132–5, 137–8, 143–5, 154
Dubtex Clothing, 9
Dufferin, Lady, 231
Dufferin and Ava, Marquess of, 238
Dukes, Alan, 342
Dun & Bradstreet, 6, 7, 11
Dundalk Bacon Company, 53
Dunnes Stores, 157

Economist, 323
Edwardes, Michael, 37
Elders, 14
Electricity Supply Board (ESB), 257, 357–8, 375
Elliott, John, 14
Emerald Star Line, 237
Enterprise and Employment, Dept of, 96
entrepreneurs
   control of, 386, 398–9
   Larry Goodman, 53–7, 75–7
   management style, 29–34
   Xtra-vision, 155
Ernst & Young, 95, 102
Esso refinery, Rotterdam, 107
Euro Disney, 13
European Community, 9, 10, 55
Evening Herald, 287, 293
Evening Mail, 302
Evening Press. see Irish Press

examiners
  Goodman group, 83–4
  GPA, 217–18
  Irish Press, 307–8
  legal role of, 95–6
  Xtra-vision, 147
export credit insurance. *see* Iraq
Express group, 287

failure. *see* causes of failure
failure prediction, 22–4
  models, 43–7
family firms, 14, 18, 25, 37–8, 388–9
  Guinness, 238–9, 339
  Irish Press, 297, 299, 305, 339
Fanning, Ronan, 346
Federal Deposit Insurance Company (FDIC), 13–14
Ferguson, Vincent, 298
Ferruzzi-Montedison group, 13
Ferry, J., 229, 243
Fianna Fail, 279, 280, 283–4, 308, 341, 342–3
Fieldcrest Ireland, 247, 253, 263, 266
Finance, Department of, 344
  and Irish Shipping, 368–72, 374, 389–90
Finance Act 1983, 90
Finance Act 1995, 395
Financial Accounting Standards Board, 198
financial ratio predictive models, 43–7
Financial Reporting Standard 5, 198, 199
Financial Times, 214, 215
Fine Gael, 283, 342–3, 359, 370–71
Finn, Jim, 110
Finucane, T.A., 360
Fischer, Gus, 39
Fish, David, 267, 268–9
FitzGerald, Dr Garret, 2, 180, 342
Fitzgibbon, 8, 10
Fitzpatrick, Bernard, 309, 311, 312, 315
Fitzpatrick, Peter, 3, 50, 80
Fitzwilton, 10, 298, 333
Flamholtz, Eric G., 29–30

Flavin, Jim, 155
Flinn, Donal P., 281, 299
Fluestox Engineering, 108
Flynn, Padraig, 342
Foley, Maurice, 2, 158, 163, 183, 386
  on collapse, 207
  Executive Committee, 181
  financial reports, 173, 180, 194
  group chief executive, 184
  joins GPA, 182
  president, 177
Food Industries plc, 48, 49, 57–8, 69, 72, 78, 92
Forbairt, 96
Forbes, 214
Ford Ireland, 14, 323
Foreign Affairs, Department of, 310
Foster's, 227
'founder's trap', 32
France, 13, 47, 55
Friel, Hugh, 70
Furer, Dr Arthur, 242
Furlong, C.J., 297
Furlong, L.S., 344, 345, 351

Gaelic Seafoods, 259
Gageby, Douglas, 296
Gallagher, Frank, 281, 285–6, 296, 300
Gallaher, 252, 253, 268, 275, 298
  compared with P.J. Carroll, 264–5
Galligan, A.G., 281, 299–300, 306
Galvin, Paddy, 228, 241, 313, 332
Gatchell family, 309
GE Capital Aviation Services (GECAS), 218
GECAS, 178
Geneen, Harold S., 340
General Electric Capital Corporation (GECC), 2, 160, 162, 177–8, 179
General Foods, 262
Germany, 13, 47, 55
G.H. Cotton Company, 258
Gilbeys Ireland, 324, 351
Glaceries de Saint Roch, 310, 311
Globe Investment Trust, 312, 322–5, 332

Goldman Sachs, 1, 190, 205, 210, 212, 215, 216
Gonda, Leslie and Louis, 186
Goodman, Larry, 128–9, 220, 397. *see also* Goodman International
    Beef Tribunal evidence, 53–4, 56–7, 69–70, 76, 78–9, 83–4
    dual role, 385
    personality, 53–5
    Tribunal evidence, 83–4
Goodman, Mrs, 67
Goodman, Peter, 67, 68, 74
Goodman International, 2–3, 15, 18, 48–93, 156, 172, 192, 217, 244, 307, 401–2
    accounting and auditing issues, 86–91
    acquisitions and turnarounds, 55–7
    age pattern, 378, 380–86, 399
    background and history, 51–7
    business and politics, 77
    business cycle, 397
    compared to Kentz, 128–30
    crisis in, 48–50
        reasons for collapse, 78–82
        speed of profit reversal, 378
    diversification, 57–8
    entrepreneur and risk, 75–7
    examinership, 83–4
    financial performance, 58–66
        warning signals, 63–6
    financial reporting issues, 394
    organisational structure, 67–75
    public interest issues, 396
    reflections, 91–3
    regulatory system failure, 400
    restructuring, 84–6
    tax liabilities, 88–91
government, role of
    export credit insurance, 77, 83–4
    Goodman, 77, 83–4
    Irish Shipping, 368–72, 400, 401
    Kentz, 96
GPA, 3, 10, 15, 18, 93, 157–221, 244, 350, 357, 369, 402
    accounting policies, 197–203

    age pattern, 378, 380–86, 399
    background, 160–65
    bank covenants, 192–3
    business cycle, 397
    capital structure and gearing, 186–90
    compared with ILFC, 167–70, 173–7, 184, 186–7, 190, 197, 201–2, 204–5, 219
    compared with Woodchester, 184–7
    dividend policy, 195–7
    financial performance, 171–7
    financial reporting issues, 391, 394
    growth and finance, 184–6
    internal plans and expectations, 193–4
    IPO
        financial losses, 1–2, 215–17
        reasons for failure, 206–15
        stockbroker analysis, 205–6
    management, organisation and culture, 182–4, 391
    overtrading?, 190–92
    product/market strategy, 166–70
    public interest issues, 396–7
    reflections, 217–21
    regulatory system failure, 400
    restructuring, 12
    shareholders and board, 177–81
    speed of profit reversal, 378–9
    stockbroker analysis, 203–6
GPG International, 237
Grace, Tom, 308
Grand Metropolitan, 227
Great Northern Brewery, Dundalk, 228
Greencore, 395, 400
Greene, Eugene, 142
Greenwald, Gerald, 180
Greer, P.H., 345, 348–9, 351, 352, 356, 370
    dominance, 359, 360
Greiner, L.E., 31
'Grey Monday', 50
Griffin, Joe, 279, 309, 311, 321
Griffin, Noel, 309–15, 320, 321, 350–51
'group-think', 36

growth, problems of, 34–5
GPA, 184–5
Guardian, 301
Guerin, Veronica, 70
Guinness. *see* Arthur Guinness Son and Co Ltd
Guinness, Arthur, 223, 224
Guinness, Benjamin, 3rd Earl Iveagh, 224, 225, 230–31, 236
  diversification, 236
  family co-options, 238
  surrenders chair, 242, 243
Guinness, Edward, 1st Earl Iveagh, 223, 224
Guinness, Hon. Finn, 238
Guinness, Peter, 238
Guinness, Rupert, 230–31
Guinness, Rupert, 2nd Earl Iveagh, 223–4
Guinness Peat Group, 160, 177
Gulf War
  and Kentz Corporation, 107
Gulf war, 55, 78, 81–2, 221
  and Goodman, 50
  and GPA, 161
  and Kentz Corporation, 98
Guy's Hospital, London, 101, 107–8
Gwilliam, D. and Russell, T., 42

Hambrick, D.C., 275
  and D'Aveni, R.A., 39–40
Hamilton, Mr Justice Liam, 50, 69
Hanrahan, Denis, 180, 181
Hardiman, Adrian, 76
Hardy, David, 312, 323
Harp lager, 224, 227, 228
Harrington, Jack, 285, 286
Harrods, 314
Harvey, General Sir Charles, 229–30
Harvey-Jones, Sir John, 2, 158, 180, 181, 183
Hatfield, M.R., 238
Haughey, Charles, 50, 83, 215, 341–2
Haughey Boland, 352, 361
Havel, Miroshov, 309
Hayes, Cecil, 272

Hayes, Joe, 298
Hayes, Paddy, 312, 313, 323, 324–5, 339
  resignation, 331–2
'Headless Firm', 41, 277, 339
Healy, Liam, 298
Heineken, 227
Heinz, 298
Heiton Holdings, 109
Hely Hutchinson, M., 239
Heron Group, 13
Hoare, David, 243
Hoare Govett, 205
Holidair Ltd, 95
Holland, 107
Holmes-a-Court, Robert, 14
Hooper, Richard, 50
Hotel des Arts, Barcelona, 98, 108, 119, 128, 382
  problems, 107, 111–12
Houston, Bill, 25, 221
Howick, Bobby, 229
Hussey, Gemma, 342

Iacocca, Lee, 37
IBI, 83, 332
IBI Nominees, 254
IBM, 14, 36–7
'Icarus Paradox', 41
ICC Bank, 126, 127
Imperial Chemical Industries, 183
'Impulsive Syndrome', 41, 93, 129, 220, 277
Ind Coope, 228
Independent Newspapers, 5, 8, 280–81, 282, 287–8
  advertising, 303–4
  developments in, 297–300
  and Irish Press, 293–4, 306–7
  lotto game, 305
  market research, 302–3
  under O'Reilly, 283–4
Industrial Development Authority (IDA), 77, 99, 100
industrial relations, 37
  Irish Press, 290, 299–301, 304–5, 338

Waterford Wedgwood, 318, 320–22, 329, 331–6, 338
Industry and Commerce, Dept of, 79, 86, 87
Ingersoll, Ralph, 306, 339
Ingersoll Publications, 282, 291, 293, 294, 306–7
Inland Revenue, UK, 95, 101, 396
insolvency, 6
Institute of Chartered Accountants in Ireland, 90, 199
institutional investors, 25
   GPA, 159, 177–81, 213, 215–20
   Guinness, 242–3
   P.J. Carroll, 263–4
Insurance Corporation of Ireland (ICI), 8, 10, 77, 87, 345–9, 360, 362
International Lease Finance Corporation (ILFC), 157, 165, 382, 385, 391
   accounting, 197, 201–2
   compared with GPA, 167–70, 173–7, 184, 186–7, 190, 219
   share valuation, 204, 205, 206
Investment Bank of Ireland, 50
investors, role of, 401–2
Investor's Chronicle, 233–4
Iran, 55
Iraq, 53, 107, 161, 382
   contracts lost, 63–4
   export credit, 62, 86
      and auditors, 87
      government role, 77, 83–4
      impact of withdrawal, 91–2, 93
      withdrawn, 67, 78–9, 81, 83–4, 87
   insurance risk, 58, 69, 75–7
Ireland
   banking, 15
   corporate collapse in, 12–15
   economic performance, 10–11
   failure prediction, 44, 47
Irish Cement, 106, 109
Irish Competition Authority, 294
Irish Congress of Trade Unions, 390
Irish Continental Line, 345, 347–8, 350, 352, 360–61, 363, 375
   sold, 372
Irish Distillers, 253
Irish Glass Bottle Company, 279, 309, 311
Irish Independent, 279, 281, 286, 301
Irish Life, 253, 254, 332
Irish Management Institute, 161, 325
Irish Marketing Surveys, 298
Irish Press, 3, 5, 18, 222, 278–80, 318, 320, 333, 377
   age pattern, 378
   background, 280–82
   business cycle, 398
   corporate reorganisation, 291–4
   endgame, 305–7
   failed rescue, 307–8
   financial performance, 288–91
   influence of history and culture, 284–6
   patterns of mature failure, 388–90
   political origins, 282–4
   product/market and competitive position, 286–8
   reasons for collapse, 294–305
      competition, 297–300
      decline in innovation, 302–3
      industrial relations, 300–2
      loss of advertising, 303–5
      management, 296–7, 298–300
   reflections, 337–9
   speed of profit reversal, 378, 379
   warning signs, 399
Irish Press Newspapers, 291
Irish Press Publications, 291, 293, 294, 307–8
Irish Shipping, 3, 18, 340–76
   background, 344–8
   big project, 354–8
   external governance defects, 368–72, 400, 401
   finance issues, 362–8
   financial reporting issues, 394, 395
   government responsibility, 374–5, 389–90
   internal control defects, 358–63
   liquidation and consequences, 372–3

mature company failure, 387–90
organisation and management, 350–52
public interest issues, 396
reflections, 375–6
speed of profit reversal, 378, 379
Tempany report, 352–4, 358–61, 363–8
trading and financial performance, 348–50
warning signs, 399
Irish Steel, 109
Irish Sweepstakes, 279, 309
Irish Times, 5, 279, 284, 287–8, 293
Italy, 13
Iveagh, Earls of. *see* Guinness
Iveagh Trustees, 240

J. Walter Thompson, 226, 240
Jack Beanstalk, 136
Jackson, Ray, 26–7, 308
Jacobs, Dr Joseph J., 105–6
Jacobs Engineering, 107, 116
    compared with Kentz Corporation, 104–6
James Crean, 10
Japan, 1, 159, 160, 161, 166, 178, 181
    banking, 159
    failure prediction, 47
    GPA investments, 212, 213, 215–17
    and IPO, 212
    Irish Shipping investments, 355, 373
    stocks decline, 211
Jefco, 107
Jeffers, Alan, 312
Jefferson Smurfit, 8
Jennings, Vincent, 282, 297, 299
Jobs, Steve, 32
John Hinde, 311, 312
John Player & Sons, 244, 252, 268

Kawasaki, 213
Kay and Searfoss, 202
Kealy, Owen, 312, 321–2, 324
Kearney, Gus, 94–5, 97, 98, 104, 109, 112–15, 117, 128–9, 386

dual role, 110–11, 385
loans to, 120–21
Keegan, Edward, 359, 365
Kelly, Noel, 97, 105, 110
Kelly, Richard, 262–3
Kennedy, K., Giblin, T. and McHugh, D., 10
Kenny, Ivor, 254
Kenny, Mary, 302
Kent, Frank, 94–5, 97–8, 104, 109–11, 113, 128, 386
Kent, Michael, 97
Kent Technologies, 109
Kentz C&M (UK) Ltd, 95, 101, 102, 108, 121, 123
Kentz Corporation, 3, 12, 18, 94–130, 147, 156, 192, 218, 307, 377
    accounting issues, 117–25
    age pattern, 380–86
    background, 97–102
    board and ownership structure, 109–10
    business cycle, 397
    compared with Goodman, 128–30
    compared with Jacobs Engineering, 104–6
    consequences of collapse, 127–8
    external governance and regulation, 125–7
    financial control, 113–15
    financial performance, 102–4
    financial reporting issues, 391, 393, 394
    management structure and culture, 110–13
    overtrading, 115–17
    product/market strategy, 106–9
    public interest issues, 396
    reflections, 128–30
    regulatory system failure, 400, 401
    speed of profit reversal, 378, 379
Kerry Group, 70, 93, 382
    compared with Goodman, 58–63, 65–6
Kilroy, Howard, 38, 313, 324, 331
Kilroy, Patrick, 323

King, James, 2, 158, 181, 182, 183
King, John, 89
Kinsella, R., 11
KLM, 166, 202
Knight, Geoffrey, 180
Kotter, J.P. and Heskett, J.L., 31
KPMG Stokes Kennedy Crowley, 26, 244, 308, 359
  and Goodman, 71–2, 76, 88–90
  and Kentz, 99, 100, 114, 117, 120–24
  and Xtra-vision, 139, 148–52
Kraft Industries, 262

Labour Court, 301, 336
Labour Party, 283, 342–3, 359, 370–71
Larkin, Jim, 281
Lavells, 237
Lawson, Nigel, 180, 181
leasing
  and financial reporting, 197–203
  groups, 10
Ledbetter, Peter, 180, 182, 183
Lee, Joe, 284
Leinster Society of Chartered Accountants, 247, 272
Lemass, Sean, 280, 281, 296, 341
Lennox-Boyd, Hon. Simon, 238
Leonard, Nicholas, 298
Lepere, John, 245, 246, 269
Leydon, John, 346
Li-Lo, 237
Libya, 107
life-cycle theory, 27–9
Limerick Steamship Company, 344, 347, 359
Lindsay, Ray, 178
liquidations, 6, 7
  Irish Shipping, 372–4
Lloyd, Paul, 97, 110
Loire Line, 237
London International Group, 326
London Stock Exchange, 33, 48
  GPA, 213–14
  Guinness, 223, 224, 231–2, 233–4
Long-Term Credit Bank of Japan, 160, 161, 178, 213

Lorange, P. and Nelson, R.T., 35–6
Lufthansa, 157
Lunny, Pat, 299
Lynch, John, 230

McAndrew, Tom, 68
Macardle Moore, 228
McElhatton, Aubrey, 345, 351–2, 360, 362
McElligott, J.J., 346–7
Macfarlane, Sir Norman, 242
McGarry, Michael, 104, 111, 113
McGing, Dan, 306
McGonagle, Liam, 359
McGonigal, Eoin, 54, 56–7, 68–71, 78–9
McGovern, J.N., 352
McGrath, Paul, 41
McGrath, Joe, 279, 309, 311, 315, 321
McGrath, Paddy, 310, 311, 315, 318, 321
  steps down, 312, 323
  succeeds father, 309
McGrath, Patrick Jr, 311, 312
McGrath, Seamus, 312, 315
McGrath family, 254
  sale of equity, 322–5
McHale, Sean, 281, 299
McKiernan, Peter, 24
McKinley, Joe, 268
McKinney, Craig, 186
McKinsey, 256
McKinsey & Co, 35
McLoghlin, Brian, 182
McLoughlin, John, 72
McMahon, Hugh, 359, 360, 361
McNeile, Robert, 239
McStay, John, 308
McSweeney, B., 322, 328
Mahon & McPhillips, 12, 94, 103, 109, 115–16, 127
Malaysia, 112
Malocco, Elio, 281, 299
management
  analytical framework of mismanagement, 390–91

445

cause of failure, 21–6
  mismanagement, 5, 11–12, 387
management culture
  Goodman, 67–75
  GPA, 182–4
  Irish Press, 295–6, 298–300
  Irish Shipping, 350–52
  Kentz, 110–13
  Xtra-vision, 138–9
Manahan, Aidan, 244, 246, 268
Mara, P.J., 215
Marais, D.A.J., 43
Marcus, Louis, 302
margin calls, 80–81
Marks and Spencer, 48
Massey-Ferguson, 13
mature organisations
  problems of, 35–9, 387–90
Maxwell group, 13
Meagher, John, 298
Menton, Colm, 145
Menton, Liam, 145
Merchants Warehousing, 57, 68
Merck, Sharpe and Dohme, 106
Merrill Lynch, 190, 197, 212, 216
Metallgesellschaft group, 13
M.F. Kent, 12, 97, 98, 104, 113, 126, 386
  debts, 127
  expansion, 106–7
Miller, D., 93, 129, 220, 277, 339, 375
  failure patterns, 41
Miller, D. and Friesen, P., 28–9
Miller's Breweries, 262
Mills, Geoffrey, 26
Mills, Maggie, 95, 102
Mills, Michael, 302
Minch Norton, 57, 68
Mitchell, Jim, 342–3, 366, 371, 374
Mitsubishi Bank, 211
Mitsubishi Trust and Banking Corporation of Japan, 160, 161, 178, 179–80, 210, 213
Mjoset, L., 10–11
Moody's, 2, 190
Mooney, Mr, 76–7

Morgan Bank, Brussels, 98, 101, 108, 121
Morgan Stanley, 163, 190, 212, 314, 323, 333
Morisson, Ian, 67
Morohashi, Shinroku, 179–80
Morpeth Committee, 272
Morris, James, 139, 142
Morris, Quentin, 312, 323
Moyne, Lord, 231
Mulroy Securities, 132, 135, 154
Murdoch, Rupert, 14, 38–9
Murphy, Denis, 359
Murphy, Richard, 135, 138–9, 143, 145, 151, 386
  entrepreneur, 155
  losses, 156
  resignation, 142
Murphy, Rodney, 298
Murphy, William Martin, 280–81
Murphy family, 283, 298
Murphy's brewery, 4, 227

Nation, 280
National Union of Journalists, 285, 300–301, 307
NCB Stockbrokers, 133, 194
  analysis of GPA, 203, 204–6
Nestle, 240, 241
NET, 106
New Hampshire Bank, 8
News Corporation, 14, 38–9
News International, 294
Nippon Total Finance, 213
Nolan, Ronan, 361
Nomura International, 1
Nomura Research Institute, 205
Nomura Securities, 211, 216
Normandy Ferries, 347
Norwich Union, 254
Nuttalls, 237

O'Brien, William, 284
O'Callaghan, Juan, 182
O'Carroll, Niall, 71–2
OC&C Strategy Consultants, 99, 108, 109, 111, 113, 114

Oceanbank Developments, 352, 361
O'Connell, Colm, 325, 330, 332
O'Connor, Stephen, 109
O'Donoghue, Redmond, 324, 325
O'Ferrall, Rory, 95, 101, 102
Ogle, M.B., 239
Ohlson, J.A., 43
Olympia & York, 13, 217
O'Malley, Desmond, 87
O'Neill, Derry, 351, 360–61
O'Neill, Captain John, 344, 345, 351
O'Neill, W.A., 345–6, 351–2, 360–61, 370
  dominance, 359
  finance, 365–9
Oram, Hugh, 286, 305
O'Reilly, Dr A.J.F., 283–4, 297–8, 303, 333
O'Reilly, John, 274–5
organisational decline, 5–6
'organisational disease', 3–5
Osborne, James, 270, 271
O'Sullivan, Terry, 302
O'Toole, Aileen, 11, 94, 104, 163
O'Toole, Michael, 285–6
O'Toole, Richard, 183
overtrading, 381–2
  GPA, 159–60, 190–92
  Kentz, 102–3, 115–17, 129
  Xtra-vision, 156
Owen, David, 149

Palgrave Murphy, 347
Panmure Gordon, 132, 153, 323
Parsons, A.C., 239
Patterson, Brian, 325
Peard, F.W., 230
Peat Marwick McLintock, 330
Penrose, E.T., 27
Penrose brothers, 308–9
Perisano, Sal, 142–3, 145
Peters, T. and Waterman, R., 12
Pettigrew, A.M., 30
Pfizer, 106
Philip Morris, 261–2
Pijper, T., 42

Pitcher, Bartle, 298
P.J. Carroll, 3, 18, 222, 231, 323, 331, 338, 369, 402
  accounting and financial policies, 272–5
  age pattern, 378, 388–90
  background, 244–8
  board structure, 270–71
  business cycle, 397, 398
  cash flow profile, 259–62
  comparisons with Gallaher, 264–5
  core tobacco division performance, 251–2
  diversification, 255–6
    aquaculture and direct marketing, 256–9
    outcome, 259
  financial reporting issues, 394
  marketing and financial performance, 248–51
  reflections, 275–7
  scapegoats and responsibilities, 262–4
  speed of profit reversal, 378, 379
  strategic and tactical errors, 266–70
  strategic dilemma, 252–5
  warning signs, 399
PMPA, 10
Polaris, 178
Polly Peck International, 13, 42
Porter, M.E., 256
Post, An, 142
Power, W., 325
Price Waterhouse, 308, 330, 334, 336, 359
Prudential Insurance Company of America, 216
Purssell, A.J., 238, 239, 240

Queen's Moat House, 13
Quinn, R.E. and Cameron, K., 28
Quinn, Ruairi, 96, 342
Quirke, Diarmuid, 109

Raftery, Captain Coleman, 352
Reardon Smith Line, 344, 345, 348, 353–8, 361

receiverships
  statistics, 6–7
recessions, 25–6
Registrar of Companies, 7, 126
regulatory system, 125–7, 400–401
Reichmann brothers, 13
Reihill, Frank, 359
research sample, 403–5
Reuters, 291, 293
Revenue Commissioners, 294, 400
  and Goodman International, 88–91
  and Kentz, 95, 126, 127
  and Xtra-vision, 147
Review Board, UK, 401
Reynolds, Albert, 343
Riada Stockbrokers, 205, 206
Ridgeway, Frank, 285
Robertson, John, 43
Robertson, Sir Lewis, 25, 220
Ross, J.E. and Kami, M.J., 21–2
Rothmans, 246, 252–3, 262–3, 270–71, 277
Roux, Olivier, 242
Rupert, Anton, 253, 263
Ryan, B., 282
Ryan, Des, 244, 246, 247, 254, 268
Ryan, Tony, 158, 160, 161, 163, 168, 194, 386
  chairman, 178
  dominance, 177, 180, 220
  dual role, 385
  Executive Committee, 181
  IPO failure, 1–2, 207, 213–14, 215
  losses, 216
  management, 182–4
  resignation, 162
  shares held, 195, 197
Ryan Commission, 395, 401

Saatchi & Saatchi, 13
Sainsbury, 48
Salomon Brothers, 164, 181, 190, 212, 216
Saudi Arabia, 106–7
Saunders, Ernest, 225, 229, 233, 237, 255, 339
  transformation of Guinness, 238, 240–44
'savings and loan' crisis, 14
Schaer, Alfred, 109
Schneider Group, 13
Schroders, 1
Scottish and Newcastle, 227
Securities and Exchange Commission, 186, 207, 242, 401
S.G. Warburg Securities, 210
Shannon Aerospace, 3
'shell' companies, 9–10
Shuttleway Holdings, 313, 333, 334, 337
Simpson Xavier, 142
Sisk group (Sicon), 118
Siuicre Eireann, 58
Sky, 38, 39
Slater, Jim, 33–4
Slater Walker Securities, 32, 33–4, 219
Slatter, S., 24
Slowey, Brian, 241
SMC software, 109
Smith, Terry, 15–16, 21, 42
Smith Group, 311–12, 314, 320, 323, 325, 398
Smithwick's brewery, 4, 228
Smurfit, Michael, 38
Smurfit Group, 1, 38, 50, 157, 210, 213, 304, 306, 324
Societe de Participations Verrieres SA, 310
Solange Ltd, 308
Somers, Bernard, 147
South Africa, 107
Southside Newspapers, 282, 296, 304, 338, 388, 398
Spain, Alex, 133–4, 139, 155
Spicer, W.A., 239
SSAP No. 6, 367
SSAP No. 9, 125
SSAP No. 12, 149
SSAP No. 13, 123
SSAP No. 19, 365
SSAP No. 21, 198–9
'Stagnant Bureaucracy', 41, 339
Standard and Poor's, 2, 190, 211

Standard Life, 254, 332
Star, 287, 302, 304
Statement of Financial Accounting Standard (SFAS), 198
Steel, Victor, 242
Stinchcombe, A.L., 282, 283
stockbroker analysts, 15–16, 42
    efficiency of, 203–6
    role of, 401–2
Stokes Kennedy Crowley, 104
Sugar, Alan, 32–3
Sun, 294, 301, 304
Sunbeam Wolsey, 9
Sunday Press. see Irish Press
Sunday Times, 48–9
Sunday World, 302
Sutherland, Peter, 2, 180, 181
Swain, Maxwell, 147
'Swimming Upstream', 41, 375
Swiss Bank Corporation, 205
Switzers, 311, 312, 314, 320

Taffler, R., 43, 44
tax amnesty, 89
tax evasion, 89–91
Taylor, Claude, 180
Telecom Eireann, 157, 395, 400
Tempany, Maurice, 341, 346
    report of, 352–4, 358–61, 363–8
Tennant, Anthony, 243
Tesco, 48
Thomas & Thomas Rodmakers, 256, 258
Thornton, Gerry, 68, 211
3i, 211
Tierney, John, 158, 180, 182
Times, 301
Tipperary Crystal, 329
TMG Group, 10
Today Tonight, 262
Tokyo Shoko Research, 11
Trade and Industry, Department of (UK), 13, 198–9, 242–3
trade unions. *see* industrial relations
Travelstead, G. Ware, 107
Traynor, Colm, 297, 299

Twentieth Century Fox, 38

Udaras na Gaeltachta, 256
Udwar-Hazy, Steven, 186
Ukraine, 107
undercapitalisation, 32
Unidare, 351
Unigate, 48, 49, 58, 67, 69, 92, 382
    investment risk, 65, 72, 79–82
United Kingdom
    banking, 15
    beef market, 55
    conglomerates, 9
    corporate collapse, 12–13
    failure prediction, 44, 47
    Goodman in, 58, 73
    GPA flotation, 214–15, 221
    Guinness weaknesses in, 234–5
    meat factories, 57
United Nations, 78
United States, 7, 38, 58
    banking, 13–14, 15
    bankruptcy legislation, 50
    conglomerates, 9
    corporate collapse, 12–15
    failure prediction, 43, 44, 47
Unlisted Securities Market, 131, 132, 136, 187

Verolme Dockyard, 345, 346, 358
'Video City', 136
Video Library, 136, 138
video market, 139–40, 147–9
Video Store, 149
Videosmith, 136, 143

Wah Kwong Shipping Company, 373
Walsh, M., 282
Walsh, Tom, 49
Waltham Holdings, 323
Ward, Sean, 297
Ward, Thomas, 242
warning signs, 36, 399
    Goodman, 63–6
    Irish Press, 399
Warwick University, 328

Waterford Foods plc, 109
Waterford Glass, 163, 253, 254, 351
Waterford Glasshouse, 308–9
Waterford Wedgwood, 3, 8, 18, 222, 278–80, 369
  age pattern, 314–16, 378, 387–90
  background, 308–14
  business cycle, 398
  crystal division disasters, 328–32
  failed turnaround, 332–4
  financial reporting issues, 394
  labour costs and competitiveness, 316–22
  public interest issues, 397
  reflections, 337–9
  sale of equity to Globe, 322–5
  second turnaround, 334–7
  speed of profit reversal, 378, 379
  warning signs, 399
  Wedgwood acquisition, 325–8
Watson, Thomas J., Jr, 37
Wedgwood group, 313, 325–8, 388, 398
Weitzel, W. and Jonsson, E., 5, 16–17
  model of decline, 40–41
Wellcome Trust, 212, 215
Wendt, Gary, 178
Westmeath Co-operative, 57
Wexford Steamship Company, 344, 347, 359
W.H. Wills, 244
Whitaker, Dr T.K., 239
Whitbread, 227, 233, 234
White, Sean, 97, 110
White Child & Beney, 237
Whyte, Gerard, 139, 142
Wilson, John, 343
Windmill Lane Studios, 139
'window dressing', 42, 364

Winkelman family, 310
Wolk, H., Francis, J. and Tearney, M., 198
Woodchester Investments plc, 10, 207, 382, 385
  compared with GPA, 184–5, 186–7
Wozniak, Stephen, 32
WPP, 13

Xavier, Anthuan, 142
Xtra-vision, 15, 18, 131–56, 192, 218, 220, 369, 402
  age pattern, 378, 380–86, 399
  background, 135–7
  bailout by Cambridge, 145–6
  board and management structure, 138–9
  business and marketing strategy, 139–40
  business cycle, 397
  financial performance, 140–42
  financial reporting issues, 147–52, 391, 394
  first financial crisis, 142–3
  flotation and expansion, 137–8
  reflections, 155–6
  regulatory system failure, 400
  role of DCC, 154–5
  second financial crisis, 143–5
  speed of profit reversal, 378–9
  on Stock Exchange, 132–5
  stockbroker analysts' reviews, 152–3
  strengths and weaknesses, 153–4
  third financial crisis, 146–7

Yamaichi Securities, 205, 216
Yeoman, 10
Yumiketa, Hiroshi, 109